TOWNS'
SUNDAY SCHOOL
ENCYCLOPEDIA

Towns'
Sunday School
Encyclopedia

ELMER
TOWNS

 Tyndale House Publishers, Inc.
Wheaton, Illinois

Unless otherwise stated, the Scripture quotations in this book are from the New King James Version ©1979, 1980, 1982, Thomas Nelson Inc., Publishers.

Library of Congress Cataloging-in-Publication Data

Towns, Elmer L.
   [Sunday school encyclopedia]
   Towns Sunday school encyclopedia : a practical guide for Sunday
school workers / Elmer L. Towns
      p.   c.m
   Includes bibliographical references.
   ISBN 0-8423-7303-9
   1. Sunday schools—Encyclopedias.   I. Title.
BV1510.T69   1992
268'.03—dc20   92-28605

Printed in the United States of America

99 98 97 96 95 94 93
10 9   8   7   6   5   4   3   2   1

Contents

Foreword

I call Dr. Elmer Towns my dear son in the ministry. I first met Elmer Towns when he came to First Baptist Church of Dallas in the fall of 1954, and we have been friends ever since. He was a seminary student, but I remember him sitting right down front and center in every service. His wife, Ruth, was always with him.

Young Towns had already served as pastor of Westminster Presbyterian Church in Savannah, Georgia, before he moved to Dallas. When he first came to our city, his wife had emergency surgery. One of our visitation pastors went to the recovery room and discovered this young couple didn't know anyone in Dallas. The pastor then arranged for the adult Sunday school teacher to go to their apartment and help them. For several nights, the ladies from our Sunday school took dinner to them. Young Towns said to his wife, "Let's go to First Baptist Church to learn how to love people like this church does, and let's get a vision for a big church." Dr. Elmer Towns told me that is where he got that vision. We were averaging four thousand in Sunday School at the time.

Later Dr. Elmer Towns wrote a best-selling book that influenced many leaders. It was called *The Ten Largest Sunday Schools and What Made Them Grow*. He came and interviewed me as our church was one of the ten largest in the world.

When Dr. Elmer Towns was Executive Secretary of the St. Louis (Missouri) Sunday School Association, he invited me to address the National Sunday School Association. People were there from all over our nation. I was doubly proud of the great throng he had gathered there because I remembered him when no one knew who he was. In our First Baptist Church here in Dallas, he helped in our visitation suppers by going out to bring people in to the church. This is an illustration of the fact that faithfulness in little things prepares a person for service in larger positions.

That night in St. Louis, we had dinner together and talked about the laws of Sunday school growth. I gave him one of my sermons and told him to preach it everywhere—and he has. It begins like this: "If a pastor will build his Sunday school, his Sunday school will build his church."

Dr. Elmer Towns shared the pulpit with me here in Dallas on Palm Sunday 1971. He challenged us to build the Sunday school. While waiting to go into the 11:00 A.M. worship hour, we looked at the crowd of people preparing to attend the preaching service. He noticed many adults were not in Sunday school. He suggested I begin an auditorium Sunday school class to get them into Bible teaching. I did just that, and the class, now taught by a gifted teacher, draws hundreds and hundreds of adults each Lord's Day.

The last time I preached at the Thomas Road Baptist Church in Lynchburg, Virginia, Dr. Elmer Towns taught the giant "pastor's auditorium Sunday school class." There were a couple of thousand people there. He still works in and loves Sunday school.

Many people have written a lot about Sunday school, but I don't know of anyone else who would write about *everything* in Sunday school. So it was only natural that Dr. Elmer Towns would do it. Most encyclopedias have many contributors, but he wrote everything here. A friend said it had to have his name on it so as not to be confused with a reference volume with many contributors. The publishers call it *Towns' Sunday School Encyclopedia*. I think the name fits, and I recommend it to you.

Dr. W. A. Criswell, Pastor
First Baptist Church
Dallas, Texas

I Love the Sunday School

I believe in the Sunday school and have had a lifelong love affair with it. Why shouldn't I? It is the foundation of my life's focus. As a five-year-old boy, I was taken to the Eastern Heights Presbyterian Sunday School in Savannah, Georgia, and didn't miss one Sunday in attendance in the next fourteen years.

In Sunday school I learned the Westminster Catechism, which structured my doctrinal thinking about God and the world.

In Sunday school I learned the Bible, even memorizing the kings of Israel and Judah in order, which gave me an appreciation for history, making me a traditionalist.

In Sunday school I was influenced not to light up my first cigarette or sip my first alcoholic drink (although my father was a chain smoker and was on alcohol). It was there I received a desire for holiness.

In Sunday school I realized Jesus Christ the Son of God was born of a virgin, died for my sins, and was raised bodily on the third day; thus, I accepted Christ as my Savior.

In Sunday school I studied those who preached the gospel and carried out the great commission, hence, when faced with the call to full-time service at age seventeen, I became a minister.

Because I love the Sunday school, I have been a Sunday school superintendent of a little Presbyterian Sunday school mission of less than fifty people and of the large Thomas Road Baptist Church in Lynchburg, Virginia, that averaged more than five thousand in attendance.

Because I love the Sunday school, I have taught small children's classes and the large pastor's auditorium Bible class at Thomas Road Baptist Church with more than 1,200 in weekly attendance.

Because I love the Sunday school, I wrote a book, *The Ten*

Largest Sunday Schools, in 1969, which became a best-seller. I also wrote many other practical books and pamphlets to help Sunday school workers.

Because I love the Sunday school, I have written Sunday school curriculum for Scripture Press, David C. Cook Publishing Company, Gospel Light, Accent Books, and Union Gospel Press, plus I wrote the curriculum at Thomas Road Baptist Church for two years. Now I write the supplement and edit Sunday School Growth Curriculum for Scripture Press.

Because I love the Sunday school, I have spoken in Sunday school conferences in all fifty of the United States and ten provinces of Canada.

Because I love the Sunday school, I researched the sizes of Sunday schools in independent and denominational groups and was the first to publish the list of the one hundred largest Sunday schools in America, and the list of the fastest-growing Sunday schools in each of the fifty states.

I am often asked, "How long did it take you to write this book?" That is a difficult question to answer. A book is written out of your total life. A book should represent all you are and know. This book represents a lifetime; it is not the kind of project that one sits down and writes. One of the first articles I ever published was "The Laws of Sunday School Growth," in 1958. I have updated and included it here. Also, I've included up-to-date topics such as "AIDS in Sunday School," "How to Reach the Baby Boomer," and "How to Reach the Baby Buster."

The articles are presented in alphabetical order to help the reader quickly find answers to their problems.

The material is not theoretical, as one might expect from an encyclopedia. It is practical, geared toward helping the reader perform a task.

The material deals with traditional issues such as "How to Lecture" and up-to-date issues such as "Reaching the Single Parent" and "How to Minister to Both Baby Boomers and Their Parents in the Same Service."

In addition to practical material, I've included other items of interest, such as the contemporary list of the one hundred largest

Sunday schools, case studies of vibrant Sunday schools, biographical profiles of past Sunday school leaders, research questionnaires, and some suggestions for programs.

I cannot take credit for this book. I am the product of many teachers and friends and the books I've read. I am greatly influenced by the organizational approach to Sunday school of Arthur Flake and A. V. Washburn. The deeper-life teaching of Columbia Bible College has influenced me. I picked up a reportorial writing style from Robert Walker, former editor of *Christian Life* magazine. My colleagues at Trinity Evangelical Divinity School in Deerfield, Illinois, motivated me to empirical research. My experience in the Baptist Bible Fellowship (BBF) gave me a passion for soul winning and a commitment to the local church. Jerry Falwell challenged me to faith and vision. John Maxwell was my role model for leadership. Larry Gilbert, president of Church Growth Institute, has given me publicity for my seminars.

Since I've written these articles over the years, all my secretaries who have typed and helped to edit each article can take some credit for this volume. I must especially thank Doug Porter, graduate assistant, and Marie Chapman, editor, for putting some of my notes and files into a format for the encyclopedia. Judy Forlano is credited with pulling together the letters, phone calls, and interviews that make this encyclopedia possible.

While I give so many credits, I must take responsibility for all the omissions and errors, and for the choice of each article that was included. May God use this volume according to its usability, and may he be merciful toward its shortcomings.

Elmer Towns
Summer 1992

Introduction

What Changes Are Occurring in Sunday School?

Sunday school is changing, and some are only seeing the tip of the iceberg. People are uncomfortable with change, but some of the changes will make the Sunday school strong in the future. Others are like a ticking time bomb that could cause the Sunday school to explode in our faces.

Attendance seems to be down in certain Sunday schools and up in others. Dry lectures seem to be out, while expressive learning activities are in. According to one observer, "The more enjoyable they make Sunday school, the fewer children seem to attend."

Some pastors are concerned when they can't get new Christians into Sunday school classes, and when those who were faithful attenders in the past seem to drop out as they get older.

Busing, which was a dominant outreach ten years ago, no longer seems effective. Not as many care about having the largest banana split in the city or being called the fastest growing Sunday school in their county. Other values are important to Sunday school workers.

There are transformational changes in Sunday school. Some changes, like termites, are eating away its foundation. Other changes are strengthening its foundation and assuring its future. Church leaders must realize what is happening and grab hold of the right ring, or they can get thrown from the merry-go-round.

1. Sunday school is changing from being the steeple to being the foundation of the church. The steeple is the most visible part of the church, and so, in the past, the Sunday school was visible in its campaigns, buses, and systematic visitation carried on by teachers. But Sunday schools no longer attract a larger attendance than the morning church service.

As a matter of fact, the average worship service attendance has 24 percent more than the average Sunday school attendance. Visitors do not usually come first to the Sunday school; usually they attend the morning service. After they come into the church by conversion or membership, they are recruited into Sunday school classes where they are grounded in their teachings and life-style of the church. Hence, the Sunday school of the future must become the foundation of the church that grounds believers in doctrine and godly living.

The year 1971 seems to be the transitional year when worship attendance passed Sunday school attendance. Prior to that year, it seemed that many pastors were constantly encouraging people to remain for the morning service. Now the reverse is true. They are asking people to come early next week for Sunday school.

The old Sunday school adage is still true: Everyone who comes to Sunday school ought to stay for church. Those who come to church ought to come early enough for Sunday school. There is a place for both in both, and if both are not in both, there is something wrong with both.

2. Sunday school is changing from the reaching arm to the nurturing arm of the church. Sunday school is defined in four points: (a) the reaching arm, (b) the teaching arm, (c) the winning arm, and (d) the nurturing or maturing arm of the church. As such, the Sunday school in the past has had a strong evangelistic outreach, primarily through Sunday school busing and Sunday school campaigns. When I used to ask a church audience how many were won to Christ through Sunday school, many hands went up. Today, less than 10 percent say that the Sunday school was influential in bringing them to Christ. Sunday school is no longer thought of as an evangelistic outreach of the church. Also, teachers do not perceive their primary role as evangelists; not many have a burden to win their pupils to Christ. They perceive themselves as educators.

The Sunday school should not throw in the towel on evangelism. Recently I conducted a survey of 649 adults at a Sunday school convention. I asked them to respond with a show of hands, how many were converted through the influence of advertising. Two percent lifted their hands. Then I asked how many were converted through the ministry of a pastor. Six percent raised their hands. Next I asked how many were saved through the organized evangelistic outreach of the church. Again, 6 percent lifted their hands. When I asked how many were saved through the influence of a friend or relative, more than 80 percent lifted their hands. Sunday school can be an effective evangelistic outreach when members will network their friends into a Bible study group where they can hear the Word of God and be saved. Then as a result of life-style evangelism and the follow-up of class members, these people are not only won to Jesus Christ, but bonded to a church through the Sunday school. Hence, the Sunday school is becoming the nurturing arm for winning them to Christ, not necessarily the reaching arm that has attracted them to the church.

3. Sunday school is changing from *front door* to *side door evangelism. Front door evangelism* is inviting people into the church where they can hear the gospel and be converted. This is also called "inviting evangelism" or it implies "event evangelism." This means people are converted as a result of a sermon or a Sunday school lesson. Statistics reveal that *front door evangelism* is not nearly as effective as *relationship evangelism.* But *front door evangelism* will get some saved. However, as Americans become more concerned about their relationship to one another, *side door evangelism* can network friends to the gospel through classes, cell groups, and special ministries for the retarded, the deaf, the divorced, the single parents or other people with special needs in the church. The key is to "find a hurt and heal it." *Side door evangelism* is reaching people through special ministry to their needs.

The churchwide evangelistic crusades of the fifties and the sixties were a successful means of getting people to Christ. Today outreach must be specialized. People can be brought under the influence of the gospel through ladies' Bible studies, recreational teams sponsored by the church, special activities, and fellowship groups. Sunday school can reflect specialized outreach by including some special purpose classes (in addition to the graded classes).

4. Sunday school is changing from its image of "children only" to a balanced ministry to children and adults. Before 1971, 39 percent of the Sunday school population were adults. But this has

changed. Today more than 51 percent of the Sunday school population are adults. You can no longer think of Sunday school as only a place for flannelgraph stories; it also is a place for adult Bible classes and fellowship groups. The tip point year was 1971, when adults finally passed children in the Sunday school population. Now that there are more adults, we should not minimize our emphasis to children but balance our endeavors to reach and teach adults.

One way to balance the outreach to children and adults is to evaluate our resources. The average Sunday school invests 70 to 80 percent of its budget, staff, and educational space on children, yet adults represent 51 percent of its population.

At a Sunday school convention in North Carolina, I asked approximately four hundred pastors their opinion as to where their Sunday school was growing. Only six pastors indicated that their Sunday schools were growing because of children. Six pastors indicated that their Sunday schools were growing because of youth. Only four pastors said their Sunday schools were growing because of senior saints' ministries. However, more than two hundred pastors indicated that their churches were growing in the young adult area. Approximately two hundred said their Sunday schools were not growing.

Young adults, ages eighteen to thirty, have been considered a hard age to reach with the gospel. However, a recent sociological study showed that young adults in this age span are going through many changes; hence they are open to the gospel. These transitions make them receptive, reponsive people to reach with the gospel. These changes include choosing a college, choosing a life partner, choosing a place to live after college, choosing a job, and deciding to have children. Usually the process starts over as they change jobs and homes again. Statistics reveal a large number of conversions in that age group, and young adults have gone to churches where they have impacted growth.

Growth oriented Sunday schools that want to reach young adults should create special classes for them. New young adult classes, unlike established classes, produce growth, and it is difficult for new members to penetrate into older fellowship circles.

In a recent study of why people choose a Sunday school class, it was shown that they first looked for fellowship, or they attended with friends. Second, they go where they can receive specific help for a felt need. In the third place, they choose a class because of a topic, the personality of the teacher, or a specific teaching technique, such as films or discussion groups.

5. Sunday school is changing from an instructional center to a shepherding ministry. Many are recruited as Sunday school teachers because of their love for teaching. However, this has a limited scope. If education were the only objective of the Sunday school, then a teacher who has taught Bible content can rightly feel that when his pupils know the lesson, he has finished his task. However, Sunday schools have a much broader objective. There is a shepherding task that must be carried out. A Sunday school teacher is a shepherd; he is the extension of pastoral ministry into the life of the pupils. Everything the pastor is to the larger flock, the Sunday school teacher is to the Sunday school flock.

When a Sunday school teacher gets a burden to shepherd pupils rather than just instructing them in biblical content, he or she will change the average Sunday school. A shepherd is first of all a leader or an example to the flock. His life modeling will do more to communicate the gospel than simply telling Bible stories. Secondly, a shepherd feeds the flock, which involves instruction, questioning, and "hearing lessons." In the third place, a shepherd tends or protects the sheep, which involves the ministry of counseling, protecting, visiting absentees, and making oneself available to talk about problems. It was Jimmy Breeland, a Sunday school teacher at the Eastern Heights Presbyterian Church in Savannah, Georgia, who cared enough to come by and take me to Sunday school in his truck. He was a shepherd for my soul.

6. Sunday school is changing from lectures to Bible study. The key to the healthy Sunday school is "Bible study with fellowship." Most think of an adult class teacher as a deacon who lectures to a class of adults in the back of the church auditorium underneath the balcony, speaking in a monotone for thirty-five minutes, then asking, "Are there any questions?" When there are no questions

they dismiss for the morning service. This typical class will not make it in the future, nor will it prepare pupils for the future.

Recently my wife attended a Sunday school class of forty-three adults in the family room of a home in a subdivision in Modesto, California. The question, "Who was Melchizedek?" was the assignment for the morning. The people entered through the kitchen, got coffee, and found a place in the family room. Even before the class officially began, they were sharing what they had found out about Melchizedek. Although a simple topic, it motivated many students to research an opinion. The class was spent in Bible sharing by many individuals before the teacher finally stood to his feet and began to give his thoughts. My wife said it was an outstanding class because everyone shared. Everyone was interested.

The modern adult Sunday school class must have three things. First, a coffee pot that allows people to fellowship before class begins and promotes informality that leads to sharing during the class. Second, it needs an overhead projector that allows people to see an outline, read a question, or focus their attention on the topic. The electronic teaching aid is a modern tool that reaches young adults who are a product of the electronic generation. Third, there must be questions to stimulate thoughts, discussion, and involvement. Even Jesus used questions in his teaching. There are 107 questions asked by Jesus recorded in Scripture. The difference between mediocrity and success in teaching is involvement by the student in the learning process.

7. Sunday school is changing from enrollment to the open hand of fellowship. There was a time in the past when enrollment figures were some of the most important statistics in a Sunday school. As a matter of record, most teachers told visitors that if they attended for three weeks in a row, their name would be placed on the roll book. Enrollment was an important figure; it was gathered and carefully kept by Sunday school secretaries and reported annually for denominational records. Enrollment meant that the pupil belonged to the Sunday school and was accepted into its ranks. Today, many of the major denominations and independent churches have stopped gathering and reporting enroll-

ment figures (except the Southern Baptists, who use it as a vital technique in their outreach). Most Sunday schools offer an open hand of fellowship to anyone who visits the class and try to make him or her feel as much a part of the class on their first visit as any other member. The open-hand approach indicates that anyone who attends is a first-class member, just as much as the person who has been there for ten years.

Perhaps the change in American society is reflected in the change of attitude toward Sunday school enrollment. Most people do not make long-term commitments to bowling teams, service clubs, or hobby groups. Most Americans make short-term commitments, so they don't ask others for long-term commitments. Like fast foods and instant everything, people become instant members of a class the first time they attend. As a matter of fact, the most important use of enrollment is as a mailing list for follow-up and for contact with absentees rather than a means of identifying those who belong to a Sunday school.

8. The teaching in Sunday school has shifted from ontology to functionalism. Ontology is the science of being, and at one time Sunday schools were primarily concerned with what a person became. However, modern American life has shifted from ontology to functionalism. Most American people are not as concerned with what a person *is* as they are about what he or she *can do*. (A Christian should emphasize both being and doing.) Following this trend, most adult classes have centered their curriculum on functionalism, such as how to balance one's budget, how to get along with teenagers, how to be a better wife, and how to discover and use your spiritual gifts. Several years ago the International Uniform Lesson began losing its popularity, as adult classes began selecting short-term lesson topics. Adult classes of four or seven weeks became popular, rather than the traditional thirteen-week curriculum. Today, classes are allowed to select their topics, and many choose functional subjects that help them live the Christian life.

9. Sunday school can't use yesterday's tools in today's world and be in ministry tomorrow. Some things must never change, while other things constantly pass away. The mature believer

must know what things to fight for and what things to give up. The Word of God never changes, and Jesus Christ is the same yesterday, today, and forever. Truth is reflected in principles, and we must never compromise biblical principles. But programs can change because they represent a technique used to reach people through the meeting of their needs. When a person's perception of his need changes, the church must use a new program to reach a person through the new need in his life.

The biblical principles of preaching, teaching, soul winning, and ministry to people never change. But programs and techniques change. The original Sunday school was conducted on Sunday afternoon and taught reading, writing, and arithmetic. But now children have public school, so Sunday school no longer meets basic educational needs of reading, writing, and arithmetic. Public attitudes have changed toward Sunday afternoons, so it is difficult to attract people to Sunday school in the afternoon. As a result, Sunday school programs have changed, but the biblical principles that make it effective have not changed.

The wise Sunday school leader will test all things by the Word of God. Some programs have served their usefulness; they should no longer receive priority treatment. Other new programs arise and demand attention. Remember the words of Longfellow, "Be not the first by which the new is tried, be not the last by which the old is laid aside." All new programs are not good just because they are new. Not all old programs are useless just because they are old. Paul tells us, "Test all things; hold fast what is good" (1 Thess. 5:21). Therefore, hold fast to biblical principles, for they are eternal, then test all programs by biblical principles for effectiveness.

Does the Sunday school have a bright future? Its historic purpose must not change. The Sunday school must reach, teach, win, and mature its pupils in Christ. As long as the Sunday school remains a channel for the Word of God, it will meet needs and have a future. As long as the Sunday school curriculum is based on the Word of God, people will attend its classes and support its programs. As long as the Sunday school is based on the Word of God, it has a bright future.

ACTIVITIES USED IN TEACHING CHILDREN

Effective teaching is like coaching a well-disciplined basketball team. The teacher knows the overall game strategy, the lesson plan. The teacher is involved with the pupils as they go through a number of plays, or activities. Sunday school is similar to the practice sessions; the game is played in the arena where the pupils apply the lessons to everyday life.

Teaching is defined as "the guidance of learning activities." Teaching, then, is not simply "telling the lesson." Teaching cannot take place unless it is accompanied by learning. Below are some suggestions for what to do, from presession until the class is over, in order that learning may take place.

Preparing the Room

Sunday school begins before the first child arrives, that is, when the teacher arrives—which should be at least fifteen minutes before the regular Sunday school time. It is the teacher's responsibility to make sure that the room is properly ventilated, that lights are on, that equipment is in place, and that everything is clean.

Welcoming the Child

Each child should be greeted on arrival in the class, first by the secretary, then by his assigned teacher, and finally by the department leader. The secretary should be seated at a desk near the entrance to the room. Here the offering may be taken, the roll checked, and other records filled out. The secretary may or may not talk to each child, depending on the circumstances. Some of

1

the records may be gained by observation, without questioning the child. However, a new secretary may need to ask for various kinds of information.

Some Sunday school teachers print each child's name on a tag and fasten the tag to the child's clothes. This makes identification easier for teachers and pupils as well. If the pupils can read, name tags on the teachers may be helpful. In some schools, children are divided into groups for various activities, and all of the children in a particular group wear tags of the same color or shape (such as birds, squirrels, or ducks).

The secretary becomes the first "friendly welcome" in the room. The secretary should be as helpful and as interested in the children as time allows. Conversation with the children may include:

1. The purpose of the offering
2. Special events in the life of the Sunday school
3. Exciting experiences in the child's life
4. The memory verse for the day
5. The worship center that will be used for children's church
6. Something interesting that will happen during Sunday school
7. A word of welcome after an absence
8. Directions for hanging up a wrap, hat, or raincoat

Presession Activities

The teacher should see that every child enters into some presession activity. Children who come early should not have to sit and wait fifteen, or even five, minutes before Sunday school begins. When teachers properly prepare a room, the environment will invite children to become immediate participants in some activity.

Presession activities do not have to teach the children new facts in order to make a significant contribution. A simple activity such as looking at a book or examining a world globe may give a child a feeling of belonging to the class. As a result of the presession activity, the way is paved for better teaching of the Word of God.

Presession activities are not designed to *prepare* children to learn. All of life is a learning experience, whether good or bad. Presession actually teaches. It provides a bridge between the child's world at home and the world of the church. The activities of presession may differ in kind and intensity from the lesson activities, but learning happens before Bible school begins.

Presession should be planned so that activities may be curtailed at any point. It should start as soon as the children begin arriving and continue until Bible school time. Presession should be exploratory and introductory in nature. Also, it should motivate to further interest in the morning lesson. For presession activities you may use:

1. A record player and some good records
2. A musical instrument (ukulele, guitar, or zither)
3. A three-dimensional viewer and picture reels
4. Story strip display of Bible verses
5. Bible activities
6. Bible games
7. Bible puzzles
8. Picture puzzles
9. A display of books on a table
10. Work on a mural of frieze
11. A small animal or pet from home
12. Pictures
13. Objects from nature
14. An interesting tack board
15. Collections of some type
16. A display of Bible money
17. Handwork from last Sunday's lesson

Large-Group Activities

Children should arrange their chairs in a circle or semicircle if at all possible. If children must be arranged in rows, they should never be placed more than three rows deep. Notice children at a street parade, before a department store Christmas display, or where the Good Humor man is selling ice cream. Each child wants to be as close to the front as possible. A circular seating arrangement helps children feel that they are part of the group, and it combats inattention, because no one is behind someone else or back in a corner of the room.

Perhaps tables will have to be moved back against the wall to make room for group seating. In planning lessons, consider the arrangement of the room and the possibilities of quick rearrangement. Avoid having more tables in the room than necessary, since they take up considerable space. Each teacher should sit in the circle with the children.

1. *Worship experiences, prayer, and Bible reading.* A child *can* worship God. Adults sometimes think of worship as atmosphere, ritual, or a "deep" Bible lesson. Actually, however, worship is simply a person's returning "worth-ship" to God, who deserves all praise. Worship is God's receiving and man's giving. Children can give praise to God, and he delights to receive praise from them. Sophisticated, earthbound adults often have difficulty centering their thoughts on God alone. But a child is single-minded; he can worship God in simplicity.

2. *Activities using pictures, the Bible, or other materials.* Children need to wiggle every three or four minutes. Do not be afraid to let them move about during group activities. During a Bible story a little boy suddenly gets up and runs to the window. He is not being disobedient, even though he was told to "sit still." He simply sees a bird outside the window. Curiosity rules a large section of a little child's mind.

   Sometimes the entire group may be taken for a picture walk and told a story in pictures as they travel around the room. The children may be taken to the window to see something God has made, or they may be engaged in some other activity requiring mass movement.

3. *Sharing.* What children are told is not nearly as important as what they tell their teacher. When the teacher verbalizes a Bible truth to the class, they may or may not learn, but when a child can verbalize a Bible truth, he has learned that truth. Learn to listen to children.

   "Show and tell" is not simply a device to take up time; it is a means of satisfying a child's social drive of "belonging." Also, "show and tell" improves communication skills, adds interest to Sunday school lessons, and indicates that the lessons are "getting through."

   Sharing may be informal conversation between the teacher

and one or more children in the large group. Visitors may be recognized or birthdays remembered. This is "sharing time." Guard against letting the regular weekly recognition of birthdays degenerate into an unhealthy amount of attention for one child or become simply a ritual.

A good way to remember a birthday is to send a card to the home or to make a birthday visit. Why just give a child a "pat on the back" for growing a year older when he had nothing to do with it? Why not remind him of God's care over him during the past year and challenge him to a closer walk with his Lord during the coming year?

4. *Members of a team of teachers.* One teacher may play a more obvious role as he or she assumes direct leadership of the class; however, each teacher should feel responsible for the entire session. The lead teacher is responsible for coordinating the entire lesson so that the pupils work together with the teachers. At times the class will be divided into small groups with each teacher responsible for leading certain activities. Even when a teacher is not in an obvious role of leadership, he should not sit back and take a mental vacation. The silent teacher should be observing the pupils' responses, evaluating an activity, or giving support to the guiding teacher. Therefore, every teacher is at all times an active part of the team.

Small-Group Activities

Throughout all of the time we spend in Sunday school, we are teaching, whether we realize it or not. We are communicating attitudes, appreciations, and values. Some of the most effective teaching is achieved in small-group situations.

Small-group work is important for success in Sunday school. A teacher cannot always interact with the children in a large group. If a child has received a mistaken idea, there is no chance to correct it. If a child has a question, he is given no chance to ask it. In a small group a teacher has a better chance to guide each child and develop his spiritual maturity.

Every pupil must feel needed in his class at church. His thinking should follow these lines: *This is my group. I really belong here. My teacher really cares about me. The other pupils care about me too. I like my class.*

Teaching is guiding learning activities. Learning activities are any exercises or endeavors that help to accomplish the aims of a Sunday school lesson. Certain characteristics of learning activities should be present in every Sunday school class, whether it is large or small, well equipped or poorly equipped, rural or urban. Some of these are listed below:

1. Activities should be related to the Scriptures.
2. Activities should be suited to the age, interests, and special needs of the students.
3. Activities should make good use of time, place, curriculum, and equipment.
4. Suggestions from the children should be used whenever possible.
5. Every activity should provide opportunities for learning.
6. Activities should encourage involvement.

Interest Centers

Activity teaching calls for greater mobility among teachers and pupils, more innovation, and more exciting interest centers than have been in the traditional Sunday school. A wide range of Christian educational media and technological help is available for use in interest centers. The interest center in the Sunday school may be geared to meet various needs: the need for independent study, the need for small-group listening and reading, the need for large-group resources, the need for small-group conferences or conversation, and the need for individual or group instruction.

The interest center, then, is also an activity center and a resource center in which equipment and materials are provided for work, study, and play. The interest centers may be made available to children for self-chosen activities during presession time or for guided small-group activities during class time. Learning is enhanced by the provision of interesting, varied activities for listening and learning by doing.

In making room arrangement, teachers should plan for flexibility and versatility. *Functional* is the key word. Virtually any room may be transformed into a delightful life laboratory with proper planning.

There are endless possibilities for resource centers that will give your room an enticing atmosphere for learning. The suggestions given here are by no means exhaustive. A resourceful teacher can always add a personal touch here and there.

1. *Library Center.* Good books about animals, birds, and flowers, Bible stories, puzzles, and pictures.

2. *Art Center.* Easels (with smocks or paint aprons nearby), finger paints, drawing paper, blunt scissors, paste, crayons, construction paper, and plenty of newspaper (to place under the easels and on tables).

3. *Activity Center.* Wood blocks, stand-up figures, building blocks, trucks, cars, airplanes, and rubber balls.

4. *Listening Center.* Record player, plastic records of quiet music for relaxation to create an atmosphere conducive to prayer and Bible study. Records containing great hymns, gospel songs, stories, and poems should also be kept on hand.

5. *Nature Center.* A garden box of potted or flowering plants, shell display, or mounted butterflies.

6. *Show-and-Tell Shelf.* Articles and objects supplied by the children each week.

7. *Worship Center.* A table covered with a plain white cloth on which is placed an open Bible along with a world globe, a lamp, a candle, or a flower. A picture may sometimes serve as the worship center.

8. *Housekeeping Center.* Appropriate size rocking chair, sofa, tea table, and toy telephone. Kitchen with a cupboard, dishes, a sink, a stove, pots and pans, an ironing board, laundry equipment, a broom and dust pan, etc. Dolls, a doll's bed, and doll's clothes.

Some people would argue that a "housekeeping center" has no place in a Sunday school, since Sunday school time is not for play. But a child often learns a lesson best by playing it out. This is his opportunity for application of the lesson truths. If he learns to "play" (live out the lesson) with others in the place where the

Word of God is taught, he will be better able to make application of the lesson at home during the week.

The biggest problem facing many Sunday school teachers is lack of space. There is often not much room for interest centers. If this is the case in your classroom, resource center space could be changed each week or every two or three weeks.

Clean-up Time

Look in on any of the children's classrooms in the average Sunday school during the last few minutes of class time and you will see one or more teachers scurrying around, cleaning up after the morning's activity. Wouldn't it be better if the children learned to clean up and put away the materials they use? Granted, a teacher may be able to clean up after activities twice as fast as the pupils would, but why lose another valuable teaching opportunity? Why not teach that cleaning up is a vital part of the activity? Learning how to clean up can become for the children a matter of pride.

ACTIVITY, LAW OF

One of the laws of learning is the Law of Activity, stated as follows: "Learning is most effective when the student is involved in the learning process." An old Chinese proverb suggests the most efficient way to learn: "I hear and I forget; I see and I remember; I do and I understand." In many Sunday school classes, teachers do not proceed past the first phrase. Someone has facetiously remarked, "In most Sunday schools, students need to possess only one of the five senses—hearing." No pictures, maps, or projected visuals are shown. Children do not feel the wool in a sheep's coat nor rocky soil. They have no idea what a pomegranate looks like, let alone how it tastes. And adults do not ask questions or share ideas.

This law of learning emphasizes the necessity of student involvement. Teaching is the organization and guidance of learning activities. Therefore, if the student is not involved, there is little if any teaching or learning. Teaching activities that encourage participation ensure 90 percent retention. It is commonly called "activity teaching." Numerous activities or experiences will help to produce learning, which occurs when the student absorbs a new truth and believes it so fully that it makes a change in his life. To learn more about specific learning activities, consult the articles on those activities in this book.

ADMINISTRATION, GIFT OF

The gift of administration includes the ability to perceive needs, to organize and administer programs, and then to evaluate the results in the light of biblical objectives. The strengths of this gift include (1) the ability to see the overall picture and think of long-range objectives, (2) the ability to delegate tasks to other people, (3) the quality of being task oriented rather than person or need oriented, (4) the ability to counsel and motivate others regarding the task and (5) the ability to judge tasks by objectives rather than by perfectionistic standards.

Among the weaknesses of this gift are (1) the appearance of wanting to get out of work (because he delegates), (2) the appearance of being insensitive to people and inflexible in God's work (because of being committed to long-range goals), and (3) the appearance of being a glorified bureaucrat. A person with this gift needs to avoid the danger of (1) becoming power-hungry, (2) using people to accomplish goals (manipulation), or (3) lowering standards to use anyone (in spite of character flaws or doctrinal errors) to get a job done.

ADMINISTRATION, LAW OF

Administration of a growing Sunday school is imperative. As the Sunday school grows in numbers, administrators must be added to give supervision for efficiency and continual outreach. The Law of Administration recommends that administrators represent 5 percent of the total attendance. The administrators are the grease and oil that keep the Sunday school machinery lubricated. Since the church is both an organism and organization, the Sunday school must have organization to keep the spiritual outreach from breaking down.

What is organization? It is the action or process of putting the right person in the right place to do the right thing in the right way, with the right tools, at the right time, for the right purpose.

ADULT BIBLE CLASS

The adult Sunday school class can be one of the most effective tools of church outreach available today. When used properly, it takes advantage of inherent principles of church growth. The adult class members, implementing the homogeneous principle, can bring new people to church, making it possible for visitors to respond to Christ with fewer barriers to cross. The class members can apply *web evangelism* to bring their friends and relatives to Christ. When the unsaved visit the class with a friend, they are coming through *side-door evangelism*. The class can also advertise and visitors will come through *front-door evangelism*.

How to Strengthen the Adult Bible Class

1. The teacher must give the class high spiritual priority. The success of any class lies in the commitment of its leaders to (a) reach, (b) teach, (c) win, and (d) mature adults in their relationship to Jesus Christ. The teacher should make this his first priority in serving the Lord. This means the teacher should not place his or her responsibilities of singing in the choir or committee membership ahead of the class. For married teachers, class leadership should normally involve both husband and wife.

2. The same room should be used each week. A classroom must be familiar and supportive to establish fellowship. Attendance is much more difficult to build if a different room is used every few months.

3. Get the members to decorate the room. Close fellowship is built through class projects. One of the best projects to foster group cohesiveness is to improve the room by wall-papering, hanging new drapes, painting the seats, or installing a small kitchen for coffee and doughnuts. Such activities make further use of talent within the class. Some adults, for example, will work diligently to improve the facilities, yet these same adults will feel inadequate to make an evangelistic call or to counsel people with spiritual problems.

4. Conduct regular class prayer meetings. God hears corporate prayer. "Again I say to you that if two of you agree on earth concerning anything that they ask, it will be done for them by My Father in heaven" (Matt. 18:19). Just as a church that prays together moves forward, so a Sunday school class that holds regular prayer meetings will win spiritual victories in the lives of its members. Perhaps a monthly Saturday morning prayer breakfast or a time of class prayer before visitation would be effective.

5. Serve the Lord as a class. Just as class projects strengthen class unity, so spiritual service will strengthen individuals. The class should learn that "we are God's fellow workers" (1 Cor. 3:9). Serving together can begin with tangible jobs such as painting, folding bulletins, or housekeeping jobs around the church. Another type of project might be raising money for missionaries, delivering church newspapers or posters, conducting meetings at a rescue mission, or visiting in a senior saint's home.

6. Give the class a distinctive name. Members will more readily identify with the class if it has a unique identity. Also, prospective members will find the class more personable. Choose a name for the class that suggests its age group, its mission or purpose, its geographic location—or one that is agreed upon by all. A contest to choose a name does not always produce one that is reflective of the class's purpose and existence.

7. Select a logo for the class. Just as a church may use a picture of its steeple or a motto on its bulletin, choose a symbol to identify the class. As an illustration, a class for young single adults entitled "Single Vision" used the logo of a young man and woman standing on a hill and looking off into the future.

8. Select a class motto. Just as a church used the slogan The Drive Is Worth the Distance, so a class could use a motto such as Where the Bible Is Taught and Fellowship Is Caught.

9. Create a distinctive letterhead and envelopes. These can be used on occasions where letters or flyers will be sent to the

class members. On some occasions the church stationary will be used, while on other occasions the class should have its own distinctive letterhead that focuses attention on the class.

10. Distribute a class newspaper or newsletter. There should be regular communication to every member on a weekly, monthly, or bimonthly basis. Some members are not regular in attendance, so a class newspaper will keep them informed of activities and be a constant reminder for them to attend the class. Whereas the actual typesetting and printing of a newspaper may be expensive, there are inexpensive ways to print a class newspaper or newsletter. A typewriter or personal computer can be used for typesetting, and perhaps a photocopying machine would print enough copies for a small class. Stationery stores have special lettering packages available to paste up headlines and titles.

At least five types of material should appear in a class newspaper. First, news of coming events; second, the names of class visitors; third, class projects; fourth, statistics such as attendance, offerings, number of visitors; and fifth, a short challenge from the teacher.

11. Elect officers and workers. Every class should have a president to take care of business. In some classes, he is called the class leader or class director. The class president is different from the teacher whose main responsibility is the ministry of the Word of God. The class will also need a secretary/treasurer (one or two persons according to the size of the class). One person may serve as a vice-president with two or three jobs, or the jobs can be divided among three people called first, second, and third vice president. The first vice-president should be responsible for outreach and visitation. The second vice-president should be in charge of ministering to the needs in the class. This involves visiting the sick, following up on absentees, and dealing with special needs. The third vice-president should handle publicity and advertisement, both of evangelistic outreach and of special events.

12. Balance evangelism and education. Some adult classes have a strong evangelistic outreach, but are weak on education. As a result, many class members drop out of the church, hence blunting their effectiveness for soul winning. On the other hand, some classes are strong in nurturing with an intensive Bible teaching program and a concentration on the devotional life. Both are good and necessary, but the key to a successful class is balance. The enemy would love to get an adult Sunday school class emphasizing one to the exclusion of the other, thus crippling its ministry.

13. Tie members to the worship service. Some strong adult classes have drifted away from the local church; a few have even broken fellowship with the church that gave them birth. This happened because members came to Sunday school but neglected the church. Sometimes all the tithes and offerings went to the class, and not to the church. On other occasions class projects took priority over the local church's outreach. Establish a "both/and" relationship. Every class member must be a member of both the church and the Sunday school. The old adage is still true: Those who come to Sunday school must stay for church, and those who come for church must come early enough for Sunday school. There is a place for both to be in both, and if both are not in both, there is something wrong with both.

14. Use an overhead projector. Adults learn in ways that are comfortable and familiar. For the most part, adults live in an electronic age. They learn through teaching aids that plug into the wall. Therefore, use the overhead projector, a practical and available tool, to communicate the Word of God. The overhead projector will make it possible for the teacher to prepare questions, outlines, quotations, and Scripture verses before class. Also, diagrams, charts, and pictures can be projected for instruction and application.

15. Provide refreshments. While some might oppose eating and drinking in church, there is a growing trend in churches to provide refreshments during the Sunday school hour. Cof-

fee and doughnuts are not a gimmick to attract a crowd, nor are they a Sunday morning substitute for the work-week coffee break that is usually taken by employees around 10:00 A.M. When Christians eat and drink together, they are fellowshipping and building class unity. As early Christians were found "breaking bread from house to house" (Acts 2:46), so refreshments produce "Bible study with fellowship." The Sunday school class should be a place to do more than just teach Bible content. Bible studies are most effective when conducted in a spirit of fellowship with other Christians. Here members ask questions, express needs, and share their lives with one another. Eating in Sunday school, then, can be regarded as a means to the end of creating an atmosphere where fellowship and learning can take place.

16. Focus on needs. It is one thing to teach the Bible, but it is entirely different to apply the Bible to the needs of class members. To do this, the teacher must know the needs of the class members. As he asks questions and gives others an opportunity to share, he learns the spiritual condition of members.

17. Be sure that someone is at the door to meet all class members as they arrive. This person could be seated at a table to take roll, meet new visitors, and create a friendly environment for people as they enter the classroom.

18. Use name tags. If everyone wears a name tag, then people will get to know one another better, and they will be able to call others by their first names.

19. Set goals for new visitors. Everyone realizes they should bring friends to Sunday school, but most people forget to invite them. Therefore, have a "goal Sunday," when everyone is responsible to bring a friend. To get 100 percent cooperation, ask each person to share the name of the person to be invited two weeks before goal Sunday. Then have them pray for that person, write a special invitation letter, or give a special invitation by phone. These people

who are made specific goals and given specific invitations will usually attend.

20. Make the class friendly. Too often Sunday school is thought of as a dull place and a boring hour on Sunday morning. Only those in charge can change that attitude. If they determine to be friendly, the class will be receptive to visitors and new members.

These twenty steps will not guarantee growth, for eternal growth comes from God. But if these twenty steps are followed, God may honor your efforts and cause the Sunday school to grow spiritually as well as numerically.

ADULT DEPARTMENT

Often a church will divide its adult department into three sections: young adults (in their twenties and thirties), middle-aged adults (in their forties and fifties), and senior adults (over sixty). Each of these groups has its own unique characteristics, which influence the way one can effectively minister to them.

Characteristics of Young Adults

Full grown and in the prime of life, young marrieds are busy with jobs, homemaking, and child rearing. Singles among them are careerminded. They are all developing hobbies, skills, and abilities.

They are still young enough to recall and relive their youth but old enough to understand life's responsibilities. Because of the drive to succeed, they often appear aggressive. They have great reasoning power and a desire to feel useful. Most are concerned about others.

Some are inclined toward feelings of failure and unhappiness or pessimism. Some are totally wrapped up in their own pursuits, oblivious to the needs or interests of others. In their preoccupation, these are hard to reach.

Because most young adults enjoy social gatherings, they may be enlisted through a social invitation.

The usual way of dividing this group is by providing one class for the singles and another for the young marrieds. Classes usually consist of a president, vice president, and secretary, with social, mission, and visitation committees.

Aims in Teaching Young Adults
1. To offer salvation and opportunities for Christian growth
2. To guide in the development of Christian life and character
3. To encourage activity in Christian service
4. To help establish both the family altar and personal devotional time
5. To help them adjust to the single life, or to married life, to the coming of children, and to the task of maintaining a Christian home
6. To help them grow within the fellowship of the church

Methods for Teaching Young Adults
A good teacher will produce teachers. This class has the greatest potential for producing other Sunday school teachers and workers. Therefore, the program should be geared toward getting these people involved in the study of the Word for themselves. It should help them mature in Christ and form convictions about Christian life and thought and about the Christian home. These convictions should be the result of research, thought, and discussion. This group learns through:

Research—biblical, archaeological, geographical

Reports—based on research previously assigned

Brainstorming—informal ideas briefly stated about a suggested theme

Lectures—talks augmented with pictures and other aids for interest and retention

Questions and answers—grab-bag questions that encourage participation

Memorization—the use of cards or signs

Discussion—group participation in a search for answers

Social events—once-a-month get-togethers to create class unity

Projects—visitation, transportation assistance to older people, preparation of visual aids for the Sunday school or vacation Bible school, and ministry to shut-ins

Teaching attitudes should make students feel wanted and comfortable. Use a vocabulary that students understand. Illustrate lessons with incidents related to the adult's everyday life. Back your teaching with Scripture. Be sincerely enthusiastic. Teach what interests your class, not what you think it needs.

Bible study should be well balanced. It may take the form of Bible survey, church history, a book study (such as the Gospel of John), Bible character studies, topical studies (such as witnessing or love), or Christian living (for example, personal evangelism, teaching Sunday school, building a Christian home, and training children).

Middle-aged Adults

Physically, while middle-aged adults generally have good health, there is a slight loss of vigor. This can be a period of great physical breakdown. To meet class needs the teachers should emphasize daily trust in the Lord for strength, help members utilize their talents with direction, and encourage them to share resources with those less fortunate. Middle-aged adults also should be encouraged to use time and energy for God's glory by facing their responsibilities as examples to younger persons. All should participate in the social life of the class without going to the extremes in sports and vigorous activity.

Mentally, some adults of middle age years tend to dread the future. Some are disillusioned over failure to achieve their goals. As parents and grandparents, they feel multiplied burdens and responsibilities. Their mental powers are keen and productive, and their minds are generally mature. Positive teaching should be a common focus of teaching to counteract the fear of the future. Show the futility of worry, and stress the power of Christ, the unfailing one. Teachers should emphasize the essentials of life, giving biblical reasons and explanations for assertions. Members should be used on committees so they can share their mature insights. Teachers should encourage discussion in order to understand how members are thinking. Reading programs should be fostered to expand their minds. Where possible, capable adults should be used as Sunday school teachers in classes to train other teachers.

Socially, middle-agers feel empty when their children are grown and gone. Some are burdened by shattered dreams. Others may feel unwanted and unnecessary. Almost all have attained economic and social prestige.

Teaching should engage these adults in constructive service, helping them develop interest in new activities. Fellowship will help enlarge their circle of friends. They should be taught God's plan of giving—and guided and challenged to help others. They should also be given opportunity to use their influence in the community. They should be encouraged to take a Christian stand on social issues.

Spiritually, middle-aged adults tend to be critical about morals, though a desire for a "last fling" may be present. Life habits are intensified. The sweet becomes sweeter, the sour more so. Some exhibit spiritual pride. Teaching should engage these adults in searching for Bible truths concerning temptation and the truth about complete spiritual restoration. The certainty that Christ is their anchor—and that he can change bad habits—are truths that should be reinforced. Adults may be won, even at this age, through visitation and church activities. The necessity of spiritual growth should be emphasized, since chronological age and spiritual age are not always equal.

Senior Adults

Many adults in this age bracket have poor health, resulting in loss of skills and abilities. They may need help in transportation and sometimes need special equipment to make them more comfortable in the church.

Intellectual growth may be in spurts. Thinking may become vague and conservative, with reluctance to embrace what is new.

This group needs more short-term studies—meditation and challenge rather than sharp, detailed analysis. Their importance should be recognized at anniversaries. They can help make scrapbooks and visual aids. Let them serve on short-term and advisory committees to prevent their feeling slighted and overlooked. Some may be critical of younger people; encourage them to pray instead.

Economically, many older adults are reaping benefits of well-invested money, while others are disillusioned because they can't support themselves on what they have saved. The teacher can inform this over-sixty group about the benefits of Christian trust funds and other resources.

Socially, many of this age group need occasions to be together with others to ease loneliness caused by friends passing away. For those who are shut-ins, one of the department teachers should take work for them to do at home, and visit them regularly. The church should also teach young people the responsibility of supporting and visiting their parents so they will not be neglected and lonely.

Spiritually, many elderly members are mature, with a well-rounded outlook on problems. Some tend to live in their spiritual past. Others have become lonely and bitter. Many begin to fear death.

The church can help older members feel needed by asking them to give testimonies of God's faithfulness in their lives. Activities and programs should foster spiritual friendships. Teaching should prepare them to accept Christ's victory over death and give them hope in his resurrection and second coming.

AGE-GRADED SUNDAY SCHOOL
The age-graded Sunday school has an organized class for each age. While this represents one class for each age in the children's departments, and usually one class for each five years in the adult department, the Sunday school usually plateaus in average attendance at approximately 750 to 1,000 pupils. This is the upper limit of growth in the closely graded or age-graded Sunday school. An age-graded Sunday school adds a department (an average of forty) for each school grade and a department of adults (each class division covering a five year span; for example, men ages thirty to thirty-four).

AIDS, MINISTERING TO PEOPLE WITH
Acquired Immune Deficiency Syndrome (AIDS) is an infection caused by the Human Immunodeficiency Virus (HIV). This virus greatly reduces or sometimes destroys the body's immune system. The immune system is the body's defense system, responsible for fighting disease. Because the immune system is weakened in a person with AIDS, infections normally harmless to a healthy

person can be very dangerous or even fatal. These normally harmless infections are called opportunistic infections.

It is estimated that more than one million Americans are HIV infected. If the symptoms of infection are mild, the individual has AIDS Related Complex or ARC. When the symptoms become severe and opportunistic infections occur, the individual has AIDS. The time period between being infected with the virus and developing symptoms is called the incubation period. The incubation period for ARC and AIDS can range from a few months to ten years.

According to the most recent research published by the Institute of Medicine, the National Academy of Sciences, and the American Red Cross, the AIDS virus spreads through infected persons to others by sexual intercourse, direct blood transfer, and intravenous drug use. The virus can also be passed on from infected mothers to their babies during pregnancy, at birth, or shortly after birth.

AIDS is caused by a virus that does not survive well outside the body. The virus is not usually spread by casual nonsexual contact. Scientists have not found any instance in which the AIDS virus has been transmitted through ordinary nonsexual contact in a family or social setting.

Ministry Opportunities in the AIDS Epidemic

Because of the nature of AIDS and its effects, not only on the one immediately infected by the disease, but also on others in the family, unique ministry opportunities exist for those concerned about effectively ministering to people and families with AIDS. The AIDS epidemic is not only a medical crisis and national public health emergency; it is also a spiritual challenge.

Some churches have responded to the unique situation of children with AIDS by establishing a "family class" for families who desire their children with AIDS to be kept under their own supervision during Sunday school. In many cases, this class may be the basis of a support group for families with AIDS-infected children.

Opportunities for ministry also exist in a visitation program to children and adults who are hospitalized or home-bound with chronic or terminal illnesses. These home and hospital visits would be means to communicate the gospel message, provide

Christian education materials from their class, or share a gift or greetings from others in the church.

Proclaiming life in the face of death has always been a primary goal for the church. The church's ministry to the dying is one that should be extended to persons with AIDS. Christians can minister to terminally ill AIDS patients through a variety of practical actions, which may include sitting at bedsides, listening to lonely people, and taking opportunities to share the gospel message to those who are suffering.

Some churches have opted to advertise their willingness to minister to AIDS victims. If this is done, it should be performed in such a way as to express the church's willingness to minister to HIV-infected persons and at the same time communicate to other families in the church and community that such a ministry policy poses no health threat to them. One church in a large metropolitan area has the following text posted in its Christian education facility:

> Parents: Christian education workers consider the well-being of your child a serious trust. While all persons who wish to participate with us will certainly be welcomed, we have instituted universal precautions as established by the Center for Disease Control to minimize the risk of spread of communicable diseases. As such, no person who has been diagnosed as being HIV positive or having AIDS will be excluded from any of the ministries or activities of the church. We are committed to keeping you informed concerning these matters and encourage your continued support.

The church ministering to HIV-infected persons may need to consider a number of practical renovations to its facilities to minimize the health risks involved in such a ministry. Some of these renovations may involve the installation of sinks with paddle-lever faucets, antimicrobial treatment in all new carpets, toilet seat cover dispensers in all toilet facilities, disposable mattress and changing-table sheet covers for the nursery and toddlers' class, and trash bags, twist-ties, and covered trash cans. Also, first-aid kits throughout the facilities should be supplemented with latex gloves, paper towels, sawdust, a dust pan and hand brush, a spray with Basic-G Germicide, plastic bags, and caution signs to be used when cleaning up blood or other body fluids.

Because of the health risks that may be associated with ministry to HIV-infected persons, all regular Christian education workers, paid staff, maintenance workers, and volunteers should be trained in communicable disease control measures. Care should be taken to ensure that these measures are administered routinely, especially when handling blood or body fluids from any child.

Procedure for Handling Blood and Body Fluid Spills

The Center for Disease Control has established a set of universal precautions for handling spills of blood or body fluids to minimize the risk of spreading a communicable disease. These should be adapted for use in a church ministry as follows:

These guidelines are to be followed by any worker with actual or potential exposure to a child's blood or body fluids. Body fluids include saliva, sputum, urine, fecal material, nasal discharge, and discharge from open skin sores, sweat, and tears.

1. Gloves must be worn for touching blood and body fluids, mucous membranes (eyes, nose, or mouth) or non-intact skin (cuts or open sores), and for handling items or surfaces soiled with blood or body fluids. Gloves should be changed after each contact.
2. Hands and other skin surfaces should be washed immediately and thoroughly if exposed to blood or body fluids. Hands should be washed immediately after gloves are removed. Careful handwashing after each contact is essential to prevent spread of infection.
3. Cleaning of body fluids on any surface shall be done with gloves. The surface on which a spill occurred (or on which a child's diaper was changed, if a nonporous barrier was not used) shall be cleaned with Basic-G Disinfectant. Where possible, the use of nonporous barriers is encour-

aged to simplify cleanup after changing diapers. The use of such barriers does not negate the responsibility of the worker to ensure that proper cleanup of inadvertent spillage has been done.

4. No worker who has an exudation or weeping skin sore shall handle any situation involving potential blood or body fluid contact.

5. All contaminated cleanup materials shall be disposed of in sealed plastic trash bags and placed in a larger trash bag out of the reach of children.

6. All wounds or open sores must be covered, in workers or children.

7. Ideally, toys soiled by saliva should never be shared and should be washed in Basic-G after each use.

8. Toileting of children with poor personal hygiene should be done by an adult wearing gloves. Gloves should be disposed of immediately.

Developing an AIDS Policy for Your Church

A growing number of churches have prepared a written statement outlining their policies and procedures related to their ministry to HIV-infected persons. The following statement represents a specimen policy statement and is based on similar statements that have been adopted by evangelical churches involved to some degree with ministry to HIV-infected persons.

It is our intention as a church not to discriminate against any person with AIDS. Therefore, no person who has been diagnosed as being HIV positive or having AIDS will be excluded from any of the ministries and activities of the church.

We desire to avoid reactions based upon exaggerated fears and prejudice. We do, however, have the responsibility to protect the health and safety of both our staff and those who attend the church. While all persons who wish to participate with us will certainly be welcomed, we have instituted universal precautions as established by the Center for Disease Control to minimize the risk of spreading a communicable disease.

Parents bringing a child to any children's ministry for the first time will be asked to complete a registration form, which will include the following question: "Is your child known to have one of the following chronic communicable diseases declared as communicable by the Center for Disease Control or State Department of Public Health? (1) Hepatitis Type B, (2) Human Immunodeficiency Virus (HIV), (3) Herpes Simplex Virus, (4) AIDS. Medical information gathered on this form will be kept confidential and be communicated only to staff directly involved with that child."

Parents bringing a child to the nursery are encouraged to bring the child's own toys from home. They will be routinely placed in a cloth bag that will hang from the crib. Cloth bags will be laundered each week. Other toys in the nursery will be sprayed with Basic-G and wiped after each use.

Children who have tested HIV positive and who are not toilet trained may not be able to be cared for by the church nursery or Sunday school program workers. Also, children with weeping sores or aggressive biting behaviors will be remanded to the parent or adult guardian. A decision on attendance shall be based on (1) the risk of transmission of the disease to others, (2) the health risk to the particular child, and (3) whether reasonable accommodations can be made to reduce health risks to the child and others.

No individual who exhibits physical evidence of a communicable disease or illness or an unbandaged wound or lesion will work directly with food preparation and serving. All individuals involved in food preparation and service shall begin by thoroughly washing their hands.

Parents who have children or youth through grade twelve who have tested HIV positive must indicate so on the registration form before their child participates in extracurricular activities that could involve risk.

Adults who have tested HIV positive must indicate on the registration form before they may participate in extracurricular activities that could involve risk.

Understanding that much research is continuing in the study of AIDS and other communicable diseases, the response of this church to these conditions may change as other circumstances change. This policy will be reviewed and updated as needed.

Additional information concerning the development of an AIDS policy for your church may be obtained from The Evangelical Free Church in Bemidji, Minnesota; Calvary Memorial Church in Oak Park, Illinois; and the Pentecostal Assemblies of Newfoundland, Box 8248, St. John's, Newfoundland, A1B 3N4.

AIMS IN TEACHING

In many respects, aims are the key to effective ministry as a Sunday school teacher. A clear aim guides Bible study; gives unity, order, and efficiency to teaching; gives teachers confidence in the classroom; helps teachers use time efficiently, helps teachers select teaching aids and methods; and helps teachers evaluate a lesson.

There are three kinds of aims a teacher may choose in a lesson. An *educational aim* focuses on what a teacher wants a student to know at the conclusion of the lesson. An *emotional aim* focuses on what a teacher wants a student to feel at the conclusion of the lesson. A *volitional aim* focuses on what a teacher wants a student to do at the conclusion of the lesson.

The aim selected by the teacher depends largely on the teacher's perceived need in the class. Three adult teachers teaching the same lesson on missions might select three different kinds of aims. One may choose to communicate statistical information about the effectiveness of the church in accomplishing the great commission. A second teacher may want his pupils to become concerned about a particular people group that is unreached. A third teacher may teach with a view to raising money for a special missions project or enlisting workers for a short-term missions project.

The aims of the Sunday school teacher are to be determined by the needs prevailing within the class. Teaching is meeting needs.

Hence, the prime and foremost aim of the teacher should be to meet the spiritual needs of pupils in the class.

General Teaching Aims for the Pupil

1. To win every person in your class to Christ. Soul winning is the primary purpose of the Sunday school. This objective may be realized by the clear presentation of the gospel in the classroom, saturated with much prayer, by personal evangelism, and by counseling. Home visitation may give opportunities for the teacher to help the pupil in spiritual matters.

2. To cause every student to grow spiritually. Conversion is only a starting point in the Christian's life. He must now "grow up into" and mature if he is to continue on in the faith and be fruitful. The learning of Bible truths, as well as instruction concerning the Christian life, daily reading of the Word, and communion with God through prayer, will cause him to mature.

3. To help the students evangelize others. Many in the community are eligible for class membership. We must not be satisfied with only the present class members; we must bring in others. God commands us to go and teach all nations and all people about him. The people of your community can be reached through visitation to the homes. Encourage your pupils to bring their friends and have a part in reaching souls who need a Savior.

General Teaching Aims of the Curriculum

The curriculum plays an important role in our teaching ministry. The teacher should therefore aim:

1. To make the best use of methods and materials. In these modern times we have access to many excellent methods and materials. We should aim to acquaint ourselves with the various materials and then seek to make the best use of them. The church library, commentaries, study helps, and Christian publishing houses offer much in this area.

2. To teach the Bible. Our aim is to get the Bible into the student and the student into the Bible. The curriculum is centered around it and in it—the Bible is the Sunday school teacher's

curriculum. God has promised that his Word will never return unto him void, and therefore, we can go forth teaching it as efficiently as we can.

General Teaching Aims of the Teacher

1. To be an example. The teacher's words have no value if they are not backed up by a consistent Christian life. A warm heart and unwavering faith will do more teaching than anything that is said. We should remember here Colossians 3:17, "And whatever you do in word or deed, do all in the name of the Lord Jesus, giving thanks to God the Father through Him."
2. To continually grow in his own life. Constant study of the Bible will help the teacher to acquaint the students with it and thus cause a love for study on their part. The teacher must assimilate God's Word before he can convey it to others.
3. To dedicate self. The teacher must accept the teaching of his class as God's work and appointment and therefore dedicate himself wholly to it. His time, talents, and prayer life should center around his work. The teaching hour should be the highlight of the week.
4. To have a heart of compassion and understanding. A genuine Christlike love is only obtainable from God himself. Through prayer, God will instill a compassion for the lost and a desire to see Christians grow.
5. To know his students' needs, as individuals and as part of the group. First, know their individual backgrounds, attitudes, handicaps, and general characteristics. Visiting their homes can reveal much for the Sunday school teacher to appropriate in his preparations and presentation.

   Second, know them as a group. People in a group act and think differently. They want to be accepted by all. As a group they will do things that each individual would hesitate doing when alone. Carefully watch their response to one another and to authority.

The teacher should aim to know his students in all circumstances. Such occasions as parties, church functions, and group endeavors will give him opportunity to observe keenly.

AMERICAN SUNDAY SCHOOL UNION (1824–1970)

The American Sunday School Union was the primary agency for the development of the American Sunday school. Founded in 1824, the ASSU was primarily a lay movement committed to using the Sunday school to teach Americans moral and democratic values. The threefold purpose of the Union was (1) to organize Sunday school leaders, (2) to publish religious literature for Sunday school, and (3) to develop new Sunday schools in unreached population centers.

As early as 1832, the ASSU organized America's first national Sunday school convention. They published the first widely used Sunday school lessons and a 100-volume Sunday school library for children. Their best known missionary thrust was the Mississippi Valley Enterprise launched in 1830. In time, this thrust led to the establishment of thousands of new Sunday schools.

Following the American Civil War, the rise of Sunday school conventions and denominational involvement in Sunday school weakened the influence of the ASSU. The Sunday School Union continued its ministry, primarily in rural communities, but lacked the successes of its early history. In 1970, the ASSU changed its name to the American Missionary Society to reflect its new focus on working primarily with multicultural and ethnic groups to form new churches.

APPERCEPTION, LAW OF

The law of apperception is stated as follows: "Learning is most effective when students integrate the lesson with that which they already know." Apperception is integration. It is more than students reproducing outwardly the truths they have been taught. While verbalizing the truth is important, it is only the first step in learning. Students must also integrate the lesson into their lives so that they grow, become healthy in every aspect of life, and become more like the Lord Jesus Christ (Eph. 4:13-16).

When a teacher introduces material with which the student is not familiar, the teacher has created a problem. When a teacher talks about tithing but has not taught the historical background from the

Old Testament, the student may be confused. All new material must be built on a foundation of previously taught lessons.

Some teachers assume that past lessons have been stored away for future use. They treat the pupil's mind like a file folder. But lessons are like tools for service rather than file folders in musty old cabinets. Every lesson is like a hammer to be used in building a house.

Another problem is that teachers do not make pupils thoroughly familiar with foundational facts before proceeding to a new lesson. Review is essential for learning.

Another threat to apperception is the failure to connect the current lesson with the whole of life. Not only must teaching tie facts together, teaching must tie the lesson to life. Part of learning is "gestalt," or the insight that the student gets connecting facts and life-style.

A further threat to apperception is thinking that teaching is filling the students' heads with knowledge as one fills a glass with water. This approach to teaching treats knowledge as isolated "things" poured into the mind, rather than treating knowledge as power, influence, and life.

Students are like a river that was moving before coming into the class and will continue to flow after leaving class. When they enter class, we must add experiences and facts to their lives and realize that they will go out from the class to continue learning.

How to Apply Teaching

All teaching must advance in some direction. Teaching that is purposeless and repetitious is not proper teaching; it is empty and does not correlate with anything else in the classroom. It is all right to repeat a lesson, but repetition must have purpose and direction. It is said you cannot get new gold out of an old mine. That may be true—unless you dig deeper. In the same vein, you can dig deeper in some old lessons by repetition and get gold for the lives of students.

Knowledge is not a mass of simple, independent thoughts or ideas. Too often, people treat knowledge like a basket of potatoes, where each potato is separated from others by a skin. In much the same way, knowledge is treated as separate bits of things to learn.

This is a wrong view. Knowledge must be interrelated to have meaning. New lessons are learned by relating them to other aspects of knowledge. Good teaching will always relate fact-to-fact, fact-to-life, and life-to-life.

We should not ask students just to reproduce lessons in our words. Students may be able to fill in the answers on an objective test and yet not really know what has been taught. They must reproduce the lesson in their own words. Teachers must use words that are meaningful to pupils to express the lesson.

Learning is much more the work of the student than the work of the teacher. Too often we think that teachers who work hard are those who communicate best. Not so. Learning is the work of the students, and their lives are changed in direct proportion to their involvement in the lesson.

Teachers can evaluate the effectiveness of their teaching by determining if learning is occurring. Educational specialists employ a variety of means to review past lessons. These strategies serve both to reinforce lessons previously taught and to evaluate what has been learned. A number of these review strategies are discussed in the article on "Review Games."

APPLICATION, LAW OF

The law of application is stated: "Learning is most effective when lessons taught in the classroom are transferred into the life of the student." One of the most difficult tasks facing a teacher is the transfer of the material from a written lesson plan to everyday life. Going from ideas to shoe leather is a constant challenge. On some occasions a lesson will have a great impact on a student. At other times the impact will be less than we desire. What causes the difference? The following points may answer that question:

1. The needs of the student. The greater the need of the student, the greater the application. Remember, this is true of "felt needs," not necessarily "ultimate needs." If the pupils want something and they know they want it, they will absorb the lesson and apply it immediately. A student wanting to drive a car will pay close attention to the drivers' education teacher and try everything explained to them.

2. The nature of the lesson. A how-to lesson may hold the student's interest more than one that tells him what he should do or know. This means students will probably listen more carefully to a lesson on how to know the will of God than to a lesson on the nature of God.

3. The method of teaching. Questions and answers may elicit a higher degree of involvement than a lecture. As a result, there is more learning and more application. Sometimes the use of a story may cause the student to identify with the results more than the use of the brainstorming method. Teaching methods that require involvement usually have greater application value.

4. The past experience of the student. The law of apperception tells us that learning is most effective when we build our present lesson on the past experiences of our students. Just as it is impossible to climb a ladder that is suspended in midair, so it is impossible to make an application on a foundation that students do not yet understand.

5. The positive role model of the teacher. Students usually identify positively with teachers and attempt to become like them. Sometimes this identification is subconscious, and the student is not aware that they have made the identification. Whether they realize it or not, the student is influenced by the life-style of the teacher.

6. A close relationship between student and teacher. A number of studies indicate that the closer the relationship between teacher and student, the greater the teacher's influence.

7. The positive role model of other authority figures in the student's life. Not only will the teacher influence the student's life; so will other authority figures (such as a mother, principal, or boss). Sometimes the teacher can bring these persons into the lesson by stories, pictures, or direct references.

Healthy Steps to Transfer Teaching

The key to practical application is integrating the lesson with the student's past experiences. Teachers can take ten steps to ensure that the lesson is practically applied in the life-style of the student. They can:

1. Relate each Bible passage to the whole of Scripture. A lesson is like a spoke in a wheel; each is necessary for the whole. Teaching should relate a Bible chapter to the context of the entire book and then relate each book to the whole of Scripture. Since the student's mind tends to close any gap left in a circle, an effective teacher completes the circle by answering any open questions.

2. Relate each lesson to the whole of the student's life. Part of the process of learning is helping the student see how things fit together. To produce insight, show how the lesson relates to aspects of the student's life.

3. Use real illustrations from modern life. Students have difficulty relating to out-of-date illustrations. Students of the computer generation may not be able to relate to horse-pulled plows and houses without electricity. When illustrations solve modern problems, students identify with people in the story and apply the answers to their lives.

4. Use positive role models from Scripture. God has communicated his principles for his people through the lives of people in Scripture. God did not just use a catechism, doctrinal statement, or propositional statement to give us principles to live by. He included the lives of people in the Bible to guide our lives.

5. Identify positive role models already in the student's life. Several factors make a person effective as a role model. First, the role model must have discernible strength in the area in which they are used as an example. Second, the student must have a positive attitude toward the role model. Third, there must be a close relationship between the student and the role model.

6. Solve problems. Teaching that is effective is functional. When we identify problems in the lives of students and give them answers, they can transfer these lessons to their lives. It has been said, "Teaching is finding a hurt and healing it."

When we help students, we show the practical application of lessons.

7. Point out relationships with the truths in the lesson. Teaching is not just giving facts, but showing the relationship between facts so students remember the connection. Look for the "glue" that is already there. There is glue that holds human relationships together, ideas together, laws together, and data together. The gospel is the glue that bonds a man to God, and confession is the glue that keeps believers in good fellowship with him. Showing the glue of relationship is the task of teaching.

8. Point out principles. God does not expect his people to live by feelings, hunches, or blind faith. God wants them to live by biblical principles. The teacher should know these principles, point them out, and help students see the relationship between them and their lesson. Finally, the teacher should help pupils see the relationship between their lives and the principles.

9. Motivate students to establish and live by principles. Teachers who want to permanently influence the lives of their students will use every motivational technique possible to get them to recognize and live by these principles.

10. Relate new principles to those already known. Again, teaching is relating things to each other. Moreover, it is guiding learning activities. One of the most effective learning activities is relating facts, principles, and concepts to life.

ARRESTED CHURCH GROWTH

Arrested church growth happens when a barrier or a combination of factors causes a church to stop growing or keeps a plateaued church from growth. Arrested church growth is caused by (1) excessive feeling of "family" spirit within the church and feelings of irritation toward "outsiders," (2) undue attention toward "Christian perfection," and (3) "bad air" generated by self-centered bickering in the congregation.

ARRESTED SPIRITUAL DEVELOPMENT (See also PATHOLOGY OF CHURCH GROWTH)

When a church stops growing internally (evidenced by a lack of prayer, the presence of sin, lack of Bible reading and study, and no vision), it ultimately stops growing externally, and begins to die. This is symptomatic of one of the church growth pathologies. Internal growth (growth in grace) becomes the foundation of numerical growth.

How to Heal Arrested Spiritual Development

1. The church should conduct a stewardship campaign to teach church members biblical stewardship of time, talents, and treasures.
2. The pastor should address known cases of unconfessed sin among members personally and (if necessary) publicly.
3. The church should be organized to pray for the resolution of church problems and the needs of the community.
4. The church should conduct a Friend Day campaign to motivate church members to reach out beyond themselves to the lost in their sphere of influence.
5. The church should institute new times and meetings for prayer and intercession. If the traditional prayer meeting has lost its vitality, perhaps a series of early morning prayer meetings (as members go to their employment) will revitalize the church.

ASSIMILATING NEW MEMBERS

Churches are too often like flow-through tea bags. New members are allowed to flow in the front door and out the back with little effective effort made to stop them. Rather, a church should be like a sponge, taking in all it can find and keeping all it gets.

The process of assimilating newcomers into the church is commonly referred to as postevangelism, but it is actually a part of the biblical and holistic process of disciple making. After a person comes to know Christ, it is imperative to get him assimilated into the church. The Bible knows nothing of free-lance Christians. Throughout the New Testament, those who were saved became active members of an existing local church; or local churches were formed, and they became active in them.

A holistic approach to evangelism requires that provision be made for the new Christian's normal growth and development. That normal growth and development requires that the new Christian become settled into, or bonded to, a local church. That is where he will be brought under the ministry of the Word of God that will result in spiritual growth (1 Pet. 2:2), victory over sin (Ps. 119:9-11), answered prayer (John 15:7), and strengthened faith (Rom. 10:17). The local church is also where the new Christian will be able to grow through fellowship with other Christians (Heb. 10:25).

When the local church fails in assimilating newcomers into the church, the new Christian stops attending church regularly (or is out of the church completely), and the growth and development process is handicapped.

Bonding is essential to the task of closing the back door of the church. Nothing is more frustrating than spending time and effort to win people to Christ and then watching them become unfaithful, join another church, or drop out of church completely. But that is exactly what happens when the task of bonding is not taken seriously. New Christians drift from one Sunday school class to another and from one social group to another, trying to find a place where they are made to feel like a vital and needed part of the church. If such a place is not found, they become discouraged and stop searching. In time, they either become casual church members, move to another church, or drop out of church entirely.

Bonding is a biblical pattern. The first church, the one started in Jerusalem on the day of Pentecost, grew more rapidly than any church since that time. Yet those early Christians were able to keep the back door effectively closed. Why? For the simple reason that new Christians were bonded to the church. Their felt needs were met by a part of the church family (Acts 2:42). Those who were already members were willing and anxious to make room for the newcomers (Acts 2:47).

It is often assumed that new Christians and new members are bonded to the church when they formally join. In practice, nothing could be farther from the truth. If such an assumption is made, the back door will always stand ajar. The key to assimilating new members is not church membership, but church ownership. Newcomers are bonded to the church only when they begin to think of the church in terms of "my church," and that only happens when they begin to feel like a vital part of the church as a whole or of some group or organization within the church.

Growing churches are not always the churches that win the most people to Christ. They are the churches that make people feel loved and accepted so that they want to become a part of the church. For a suggested bonding strategy to help assimilate new members, see the article "Seven Touches, Law of."

ATTENDANCE CAMPAIGNS

A Sunday school campaign can be one of the greatest tools to revitalize the Sunday school and keep a church growing. As the spring approaches, this is a time when the secular culture gives energy to the church program. People are glad to get over winter, and they join in the new life of spring.

A Sunday school campaign is not an old-fashioned contest. In the old days Sunday schools had contests, but these are not as effective now as they used to be. A contest gave a prize when a pupil brought a friend. A Sunday school contest was some outward reward or stimulus to motivate people to bring visitors to the Sunday school. Over the years, rewards such as a bicycle for those who brought the most visitors, or an American flag for all those who came on the Fourth of July have been effective. However, in today's Sunday school, many complain that gimmicks are not consistent with the biblical message. They think a Sunday school contest cheapens the gospel and turns the student's attention away from learning the Bible and spiritual growth.

In a Sunday school campaign people are organized to carry out the objectives of the Sunday school so there is shared goal setting, shared problem solving, and shared implementation. A Sunday school campaign involves outreach by everyone because of the great commission, which is the purpose of Sunday school.

The Biblical Basis for a Sunday School Campaign

1. To reach people for Christ. A new member to the Sunday school or a new convert to Christ is kept in the church by the way you bring them into the church. A contest that gets attendance by offering prizes will have difficulty keeping visitors. But in a Sunday school campaign, people are reached by friends with an emphasis on establishing a relationship to the unchurched. When a prospect is bonded to the Sunday school through relationships, he is more likely to stay in the church.

   The purpose of the Sunday school is the great commission. "Go therefore and make disciples of all the nations, baptizing them in the name of the Father and of the Son and of the Holy Spirit, teaching them to observe all things that I have commanded you; and lo, I am with you always, even to the end of the age" (Matt. 28:19-20). Three verb forms are the objectives of a church and should be the direction of a Sunday school campaign.

   First is the phrase "make disciples." Since a disciple is a follower of Jesus Christ, we want to do more than just get a visitor to attend our Sunday school one time. We want every visitor to enroll in the Sunday school, study Jesus Christ weekly, and become his disciple. The Greek word for "make disciples" reflects the modern term *bonding*.

   The second word is *baptizing*. The historic church's interpretation for baptizing was *churching*. The second objective is to get new converts into the church.

   The third word is *teaching*, which means instructing people in biblical content. This is the task of the Sunday school.

2. Biblical motivation. A Sunday school campaign will organize people to carry out the great commission. Remember, whatever God commands his workers to do, God expects his leaders to motivate the workers to do. Since God expects the Sunday school to reach the lost, he expects Sunday school teachers to motivate pupils to reach their friends and neighbors with a view of getting them into the Sunday school, where they can hear the Word of God.

3. The division of labor. God will not do for his workers what he has commanded them to do. In reverse of that principal, his workers cannot do what God has reserved as his duty. In the first place, God has commanded us to go and to motivate all people to become disciples of Jesus Christ. Our task is to reach people and give them the gospel so that they can become saved. Our part of the law of the division of labor is to get unchurched people to hear and respect the gospel. When Sunday school teachers do their part in getting people to visit and learn the Bible, then God will convict them of their sin and convert them.

4. An active faith. Faith is affirming what God has said in his Word. God has said he will bless his Word. It will grow when it is sown as seed. When Sunday school teachers obey the biblical command to sow the Word of God into the hearts of the unconverted, they are exercising faith. Because they believe God will work in unsaved pupils, they will use a number of means to attract them and to reach them for Christ.

Foundational Principles of Attendance Campaigns

Several practical principles can help Sunday school leaders plan a campaign. These principles will lead to a successful outreach program.

1. The law of the two-humped camel. Sunday school attendance generally goes up in the fall and the spring, then declines in the winter months because of severe weather, early morning darkness, and sickness. Attendance also declines in the summer because of vacations, weather that attracts people to outdoor activities, and holidays. The principle of the two-humped camel means that Sunday school leaders should plan a campaign in March and April because attendance will naturally be up. There will likely be two classes of people present in the fall and spring. First, the casual church attender will be present, and second, new visitors will attend the service. Therefore, a Sunday school campaign will work better in the fall and spring than at other times of the year.

2. The law of planting. There is a season on the calendar when

farmers should plant their crops. Also, there is a season for harvest. Between these two seasons, there is a season for rain, sun, and growth. A good farmer does not work against the seasons but takes advantage of the seasons. The same applies to Sunday school leaders. Plan to reach unchurched prospects when they are inclined to come, such as March and April.

In the fourth century A.D., St. Augustine used the phrase "the seasons of the soul." He meant there are times in the life of people when they are more open to the gospel than at other times. These are times when people go through severe crises, changes of life-style, or factors that cause a disequilibrium in their personality. The "seasons of the soul" could be when there is a birth in the family, severe sickness, loss of a job, or when people move from one culture to another (culture shock). When people go through a crisis or a disruption in life, they usually turn to God and are willing to be converted. The aggressive Sunday school leader will plan a Sunday school campaign at the right season, when there is a season in people's hearts to respond to the gospel.

3. The law of creek jumping. When a person is trying to jump across a creek, he has to get a running start to clear it. This is called the law of momentum or credibility. There is a principle that the wider the creek, the faster the person must run to jump over the creek. In the same way, when planning a Sunday school campaign, the more people you expect to attend, the longer time you must spend making your plans. A Sunday school leader must build up momentum or build credibility.

4. The law of target shooting. When beginning a campaign, Sunday school leaders should know what they want to accomplish. They should set good, reachable goals. Just as an archer is more likely to hit a target that he is aiming at, so Sunday school leaders are more likely to reach a clear, established goal.

How to Plan an Attendance Campaign

Goal setting. Do not emphasize numbers in a campaign for the sake of numbers. However, every person counts, so interpret goals in terms of people. In the business world, they speak of "management by goals." Goals give direction to a campaign and help evaluate its effectiveness.

It is better to set a small goal and reach it successfully than to miss a large goal and be a failure. Therefore, set small individual goals in a Sunday school campaign, and help Sunday school pupils be the winners.

Input goals. An input goal is a step toward accomplishing the overall campaign goals. Like rungs of a ladder, input goals help pupils walk Sunday by Sunday through a Sunday school campaign. When an input goal is accomplished, it will move the pupils toward the final goal. An input goal may involve enrolling a friend in Sunday school, enlisting prayer support for the campaign, or getting the church to fast together for the campaign. Other practical input goals are to get people to phone all the prospects, to mail a personal postcard to all prospects, or to visit all of the prospects.

Output goals. This is the end result of the campaign. The output goal is how many you want to attend, how many families you expect to reach, or how many conversions you want to achieve. The output goal is reaching the top of the ladder, while input goals are taking one rung at a time.

Goal education. People have to be educated about the goals of a Sunday school campaign. There are several practical ways to do this: (1) put signs or posters around the church, (2) use a motto with the campaign, (3) send a newsletter to everyone telling them about the goal, (4) use church bulletins and pamphlets to get people excited about the goal, (5) have individuals give testimonies to help generate excitement, and (6) use a progress chart, such as a thermometer or a graph in the church auditorium to help communicate a goal.

Goal evaluation. There is a principle of leadership that says, "People do not do what you expect; they do what leaders inspect." Therefore, to get everyone involved in a Sunday school campaign, check up on them. Use the following ideas for accountability: (1) report forms (ask people to report on their work), (2) post totals so everyone can see them, (3) announce the results of input goals (what people are doing to get ready for the campaign), and (4) magnify workers. Those who have done a good job should be given public commendation, not to appeal to the ego, but to indicate their faithfulness to God.

ATTENDANCE GOALS (See GOALS)

AUDITORIUM BIBLE CLASS

During the early seventies, the Auditorium Bible Class (ABC) or Pastor's Bible Class was one of the techniques in building a growing Sunday school. At that time many Americans sat in small Sunday school classes that were drab and uninteresting. But excitement was generated when adults were moved into the large auditorium and exposed to an exciting master-teacher. Many adults who were well trained in their small discussion classes got caught up in the excitement of the large class. They became involved in reaching other adults, and the whole auditorium Bible class grew. But now, after twenty years of emphasis on the auditorium Bible class, apathy has set in. Teachers have found it is easier to lecture than to prepare discussions and use the overhead projector. As a result, many of the large auditorium Bible classes are declining in attendance. To offset this trend, many Sunday schools are dividing the large class into smaller adult classes designed to meet their needs. However, the concept of the auditorium Bible class should not be completely eliminated.

Many Americans do not want to become involved in small groups. They want to visit a church and hear the message, but they do not want to become involved. The auditorium Bible class is the place where visitors can make a first contact with Bible study. As such, the ABC can become the handshake of the Sunday school. After visitors become involved with the master-teacher in the auditorium setting, they can become involved in the smaller classes that meet their needs.

The Auditorium Bible Class, as well as all classes, should include a maximum use of visuals including the overhead projector, charts, blackboards, tack boards, and other means of visual aids. America has become a visual society, and young adults have grown up learning many of their attitudes toward life from television. It is said that more than 75 percent of all their learning endeavors come through visual channels. As a result, the church cannot resort to the audio channel exclusively and expect people to learn and grow in Christ.

AWARDS

Awards will not attract people to your church, but awards will reinforce an exciting Sunday school class. The pastor of one superaggressive church sums up his rules for promotions that bear fruit: (1) maintain high standards for advertising material, (2) follow through on what has been announced, (3) do not give awards or rewards that are not earned, (4) use prizes that cannot be gained in any other way, (5) learn the best time to give out promotional items (usually the end of the service), (6) use variety, (7) be willing to invest funds to adequately promote, and (8) inspire leaders to support the contest, or it will not work.

Awards generate excitement, and excitement generates Sunday school growth and attracts visitors. Most people do not come just to get an award. Awards are only a means to an end. The award can be used as a reinforcement for excitement but they can not in themselves produce enthusiasm.

It is not the award given but how it is given that really counts. It is possible to give a bookmark with great results if it is given correctly. Some churches have spent a great deal of money on prizes that have not produced results but in fact have backfired on them. While some awards are wrong, it is usually the way they are given that makes them wrong.

Should churches use external rewards to motivate members in a Sunday school contest? Christian educators do not agree on the answer. Working for awards appears to have a scriptural foundation (see 1 Cor. 3:11, 14). Also, churches that use awards as part of their Sunday school contest claim they (1) unify the church,

(2) attract crowds, (3) get more church members working, (4) stimulate teachers, (5) emphasize evangelism, (6) reach the community, (7) encourage visitation, (8) bolster the entire church, (9) boost attendance permanently, and (10) spur church building and expansion.

But there are also weaknesses with awards. Just because no one can prove an award is not biblical (negative) does not make it acceptable (positive). The liabilities of awards are: (1) they can cheapen the gospel, (2) they can detract from a worship service, (3) they can offend some people, (4) they can be compared to a worldly motivational technique, (5) they can motivate people to work for wrong motives, and (6) they can be costly.

A word of tolerance to the wise: don't be against all awards just because you are uncomfortable with them; the next Christian may be comfortable with them and feel they are of God. Both of you are basing convictions on feelings. Don't be quick to endorse every award because it works or because someone else used it. Use only that which fits the "philosophy of ministry" for your church.

Practical Suggestions for Awards

Keep the award presentations out of the church worship services. This will prevent unnecessarily offending members of the congregation who may be opposed to the giving of awards. Also, such presentations could become a barrier to the unchurched. Presentations during a church service could have the effect of turning the sanctuary into a carnival or circus tent. The best place to give awards is in the Sunday school. In this setting, the winners are being honored before their peers. Also, as the contest was promoted through the Sunday school, it is fitting that it should conclude in the Sunday school. Seeing the awards being distributed could also motivate other class members to do more in the next campaign.

Results of contests should not be directed toward making the pastor look ridiculous. While it may be great fun to throw a pie in the face of the pastor if a goal is met, it will not help the pastor to meet a spiritual need in the life of a visiting family. Just because the pastor is willing to do anything to reach people, he must not put up barriers that will make his ministry ineffective. A visiting family may hesitate seeking spiritual counsel they need if they have come to view the pastor as a clown who gets a pie in the face. Remember, the pastor should be esteemed as a man of God.

BABIES, HOW TO REACH FAMILIES THROUGH THEIR BABIES

The cradle roll is more than booties hanging on a chart in the nursery. The cradle roll is a strategy to reach the nonchurched family through a new baby. It is a continuing ministry of one to two years during which time visits, phone calls, and mailings are made to a family. With each visit, the family is given literature that parallels the developmental age of the child that will help the new father and mother understand the growth of their baby. With each contact, the family is reminded that the baby is from God, and they are taught how to raise their baby for God's glory.

The cradle roll is the handshake of your church. It communicates to young couples that your church has a program and adequate facilities to train and care for their child.

In a nutshell, the Cradle Roll Department is a list of potential members of the church. Newborns are its special outreach, with constant ministry until each baby is transferred to the roll of the Nursery Department.

Why a Cradle Roll?

1. To reach parents. Young couples who have given little thought to church or God often have tender hearts after the birth of the new life entrusted to them. The arrival of the baby provides a reason to go to the home and express interest and concern.

2. To give aid. More than just adding a baby's name to the ribbon hanging from a cardboard cradle on the wall, the Cradle Roll Department seeks to render aid to the new parents as they begin to train their little one. Through personal

visits, printed booklets and books are delivered from the church library to parents.

3. To reach children. If the Sunday school waits until babies are old enough to choose to come to Sunday school, they may never come. A cradle roll program is designed to reach a reachable family through the new baby. Cradle roll workers constantly keep in touch with the child and encourage his being brought to the nursery as soon as possible.

The Scripture Press Cradle Roll Course contains literature for the first two years of the baby's growth. This material was written by Bernice Cory, founding editor of Scripture Press approximately three decades ago and has more than a million copies in print. Since babies are timeless, the principles of their development never get old. This program by Scripture Press is as workable now as when the first church used it.

Who Staffs the Cradle Roll?

1. The superintendent. In a small church, there may be no other person on the cradle roll staff besides the superintendent. A lady who is too shy to teach a class may be willing to visit homes and talk with young mothers on a one-to-one basis. A young woman would have much in common with the age group of cradle roll parents. At the same time, an older woman might have more leisure time to visit, and more experience with which to aid the new parents.

2. The secretary. As in any other department, the secretary should keep a record of all the names, addresses, and birthdays of the babies on the roll. If a card is kept for each baby, facts should be added after each contact by a visitor. The secretary also should mail birthday cards to the babies each year, until the Nursery Department takes over. Supplies for the department should be ordered by the secretary.

3. Home visitor. This may be the superintendent, or a pair of ladies may like to visit the homes. The more visitors involved (at least one to every eight babies), the more people will be seeking new babies to visit.

Duties of the Cradle Roll Staff

1. Visit homes. As names of new babies or new families are presented to them, visitors should go to homes and make a friendly visit, seeking to enroll the baby in the cradle roll. Leaflets and an appropriate symbol or certificate should be given to the parents to make the event an important one.

2. Counsel with parents. While a visitor may not know all the answers, she should be aware of any special needs in the home. If there are any questions she cannot answer, she should assure the parent that (1) she will get the answer and report it, or (2) she will refer the question to the church staff member who can provide the needed assistance. Sometimes there are medical or emotional problems, and the pastor would know what professional help is available to the parent.

3. Provide an adequate church nursery. The crib nursery may be one of the most important rooms in the church. Whether or not it is clean, cheerful, and well-staffed may determine whether the parents eventually attend church themselves.

4. Plan a mothers' meeting. Some mothers may not be able to bring their baby to church and attend themselves. Some kind of meeting with mothers during the week might be the answer to reaching these otherwise unchurched mothers. An informal home meeting would allow discussion of mutual problems and a brief Bible study relating to those needs.

5. Discover prospects. In a city area, contact of homes with new babies may be established through regular calls on diaper service firms or the corner grocer; the newcomers' list from the welcome wagon; or birth announcements in the newspaper. And if your church has door-to-door visitation, they should report new babies discovered.

6. Annual Baby Day. Emphasize the importance of the baby in the home and the responsibility of parents during an annual Baby Day celebration in the church. All the new babies for the year are presented to the church at a special service, where a charge is given to the parents by the pastor.

7. Discover needs. In the course of a visit, the cradle roll workers may find that medical help, which the family is

unable to get, is needed for the parent or child. The worker may (1) refer the problem to an agency of the church to give that aid, or (2) refer the problem to the pastor, who will put the family in touch with a social agency that can provide the aid. A friend in need is a friend indeed. Otherwise disinterested parents may become interested in another church that cares more about them. Occasionally the need for clothing or food becomes evident. The visitor may alert a church group to deliver the supplies to the home.

8. Secure an adult class sponsor. An adult class may sponsor the cradle roll nursery by providing crib sheets, toys, bottle warmers, and other necessary equipment, and by being responsible for washing the linens each week.

This sponsor might also provide emergency baby-sitting so a parent can go to a doctor or to a revival meeting; maintain a supply of church-donated, used clothing for families; or wash clothes for or take food to a mother who has sickness in her home.

Conclusion

The cradle roll program is a tool that will touch young families. They can be reached through their need, and their greatest need is spiritual guidance to help their baby develop to the glory of God.

BABY BOOMERS (See also BABY BUSTERS)

Church leaders are becoming aware of the influence of the baby boomers in American society. Business and industry have been researching the needs and values of this unique group of people ever since the explosion of babies after World War II. Based on this research, the business community has adapted its marketing strategy to reach the baby boomer with its products.

Now the boomer influence must be faced by the church. Within ten years they will take over the leadership of local churches and denominational headquarters. Within the present business community, boomers are junior executives or middle managers; however, they will soon be executives at AT&T, IBM, and other industries of America. Within ten years they will control CBS, NBC, and ABC. When they take over the leadership of Christian organizations, they will functionally operate the church differently. To properly reach them, we must recognize the unique needs they bring to Christianity. Just as the church cannot reach the Chinese without understanding Chinese culture, values, and language, so the church must understand the boomer to develop a cross-cultural strategy to reach and minister to the baby boomers in America.

Called the "critical mass," the numbers of boomers make them unique. Nine months after the end of World War II, there were 233,454 births. More were born in that time period than at any other time in American history. The explosion in fertility continued for twenty years until 1964. This bulge of births in the demographic graph has been described by sociologists as a pig in a python. There are 75 million baby boomers, plus their children, called *the boomers busters,* or *the boomerangs.*

The baby boomers went into the adolescent subculture but were different from teenagers of previous generations. Usually, young people are assimilated into adult culture as they grow older and society goes on. However, the baby boomers have remained a distinct subculture. Rather than becoming like adults, the reverse has happened. The older male drives a sports car to keep his youthful image. America has become a nation ruled from the bottom, or controlled by her young.

Newspaper articles tell us that the boomers are more conservative than most previously thought. They are returning to the church. The Gallup poll released in 1989 indicated that 76 percent of all new American church members are between the ages of eighteen and thirty-six. Those churches that ignore the baby boomer have realistically cut off 76 percent of their potential market outreach.

In the book *Ten Innovative Churches,* most of the congregations referred to are led by boomer pastors, usually under forty years of age. These growing churches are reaching young adults. One of the boomer pastors said to reach the baby boomer you must have (1) a synthesizer, (2) a young adult Sunday school class for them, and (3) practical sermons on parenting, spouse relationships, and financial management.

The negative influences of the boomers are that they tend to be (1) antitraditional, (2) narcissistic, (3) weak in personal separation from worldly activities, (4) pragmatic, (5) geared to change, and (6) materialistic. The positive influences they are bringing to the church are (1) honesty and transparency, (2) efficiency in ministry, (3) caring and relational attitudes toward people, (4) functional Christianity, (5) less guilt-ridden motivation, and (6) equipping ministry for every lay church member.

Those churches that refuse to reach the baby boomer will become hibernating churches. Those that effectively reach them will be churches that influence culture.

Why Boomers Lack Loyalty to the Church

1. They have not been conditioned to commit themselves to social institutions. The experiences of a generation tend to condition that generation to adopt certain presuppositions in life. Parents of boomers lived through the Great Depression (don't trust the economy) and fought World War II (trust the government). Boomers were born during an economic boom (trust the economy) and lived through Vietnam and Watergate (don't trust the government). As a result, boomers have not been conditioned to commit themselves to the government or to other social institutions, such as the church and family.

2. They have a personal philosophy of life contradictory to committing themselves to social institutions. Boomers live in a self-centered world of their own making, and many have adopted a self-centered personal philosophy of life, which might be summarized in the question, What's in it for me? When any institution, including the church, fails to convince the boomer it has something of value to offer, the boomer will not commit himself or herself to that institution.

3. Boomers are consumers who have learned to distrust their world. They are not honest with their world because it is not honest with them. In their world of television, advertising is based on image, not necessarily truth. This, coupled with the

continuous introduction of new products and product lines to replace old ones, naturally results in a lack of loyalty. Boomers are now being referred to as "the over-the-thrill crowd" as they mature and become increasingly suspicious of image advertising.

4. Relational problems in the home, the basic social institution of society, impacts the way boomers relate to other social institutions. Studies indicate an increasing number of boomers live in nonfamily units (about 9.1 million). Despite this statistic, 90 percent of boomers believe marriage is the best life-style. They tend to be very relationship-oriented and most hope to remain married to the same spouse for life. But statistically, 50 percent of boomer marriages end in divorce. Despite this, 8 percent of those who divorce will choose to remarry.

5. The boomer life-style leaves little time for church. Only one percent of boomers believe the childless family is ideal, and 90 percent of boomers claim family life is the most important thing in their lives. Yet few boomers have made career sacrifices for their families. Sixty percent of mothers are back at work within a year of the birth of their children. Often, these women work primarily to pursue personal interests rather than supplement the family income. These dual career couples tend to think of evenings and weekends as family time. The long hours at work and growing pressures of family life are also impacting other traditional support systems, such as neighborhood and the extended family. These support systems that tend to build loyalty tend to be absent in the boomers' social network.

6. Boomer mobility tends to discourage boomer loyalty. Many are working for businesses that are likely to transfer them as often as every two years. Others spend a great deal of time traveling for business reasons or commuting long distances to work daily. A well-developed transportation network provides them with mobility, so they become rootless. One of the primary reasons people are loyal is related to their perception of established roots in a community, company, or

church. When boomers have not established these roots, they lack this dimension of loyalty.

7. Redemption and lift tends to encourage boomers to move up in churches. After a person is converted, the stabilizing influence of the Christian life will elevate him in the socialization process. This upward social mobility often results in people looking for new churches. With the boomer, this tendency is strengthened by the appearance of affluence that surrounds the boomer at work but is often absent in the traditional church.

8. Religious trends that erode denominational distinctives impact boomer loyalty to a church. Such things as denominational mergers or the merger or union of seminaries for academic strength or financial constraint have produced a blurred theological focus. This has also resulted in a greater ecumenical spirit in some denominations. This, along with the rapid growth of interdenominational agencies, such as camps, conferences, seminars, magazines, etc., to service individuals has also led many boomers to be more open to changing denominations. Youth attending Christian colleges tend to choose interdenominational schools rather than denominational schools. Marriage across denominational lines has become more common.

9. Television encourages boomers to be more selective in choosing their church. Just as television has shaped boomer values in many areas of life, it has also begun to impact boomers' attitudes toward church. Many perceive the ministry of the televangelist's media church as more attractive, meaningful, and exciting than that of their local church. Because of their increased mobility, boomers will drive across town to attend the church they were introduced to on radio or television rather than attend the church in their own community.

Why Boomers Are Returning to the Church

1. Boomers are returning to the church out of a concern for their children. Seventy-six percent of all boomers have children. As these new parents have children, they will return to

church, as other generations before them have, to teach moral values to their children, provide services for family, and relate to other parents of like goals and like problems. Boomer parents striving to build strong families tend to turn to the church for help.

2. Boomers are returning to the church because they perceive church membership as a symbol of belonging, acceptance, and identity. As society becomes increasingly individualistic in its approach to life and relationships, many boomers are looking to the church to provide the sense of community that is lacking in other areas of their life.

3. Boomers are returning to the church because they are burned out on their popular culture. Like the writer of Ecclesiastes, many boomers have tried what is offered by their popular culture and have failed to find significant meaning in their life. Others have recognized their life has been a failure and are seeking to identify with something of enduring value.

4. Boomers are looking for spiritual reality. As boomers begin to get mystical in their faith, they may express it through Eastern religions, the New Age movement, a traditional church, or the new emerging conservative churches. They are looking for a religion that is supernatural and will bring them experientially into contact with God or a spiritual reality beyond the norm.

5. Boomers may also be returning to church for economic reasons. They work harder and longer than their parents but appear to have less as a result. This generation raised in an economic boom tends to place strong faith in the ability to perform, but that faith has been buffeted as they have worked their way through economic recessions and market corrections. Some are beginning to feel insecure about the economic prospects. In the past, economic uncertainties sometimes caused people to turn to the church in their fear and/or confusion.

Five Questions to Ask as You Prepare to Reach Boomers

As you begin to develop a ministry to reach the baby boomer, ask the following questions to get the data you need to make a good decision.

1. What percent of your church are boomers?
2. What percent of your boomers have children?
3. What percent of your boomers hold leadership positions?
4. What is the attitude of your church toward boomer values?
5. How can your church develop a strategy to reach boomers?

Seven Things a Boomer Looks for in a Church

Research into the attitudes of boomers that impact their choice of a church suggests seven things they want in a church. When these are present, they will commit themselves to its ministry both financially and to some degree through involvement in some aspect of ministry or service in the church. When these are absent in a church, so are boomers. The church that will be effective in reaching the boomer in the nineties and on into the twenty-first century needs to consider what is important to the boomer.

1. The church most attractive to boomers is the one that is functional in its approach to their faith. They will commit themselves to things that will help them function in life. They differ from their parents in that they will not attend church meetings because of tradition or guilt or to meet someone else's expectations. They want their Christianity to work in the marketplace. They are looking for functional sermons that will help them cope with the problems of life and living.

2. Boomers are concerned with form or excellence. They want things to be as perfect as they see on television. They want their church to use the latest tools to do a job (such as personal computers, fax machines, seminars, overhead projectors, VCRs). They believe you can't use yesterday's tools in today's ministry and meet the challenge of tomorrow. Boomers know that using the right tools is more efficient, and they don't want their church to waste their time. They will serve in the church, but they want their church to use them at their strength.

3. Boomers will commit to churches that are characterized by team ministry. Boomers respond to a new style of leadership. They want a church that provides opportunities such as

(1) shared goal setting, (2) shared problem solving, and (3) shared decision making. The business model for boomers is corporate management, which is also identified by such terms as the management team or shared leadership. Their parents worked or managed in isolation from others, but networking is important to boomers.

4. Boomers are looking for churches that are both innovative and conservative. Boomers are antitraditional, but they are also conservative and institutional. Boomers are generally perceived as anti-institutional because they were involved in the protests of the 1960s. This conclusion is based on a misunderstanding of what boomers were attempting to do during those years of college unrest. They were not against the institutions themselves, but against their hypocrisy and abuses. Boomers are for the five basic institutions of society—including the family, the church, good government, schools, and business.

5. The church that reaches the boomer is the church that is businesslike without becoming a business. Boomers want to be part of a successful church that meets their needs with quality ministry. They want to accomplish goals. They want form: dress, tools, job description (what must I do?), and job objective (what must I accomplish?). Again, this is one of the areas in which boomers differ from their parents. The motto of their parents was, "Do the best you can with what you have." In contrast, boomers believe "A job worth doing is worth doing right." Their parents worked for the sake of work and worked out of habit, viewing their work as a means to an end. Boomers work hard—some think even harder than their parents—but they do it for different reasons. They are more likely to take pride in both process (their work) and product (their goal).

6. Churches that reach boomers are relational in their outreach strategy. The boomers consider relationships important. Their music reflects the intimacy of relationships. Boomers tend to have a series of deep relationships with members of the opposite sex before marriage. Relationship is an imperative factor in seeking a marriage partner. Also, boomers tend

to have more difficulty with broken relationships than do their parents. For the boomer, the quality of life is measured by relationships.

7. Finally, boomers are looking for "Christian behaviorism" in the churches they attend. While the school of psychology known as behaviorism tends to be anti-Christian, behaviorism as a philosophy of life and ministry does not have to be anti-Christian. Every church must remain an island in that it remains different from the world. But the church should adopt a philosophy of behaviorism to encourage its people to experience their Christianity and apply the principles of biblical doctrine to their life-styles.

Boomers want to experience their Christianity. They want to love, laugh, talk, pray together, share with, and care about others. They will reject correct doctrine if it is presented with manipulative methods, but they will accept it when they understand how it can impact their life positively. They expect Christian experience to grow out of the essentials (the fundamentals). They are more tolerant about deviation in secondary doctrinal issues than deviation in life-style issues. This means church leaders should teach doctrine from the perspective of how to live.

How Should the Church Respond to Boomers' Expectations?

First, the church should not indiscriminately seek to copy their world. The gospel that saves is not always the gospel that sells best. The workable principles discovered in a market survey may not be eternal truth, but only public opinion. While public opinion is important to know in making decisions concerning the emphasis of a church's ministry, that ministry must be based on the eternal principles of the Word of God.

The church can respond to boomer expectations by applying cross-cultural principles in the development of a strategy to reach the boomer for Christ. Just as the gospel must be communicated cross-culturally to reach and win the Chinese, so the gospel must be communicated cross-culturally to reach the boomer.

This means the pastor and church that reaches boomers should be aware of the carriers of their culture and correctly interpret them. The boomers are relatively sophisticated in their knowledge of films, music, drama, performers, art, and the topics on talk shows. An uninformed and nonrational negative attitude to their culture will alienate them, but if their culture is correctly interpreted, it will be easier to reach them. There is evil in their culture as in all cultures, but there is much that is neutral, and some that is good. Knowing the difference is one key to ministering to boomers.

Churches who want to be effective in reaching the boomer for Christ need to create a ministry based on biblical objectives. "Thus saith the Lord" is still true, although it may read slightly differently in the new Bible translations used by the boomer. God did not say, "Thus saith the Lord until the boomer comes." This means the church needs to give the boomer biblical principles to live by and base church strategy on Scripture, not tradition. The pulpit should continue to communicate God's standard of perfection for living and ministry.

There are other things the church can do to help boomers that reflect this balance of remaining strongly committed to unchanging eternal principles and adapting them to their culture. Church leaders should involve boomers in ministry, giving careful consideration to their spiritual gifts. Also, they should provide help so boomers can correctly interpret the Bible for themselves. When planning church programs, remember boomers respond to feeling, thinking, and doing. Transparent Christianity should be built into every program.

Developing a Bible-based Data-driven Strategy to Reach Boomers

Churches that are effective in reaching the boomer for Christ understand the eternal principles of ministry revealed in Scripture, have collected data about boomers they have targeted to reach, and have developed a Bible-based, data-driven strategy to reach them.

Developing such a strategy to reach the boomer begins with understanding the nature of church growth. Studying church growth as a behavioral science, like any other scientific study, involves a number of steps in the scientific process. First, data must be gathered. Then it is examined by the church growth specialist. Third, from this examination certain hypotheses are developed. Fourth, the proposed law must be tested. When this is completed, the law can be established.

But the study of church growth is more than a behavioral science. It is also a branch of systematic theology. The process of theology is described as the gathering, analyzing, arranging, displaying, and defending of all facts about God and his world. This description recognizes the scientific nature of the theologizing process. Historically, theology has been viewed as the queen of all sciences.

Because church growth is both a behavioral science and a branch of systematic theology, the principles of church growth derived from sociological study must be based on biblical revelation. This means the eternal principles upon which a church develops a data-driven strategy to reach the boomer must be Bible based. The principles of strategy come out of Scripture. Specific methods are the adoption of these eternal principles to changing culture.

It is important to recognize that although the eternal principles of ministry drawn from the Bible do not change, specific methods will often change as they lose their effectiveness. Any church leader who has ministered for long has seen this take place in his or her own ministry. Some of the methods that were extremely effective in reaching people during the sixties and seventies—such as busing, revival meetings, vacation Bible school, and Christian camping—are not as effective today as they once were. On the other hand, things like the Saturday seminar on topics such as divorce recovery, Bible survey, spiritual gifts, life conflicts; "Friend Day"; and social services are extremely effective in reaching people today, but these methods may lose their effectiveness in the years to come.

In developing a strategy to reach boomers, churches need to take seven steps:

1. Develop a strategy to gather data.
2. Appoint a committee to gather and interpret that data and make specific recommendations.
3. Consider the use of think tanks in developing aspects of their ministry.

4. Develop an entrance map that charts how individuals come into their church and are assimilated into the church.
5. Collect data about the community they are attempting to reach.
6. Collect data about the public opinion of the community toward the church.
7. Collect data about member attitudes toward the church.

How to Use the Worship Service to Reach Boomers

Many churches have demonstrated that boomers can be attracted to Christ and the church through the worship service, but boomers will not attend simply because a worship service has been announced and convened. The worship leader needs to be careful of empty traditionalism that has no meaning to the boomer, is not biblically based, and represents the rural values of the 1950s rather than the urban values of the 1990s.

The worship leader who wants to attract and involve boomers through the worship service must also emphasize excellence. He will plan well, study well, execute well, and deliver well. Boomers live in an age of accountability. In the church of the boomer, everybody, including the pastor, is expected to submit to the accountability of others. Therefore, after the worship service, those involved in leadership roles should evaluate. The best evaluation session will involve all responsible leaders and be willing to deal with the tough questions others may overlook. Consider the following questions as you evaluate your worship service:

1. What was done right?
2. What was done wrong?
3. On a scale of one to ten, how poorly?
4. Using the same scale, how well?
5. What can be done better next time?
6. What new things should be tried?

Good decisions are based on good information. If you want to make good decisions about your ministry of worship, you need to have an effective means of collecting data. Conduct surveys to gather input from the congregation. These surveys may poll such things as the type of songs that should be used, message topics that would best address the specific problems of the boomer in the pew, the best times to conduct church services, and new ideas being considered, such as drama or special programing.

Boomers tend to choose a church by its style of worship. Six worship styles have proven effective in reaching boomers. Each of these styles can attract boomers, but they do it in different ways. The way a church or pastor chooses to reach out to boomers depends to some degree on the gift mix of that church and pastor. While all pastors should have the spiritual gift of shepherding, there is a supportive spiritual gift that becomes the glue to characterize these six worship styles.

The pastor with the spiritual gifts of *evangelism* and prophecy tend to function best in what might be described as the *evangelistic church*. This is the church that stresses things like personal soul winning and door-to-door visitation. It is most likely the church that gives a regular public invitation in its services or runs a fleet of buses through the city. Its program is governed by an overwhelming desire to reach the unchurched people in the community, and anything that might offend an unchurched visitor is carefully avoided.

Pastors with a strong gift of *teaching* tend to function best in a *Bible expositional church*. These churches are characterized by a strong teaching emphasis in the pulpit and great concern for discerning what the Bible says. These churches are often led by pastors who use teaching aids with their sermons such as printed notes and overhead projectors to help them communicate their strongly biblical sermons. Christians who attend these churches tend to carry reference Bibles, which in course of time become well marked. Most often, the pulpit ministry consists of a week by week exegesis of consecutive passages through a particular book of the Bible.

Pastors with a strength in the spiritual gift of *exhortation* tend to function best in what may be described as a *charismatic renewal church*. When we use this designation to describe a church, it does not mean these churches are necessarily charismatic in theology, with an emphasis on signs and wonders. However, many churches that are charismatic in theology are also charismatic renewal churches. These churches have a strong emphasis on personal revival and the corporate worship of God. Most often this worship involves the singing of contemporary praise choruses and physical manifestations of worship such as lifting hands.

Pastors with a strong gift showing *mercy* tend to function best in the *body life church.* These churches have a strong emphasis on building meaningful relationships and living a transparent Christianity. They are most likely to be the church that encourages the development of *koinonia* through the use of small groups and home cells.

While some church types or worship styles are related primarily to the impact of a gifted pastor, others have historic roots. The last two worship types have existed in historic Protestant Christianity and represent the liturgical and congregational churches. The first four church types are effective because of the spiritual gifts and ability of the pastors. The strengths of the following worship types are the members who are the worshipers and workers in the church.

The *liturgical church* is more likely to be affiliated with one of the mainline denominations (Presbyterian, Lutheran, United Church of Christ, Episcopal). It is the church that worships according to a prescribed liturgy or order of service, which may include the singing of the Doxology and Amen refrains; the recitation of the Apostles' Creed, church covenant, or some similar confessional expression of faith; responsive Scripture reading; and the singing of anthems. The people who attend these churches are often characterized by the spiritual gift of *helps.*

The *congregational church* (Baptist, Free, Community) tends to be less formal in its approach to worship than the liturgical church, but more restrictive than the charismatic renewal church. These churches sing gospel songs rather than hymns and have a more devotional approach in pulpit ministry. This is the church that may encourage spontaneous reactions in the services such as saying "Amen" at appropriate places or the sharing of a testimony when called upon. They tend not to have seminary trained pastors and may be led by lay pastors. This church is more of a people's church rather than a pastor's church. Every member is a minister. The pastor who functions best in this church has strength in the spiritual gift of *administration*.

How to Minister to Boomers

If the church is going to reach boomers, it must reach them at their point of need. The church should develop new ministries and counseling to help boomers cope with the problems they are facing in life, such as alcoholism, drug addiction, homosexuality, divorce, stress, relationships, unemployment, and financial management. These issues should be addressed through shorter classes than the traditional quarterly approach to Sunday school. Workshops and one-day seminars are tools that are becoming increasingly effective with boomers.

Churches need to encourage participatory worship. Have more congregational singing in your church. Provide a service that will allow for a contemporary expression of worship. Be open to allowing boomers to respond with applause. Do things that involve more action than simply sitting and watching a preacher. Many churches use overhead projectors, videos, films, and tapes in their study groups. Many boomers are intensely interested in their study groups. Many boomers are interested in sports, recreation, athletics, and music.

Churches should make the Bible "user-friendly" to boomers. Boomers are more likely to use a newer, easier-to-understand translation of the Bible. Encourage questions and respond to them honestly. Don't send people on guilt trips that will only turn them off, but rather seek to change opinions by helping boomers get a better grasp of the Scriptures. Use competitive teaching methods to teach biblical truth to boomers.

Boomers are more open to women being involved at every level of ministry than other generations. Help women find their gifts and abilities, and lead them into involvement in the ministry in the area that God would have them be. Help them understand the importance of the shepherding ministry of the church. Look for ways to minister to the specialized needs of certain groups of women, such as the single parent and the working mother.

Churches that reach boomers will limit confrontational evangelism. Instead, there will be a greater emphasis on relational evangelism. Use creative side-door approaches to evangelism to get boomers into the church. Don't try to turn every boomer into an evangelist.

Churches should use a variety of different ministries, activities, and groups to strengthen relationships among the members of the church. Trends in adult education show boomers believe in continuing education. Churches would do well to offer institutional classes that would gain the attention of the community. These classes should be held outside the church facility yet remain church sponsored. Also, boomers are open to home cells and Bible study groups. Boomers grew up with shopping centers, television, and fast food restaurants that offered them choices. Give boomers choices in ministry as well.

Remember, boomers are committed to excellence for both themselves and their family. They will not stay in a church that does not have adequate nursery facilities or workers with whom they do not feel comfortable leaving their children. Often when boomers step into a church, they think they are stepping into the past. Upgrade your church facilities to insure the parking lot is paved and striped, lighting is adequate both inside and outside, and the sound system helps rather than hinders communication.

Boomers must know the reason why they are doing something. Challenge the boomer with ministry. Boomers will rise to a challenge and fight for a cause they have come to believe in. Give them a vision and understanding of the purpose for your church through required orientation classes and discipleship classes. Emphasize a team approach to ministry and provide opportunities for lay involvement in ministry. Show the importance of the individual, but remember the individual is a part of the whole. Help boomers find and develop their spiritual gifts and then exercise them through ministry in the church.

Church programs should be highly organized and structured, but loosely controlled. Boomers do not like rigid controls where they have no input. Be flexible in ministry. To hold the attention of the boomer, an hour-long teaching program needs to be fast moving, innovative, and productive. Stress principles of practical living in your messages, but never give a boomer a principle without giving him the application of the principle. Issues that boomers need to have addressed include biblical doctrine, the Christian family, finances, spiritual gifts, interpersonal relationships, problem solving, decision making, and evangelism.

Research suggests boomers value anonymity when visiting a church and do not like to be embarrassed by being publicly identified. Many churches provide a visitors' center where a guest to the church can be met on a one-on-one basis and be given information about the church and all its ministries. Avoid having visitors publicly identified in the church, which may create a barrier to their returning.

The church of the twenty-first century will be a niche church. Trying to be all things to all men will probably mean that you will reach none. To reach the boomer, find the areas in which your church is strongest and build on your strengths.

BABY BUSTERS

The baby busters are a generation of children born between 1965 and 1976. The title originally came from the downturn in fertility in 1965; the explosion of babies after World War II finally went bust in 1965. Sociologists claim that the pig was moving through the python, and fertility in America returned to normal. The baby boom generation was now launched, and the demographic bulge would get older until the baby boomers passed off the scene some time after 2020 A.D. After the baby boom, American families had fewer children; there were fewer live births per capita in the United States. As a result, baby busters grew up in smaller families and attended school in smaller classes. In contrast to their parents, there was more of everything to go around for the busters.

Their parents are called baby boomers and got this label from a *Life* magazine article in 1946 showing a nurse in a Cleveland, Ohio, hospital holding two babies surrounded by cribs of babies. When the magazine entitled them a baby boom, the label stuck. During World War II the birth rate declined because the soldiers were away from their wives, fighting to protect their country. But nine months after V-J Day, the official end of World War II, there were more babies born than any other month in the history of

America. Sociologists identify an overwhelming group of people as massive as the baby boomers as a "critical mass." The sheer amount of babies changed America drastically. The nation has never been the same since.

COMPARATIVE CHART OF THREE GENERATIONS

NAME	Depression Babies	Baby Boomer	Baby Busters
BORN	1925–1945	1946–1965	1966–1976
LABELS	Consumer generation; The man in the gray suit	Me generation; Spock generation; Woodstock generation; Pepsi generation	The Boomerang generation
MALE HERO	John Wayne	John Lennon	Bart Simpson
FEMALE HERO	Betty Grable	Gilda Radner	Madonna
STRUGGLES	With the elements (housing, roads, air-conditioning, food)	With the issues (race, feminine rights, student rights, etc.)	With relationships (parents, boy-girl, employer)

The parents of baby boomers were the *depression kids*. They grew up when everything was scarce: no jobs, no money, not even a prospect of a bright future. The depression kids were realists, so they worked hard—even moonlighted to give their kids every luxury they never had. America continued to prosper as business, education, the housing industry, and the nation in general serviced this "critical mass" of consumers. The baby boomers had their own room, their own television, their own baseball uniform, and the best of schools, playgrounds, toys, and education experiences. Because of the "blue sky" idealism after World War II, baby boomers grew up idealists. This generation of children grew up expecting the best of everything. They personified the popular song written during their growing years, "To Dream the Impossible Dream."

The first baby buster turned twenty-five years of age in 1991, but busters do not march to the same drumbeat as their boomer parents. Their boomer parents were fighters and winners—fighting for women's rights, nuclear freeze, and the Peace movement. Boomers hated Vietnam and the Cold War, and they loved the "Camelot" Kennedy Years in the White House. But their baby busters are different. They have no great dreams, no battles to win, no mountains to climb. They are a generation with busted dreams, busted ambitions, and busted trust.

The baby boomers smoked pot to escape the realities of the world and loved it; the baby buster smokes crack and dies. The baby boomers experimented with free sex and brought in a wave of sexual revolution; their baby buster kids go to bed with a partner, end up with AIDS, and die.

The hero of the baby busters is Bart Simpson, the irreverent smart-mouthed cartoon kid who does not respect adults, calling them "dude." Bart Simpson is equally irreverent with his father, calling him by his first name, "Homer." The ultimate dream of Bart Simpson is to be "an underachiever" in school. He complained when awarded a C+, saying it was disgracefully high. Bart's boomer parents dreamed of landing on the moon and finding a cure to the ills of inner-city poverty, and a larger percent graduated from college and graduate school than any generation before them. But Bart Simpson has no dreams, no tomorrows, no mountains to climb, and no wars to win.

How to Understand the Baby Buster

The following labels describe the baby buster generation. They do not come from popular usage, nor are they intended to coin new terms. They are functional designations intended to help understand this perplexing generation.

The entitled generation. Psychological entitlement happens when privileges become rights demanded by those who don't understand the struggle to get them in the first place. As an illustration, air-conditioning in cars was originally sold to the elite, then it was offered in the family station wagon. Today, the high school student needs air-conditioning in the car he drives to school. The baby busters' grandparents, the depression kids, had to fight the elements for the basic necessities of life. Their grandparents had marginal running water, perhaps no hot water in the house, no hot lunches in the schools, no interstate travel, no school buses except for rural routes, and perhaps only the wealthy went to college or became a physician. But most privileges have trickled down to the poor, and busters feel they are entitled to them all.

Sociologist Richard Niebuhr described the family cycle from rags to riches in three generations. The first generation sacrificed and disciplined themselves to rise out of poverty to make money. The second generation lived off their parents' values and enjoyed their inherited wealth, but they communicated their second-generation values to the grandchildren, not the values that made the original fortune. The third-generation without character and discipline can't maintain the sociological level. They blow it all and return to rags. The busters are third generation children who have had everything given to them, yet they cannot appreciate luxuries without entitlement.

Things are important to the third generation busters, things like cars, CDs, televisions, $200 gym shoes, and the best in entertainment. The parents of boomers had things provided for them by their parents, primarily because the first generation sacrificed as children. But last come the busters; things are almost forced on them as a way of life.

The second-generation baby boomers are competitive. Perhaps their winning nature can be blamed on their first-generation parents. The boomers were given baseball uniforms, a ball field almost as good as Yankee Stadium, coaches, and everything to enjoy the games—things that their parents, the depression kids, did not have. Then these first-generation parents yelled at their little baby boomers to hit, slide, score, and win. Children can learn to be overachievers. The driving compulsion to overcome the great American financial depression forced them to make winners out of their boomer kids. What about the baby busters? Are they less competitive because things have been given to them?

The psychology of entitlement has affected the busters, the generation of busted dreams. They expect government subsidies, and they know they are entitled to welfare, for the courts told them so. The *entitled generation* expect scholarships, grants, and loans to get through college. No one works his way through college anymore.

The buster does not go looking for jobs; jobs have always come looking for them. Since there were fewer busters, the workplace needed them at McDonald's, where they got their first job (they saw the want ad on the placemat). Next they were sought for summer jobs. Therefore, they feel entitled to a good job at a good wage with good conditions and good benefits.

Depression kids worked their way through college by washing dishes, waiting tables, or holding down a midnight job. Back then, college was inexpensive, and a student could work his way through. The second generation, the baby boomers, were put through college in the golden years, paid for by hardworking parents. They were the golden years because a college education was inexpensive and available to all who would work and study. But now, on the downside of inflation, a college education is too expensive for most parents, so the buster goes through on loans. Few busters will graduate from college without owing $20,000 to $30,000. They do not value the future and borrow against it.

The it generation. The second generation baby boomers were the "now generation," they wanted everything in the present tense, but their children, the busters, don't have the same time quality evaluation; they just want "it." They are the instant generation—instant cake mix, instant loans, instant replay, and instant tea. The buster stands impatiently beating on the microwave because it takes ninety seconds to cook his frozen dinner. Yet the depression kids remember waiting five hours for the oven to cook a turkey.

It was the depression kids who lived by the value of postponed gratification. Their motto was pay now and play later. When they were teens, weeknights were study nights and weekends were for dating. They worked all week so they could have fun on the weekend. They worked a lifetime to have fun in retirement. Not so with the boomers and busters. The motto is "instant gratification." They want to pay now and play now. To them, every night is date night.

The busters are a product of the advertising and marketing that pours into their lives through television. The television says, "Buy"; the key words are *you* and *now*. You are important; "Have it your way." And buy now, don't worry about the future; "You deserve a break today."

The isolated generation. When the buster joins a crowd with a Walkman plugged into his ears, he doesn't relate, talk, or interact. He listens to music by himself and remains isolated in the midst of the crowd. To understand the isolated generation, compare the way different generations danced. The first generation, depression kids, listened to the big band sound and hugged and squeezed one another on the dance floor. Dancing was relationship, and they whispered into one another's ears as they suggestively held each other in their arms. The depression kids idolized dancers Fred Astaire and Ginger Rogers for the grace and flair that represented two people in perfect harmony. Then came their kids the baby boomers. They listened to Dick Clark and the American Bandstand. They did the twist, the swim, and a number of other dances whereby two couples danced together but seldom touched. Boomers did not have the intimacy, relationship, or interpersonal involvement in their dance routine. This generation is now followed by the busters, who dance alone. They idolize Michael Jackson and Madonna, who dance with themselves; no one else is even on stage. Their idols are the perfect expression of the isolated generation.

Many busters are children of divorce. Many grew up in isolation, perhaps without the intimacy of a father and a mother in the nuclear family. They felt alone in this world, and it is hard to dream with no one to share your intimate thoughts.

The devalued generation. The very fact that there were fewer children born during the baby bust implies that babies were not valued as highly as before. But notice other things that crept onto center stage during their childhood. First came *Roe v. Wade* (1973), resulting in rampant abortion, the ultimate act against devalued children. Because children are no longer valued as in the past, America slaughters over 3 million unborn babies a year.

Also, the busters have been the target of an explosion in child abuse. While some feel that it was going on for years but not reported by or to the police, others feel that family restraints were lifted by changing family values. Adults took their hostilities out on their children, surely suggesting children were devalued in their parents' thinking. Many parents did not want children, evidenced by their use of the pill or other means of birth control. When many of the busters finally went off to college, many parents said to them, "Don't come back." In many homes they were not wanted because of parents' mid-life divorce. Busters were children left to work out their own problems; they could not go to Mom and Dad to talk about them.

Another reason that produced the devalued generation is the nature of their parents, the baby boomers. Boomers have been called the "me generation," which meant that they were proud, egotistical, or at best self-centered. Those who are too concerned with themselves don't have time to give to their children, which devalues the child's relationship to his parent and devalues the child's self-perception.

The self-proclaimed generation. The baby busters grew up with parents who told them, "You are important," but many of the parents denied by actions the words that came out of their mouths. They were too busy with their own pilgrimage in life. As a result, the busters felt they were important, but did not feel importance coming from other people. Since healthy ego development comes from proper self-recognition, they had to blow their own horn. They are characterized by self-proclamation, or to express it another way, busters are self-absorbed.

The lengthened adolescence generation. One obvious thing about the still-emerging baby buster generation is that they are slow to grow up. They seem to grow into maturity later than previous generations, which means they take on the role and responsibility of adulthood later than their parents or grandparents did.

Adolescence is a transition between childhood and adulthood.

Generally, it is a protected time when the child is allowed to find itself, develop some maturity, choose a vocation, choose a partner, and learn how to make his way in the world. Traditionally, adolescence has been called by sociologists a time of "passages" or the "season of the soul," when the personality ripens into maturity.

Historically adolescence has lasted from age thirteen to seventeen or eighteen—at least it took that long for the depression kids. In her 1986 article entitled "The Postponed Generation," Susan Littwin indicated that adolescence now lasts from age eleven to twenty-eight. Adolescence has been lengthened on both ends. Kids enter it earlier and leave it much later. Whereas the first generation took four or five years to transition to adulthood, it takes the buster fifteen to seventeen years. First the boomers lengthened adolescence on the front end, entering it earlier because of their general sexual freedom and the sexual revolution they introduced to the world. Now the busters are lengthening adolescence on the exit end. They are refusing to grow up. Like Peter Pan, they seem to desire perpetual adolescence—freedom to make mistakes, goof off, and mess around, all without consequence. Disturbingly, busters come out of adolescence about ten years later than their parents did. What we see are young people in their twenties who have all the characteristics of a teenager. We are not talking physical characteristics, but the emotional outlook and commitment to handle the pressures of life.

The postponed generation people know more because of television, have experienced more in the realm of sex, and have traveled farther, yet they usually do not accept responsibility and usually cannot act upon what they know.

At one time there was a clear line between adolescence and adulthood; adolescence ended when you left high school, joined the military, or graduated from college. At other times it ended when you got married or got your first job. But now a baby buster can work for five years and still live like an adolescent at home, or he can earn a Ph.D. and marry—and still not accept the responsibility of adulthood.

What are some results of postponed adolescence? They marry

later and are not in a hurry to get through college, but they will reduce academic loads, change majors. If and when they graduate, they will switch jobs, switch mates, change apartments, make short-term commitments to sports teams, duck responsibilities, and float from one hobby to another, or from one singles bar to another.

The noncommitted generation. Busters seem overwhelmed by life. Since they know more and have experienced more from the multitude of television advertisements, media information, and the possibilities of travel, work, and an open-ended life, they seldom know how to handle any of it. So they don't commit to anything. The busters feel they must try everything before making a decision. That is life in a consumer market. They leave their options open. Rather than buying a computer, they shop around but do not make a commitment because next year the model may be cheaper and have more options. Because they live in a changing world, they do not commit to the present because it may be out of date tomorrow.

The buster shops for a car phone but puts it off for ninety days and the price drops from eight hundred dollars to one hundred and fifty dollars. So he felt he learned a way to get along in life. Don't make a deep commitment to a girl; a better wife will come along. Do not make a deep commitment to a job; a better offer will seek you out when a head hunter phones you with an attractive offer. Do not make a deep commitment to anything because everything is transitory.

The nonfocused generation. The busters have difficulty focusing on anything for a long period of time. Their life is like a news story presented on the evening news. Everything is instant—an instant war, an instant crisis, an instant political drama. For fifteen minutes busters give rapt attention to earthshaking danger, then back to pizza or the football game.

Television has produced dysfunctionalism more than anyone is willing to admit. The way television makes us experience information and feelings is the way we relate to others and to our culture. Television presents news in nice "bite-size," thirty-second modules of time. So busters drift through life unconnected from one experience to the next. He is dysfunctional.

Television never moves to closure on anything. The soaps never end; they just keep on going. When the baby buster gets wrapped up in the famine of Africa, before he knows it, it is no longer a news item. Suddenly its Grenada, then herpes, then the nuclear freeze. Before long, the flow of news makes it difficult for him to commit to any issue, so life becomes an existence of nonissues. They are the nonfocused generation.

The unisex generation. The busters are the first generation that is the product of America's growing unisex orientation to life. Unisex is a movement towards the center; both boys and girls wear jeans and T-shirts and have the same length hair. Outward adorning is not the issue; it is crossing the ontological bridge between the sexes that becomes the issue. There seems to be no mystery in the boy-girl relationship. Buster children have grown up with sex education. They have seen nude pictures, can identify the anatomy, know what they are expected to do in copulation, and can explain it with proper identification of the organs. But they don't know the mystery of the sexual relationship. Even in marriage, there is often a contractual agreement. They have not genuinely experienced what Jesus meant when he said, "The two shall become one flesh."

The growth of women's rights has resulted in both men and women doing all the roles at an airline—pilots, computer operators, luggage handlers, and even mechanics. This is not wrong in itself, because in many of these tasks previously relegated to men, women are performing observably better. The issue is that in the middle of America's social struggle to correct a historic wrong, busters seem to be swimming in a stream in which they can't find bottom.

When it comes to the church, busters have difficulty understanding the traditional arguments of the fundamentalists against women in ministry. The issue is not whether women should be ordained or whether they should be the senior pastor in a church. That issue is explained in 1 Timothy 3. The issue is, Should women have ministry in the church? The busters speak unequivocally, while depression kids equivocate.

The "anomaly" generation. Anomaly means you are hot and cold at the same time, or you are happy and sad, or depressed and vibrant. *Anomaly* means you are both extremes without coming to a middle synthesis. The busters are the "anomaly" generation, at least to their parents and grandparents. They wear a five-hundred-dollar suit and sneakers to work. They want to be comfortable yet present a good image. They wear shoes without socks. They drink a diet cold drink for breakfast rather than the traditional coffee. The anomaly buster Christian wears a T-shirt with a rebellious slogan, or even a silkscreened ad for beer not caring about the antichurch implication to their parents or grandparents.

Busters are tolerant of change, expect change, and embrace change with affection. They can take charge in stride because they are nontraditional. But their parents, the baby boomers, and their grandparents, the depression kids, look at moral situations through the eyes of tradition. Their parents interpret by the standards of consistency, and when things are not consistent, they get uptight. But busters don't agree. They hold contradictory beliefs and have no trouble with them. They may not believe in losing one's salvation (eternal security), yet attend a Pentecostal church that says they can. They may speak in tongues, yet attend a Bible church that preaches against sign gifts.

The buster generation says contradictory things, and it does not bother them because consistency is not a rule of thumb. Their view of Christianity has choices like a cafeteria, so they load up their tray with a little Mexican food, southern black-eyed peas and Italian pasta and drink a little wine that is opposed by their pastor. The "anomaly" buster quips, "What's the big deal?"

The first atheistic generation. The buster generation is a product of Madalyn O'Hair, who got the Supreme Court of the United States to kick the Word of God, recognition of God, and the symbols of God out of the public schools. So buster children were reared without knowledge or training of an absolute Deity, either Jewish, Catholic, or Protestant. Supposedly, they were reared in a neutral environment with no reference to God. They were supposed to be reared free of all moral restraints and choices. But that is not the way it happened. Since nature abhors a vacuum, anti-God forces rushed in under the guise of neutrality, and public schools became humanistic and atheistic. The result is not just "no god," but "anti-God." What do they think about God? Their orientation is secular and humanistic, and they will not allow the church to run their moral life.

The busters do not get their theological views from the church or organized religion; rather, they get their views about God from films and music. As a result, they have a watered-down view of God, the church, and ministers. Their pluralistic viewpoint of life makes them antidoctrinal and antiorthodox. Yet they are not theologically liberal but are against the liberalism of the mainline churches. Busters believe in supernaturalism because in the movies they see demons and supernatural events. They have seen the realism of *The Exorcist* and the surrealism of *Ghostbusters*.

BARNETT, J. N. (1893–1957)

J. N. Barnett became the secretary of the Sunday School Department of the Southern Baptist Convention, Nashville, Tennessee, in 1943, serving until 1957. Prior to his appointment, Barnett was assistant to Arthur Flake, serving in several capacities. During his leadership, Sunday school enrollment grew from 3,188,341 to 6,8247,713 or a net growth of nearly 4 million. His books *The Pull of the People* (1953) and *One to Eight* gave crystallization to the laws of Sunday school growth. He organized the local associations and churches through which Sunday school methods flowed to each church, resulting in the growth of the Southern Baptist Convention.

BARRIERS TO SPIRITUAL GROWTH (See also E-0 EVANGELISM)

Dr. Ralph D. Winter has established four very helpful classifications for the barriers to evangelism.

E-0	Internal barrier
E-1	Stained glass barrier
E-2	Class and cultural barrier
E-3	Language barrier

E-0 stands for evangelism that is carried on among people who are already church attenders. The "0" represents those already in the church, so there are no barriers for them to cross. The "E" represents evangelism, which means these people in the church need to be evangelized. This includes the evangelization of un-saved members, the children born to church members, children and young people brought in by bus, and any other unsaved people who might be attending the church.

E-1 is evangelism that crosses the stained-glass barrier; that is, the church building becomes a barrier to getting people saved. E-1 evangelism is carried outside the church setting, but it does not cross any linguistic, ethnic, or cultural barriers. This would be near-neighbor evangelism, reaching people who do not attend church.

E-2 evangelism crosses cultural or class barriers. E-2 evangelism reaches out to people who are separated by ethnic, cultural, and class barriers.

E-3 evangelism crosses the linguistic barrier. This is usually thought of as foreign missions because the missionary who goes to another country has to learn another language or dialect. But there are diverse speaking groups in most cities of America. There are cultural barriers and language barriers in the United States. Since the principles of reaching people in foreign countries are the same that are used in some places in this country, E-3 evangelism is now usually called cross-cultural missions.

The stained-glass barrier refers to the imagined barrier be-tween the church and those on the outside. Obviously, it does not mean that a stained-glass window is wrong, nor is it a barrier to getting some saved. This phrase is used only as a symbol. A stained-glass barrier is usually a wall of fear that outsiders have about what goes on in the church, and it has no real foundation in fact.

This barrier is built by both Christians and the unsaved. Christians build the barrier from inside the church. Some con-struct it with the fear of being contaminated by the influence of the world. Sometimes they hide behind the wall of fear. Even though the Christian should be separated from sin and the influence of the ungodly, he must cross the stained-glass barrier to share Christ.

The unsaved build the barrier from the outside. They make their bricks from fears of what they do not understand. Sometimes their barrier is the conviction of sin they experience in the presence of the people of God. These fears are to be expected. Paul indicated that the unsaved man understands neither the things of God nor the people of God (1 Cor. 2:14-15). Furthermore, being in the presence of Christians is a reminder of God's impending judgment (2 Cor. 2:15-16), and that produces both fear and discomfort.

Most Christians are probably more comfortable remaining behind the stained-glass barrier in their attempts to evangelize the lost. They want the outsider to come in the front door and respond to the gospel. The unsaved prefer to remain outside where they can go on with their natural life without the convicting presence of the people of God. Also, outside the church they are not faced by truths that they do not understand.

Fear is a very real barrier to evangelism. Christians are often reluctant to witness because they fear rejection. To be accepted and liked is a basic human need. The very possibility of rejection strikes fear. Other Christians are reluctant because they fear failure, especially in serving God.

No one is immune to the barriers built by fear. Even the great apostle Paul had to deal with the problem of fear. In his first letter to the church of Corinth, he wrote, "I was with you in weakness, in fear, and in much trembling" (1 Cor. 2:3). Fear was an apparent barrier to Paul; he requested of the Ephesians that they would pray for him that he might preach the gospel without fear (Eph. 6:19).

Christians often create a barrier between themselves and the unsaved by their judgmental attitude. This often occurs because Christians tend to measure the unsaved by their own list of acceptable and unacceptable behavior, which many times contains a mixture of the commands of God and the traditions of men.

Non-Christians begin to sense their disapproval. Often they will even apologize for their conduct, but such apologies are only words. In reality, many resent having been censured. Instead of Christ attracting the sinner to himself, the Christian has used his legalism to drive the sinner away. Remember, the law brings conviction of sin, but the law never saves. The law when wrongly presented is a legalistic barrier to presenting the gospel.

Are the barriers real? Most barriers to evangelism have no more basis in fact than the chicken-wire fence used to restrain the buffalo in Florida. They lack any true restraining qualities, but they remain barriers because they are perceived to be barriers. Even the most formidable barriers—those of culture, language, and ethnicity—can be overcome by a determined effort to bridge the culture, language, and ethnic background of another person.

Overcoming Barriers

Identifying the barriers. The first step in overcoming barriers is to identify them. The Christian has the responsibility to make that step. Paul said, "I have become all things to all men, that I might by all means save some" (1 Cor. 9:22).

In the treatment of any physical sickness, the first step is always diagnosis. This process may require days and even weeks of testing, but it is essential to proper treatment. Viruses are treated differently than bacteria, and even among bacteria, one particular drug may be more effective than another. So it is with the barriers to evangelism. It is needful to identify the classification of the barrier (E-0, E-1, E-2, or E-3).

People are all different, and the barrier standing in the way of each one is different. The key is to identify the specific barrier and tear it down. If it is one the prospect has erected in his own mind, you have to take the initiative and cross the barrier. If the barrier is in your church, again you must take the initiative to change it.

You may not have erected the barrier, but you must remove it. Do not let your fears keep you from being a witness. The task begins with gaining victory over fears. While the world, the flesh, and the devil are enemies, they are not to be feared. Jesus prayed that believers (John 17:15-26) should not be taken out of the world but that they should be insulated against it. His petition was, "but that You should keep them from the evil one" (John 17:15). Victory is available to the believer by his walking in the Spirit rather than in the flesh. "Yet in all these things we are more than conquerors through Him who loved us" (Rom. 8:37). For the believer, the key to victory over fear is faith in God and his promises.

Once Christians have overcome their own fears, they are free to begin tearing away the fears of the unsaved. This is done by establishing redemptive friendships. This exposes them to Christians, the Christian life-style, and the joys of the Christian life. In Luke 14:12-13, Jesus suggested that when believers give a dinner, they should not invite only friends and relatives because they will only feel obligated to return the hospitality. Instead, he said to invite the poor, maimed, lame and blind. (This means those who are rejected by others.) When they begin to see that Christians are people much like themselves, the stained-glass barrier begins to dissolve.

We must not be judgmental. Christ alone is the righteous Judge, and Paul indicated that he will judge his own servants (1 Cor. 4:4). Our task is to accept the unsaved man as he is and win him to ourselves, so that we can lead him to a saving knowledge of Jesus Christ. Once he has become a new creation in Christ (2 Cor. 5:17), the Holy Spirit will work through the Word of God to bring about the needed changes in his conduct and life-style.

BASE
The *base* is the term used to define the average weekly attendance of a Sunday school. It is a new term, as opposed to the older measure of defining Sunday school by its enrollment. Before deciding how large to build a class or a Sunday school, you need to know the present average attendance. Before setting an attendance goal, first determine the base. The base is the average weekly Sunday school attendance. A base is not measured during the spring when attendance is high, nor during the summer when attendance is down. Add attendance for all the weeks into a total and divide by the number of Sundays. The Sunday school base is a realistic figure on which to plan growth and make calculations for outreach.

BEGINNER DEPARTMENT
This age group cannot be lumped into the "average" or "norm."

Some four- and five-year-olds are nervous and easily over-stimulated, while others are quiet and slow to respond. Some appear to have boundless energy, but others are listless. Some have seemingly limitless endurance, while others tire easily.

In the realm of mental capacity and development, a child's vocabulary and reasoning ability depend upon his out-of-church surroundings, experiences, and learning stimulation. Some exhibit self-control and self-direction: they control crying and bathroom needs and show patience, courtesy, and (usually) kindness. They obey directions.

All normal beginners can be trained to take off their own coats and hats, put away toys, help take care of equipment, and remember behavior suitable in Sunday school.

Their attention span for a story is only three to four minutes. They may be interested in a self-chosen activity for eight to ten minutes, and in a game much longer. Beginners are interested in the things of God and show remarkable depth of understanding.

Beginners may be bossy, "show-offish" or interested in things that belong to others. They need to learn cooperation. Their range of interests tend to be restricted to home, Sunday school, and natural surroundings. They are full of questions: Who? What? Why? Their teacher's answers to these questions may become their lifelong belief. They have some concept of time and are natural mimics with good imaginations. While they follow literal suggestions, symbolic expressions have no significance for them.

A beginner can learn that: (1) God shows his love to us by his gifts and care, (2) Jesus is our best Friend, (3) God sent Jesus to die for sin, (4) Jesus is now living, (5) God will forgive sin when we ask him, (6) God created everything and everyone, (7) God is always with us, (8) the Bible is God's Word and he speaks to us through it, (9) prayer can be made at any time or place, (10) Jesus helps us do right things, (11) Jesus is God's own Son, (12) God can do anything, and (13) Jesus wants us to love him.

How to Work with Beginners

The teacher of beginners needs to love children, be sympathetic and understanding, have a happy, childlike spirit, and have a controlled emotional life. Also, this teacher should have an open mind and a vivid imagination. As he prepares to work with this group, six elements should be a part of his preparation.

1. Study the lesson. See each lesson in relation to the unit, as well as to the one topic, and decide what the lesson ought to accomplish.
2. Make a list of teaching materials. Make a checklist, so hard-to-get items may be located well in advance of need.
3. Plan possible activities. Plan for variety in activities. This will care for each child's individual interests. Be sure all activities relate to the aim of the lesson. Avoid monotony and over-stimulation.
4. Outline the program. Have a uniformity in program for the security it provides. Maintain an atmosphere of freedom and informality. Be orderly, yet have flexibility enough to anticipate interruptions.
5. Choose songs carefully. Use songs about their home situations and experiences—glad songs with short sentences. Teach new songs to correlate with the lesson. Singing meets program needs, socializes a group, gives a sense of unity, and reinforces biblical information.
6. Include essential elements. Fellowship, learning, and worship are important. Use an activity time for friendly greetings, recall of Bible stories, and an activity. Have a group time for songs, birthday recognition, prayer, offering, rest and relaxation, and the Bible story.

Beginner Suggestions and Ideas

Activity time. Exchange friendly greetings; give needed help with hats and wraps. Recall Bible stories and verses.

Group time. Sing a familiar greeting song, share activity time experiences, and recognize visitors and new members, those with new brothers or sisters, or those with birthdays.

Teach giving. Help children learn to give to the Lord by naming things money will help to buy, singing about it, and praying to God about giving.

Provide rest and relaxation. Take a picture walk. Fly like birds. Skip to rhythm. Sing and march to songs, or take a short nap.

Retell the Bible story. Have children repeat the story in their own words, place the story pictures on flannelgraph, draw or show pictures about it, or examine the story in leaflets or story papers.

How to Maintain Control in a Beginner Class

Certain principles must be followed if the Beginner class is to be properly controlled and disciplined.

1. Qualified Teachers. Each teacher must be a consecrated Christian who sets a good example by a godly life. He or she must be a good disciplinarian, be dependable and punctual, and be adequately prepared.
2. Trained Teachers. Each teacher must win the hearts of the children by being sincere and warmhearted. He should be kind and calm at all times. He also should know the background and home situation by contact with parents. He must be specially instructed concerning the needs and goals of that department. He should know what is expected, and he should attend workers' meetings that engender unity of purpose among teachers.
3. Ideal Ratio of Teachers. There should be one teacher for five to seven pupils; two teachers for ten pupils; three teachers for eleven to fifteen; five teachers for sixteen to twenty; seven teachers for twenty-one to twenty-five; and eight teachers for twenty-six to thirty pupils.

How to Maintain Discipline

1. Establish a pattern of conduct. Set rules that are always followed. This fosters in children a sense of security.
2. Establish set routines for activities.
3. Make suggestions; don't scold. Don't force children or yell at them.
4. Divert attention by changing interests.
5. Encourage home cooperation. Parents should instruct children concerning conduct. They should not interfere with the class or stay to watch the children.

Suggested Activities to Keep Beginners' Interest

1. Have presession activities. When the child arrives, help him choose from available activities.
2. Provide various interest centers. Establish a book center,

nature center, handwork center, housekeeping center, and others, as room and materials allow.

3. Make the Bible lesson interesting. Use slides and filmstrips, drama, puppets, object lessons, pictures, and other visual aids.
4. Observe special days and occasions.
5. Stress Bible memorization through games and drama.

BELL—SUNDAY SCHOOL SCHEDULE

Every Sunday school needs a bell to help keep everyone aware of the schedule. When leaders add a bell, chime, or buzzer to their Sunday school, they are leading it to begin and end on time. Ring the bell at 9:30 (or at whatever time every teacher needs to be in his class), 9:45 (or the time the Sunday school lesson should begin), 10:45 (or the time the Sunday school lesson should end), and 10:50 (or the time the class should be dismissed to make their way to the morning church service). Obviously, these times will have to be adjusted if the Sunday school operates on a different time schedule. The old-fashioned bell that is rung by hand is only symbolic of its continuing effectiveness. The modern Sunday school should use an automatic timer and an electronic bell.

BIBLE, INTERPRETING THE

Interpreting the Bible is the primary task of Bible study, but that task is twofold in nature. First, because the Bible is a spiritual book coauthored by holy men of God and the Holy Spirit, the believer must use spiritual principles of interpreting the Bible, including prayer, cleansing from sin, and comparing Scriptures. Also, because the Bible was written for common men and women in language they could understand, the believer must use literary principles of interpreting the Bible. This is interpreting the Bible according to the face value of words in their setting and context. Both spiritual and natural principles are important. The man who is spiritually right with God but who fails to give attention to the normal rules of language interpretation will miss out on the message of Scripture. The man who follows these principles of interpretation exactly but is not walking in fellowship with God will also miss important lessons when he attempts to interpret the Bible.

Spiritual Principles of Interpreting the Bible

If God used holy men of God to write his Book, he wants holy men of God to interpret his Book. If one is not in a proper relationship with God, it is not realistic to think he will be able to interpret the Bible correctly.

Every Christian needs to pray as he comes to study the Bible. The Bible is God's revelation to man. As we come to hear what God has to say, we need to talk to God. David prayed, "Open my eyes, that I may see wondrous things from Your law" (Ps. 119:18). This ought to be our prayer as we come to interpret the Bible.

Sin in the life of a Christian will hinder the Holy Spirit from illuminating the Scriptures. It is important that we are not harboring unconfessed sin in our lives if we expect God to teach us through the Bible. Because no one is perfect, we need constantly to apply the principle of 1 John 1:9 to maintain our fellowship with God. "If we confess our sins, He is faithful and just to forgive us our sins and to cleanse us from all unrighteousness." Naturally, the Christian must strive to live a pure life, but when we fail, God is willing to forgive if we will confess.

No one can have a cleansed life until he first receives Christ as personal Savior. Jesus told his disciples, "Unless your righteousness exceeds the righteousness of the scribes and Pharisees, you will by no means enter the kingdom of heaven" (Matt. 5:20). The righteousness Jesus requires of his disciples is not a superior list of standards or perfect life-styles. Rather, everyone should receive the righteousness of God by faith (Rom. 3:24-25).

At salvation, we are first cleansed, but as we live in this world we are contaminated by the affairs of life. When we sin, we need to be cleansed so we can restore our broken fellowship with God. Jesus said, "He who is bathed needs only to wash his feet, but is completely clean; and you are clean, but not all of you" (John 13:10).

The Bible is the best interpreter of itself. As we study the Bible, we should learn to compare the Scriptures we are studying with other relevant passages of Scripture to interpret the Bible.

Literary Principles of Interpreting the Bible

Conservatives believe in a "historical grammatical" interpretation of the Bible. This basically means that we study the Bible within its historical context. In other words, we interpret the Bible as we would normally interpret any literary work, using the normal rules of grammar.

As we come to interpret a passage, we must consider its historical context. Since the author spoke in a historical setting, we must understand something about that background to interpret the text.

Also, the more we know about the author, the easier it will be to determine what he wanted to say in the passage. The Bible was written by men to other individuals or groups. The good interpreter of the Bible will also interpret a passage in light of the recipients of the message. We should also consider the place of the passage in the context of the total message of the book in which it is found.

Words are important, so we also interpret the Scriptures in their grammatical context. God inspired the words of Scripture. When both the Old and New Testaments were being written, God chose to use Hebrew and Greek, explicit languages in which to write his Word. God chose to give his Word first to people in a culture that was very careful about the words used. When we interpret the Bible, we should use our knowledge of grammar to interpret the passage.

The Bible should be interpreted literally, which means we should seek the obvious meaning of words, context, and language. When we interpret literally, we seek the literal meaning of the author when he wrote or spoke the message of God. We should not seek for a hidden or mystical meaning. If God had written his message in esoteric pictures, there would be no objectivity to Christianity. Anyone could make a passage mean anything he desired. Hence, there could be no Christianity.

Do not stumble over the word *mystery* in Scripture (Eph. 3:9). A mystery was part of the message of grace that was hidden in the Old Testament, but revealed in the New.

The Bible contains much figurative language, such as metaphors, similes, parables (extended metaphors), and many other figures of speech. It is generally clear when figurative language appears that a clear understandable message is being taught. To interpret the Bible, the reader must search for the literal meaning the author had in mind when he used the figurative language.

The principle of interpreting Scripture according to the meaning of the author should remind us that the Bible's authorship is both human and divine. Therefore, we must follow human laws of interpretation to understand the Scripture. But we must also follow the spiritual principles of illumination to understand the mind of the Holy Spirit.

BIBLE SEARCH

Bible search is a method of teaching where the students learn by searching the Bible rather than listening to a lecture. With the presentation of a statement, the class is to search the Scriptures to find the reference and explanation for the statement presented. The following rules should be observed by the class for effective use of Bible search.

1. Each person is to find two references for each statement made.
2. Each person may use all available resource materials to find these Scriptures.
3. Class members may work in pairs, sharing the work and pooling their knowledge. Each pair should present a common conclusion.
4. The conclusions must be written on paper to share with the class. Have a number of concordances and commentaries available to aid the search for Scripture references. Arrange also to have pencils, paper, and extra Bibles handy.

Use the chalkboard or a felt-tipped pen and a flip chart to place statements relevant to the topic. Place only one statement on each side of each page of your flip chart or section of the chalkboard. The class should be working on only one assignment at a time. First, show the statement to the class and read it to them. Second, give them about two minutes to search for the scriptural source of each statement. Finally, let the students report on their findings. Be careful that they do not simply read back the phrases of the Scripture verses they have found. Ask them to tell the meaning of the verses. This way, one student teaches the others as he explains and interprets the Word of God.

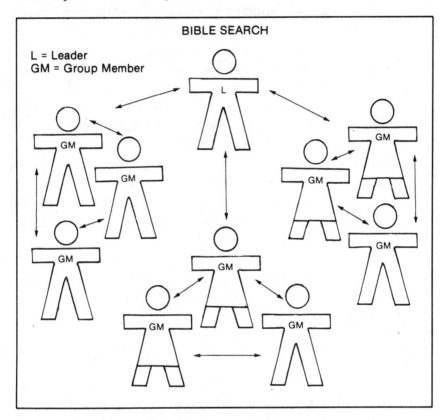

BIBLE SEARCH

L = Leader
GM = Group Member

BIBLE STUDY AND LESSON PREPARATION

The Bible is the Word of God, which brings the revelation of God's will to men. If we are to teach God's message, we must first comprehend what he says. Here are some practical methods for Bible study as you prepare your Sunday school lesson:

1. Read the text. Before reading commentaries in quarterlies or lesson aids, read the Bible lesson passage thoroughly several times. Write down all questions that come to mind. Put yourself in the pupil's place. What does he need to know? What bothers him? Note possible answers.

2. Read the context. Read the entire chapter, section, or book of the Bible in which the lesson passage occurs. Some passages of the Bible seem self-contained, but seen in the light of the whole book, they look different. Try to understand the setting by the circumstances under which the passage was written, the line of thought with which it is connected, and the main emphasis of the section where the passage appears.

3. Study the details. Who are the persons mentioned? What does this book say about them elsewhere? What does the Bible as a whole teach about them? Use a concordance or Bible dictionary and center references. Exactly what events occurred? Name them in order. Is there a similar event elsewhere in the Bible? Locate places in an atlas.

4. What does the text teach? The teaching of the Bible is called doctrine. Determine the doctrine by asking, "What is the main principle of this text? What do the words mean? How is it illustrated? How is the teaching of this passage linked with the general teaching of the Bible?"

5. How is the teaching applied? How is this to be applied to the pupil's life? Completion of a Bible story is not the end of the lesson. Its carryover into life must be determined by application.

How to Read and Apply the Bible in Your Personal Study

As you study the Bible in your lesson preparation, follow these nine steps to make the lesson more meaningful in your own life before attempting to teach it in your class.

1. Begin reading by yielding yourself to God. Before seeking to hear from God, take a moment to consciously and intentionally yield yourself to God, asking him to make the lesson real in your life. Pray, "Open my eyes, that I may see wondrous things from Your law" (Ps. 119:18).

2. Listen to the voice of God as you read. Chiang Kai-shek, former President of the Republic of China, testified, "The Bible is the voice of the Holy Spirit to me." Let God speak to you as you read his Word, and let it accomplish its objectives in your life (cf. 2 Tim. 3:16).

3. Read the Bible before you read books about the Bible. Study-

ing other books is not wrong unless they are books containing false teaching. But study the Bible first to get a foundation upon which you can add the insights of other writers (Acts 17:11).

4. Read with your whole attention on the Bible. Christians should meditate on the words of Scripture and allow them to become a part of them (Ps. 119:15). When a man asked R. A. Torrey to tell him in one word how he studied the Bible, Torrey responded, "Thoughtfully."

5. Read with attention to words and their meaning. Christians believe God inspired the very words of Scripture, so the words of Scripture are very important. The Bereans "searched the Scriptures" (Acts 17:11). The word *search* means to investigate, inquire, scrutinize, or sift. Originally this word referred to the sifting of chaff from the grain. As we study the Bible, we should "search the Scriptures," which means to separate every word and study every word carefully and individually.

6. Read to understand what the Bible is saying. Don't read the Bible to find a proof text for a particular theological system. Rather, be diligent in your study of Scripture to understand what the Bible is saying (2 Tim. 2:15). Someone once said, "The Bible is twenty-one; it can speak for itself." Let the Bible speak for itself as you read it.

7. Read some every day, but plan to read the whole Bible. Some people just read parts of the Bible, but the Christian should study the whole Bible from Genesis to Revelation. The whole Bible has something to teach us about the person and work of Jesus and how to live the Christian life (Luke 24:27). Jesus taught the whole Bible and urged his disciples to do the same (Matt. 5:17-19).

8. Read the Bible systematically. The early Christians read the Scriptures daily, setting a good example for Christians today (Acts 17:11). Reading the Bible systematically implies reading the Bible (1) every day, (2) at the same time every day, and (3) following the same pattern or reading schedule every day.

9. Read the Bible to apply it to your life. James urged the early

church, "But be doers of the word, and not hearers only, deceiving yourselves" (James 1:22). As you read the Scriptures, ask yourself the following questions: (1) Is there some command to obey? (2) Is there some promise to claim? (3) Is there some sin to avoid? (4) Is there some prayer to pray? (5) Is there some challenge to accept?

BIBLE USE IN CLASS

Pupils should bring their Bibles not only to earn points or for a contest, but to use them. Each should be encouraged to own a Bible. If any cannot afford it, the church should provide one. Each age group should use the Bible. Some ideas on how to use the Bible in class for various age levels follow.

1. *Preschool.* Teach that the Bible is a special book. It is God's book. It tells about Jesus. It tells what is right and what is wrong. All the stories of the Bible are true stories. Children should see older persons carefully handling the Bible and studying it.

   Children should know which stories you tell are from the Bible and which are not. Always hold the Bible when telling a Bible story, but not for other stories. Show Bible pictures. The Bible story for the preschool child should be less than five minutes in length, free from much description, full of repetition, and free from fear-producing elements. There should be a Bible in the department.

2. *Primary.* Encourage the child to bring his Bible and to use it. Point out the differences between the Old and New Testaments. Study the children of the Bible. Help the child locate memory verses and Bible stories in his own Bible. Let the child read carefully selected verses aloud, especially the third grader. Tell the Bible story from the Bible, not from a quarterly.

3. *Junior.* Teach that the Bible is inspired by God, that it is God's revelation to us, that God expects us to obey its teachings, that the Bible is the final authority in all matters, and that the Bible helps us to solve our everyday problems.

   The junior should learn the books of the Bible in order; he

should learn the chronology, the history, and the geography of the Bible. He should form the habit of daily reading, and he should memorize Scripture.

Encourage juniors to read their Bibles by having some form of group reading in every class session: Unison, responsive, antiphonal (boys vs. girls), or by rows. Have sword drills and treasure hunts (where references all contain a certain word, the "treasure") and notebooks in which to copy verses and illustrate. During teaching, pause to ask questions about the Bible passage. To answer, pupils must read the verse silently and answer in their own words.

4. *Youth.* Young teens should be learning to use Bible study helps such as a Bible atlas, dictionary, and harmony of the Gospels. Provide for participation in direct Bible study. Provide a variety of studies—Bible survey, doctrines, the Bible and science, and other topical studies. Allow opportunity for paraphrasing and Bible search (see separate articles).

5. *Adults.* Provide for participation in direct Bible study. Use Bible study guides that can be applied to many passages of Scripture to encourage daily Bible reading. Make use of book studies and topical studies.

Let pupils make their own application when possible. Teach from the Bible, not from an aid. Have an aim for each lesson. Evaluate each lesson.

In all Bible study, look for something. Write down what you find. Ask yourself the following questions:

What does this mean to me?

Is there an example for me to follow?

Is there a command for me to obey?

Is there a sin for me to avoid or forsake?

Is there a promise for me to claim?

Are there conditions to that promise?

What does the chapter teach me about God?

What does it teach me about Jesus Christ?

What does it teach me about the Holy Spirit?

What does it teach me about sin?

What does it teach me about Christian living?

What is one practical verse for me to apply to my own life?

Is there anything in this chapter that should be my prayer for today?

Try to think of a song that expresses the teaching of this chapter.

BIBLICAL BARRIERS

There are both biblical and natural barriers that cause a church to stop growing or prevent it from growing. A biblical barrier grows out of the nature of Christianity.

Biblical barriers to church growth include: (1) the offense of the cross, (2) the need to repent of one's sins and turn from them, and (3) the need to confess Christ before others and be baptized.

BILLINGTON, DALLAS FRANKLIN (1903–1972)

Born in a log house in western Kentucky and raised in a devout Christian home, Billington responded to the gospel at the age of twenty-one, when he was converted in a tent meeting in Paducah, Kentucky. In June 1934, he organized a group of people into the Akron Baptist Temple, Akron, Ohio. Beginning with thirteen people meeting in an elementary school and an offering of $1.18, the Akron Baptist Temple was born. Under his ministry over the next thirty-eight years, the church grew to more than sixteen thousand members and physical assets of several million dollars. The church was among the first to have its own television studio. Its radio, television, and missionary outreach made its ministry worldwide. In 1968 the church was recognized by *Christian Life* magazine as having the world's largest Sunday school.

BIOLOGICAL GROWTH

Biological growth is the numerical growth of a church resulting from babies born to church members and added to the church membership and attendance.

BOARD OF CHRISTIAN EDUCATION

As a church grows, pastors and church boards will need help in coordinating the educational program. One means of accomplishing this task is to establish a board of Christian education or committee to help ensure the continued growth and efficiency of the church.

Why Have a Board of Christian Education?

There are several reasons for organizing the church's educational program under a board of Christian education including: (1) to help the church carry out the great commission, (2) to fulfill the model of representative government in the local church, (3) to prevent omissions, overlapping and overemphasis in the local church, (4) to provide educated leadership in the local church, (5) to effectively correlate and coordinate Christian education, (6) to avoid duplicating services and (7) to follow biblical principles.

How to Set Up a Board of Christian Education

There are several steps involved in setting up a C. E. board for a local church. Begin by appointing an investigating committee to determine the need. This committee serves temporarily and is dissolved when its final recommendations have been submitted to the governing church board. It should be composed of individuals committed to improving the quality of their church's C. E. program. It is best to give this investigating committee three specific responsibilities. First, they should establish a standard by which they can evaluate the existing program. This standard can be established by visiting another church with a good educational program or in consultation with denominational leaders of the C. E. department of a local Bible school, seminary, or Christian school. Second, they should study the existing program of the church. Third, a comparison should be made between the existing program and the ideal or prospective program of the church.

Once the decision has been made to establish a C. E. board, the area of responsibility and authority of the new board should be clearly defined. Members of this board should know how they relate to the official church board and the congregation. Also, the number of people who should be members of the C. E. board should be determined at this time. It would be best to establish the qualifications of those who serve on the board at this time.

Next, the proposed new board should be taken to the church congregation for their approval. This may involve additional steps such as a constitutional amendment or new bylaw to be added to the governing documents of the church. Finally, the members of the new board should be selected and appointed to serve. In many churches, these members are appointed at the annual meeting when the nominating committee recommends other appointments. Other churches prefer to appoint these members at a workers' conference or have them appointed by the official church board.

Duties of the Board of Christian Education

The duties of the board of Christian education are:

1. To establish all policy for the educational programs of the church with respect to materials, personnel, meeting times and meeting places of classes, and groups within the program
2. To select and approve all educational literature
3. To coordinate teaching methods among the various programs, outlining the goals and objectives of those programs
4. To select, train, and approve leaders and teaching staff
5. To evaluate and plan for future Christian education needs
6. To plan all educational outings and activities
7. To prepare and submit an annual budget for approval by the church
8. To appoint the minister of Christian education

Qualifications for Members of the Board of Christian Education

Members of the C. E. board should have the capacity to grow and the willingness to continue to study the work, plans, and educational materials of Christian education. Also, they should have a deep interest in the work and a willingness to spend time on the designated responsibility. Third, they should have some practical experience in the field of Christian education. Also, they should have the ability to work with others and possess good judgment and intellectual ability.

BONDING (See ASSIMILATING NEW MEMBERS)

BOOMERS (See BABY BOOMERS)

BRAINSTORMING

Brainstorming is a creative method of teaching that allows the students freedom to express their opinion or knowledge about a topic so that they learn in the process. Give each student a three-by-five-inch card on which you have written a word to be discussed. Have each write down the first thing that comes to mind concerning the word. Discuss contributions later. First, get students to think creatively. After each has written something on a card, give opportunity to share the ideas. The ground rules for brainstorming are simple. Each person says what is on his card or whatever comes to mind that he may not have written down. As he reacts to what is said by others, he should not question the validity of their contributions. When such questioning and refutation begins, creativity generally stops. The aim of brainstorming is creativity.

Encourage members to amplify what is said by other students. This is called "hitchhiking" on someone else's thoughts. The contribution of one student may bring to another person's mind a further thought on the topic. This person shares his new or expanded thought.

BRIDGING GROWTH

Bridging growth refers to the increase of a church's (denomination) membership through the process by which new churches are planted in cultures different from the culture of the base church. This growth is represented in two degrees: first (designated as E-2 evangelism), in cultures somewhat different from the original church, and second (designated as E-3 evangelism), in cultures with a different language from the original church.

BUDGET, PRINCIPLES OF THE CHURCH

Several principles should govern the church budget:
    1. It should be practical and reliable, tailored by the administrator to fit the operation of the church.

2. It should eliminate wasteful expenditures, yet it should not promote false economies by failing to provide for minor repairs that soon become costly major repairs.
3. It should be properly constructed to achieve the important ministry goals of the church.
4. The ratio of expenditures to various operations is spelled out and adjustments made from year to year.
5. A projected budget must be based on accurate past financial records.
6. It should be prepared and adopted prior to the end of the fiscal year, to be in effect by the first of the year.

BUILDINGS (See also PROVIDING ADDITIONAL SPACE)

The psalmist wrote, "I was glad when they said to me, 'Let us go into the house of the Lord'" (Ps. 122:1). Besides the inner strength he received from going, there also must have been something in the appearance of the temple that made him glad for the opportunity to worship the Lord. It must have been attractive, appealing, and inviting.

For years Christian education's effectiveness was hindered because of limited facilities and equipment. Now we realize that the building sets the pattern for the type and quality of Christian education. It is important that as we think of "equipment" for Christian education, we think of the building in which the work is to be done.

1. The Equipped Church Building. A church must begin its teaching ministry in the existing building, even though facilities may be limited. However, rooms can be clean, neat, and attractive. A well-kept building says to outsiders, This church has vision and is interested in progress. The building indicates that those who attend have spiritual values because they care for the place where they worship God. The world may not know much of the Bible's teaching, but they're acquainted with the axiom, Cleanliness is next to godliness. A nicely painted building, with shrubs trimmed, grass mowed, and signs properly marked, is a silent sermon. A building with such appeal says to some, Enter.

The church needs a committee to see that its equipment is kept in good repair. This committee also should see that equipment and facilities are adequate for the growing educational ministry. This indicates vision.

If possible, the pastor's study should be at the church. In addition to the church name sign and schedule of services, there also should be a sign indicating where the pastor's office is located so that visitors, business people, church members, and people with problems can locate it.

The pastor's study should have the equipment necessary to carry on the pastor's work. It should be attractive, well lighted, ventilated, and painted, with desks, chairs, filing cabinets, and seating for visitors.

When the church can have a separate church office, this should accommodate visitors so the pastor can have more privacy in his study. The business office (with its telephone, desk, chairs, typewriter, and other necessary furniture) may be used for the duplicating work of the church such as church bulletins.

If the church is large enough to have a director of Christian education, a minister of youth, or an associate minister, they should have their own offices. It should be equipped with the necessary items to carry on this ministry and perhaps large enough for chairs and a table for conferences with teachers and officers of the church. The Christian education building should have rooms for the various departments in the Sunday school. These departmental rooms should be accessible for the age groups meeting in them and well marked so visitors can be directed or taken to them easily.

When the building and equipment are examined, many miscellaneous items should be checked also: coat racks, toilet facilities, drinking fountains, chorus and hymn books, pianos, chalkboards and chalk, pulpits, flannelboards, tackboards, and other equipment.

While equipment alone is not the answer, it helps produce answers.

2. The Equipped Administrative Area. In an effective Christian

education ministry, the heart and most active area will be the Christian education office and the Christian education director's office.

The church having a director of Christian education should provide him with the necessary equipment for his office. The office should be accessible to those who need to visit with him for the work and should be equipped with a good desk, chairs, adequate lighting, the necessary filing cabinets, and, if there is room, a table for working over plans with leaders in the department as well as for conducting conferences.

If there is only the office for Christian education or the Sunday school—with no particular office for the director—this office should be equipped with the records, the filing cabinet, and the other materials necessary for the work. In this office it would be well to store the projectors, screens, tape recorders, record players, and other audiovisual equipment. This office is important and, like the other offices, should be properly marked so people will know where it is. It also should be rather central in its location so the reports on Sunday can be brought there for the tabulation of attendance, etc.

The administration area will be worthy of adequate furnishings: work area, desks, filing cabinet facilities, duplicating facilities, and storage. The continued planning for an extended outreach in ministry, as well as the record keeping, is done from the administrative area of the Christian Education Department. There should be the necessary equipment for this in the well-planned church program.

BUILDING FOR TEAM TEACHING

Far too often, churches are content to let Christian education people struggle with all but impossible handicaps. If leaders are to cope with changing situations, they must have sound curriculum content and good teaching facilities and equipment. We need to do some penance for the lack of encouragement given those willing to teach whom we needlessly handicap by not providing the tools. The improvement of the educational programs of churches rests upon the parents and the church leaders charged with local church administration.

For those concerned with the educational programs, there should be an immediate evaluation of buildings, equipment, teachers, and the newer methods of teaching suggested by contemporary leaders in the field of religious education. These newer methods envision teachers functioning cooperatively as a team under the direction of an experienced master.

This calls for classrooms considerably larger than those to which many have been accustomed. The number of pupils in each room is considerably greater than that which formerly assembled in a ten-by-twelve-foot class space. The number of pupils and the size of the classroom should not be determined exclusively by an architect, the building committee, or the building budget, but should be designed by those involved in teaching. It should provide the best possible learning situation for the age group involved. The younger the pupils, the more floor space needed to avoid crowding and overstimulation, and to permit room for activities. The younger the pupils, the fewer there should be to a given classroom, so they may have personal attention and guidance.

The concept of team teaching, unfamiliar to many, often is rejected by Christian education committees that do not understand its purpose or do not visit churches using this method successfully.

This method was evaluated through experiments in our vacation Bible school years ago. With a good lead teacher and three or four less-experienced persons assisting, there were better results than when pupils went into small classes.

Why not use your vacation Bible school to test group learning? Use two or three trained teachers in each of the various age groups of VBS. Put with them persons with aptitude for guiding young children.

Such learning procedures do not call for a frightening or drastic revolution in teaching methods. The basic premise is that teachers work cooperatively on a planned program within a given room with a larger number of pupils. Those who have successfully used this method find that the larger room and team of teachers make possible a greater variety of teaching experiences, and that learning can take place in such an environment much more effectively than in a small, crowded room.

This group learning is not restricted to "sitting and telling," but also includes creative, purposeful activities of considerable variety. In all of this, the children learn how to adjust to and appreciate others who come from different backgrounds and who have different tastes and personalities.

During the last ten or fifteen years, there has been a commendable increase in the size of classrooms. However, most rooms still lack inspiration and stimulation. They are devoid of those qualities that evoke a sense of pleasure in their appearance, such as nice furnishings, a good arrangement, and attractive colors.

Too many church classrooms offer little beyond four walls and rows of chairs. They are stark, unadorned, and "faceless." This need not and should not be. Walls can be made sources of inspiration and can aid in teaching. Make inexpensive display areas of perforated panels with pins or wire brackets for hanging items of interest. Mount pictures with Plasti-tak.

Why should the classroom look the same every Sunday morning? Why not occasionally change the decor, rearrange the furniture, or introduce different learning procedures? You cannot find an easy way to good teaching, but you can make it more effective by adding variety, beauty, inspiration, and elements of surprise.

"The navy has a saying, 'If it doesn't move, paint it,'" one architect said. School executives now are saying, "If it doesn't move, we don't want it." Generally speaking, this applies to church school classrooms also. Not only are classrooms with large floor areas pleasing and inspiring, but they permit flexibility in teaching methods, and the furnishings and equipment can be adjusted to implement those teaching methods.

BULLETIN BOARDS

Bulletin boards may be used for both advertisement and education. The materials should be attractive and relevant to the needs and interests of the group. Bulletin boards in classrooms, assembly rooms, or central places in the church can provide valuable training and teaching aids or be used for advertising. To be effective, longer-term displays must be attractive, neatly arranged, and kept current. During a teaching session a bulletin board might hold a time line of yarn and thumbtacks.

BUS MINISTRY

Bus evangelism is a method of establishing a bus route and visiting people along that route to invite them to attend the Sunday school with a view of reaching them for Christ. It is more than convenience busing; it is intentional evangelism, using a bus as a tool to reach people. Bus evangelism has been declining in recent years but is now stabilized. The reason Sunday school busing has declined is because of increased cost of gasoline, insurance, and maintenance on the vehicles. Some churches got into the bus ministry for the wrong reasons (just for numbers or to keep their children from going to other churches). The high cost of running buses has been enough to force these churches out of the bus ministry. Also, the nurturing aim of some Sunday schools was at cross purposes with the implied evangelistic nature of bus ministry.

Every church should consider running at least one Sunday school bus as part of its total evangelistic strategy. A bus ministry will bring outreach, soul winning, and excitement in the church. If the bus workers reach out in faith, it could bring revival to the church.

Those opposed to busing will question if the church really wants all the excitement associated with Sunday school busing when "bus kids" damage the church property and facilities, get into fights with the church leaders' kids, and stuff rolls of toilet paper down the commode each Sunday morning. Look beyond the problems. The real excitement of bus ministry is when children are actually won to Jesus Christ. When that happens, there is not only rejoicing in heaven, but also among the bus and Sunday school workers who are involved in bringing boys and girls to a saving knowledge of Christ through this ministry.

Busing is an excellent tool for reaching families for Christ. After a child who rides the bus is won to Christ, the workers can use that leverage to reach the parents. Through side-door evangelism families are brought into the church.

Bus Ministry Essentials

The key word is *evangelism*. The church bus is not new to this generation. Churches have provided alternate transportation for various reasons for many years: for children whose parents could not or would not bring them to church, and for aging persons who could not drive a car. The bus was a means of meeting the needs of the riders.

More recently, the church bus has come into its own as one of the most effective tools for Sunday school outreach. But it is more than a vehicle to swell the numbers on the attendance record board. It is a recognized means of evangelism. Therefore we place high on the list of essentials that purpose.

1. Evangelism. Sheer arithmetic leads to the inescapable conclusion that the greater the number of people who hear the gospel, the greater the number of people who will be saved. People who are not brought under the sound of the gospel have little chance of being reached and won. The church bus evangelism ministry should be equated with every other phase of church work. No one form of outreach can be considered the only way to evangelize. In actuality every facet of the church's outreach should be considered as a means to win souls. The music, the teaching—even the baseball team should be considered as yet another way to obey the great commission. When the bus ministry is viewed in its proper light—as one of the really effective ways to win souls—it will have the unqualified backing of the church. When it is considered vital, no amount of discouragement can cause it to be abandoned. Bearing in mind that each one who is reached probably will influence five or more people, workers will strive to bring them in.

2. Sincere commitment. Personnel who have been called by God cannot be easily swayed by difficulties. Prayer and careful consideration are needed before one is committed to any task in the church. Some less visible service in the bus ministry (such as keeping the engine in running order)

is not often given the recognition it deserves. Anyone serving with the hope of praise will quickly give up in the face of adversity. It is always true that when God calls, he supplies. Certain of the value of his calling, the bus ministry worker in any capacity will wait upon the Lord for that supply so definitely promised in Philippians 4:19, "My God shall supply all your need."

3. Real love for people. Many of the riders on the bus will be children—little children, unkempt children, vocal children, and sometimes children with violent tempers. It's fairly easy to love a clean child in Sunday-best clothing, but it's not always easy to get near an unwashed, disheveled one. Yet in her heart-baring, soul-searching book, *Climbing,* Rosalind Goforth pointed out one of her lessons in loving the unlovely. In a Chinese home where the beds were rolled mats on an elevated brick platform, Mrs. Goforth sat down to talk with a weeping Chinese mother. "I am so anxious and heartsick," the woman confessed to her. "The place is crawling with lice, and I have so much work to do I cannot get rid of them." Mrs. Goforth's instinctive reaction would have been natural—but she did not carry it out. Instead of recoiling, she slid closer to the weeping woman and put her arm around her. That's love for people.

4. A qualified director. People will follow a man who knows where he is going. In any area of activity, there must be a general who can show (not tell) others the way to go or to do. The successful bus director will be one who is in his position because he has himself been a bus ministry worker. He has experienced the problems.

   A qualified leader must know more than the techniques of his task. He must have a good relationship with his followers. He can say with Paul, "Do as I do." His own unbounded enthusiasm—born of experience with results—will transfer itself to his workers. He can say with authority, "I know it works, because I've done it."

   Often at least a part-time employee of the church, the efficient bus director will prove to be a good investment of the church's money. The busing program will bring in more unreached souls than probably any other single outreach.

5. Visitation. Like the director, the bus workers must be dedicated to the task of reaching people. They should not be dissatisfied or discouraged if every visit does not produce a rider. They should not scratch a child off the list if he fails to be ready on time. They should go back to the home and try again and again. (The record set by one outstanding bus director was eighty visits to one elderly man before the man was brought to church and subsequently won to Christ.) Just as the Good Shepherd sought till he found the lost sheep, the good church bus worker keeps on seeking little lost lambs until he finds them.

One noted bus director estimates that for every ten riders, an hour of visitation is required. In many churches, bus captains and other workers meet at the church for breakfast on Saturday, then go out and visit at least until noon. Some make a day of it. There is no instant success for the bus worker. He must be just that—a worker.

6. Getting riders. Robert Raikes, the founder of Sunday school, originally followed his editor-father's plan of trying to reform the delinquent adults in Gloucester, England. One day, on a chance encounter with young ruffians, he recognized that his efforts at changing lives must start with the children. Thus began the first Sunday school. A noted bus leader, William Powell, had a similar experience: "I approached the adults first. 'That is a wonderful thing you are doing, but we are not interested,' they would say. Then I learned to go to the children first. . . . I simply ride around in my bus looking for children. When I find them out playing, I get out of the bus and ask them if they want to see a magic trick. After I show them the trick and give every child a pair of the cards with Bible verses and church information, I find out which children are not attending church. Then I get them excited about riding that big bus with all the other boys and girls to my wonderful church." Then he fills out a prospect card for all unchurched children and makes a visit

to the parents to be sure the child may ride the bus the next day.

7. Program while riding. The bus captain is often responsible for planning and conducting a program for the riders. While the driver's attention is focused on the road, someone may direct the attention and activity of the boys and girls. If there is no plan, the riders will quickly devise one.

   A lively, interesting program will preclude any mischief making. An enthusiastic, strong-voiced singer can teach short choruses that will assure riders of carrying home that much truth in their hearts. (He will be sure the choruses are understood and scriptural.) Games can be used to teach memory verses, and Bible stories can be presented in a variety of interesting ways: puppets, flannelgraph, and pictures. A pastor in Poway, California, was so sold on the value of the bus program that he discouraged riders from driving their own cars to church.

8. Effective Sunday school teaching. Boys and girls may happily ride the bus one Sunday, anticipating an interesting morning at the wonderful church described to them. If they are bored by unprepared, untrained teachers (who can in no way meet the competition of our television cartoons), they will not come again. If they do, they may come prepared to "add some life to the class."

   The truly effective teacher is one who loves the children regardless of their status or condition. Frequently using "Honey" as a substitute for a name does not deceive a child. Some churches have classes totally devoted to bus kids, and for them it has proven successful. Teachers especially qualified to deal with undisciplined children are in charge of the bus classes. The result has been less disruption in the regular teaching program and better outreach to the unchurched.

9. An interesting children's church. Children's church and interest do not necessarily go together. In one church this was demonstrated by the junior boys who were brought in the front door of the church, then made their way out the

bathroom window to escape the boredom of the program offered them.

We must begin where they are in order to bring them where they need to be. If it is children's church, the music, stories, and "sermon" must be geared to the age group that will be there. In a young bus ministry in which there may not be a sufficient number of Juniors (ages nine to eleven) to warrant a separate group, the church can combine these two successfully. (Browse at the Christian bookstore for books to guide a children's church program.)

10. Trained personal workers. Christian workers in any field today have been made aware that severe problems exist in the homes of many of the children in their charge. Nowhere is this more apparent than in the lives touched by the bus ministry. Some training should be extended by the church to help these people know some ways to deal with the hurts and needs they will encounter. When boys and girls make decisions for Christ, the personal workers need to know how to deal with them and how to visit their parents.

11. Soul-winning visits. Not all visits are made with this purpose in first seeking riders. However, when the workers have sincerely and consistently shown interest in the children of the family, a door is open to reach the parents. As it was in the first Sunday school, when the children's lives and attitudes were changed, parents began to examine the reason for it. The purposeful bus visitor will visit with a goal to lead the parents to Christ.

An experienced visitor stated, "It is ten times easier to reach a child than to reach the parent. But it is ten times easier to reach the parent after we have reached the child."

12. Fun times. Church recreation leaders long ago learned that one way to establish good rapport with their charges (young or old) is through enjoying a fun time together. This may take the form of a picnic at a nearby park after church or in some cases, a potluck dinner for them right at the church. It can be a special Saturday activity once a month, like a trip to the zoo or a museum, or some other commu-

nity opportunity. The children may then view their leaders as people who can be happy and laugh as well as be stern and sober in class.

13. Church support. No matter how wholeheartedly the bus workers may enter into their task of visiting and transporting children or adults to services, they need the support of the church membership. The support is not simply monetary, although the budget should allow for the finances necessary for maintenance and gasoline. But the church should also show approval by willingness to adapt to the changes that might be incurred because of added numbers in attendance.

"Our little church is getting too big," some staid old-timers complained in one bus explosion promotion. "We liked it the way it was," one said. The church must be constantly aware of the values of a bus ministry. Testimonies from those won, reports of numbers reached, descriptions, and updates all help to let members know that the time and money investment the church has made has been worthwhile.

In a greater way than ever before, people want something to show for their money. Carried on in the proper, effective manner described here, the bus evangelism ministry will produce the desired results.

Bus Ministry Failure

While many churches have practiced proper bus evangelism procedures with great success and booming attendance, others have experienced failure and actual financial loss. There are variables, both spiritual and material, which account for this deep disappointment. Bearing in mind that "the battle is the Lord's" and that the foes are "principalities and powers" and not flesh and blood, let us examine some of the factors that can make reaching the unchurched through bus evangelism a failure.

1. Failure to obey the great commission. Taking the gospel to every person is God's command.
2. Using the "drop-in" policy. As some businesses erroneously do, the church may put up a sign and expect people to just

drop in. They permit this concept to replace God's clear command to go and bring them in.

3. Business as usual. Satisfied with the program of the church, the leaders compare themselves to themselves and shrug off their laxity saying, "We're doing about as much good as most of the other churches."

4. Limited vision. Failure to see the needs and possibilities around them.

5. Spiritual nearsightedness. There is no awareness that "the fields are white already to harvest."

6. Lack of faith. "This might work for some churches, but we have an unusual situation."

7. Doubt that the number of people won is determined by the vision, attitude, and commitment of the pastor and possibly the staff. This contingent does not recognize that space, population, and finances do not control church growth.

8. Minimizing the importance of children. "Only a child," they say. Jesus spent time and attention on children, illustrating spiritual truths by their lives. In reality, winning the children is the most effective way to evangelize your community. And regular church bus outreach is the best way to win those children.

9. Spreading yourself too thin. "If you chase too many rabbits at once, you cannot catch even one," a wise man observed. There are a multiplicity of duties and activities a church could be involved in doing, but there is one main priority: Get the gospel to every creature. For this purpose, Jesus promised his blessing: "Lo, I am with you always" (Matthew 28:20).

10. Doubting God's ability to use you and your church. "I know he can do it, all right . . . but will he do it for me?" The Bible is clear that God will not bless this lack of faith, for "he who comes to God must believe that He is, and that He is a rewarder of those who diligently seek Him" (Heb. 11:6). Activity is often easier than trust.

11. Lack of personal commitment that would make possible establishment of right priorities and emphases.

12. Failure to undergird all activities with prayer. Failure to pray

for that "wisdom from above" that is promised to those who do not doubt and waver, but who ask for God's help. Failure to pray for the strength promised for whatever God directs us to do (Phil. 4:13).

13. Waiting for unanimous support. Sometimes one or two outspoken persons can prevent action on a vital issue. It should be remembered that a majority should determine what the church does on any given decision.

14. Failure to plan ahead. Failure to consider the inevitable changes and needs in a bus ministry will render it ineffective. The church should be aware in advance that classrooms and teaching procedures may have to change to accommodate the large numbers.

15. Unwillingness to make changes. When they do come, changes are deeply resented by church members with no vision. They grumble, "We've never done it that way before."

16. Conflict over revised space and personnel. It may be impossible to have the ideal ten people to one teacher.

17. Failure to recruit and prepare an adequate number of workers for additional pupils. The meaning of the word *adequate* is, of course, dependent on the quality and effectiveness of a given worker. Regardless of philosophy about the ratio of pupils and teacher, plans must be made in advance to have workers on hand to take care of the pupils who come.

18. Sacrificing quality for quantity—and vice versa. The two must go hand and hand; it is not either/or.

19. Failing to keep bus workers motivated. Make sure they are duly recognized for faithful service and for special outreach. Provide funds for their reasonable needs and activities.

20. Placing the bus director under supervision of a committee. No one in a place of authority can function at his best with his hands tied. He will not fight for his vision, but give up.

21. Viewing the bus outreach as merely a convenient form of transportation for persons without cars.

22. Use of high-pressure methods of child evangelism. (This reflects upon the need for trained counselors.) Scripture sets no age limits on salvation, and it does clearly direct

that children should be taught and guided "in the way they should go." Careful counseling will make sure the child understands his decision. Subsequent good teaching will help him to grow.

23. Wrong concept of the use of contests, gifts, and awards. These may result in numerical gain for a few weeks, but they will never sustain the growth over a period of time.

   Overemphasis on gimmicks and rewards or gifts has been called paying too much attention to the peanuts and letting the elephants get away. ("We can't afford the take-home papers you suggest for the unsaved kids to carry into their homes, because we're spending all our money on buses.") In a word, they have gotten all the "elephants" there, but the means has hampered the end.

The above causes of failure may be considered as nonmeasurable. More foreseeable and more visible are the following items:

1. Wrong choice of a director. Careless, unpremeditated choice of an inexperienced person can result in disaster. One who lacks training and dedication to the task will be unable to cope with problems. The church should prove a prospective director by considering his past record. What are the projected goals for the outreach by the bus? Does this prospect's record show that he can accomplish this goal or lead the bus workers in doing it? He should have "walked in the moccasins" of the bus captain, thus becoming acquainted with what lies ahead.

2. Too few visits. There is no substitute for visitation. This is one factor that can be remedied. Set out to increase the time spent from door to door until each bus captain is spending at least four hours a week visiting those on his route.

3. Poor recruitment. One bus captain cannot do the job of three of four persons, such as are needed to effectively carry out the ministry each week. Besides a safe and dependable driver, he needs a cocaptain and some young people to conduct the riding program.

4. Too few workers and materials. Here come the "elephants."

They are brought in, expecting to be fed, but all the "peanuts" have gone to entice them there. Keep them coming back. Make sure there are good teachers who are provided with teaching materials to ensure interest and real learning.

5. Failure to provide good programs on the buses. Consideration has been given to the program en route to church, but little is said about a program on the return trip. Certainly the best workers available ought to be reserved for this time if it is to be of value. The riders have had a full morning and either enjoyed or endured three separate programs already. This one should be of lighter substance and leave a feeling of real pleasure.

6. Failure to provide a fun time for the riders after church once a month.

7. Inadequate training of bus workers, counselors, and soul winners. Advance thought and planning will reveal the wisdom of starting a training program before the first bus is running. Thorough preparation ensures doing a task right the first time, not bumbling though it.

8. Failure to reach the parents of riders. Such lost opportunities are hard to retrieve. The time to contact those parents is while the church is ministering to their children. Showing genuine interest in and love for the boys and girls is usually the way into the hearts of the father or mother.

Rev. Jim Vineyard, former bus director of the First Baptist Church in Hammond, Indiana, calls attention to a resource often overlooked by bus ministry personnel. He suggests, "Assign to each family of the church ten homes of folks living on the bus routes. They should pray daily for those unsaved parents. After they have been praying for them for a couple of months, ask them to go and visit the unsaved parents. Then, after they have visited them off and on for a few weeks, approach them with a request to visit them every ten days." He found that such a plan guaranteed the concern and interest of the church people, for they have invested their prayers in those unsaved parents and then invested their time.

9. Too few buses at the start, or not the right size for the area to be covered. William Powell advocates, "Every church should begin with at least two buses." Consideration of the territory is necessary for a wise choice.

10. Failure to provide adequate Sunday school space. Some of the largest churches successfully challenged their adults to combine individual classes into one large one in order to release smaller classrooms for the expected bus riders. While it was hard to give up a long-enjoyed habit of worship and study, the adults agreed it was a good move. They grew to prefer their larger class, while the new pupils had space for an interesting and profitable class session.

If your church bus program is not all it was expected to be, perhaps the answer to the problems will be found in the areas discussed here. Analyze them. When you recognize an area of weakness or failure, set about to remedy the situation.

BUZZ GROUPS

Buzz groups are a method of teaching whereby a class is divided into small groups for discussion and interaction. This is one of the favorite types of teaching methods for young people and adults because it gives more people opportunity to take part. It also provides for an introductory presentation of the subject by someone well versed on it. The advantage of small-group discussion is that each participant has a chance to test his thoughts in an informal and unthreatening atmosphere. Ideas unworthy of presentation before the entire group are weeded out in the buzz group. This saves valuable time. Also, when a group of sixty is divided into ten buzz groups, ten people can speak at once. During these sessions surveys of the different opinions within the group can be taken quickly by the recorders. The result is a multiplication of information on a particular topic. This method of group involvement taps the resources of everyone present.

Another advantage of the buzz group is that it allows for the spotting and utilizing of leadership within the group. Those who contribute new ideas to the group can be consulted in the future as resource persons. The contributions of these people would have been forever lost under the traditional speaker-listener method. The buzz group has proved itself a highly effective tool for communication within a group and can be counted on to stimulate creative and purposeful activity in any gathering.

The buzz group also has disadvantages or problems. The first problem can result from the method used to organize the buzz group within the meeting. If done improperly, the meeting can dissolve into mass confusion. Then, too, this teaching technique seldom works with younger age groups. Their attention span is short, and their ability to grasp concepts has not developed. Even the junior high student sometimes has difficulty in the buzz

group because the internal authority of the group is not strong enough to maintain purposeful activity. When the leader is working with these younger age groups, he should be certain no one is left out of a buzz group and that each group understands what is required.

Another problem is repetition in the reporting sessions. If the scope of the subject has been too narrow, the various groups will overlap. This results in a boring report session because all the reporters say the same things. Give each buzz group a particular phase of the problem or topic, and have them focus attention only in that area.

Even if the previous dangers are avoided, it is still possible to overuse this valuable teaching technique. Every situation does not call for buzz groups. This teaching technique and instrument of communication should be used economically, not as a quick substitute for an unplanned and unorganized meeting. Success with buzz groups requires organized leaders, adequate time for completion, and mature participants.

How to Use Buzz Groups

Buzz groups can be effectively used to stimulate discussion and enhance the learning process in a variety of situations. For example, if a group is assembled to listen to a lecture, they may break into small groups to list questions they would like the speaker to answer. After he has spoken, they may reassemble to the small groups for further discussion.

Buzz groups can be used to start a meeting. For example, suppose a speaker does not show up in time. Those who come can informally be put into small groups to discuss the topic of the speaker. By the time the speaker arrives, they will be warmed up on the subject and may have listed points they desire the speaker to cover.

In a small group studying the Bible, each group may read the passage silently and discuss findings. Their findings may later be compared with other group discoveries, resulting in the pooling of many individuals' efforts.

Buzz groups may be employed to overcome people's feelings of apathy or helplessness and to redirect a group toward action. A good preliminary for buzz groups is role play, where the audience has opportunity to see the problem and gain the facts. When they break into small groups, they can act as a team, often simply blowing off steam. Yet here they reassure each other through discussion that something can be done about the problem. People get involved when the groups are small.

Divide the class into groups of three to six persons. Give the groups a brief time to discuss assigned questions. Write out questions on file cards and give one to the leader of each buzz group, so the members can refer to the questions at any time. Ask each group to appoint a representative to report the findings to the entire class. Direct the groups to different sections of the classroom. No group needs to leave the room, for the voices of each group will merely add to the background hum.

Give a two-minute warning signal for termination of discussion, and then direct the class to reassemble. After all groups have reported, the teacher is responsible for summarizing the findings and concluding the lesson.

CALDWELL, ESTELLE JONES (1898–1980)

Estelle Jones Caldwell was born in St. Louis, Missouri, in 1898 and was a pioneer in the Sunday school of the International Church of the Foursquare Gospel. She graduated from LIFE Bible College, Los Angeles, California, in 1925 and served as a faculty member for twenty-five years in Sunday school organization, evangelism, and voice. She served in the Sunday school department and was director of children's ministries. She held a Saturday children's church with more than 1,000 in attendance and directed Sunday school at the headquarters church of the Foursquare denomination.

CAMEO CHURCH—A BABY BOOMER CHURCH

What is a baby boomer church? There are approximately three thousand to four thousand churches in America that could be called baby boomer churches or CAMEO churches (contemporary approaches to ministry, evangelism, and organization—as described by Rick Warren). These churches are revolutionary in methodology, but traditional in conservative theology. They are pastored by boomers who effectively reach boomers. Their effectiveness is ministering cross-culturally to the "now generation." Note the following characteristics of the boomer church:

High Touch and High Feel

Boomers like participatory worship with praise choruses, hand clapping, and raised hands. They like hugs, affirmation, and high fives.

Contemporary Music

A boomer church has a band with an electric guitar, an electric piano, and drums. Church attenders want to worship God on Sunday with the sound that fills their ears during the week.

Pastoral Leadership and Every Member a Minister

They have reversed the role, putting ministry in the hands of the people. The pastor is a leader of the people who do the ministering.

Businesslike without Being a Business

Many of their churches worship in rented convention rooms or public schools. The pastor operates out of an office complex like an insurance agency. The church uses up-to-date tools for efficiency and economizes work, energy, and time.

Cells, But No Sunday School for Adults

Adults attend worship for two hours while their children attend Sunday school. The adults attend cells in homes for Bible study and fellowship. Adults do not attend Sunday school.

No Sunday Evening Church Service

The Sunday evening service does not fit the boomer's schedule and is not included in the church calendar.

Low Giving

Boomers will not give unless there is a quality return on their investment. Whereas the average American church attender gives $525 per year to his church, or 10 percent weekly, the boomer church received $400 per year, or 8 percent per week, from each attender.

Fix-It Sermons

The boomer is functional and wants the sermon to help him in everyday life at home or in the market place. As a result, the boomer preacher delivers practical sermons to meet a need or fix a problem.

CAPITAL FUND-RAISING

As a church grows, it must provide expanded facilities to accommodate the growth. With the high costs often involved in church construction, most churches engage in some sort of capital fund-raising program for money to build or renovate facilities. Several principles should be considered before launching a capital fund-raising program.

1. Before beginning a building program, determine the giving potential of the church.
2. A building program should be presented as an incentive for many to give half again as much as previously.
3. Keep the congregation fully informed of the needs and progress.
4. It is easier to raise money for a building than for missions, staff, or for any other purpose. Therefore, make sure the giving level for missions and for current expenses is where it should be before beginning a building-fund drive.
5. A church normally begins to develop a building program in response to needs. But the amount of money available often determines the final size and nature of the building.
6. During the first building-fund drive, anticipate several large cash gifts.
7. It is easiest to raise money for a building under construction; it is much harder to raise money to pay off a mortgage. The older the building, the harder it is; therefore, keep the term of the mortgage as short as possible.
8. Do not bind the hands of the future decision makers of the church by building more than could be paid off in about five years.

CARTER, LINDEN J. (1881–1962)

Linden J. Carter is considered a founding leader of the Advent Christian Sunday School movement. Linden Carter was a Canadian, born in Quebec on October 28, 1881. He accepted Christ as Savior during a Methodist revival in the mid-1890s, then began preaching while in college at McGill University. Eventually he transferred to what is now Berkshire Christian College and was ordained to the ministry in 1906. Despite the hours spent in writing and editorial work, Linden Carter was widely loved as a faithful pastor. He served churches in Ontario, Maine, and Massachusetts, before going to East Norwalk, Connecticut, where he spent fifteen fruitful years. At the time of Dr. Carter's death at Vernon Home in 1962, publications officials computed that more than 2 million copies of *The Blessed Hope* quarterlies were distributed during his years as writer-editor of the International Sunday School lessons. More than one million pages of Dr. Carter's tracts and pamphlets were distributed worldwide.

CASE STUDY

The case study is a method of teaching that involves allowing students to apply the principles of the lesson to the solving of a problem from real life that relates to the objective of the lesson. The aim of the case study, like that of all teaching methods, is to stimulate learning. Its value as a teaching method has been largely overlooked or limited within the church. Although case studies require skill in handling, a properly presented case study can bring excellent results.

Choosing the Proper Case Study

As a matter of good common sense, select one familiar to all. If one wanted to do a case study on stealing for second graders, he would not depict teenagers stealing hub-caps. By the same token, stealing chocolate pie would hardly be appropriate for teenagers. The teacher using a case study must consider the cultural and educational background of his students. Students must identify closely with the case study to ensure its effectiveness.

Students will more readily identify with a contemporary case study. This type hits the student where he lives. It must, however, be accurate in its application to the lives of the students. If a teacher wants to use a case study from the past, he should be sure it is relevant to the students. In this type of study the class can observe solutions people have already found to problems.

The case study is usually not a lesson in itself but a means to teach a certain lesson. Therefore, the case study must be interesting and relevant enough to evoke an enthusiastic discussion at its conclusion. It should have a climactic ending. The teacher should not offer a solution or even a choice of solutions. Allow students to work out the problem themselves.

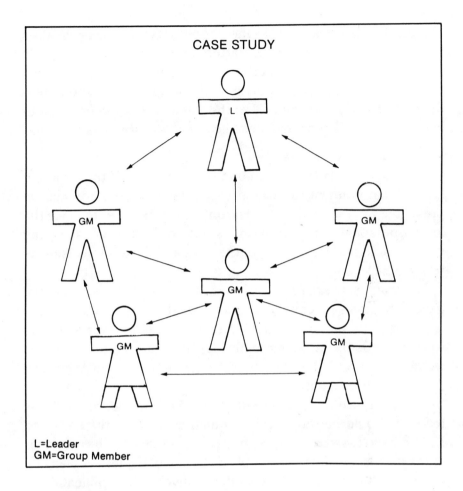

CASE STUDY

L=Leader
GM=Group Member

Preparing a Case Study

The bulk of the preparation for a particular case study must be done by the leader, though he may delegate research to others. The leader is responsible to prepare the case study by researching and recording information factually, accurately, and objectively. He should consider (1) the people involved, (2) the historical background of the situation, (3) the relationship between persons or groups involved, (4) the religious background and perspective of the situation, (5) the sociological factors involved, (6) the economic factors involved, (7) the educational backgrounds of persons involved, (8) the ethnic origins of persons involved and (9) the tensions causing the problem.

Once the leader has researched the subject thoroughly, he then has to organize his material. Matters superfluous to solving the problem should be eliminated. The remaining information is then organized to arouse the interest of the group, reveal the importance of the problem, and show the relevance of the problem to life. The leader is then ready to begin the case study itself.

Presenting the Case Study

If the case study is presented at the beginning of the lesson, it is the focal point of the whole lesson. Or a case study can be presented after the aim of the lesson is clear, in order to make the lesson personal. The case study is not an illustration, since the group discusses the aspects of the case and makes a decision as to the outcome.

The teacher presents the case study by relating the essential facts. If he gives no conclusion, he leads the students to pull the facts together and come up with a solution. If he gives a conclusion, he leads the students to discuss its value and tell how they would have decided. Either way, the case study involves presentation and discussion.

The key question in a case study is, What would you do? The teacher should be thoroughly acquainted with all the facts and should have answered the key question for himself. The purposes of the discussion are to accomplish the aim of the lesson plan and to apply the lesson to the students' lives. The application is inherent in the key question, What would you do? The closer the case study is to the students' lives, the more clearly do the students apply the solutions to themselves. If the case study deals with a problem that the students have not as yet seriously considered, they should be led to exercise empathy, forcing them to consider the new situation or problem.

A notable value of the case study is that it allows the student to involve himself in a real-life situation without really ever taking part in it. A student can imagine, through the case study, being confronted with an "honest versus dishonest" decision. The case study is sort of on-the-job training. Second, since most everyone likes a good story (especially if he can identify with it), the case study is an excellent attention-getting device. Third, the case study prompts discussion and stimulates thinking. Finally, the case study permits the student to take an active part in the class.

This method is not without its weaknesses. The student may not be able to identify sufficiently with the case. He might tell himself, *That could never happen to me.* Another potential problem is that the students might tend to give "the proper Christian answer" rather than their true feelings. The students may simply not be interested in the problem that a particular case study presents. The case study cannot succeed without a good discussion. The group may not solve the problem, or some students may be led into wrong actions or attitudes.

CELLS

In the past two decades, the American church has become aware of the growth of the Korean church, realizing one of the primary growth methods has been the use of the small home cells. However, this is not just a Korean phenomenon. As one studies the pattern of church growth in the early church, there appear to be two aspects to apostolic church life. First there was the cell, which was a small group meeting together for fellowship (Acts 2:42). Second, there was the celebration that was a gathering of a larger group for some corporate activity (Acts 4:32; 5:14).

Evidence for the existence of cells and celebration as part of church life exists in the New Testament apart from the church in Jerusalem. In the city of Corinth, the church in that city was apparently composed of a number of Gentile cells (Rom. 16:4) and a number of Jewish cells (Rom. 16:16). It is significant that in writing to the Romans from Corinth, the apostle sends greetings from "the whole church" in Corinth (Rom. 16:23).

Cells provide the infrastructure needed to build a larger church. Most people will be bonded to a cell group in the church before they will become a part of a larger ministry. But there must also be a place for large group activity. The activity of the corporate church is called *celebration.* The two (cell and celebration) are complimentary, not contradictory. What is learned in cells is expressed in celebration. What is gained in celebration should strengthen the cell experience.

Cells have been called many things over the years. Zinzendorf and the Moravians spoke of their choirs. Wesley and the early Methodists had their class meetings. The Southern Baptist Convention has traditionally called them Sunday school classes.

The primary analogy for the church in the New Testament is that of the body (1 Cor. 12:27-28). This being the case, we need to understand church growth in these terms of cells and celebration. Just as the body grows by the division of cells, so the church grows by the division of cells. The secret of Sunday school growth is adding ministries, adding ministers, and adding places of ministry. We must add classes, add teachers, and expand our base for growth. If the physical cell in the body grows without division, it is called cancer. The same sort of cancer happens in the body of Christ.

To effectively reach adults, churches must create classes in structure for adults (age-graded and gender-graded classes). Many churches begin this strategy for growing by grading adults into classes for each decade of chronological age, such as twenties, thirties, and forties. But we must also create open classes. The structure is like a skeleton that gives strength to the body. But the open class is like the heart that gives feeling to the body. While we must organize adult classes according to the principles of age grading to effect a structure that best meets the unique needs of adults at various times during their maturing, we must not forget the auditorium Bible class that is open to all.

In starting new open Bible classes, we are thinking psychographically rather than demographically. Many churches have begun open classes for single adults, single again (divorced persons), newly married, college, single parents, young married couples, expecting couples, young couples, business and professional women, senior saints, teacher training, new members, choir, widows, the hearing impaired (deaf), and mentally retarded. These classes complement the traditional auditorium Bible class and classes for men and women.

CHALKBOARDS

A traditional chalkboard has a dark, waterproof surface, smooth enough to mark with chalk without distortion, grainy enough to hold chalk. The new models are usually white (teflon-like) for use with a marker. Chalkboards may be composed of slate, porcelain, or several types of wood and paper materials. The most practical type is a composition board with a dull green finish. (The change from the previous blackboards resulted in the present term *chalkboards*). Chalkboards may be made by applying a special type of paint, made up of ground slate and iron oxides, to any paintable surface. The size of the board usually depends on its purpose and the size and shape of the area where it will be used. Some special boards are permanently marked with grids, staff lines for music, or some other feature, for specific purposes. Chalkboards may be movable or stationary, but they should always be clearly visible to all students.

The chalkboard has a number of advantages:

1. It uses both verbal and visual communication.
2. It is accessible.
3. It is economical (inexpensive, easy to use, reusable, minimum space needed).
4. It is versatile.
5. It allows for group participation and involvement.
6. It allows for closely supervised instruction and evaluation.
7. It makes learning more accurate.
8. It speeds learning.
9. It makes learning more enjoyable than verbal method alone.
10. It acquaints pupils and professor with each other.
11. It motivates action and interest.
12. It stimulates creative thinking.
13. It deepens understanding.
14. It aids memory.
15. It focuses attention and provides summary reference.
16. It aids vocabulary growth.
17. It teaches organization and leadership.
18. It can help develop stronger personalities and overcome fears.
19. It changes attitudes and opinions.
20. It provides relief from looking at the teacher's features.

21. It can reproduce material and illustrations not presented in textbooks.
22. It can serve as a bulletin board or projection screen.

Disadvantages of the chalkboard:
1. Its usefulness may be overlooked because it is common.
2. Usage often ignores proper techniques.
3. It may be made a substitute for preparation.
4. Lesson may be made to fit board, not vice versa.
5. Size of board may limit application before erasure.
6. Material on board is not permanent.
7. Board may become cluttered or may not be cleaned properly.
8. Teacher's or students' poor writing may confuse others.
9. Poor chalk detracts.
10. Board may adversely affect acoustics.
11. It has limitations caused by size, location, or material.
12. Pupils may have to change positions to see.
13. Time may be wasted when students travel to and from the board.
14. An error may be permanently impressed on students' minds.
15. Material may be obscured by someone standing in front.
16. Chalk dust may cause throat or skin irritations and damage clothing.

How to Use a Chalkboard
1. Use clear, firm lines.
2. Put work high enough for everyone to see.
3. Write large.
4. Organize work.
5. Erase the board after use.
6. Keep the lines horizontal when writing.
7. Stand sideways when writing.
8. Hold chalk between thumb and forefinger and write at a 30 degree angle to prevent squeaking.
9. In lecturing, write difficult names, formulas, and dates to be remembered and copied.

10. In discussions, write the subject clearly for the class to see. Write down the problem. Write down the partial solutions as suggested. Modify and rephrase as necessary. Be careful to arrange problem and solution in clear and forcible logic. List conclusions.

11. Draw stick figures rather than trying to draw full-bodied people.

12. In outlining, use minimal details.

13. In geometric drawings, use colored chalk for overlapping lines.

14. Label all diagrams clearly.

15. Use perforated paper to draw maps and other sketches. Trace the pattern on a large sheet of drawing paper. Punch holes along the outlines. Tape the paper on the chalkboard and rub or pat a chalky eraser over the holes several times. Remove the paper, and the outline of the drawing remains on the board. Use chalk to fill in the outline.

16. Put meaningful and important vocabulary words on the board.

17. Permit children to use the board to enhance learning.

18. Create suspense by placing a series of drawings or ideas on the board and covering with paper. Uncover each as it is discussed.

19. Use special chalkboard wax to stick paper and other materials to the board to prevent damage to the board.

20. Do not use the chalkboard to the exclusion of other visual aids.

CHARTS

Charts are used in teaching chiefly as a visual presentation of the lesson. Charts present titles, labels, columns, lines, arrows, numerals, colors, varied type, diagrams, illustrations, pictures, maps, notes, and other devices to help clarify the material and make it more readable and meaningful. Charts are less flexible than chalkboards. Once a chart is finished, you can highlight it or add to it, but you cannot change what is already written on it. Charts require some skill in preparation.

Charts have many advantages:
1. Charts attract attention and communicate to the eye.
2. Charts can be prepared in advance and are easy to use in teaching.
3. Charts help to make the lesson clearer and visual to the student.
4. Charts save teaching time, allowing more time for group discussion.
4. Charts add variety to a lesson and increase retention by students.
6. Most charts are inexpensive and may be used repeatedly.

Kinds of charts include flash cards (several charts in sequence), flip charts, pocket-sized cards (as for memory work), strip charts (cover certain words with a taped-on strip and remove at proper time), sleeve (slide a paper sleeve over words to cover those not under discussion), shaped (a question mark–shaped chart to ask a question), or link (sectional, linked with paper clips as discussed).

CHURCH GROWTH

Church growth is that science that investigates the planting, multiplication, growth, function, health, and death of churches. It strives to apply the biblical and sociological principles in its gathering, analyzing, displaying, and defending of the facts involved in implementing the great commission. Church growth is a behavioral science. As such, it follows the scientific method of inquiry as do other natural sciences, such as psychology or sociology. The scientific method involves five steps. First, data must be gathered by the church-growth researcher. This involves finding all of the facts about one source of church growth, or all the facts why there is no growth. Second, the data is examined for causes or effects. At this place the researcher determines if the facts are repeated, whether they will bring about the same results in growth. If it does, it leads to the third step, the point at which the researcher suggests a hypotheses. This is a suggested principle or law that causes church growth. (The word *hypotheses* comes from *hypo* meaning "to propose" and *theses* meaning "an unproven law.") The fourth step is to test the suggested law to see if it is observable, workable, and if it produces the same results in all situations. When the results are consistent, the fifth step leads to establishing the results as a law or principle stating what will produce evangelism and church growth and what will cause a church to plateau or deteriorate.

There are two basic types of growth affecting churches. First, there is external church growth, which means the church grows outwardly in numbers. This is measured by growth in membership, attendance, enrollment, baptisms, or financial offerings. These growth phenomena are observable, repeatable, and measurable. The second is internal church growth. This involves spiritual growth in individuals or in the church. Other synonyms to describe internal growth are growing in the Word; growing to maturity; growing in love, hope and faith; or growing spiritually.

Since church growth falls under the broad category of theology, it must be consistent with the methodology of systematic theology. The definition of systematic theology is "the gathering, analyzing, arranging, displaying, and defending of any and all facts about God and his world." Implied in this definition is the inductive method of inquiry; that is, the gathering of facts from two sources: Scripture and the observable world. Therefore, to understand why churches grow, the researcher must examine the principles found in external methods of growth (programs, culture, and history) as well as examining internal methods of growth that come from the Word of God (the influences of prayer, revival, and spiritual life).

The church is both an organization and an organism. As an organization, it is outward in its programs and committees. But the church is also the body of Christ. It is an organism with inherent life. It must grow internally. Those who work in the church must recognize that both external and internal growth is an affirmation that the church is an organization and an organism.

CHURCH GROWTH WHEEL
(See also DISCIPLESHIP AND CHURCH GROWTH, LEADERSHIP AND CHURCH GROWTH, ORGANIZATION AND CHURCH GROWTH, OUTREACH AND CHURCH GROWTH.)

The relationship between church growth and those factors that tend to cause church growth can be described through use of the Church Growth Wheel (see diagram). The inner circle indicates the priority of growth (spiritual factors). The outer circle indicates the human or numerical aspects of growth. Some pastors give all their attention to spiritual factors such as prayer, Bible teaching, and holiness, but they neglect organization, outreach, and wise administration. Other churches give all of their attention to programs, leadership, outreach, and attendance campaigns, but they neglect the spiritual dynamics.

Just as the rock thrown into the lake produces the highest waves at the center of impact, the spiritual dynamics of church growth have greater priority than the natural principles. In the New Testament church, spiritual principles always should override natural principles; human factors should never override the spiritual factors.

The traditional laws of Sunday school growth have concerned themselves with organization and administration. On many occasions, a church has adhered to these "laws" only to stagnate. Other churches have experienced growth without following these laws. There were other factors that caused their growth. Some of these were spiritual dynamics and new organizational methods to meet needs and solve problems that prohibited expansion.

For a discussion of the spiritual and natural factors of church growth at work in the church growth wheel, see the articles on Discipleship and Church Growth, Leadership and Church Growth, Organization and Church Growth, and Outreach and Church Growth.

CIRCULAR RESPONSE
Circular response is a method of teaching that allows all students in a class to make a contribution to a suggested topic.

OUTREACH

PROGRAM
1. Advertising/Media
2. Canvassing
3. Busing
4. Organized Visitation
5. Psychology
6. Promotional Campaigns

NATURAL — Outreach Necessitates More Leadership Leadership Sets the Pattern & Provides the Vision

FACTORS — Results Motivate Discipleship / Discipleship Leads to Outreach

A (See copy below)

SPIRITUAL

FACTORS

LEADERSHIP

DISCIPLESHIP

NATURAL FACTORS
1. Gifted
2. Multiplication of Ministry
3. "Hot Poker"
4. Formal Training
5. Weekly Interaction
6. Standards

D

CHURCH GROWTH

B

NATURAL MOTIVATION
1. Sense of Accomplishment
2. Recognition
3. Reward
4. Challenge
5. Personal Involvement
6. Competition
7. Exposure

CONTRIBUTING — Organization Depends on Leadership / Leadership Values & Promotes Organization

C

TO GROWTH — Needs Necessitate Organization / Organization Promotes Discipleship

CONTRIBUTING

TO GROWTH

WISE ORGANIZATION
1. For Business Matters
2. For Educational Effectiveness
3. For Building Utilization
4. For Efficiency
5. For Involvement

ORGANIZATION

A

PERSONAL
1. Personal Soul Winning
2. Spiritual Growth
3. Saturation Evangelism
4. Revival
5. Preaching/ Teaching
6. Prayer
7. Purity

B

SPIRITUAL MOTIVATION
1. Love of God
2. Commitment
3. Eternal Reward
4. Word of God
5. Prayer
6. Fellowship
7. Sacrifice
8. Spirit Filling

C

BIBLICAL
1. What a Church Is
2. Pastor
3. Deacons
4. Committees

D

SUPERNATURAL FACTORS
1. A Call from God
2. Character/ Meets Biblical Requirements
3. Empowered by H.S.
4. Attributes of Biblical Leader

Some teachers feel that circular response merely consumes class time. They believe students are not learning because specific lesson content is not being presented. However, teachers should think in terms of meeting the needs of students. Discussion and involvement by individual members of the class may provide just the needed motivation for serious consideration of the Christian faith. Student involvement in the class is the key to personal growth.

If possible, have the class seated in a semicircle. Go around the group clockwise, giving each person an opportunity to contribute. If the class is seated auditorium style, have each one in a row contribute, going from left to right through all the rows.

Ask each student to contribute the first thing that comes to his mind on the topic. His contribution may be an illustration from life, a question, a fact from the Bible, a question based on a previous contribution by another member, or a personal insight regarding the topic. Do not evaluate contributions made, or the shy person who only asked a question or read a verse of Scripture may be embarrassed. Stand by the chalkboard and be prepared to write down questions the students ask during the response. Do not try to answer the questions at this time. After all students have contributed, discuss the questions.

CLASS, BEGINNING A NEW

The first step in beginning a new class is to find and recruit a teacher. Remember, you are looking for more than a person with teaching skills. You are looking for someone to lead the class. A spirit-filled Sunday school teacher can revitalize a class and ultimately a church. (See Enlisting Workers for suggestion for recruiting a teacher.)

The second step in beginning a new class is to get some seed members to help the new teacher get the class started. Sometimes seed members come from dividing another class. Do not divide a class too often because it tends to discourage members who rebuild their class, only to have it divided again. On other occasions, ask for volunteers from all adult classes to be the "seed" to help begin a new class. It is difficult to begin a new class with just a teacher. When the teacher goes into an empty room, he can become discouraged and quit. However, if he has a core of people to help him build the class, he is less likely to get discouraged.

The biggest problem for some churches in beginning a new class is finding a room for the class. This problem is not insurmountable, even if you are already using the pastor's study and several halls and Sunday school buses in the parking lot. More and more Sunday school classes are meeting off campus than ever before. Classes are meeting in homes, schools, restaurants, and many other nontraditional settings.

To begin new classes, leaders need to get others in the church to accept their existence. Expansion begins when the goal and contribution of new classes are accepted and supported. If the new class is an open class, then other teachers may view it as a threat or competition, taking away members or potential members.

Next, expand by appointing class officers for the new class to help in reaching others with the gospel. Finally, the ushers, secretaries, and other administrators in the Sunday school will need to know of the existence of the new class and how it fits into the scheme of things.

Ultimately, beginning a new class will involve going out after new people. There is only one way to build a church. That way is through reaching new members. Within that one way, there are many strategies and steps.

CLASS, LAW OF THE (See also GROWTH, LAWS OF SUNDAY SCHOOL)

The law of the class is one of the traditional laws of Sunday school growth that states there should be one teaching center class for every ten pupils. This does not mean one classroom, because in some rooms there are three or more teaching centers, especially among the smaller children's departments that use the activity teaching centers. The law of the class is a general statement that applies to the total Sunday school. Some adult classes will have fifteen to twenty-five pupils, while other children's classes will have four or five pupils.

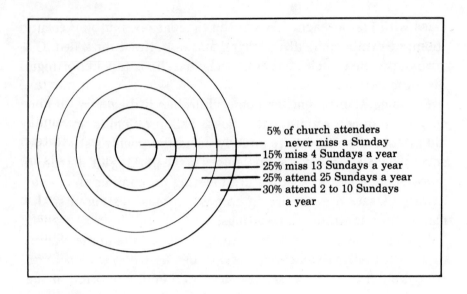

5% of church attenders
never miss a Sunday
15% miss 4 Sundays a year
25% miss 13 Sundays a year
25% attend 25 Sundays a year
30% attend 2 to 10 Sundays
a year

CLASS SUNDAY SCHOOL

The class Sunday school is found in a single cell church where the Sunday school is organized around individual classes. This type of Sunday school is called the one-room Sunday school or the class Sunday school. That is because everything is organized around individual classes, or everyone meets in the auditorium (one room) for opening exercises or opening worship.

Why a Class Sunday School Stops Growing

The first plateau of Sunday school growth comes when attendance reaches beyond the average attendance of 66 pupils and stops growing at approximately 100 to 150. Just like a house plant will outgrow the pot in which it was planted as it grows, so the number of pupils will outgrow the facilities and organizational structure as it grows. If the Sunday school is not reorganized to take care of more pupils, both the plant and Sunday school will become root bound and begin to die without growth. A root-bound plant chokes on its own roots.

Why do Sunday schools get root bound at the 100 to 150 plateau? There are three primary reasons. First, they simply run out of space or classrooms. New classes cannot be started for growth because there is nowhere to meet.

The second reason for this natural plateau in growth is related to the basic management principle of span and direction. One manager should never have more than seven people reporting to him. A superintendent cannot give effective direction nor take responsibility for more than this number of workers. By the time the class Sunday school has reached 100 to 150, the Sunday school superintendent is probably trying to manage ten to fifteen teachers, and everyone begins to wonder why so many details are falling between the cracks.

A third reason for this danger level of 100 to 150 is that when the average Sunday school reaches this level, the leaders usually cannot think of other new classes to begin. These Sunday schools tend to have developed about fifteen classes, one or two for each grouping in a departmental Sunday school.

This danger level is perhaps the most serious simply because it is the one that so many churches face in their present situation. There are steps that can be taken to break the "100" danger level. The Sunday school should probably consider changing its organizational structure to a departmentally organized Sunday school. Also, the church may need to find more room to grow. But the real key to breaking this danger level is to begin new classes.

How to Break the First Barrier of Sunday School Growth

1. Begin new classes.
2. Find additional administrators.
3. Find additional space for new classrooms (perhaps off campus).
4. Consider going to a split-level Sunday school.
5. Change large classes taught by one teacher into a team-teaching situation with several teachers.
6. Organize large classes or team-taught classes into a department.
7. Appoint one teacher as a departmental superintendent to supervise and coordinate the other teachers.

CLASSROOM, LAW OF THE (See also LAWS OF SUNDAY SCHOOL GROWTH)

There must be educational space for growth. Growing Sunday schools must have classrooms if they continue to grow. But Christian educators differ in their conclusions as to how much room there must be for Sunday school growth. The traditional laws call for ten square feet per pupil. Those who conduct an activity-centered Sunday school, however, must have twenty-five square feet per pupil. Your space and building will to some degree dictate your approach to Sunday school teaching.

CLENCHED FIST, LAW OF THE

The law of the clenched fist is built on the law that pressure builds the body. That is why runners put pressure on their legs and lungs, to strengthen their bodies for the race. Weight lifters do the same thing. They pump iron, putting pressure on their bodies to build them up.

Pressure also builds the body of Christ. Sharing the vision of reaching people puts pressure on church members. A goal of placing a Bible in every home is another way to create pressure. A Sunday school campaign puts pressure on all who are involved.

Growing Sunday schools should plan two attendance campaigns per year, one in the spring and one in the fall. The campaigns should not be longer than six or seven weeks, as people get tired of them. If you have too many campaigns, the people will not work as hard as they can during the next campaign to find prospects, excite students, phone, write, and visit. Relax the attendance drive during the Christmas holidays, the cold weather of January, and again during the summer.

A man can keep his fist taut only so long, then the muscles give out. Likewise, a Sunday school leader can put pressure on his workers for only a short time. Just as a runner who puts too much pressure on his body causes a stroke, too much pressure on the body of Christ builds up resentment or resignation in workers.

Too much exercise can lead to a heart attack or stroke in the physical body. In the spiritual body it can lead to discouragement or other more serious problems that become counterproductive in the cause of Christ.

COLLOQUY

A colloquy is a modification of the panel discussion as a method of teaching. Less formal, the colloquy utilizes several representatives from the audience and several resource persons familiar with the problem. The audience representatives present the problem, and the resource persons comment on various aspects of it. The audience and its representatives participate under the guidance of the moderator. The moderator develops the discussion of the resource persons, group representatives, and the audience.

The moderator should be skilled in the techniques of handling discussions. The moderator (1) plans with panel members prior to meeting; (2) plans for audience participation prior to meeting; (3) informs audience of the nature of the colloquy and of their responsibility; (4) encourages and develops audience participation; (5) restates and clarifies audience questions to panel; (6) develops a friendly and informal atmosphere, controls tempers; (7) keeps discussion within time limit; (8) recognizes speakers from the audience, one at a time; (9) makes practical application; (10) changes tactics of discussion to fit the problem; (11) avoids taking sides; (12) avoids talking a lot; (13) prevents monopoly; (14) keeps discussion on the point; (15) allows those who haven't participated to speak first; (16) occasionally summarizes, and (17) then gives a final summary.

The resource persons are chosen for their knowledge and interest in the subject to be discussed. The resource persons (1) contribute when their opinion is needed, (2) keep to the subject, (3) keep remarks short, and (4) speak in nontechnical language.

The audience representatives are chosen for their interest in the subject and the ability to ask questions and make intelligent comments. The audience representatives (1) prepare themselves; (2) present the problem; (3) ask questions of the experts; (4) clarify discussion for the audience; and (5) stimulate audience participation.

The topic should be chosen to fit the needs and interests of the audience. The audience (1) studies material pertaining to the topic before meeting; (2) presents the problem; (3) arranges further discussion and future action; (4) recognizes its part as participants; and (5) uses resource persons as specialists.

A colloquy (1) permits direct representation and participation by the audience; (2) permits the audience to question a vague statement made by a resource person; (3) makes the experts consider more closely the needs of the audience; (4) stimulates the audience through those representing it to listen more carefully and participate more freely; (5) offers an opportunity for those audience representatives to challenge the resource persons; (6) provides the stimulus for the resource persons to get accurate information; and (7) gives the audience an intimate feeling of association with the members on the platform.

On the other hand, a colloquy (1) often does not allow sufficient time to present all views; (2) requires a skillful moderator; (3) may let resource persons assume a dominant role; and (4) is most effective for a controversial issue.

COMMUNICATION

The word *communicate* means to make some information common to two people. When a person communicates the request, "Give me a cold drink," we know they have effectively communicated when the person to whom they are speaking gives them a cold drink. Both the speaker (the person who encodes the message in words) and the hearer (the person who decodes the message) have understood the message.

The teacher must communicate with the student. The teacher must teach the lesson (encode it in words), and the student must understand what is said (decode the words).

But communication is not a one-way street from the teacher to the student. There is feedback in the classroom. The student must respond. The teacher must use words that are understood by the student, and the teacher must understand the words used by the student. When they understand each other, communication occurs.

What Is the Communication Process

The parts of the communication process are as follows:

1. The sender-encoder (teacher). This person has three duties. First, he must choose words. Second, he must give meaning to the words. Third, he must use the words properly.
2. The receiver-decoder (student). This person has three du-

ties also. First, he must recognize words. Second, he must interpret the words. Third, he must relate the words' meaning to what he already knows.
3. The message. This is the lesson the teacher wants to teach.
4. The channel. This is the method the teacher uses to communicate the lesson.

The message is in the mind of the teacher who is the sender-encoder. The teacher gives to words the meaning he wants to convey to his pupil. The message is placed in a channel to communicate to the pupil. A channel is the way the teacher communicates a message. The pupils (receiver-decoder) must receive the message and interpret it. When they hear the words of the teacher, they have to know what is meant. This is the process of interpretation. They must apply it to their lives.

The Function of the Teacher/Communicator

Teachers have many choices in the use of language. They cannot use just any word; they must use an appropriate word. Also, they cannot use all of the words at their disposal. They must follow certain rules in word choice, and they must:

1. Know the message to be communicated. When they are teaching the Word of God, they must choose the words that correctly communicate God's message to the class.
2. Know which words are commonly used by the students. This means that teachers must understand their students, the terms they use, and why they use them. Not everyone can teach high school students because teenagers have their own subculture, and with it their own language. Not that high school teachers use the slang of the students, but they know what to avoid and what to choose.
3. Choose words and the channel. In the final analysis, words give life to lessons, or they put students to sleep. The correct choice of words will set a heart on fire or will burn it up with rage.
4. Relate the message through words. Christianity was communicated in words. God does not speak in vague concepts, nor abstract thoughts. God used the common words of Bible

times, and through these words he communicated his eternal truth to men. The Scriptures were literally inspired by God to give authority and credibility to the message of God. When Jesus came, he was called the Word (John 1:1, 14). Just as the Bible is the written Word, Jesus is the incarnate Word. He communicates the message of God to us.

CONGREGATIONAL SINGING

Congregational singing is an important part of the worship program of any church or agency within the church and provides an opportunity for everyone to express worship to God in song. People will engage in group or congregational singing more than any other type of singing. The purpose of group music and music in general is basically fourfold:

1. Singing is a musical outlet. People desire to express themselves through music. Not everyone can sing well enough to perform as a soloist or musical group, so congregational singing is especially appealing because everyone can participate.

2. Singing is an emotional outlet. A happy person will probably sing something that depicts his mood. The same is true when a person is unhappy. The songs people sing in the church tend to express one of these moods—joy or sadness. Most songs people sing display joy and gladness. The Word of God has instructed the Christian to be joyful.

3. Singing is a social experience. Singing produces an atmosphere of fellowship. Group participation levels barriers and gives to all those participating a sense of belonging, sharing in the true Christian experience. Singing can produce this experience among non-Christians, and infinitely more so among Christians (with God the Father, God the Son, and other Christians through the Holy Spirit).

4. Singing is a spiritual necessity. People can worship God through singing. If the music during a service has produced worship, there will be (a) a realization of the presence of God, (b) a consciousness of one's dependence upon God, (c) a contemplation of the ideal or Christian way of living, and

(d) a dedication or commitment of one's life to the Christian way of living.

How to Choose Appropriate Music for Worship

It is usually best to correlate your music with the central theme of the worship service (the sermon or lesson topic) and the Scripture being used. There are at least two reasons for doing so. First, this enables people to focus on a single thought or emphasis as they are involved in the worship service. Second, it assists the pastor or teacher in communicating his message and the people in learning if the music reinforces the lesson or sermon theme. God has created man in such a way that music enables a person to integrate truth into his being faster and more effectively than other methods.

When choosing music for the worship service, consider the nature of the congregation's experience with God. Music should be planned to build to a climax and then bring a person back down without interrupting the worship experience. As songs are selected for the worship service, they should not only communicate an appropriate message, but their music should also fit in with the overall plan and flow of the service. Also, the worship leader should check congregational music to ensure it is not too difficult for musicians in the church to play or for the congregation to sing.

CONTESTS

Sunday school contests are as old as Sunday school. The founder, Robert Raikes, gave clothes and money as prizes for attendance, memorization, and other achievements. Sunday school promotions and contests have their place, but should a minibike be ridden down the aisle of a church sanctuary to coax kids to invite their friends to Sunday school? Or should a church set up a shopping center–style carnival, where children ride with tickets earned by "each one bringing one"?

Some believe we ought to eliminate all Sunday school contests and promotions because they are unbiblical. But are they? A contest is simply an external stimuli to attract people to hear the gospel. The miracles performed by Jesus (external stimulus) attracted crowds and caused people to listen to the message. Many times Jesus used miracles as a prelude to his sermons.

The gospel of salvation never changes, but as the Good News gives a man eternal life, that man must live for God within his culture. Christianity often adapts to the socioeconomic society in which it finds itself. In other words, God meets a man at his own level and lifts him to the divine level. Contests and gimmicks are a way of life for America. The First National Bank gives T-bone steaks to those opening a new account, and gas stations give a free glass or kite to those who fill up. Sunday school contests simply are an adaptation of the American way of life.

How to Choose a Good Contest

Where is the line between a biblical incentive and a gimmick that smacks of tasteless entrepreneurism? The following three questions will guide Sunday school workers in choosing good contests.

1. Will the contest accomplish a biblical aim? A Sunday school contest is biblical when it accomplishes the aims of the Scripture. The first aim is to reach people with the gospel— the Good News of salvation through Jesus Christ. Paul identified this principle: "And to the Jews I became as a Jew, that I might win Jews; to those who are under the law, as under the law, that I might win those who are under the law; to those who are without law, as without law (not being without law toward God, but under law toward Christ), that I might win those who are without law; to the weak I became as weak, that I might win the weak. I have become all things to all men, that I might by all means save some" (1 Cor. 9:20-22). The "all things" that Paul will do to reach people with the gospel was governed by the phrase "to win." But before we can win a man to Jesus Christ we must reach him; we must motivate a man to turn his attention toward the gospel so that he may give a sincere hearing to the Good News.

   After a person is brought to church or Sunday school, he must be evangelized. Evangelizing a person is simply giving him an understanding of the plan of salvation, then motivating him to make a decision for God. A biblical Sunday school contest first gets students "under the sound of the gospel." Second, it motivates them to give an honest hearing to the gospel. Finally, it provides an opportunity to properly present the plan of salvation.

2. Will the contest accomplish a biblical goal? Educators define a goal as "that outcome by which educational activities are judged." The biblical goals of Scripture are building aggressive churches, maturing (completing) saints in Jesus Christ, and bringing glory to God. The goal of evangelism in the New Testament is to gather people into an *ecclesia,* "an assembly" or "summoned assembly."

Another biblical goal for Sunday school contests is to communicate the glory of God. What do people think of God after a contest is completed?

3. Are numbers the mania of your Sunday school, or are numbers the outgrowth of soul winning? There is nothing wrong with numbers. Making disciples first implies winning people to Christ and, second, getting them to follow Christ. When you have done this, then you can count the heads of those who follow Christ.

But Sunday schools hurt their ministry when they put more emphasis on the measure than on the measured. The question is not the number in Sunday school, but whether the Sunday school attendance figure represents (a) souls that are being reached for Christ, (b) people that are studying the Word of God, and (c) individuals who are becoming disciples of Jesus Christ.

Some Sunday schools have confused means and ends. The end result is winning souls and building strong New Testament churches. The means includes an emphasis on numbers. Let us not reverse the two. (For specific contests and campaigns discussed in this encyclopedia see Election Campaign, Everybody-Can-Win Contest, Fall Roundup, Friend Day (under F.R.A.N.gelism, March to Sunday School in March, Room Decoration Contest, and Twin Sunday.)

COOK, DAVID C. (1850–1927)

David C. Cook was one of the early Sunday school leaders and first publishers of Sunday school literature. In 1875, he founded the David C. Cook Publishing Company, which continues to this day as one of the leading interdenominational publishers of Sunday school literature.

CORY, BERNICE T. (1900–1973)

Bernice T. Cory was a cofounder of Scripture Press Publications, Inc., Wheaton, Illinois. She and her husband, Victor E. Cory, began work on the All-Bible Graded Sunday School lessons in 1932. This grew into Scripture Press, which now has a worldwide ministry of Christian education materials in seventy languages, 120 countries, and to more than seventy denominations.

From the beginning of Scripture Press, Mrs. Cory wrote and edited Sunday school lessons, vacation Bible school lessons, flannelgraph visuals, a cradle roll course for the Sunday school, and children's educational books. She was used of God to influence many evangelical interdenominational organizations and was frequently a speaker at Christian education conferences.

CORY, VICTOR E. (1896–1968)

Victor Edwin Cory, cofounder and chairman of the board of Scripture Press Publications, was the business and organizational force behind the worldwide ministry of Sunday school outreach to more than seventy denominations distributed in seventy languages and in 120 countries. His wife, Bernice, was the writing and editorial force of the company's success.

Victor Cory was used of God to pioneer and establish a number of Christian organizations in addition to Scripture Press. He was the founder of the Greater Chicago Sunday School Association and was one of the main founders of the National Sunday School Association.

For years he served actively on the boards of fourteen organizations. At his homegoing he was an active member of GCSSA, NSSA, Evangelical Teacher Training Association, Pacific Garden

Mission, The Lightbearers, Winona Lake Corporation (president), and the Great Commission Prayer League.

COUNSELING YOUTH

Counseling is guiding a person through his problems to a better understanding of his potential. Here we are talking about helping average people with average problems. Psychological or therapeutic counseling is not the intent.

There are several types of referrals in counseling. Self-referral is when the person himself seeks the service of a counselor. Teacher referral is when the person is referred to the counselor by somebody else in the church, such as the Sunday school teacher. A third type of referral is when the counselor sees the person in trouble and calls him in for counseling.

How to Counsel

Relaxation. The person must be put at ease so that a healthy interview may be held. The first few minutes of the counseling situation are most important. There are several foundational stones for good counseling that should be followed:

1. The person should be told that the counselor does not know all the answers to his problems, but that the Word of God will be searched to find solutions to problems.
2. The person should be informed they will work on the problem together.
3. The person must be told that anyone who is striving to live for Christ will have problems because of the flesh, the devil, and the power of the world against him.

Rapport means a "relation characterized by harmony, conformity, accord, or affinity." It is "an intimate harmonious relation as applied to people having close understanding." A permissive atmosphere must prevail. The counselor must be careful to respond to feelings in such a way as to build confidence in the teen and build up rapport. The counselor must have warmth and understanding but controlled emotions.

Revelation does not deal with the solution of the problem but only a clear understanding of the problem itself. Youth counselors must realize that many times people bring up a problem that is not the true source of their difficulty. Therefore, do not answer the "fruit" problems and neglect the "root" problems. When the counselor feels he understands the problem, he should determine whether the person understands the problem. Questions, restatement of facts, and introduction of other materials should be used to make sure the person understands his problem. Once the counselor feels the person understands the problem, then the problem should be clearly stated.

Results have to do with helping youth with their problems.

1. Determine the alternatives. The alternatives may involve many solutions that can be applied to the problem. The person should understand all the different alternatives he may choose. The counselor and counselee should attempt to explore all possible solutions before making any decisions.

2. Scriptural insight phase. The counselor must not give advice. He must guide the person to the Word of God and to Jesus Christ. Here the counselor assumes the role of teacher.

3. Confession of sins to God. The confession of sin is the admission of failure in our responsibility. The purging and releasing of guilt and tensions through confession results in happiness.

4. Making decisions. This is the place for the counselor to guide a person into the Word of God and to the apparent solutions. The counselor should be warned that the solution must be the teen's suggestion. Decisions come hard. Each person must learn to make independent decisions gradually, realizing he needs the help of the human counselor as well as the divine Counselor.

The problem is solved as it is worked out in life. The counselor should pray with the person, then map out an attack on the problem. A daily plan of Bible reading, Scripture memory, suggested books to read, and quiet time can be planned. The counselor should frequently check up on the spiritual progress of the person. Resist all temptations to share with others what a person has given to you in confidence.

Every counseling situation will take a different shape. Problems are different, people are different, circumstances are varied, and solutions are complex. The general approach suggested here will be used in an ideal situation, but there is no ideal situation. Even though this approach can't be fully employed in every situation, the general guidelines and attitudes of approach can be used in every situation. In some counseling situations the problem is evident and relaxation can be skipped. In the next situation, the counselor and the person will have to give attention to relaxation and rapport. In a further counseling situation, results may receive all the attention.

The goal, not the technique, must be kept in sight. The counselor must be person-centered, not technique-centered. The wise counselor will choose these techniques in the required order to lead people to a solution of their problems and a proper adjustment in life.

COVENANT, SUNDAY SCHOOL TEACHER'S

A Sunday school teacher's covenant could be used to improve the quality of teaching in your Sunday school. The covenant could not only be used as part of the annual teacher's dedication service; it is also an excellent tool in recruiting quality teachers for your Sunday school. A Sunday school teacher's covenant communicates the standards, aims, and expectations for new workers. The following is a sample teacher's covenant.

Suggested Teacher's Covenant

Recognizing the high privilege that is mine to serve my Lord through our Sunday school, and trusting in the help and guidance of the Holy Spirit, I earnestly pledge myself to this covenant.

1. I will live what I teach about separation from the world and purity of life, "avoiding all appearance of evil," setting an example in dress, conversation, deportment, and prayer (1 Tim. 4:11-12).
2. I will be faithful in attendance and make it a practice to be present at least ten minutes early to welcome each pupil as he or she arrives. If at any time, through sickness or other

emergency, I am unable to teach my class, I will notify my superintendent at the earliest possible moment (1 Cor. 4:2).

3. I will at all times manifest a deep spiritual concern for the members of my class. My first desire shall be to bring about the salvation of each pupil who does not know the Lord Jesus and to encourage the spiritual growth of every Christian (Dan. 12:3).

4. I will carefully prepare my lessons and make each lesson session a matter of earnest prayer (1 Thess. 5:17).

5. I will regularly attend and urge members of my class to be present at the church services, recognizing that the church and Sunday school are inseparable. Believing in the importance of prayer, I will also endeavor to maintain regular attendance at the midweek prayer service.

6. I will teach, according to the doctrines of our church, Christ as Savior, Sanctifier, and coming King (Acts 20:27).

7. I will wholeheartedly cooperate with the absentee program of our school and will strive to visit the home of each pupil at least once a year (Matt. 18:12).

8. I will heartily support the Sunday school program, attending at least nine of the twelve monthly teachers' meetings and training classes (2 Tim. 2:15).

9. I understand that my appointment as a teacher is for the twelve-month period beginning the first Sunday in October. Whether my appointment is made then or later in the Sunday school year, I understand that it automatically terminates September 30 and that decisions regarding reappointment are based on my fulfillment of this teacher's covenant.

10. I will cheerfully abide by the decisions of my church and Sunday school, cooperating with my fellow workers in bringing our work to the highest possible degree of efficiency as one of the teaching agencies of the church (Matt. 28:19-20).

CONVERSION

Conversion is participation by non-Christians in a genuine decision for Christ, a sincere turning from sin, and a determined purpose to live as Christ would have people live. Individual conversion is the evangelization of one person at a time. Multi-individual conversion involves many people participating in the act, although each individual makes up his own mind, debates with others, and decides to either accept or reject Christianity. Mutually interdependent conversions occur when all those making the decision are intimately known to each other and take the step in view of what the others are going to do.

CONVERSION GROWTH

Conversion growth is numerical church growth resulting from winning lost people to Jesus Christ and bonding them to the church.

CRADLE ROLL

The Cradle Roll Department is the agency or organization that ministers to the babies in the church. "Newborns" are its special outreach, with constant ministry until that baby is transferred to the roll of the Nursery Department.

There are several reasons why a church should include a Cradle Roll Department in the Sunday school. First, it can be an effective outreach to new parents. Young couples who have given little thought to church or God often have tender hearts after the birth of the new life entrusted to them. The arrival of the baby provides a reason to go to the home and express interest and concern.

Second, this department can give aid to new parents. More than just adding a baby's name to the ribbon hanging from a cardboard cradle on the wall, the Cradle Roll Department seeks to render aid to the new parents as they begin to train their little one. Through personal visits, printed booklets, and books from the church library, the cradle roll visitor can minister to the home.

Third, the cradle roll reaches children. Even if the Sunday school waits until a child is old enough to choose to come to Sunday school, at least the baby's name on the cradle roll is symbolic of the church's concern for that life. It is a reason to keep in touch with the child and encourage his being brought to the nursery as soon as possible.

Staffing the Cradle Roll

In a small church, there may be no other person on the cradle roll staff besides the superintendent. A lady who is too shy to teach a class may be willing to visit homes and talk with young mothers on a person-to-person basis. A young woman would have much in common with cradle roll parents; at the same time, an older woman might have more leisure to visit and more experience with which to aid the new parents.

As in other Sunday school departments, the secretary should keep a record of all the names and addresses and birthdays of the babies on the role. If a card is kept for each baby, facts should be added after each contact by a visitor. The secretary also should mail birthday cards to the babies each year until the Nursery Department takes over. Supplies for the department should be ordered by the secretary.

A third person involved in the cradle roll is the home visitor. This may be a pair of ladies who like visiting in homes. The more visitors involved (at least one to every eight babies), the more people involved in seeking new babies to visit.

Duties of the Cradle Roll

The cradle roll staff should accomplish the following responsibilities: (1) visit homes, (2) counsel with parents, (3) provide an adequately staffed and supplied church crib nursery, (4) organize a new mothers' club, (5) discover prospects, (6) organize an annual (or quarterly) Baby Day, (7) discover needs, and (8) enlist others to help meet those specific needs uncovered.

CREEK JUMPING, LAW OF

The law of creek jumping is a description of the momentum and credibility a leader needs to successfully launch a new program. The law of creek jumping states the wider the creek, the faster you have to run to clear it. Getting a running start before jumping a creek is illustrative of building up momentum or credibility before an attendance campaign. In Sunday school, the larger the goal, the longer it takes to convince workers they can reach it. The problem is not that the leader must convince himself; he must build up confidence in others. A church leader must build believability in the program and the church's ability to reach a goal.

Plan a six- or seven-week spring or fall campaign with the high Sunday as the last day. Take time to pray to grow, plan to grow, and promote to grow. A teacher can't lead if his class won't follow, and pupils won't work to double their class unless their teacher takes the time to convince them it can be done.

The obvious application of the law of creek jumping is not to attempt high goals before the people have a basis to trust the new program or believe in your leadership.

CRUSADE EVANGELISM

Crusade evangelism refers to that method of reaching people with the gospel in the context of a public meeting place, in which an evangelist delivers a message and people are asked to respond, with follow-up being the responsibility of the local churches. This is sometimes called event evangelism.

CURRICULUM

The word *curriculum* is derived from a term meaning "racetrack." It was a course that guided the runner to the goal. Technically, a curriculum is a course of study that is organized to guide the pupil to specific objectives by the proper use of content, experience, teaching aids, teacher influence, application, and motivation. Therefore, a curriculum in Sunday school is a course of study of the Bible and related subjects that leads to and accomplishes the great commission.

The curriculum of Christian education begins with a Christian purpose. The doctrine of revelation is the foundation of our curriculum. The content of God's revelation to man is found in the Bible. God's personal, direct revelation of himself is the person of his Son, Jesus the Messiah. The divine element also enters into our curriculum with the illuminating power of the Holy Spirit. The result is a curriculum in Christian education that is supernatural.

A good curriculum results from carefully planned organization. Care must be given to placing the various elements in the sequence that will contribute most to the development of Christian faith and character. Some progression must be assumed on the part of the learner and teacher. It is not necessary to repeat everything at every stage. The timing of emphases will utilize seasonal interests to the best advantage. The placement of units or courses will observe the need for variety and freshness of approach. Closely related areas of curriculum will be placed to make use of the possibilities of cumulative learning. There will be frequent cumulative learning, providing incentive to commitment and action consistent with the developmental level of each age group.

How to Choose the Right Curriculum for Your Sunday School

There are essentially four kinds of curriculum materials with various methods of covering Bible content. If a student visited four different churches on four successive Sundays, he might encounter four different series of lessons in his own age group. This is one of the most effective arguments for a student's regular attendance at the same Sunday school. When he skips from one Sunday school to another, he gets only a smattering of unrelated biblical knowledge because of the different curriculum plans used.

Publishers and constituents of the *uniform grading* curriculum maintain that it unifies the family because everyone has the same emphasis at Sunday school. Thus, more opportunity is available for united Bible study in the home. Because of the same basic lesson, interest is mutual. Such lessons are often limited in scope because all age groups must cover the same material. The material is usually adapted to the various younger age groups, leaving much of the Bible not studied by young people and adults.

The *unified grading* curriculum has a central theme for the whole Sunday school; each class may have different Bible content. The strength of this curriculum is the unity it gives to the family and the church. It has the same weaknesses as the uniform grading curriculum.

The size of a Sunday school will often dictate which plan is most feasible. The *departmentally graded* material is sometimes considered best suited for Sunday schools with 150 to 400 in attendance. Sunday schools with over 400 in attendance can better adapt

MODERN CURRICULUM PLANS

UNIFORM GRADING	UNIFIED GRADING	DEPARTMENT GRADING	CLOSE GRADING
The same Bible portion is taught to each age-group.	Different Bible content, related by a single theme, is taught to each age-group.	Different Bible content is provided for each department group (Primary, Junior, etc.).	Different Bible content is provided for pupils in each public school grade.
(1) A small church can unite all pupils in a single lesson-related worship service. (2) All family members can discuss their common lesson at home.	(1) Several age-groups can meet in a single theme-related worship service. (2) At-home discussion of the theme is possible.	(1) All activities are closely related to the Bible lesson in each department group. (2) Lessons can be geared to the social, psychological, emotional and mental level of all pupils.	(1) Curriculum can be planned to fit the stage of development of pupils.
(1) Lessons are repeated on a 5-7 year cycle, provide limited Bible coverage. (2) Bible content often not suitable for pupils of all ages.	(1) Limited number of themes make it difficult to give complete Bible coverage. (2) Lessons taught in each department determined by theme, rather than pupils' developing needs.	(1) Common at-home discussion is limited, since parents and children study different material.	(1) At-home discussion limited. (2) Hard to relate all activities in SS hour (songs, worship service, etc.) to theme, since each grade has a different lesson.

Here are the four basic plans evangelical publishers follow in grading their lesson materials. To evaluate curriculum, you need to study the advantages and disadvantages of each curriculum plan when applied to your needs and goals.

closely graded materials into their program. Of course, any of the curriculums can be adapted to any size Sunday school.

A great deal of informative study and prayerful consideration must go into the choosing of a curriculum for the Sunday school. The board of Christian education should have the responsibility of choosing the curriculum, if such a board exists. If there is none, the pastor and the Sunday school superintendent may make the decision. It may be done after the Sunday school superintendent meets with the department superintendents, or in smaller churches, with individual teachers.

How to Evaluate Curriculum

In evaluating curriculum for any aspect of your C. E. program, there must be criteria for deciding which materials should be adopted for regular use in the Sunday school. Some curriculums may be theologically sound, yet not meet the personal needs of pupils. The next curriculum may be geared for a denomination other than your own. Still other materials may be too expensive for the budget of the church. The following are several questions one should ask in evaluating curriculum:

1. Is the curriculum in line with the doctrines that the Bible teaches?
2. Is the curriculum correlated in content so that students receive a complete program of Bible education, beginning with cradle roll and progressing to the home department (shut-ins)?
3. Are the materials properly age-graded?
4. Is the teacher's guide adapted to the aim, experience, and needs of the class?
5. Is the pupil's guide likewise adapted and interesting?
6. Will the planned lessons lead to decisions for salvation, spiritual growth, and Christian service?
7. Are the materials up-to-date and attractive?
8. Does the format of the books appeal to teachers and pupils?
9. Are the pictures contemporary and colorful?
10. Are the materials durable?
11. Is there an outline or general guide for aid in preparation?
12. Do teaching resources encourage the use of the most effec-

tive variety of teaching materials as opposed to the monotony of the same approach for every study?

13. Are there suggestions for displays and illustrations?
14. Is provision made for emphasis of special days such as Easter, Christmas, Thanksgiving, Mother's Day, and Father's Day?
15. Do the stories include character building as well as Bible facts?
16. Do the lessons challenge dedication of life on the part of the pupil?
17. Is adequate learning material provided for the pupil, such as pupil books, activity sheets, take-home papers?
18. Does the written work encourage active Bible study?
19. Do learning assignments challenge the pupil's interest and knowledge?
20. Do the paperwork assignments relate to the pupil's experience and age level?
21. Are illustrations authentic and pertinent?

Evaluators of Sunday school curriculums may find that no one curriculum provides all the above desirable features. Aim toward choosing the curriculum that gives the best balance of Bible content, learning activities, and application of truths to life.

CURRICULUM SECRETARY

The curriculum secretary is a person appointed by the board of Christian education with the sole responsibility of securing all educational materials needed in the C. E. program of the church, distributing those materials before the date they are needed, and keeping a file of quarterlies and student books for use by substitute teachers and new students. Because of the nature of the task associated with this position, it is generally best if the curriculum secretary has the gift of administration and has developed that gift to some degree.

DEAF, MINISTRY TO THE

A church sometimes uses the idea that there are not enough deaf people in the community to have a class for them to excuse its lack of ministry. How many constitute enough for a class? Recall that Mark Hopkins's definition of a school was "the teacher at one end of a log and the student at the other."

Consider first the church where several deaf people attend.

The Class for the Deaf

1. *Equipment.* The usual comfortable, lighted, ventilated room is necessary. Furnishings should include a chalkboard, an easel for flannelgraph or charts, Bibles, pencils, paper, and pictures.

2. *Curriculum.* Teaching materials to be read by the deaf in preparation for their lesson should be written especially for them. Their language is less complex at the same age and grade level than that of hearing persons. Denominational publications often make provision for such literature. If a church writes its own materials, a deaf Christian or one who understands the language limitations should prepare it.

   Subject matter will depend upon the spiritual and biblical progress of the deaf person. Some deaf people are not exposed to Christian teaching at an early age in the home. They may come to church with no understanding of stories and truths that other children absorb without effort. A good place to begin is where Paul began in dealing with the people of Athens—God who made heaven and earth and everything also made you, and he has a plan for you.

3. *Procedure.* Use sign language. This may seem to be a simple description of procedure, but those who teach the deaf regularly have discovered it is not simple. Sometimes there are distractions. Since the deaf hear with their eyes, when their attention is distracted for any reason, they miss what the teacher is "saying" with signs. Also, among the deaf, as among the hearing, there may be boredom. If a deaf person wants to turn off the teacher and the teaching, he needs only to lower his eyes. This shuts out communication.

The concerned teacher of the deaf will not be content with merely using the sign language. To enliven interest and clarify difficult points he will use:

a. *Chalkboard.* "I use the chalkboard to write a question for the class to think about, or a Bible verse to be stressed or learned," said Mrs. Pepper Moore, for many years interpreter and teacher of the deaf at First Baptist Church, Nashville, Tennessee.

b. *Flannelgraph.* The intrigue of pictures adhering to the board will capture attention and focus eyes on the explaining signs.

c. *Drama.* Signs may spell out words for which the deaf have no basis on which to build understanding. "David hit Goliath with a stone from his slingshot, and the giant fell down." The teacher may state the facts with signs and then literally act out the facts. (Actions are the oldest international sign language.)

d. *Puppets.* With interpretation, the deaf can and do follow the meaning of a Bible puppet presentation.

e. *Charts.* A chart may hold the outline of the principal points of a lesson. For greatest attention, the strip chart or link chart, revealing one point at a time, will be most effective.

f. In more advanced classes, the deaf can participate in *role play.* The entire drama may be pantomimed without the need for sign language.

A Class with One or Two Deaf

Should the deaf child who comes home from a school for the

deaf be ignored in a Sunday school class? Should he be treated as though he were hearing? The problem is not one to be ignored. Ministering to the spiritual needs of a deaf child may mean winning a family.

1. Form a church class in sign language. In areas where deaf children are present occasionally in classes, a church may form a Sunday night class in sign language, taught by an interpreter from a church that has a ministry with the deaf.

2. Seat the child with an interpreter. When the deaf child is present in class, allow space beside him for the interpreter. This helps him understand what is going on, even though the interpreter may not be an expert.

3. Use visual aids. Use the chalkboard to write out unusual names, places, Bible references. Show pictures that tell the essence of the story.

4. Encourage participation. In playing review games, allow the deaf child to respond, through the interpreter. Let him feel he is part of the class. He will enjoy participating in role play.

Special Services to the Deaf

Often a teacher of the deaf will discover he is the only link between the deaf person and the complicated world about him. He will have occasion to render him many special services, such as:

1. *Medical.* Few doctors are prepared to understand the symptoms of the deaf. An interpreter is necessary to help the doctor know what is needed and to help the patient understand the treatment prescribed and be able to follow it. In some cases he will also have to interpret to the patient's family.

2. *Legal.* A deaf person may need to draw up a will, to buy a house or a car, or face some other legal problem with which he cannot cope alone. A Christian teacher-friend who is concerned about him can make sure those involved have full and correct understanding of the case.

3. *Emotional.* Deaf persons meet problems of life, just as hearing persons do. In case of serious illness, death in the family, grave injustice, lies, or other hurtful experiences, the deaf

need someone to guide their thinking toward the Christian view of the problem. Deaf youth have the same need for counsel in friendships as hearing youth do.

4. *Shopping.* A deaf person may need assistance in making large purchases. He cannot make himself understood to the sales clerk; nor can the clerk explain style, colors, materials, or costs to him.

5. *Spiritual.* While a deaf person may "hear" the preacher's message via an interpreter and respond to the invitation, very often winning the deaf is done on a one-to-one basis. Knowing, trusting, loving the teacher, the deaf person has confidence in the teacher's concern for his soul. When he understands his spiritual need, he seeks the help of the one who cares. It is imperative for the teacher of the deaf to know how to lead a soul to Christ.

DEBATE

The debate is a teaching method that is seldom used in the church to communicate the Word of God. However, on certain occasions it can be used effectively. A debate can engender objective thinking. It can cause students to compare scriptural truth with man's ideas.

Print on the chalkboard: "Resolved, that Jesus offered the Davidic kingdom to Israel, but the nation rejected him in unbelief." Several days before the debate, assign two students to study the Scripture portion and defend the resolution, and two students to oppose the resolution. Debate demands thorough knowledge of the subject. Preparation should include analysis of the topic from opposing points of view. The teacher should help students prepare by making research material available to both sides. Arguments for and against Jesus' offer of the kingdom should be shared with the debaters. Type these reasons out and give them to the four debaters. Challenge those helping in the debate to find true solutions to the problems. They should do more than attempt to win the debate; they should also try to find the correct answers to any questions. Ask each debater to continually prove his point by Scripture references.

Before the debate begins, read the Scripture portion for the lesson to the class. Ask them to look up and read each Scripture reference made by those taking part in the debate. Ask them to analyze Scripture used by debaters to determine whether the speakers have interpreted correctly. The class should see the full implication of the problem if the debate is properly done. But do not be alarmed if some members are left in doubt, because a debate is a factual presentation with persuasion. If there are questions in the minds of some class members, clear them up in the summary.

Each speaker should be given three minutes to make his first presentation. A timer should be appointed and provided with a bell. Remind debaters they will be interrupted if they run over the allotted time.

Use the following sequence of presentation:
1. First affirmative speaker
2. First negative speaker
3. Second affirmative speaker
4. Second negative speaker

During the rebuttal use the reverse order:
1. First negative speaker
2. First affirmative speaker
3. Second negative speaker
4. Second affirmative speaker

Allow each person in the debate two minutes for rebuttal.

Arrange for two tables at the front of the class, with two affirmative speakers at one and two negative speakers at the other. Prepare a large name card to identify each speaker to the class. Ask each debater to stand and address the class when speaking. The teacher presides over the debate at a small table between the two larger tables.

At the close, ask the class for a vote on the conclusion. If the class is given opportunity to vote on the winners of the debate, use the following criteria for declaring the winners:
1. The presentation of facts or content

2. The substantiation or proof of their statements
3. Ability to answer (the rebuttal)

There may be danger in voting on winners in a Sunday school class. This added pressure may motivate a debater to try to win rather than to present the facts.

DECLINE IN ATTENDANCE

Historically, Sunday school has been a growing institution as it emphasized reaching and teaching people, but some Sunday schools have experienced a decline in attendance. The following reasons are suggested for Sunday school decline. (No statistical proof is offered to substantiate these reasons for decline. The observations are based on the author's study of fast-growing Sunday schools.)

1. Evangelism is neglected. The church boom years immediately after World War II are over. People are no longer pressured by peer status to attend Sunday school. Sunday school is no longer the "in" place to be on Sunday morning. Friendly invitations to "come and hear our pastor" also have lost their appeal. But those Sunday schools that are growing usually have an aggressive evangelistic approach. Southern Baptists, for example, built the largest Protestant denominations on the premise that the Sunday school is the evangelistic arm of the church.

2. Facilities are inadequate. Just as a quart of water will not fit into a pint jar, 200 people cannot fit into a Sunday school designed for 100. Growing attendance continually needs more space, and if the leadership lacks vision and stops adding educational space, attendance levels off.

3. Quality is emphasized to the exclusion of quantity. Sometimes Sunday schools stop growing because no emphasis is made on numbers. Spurgeon said more than one hundred years ago, "The minister that will not emphasize numbers will not have them."

   Many a Sunday school leader follows the unspoken rule that if we have quality education, we will attract great crowds, but I have observed outstanding small Sunday schools that have never grown. Therefore, I believe that quality alone will not lead to a growing attendance. Some hold the opposite opinion—that large Sunday schools must be good because people are attending. I also have observed crowds flocking to Sunday schools offering poor education. The conclusion is simple: Quality does not produce quantity or vice versa. A Sunday school must work at both quality and quantity to have large crowds and effective education.

4. Inadequate administration hurts attendance. Dr. Lee Roberson built the second-largest Sunday school in America (attendance 7,453) at Highland Park Baptist Church, Chattanooga, Tennessee, on the principle that the Sunday school rises or falls on leadership.

5. Antiquated educational environment kills growth. Public school children today are given the finest education in history. It is built on enjoyment, involvement, and experience. But a credibility gap can arise when in Sunday school they sit in furnace rooms, study from quarterlies with small type and out-of-date pictures, and endure boring lectures.

DIORAMAS

A diorama is a teaching tool to aid learning. It is a three-dimensional scene that tells a story. It is adaptable to any age level and almost any subject. Students can build dioramas in any box or frame—a shoe box or corrugated carton, a windowsill, a bookcase shelf, a mantel, or a sandbox or sand pan.

Suitable Subjects

1. A scene from a Bible story, such as Andrew bringing Peter to Jesus
2. Bible customs, e.g., a diorama of a woman getting water from a well
3. Illustrations of Christian growth and conduct
4. Missions, with a scene from a mission field
5. Church history, depicting an early church scene or event

Advantages for the Students

1. Affords benefits of learning cooperation, sharing, and friendliness
2. Offers opportunity for the shy person to participate and the aggressive one to use his energy constructively
3. Gives opportunity for class members to do research and use information
4. Teachers discover understandings, feelings, and skills of the group. This knowledge enables teachers to guide the class to better knowledge, attitudes, and habits by further conversation and aids during a project.

Materials

1. Permanent box frame. This can be reused by placing in it new figures and scenes. May be a wood or corrugated cardboard carton.
2. A three-part cardboard background. Cut three pieces of heavy cardboard, the middle about two feet long and a foot high, side pieces about one foot square. Hinge together with tape or lacing. Cover with shelf or wrapping paper, on which background scenery is drawn. Reuse by making new background covers.
3. Figures. Wind two pipe cleaners together by using a third. Glue or tape on a construction paper head. Add facial features. Dress the figure to fit the character. Place feet of the figure in clay to make it stand up. Or use clothespins and dress as above. Other figures may be drawn on cardboard and cut out, made of plywood, pápier-máchê, or modeling clay.
4. Palm trees. Palm trees may be made by rolling brown construction paper into a tube the desired height and diameter for the scene. Glue. Fold nine-by-twelve-inch green crepe paper into a fan, about an inch for each fold, then fold in half. Draw pattern of palm leaf on folded fan, with base of palm on the fold. Cut out and arrange leaves in a bunch. Tie with thread or string. Glue leaves inside the top of the brown paper tube. Cut up the base of the tube a half inch in four places; fold back to make the tree stand up.

Apple trees may be made by hole punching colored tissue paper and gluing the resulting confetti to the stems of twigs. Use spools for trunk. Large weeds with small dried flowers or pods painted green will resemble trees. Live evergreens will serve as pine trees.

5. Oriental houses. Use brown construction paper with a sixteen-square fold. Cut and paste as for a box. Invert, making open side down. Add a railing around the flat top, and accordion-fold stairs leading to the roof. Cut out a window and door.

6. Variations. Curtains across the front of the scene may be used as a screen for shadow pictures. Flashlights may light interior through holes in each side of box. Cellophane in front will give an unusual and beautiful effect. Make a peep show with a scene inside a shoe box. Slit an end of the box through which to view the scene. Cut a rectangular opening in the top cover of the box to let in enough light to see the three-dimensional scene.

Procedure

1. Tell the story.
2. Discuss the subject with your class.
3. Smaller children may each draw a picture to illustrate the theme. Comment on good points of each and hang up all pictures.
4. Let class choose scene for illustration.
5. Plan together, with reference materials on hand—pictures, books, maps, handwork books on dioramas.
6. Divide class into committees, each to work on certain aspects. One may decide upon the box or frame. A second might make the background and fit it into place. The third would work on the "floor" of the box to simulate the interior of a building, or the trees, roads, water, and hills of the outdoors. Another committee could make the figures.
7. Arrange and rearrange figures and background to best advantage. Display most important figures and objects in foreground.
8. Retell the story, using the diorama, with group participation.
9. Evaluate the project.

DIRECTOR OF CHRISTIAN EDUCATION

The director of Christian education is not the Christian educator for the congregation, but rather the director of the church's educators. Sometimes he is called the minister of Christian education to indicate he is a part of the pastoral staff of the church. Usually, the need for this staff position comes at or near the time when the church is financially able to fill that position. Often, this person is the second major staff position hired by the church. However, the membership must also be spiritually ready to turn the educational leadership over to this person and to accomplish the work of Christian education under his (or her) direction.

How to Call a Director of Christian Education

If the need for a director of Christian education has been determined, the congregation must be properly informed of this person's duties and qualifications. By knowing this, the congregation is being prepared for an additional paid staff member. The church must know the status of the director of Christian education and the line of authority. Knowing this alone would avoid making the director of Christian education an errand boy or girl. If there is a director of Christian education in a neighboring church, it would be wise to invite this person to explain his duties to the congregation.

Usually a church hires a man from its own denomination because it expects him to be in accord with the church's statement of faith and government. Nevertheless, it is a good policy to question the prospective leader concerning his doctrinal position.

After the congregation has been informed about the need for a director of Christian education, each prospect should be invited to the church. Each should receive a letter outlining the educational needs of the church, the working conditions, financial arrangements, and a complete job description.

The director of Christian education, if interested, must interpret his educational training, experience, and philosophy in light of the needs of the prospective church.

When the candidate visits the congregation, he or she should be introduced to the pastor first, the board of Christian education next, then the official board, and finally the congregation. The church should underwrite the expenses of the candidate for this visit.

The senior minister and the candidate should spend time in prayer, in fellowship, and talking in detail about duties, working conditions, and financial arrangements. This prevents later difficulties in their relationship. In the final analysis, the director of Christian education is hired by and works for the pastor. If both parties feel this is the Lord's leading, then a definite salary offer should be made, required duties outlined, and, in some cases, a plan for retirement mentioned.

The best time for the director of Christian education to begin his work is in the summer before secular schools resume classes. Early August is suitable, although earlier in the summer may be even better. The educational program can then be in full swing for fall.

Of course the first Sunday the director of Christian education is on the scene, the senior minister should explain again the educational program to the congregation. The morning service may conclude with an installation or dedication ceremony. Some churches also plan a congregational dinner to welcome the new director of Christian education, so he could bring a challenging message on the task of Christian education for that local church.

What to Look for in a Director of Christian Education

When looking for a director of Christian education, the church should consider five major areas for evaluation. These include (1) character, (2) decorum, (3) training, (4) philosophy, and (5) spiritual gifts. If a prospective director of Christian education can qualify in all four areas, the possibility is great that he will prove to be a success.

Character. The first impression, based on personality, is only a hint as to the true nature of the individual. The individual must be examined on the basis of inner character rather than outer personality. The director must be a born-again believer who is attempting to live the Christian life. The prospective director of Christian education must be a true child of God. Beyond this, there must be evidence of a growing and advanced yieldedness to

God. This person's spiritual maturity will largely determine his success with the entire Christian education staff. Personality traits play a secondary part. These traits must be largely positive. However, in selecting a director of Christian education, a church cannot afford to concentrate on outer personality and overlook the inner man, the true character of the child of God.

Decorum means the director uses good taste in personal conduct. Any person attempting to serve God as a leader of people should be aware of the need to cultivate decorum. It cannot be described only as the presence or absence of any one or more personality traits. Therefore, no prospective director of Christian education should overlook the importance of strengths or underestimate the handicap of weaknesses. Nor should the director fail to cultivate the former or improve the latter. If a person is by nature outstandingly friendly, he should use this ability to relate to people for the glory of God. If bitterness or anger is a weakness, one should exercise constant vigilance to guard against losing one's temper.

Beyond personality, decorum enters the realm of habits, mannerisms, and cleanliness. A person should survey himself totally for negative points along these lines. By virtue of the office, the director of Christian education holds a privileged position before God. Any bad habit, distracting mannerism, or untidiness may cause this servant of God to be a reproach instead of a blessing. The Christian leader should strive for tasteful conduct of the highest degree.

Training. Some churches set strict educational standards for a candidate for director of Christian education. Most now require a bachelor's or master's degree. This is a beginning, but such a standard is by no means sufficient in itself. A person with a degree is not always a good prospect for director of Christian education. This person needs training and experience in church education, otherwise academic teaching might be stressed over the actual spiritual results of teaching. Possession of a degree merely means that this individual has been exposed to a certain set of standard requirements and has responded as well as an average student. A college degree alone does not mean that the individual is automatically capable of leading a church. It is therefore recommended that the director be evaluated on the basis of an all-around Christian education, training, experience, and past performance as a leader.

The person with an advanced degree in Christian education can legitimately claim that a group of authorities in this field has placed its stamp of approval on him or her. But remember, God calls the person, not his degree. The prospective director who has quit school prematurely may also be expected to drop other tasks prematurely.

A career as director of Christian education hinges on how well a person knows the Lord and the principles by which he or she is supposed to be living and teaching. Knowledge of the Bible will help him be a good counselor, leader, and teacher. It also will help the director to recognize biblical preparations in prospective Christian education personnel.

Philosophy. The word that best describes the DCE's total outlook is *philosophy.* It refers to the mental outlook, ambitions, and presuppositions he brings to his office. The DCE's mind must be reconciled to the mental as well as physical hardships that await those who dedicate themselves to the work of God. Every Christian worker must face the reality of unpleasant experiences and disappointments. If a person is unwilling to face these circumstances for Christ's sake, there is little chance that he or she will ever be a successful director of Christian education.

Every person naturally has ambitions. The heart of the director of Christian education must be ambitious for the work of Christ. If the potential director of Christian education has a deep-seated, secret ambition for anything other than serving in the local church, this person will have severe problems. Christian joy comes from serving God in the best way possible. If a candidate does not firmly believe that the director of Christian education has the greatest opportunity to reach young hearts for Christ, it is doubtful that he or she should serve in such a capacity. The director of Christian education who can visualize a lifetime of service in this field can trust God to supply his need to achieve personal and professional fulfillment. Emotions can lead a person astray in the choice of a career, but God never will.

Spiritual Gifts. When looking for a director of Christian education, the selection committee should also consider the candidate's spiritual gift mix. Because of the nature of this position, the ideal candidate should normally evidence giftedness in teaching, exhortation, and administration. Consideration should also be given to the gifts of the pastor with whom the candidate will be working to ensure the two individuals will complement each other for the good of the church. The unique circumstances of a particular church may suggest additional spiritual gifts that the director of Christian education should have.

The Relationship between the Senior Pastor and the DCE

Normally there is a direct relationship between the pastor and the director of Christian education. The DCE is hired by the pastor and receives direction from him. The pastor is ultimately responsible for the educational program of the church but delegates this duty to the director of Christian education. The director of Christian education has not been hired as an assistant minister, although he should be willing to help in every area of the work. The DCE does not usually preach, nor does this person make hospital or home calls in a pastoral capacity, but he should be willing to do so. The time of a DCE should center on leading the Christian education program of the church.

When the pastor has enough confidence in a candidate to hire him or her as the director of Christian education, he should then be able to rely on that staff person to fulfill his or her responsibilities as part of the ministry team. The pastor should encourage and support the DCE. Just as the DCE looks to the pastor for leadership, the pastor should look to the DCE for input as he makes decisions that may impact the educational ministry of the church.

The Duties of the Director of Christian Education

There are seven main duties of the director of Christian education.

1. To counsel and guide the Christian education board in much the same manner as the pastor guides the general board.
2. To coordinate the youth program and weekday clubs. This includes:

    a. planning meetings with officers and sponsors

    b. recruiting sponsors

    c. providing in-service training

    d. organizing deputation teams

    e. planning retreats

    f. planning for publicity and record keeping

    g. visiting youth members and prospects

3. To recommend sponsors and leaders for children's church, local summer camp program, senior citizens' group, and the nursery school program.

4. To give direction to the Sunday school. This includes:

    a. advising at superintendents' meetings

    b. assisting in recruiting and training workers

    c. advising on enlargement of activities such as visitation, contests, and publicity

    d. advising on visual aid selection

    e. encouraging good record keeping and systematic review

    f. continually reevaluating curriculum materials

    g. recommending nominees for superintendents

5. To be responsible for training leaders. This includes:

    a. finding and selecting workers

    b. training new and existing workers

    c. promoting the spiritual maturity of the workers

6. To provide vision for the total program of Christian education in the church.

7. To teach the Word of God. The director of Christian education must strive to maintain a balance between the two extremes of teaching too much (letting his administrative duties slip) and retreating into his office (becoming exclusively an administrator and not using his teaching gifts).

DISCIPLESHIP AND CHURCH GROWTH (See also CHURCH GROWTH WHEEL)

No work is effective for God unless the people are willing to follow God and the leader that he has placed over them. Jesus said, "And whoever does not bear his cross and come after Me cannot be My disciple" (Luke 14:27). The effectiveness of the church is measured by the degree to which the people follow the Lord.

Spiritual Factors of Discipleship

1. Growing churches are characterized by people who love God. Even though this is an intangible factor, an individual's love will cause him to endure hardships, visit on a bus eight hours on a Saturday, stay up and pray all night, or endure any other hardship for the cross of Christ.

2. Growing churches are characterized by people with commitment and yieldedness. To be a disciple of Christ, a person must yield himself to do God's will. This involves (a) a total commitment of one's conscious endeavors and (b) daily yielding of one's self to God.

3. Growing churches are characterized by people who pray. The effective disciple spends time (a) worshiping God (John 9:31), (b) fellowshiping with God, (c) asking for power (Luke 11:13), and (d) praising.

4. Growing churches are characterized by people who know and live by the Word of God. A disciple must continue in the Word of God (John 8:31).

5. Growing churches are characterized by biblical fellowship among their members. Disciples must want to fellowship with other disciples. They spend time together in order to grow through fellowship.

Natural Factors of Discipleship

1. Growing churches reach a person as and where he is. We cannot expect a lower-class person to attend a church with highbrow music. The man from the housing project cannot feel an affinity with people who have a different value system. God will reach certain people through a Pentecostal-type church, while others will be reached through a more intellectual Bible study. This principle reflects Genesis 1: "like produces like."

2. Growing churches spend time and money on those who will respond most readily. Jesus taught his disciples that if they were not received in a town, they should shake the dust off

their sandals (Luke 9:5). By this, he implied that they should spend time on those who would respond to the message. Therefore, a Sunday school should invest most of its energy on those who will attend rather than those who won't. This does not mean that we should neglect any segment of the population. Sunday school buses are more successful in the slums, housing projects, and among the poor than among the rich. The rich have transportation to bring their children to Sunday school or won't allow their child to ride a Sunday school bus. The poor are willing to send their children to the church that cares for them.

3. Growing churches have more people making a profession of faith, hence they have more who can become disciples. The criticism often is heard that fast-growing churches need a backdoor revival. They have many coming down the aisle to receive Christ, yet not everyone continues to grow in faith. However, let us not criticize the churches getting many decisions. Two points should be made. First, we want every person saved that we can possibly reach. Second, we want those saved to go on with Christ. This is discipling. However, emphasizing just discipleship is not the purpose of the church, although the church that has the most professions of faith is most likely to be effective in discipleship.

4. Growing churches involve new Christians in service. God wants a new Christian baptized so he feels the obligation of going on with Christ. The outward confession of baptism can be a stimulus to motivate the young Christian to faithfulness. When a person receives Christ, immediately tell the church. Their expectations also motivate him to service.

5. Growing churches stress salvation of the whole person. Salvation involves intellect, emotion, and will. For a person to be saved, he must know the gospel content, feel the conviction of sin and the love of God, then respond by an act of his will. This is believing. Since the end product determines the process, plan Sunday school to appeal to the intellect, emotions, and will of the individual. He must know the content of the gospel, so communicate Bible content. He must feel

hatred for sin as well as love for God. Sing songs to stir emotions and use humor, testimonies, pithy sayings, and activities to motivate pupils. Since salvation involves a decision of the will, get the pupil doing things in the class that will immerse him in the Word of God.

6. Growing churches have disciples that assume the attitudes and practices of their leader. If the people are not soul winners, it's often because the pastor is ineffective in his outreach. When the people do not sacrifice, it is usually because of their pastor's attitude. Jeremiah the prophet said, "Like priest, like people." He cannot get the people to do what he himself is not willing to do.

7. Growing churches realize the power of an educated disciple. The effectiveness of a worker is in direct proportion to his education. Some workers are not successful because they have not been trained. Others fail because they have enough "education" but don't know the right things (their theology is wrong). Therefore, the leader must reinforce the primacy of the church; this is the cornerstone of Christian education. They also must reinforce the primacy of the church's methods; disciples must be convinced that the method they use is the most effective to reach a lost world. And the leader must continually reinforce loyalty to the cause. The rededication service is effective for growth. Workers need to come to the altar and renew their pledge for church growth.

8. Growing churches realize the power of the motivated worker. Bus workers without formal education have brought hundreds of children to Sunday school. Dwight L. Moody never finished high school but shook two continents for God. Fast-growing Sunday schools have been built on the shoulders of motivated workers. Therefore, the leader must make the following assumptions: (a) People do not naturally want to serve God because they are sinners. (b) Because everyone has a gift (ability to serve God), everyone should be serving God. (c) Therefore, the leader should motivate everyone to serve God. To magnify the motivated worker does not lessen our emphasis on the trained worker, for God uses both. But

the worker who is trained and motivated is the most effective disciple of all.

DISCIPLINE, HOW TO SECURE GOOD BEHAVIOR

A new problem is erupting in Sunday schools. It's discipline—on a larger, more frightening scale that ever before.

Pupils "shake down" offering money from other pupils in the washroom or slash cushioned pews when ushers aren't looking. They slap around younger children when bus workers aren't present, and they rip anything that is not nailed down from Sunday school rooms.

The discipline problems of the past—when pupils wouldn't share crayons or found it hard to keep still while waiting in line—were simple compared to those of today. The exasperating new tensions come from children who throw around four-letter words, use their fists, spit, bite, or defiantly stare down meek teachers.

How have teachers reacted? Some have whipped inner-city boys, but striking a child is against the law. Some teachers yell at pupils, who only yell back. Other teachers grit their teeth, cry, or quit.

What causes this severe disorderly behavior? For one thing, permissive public school behavior is spilling over into the Sunday school, but this is not the whole problem. Children from Christian families usually are better behaved than their public school counterparts, so it is more than just the influence of our society on Sunday school scholars.

What can be done? Teachers are finding that gimmicks can't keep a twentieth-century student quiet. In the past, teachers have awarded prizes for the quietest or used the mystery chair. But that doesn't always work. Today's pupils are involved in the learning process, and most Sunday school teachers are not ready or equipped to share classroom control. At school, pupils have a voice in discipling fellow students. Should they have the same authority in the house of God?

The authority of the Sunday school is the Word of God, whereas the authority of public school is the democratic process. Therefore, teachers should usually handle problems differently on Sunday. Since God is love, teachers must communicate love. Since the Bible upholds what is right, teachers can't let pupils continue in wrong behavior. Since the Ten Commandments prohibit taking God's name in vain, teachers can't allow cursing.

The Sunday school must work with the home to secure good behavior. Since the Sunday school worker must never touch a pupil in discipline (the local and state laws prohibit it), and the negative means of discipline will be misunderstood, the Sunday school must work in harmony with the home. The first premise of discipline is that the mother or father has the right and obligation to discipline a child. Therefore, the home must be involved in the whole process of teaching, not just negative discipline. The second premise is the Sunday school must be a place of love and acceptance. Therefore negative discipline must be approached with care.

What can teachers do? Good class discipline begins with self-discipline. Teachers must prepare well, plan class activities, master content, and give attention to interesting teaching techniques. They must remember that listening is not learning, therefore teaching is not telling. Pupils must stand, s-t-r-e-t-c-h, yell, march, and act out Bible stories. The primary department at Welsch Avenue Free Will Baptist Church, Columbus, Ohio, directs the little ones in spontaneous calisthenics at the beginning of class. They are able to jump all over the place. "It's getting the wiggles out," explains the teacher.

Sometimes students are disruptive because of room conditions. The room is too crowded, too stuffy, too cluttered, too hot, or too dark. Adequate facilities won't guarantee good behavior, but poor facilities will produce the opposite.

Teachers can defuse class explosions by getting to know their students, then coming early on Sunday to talk with them before class. When a child is rebellious, ask him why and remind him Sunday school is a place to learn about Jesus Christ. By sharing love and attention a teacher may meet the very need that causes the child to rebel in class.

A classroom is a threatening situation to many pupils, therefore they retaliate and strike out at the teacher. Remove some of the threat by giving instructions carefully. Pupils will respond better when they know what is expected of them.

Don't respond to your students out of bias or prejudice. Some teachers don't like long hair on boys, certain minorities, dirty dresses, runny noses, or laughing, pushy girls. If a teacher reacts personally, behavior degenerates into a shouting match. When a teacher corrects a disruptive student, it becomes an argument, even though the teacher is in the place of authority. Make sure that student discipline is the result of broken rules, not personality dislike.

Other positive steps toward achieving good discipline include praise for good behavior, recruiting enough helpers, teachers sitting among pupils, attractive visuals, and concentrated prayer for problem students.

However, in certain cases, negative steps will be in order. Some excellent teachers have captivated the interest of all the juniors but one. A rebellious boy laughs as the flannelgraph story is told. Good teachers have followed every suggestion only to be thwarted by a pseudodelinquent who laughs at the things of Christ or giggles during prayer. The majority of the class who want to hear the lesson should not be sacrificed to one lawless pupil.

Remove the belligerent student from the class. Put him in the secretary's office or sit him in a chair in the hall. In doing so, he loses his platform to perform for the kids, you reduce pressure on him, and when he is out of the room, you can counsel him individually. (Some of you may remember being sent to the principal's office because of bad behavior.) First, let him sit quietly and wait. This gives him a chance to think. When talking with the pupil about his behavior, appeal to proper motives and place responsibility back on the pupil to reenter the class and practice good behavior. The teacher's attitude toward behavior is important. Always keep the goal of good behavior before the class.

DISCUSSION

While discussion may be one of the easiest and most interesting methods of teaching, it holds complications and pitfalls the alert teacher must avoid. Pupils may go off on a tangent and never get back to the original subject. The conversation will take off wildly once they hit on last night's game or "Mary and Bill are going steady." The teacher must keep a firm hand to maintain control of the discussion.

Preparation for discussion cannot be too extensive. The teacher needs preparation for starting the discussion. Once discussion is underway, the teacher must guide it constantly toward its goal. The teacher should set up a definite goal, propose a way to get there, and give guidance on that way.

There are two particular difficulties with discussion, one of which the teacher will be sure to encounter in almost any discussion. First, "No one will talk; I can't get anyone to discuss." By introducing the subject in terms interesting to the group and using some incident pertinent to their experiences, a teacher can stimulate almost any group to participate in a discussion. Give pupils opportunity to get used to each other, to know each other. If they are accustomed to lectures on Sunday morning, begin by asking questions you know they can answer, to gradually break the ice.

Second, "Everyone wants to talk at once, and I can hardly control them." This is probably not as common a difficulty as the first, but will be found in junior high and high school groups. These pupils are getting a first taste of freedom in class. A firm hand will be needed. Don't be afraid to teach a few lessons in common courtesy. The teacher will even need to take over the discussion at times, to keep it in hand. But this is better than letting it run wild. A mixture of diplomacy and a knowledge of the subject and of human nature will usually overcome the difficulty.

DISCUSSION GROUPS (See BUZZ GROUPS)

DOUBLING YOUR CLASS ATTENDANCE

You can double the attendance of your Sunday school class. Sound impossible? Well, it isn't. Hundreds of teachers have used the principles included here and have had results. Read all the points carefully—then discuss them with the other teachers in your Sunday school. Think how much could be accomplished for the Lord if every class in your school doubled in size this year.

1. Set an overall goal. If your class has been averaging fifteen, set a goal of thirty. Prepare a poster with a goal of thirty. Write "30" on the chalkboard. Saturate your pupils with the goal.

   Goal-setting works. A junior class in the Florence (S.C.) Baptist Temple hung a large sheet of paper from one wall to another, then had each of the twenty-six boys write his name on it and sign "52" by his autograph. In that way, each student reinforced the class goal of fifty-two. The total Sunday school set a goal of 1,225. Posters were put on walls, bulletin boards, and doors. Every poster announced the goal of 1,225, but each differently—in German, Spanish, Greek, upper and lowercase letters, gothic, and roman numbers.

2. Set a goal for finding new prospects. In order for your class to double, attempt to get twice as many prospects as your average attendance. This means that each member should suggest two names for your prospect list.

   An adult class at the Berean Baptist Church, Salem, Virginia, distributed blank cards to members and asked each to submit names of friends he or she would like to see in the class. After two weeks of listing names, the goal still was not reached. Therefore, three ladies were delegated to phone members of the class and write down the names they suggested. They worked until 100 new names were gathered.

   To have a growing Sunday school class, put as much emphasis on finding prospects as on recruiting them.

3. Assign prospect responsibility. Many growing classes type the names of all prospects on sheets of paper, then distribute photocopies in the class, assigning prospects to be contacted before the next week. The Calvary Baptist Church in Ypsilanti, Michigan, printed a motto over its visitation board, People Expect What You Inspect. Many members work in the automobile assembly plants in Detroit, where they are taught by GM that people work accord-

ing to how closely the foreman supervises them. The same rule applies to Sunday school. Therefore, give each of your class members a prospect to contact, then check up on them the following Sunday to see if they have made the contact.

4. Phone every prospect. During the fall campaign, phone every prospect on your list every week. Extend to each a friendly welcome, giving the time, place, and lesson topic.

5. Send mail to every prospect. During your campaign, mail every prospect a postcard or letter inviting him to Sunday school. A housewife can write a personal note to thirty prospective students in two hours. A first-class letter to thirty prospects costs less than $10—and eternal benefits will result.

6. Visit every prospect. Visitation puts the *go* in *gospel,* carrying the message to every person. After you have phoned every prospect, a visit to his home will convince each of your love. In fact, visit every prospect every week during your attendance campaign.

7. Start a class newspaper. During your campaign, start a one-page (or larger) class newspaper. The junior class at the Crestwicke Baptist Church, Guelph, Ontario, distributes an eight-page paper, *The Roadrunner,* to every junior. Since it is a large class, the teachers spend time writing articles about juniors who have recently committed their lives to Jesus Christ. The paper also includes crossword puzzles, homework, stories, and news about the attendance campaign. The attendance motto and logo also are printed there, reminding the kids of their attendance goals.

The average Sunday school teacher with less than ten pupils cannot publish a newspaper every week, but he can do it at least twice during each attendance campaign. A class newspaper is not hard to prepare. If you've never issued one, simply write a one-page letter giving the news of the class. Then type the letter in two columns to make it look like a newspaper, and put a headline across the top. Fill in the newspaper with the names of students, their accomplishments, and what you expect to do for God.

8. Name your class. Bill Newton took the fourth grade boys class at the Thomas Road Baptist Church, Lynchburg, Virginia, and called it "The Treehouse Gang." A massive cardboard tree, with a door, was used at the entrance of the room. Two more large trees, reaching from ceiling to floor covered the inside walls. Later, a stockade was put in the hall surrounding the doors. Bill Newton started his class in September. His goal was to average fifty-four before the year was out. With enthusiasm, ingenuity, and determination, Newton pushed the average attendance to ninety-four.

9. Post attendance. A junior boys' class at a Baptist church called their campaign "Spring Training." A massive box score chart marked hits, runs, and errors so that students could follow their progress each week. The class was divided into two sides, and at the beginning of each class they "batted around," adding up visitors, attendance, and Bibles.

   Since pupils tend to value those things that are important to teachers, make sure to call the roll carefully. This tells each student it is his duty to be in class every Sunday. The extra pressure of some kind of a wall chart gives added motivation.

10. Get a motto. The high school class at the Bible Baptist Church, Savannah, Georgia, had a "Fat Is Beautiful" campaign. Instead of awarding stars or rockets or putting names on the wall, they weighed in each week. The teams began with an equal total weight. Visitors tipped the scales for the winners, while absentees dragged the losers down.

11. Get a logo. A Baptist church celebrated its twenty-fifth anniversary with a huge silver seal hung all year in the auditorium with the motto, The Twenty-fifth Year of Redemption. Under the motto was their goal: 2,500 Souls Won to Christ. The entire seal was their logo. The large seal was fashioned into small silver seals, which they affixed to envelopes and letterheads. It was also printed on all the literature of the church.

12. Give out buttons. Dr. Bob Gray, Trinity Baptist Church, Jacksonville, Florida, set a Florida record of more than five thousand in Sunday school on the church's twenty-fifth anniversary. Each person was given a button that said, "I Am One of 5,000" to remind him to be faithful in attendance.

13. Stretch their faith. The First Baptist Church, West Hollywood, Florida, planned to beat the Jacksonville record and have the largest Sunday school in the history of Florida. To do so, attendance had to double from 2,700 to 5,400. In a three-day workers' conference, their faith was stretched.

On the first night of the conference, everyone was pinned with a "5,000+" button and asked to pray for five thousand plus every time he ate a meal during the next week. Since most eat three meals a day, every person would pray twenty-one times for five thousand plus. Pastor Verle Ackerman called it "Fast or Pray," reminding his people that if they didn't pray for five thousand plus, they should not eat.

The second night, each worker signed a pledge card saying, "I will work for five thousand plus."

On the third night every teacher made a numerical commitment of a goal for his class on five-thousand-plus Sunday.

When the tally was in, they had pledged to reach 5,400. Later they reached 5,427, the largest Sunday school in the history of Florida.

14. Choose a good day. Don't plan a Sunday school campaign for Labor Day weekend, or during the Fourth of July holiday when there is a natural dip in the attendance. The minister who tried to have his largest attendance on Labor Day weekend and the Sunday after Easter, claiming, "Anybody can get a crowd on Easter, I want to build an attendance to show our people love God," has missed the whole purpose of an attendance campaign. A high attendance should do more than demonstrate the loyalty of the faithful. It should bring visitors; electrify everyone when the attendance is doubled; and bring men, women,

and children to a saving faith in Jesus Christ. So plan for Sunday school growth when the best results are possible. Then you will be a good steward of your time, energy, and money. Therefore, plan to grow on those days when attendance can be largest.

15. Remember the clenched fist. A man can keep his fist taut only so long, then the muscles give out. Likewise, a Sunday school class can pressure itself for expansion for only a short time. Therefore, growing Sunday schools plan two attendance campaigns for six or seven weeks each spring and fall. They work hard during a campaign to find prospects, excite students, phone, write, and visit. The attendance drive is relaxed during the Christmas holidays, the snows of January, and again during the summer.

16. Get a running start. Before jumping a creek, a boy runs faster if he has to jump farther. In Sunday school, the larger the goal, the longer it takes to reach it. Plan a six- or seven-week fall campaign with the high Sunday as the last day. Don't read this article and plan to double your class next week. Pray to double, plan to double, and promote to double. But remember this: A teacher can't lead if his class won't follow, and pupils won't work to double their class unless their teacher takes the time to convince them it can be done.

17. Plan a high day. Plan a high attendance Sunday on the last Sunday of your campaign. Some criticize this, saying that it only gets a crowd and makes small-class teaching impossible. However, the "high day" really is only a return to the old-fashioned rally day, where all pupils assembled in the auditorium to "rally" enthusiasm for Sunday school. Most teachers need to break lethargy and infuse the pupils with expectation. A "double day" convinces the pupils it can be done again and again, until the class is permanently doubled.

18. Pray. God answers the prayer of those who ask for their ministry to be enlarged, but prayer alone cannot build a Sunday school. God will not do what he has commanded us

to do. We are to go and reach people. Classes grow when teachers are busy visiting, phoning, mailing, and praying all week.

19. Feed them the Word. People go to restaurants where they get good food, then they tell their friends. Books are sold by word-of-mouth advertisement. The satisfied customer is still the best salesman for any product. The basis for growing Sunday school classes is still good Bible teaching that causes students to bring their friends. The Bible must be made interesting, captivating, and relevant.

20. Try super saturation. The disciples went everywhere preaching the Word, reaching men by all means. A Sunday school teacher should use every technique to excite pupils about coming to Sunday school. Extra promotion, contests, and taking pupils to a ball game show that a teacher cares. Extra preparation, visitation, and prayer will get results. The work of God is still spelled W-O-R-K. Any class will grow in direct proportion to the energy expended by the teacher.

DYAD

This method of teaching is also called Neighbor Nudge. It is done by dividing the class into pairs and assigning them a topic for discussion. Start at the left side of each row, and have the students number off for discussion. If the room is crowded, have the partners turn their chairs toward each other. This will help to minimize the sound of the discussions. Set aside approximately three minutes for the activity. Have each individual share with his partner one particular practical application of material just presented to the group. Remind students that every person should contribute to the discussion.

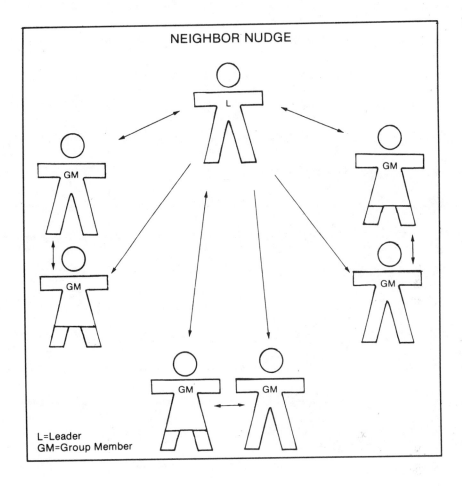

E-0 EVANGELISM

E-0 evangelism is evangelism of unsaved members within the church congregation. These unsaved are children born to Christians who are not saved, or they are members who profess salvation but are not saved. This evangelism overcomes the spiritual barriers that cannot be removed without compromising the gospel. Some will never be saved because the message of the cross, which is an intricate part of the gospel, is offensive to them. Grace is also a barrier to some, for they want to do good works to be saved and resist being saved by grace alone (Eph. 2:8-9).

E-1 EVANGELISM

E-1 evangelism is evangelism that crosses the perceived barriers related to the church or church building in the minds of the unsaved. It seeks to overcome what has been called "the stained-glass barrier." *Stained glass* reflects more than windows or church sanctuaries. It is symbolic of all that stands between those standing outside of the church and the church bringing them inside to hear the gospel. These barriers make it difficult for a person to attend a Sunday school or church service or continue to attend. The stained-glass barrier includes such things as poor location, inadequate parking, and unkept or poorly maintained facilities, but there are others.

When the parking lot is full, it is a barrier for the visitor to find a parking place in the street. Some think that adequate parking or eliminating other barriers will cause church growth. Not so! There must be a dynamic that draws people to Jesus Christ. The church must have warm services, and the pastor must preach with power. A barrier just makes it harder to reach people; it does not make it impossible to reach people. Eliminating barriers makes it easier to reach people.

Stained-glass barriers also include perceptions, such as a lost person's dislike for a denomination's name, or what an unchurched person remembers about a particular church. Some have had a bad experience with a church member from a certain denomination, hence the church name is a barrier. A church split becomes a barrier to the neighborhood, making it harder for both halves to reach people for Christ.

E-2 EVANGELISM

E-2 evangelism crosses cultural and class barriers. Such barriers hinder the evangelistic outreach of some churches. E-2 evangelism recognizes members of certain cultures who may not wish to attend a church made up predominantly of members of another culture. It is not a matter of liking the people of another culture or class; it is a question of being comfortable with their different values. While the church must be the church of the open door, willing to admit members of any culture, such people will have difficulty becoming assimilated into the social life of the congregation.

Class barriers present the same problems as cultural barriers. The difference among classes is not primarily how much or little money people have but rather the values they hold. Music, for example, expresses the heart in the worship of God. Just as music unites, it can also divide. Music often expresses the values of different classes of people. Members of lower classes do not usually like the "long-hair" music of the classics, and upper classes often fail to appreciate the twang of the country and western sound, even when the words are biblical. Never make the mistake of concluding that the music enjoyed by one class is superior or inferior to music enjoyed by another class. Music affirms the soul and is one way people magnify God in worship. Since "the Father is seeking such to worship Him" (John 4:23), who of us can say that God doesn't enjoy the Nashville-type gospel music of an unsophisticated church just as much as he enjoys a Bach chorale from a church with a full pipe organ, if the music comes from the heart of the worshiper?

E-3 EVANGELISM
E-3 evangelism attempts to cross linguistic barriers, which are perhaps the most obvious barriers to evangelism. People like to hear God in their heart language (the language in which they think) even when they themselves speak a second language.

ELECTION CAMPAIGN
A strategic time for an election campaign contest, to encourage Sunday school growth and attendance, is during a political campaign period, when attention is focused on campaigning. The ground rules are based on election procedures:
1. Smaller departments or classes are divided into two "parties," such as the Amen and Hallelujah parties, and larger departments into four groups, each with a name.
2. Each party selects a candidate to be elected as class president.
3. Each party selects a secretary to keep records.
4. Points are earned for the candidate as follows: each person present, 100; each visitor, 150; and each absentee, -100.

Party members get full credit for bringing visitors to any department of the Sunday school; however, new members get full credit only for joining the sponsoring class.

ENCOURAGERS (See also F.R.A.N.GELISM)
Encouragers are those on the evangelism team with the spiritual gift of showing mercy (Rom. 12:8). They use their gift to encourage people. On visitation night, they are given a list of absentees who may need encouragement. Also, they are given the names of those who are sick or shut-in or who have a special need. The encouragers are not expected to make soul-winning calls, though at times they may be directly responsible for leading people to Christ. As they encourage some and help others, they build the body. They

allow the evangelist to give priority time to prospects. This allows both to be successful.

ENLISTING WORKERS

How can a church enlist teachers for the Sunday school? Whose task is it to do the enlisting? From what sources may workers be recruited? Answers include the following:

Sources of Prospective Workers

1. Churchwide survey. Discover talents and interests of members. Include questions such as: Have you ever taught Sunday school? If so, what age group? What age group do you prefer to work with? What is your favorite form of recreation: Reading? Music? Sports? Art? Other? Do you play and instrument? Which? File a card for each potential worker.
2. Visit. Call on the persons who show teaching potential. Talk with them and note on their cards any teaching experience, special aptitudes in a craft or profession, or college training in the teaching field.
3. Observe. Note the faithful attenders in youth and adult classes. Talk with their teachers about their participation and ministry potential.
4. Vacation Bible School. The list of vacation Bible school workers will turn up names of some who serve regularly as assistants in a department. Their interest and abilities may be further explored.
5. The invitation. Those who respond to an invitation for dedication of life for whatever service the Lord opens.
6. Spiritual Gift Inventory. A tool such as a spiritual gift inventory test may help individuals discover spiritual gifts that may indicate ministry potential in some particular area.

Who Does the Enlisting?

1. A nominating committee. Many churches have a nominating committee elected or appointed annually. It is the task of this committee to secure workers for every office and teachers for every department. (Those who have served on the committee often are glad to be released from duty as the year

expires, because of the difficulty in getting the consent of persons capable of doing a specific task.)

2. The director of Christian education. If there is no such director, the superintendent of the Sunday school usually is responsible for enlisting workers. During visitation he always should be aware of potential colaborers in the educational work of the church.

3. The pastor. Since he contacts all the membership of the church through home and hospital visits, he is in the best position to know the person behind the face. In the home, he can see the character and personality of the men and women on the roll. He can observe in the lives of the children the type of home training given. Conversation will show him the interests and activities of the people. He can make the initial contact for the nominating committee, or he can refer names to them.

How Can Workers Be Enlisted?

1. A visit. This is perhaps the best way to discuss such an important and often life-changing decision. A casual church hallway chat does not allow for real thought about the seriousness of the request. Time spent in a personal visit emphasizes its importance to the potential teacher.

2. A letter. Because a letter may be read and reread, studied and prayed over at leisure, the request for service may be stated on paper. The need often is presented more clearly in writing, and the force of the visitor's personality does not stand between the visitor and the prospect. The force of the request itself makes the impression.

3. A telephone call. Again, face-to-face reaction does not distract, and a heart-to-heart call may accomplish what a visit could not. Unable to see the quick negative response often registered at first, a timid superintendent or committee member continues to talk on the telephone without having his enthusiasm dampened. And the prospective teacher cannot see the worried frown of concern on the face of the caller as excuses are given.

4. A pulpit plea. Occasionally a pastor feels God would have

CHRISTIAN SERVICE SURVEY

Name _____

Date _____

Residence _____

(Street - RFD)   (City)   (State or Prov.) (Zip Code)

Occupation _____   Telephone _____

Business Telephone _____

Business Address _____

(Street - RFD)   (City)   (State or Prov.) (Zip Code)

Age Group Youth ☐ Young Adult ☐ Middle Adult ☐ Older Adult ☐
12-24   25-35   35-60   60 plus

Special Training _____

Key to Categories: Past (I have served), Present (I am serving), Future (I am willing to serve).

Boards – Committees – Officers	Past	Present	Future
Board of Deacons & Deaconesses	☐	☐	☐
Board of Trustees	☐	☐	☐
Board of Christian Education	☐	☐	☐
Church Moderator	☐	☐	☐
Church Clerk	☐	☐	☐
Church Treasurer	☐	☐	☐
Financial Secretary	☐	☐	☐
Sunday School Superintendent	☐	☐	☐
Sunday School Secretary	☐	☐	☐
Children's Church Director	☐	☐	☐
Training Hour Director	☐	☐	☐
Finance Committee	☐	☐	☐
Music Committee	☐	☐	☐
Visitation Committee	☐	☐	☐
Transportation Committee	☐	☐	☐
Missionary Committee	☐	☐	☐
Ushering Committee	☐	☐	☐
Publicity Committee	☐	☐	☐
Flower Committee	☐	☐	☐
Kitchen Committee	☐	☐	☐
Recreation Committee	☐	☐	☐
Auditing Committee	☐	☐	☐

Services	Past	Present	Future
Prayer Partner	☐	☐	☐
Organist	☐	☐	☐
Pianist	☐	☐	☐
Choir Director	☐	☐	☐
Song Leader	☐	☐	☐
Instrumental Player	☐	☐	☐
Choir Member	☐	☐	☐
Library Worker	☐	☐	☐
Audio Visual Worker	☐	☐	☐
General Office Worker	☐	☐	☐
Typist	☐	☐	☐
Mimeographer	☐	☐	☐
Telephone Caller	☐	☐	☐
Poster Work	☐	☐	☐
Nurse	☐	☐	☐
Recreational Worker	☐	☐	☐
Pageants - Dramatics Worker	☐	☐	☐
Crafts Worker	☐	☐	☐
Painter	☐	☐	☐
Manual Worker	☐	☐	☐
Electrical Worker	☐	☐	☐
Seamstress	☐	☐	☐
Others	☐	☐	☐

(continued on next page)

Children's Work	Past	Present	Future	Youth Work	Past	Present	Future	Adult Work	Past	Present	Future
Sunday School:				Sunday School:				Sunday School:			
Department Supt. --	☐	☐	☐	Department Supt. --	☐	☐	☐	Department Supt. --	☐	☐	☐
Department Sec. --	☐	☐	☐	Department Sec. --	☐	☐	☐	Department Sec. --	☐	☐	☐
Department Pianist	☐	☐	☐	Department Pianist	☐	☐	☐	Department Pianist	☐	☐	☐
Teacher ----	☐	☐	☐	Teacher ----	☐	☐	☐	Teacher ----	☐	☐	☐
Children's Church:				Training Hour:				Cradle Roll Visitor --	☐	☐	☐
Leader ----	☐	☐	☐	Sponsor ----	☐	☐	☐	Home Dept. Visitor --	☐	☐	☐
Pianist ----	☐	☐	☐	Pianist ----	☐	☐	☐	Training Union:			
Training Hour:				Officer ----	☐	☐	☐	Adult Group Leader	☐	☐	☐
Leader ----	☐	☐	☐	Weekday Club:				Leadership Education			
Worker ----	☐	☐	☐	Steering Committee	☐	☐	☐	Instructor ----	☐	☐	☐
Pianist ----	☐	☐	☐	Boys ----	☐	☐	☐	Group Bible Study			
Sponsors ----	☐	☐	☐	Girls ----	☐	☐	☐	Leader ----	☐	☐	☐
Weekday Club:				Club Leader				Women's Society			
Leader ----	☐	☐	☐	Boys ----	☐	☐	☐	Officer ----	☐	☐	☐
Worker ----	☐	☐	☐	Girls ----	☐	☐	☐	Group Chairman	☐	☐	☐
Vacation Bible School:				Club Helper				Men's Fellowship			
Dept. Supt. ----	☐	☐	☐	Boys ----	☐	☐	☐	Officer ----	☐	☐	☐
Dept. Sec. ----	☐	☐	☐	Girls ----	☐	☐	☐	Family Life Committee	☐	☐	☐
Dept. Pianist ----	☐	☐	☐	Vacation Bible School:				Senior Citizens:			
Teacher ----	☐	☐	☐	Dept. Supt. ----	☐	☐	☐	Leader ----	☐	☐	☐
				Dept. Sec. ----	☐	☐	☐	Worker ----	☐	☐	☐
				Pianist ----	☐	☐	☐				
				Teacher ----	☐	☐	☐				
				Youth Counsellor ----		☐					

I am especially in-
terested in the
Cradle Roll, 0-2 yrs.
Nursery, 2-3 years
Kindergarten, 4-5
Primary, grs. 1-3
Junior, grs. 4-6

I am especially interest-
ed in:
Jr. Hi's, grs. 7-9 --
Sr. Hi's, grs. 10-12
Post High School

Signature

I believe that every church member should share in the church life and work. I intend to serve as I am able when the opportunity is presented to me.

3M–2-67   Printed in U.S.A. by North American Baptists, 7308 Madison Street, Forest Park, Illinois 60130.

him give an altar call for a task for which volunteers are needed, leaving it to the Lord, so to speak, to bring forth his chosen workers. A decision made publicly usually proves valid.

5. Gift counseling. People are most eager to serve God when they can use their spiritual gifts in effective ministry. The best time to enlist a new worker may be during a gift counseling session as you discuss where a person with his or her particular gift mix could best serve in the church.

How to Recruit Sunday School Workers

1. Know exactly what you need and want. When looking for workers, don't just ask for warm bodies or volunteers. First, know how many teachers, secretaries, or other workers are needed. Then, you must know what jobs there are to fill. This involves knowing how many children, youth, or adult classes need a worker. This also includes knowing exactly how many administrative responsibilities are needed. Also, if growth is planned, you should know how many workers are needed for the expansion planned.

2. You must get prayer support. First pray that God will provide the exact number of workers you need. But more than your own prayer, make requests in prayer meetings and in other places where spiritual people can make this a matter of intercession before God.

3. You must create a *great commission* attitude. The marching orders of the church are to "make disciples of all the nations" (Matt. 28:19). This involves using all Christians to take the gospel to all people because Christ died for all. Since we are told to reach every person, and since the time is short and our resources are limited, we must be more aggressive in reaching the lost; we must be superaggressive.

A *great commission* atmosphere is a serving atmosphere. This means that every person in the church must be willing to serve somewhere in the church. When this is accomplished, people will come to church with their cups just to have them filled. They will come to take the Water of Life to other people. Church is a place of service, and every Christian should be involved in service.

We need to create two atmospheres: first, it is usual when every Christian is involved in service, and second, the church is unusual when people are not serving Christ.

4. You must know what you want workers to do. Before your recruit a teacher, you must have a job description. This answers the question, "What do you want me to do?" A job description is the first tool to place in a person's hand when you ask him to consider a position.

One weakness that hinders quality teaching in Sunday school is traditionalism. We think everyone else knows what a teacher should do, and that is not the case. One of the reasons for inconsistency or lack of production is that teachers do not know what is expected of them. A job description gives them direction for more effective work.

5. You must know what they are to accomplish. This is called job objectives or job expectations. People should know more than what is their task; they should be goal-oriented. They should know what they are expected to accomplish. When you give a potential teacher a goal, he is much more likely to work with dedication, precision, and accuracy.

6. Transform a "slot" attitude into a "spiritual gift" attitude. Often when we begin recruiting people for tasks of the church, we are filling slots. Therefore, we begin with wrong attitudes toward recruitment. We end up trying to talk people into jobs, rather than trying to employ people to work according to their talents. Because a person's spiritual gift is simply his ability to perform tasks of the church, we should recognize what he is able to do and attempt to "use him where he is usable."

A wise pastor once talked about the "tyranny of slots." He described people who would come up to him before the church service asking him to make an announcement to recruit people to teach in vacation Bible school, work in a woman's missionary society, or take a position in children's church. Because the positions were empty and the programs needed people, pastors usually turned up the thermostat, putting heat on everyone to take a job.

The tyranny of slots ends up in the manipulation of believers. When a person takes a position for the wrong motives, many times ill-equipped people serve with a bad attitude because they have been manipulated to do what is against their nature and talents.

When you try to force round pegs into square holes, both are stripped of their usefulness. Be careful of the tyranny of slots because when good people are manipulated, they can be ruined for life and harm others in the process.

7. You should administer a spiritual gift test to everyone. Begin with the premise that every person in your church is gifted to minister for Jesus Christ (Eph. 4:12). Then administer the inventory to all members so you can put them to work where they are most gifted. Suggest to the pastor that he should teach or preach on spiritual gifts during the Sunday evening service or during the Wednesday night prayer meeting. In these series of messages, he should explain the different gifts, their functions, and the characteristics of those who have them. Then administer a spiritual gift test so that each person can find his or her spiritual gift. Obviously, not everyone in the church will be present to take the inventory; some are unwilling, some are fearful, and others just can't be reached. However, try to get everybody to take the inventory.

Next, initiate a program to give the spiritual gift test to all new incoming members. This could be done during the new member orientation. This is done with the conviction that everyone should know his gift and every person should have a ministry. As people come into church membership, make them aware of their spiritual gifts and of the ministry opportunities in the church that correlate with their spiritual gift. All new members coming into the church should not only sign up for membership but also commit themselves to a place of service.

8. Create a Spiritual Gift Inventory Bank. When you begin to recruit people to serve in the church, don't just call your friends or go to those who are already busy. Rather, create an information bank on every person in the church, listing each person's three major spiritual gifts. Then when you are looking for a Sunday school secretary, check the list of those with the gift of helps or the gift of serving. Or, when you need a departmental superintendent, look for those with the gift of administration.

9. Talk personally with them. Try to keep all recruitment away from pulpit announcements or want ads in the church bulletin. Go to people personally and challenge them with the responsibility of teaching so that they understand the greatness of the challenge. If you treat your request with importance and dignity, they will respond in like manner.

    Make an appointment. Let them know you have an important item to share with them. When you make an appointment to talk with them concerning an important item, you elevate the task. When you just catch them walking down a church hall, you make it seem casual and unimportant.

10. Let them know why you have chosen them for the position. They need to understand that this is not a frantic appeal for help, but a professional approach to ministry. Let them know you have evaluated their ability and prayed over this request.

11. Take a job description and a job objective with you. Go over the requirements of the position and your expectations. Leave it with them to study.

12. Ask for careful consideration. Do not press them for an immediate answer; rather, ask them to pray about the matter and give it serious consideration. The task of teaching Sunday school should be accompanied by a deep burden from God that teaching is his will. Such a response only comes from prayer.

13. Invite them to observe the task. Sometimes people are fearful of assuming responsibility for a job they do not understand. Certain people do not know what goes on in a

classroom, so they would immediately say no. However, they could receive a burden for the job by visiting a classroom, talking with other teachers and the superintendent, and seeing the room where they would teach. A visit to their place of service could be the determining factor that gives people a burden to teach a class.

14. Promise them training. If Sunday school teaching is an important task (and it is), then teachers must be trained for the responsibility (and they should be). Do not thrust a new teacher into a classroom without adequate preparation. It is not fair to the teacher or to the pupils. A church should provide teacher training for its prospective teachers. These classes can be conducted during Sunday school or another hour during the week. The training given to a new teacher and his qualifications will probably determine his success or failure.

15. Begin with an internship. Again, do not thrust a new teacher into a classroom without preparation. Perhaps the best preparation is an internship, whereby a prospective teacher serves with an experienced teacher. First, he can observe how an experienced teacher conducts a class. Second, he can take part in the teaching responsibilities, such as telling a story, presenting a flannelgraph lesson, or handling the questions and answers. A third responsibility might be to deal with some of the mechanics, such as taking roll or supervising presession activities. In this capacity the new teacher gets to know the pupils and the routine; also he becomes familiar with the physical aspects of the class.

16. Promise him support and help in solving problems. Every teacher will encounter difficulties from room problems to behavior problems. Let him know that you are there to help him solve problems and to make the teaching run smoothly. When he knows he is not in it alone but is a part of a team, he will more likely respond.

17. Promise in-service training. All teachers need to sharpen their skills on a constant basis. The church that is going to recruit is the church that will encourage its teachers to

keep up-to-date by attending conventions, attending seminars sponsored at the church, or even watching videos or films on improving teaching.

Right Motives in Recruitment

1. To use people's spiritual gifts. When people are gifted, they want to use their gift and get satisfaction from doing it. More than that, they grow closer to God when they let the Holy Spirit work through their spiritual gift. Tie spiritual gifts to recruitment.
2. To invest in others. By investing money we get dividends on returns. By investing in others in ministry, we get spiritual dividends that are much greater than this world has to offer.
3. To help those serving to fulfill their calling. Everyone has a calling to some form of Christian service. Find out those who are called to teach Sunday school.
4. To encourage spiritual growth. Teachers always learn and grow more than their students do.
5. To provide spiritual help to others. A person who teaches Sunday school helps others to grow in Christ or to come to salvation.
6. To glorify God. God is glorified by many means, both direct and indirect. When a person teaches Sunday school, he is obeying God, broadening his kingdom, and helping others to grow into the likeness of the Lord Jesus Christ. All of this is a way of glorifying God.

Wrong Motives in Recruitment

1. Recruitment based on guilt. Often leaders try to make people feel guilty for not serving in the church. Guilt is an accusatory sense of failure. Some try to show people that they are inadequate Christians if they don't volunteer for service. At other times, leaders might even go so far as to say, "If you don't volunteer, the people's blood will be on your hands."
2. To do someone a favor. Some leaders go through the congregation asking their buddies to teach a Sunday school class and "do me a favor."

3 "You owe me one." Sometimes leaders go to people and use the leverage of obligation. It might follow this approach: "I helped you on the bowling team; why can't you help me in Sunday school class?" Such leaders, by calling in the IOUs, use the wrong motives in recruiting workers.

4. To fulfill tradition. Some people use tradition as leverage, for example, by saying, "Your father was a good Sunday school teacher." Other times they create the attitude that it's expected of you because everyone is doing it.

5. "If you don't help me I'll scream." Some leaders go around in a panic mode, telling others that they are about to have a breakdown, about to give up, or about to scream. They put the strong arm on recruits based on their lack of emotional adjustment or other psychological needs.

ENROLLMENT

The contemporary Sunday school has lost a powerful means of growth. About twenty years ago, Sunday schools stopped emphasizing enrollment, and teachers stopped promoting the enrollment of new students for Bible study. If the Sunday schools of the nineties would like to be strong and have a powerful outreach, they should return to an emphasis on enrollment as one powerful, yet forgotten, means to grow a Sunday school.

In the old days a teacher would say, "After you attend for three weeks, we will add your name to the roll." That was the teacher's way of challenging a student to be faithful so he would belong to the Sunday school class. Enrollment simply meant that a person was no longer a visitor, but he was a member of the in-group. The visitor now belonged with the other pupils and was one of the gang. Sunday school enrollment did not afford all the privileges of church membership but gave one a higher status than that of just a visitor or stranger. Sunday school enrollment meant "sub-membership" to the local church.

Many times businessmen want to identify with a local church, but because of their life-style or unscriptural beliefs, they cannot be accepted into the membership of the church. So they join the men's Bible class, which means that their name is added to the roll. As a result, they can make business contacts and move into the stability of the neighborhood. They have the privilege of church membership without meeting all the requirements. While we do not condone all that this implies, we recognize the desire people have to associate with the positive benefits of the local church.

Sunday school enrollment is the "handshake" that welcomes the outsider into the fellowship of the class and makes that person feel like an insider. When people are enrolled in Sunday school, they no longer have a barrier to attending church services or to hearing the gospel. They network with other believers in a Bible study fellowship where they can learn from the Word of God.

A recent survey indicated that baby boomers do not like the term *church membership.* They identify hypocrisy with the phrase because of all they have heard and seen in people who claim to be church members, but whose lives deny being truly Christian. Surveys tell us that baby boomers are coming back to the church; yet they find the term *church membership* a stumbling block. They have said they would like to be a part of the family of believers, or they would like to be in a church fellowship; they just do not want to be identified with membership or joining a church. Could Sunday school enrollment be the open arms to reach the baby boomers for Christ? They are coming back to Sunday school because they want teaching and because they want to instill in their children the values of Sunday school. Therefore, enroll them in Sunday school to help them identify with a local body of believers where they can learn about church requirements and benefits of being a member of God's family.

Another phrase that is now being used with reaching baby boomers for Christ is the "seeker service." This is a church service designed for the comfort of an unsaved person who is honestly seeking knowledge and experience about God. The seeker service helps them come to Christ without crossing too many cultural, man-made barriers. One pastor said, "I don't ask unsaved people to pray the Lord's prayer because they can't pray, 'Our Father.'" The pastor went on to say, "I'm not an expositional preacher because the unsaved will not listen to Bible lectures." A seeker service has contemporary Christian music and drama and is issue-oriented to meet the needs of modern people. The desire to reach the baby boomer through the seeker service could be met by enrolling them in Sunday school. The baby boomer will make friends with those in his class, providing them with a friendly environment where they can seek God.

Southern Baptists have long known the strength of enrolling people in Sunday school. Their formula indicates that 40 percent of Sunday school enrollment will be present in Sunday school attendance. As a result, they go out and ask people to enroll in the Sunday school. Many times they ask a friend, "Can I enroll you in my Sunday school?"

Neil Jackson, a consultant with the Southern Baptist Sunday School Board, was eating in a Nashville restaurant. The waitress was obviously pregnant, almost ready to deliver. When the friendly waitress brought the food, Neil Jackson asked, "Can I enroll your baby in Sunday school?"

"What do you mean?" she questioned.

"The baby you are going to have ought to go to Sunday school where he can learn about God, learn to pray, and get a purpose in life." Then Neil Jackson said to her, "God loves your baby."

When the waitress came back with the check she said, "Enroll my baby in your Sunday school. I am interested in anyone who is interested in my baby."

The waitress did not live near Three Rivers Baptist Church in Nashville where Neil attended. She lived on the other side of town. Jackson phoned a pastor friend who visited her that same afternoon and enrolled the baby, mother, and father in Sunday school. When the baby was born, she was brought up in the house of God.

Action Enrollment is a relatively recent Southern Baptist program designed to provide growth in Sunday school attendance through increased Sunday school enrollment. Andy Anderson, while pastor of the Riverside Baptist Church of Fort Myers, Florida, came to the realization that even given his best efforts or the efforts of others, his church would always average about 40 percent of its Sunday school enrollment. He devised a simple formula to depict the relationship between attendance and enrollment: E = P + A (Enrollment = Present + Absent).

Briefly summarizing, the number of people present and the number absent will remain relatively constant in a ration of 40 percent (attending) to 60 percent (absent). As enrollment rises, so does the number of those attending the class.

Southern Baptists are taking the positive approach and moving with renewed zeal toward building Sunday school via the "action" method. This approach has demonstrated that of all persons enrolled by door-to-door canvasing, approximately 20 percent will never attend, 40 percent will come at least once but will not become active, and the remaining 40 percent will become active attenders.

How to Get New People to Enroll

The teacher must take the initiative to get new people to enroll in the Sunday school. However, this task can be delegated to an outreach class officer. The following are some ideas to get people to enroll in Bible study.

1. Join One, Join All. Initiate a campaign in your church so that when someone joins the church, they also join a Sunday school class. Assign someone in the class to enroll new members in the Sunday school class.
2. Go through the list of those who came to vacation Bible school. They are excellent prospects to enroll in Sunday school.
3. Ask the youth to do a block survey in the neighborhood to determine those who are not church members or enrolled in Sunday school.
4. Request church members to identify neighbors who are unchurched.
5. Find unchurched parents who send their children to the church's day-care center.
6. Go through the visitor cards that have been turned in to the church in the last six months.
7. Survey local newspapers for information on newlyweds.
8. Glean local newspapers for information on newborn babies.
9. Check the guest book in the church lobby to identify any

visitors who have attended weddings, funerals, and other meetings at the church.

10. Survey your church members to find the names of their friends who are prospects for Sunday school enrollment.
11. Subscribe to newcomer services for information on prospects such as hookups for gas, water, and electricity.
12. Do a survey in the church foyer after a worship service. Ask each attender to give you the names of those who would be good prospects for the Sunday school.
13. Ask the pastor to add the statement, "Enroll me," when making church announcements. The pastor can ask all those signing a visitor card on Sunday morning to add the phrase "Enroll me" if they are interested in joining an adult Bible study. This small invitation seems so trivial, yet prospects can be enrolled in Sunday school by showing an interest in them.

How to Get Enrollees to Attend Sunday School

Attach to each chair a card with the name of a person on your roll. Then, contact every class member and let them know their name will be attached to a chair for "be there Sunday."

Another way is to write the names of all class members on a card large enough for everyone to read. Post the names on the wall, and ask class members to call on absent members with the view of getting them in the Sunday school.

The Sunday school teacher can become the "Saturday night caller." In less than an hour, a Sunday school teacher can phone everyone on his Sunday school roll, reminding them of Sunday school. The Saturday night caller can ask his class members, "I am trying to determine how many will be present Sunday. Will you be there?" If they are going out of town, do not put them on a guilt trip. Everyone needs time away for a vacation. Then say, "I will see you in Sunday school when you get back in town." People want to know that you care about them, and your phone call tells them that. People do not care how much you know until they know how much you care.

Use the big three: phone, mail, and visit. Go through the names of your Sunday school roll and contact everyone of them three times.

Plan a "double your enrollment month." During a certain month get everyone in your class to: (1) pray every day for every person on the roll, (2) take time out of class to have five pupils write a postcard or a personal note to nonattenders, (3) have everyone phone someone on the roll, and (4) have everyone drop by and see someone on the roll. While this is a gigantic task, it will pay gigantic results.

ENTZMINGER, LOUIS (1876–1958)

A converted lumberjack who served successfully as educational director of First Baptist Church, New Orleans, Louisiana. In 1913 J. Frank Norris persuaded him to become superintendent of the First Baptist Church, Fort Worth, Texas, with a membership of 1,200. By 1928 the church had grown to 12,000 members and claimed to have the world's largest Sunday school with an attendance of 5,200. His organized visitation programs, learned from his Southern Baptist roots, are credited for the growth, along with the dynamic preaching of Norris.

Entzminger organized and taught in the Fundamentalist Baptist Bible Institute in the church, later known as Bible Baptist Seminary. He is credited with originating the six-point round system for Sunday school. He had Sunday school clinics in many of the largest churches in America, motivating them to attendance growth.

EQUIPMENT STANDARDS

When one looks at Sunday school equipment and buildings, he or she sees every conceivable type of facility being used. Some Sunday schools have streamlined buildings of steel, brick, and glass constructed on a well-landscaped lot. These Sunday schools are as up-to-date as any public school. On the other end of the spectrum, some Sunday schools meet in dilapidated buildings constructed more than one hundred years ago. Children are packed into basements, hallways, and some classes even meet in Sunday school buses. Some Sunday schools have modern molded plastic chairs in bright colors. Others still use the slat-back folding chairs from which children's feet never touch the floor. Some Sunday school rooms have wall-to-wall carpet and indirect lighting. Others have concrete floors, and naked light bulbs hang from the ceilings.

Obviously, the Spirit of God can illuminate the student's heart through the Word of God in any situation. Mark Hopkins said, "Education is a teacher on a log facing the pupil on the other end of the log." He was emphasizing the educational relationship between teacher and pupil. But notice there was a log. So there must be a classroom in which learning takes place.

Four principles should be remembered. The first is that Sunday schools can be effective with any building and equipment. Jesus taught in a boat, on the mountaintop, and on the highway. The second principle is that modern facilities and equipment will not guarantee good education. Many Sunday schools prospered in old facilities yet began to decay when they moved into new buildings. However, it was not the buildings that caused the decay. Beware of claiming, like medieval monks, that comfortable surroundings destroy one's godliness. The third principle is that good facilities will enhance teaching. As a matter of fact, good facilities will become an assistant teacher. The final principle is we should be thankful for the facilities we have, whether they resemble the little red schoolhouse out on the prairie or the basement of an inner-city church.

But at the same time, every Sunday school should attempt to upgrade its buildings. We should constantly paint, put down carpeting, or decorate walls to make teaching more effective. Our children live in air-conditioned homes and attend modern public schools with all of their conveniences. The Sunday school should not lag behind. An old building says to the child, "God is out-of-date." A new building will tell the pupil, "Come in and learn."

Buildings and equipment are more than teachers—they advertise our purpose to the world. Outsiders form opinions of the quality of our Sunday schools by the appearance of our buildings.

We never get a second opportunity to make a good first impression. Therefore, we need the finest possible buildings, equipped with the best possible furniture, to give an opportunity for the best possible teaching. Our aim is to produce the greatest change in the pupils' lives, conformity to the image of Christ.

GENERAL EQUIPMENT STANDARDS *

Department	Chair Height	Chair Rail—floor to top of rail	Table Size*	Storage	Chalkboards in Assembly Rooms	Chalkboards in Classrooms—Height above floor	Tackboards—Height above floor	Piano	Picture Molding (concealed) Height above floor	Picture Rail—Height above floor	Coat Racks—Refer to specific department section
Nursery	10"	—	24"x36"	Cabinets above heads of children	No	—	—	—	—	—	Movable
Beginner	10"–12"	20"	24"x36" and 30"x48"	Cabinets above heads of children	No	—	1'8" to 2'0"	Studio	—	2'0" to 2'3"	Movable
Primary	12"–14"	24"	38"x48" or 36"x54"	Cabinets above heads of children	Portable	—	2'4"	Studio	7'0"	2'4" to 2'8"	Movable
Junior	15"–17"	28"	Trapezoid	Closets or cabinets	Portable	2'8"	2'8"	Studio	7'0"	2'8"	In assembly
Junior High	16"–18"	32"		Closets or cabinets		3'0" to 3'2"	3'0"	Studio	7'0"	No	In assembly
Senior High	18"	32"		Closets	Portable	3'4"	3'4"	Regular	7'0"	No	In classroom
Adult	18"	32"		Closets	Portable	3'6"	3'4"	Regular	7'0"	No	In classroom

*Height of tables should be ten inches above chair height
Coat racks for workers should be at same height as for Adults

Nursery Department Standards

	Babies	Toddlers	Two-Year-Olds	Three-Year-Olds
Baby's Schedule (card)	x			
Babee-Tenda Safety Chair	x	x	*	*
Ball (7" or 9" diameter)	x	x	*	*
Beds (hospital cribs, 27"x42")	x			
Bible (No. 1450 BP)	x	x	x	x
Blockbusters (set of 12)		x	x	*
Blocks			*	x
Blocks (large, wooden, hollow)			*	*
Block accessories			x	x
Books (as recommended)	x	x	x	x
Bookrack (28" long and 27" high)		x	x	x
Cabinet for supplies (on wall, 50" from floor)	x	x	x	x
Chairs (seat 10" from floor)			x	x
Changing diapers, provision for	in bed	x		
Diaper-bag holders (pigeonholes on wall)	x	x		
Dishes (soft plastic)		*	x	x
Doll (rubber, molded head)	x	x	x	x
Doll bed (16" x 28", 16" high)		x	x	x
Easel (for painting)			*	x
Finger paints			*	x
First-aid kit	*	x	x	x
Modeling dough (water clay or homemade dough)			x	x
Nature materials	x	x	x	x
Newsprint paper			*	x
Open shelves (2 sets, 12" deep, 30" long, 26" high; movable, closed back)		x	x	x
Paints and brushes			*	x
Pictures (selected and mounted)	x	x	x	x
Playpen	x	*		
Pull toys		x		
Puzzle rack			x	x
Puzzles (wooden)			x	x
Record albums (Broadman)	x	x	x	x
Record player	x	x	x	x
Resting cots or mats (for extended session)		x		
Rocker (adult)	x			
Rocker (child)		x	x	x
Rocking boat and steps combination		x		
Smocks or uniforms for workers (pastels)	x	*		
Sterilizing solution (Zephiran chloride concentrate, or others)	x	x		
Stove (24" high)			x	x
Sink-refrigerator combination (28"x30", 40" high)	Convenient to all Nursery rooms			
Swing (Cosco)	x			
Table (utility, Cosco)	x			
Table (24"x36", 20" high; usually two)			x	x
Thermometer (room)	x	x	x	x
Toilet (flush bowl or other)	x			
Toilet (juvenile fixtures)		x	x	x
Transportation toys (interlocking trains, boats, cars, trucks)		x	x	x
Wastepaper basket (plastic)	x	x	x	x

*OPTIONAL

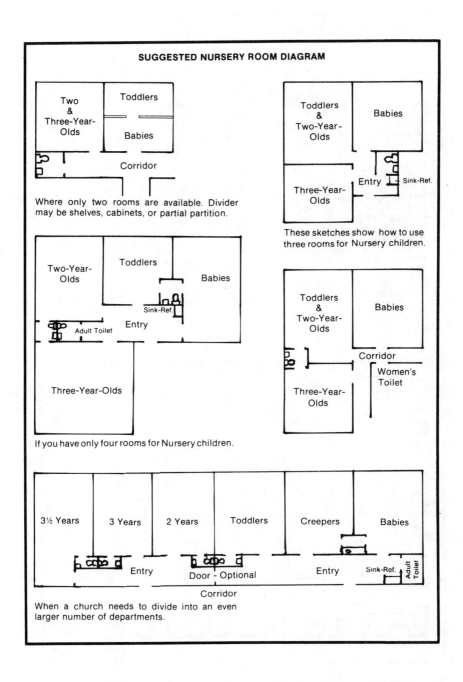

SUGGESTED NURSERY ROOM DIAGRAM

Where only two rooms are available. Divider may be shelves, cabinets, or partial partition.

These sketches show how to use three rooms for Nursery children.

If you have only four rooms for Nursery children.

When a church needs to divide into an even larger number of departments.

SUGGESTED BEGINNER ROOM DIAGRAM

This room is designed to accommodate 25 children and 5 workers. It will accommodate 20 children for weekday kindergarten.

1. Overhead Storage Cabinet
2. Table for Reports
3. Rack For Children's Wraps
4. Table For Puzzles
5. Table For Art Activities
6. Art Shelves
7. Puzzle Rack on Shelf
8. Table For The "Home"
9. Stove
10. Cabinet-Sink
11. Chest of Drawers
12. Doll Bed

13. Rocking Chair
14. Nature Shelves
15. Bookrack
16. Piano
17. Picture Rail
18. Table-Cabinet and Record Player
19. Block Shelves
20. Tackboard
21. Painting Easel
22. Drying Rack
23. Rack for Adult Wraps
24. Bathroom (connecting another room)

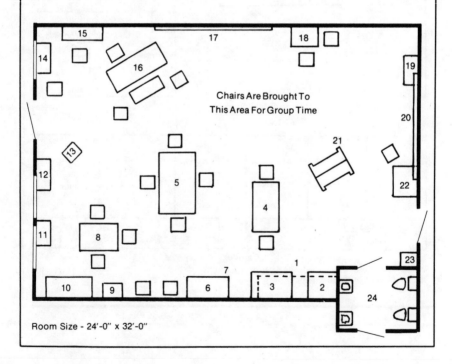

Chairs Are Brought To
This Area For Group Time

Room Size - 24'-0" x 32'-0"

Beginner Department Standards

Ample floor space for beginner children is needed. From 16 to 25 square feet or more is suggested for each child. It is desirable to provide 25 square feet or more per child.

Rooms to accommodate an attendance of up to twenty-five children in each department are suggested. More than twenty-five children enrolled would indicate the need for two or more beginner rooms. A rest room should be accessible, preferably adjoining the room. If there are as many as two beginner departments, they may be connected by a rest room.

Try to have:

1. Department room off main corridor; entrance at rear of room
2. Room located above ground
3. Movable racks for hanging children's and workers' wraps
4. Ample low windows (22 to 24 inches from floor)
5. Floor covering—asphalt tile, rubber tile, or vinyl tile
6. Soundproof, plastered, soft colored walls; acoustical ceiling
7. Picture rail, tackboard(s)
8. Suitable furniture for workers and children
9. Cabinets for storage of:
   Children's books
   Department Bible
   Dolls
   Nature materials, such as birds' nests, cotton bolls, seeds, flower containers
   Puzzles
   Scissors, crayons, paste, paint, paint brushes, modeling clay
   Smocks for painting
   Drawing paper, construction paper, newsprint paper
   Block accessories
   Record materials
   Record player, recordings
   Musical instruments
   Printed curriculum materials for Sunday school
   Beginner music activity, band, kindergarten, etc.

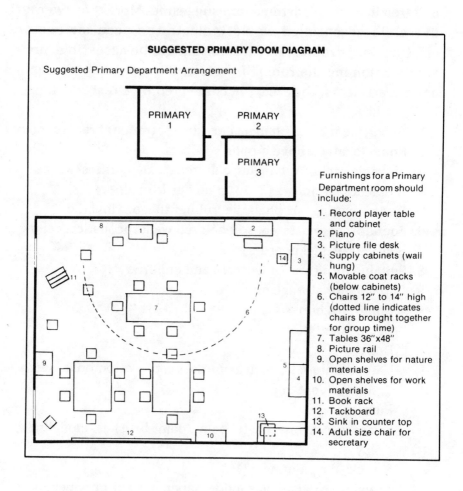

SUGGESTED PRIMARY ROOM DIAGRAM

Suggested Primary Department Arrangement

PRIMARY 1

PRIMARY 2

PRIMARY 3

Furnishings for a Primary Department room should include:

1. Record player table and cabinet
2. Piano
3. Picture file desk
4. Supply cabinets (wall hung)
5. Movable coat racks (below cabinets)
6. Chairs 12" to 14" high (dotted line indicates chairs brought together for group time)
7. Tables 36"x48"
8. Picture rail
9. Open shelves for nature materials
10. Open shelves for work materials
11. Book rack
12. Tackboard
13. Sink in counter top
14. Adult size chair for secretary

Primary Department Standards

A good environment for learning is vital to the success of a Primary department. Good work can be done in a room that is less than ideal, but a church should strive for the best in space and equipment for its children. A Primary room should be equipped by the church for all the organizations—Sunday school, band and choir.

The following are some recommendations for a good Primary room:

1. Located above ground
2. Planned for thirty to forty children to be enrolled in the department
3. An open room providing 25 square feet or more per person; 16 to 20 square feet is recommended minimum
4. Ample low windows with clear glass and good screens
5. Asphalt tile, vinyl tile, or rubber tile floor covering
6. Walls that are soundproof, plastered, and painted a soft color
7. Acoustical tile or acoustical plaster ceiling
8. Tackboard (preferably cork) 24 to 30 inches wide, beginning 30 inches from the floor, and as long as space permits; on one or more sides of the room
9. A picture rail 30 inches from the floor, at least 12 feet long, at the front of the room
10. Ample cabinet space—at least three separate cabinets, preferably wall hung, 18 inches deep, with locks
11. Rest rooms nearby; a sink in room desirable (29 inches above floor)

Furnishings for a Primary Department room should include:

Department Bible

Piano

Record player and cabinet

Chairs 14 inches high (12 inches chairs for six-year-olds)

Tables 10 inches higher than chair seats (rectangular tables about 36 by 48 inches or 26 by 54 inches are a usable size)

Movable rack(s) for hats and wraps; rods approximately 3 feet 6 inches to 3 feet 10 inches above the floor

Picture file desk and chair for secretary

Book rack

Open shelves (two sets)

Shades and draperies (as needed)

Junior Department Standards

Each department should have a large assembly room. It is desirable to provide at least 18 square feet per person (14 square feet per person would be a minimum).

Most Junior Departments have an average attendance of forty to fifty. When attendance reaches fifty, consideration should be given to the creation of two departments. If multiple departments are necessary, they should be in the same area of the building.

Recommendations for Junior Department facilities:

1. Department room off main corridor; entrance at rear of room
2. Located above ground
3. Classrooms
4. Unbroken wall space at front of assembly room
5. Windows required
6. Floor covering—Asphalt tile, rubber tile, vinyl tile, or hardwood
7. Soundproof, soft colored walls; acoustical ceiling
8. Picture molding
9. Combination chalkboard and tackboard
10. Suitable furniture for workers and for boys and girls
11. Adequate storage space for materials used by all Junior organizations; if desired, this may be divided into separate compartments for each organization; may be close or wall-hung cabinet(s)
12. Robe storage within assembly area; or use portable robe racks placed in an area adjacent to department
13. Movable rack for wraps

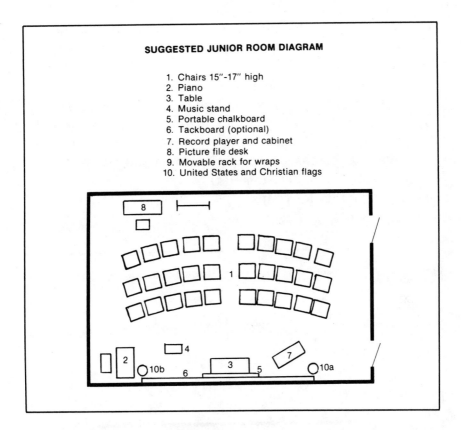

SUGGESTED JUNIOR ROOM DIAGRAM

1. Chairs 15"-17" high
2. Piano
3. Table
4. Music stand
5. Portable chalkboard
6. Tackboard (optional)
7. Record player and cabinet
8. Picture file desk
9. Movable rack for wraps
10. United States and Christian flags

Junior High Department Standards

This department also should have a large assembly room with at least 18 square feet per person (minimum 14 square feet per person).

No Junior High Department should have more than sixty-four in average attendance. At that point, consideration should be given to the creation of three departments, one for each age level. Multiple departments should be in the same area of the building. Movable doors between alternate classrooms provide for multiple use.

Recommendations for Junior High Department facilities:

1. Department room off main corridor; entrance at rear of room
2. Located above the ground
3. Assembly room as a classroom
4. Unbroken wall space at front of assembly room
5. Windows required

6. Asphalt tile, rubber tile, vinyl tile, or hardwood floor covering
7. Soundproof, soft colored walls; acoustical ceiling
8. Picture molding
9. Combination chalkboard and tackboard up front
10. Suitable furniture for workers and for boys and girls
11. Storage space, adequate for materials used by all junior high organizations; if desired, this may be divided into separate compartments for each organization; may be closet or wall-hung cabinet(s)
12. Movable rack for wraps

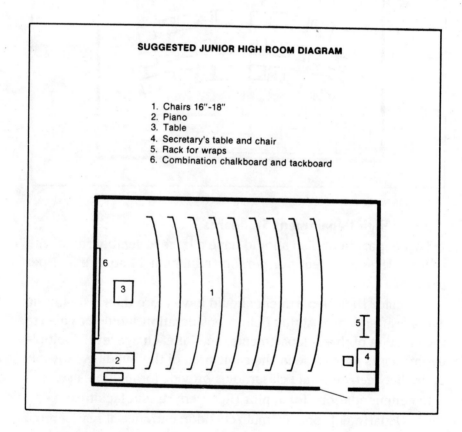

SUGGESTED JUNIOR HIGH ROOM DIAGRAM

1. Chairs 16"-18"
2. Piano
3. Table
4. Secretary's table and chair
5. Rack for wraps
6. Combination chalkboard and tackboard

Senior High Department Standards

An assembly room will be needed for each Senior High Department, with a minimum of 14 square feet of floor space per person.

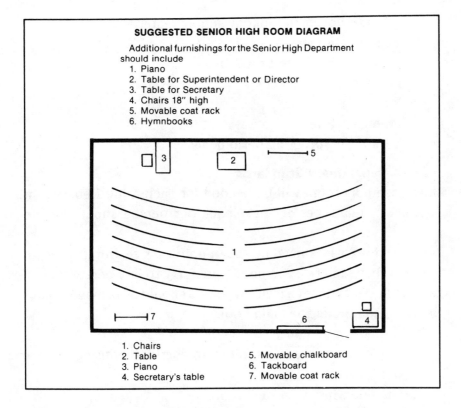

SUGGESTED SENIOR HIGH ROOM DIAGRAM

Additional furnishings for the Senior High Department
should include
1. Piano
2. Table for Superintendent or Director
3. Table for Secretary
4. Chairs 18″ high
5. Movable coat rack
6. Hymnbooks

1. Chairs
2. Table
3. Piano
4. Secretary's table
5. Movable chalkboard
6. Tackboard
7. Movable coat rack

Movable partitions between alternate classrooms will provide for multiple use.

Basic considerations and provisions:

1. Classroom off main corridor; entrance at rear of room
2. May be located on any floor
3. Ample wall space at front of room
4. Windows required
5. Asphalt tile, rubber tile, vinyl tile, or hardwood floor covering
6. Soundproof, plastered, light-colored walls; acoustical ceiling
7. Tackboard near exit door of assembly room; picture molding
8. Combination chalkboard and tackboard at front of classroom; movable chalkboard for extra groups
9. Suitable furniture

10. Storage closets for Sunday school materials:
    Record supplies
    Assembly program properties
    Erasers, chalk, pencils
    Posters
    Free literature
    Lesson and program periodicals

Adult Department Standards

An assembly room will be needed for each Adult Department. Again, 14 square feet of floor space per person should be provided.

Rooms for classes need not be of uniform size, but it is recommended that each one accommodate forty to fifty persons. Separate Adult Department assembly rooms should be provided. Adult Departments prefer the main floor.

Additional suggestions:

1. Department classroom off main corridor; entrance at rear of room
2. Outside window in each room
3. Ample wall space at front of assembly room
4. Asphalt tile, rubber tile, vinyl tile, or hardwood floor covering
5. Soundproof, light-colored walls; acoustical ceiling
6. Suitable furniture
7. Picture molding
8. Bulletin board near exit door of assembly room
9. Separate chalkboard and tackboard in the classroom
10. Storage closets for Sunday school materials:
    Record supplies
    Program properties
    Erasers, chalk, pencils
    Current posters, charts, other learning aids, curriculum supplements
    Promotional literature
    Lesson and program periodicals

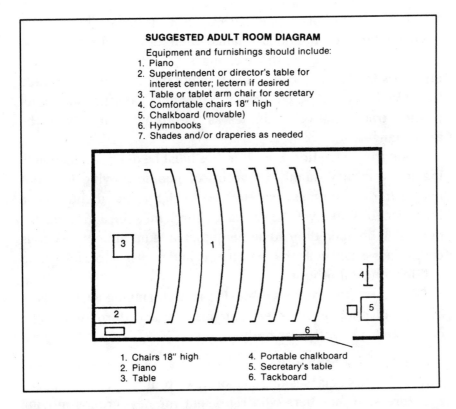

SUGGESTED ADULT ROOM DIAGRAM

Equipment and furnishings should include:
1. Piano
2. Superintendent or director's table for interest center; lectern if desired
3. Table or tablet arm chair for secretary
4. Comfortable chairs 18″ high
5. Chalkboard (movable)
6. Hymnbooks
7. Shades and/or draperies as needed

1. Chairs 18″ high   4. Portable chalkboard
2. Piano   5. Secretary's table
3. Table   6. Tackboard

EQUIPPERS (See also F.R.A.N.GELISM)

Equippers are those on the evangelism team with the spiritual gift of teaching or shepherding. On visitation night, they are given names of those who have joined the church or have made a recent public profession of salvation. The equippers meet with a new convert to disciple him in the faith. Equippers are not soul winners, though they may have some success in that area. They teach one-on-one, or two equippers meet with a couple. This discipling relationship exists for eight weeks, making sure the new convert is grounded in the faith and "bonded" to the church. After an equipper has finished the eight-week lesson, he is given another new convert to teach.

ETHNIKITIS (See also PATHOLOGY OF CHURCH GROWTH)

Ethnikitis is one of the pathologies of church growth and represents an inbred allegiance of the church to one ethnic group and a lack of adaptation or openness to other groups. This disease occurs when communities change their ethnic character and churches fail to adapt to those changes. Sometimes a symptom of ethnikitis is what has been called "white flight," where the traditional WASP (White Anglo-Saxon Protestant) churches move out of their traditional communities as the ethnic character of the area changes.

In our growing nation, our churches must be multiethnic, reaching to every new family or group of people moving into our neighborhood. In one sense, the small neighborhood church is a homogeneous unit, yet the growing church must be a heterogeneous unit (the open door to all people), made up of homogeneous cells (classes and cells that will attract and minister to each group within its neighborhood).

The church that suffers ethnikitis is first, sinning against God, second, disobeying the great commission, and third, allowing a cancer to fester within its body.

How to Solve Ethnikitis
1. Begin Bible classes or cells for new groups.
2. Hire staff members who represent the new groups moving into the neighborhood.
3. Begin a second-language preaching service.
4. If the church moves to another neighborhood, dedicate the building to spawn a continuing church.
5. New groups do not automatically visit existing churches; they must be aggressively sought and brought into the church fellowship.

ETLING, HAROLD HARTZ (1905–1977)
Harold H. Etling was a Sunday school pioneer in the National Fellowship of Grace Brethren churches. He was born in Akron, Ohio, on February 14, 1905. He graduated cum laude with the second class of Grace Theological Seminary in Winona Lake, Indiana, in May 1939.

Prior to his pastorate he served five years as president of Summit County (Ohio) Christian Endeavor Union, and during these years also served as music director in the First Church of Christ, Akron, Ohio.

Mr. Etling served twenty years in three pastorates: two in the Evangelical United Brethren Church in Ohio, and one as pastor of First Brethren Church, Akron, Ohio. He was ordained to the ministry August 25, 1939, in the Fellowship of Brethren Churches.

In 1948 he was elected by the National Conference of the National Fellowship of Brethren Churches as a member of the FGBC Sunday School Board. In January 1954 he was chosen to become the first Sunday school board director. In September 1966, the National Sunday School Board and the Brethren Youth Council merged and became known as the Christian Education Department. Mr. Etling was director of this organization until 1972.

Mr. Etling served as moderator of the National Conference in 1959. He is the author of eight textbooks used in connection with the Christian Worker's Training Course of Brethren Sunday Schools. He also wrote for the quarterlies for the Adult Department of Brethren Sunday schools.

For a number of years, Mr. Etling lectured at Grace Theological Seminary in the field of Christian education. He also was a speaker and lecturer at numerous Sunday school conferences and conventions, national, state, area, and denominational.

In 1962, 1966, and 1967 he served as president of Indiana Sunday School Association. From 1962 to 1964 Dr. Etling was president of National Sunday School Association, and in October 1966 he was elected to the office of treasurer in NSSA.

An honorary doctorate degree was bestowed upon Mr. Etling in May 1962 by Grace Theological Seminary, recognizing his accomplishments in the field of Christian education.

Harold Etling also served in curriculum development and promotion for Gospel Light Publishers. He was the author of the following books: *Our Heritage, Brethren Beliefs and Practices,* and *Emmanuel, God with Us* (studies in Matthew). He and his wife, Ada, had two daughters and seven grandchildren. Harold H. Etling went home to be with the Lord January 3, 1977.

EVALUATING THE LESSON

How well did you do on the last lesson? Before you can prepare your next Sunday school lesson, find out your mistakes and strengths from last week. If you can overcome mistakes in your teaching, this is an indication of professional growth on your part.

The best time for evaluation is immediately after teaching. Usually a teacher attends church after the Sunday school class. Therefore, Sunday afternoon is the earliest time at which he can evaluate his past lesson. Start your evaluation by viewing your strengths. You need the encouragement. What did you do well? Make a list of your strong points, those things you think went well today. At what point were the students most interested in your lesson? If you find out why they were interested, you might find one of your strengths.

Next, let's look at your weaknesses. Every teacher has some weak points, so don't get an inferiority complex. Honestly now, at what point did your students "turn the lesson off"? At what point was there student unrest? Some of the weak factors you can change; others you can't. But one thing is for sure: you are responsible for the weaknesses.

After you've found your weaknesses and strengths, make a list of things you are going to do differently. If you feel that you don't have the teaching background to even recognize your weaknesses, call in a fellow teacher or the Sunday school superintendent. Have him sit in your class, and ask him to give you honest constructive criticism.

EVANGELISM, DEFINITION OF

Evangelism is communicating the gospel to people in an understandable way and motivating people to respond to Christ and become a member of his church. A survey of the literature written on evangelism suggests three common views of evangelism. These views have been classified as follows:

P-1 Presence Evangelism. In presence evangelism, the goal is perceived as getting next to people and helping them or doing good works to open the door of opportunity to present Christ to them.

P-2 Proclamation Evangelism. In proclamation evangelism, the goal is perceived as presenting the gospel, i.e., the death and resurrection of Christ, so that people can hear and respond.

P-3 Persuasion Evangelism. In persuasion evangelism, the goal is perceived as making disciples and incorporating them into the body of Christ, i.e., a local congregation of believers. The church must go beyond P-2 evangelism (just preaching the gospel). It must use every available means to reach every available person at every available time. It goes beyond the mind of the candidate; it also focuses on the will.

EVANGELISM, EXPLICIT TYPES OF

Crusade evangelism (see Crusade Evangelism)
Front-door evangelism
Friendship evangelism
Inviting evangelism
Life-style evangelism (see Life-Style Evangelism)
Oikos evangelism
Personal evangelism
Relationship evangelism (see Saturation Evangelism)
Superaggressive evangelism

EVANGELISM, GIFT OF

The person with the gift of evangelism has the ability to lead people beyond his own natural sphere of influence to a saving knowledge of Jesus Christ. In the exercise of this gift, the evangelist is the aggressive soul winner who seeks the lost. While everyone has the obligation to witness for Christ (Acts 1:8) and everyone should try to win people to Christ, those with the gift of evangelism are better able to get decisions for Christ.

The strengths of this gift include (1) a consuming passion for lost souls, (2) a clear understanding of the gospel and what it can do in one's life, and (3) a desire to improve his effectiveness through Scripture memory.

The common weaknesses of an evangelist include (1) a belief everybody should be an evangelist, (2) a tendency to go after decisions even when people are not ready to respond, and (3) a tendency to be confrontational in his evangelism.

Those with this gift may (1) fall into pride or (2) become numbers-oriented rather than people-oriented.

EVANGELISM IN THE SUNDAY SCHOOL CLASS

The goal of Sunday school is (1) to reach people, (2) to teach them the Word of God, (3) to win them to Jesus Christ, and (4) to lead them to spiritual maturity. When the initial focus of the Sunday school is on evangelism, the entire Sunday school is revitalized.

The gospel is the Good News of Jesus Christ. It is the (1) death, (2) burial, and (3) resurrection of Jesus Christ (1 Cor. 15:1-4). A person must believe the gospel to be saved. There is no other message by which people can be saved. Jesus said, "I am the way, the truth, and the life. No one comes to the Father except through Me" (John 14:6). Even though there is only one way to be saved, there are many plans that Sunday school teachers use to present the gospel to the pupil.

How to Present Salvation to Students

1. Public invitation to pupils to invite Christ into their hearts. At the end of the class period, have all the pupils bow their heads in prayer. As they are praying, rehearse with them the plan of salvation: that (1) God loves them, (2) Christ died for them, and (3) Jesus will save them from their sins. While their heads are bowed, challenge them to receive Jesus Christ into their hearts. Let them know that you are going to help them in the prayer of conversion. Then ask them to pray in their hearts as you lead them outwardly: "Dear Lord Jesus, I want you to come into my heart and be my Savior. I am a sinner and am sorry for my sins. I want to turn from my sins and turn to you. Cleanse me from my sins with your shed blood. Make me your child and help me to follow you. Amen."

   After the pupils have prayed this prayer, ask them to remain after class so you can counsel them on the first steps of growing in Jesus Christ. Some teachers may want the pupils to make a public profession immediately (Rom. 10:9). Some teachers may want the pupils to either raise a hand, stand, or make some visible sign to the class that they have just received the Lord Jesus Christ as their Savior.

2. Remain after class. As you come to the end of the lesson, invite students who want to be saved to remain after class and talk to you about the gospel. At this point instruct all the students to leave and not to remain in the room to visit with each other. In this way, those who remain make an intentional effort to be saved. Hence, the teacher is able to go through the plan of salvation and present the gospel to them.

3. Present the "Romans road of salvation." Man must follow God's road to heaven, just as the travelers followed the Roman roads during the time of Christ. The Romans road of salvation is often used to illustrate this fact. This term is also used because the verses used are chosen from one book in the Bible, Paul's Epistle to the Romans.

Step One: Know your need. "For all have sinned and fall short of the glory of God" (Rom. 3:23). It makes no difference how good we are. Even if we were almost perfect, we still fall short of God's holy standard of perfection. The teacher should quickly clarify that he also is included, for all have sinned.

Step Two: Know the penalty of sin. "For the wages of sin is death, but the gift of God is eternal life in Christ Jesus our Lord" (Rom. 6:23). This refers to both physical and spiritual death. Physical death occurs upon the separation of the body and the spirit of man (James 2:26). Spiritual death occurs when one is eternally separated from God.

Step Three: Know God's provision. "But God demonstrates His own love toward us, in that while we were still sinners, Christ died for us" (Rom. 5:8). While the wages for sin is death, Christ died in man's stead. He died for our sins because we could not pay the price for our sins. This provision gives the sinner the option to receive or reject God's gift of eternal life.

Step Four: Know how to respond. "If you confess with your

mouth the Lord Jesus and believe in your heart that God has raised Him from the dead, you will be saved" (Rom. 10:9). To believe in Christ is the same as receiving Him. "But as many as received Him, to them He gave the right to become children of God, to those who believe in His name" (John 1:12).

Step Five: Make a decision. Having heard the way of salvation, a person should not be left with head knowledge. An opportunity for decision should be given. Ask the person to pray simply for Christ to come into his life.

4. The Four Spiritual Laws. The teacher should explain that just as the physical laws govern the physical universe, the spiritual laws govern our relationship with God.

Law One: God loves you and offers a wonderful plan for your life. "For God so loved the world that He gave His only begotten Son, that whoever believes in Him should not perish but have everlasting life" (John 3:16).

Law Two: Man is sinful and separated from God. Therefore, he cannot know and experience God's love and plan for his life. "For all have sinned and fall short of the glory of God" (Rom. 3:23).

Law Three: Jesus Christ is God's only provision for man's sin. Through him you can know and experience God's love and plan for your life. "Christ died for our sins. . . . He was buried. . . . He rose again the third day according to the Scriptures. . . . He was seen by [Peter], then by the twelve. After that He was seen by over five hundred . . ." (1 Cor. 15:3-6).

Law Four: We must individually receive Jesus Christ as Savior and Lord: then we can know and experience God's love and plan for our lives. "For by grace you have been saved through faith, and that not of yourselves; it is the gift of God, not of works, lest anyone should boast" (Eph. 2:8-9).

5. Evangelism Explosion. The Evangelism Explosion plan suggests an introduction to lead people to Christ. Rather than beginning by accusing the person of being a sinner, it pre-

sents the results of sin. Begin by asking first, "Have you come to the place where you know for certain that if you were to die tonight you would go to heaven to be with God?" The second question is, "If you were to die tonight and stand before God and he were to ask you, 'Why should I let you into my heaven?' what would you say?"

The EE presentation is:

Grace: Heaven is a free gift; but

Man is a sinner and cannot approach God.

God is merciful and does not want to punish us, but he is also holy and must punish sin.

Christ, the infinite God-man, died to purchase heaven for us—the gift of eternal life.

Faith: We must receive the gift by faith.

6. The wordless book. The wordless book has been used for many years by teachers to present the plan of salvation. It is easy and quick for the teacher to make such a book from construction paper. Obviously there are no words in the wordless book. The teacher should explain each colored page and its spiritual meaning as he shares the pages with the pupils.

Page one—black. This black page is used to show the pupils the blackness of sin in our hearts (Prov. 4:19). Talk about the things that we do wrong that make our heart black with sin. The punishment of this sin is death (Rom. 6:23).

Page two—red. The red page tells how God made a way for us to have our sins forgiven. Explain that the blood of Jesus Christ, God's Son, cleanses from all sin (1 John 1:7).

Page three—white. Explain to the pupils that our heart can be white as snow when Christ takes away our sin (Isa. 1:18).

Page four—green. This color represents growth. When we receive Jesus Christ, we have everlasting life (1 John 5:12-13).

Page five—gold. Explain that gold represents the streets of heaven, where we will all spend eternity (Rev. 21:18).

7. The white heart. The teacher should cut a heart from white cloth. Hold the white heart before the students and tell the pupils that their hearts must be clean to get to heaven. As the teacher illustrates a sin, he should put a blot on the white heart with iodine or a water-based felt pen. Show how the iodine or ink messes up the heart. Mention such sins as disobedience, lying, stealing, thinking dirty thoughts, etc. With a bowl of Clorox for the iodine or a bowl of water for the ink spots, wash the heart free from the blotches. Tell how receiving Jesus Christ as Savior washes away all sins.

8. The gospel hand. The gospel hand is presented with much of the same message as the wordless book. To make the gospel hand, the teacher should take a plain, light-colored glove and with colored marking pens, color the fingerprints of each finger. The thumb will be colored black, the index finger colored red, the middle finger white, the ring finger green, and the little finger gold.

9. The handshake invitation. On several occasions people know the plan of salvation but have difficulty moving beyond their awareness into a decision. After presenting the gospel, hold out your hand as an invitation. Offer to shake hands with them as they respond to Christ. Tell them, if they mean business and are ready to receive Jesus Christ, to reach out and shake your hand. This symbolic action is an outward manifestation of inner reality. When they take your hand, remind them that shaking hands does not save anyone. Then lead them to receive Jesus Christ.

In dealing with adults, use the Four Spiritual Laws, the Evangelism Explosion, or the Romans road of salvation. These are not always comprehended by children. However, children seem to always understand the analogy of inviting Christ to come into their heart. Show them that salvation is tied to the Savior, who is Jesus Christ. If they want to be saved, they must ask Jesus Christ to come into their hearts. "Behold, I stand at the door and knock. If anyone hears My voice and opens the door, I will come in to him and dine with him, and he with Me" (Rev. 3:20). Explain to the child that the word *dine* means having a meal or having fellowship. When we ask Christ to come into our heart, he comes in and has fellowship with us. As the pupil bows his head, help him pray in his heart the following words: "Dear Lord Jesus, come into my heart and save me. I want you to live in my life. Take over my thoughts, my hands, my eyes, and my mouth. Live your life through me and take control of me. Help me to be a Christian who can live for your glory. Amen."

EVANGELISM, TEAM (See also F.R.A.N.GELISM)

This approach to evangelism views evangelism as a team ministry in which the conversion of others is achieved through the cooperative efforts of various individuals with different gifts using their gifts to reach others. A program of team evangelism divides workers into five general tasks representing five areas of spiritual gifts: (1) evangelists, (2) equippers, (3) encouragers, (4) helpers, and (5) intercessors. Each of these tasks is discussed in separate articles in this book.

EVANGELISTS (See also F.R.A.N.GELISM)

This term is used here as a technical definition of those who are involved in the soul-winning outreach with the program known as F.R.A.N.gelism. Evangelists are those on the evangelism team with the spiritual gift of evangelism. On visitation night they are given the names of prospects to visit that evening. Because they have the gift of evangelism, they want to meet strangers and do the work of winning others to Christ. They are usually effective in this ministry because it is their spiritual gift. Also, they probably have greater success than those who visit from other churches because they are going to see prospects who have visited the church. The prospects (receptive-responsive people) they go to see usually have a relationship with someone in the church. Hence, because they present the gospel to prospects with greater interest, they have a higher number of decisions for Christ.

EVERYBODY-CAN-WIN CONTEST

Motivation determines priorities—even of Sunday school boys and girls. All children cannot be expected to visit an "I Love Jesus" Sunday and abandon all other projects, particularly without parental push. So teachers need to turn to extrinsic (not inherent) motivation in various forms:

1. Periodic prizes for each pupil who maintains a specified attendance level for a month. (This may take the form of an award for attendance three out of four Sundays, or perfect attendance may be the standard.)

2. An award or gift for the pupil with perfect attendance for three months, six months, or a year. Graded in value, each lesser prize must be attained before the grand prize for the year can be received.

Does it work? Teachers who have tried attendance recognition have, for the most part, praised the results. Boys and girls from indifferent homes come of their own volition—sometimes with uncombed hair and unwashed faces, sometimes having gotten their own breakfast—but they are there, hearing the Word of God. As with adults, some boys and girls are not motivated as much by the monetary value of a gift as by recognition for having had perfect attendance.

Of course, a child's presence in a classroom does not guarantee that the teaching will penetrate his heart. And an attendance habit built on the desire for gifts may be broken when objects no longer are given. The time to reach the heart and soul of a child is the Sunday that the pupil is sitting in the class, eyes upturned, measuring both teacher and lesson against his home values.

EXHIBITS

Exhibits are used as a method of teaching to enhance learning. An exhibit is shown to the students in the process of teaching. Bible stories frequently refer to objects and clothing unfamiliar to hearers. Pictures aid understanding, but reality is best. If the objects are available from Holy Land tourists, display them. If the widow's mite is mentioned, show one. If you refer to the Kaffia headdress, exhibit one—preferably on someone. If flowers are mentioned, show a flower card of pressed flowers from Bethlehem. Missionary stories are often clarified by exhibits of regalia from the land under study.

EXHORTATION, GIFT OF
The person with the gift of exhortation has the ability to stimulate faith in others and motivate others to a practical Christian life. The strengths of this gift include (1) a tendency to be encouraged by results in the life of another, (2) an excitement over practical principles of life, (3) a tendency to interpret his experiences into principles and then validate them with Scripture, (4) a tendency to be comfortable ministering to both groups and individuals, and (5) a grief over sermons that are not practical.

Among the weaknesses of this gift are (1) a tendency to give direction to those unwilling to receive it, (2) being sometimes accused of taking Scripture out of context, and (3) a reluctance to win souls if follow-up is not assured.

The individual with this gift needs to avoid the danger of (1) being discouraged with a lack of progress in listeners, (2) ministering for selfish purposes or (3) ministering to the symptoms rather than the real problem of a person.

EXPANSION GROWTH
Expansion growth is the growth of Christianity by planting new Sunday schools or churches. Expansion growth takes place when a similar church is planted in a similar culture, as opposed to extension growth, which plants a church cross-culturally in a different type of culture.

EXTERNAL GROWTH
External growth consists of numerical growth in attendance, offerings, membership, finances, or enrollment. External growth is observable, measurable, and repeatable.

FAITH AND CHURCH GROWTH

In the early eighties, I published an article entitled "I Visited the Ten Largest Churches in the World." I studied these ten churches to determine the reason for their massive growth. I was looking for principles of methodology that made them great, but found little commonality in the structure that caused their growth.

The one common denominator I found was that the faith of the pastor or leader was the primary cause for the massive power and strong evangelistic outreach of these large churches. It was the pastor's faith that caused them to grow. The faith of a Sunday school teacher can cause growth in a Sunday school class.

How to Use Faith to Build a Sunday School

Knowing it was in response to faith that the power of God was displayed, I began a study of faith in the Scriptures to understand how to trust God. This study led to six expressions of faith in the New Testament. Even though I speak of six expressions of faith, there is only one definition of faith. Faith is affirming what God has said in his Word. This definition is expressed in the popular statement, Faith is taking God at his Word.

Six Expressions of Faith

To have a great faith and move mountains, a person must move through all six expressions of faith.

1. *Doctrinal faith.* If we want faith, we must begin with a correct understanding of the Word of God. The more we know of the Bible, the more faith we can have; and the more correctly we know the Bible, the more effective our faith will be. Through-

out the New Testament the phrase *the faith* and *doctrine* are used interchangeably. When faith has an article preceding it as in *the faith,* it means "the statements of faith." Therefore, to have correct faith, we must have an accurate statement of doctrine.

The apostle Paul certainly recognized the importance of correct doctrine. He constantly opposed those who sought to change the faith; perhaps he was concerned about accurate doctrine because of his own experience. When Saul of Tarsus was persecuting the church, he thought his doctrine was accurate and that he was serving God. Yet later, when he met Christ on the Damascus road, he gained a living faith that changed what he believed and how he lived. Paul talked about those who "depart from the faith" (1 Tim. 4:1) and those who had "denied the faith" (1 Tim. 5:8). At the end of his life, the apostle was able to say, "I have kept the faith" (2 Tim. 4:7). Jude challenged his readers to "contend earnestly for the faith" (Jude 3).

If we want to have a growing biblical faith, we need to ground it upon a correct knowledge of God. A certain woman once heard someone compliment her great faith. "I have not a great faith," she responded, "I have a little faith in a great God."

Someone may ask, "How can I get more faith?" Paul wrote, "Faith comes by hearing, and hearing by the word of God" (Rom. 10:17). The source and foundation of all faith is the Bible.

Doctrinal faith is both the beginning and the test of our Christianity. If our statement of faith is wrong, then our personal faith is misplaced. We must begin with a correct statement of faith and build saving faith thereupon. It is at this point that we are meeting some of the important conditions to correctly experience a life of faith and continue to learn about doctrinal faith.

2. *Saving faith.* A person becomes a Christian by faith. "For by grace you have been saved through faith" (Eph. 2:8). When the Philippian jailer was troubled about his salvation, he was

exhorted to exercise belief, the verb expression of faith. "Believe on the Lord Jesus Christ, and you will be saved, you and your household" (Acts 16:31). When Nicodemus failed to understand how he could enter into a relationship with God, Jesus said, "For God so loved the world that He gave His only begotten Son, that whoever believes in Him should not perish but have everlasting life" (John 3:16). Apart from faith, personal salvation is impossible.

Personal salvation is experienced by the inner person. Since humans are composed of intellect, emotion, and will, faith comes through a proper exercise of these three aspects of personality.

Our faith must be grounded on correct knowledge. A person cannot put his trust in something he does not know about; nor can he honestly trust something that is proven false to him. A person must first know the gospel, which means he has an intellectual knowledge of salvation. But knowledge alone will not save him.

The Bible seems to make a distinction between "believe that" and "believe in." In the first place, one can believe that his team will win or believe that a job is superior. The belief is opinion, but is not deep conviction, based on the object of his faith: Jesus Christ. When a person "believes in," the belief is based on a careful weighing of the evidence. When we say "believe in," we are speaking of a moral expression or a moral experience.

The Gospel of John uses the word *believe* ninety-eight times and ties faith to the object of belief. We are exhorted to "believe in Jesus Christ." As a result, the important aspect of belief is what you believe, not just the measure of your belief. Therefore, to have saving faith, a person must believe that God will punish sin (Rom. 6:23) and that Christ has made a provision for his salvation (Rom. 5:8). A person must believe these truths, which means he accepts them intellectually, but mere intellectual assent to biblical truth is not enough to save him.

Our faith will have an emotional expression. Knowledge

about God is the foundation of saving faith, but such faith will extend to the individual's emotional responses as well. Solomon wrote, "Trust in the LORD with all your heart, and lean not on your own understanding" (Prov. 3:5). Jesus repeated this truth, "You shall love the LORD your God with all your heart, with all your soul, and with all your mind" (Matt. 22:37). This means that intellectual belief is not enough. A person cannot trust his own understanding about God. Although emotions are involved in faith, faith is more than emotional feeling. Our emotional response to the gospel must be founded upon an intellectual understanding of the Scriptures.

Your faith must be a volitional response. A third aspect of saving faith is an expression of volitional faith. A person is saved as a result of an act of his will whereby he relies on Christ, as proclaimed in the gospel. Paul told the Roman Christians, "You obeyed from the heart that form of doctrine to which you were delivered" (Rom. 6:17). When a person accepts Jesus Christ as his Savior (John 1:12), it is a conscious act whereby he invites him into his heart (Eph. 3:16).

3. *Justifying faith.* Whereas saving faith is an experiential encounter with Jesus Christ, the next expression, justifying faith, is nonexperiential. Justifying faith is belief that we have been justified or declared righteous. Justification is not something that we feel with our senses. It is something that happens to our record in heaven. God is the one who performs the act of justification (Rom. 8:33). Man is the one who receives the action and is justified (Rom. 5:1). Justification is the judicial act of God whereby he justly declares righteous all those who believe in Jesus Christ.

Abraham was the first person in the Bible described as having been justified by faith (Gen. 15:6). This is not to say that he was the first person to become a child of God. God made a promise to Abraham that he accepted as possible, and God rewarded him for his faith.

Justification is an act whereby our legal position in heaven is changed. Being justified is similar to the act whereby the

U.S. government declares that an alien becomes an American citizen. The moment the person is pronounced a citizen, nothing happens to him internally. His thought processes remain the same as do his personality and speech pattern. The only actual change is his legal standing. As he becomes aware of the benefits of an American, he may shout, cry, or break into a grin. It is simply an emotional reaction to a legal action.

In the same way, justification changes our legal standing in heaven. We become children of God. In response to this new relationship, the new Christian may respond emotionally.

The basis of justifying faith is a double transference that happens at salvation. Our sin was transferred to Jesus Christ; he became our sin. The preposition *for* is the key word, indicating Christ died for us (Gal. 2:20), he gave his life for the church (Eph. 5:25), and he gave himself for the sins of the world (John 1:29). The second transference is that the perfection of Jesus Christ was credited to our account. When God looks at us in judgment, he sees the righteousness of his son. "For He made Him who knew no sin to be sin for us [the first step of transference], that we might become the righteousness of God in Him [the second step of transference]" (2 Cor. 5:21).

4. *Indwelling faith.* The Bible teaches that a person cannot overcome sin and sinful habits by himself. Faith is the secret of the victorious Christian life. "This is the victory that has overcome the world—our faith" (1 John 5:4).

Even beyond living a triumphant life, a person can walk in moment-by-moment communion with God. A medieval monk described this victory as "practicing the presence of God." This life of victory and fellowship is made available by the indwelling of Jesus Christ. When a person becomes a Christian, Christ comes into his life. The believer has union and communion with Christ (John 15:5). Not only does Christ dwell within the believer; the power of Christ is available to him. Paul testified, "Christ lives in me; and the life which I now live in the flesh I live by faith in the Son of God" (Gal.

2:20). The secret of victorious living is allowing the life of Jesus Christ to flow through us. The believer must surrender his fears and rebellion to Christ. In so doing, he finds new faith to overcome his problems. Paul described this "new faith" that comes from Christ as "the promise by faith in Jesus Christ [that is] given to those who believe" (Gal. 3:22).

Every Christian has access to the "faith of Jesus Christ." Yet many Christians are defeated and discouraged because they have not allowed Christ's power to flow out of their lives.

To get this victory, a Christian must first recognize that faith comes from Christ and is described as faith *in him* (Gal. 2:16; Eph. 3:12; Phil. 3:9). Second, a person must yield (the nature of faith is trusting) and allow Christ to work through him. In addition, the Christian must constantly obey the direction of the Word of God so that he can continually have power for victory.

5. *Daily faith.* When we live by faith we are being set apart to God, which is the meaning of *sanctification*. The Bible teaches that positional sanctification is a past action on Calvary. Progressive sanctification is being carried out daily, and future sanctification will take place when we arrive in the presence of God. Daily sanctification requires an exercise of faith, "For we walk by faith, not by sight" (2 Cor. 5:7).

As we live by faith, God is able to use us and cause us to grow in grace. Sometimes daily growth seems minute or even nonexistent to a casual observer. We may sometimes become frustrated with the apparent lack of progress, not able to see the forest for the trees. It is good from time to time to look back and see how God has been working in our life.

As a bricklayer places one brick upon the other, building a large tower, he may feel his progress is insignificant. Yet the tower will be built one brick at a time. It is the same in our Christian life. God makes the big changes through a series of little ones. We must learn to trust God for the little things so we can enjoy great growth. We must trust God daily so we can enjoy yearly gain. Like any other growing experience, living by faith is taking one step at a time.

We grow in faith through the Word of God. As we make the Word of God a part of our life by reading, studying, and memorizing, we begin to grow in faith (1 Pet. 2:2). Every Christian needs to hear the Word of God taught and preached regularly (Ps. 1:1-3).

We grow in faith by following biblical principles. A growing faith is an obedient faith. Usually the exercise of faith will be rational and in keeping with what God wants done. We must put complete trust in the principles of the Bible and not trust our feelings. Faith is not a blind leap into the dark; faith is following the light of God's Word.

We grow in faith through seeking the Lord. The doctrine of seeking the Lord is not usually emphasized, but it is biblical to search for God. "When You said, 'Seek My face,' my heart said to You, 'Your face, LORD, I will seek'" (Ps. 27:8). Our faith will grow as we seek God. First, we will begin to recognize the issues that keep us from God. Then, as we search for a better relationship with the Savior, we will come to know God experientially.

We grow in faith through confessing our sins. No Christian will live a sinless life, but God is constantly cleansing us through the blood of his Son. "If we walk in the light as He is in the light, we have fellowship with one another, and the blood of Jesus Christ His Son cleanses us from all sin" (1 John 1:7). When we as Christians do sin, God will forgive and cleanse us if we confess our sins to Him (1 John 1:9). Every time we recognize sin in our lives and rid ourselves of its hindrance, we grow in faith.

We grow in faith by surrender. The Christian must constantly surrender to the lordship of Christ. We do this once when we are saved, but there are also subsequent times to surrender to Christ. As we yield our lives to the Lord, we are growing in grace (Gal. 3:3; Col. 2:6). Paul challenged the Romans to "present your bodies a living sacrifice, holy, acceptable to God, which is your reasonable service" (Rom. 12:1).

We grow in faith through constant communion. If we want

a growing faith, we must have constant communion with Jesus Christ. As we spend time in prayer, Bible study, and fellowship with Christ, we will develop our faith more fully. Jesus recognized that we would become like those we spend time with (Matt. 10:25). As we spend time with the Lord, we will become more Christlike in our faith.

We grow in faith through the testing of difficult experiences. Once we are saved, our faith is nurtured as we grow from victory to victory. Paul describes this as going "from faith to faith; as it is written, 'The just shall live by faith'" (Rom. 1:17). God wants us to have faith in himself because that pleases and glorifies him. Living faith is not something we receive as one takes a vitamin pill. With the opportunity of taking a step of faith, there is the risk of success or failure. When we successfully trust God, we should learn through the experience and grow thereby. Faith must come from man's heart, which is governed by his free will. Therefore, to develop a person's faith, God will sometimes maneuver man into a corner so that the creature is forced to look at his Creator in faith. Through such experiences, man has an opportunity to grow in his faith.

6. *The gift of faith.* The gift of faith is one of the gifts that the Holy Spirit supernaturally gives men to serve God (Rom. 12:3; 1 Cor. 12:9). This faith that is called a gift is more than saving faith. The gift of faith is considered to be a serving gift, or an ability whereby a person serves God by exercising faith. No one has all of the gifts, so not everyone has the gift of faith. Paul explained that the gifts differ "according to the grace that is given to us" (Rom. 12:6). God has given some this special gift of faith to enable them to carry out their ministry in a more effective way.

If God has given us the gift of faith, we need to exercise it faithfully in keeping with well-balanced Christianity. Paul said, "Though I have all faith, so that I could remove mountains, but have not love, I am nothing" (1 Cor. 13:2).

The Bible teaches that the proper use of our gifts increases the effectiveness and usefulness of those gifts (Matt. 25:14-

30). It also teaches that we can desire and pray for more gifts (1 Cor. 12:31). Therefore, it is possible for us to have more faith to trust God for bigger things than we have now. If we are faithful in small things, God will give us more faith. Note that Abraham grew from being weak in faith to one who was strong in faith (Rom. 4:19-20).

The ultimate human expression of Christianity is an act of faith. To the casual observer, *faith* is simply defined as "reliance, trust, or dependence." Yet to the careful students of the Scriptures, faith has at least six expressions. First, we must know correct doctrinal faith, which is called a statement of faith. Second, we become a Christian by experiencing saving faith in Jesus Christ. Third, we must have justifying faith. Fourth, we must let the faith of Christ flow through us (indwelling faith). Fifth, we must live the Christian life by daily faith. Finally, as we grow in our spiritual gifts, we may be given the special gift of faith by the Holy Spirit, whereby some serve God and magnify him by the expression of great faith for accomplishments in their Christian service.

FALL ROUNDUP

Fall Roundup is a program often used to enhance Sunday school enrollment and attendance.

On a poster for each department in Sunday school draw a cow for each member of every class, with name affixed. In the center of the poster, draw a horse, representing the teacher. As each pupil is signed up, a picture of a cow is pasted over the drawing. When all members have signed, the roundup is completed. (Men's classes use steers instead of cows.)

A big poster in the auditorium will feature a picture of horses with teachers' names, showing they have completed their roundup. Scatter a few cows and steers around the edges.

At the end of the campaign, a picnic may include a pony and wagon rides for all the children. Toy horses may reward children who brought the most visitors, a radio may reward teenagers, and a Bible may be given to the adult who brought the most visitors.

FASTEST GROWING SUNDAY SCHOOL ANNUAL RECOGNITION

Christian Life magazine determined its annual listing of the largest Sunday schools had motivated Sunday school growth, especially among large churches. When it was determined that public interest was declining, the author determined to find and print the fastest growing Sunday school in each state. Many of these were smaller Sunday schools; hence, all churches would be motivated to outreach. The first listing occurred in 1974 with the church experiencing the largest growth. To locate the fastest growing Sunday school, mainline and evangelical denominations were contacted, as well as Sunday school convention personnel. Ads were published to search for the fastest growing Sunday school. Also, the author had research assistants in each state to help locate Sunday schools with rapid growth.

The listing occurred for years, ending in 1984. From 1974 to 1980 *Christian Life* printed the results, from 1980 to 1982 *The Sword of the Lord* printed the results, and from 1983 to 1984 *Moody Monthly* printed the results.

Each year the recipients were invited to the International Christian Education Convention, Cobo Hall, Detroit, Michigan, to receive their reward—a large two- by three-foot banner. The banner was personalized for each state, indicating the church that had the fastest growing Sunday school in that state.

FIELD TRIPS

A field trip is a method of teaching that capitalizes educationally on the wandering and exploring instinct of the pupils. A field trip can acquaint pupils with their environment and interpret, supplement, and enrich curricular experiences. Before going on any trip, plan what to observe and have definite questions in mind. The teacher should visit the place beforehand to be well informed as to what the pupils will see. At the destination, the teacher should wait till all are assembled and should speak so that all can hear (always difficult in a large group, but absolutely necessary to effective learning). On return to class, ideas learned should be reviewed.

1. Local trips. This is the simplest type, in which the group visits points, parts, or sections of its own building and grounds. Primaries or beginners may visit the church sanctuary to learn the meaning of the *pulpit, pew,* and *organ.*

2. Community trip. This is the usual field trip to some point of interest outside the local place of teaching, such as when the high school class visits a college or the college class visits a Jewish synagogue to observe worship. A class of prospective Sunday school teachers may visit and observe public school classes. Or the Sunday school staff may visit another church to observe architecture, planning of space, furnishings, and equipment.

3. Tour. The tour or journey is a trip lasting several days, a month, or even longer.

4. The imaginary tour. All the details of the trip are investigated, studied, and planned, just as though the group were actually going. This is an excellent technique for missionary programs.

5. The individual trip. The pupil may take a trip by himself because of an assignment or some particular responsibility in connection with curricular work or because of his own specialized interests.

FILING LESSON MATERIALS

Some people are string savers, squirrels, or pack rats by nature. They store every article they feel might have some future use. The practice is not without merit, depending on the place and manner of storage. Probably everyone at some time experiences the frustration of "carefully putting away" a clipping, a picture, or an article deemed of value, only to forget where it was placed—or to spend an hour searching for it in a miscellaneous collection in a drawer. The simple expedient of an alphabetical file will save valuable hours of fruitless searching.

How to Organize a Christian Education File

1. Biblically. The best way for a beginning Sunday school teacher to start a file is by Bible reference. Secure sixty-six file folders, then place the name of one book of the Bible on the tab of each folder. At first, file lessons by Bible books. After all, Sunday school lessons should be based on Scripture, so file each lesson by its primary Scripture reference.

   One can supplement this file by taking notes in Bible conferences, teacher training classes, and during the pastor's weekly sermon. These notes can be filed along with the Sunday school lessons for future reference.

   As the file grows larger, add file folders for individual chapters of a book. This will force one to center Sunday school teaching on the Bible. Also, for future lessons a teacher can quickly refer to previous research on a given passage. (Note: Illustrations, teaching aids, pictures, and materials used in teaching should not be filed under the biblical file. These should go in the alphabetical file.)

2. Alphabetically. Initially, a file may fit into a single drawer. (A transfer file box or corrugated packing box accommodating letter-size file folders may be used.) Folders may be labeled as needed, depending on the teacher's personal collection of material. Possible subjects include archaeology, Easter, Christmas, poetry, puppets, animals, and visual aids. These should be arranged alphabetically.

3. By subject. The file remains alphabetical, but subdivisions are made according to subject within the alphabetical frame, instead of filing by names, as in the case of business correspondence or student files. For example, a teacher may have a special interest in archaeology. Under the A division, a divider may be labeled Archaeology. Folders alphabetized behind that divider may include Africa, books, Holy Land, Indian, marine—and any other aspects of archaeology on which the teacher has collected information. When a file is first organized, ample space may allow filing of entire copies of magazines with significant articles. As space fills up, clipping will be necessary, or a magazine shelf file.

4. Numerically. Some teachers and Bible students prefer to number their subjects and file according to number. Only the person filing the material will know the key, and quick reference is difficult for anybody else.

What Goes in the File?

The answer is: everything a teacher wishes to keep—everything that has potential value for teaching or personal study. The variety is as great as the teacher's personal interest. Some useful subjects include teaching methods (separate folders on each method on which information has been collected), Bible studies, Bible background (archaeology and history), Bible geography, cults, vacation Bible school, teacher training, church history, special days (such as Easter, Mother's Day, or Christmas), recreation and social activities, publicity, pedagogy, psychology, stories, quotations, biography, handwork ideas, patterns.

1. *The picture file.* Pictures can be filed by subject or by size. When filing by subject, alphabetize carefully for quick location—animals, children, family, friends, life of Christ, missionary, nature, Old Testament—whatever subjects are necessary for the teacher's regular use.

   The sizes of pictures varies according to their source. Teaching pictures purchased regularly with the lesson study aids may be filed in a special drawer that accommodates their larger size. They should be filed according to subject and\or unit of study. Extremely small pictures (useful in scrapbooks and with an opaque projector) may be filed in folders according to the quantity—one folder for Old Testament, one for New Testament, one for children (or whatever the age group taught).

2. *The flannelgraph file.* Flannelgraph materials may be filed alphabetically or by Bible reference. If the stories are labeled according to character or subject, alphabetize in filing: Abraham, Creation, Daniel, Easter. Use separate files for missionary stories, character stories, or Bible verses or songs. Alphabetize the folders or titles under each category. When the file grows, file flannelgraph by Bible references.

3. *Catalogs.* Request and file catalogs from Christian publishing

houses, for reference when materials are needed. A large accumulation can overflow a filing cabinet. They may be filed on bookshelves.

Maintaining Your File

Occasionally, an article you want to keep will appear on the reverse side of another subject equally valuable. In this case, you should either make a photocopy of one side or cross reference the articles. The paper may be placed under one title, but a plain white sheet of paper should be filed under the other title, telling where the article is to be found. When an article is temporarily removed from the file and placed elsewhere, the fact may be noted on a sheet of paper and placed in the folder.

From time to time your file will need weeding. This doesn't have to be a big project. A home owner may run across a weed when he is on the way to pick peas. So he pulls it up. As a teacher searches for an item in the file, he may run across an article about a method or fact that is obsolete, so he discards the article. If the file drawer is getting too full for easy filing, time should be taken to check several folders to find items that have served their purpose and are no longer useful. They may be removed to make room for more current material.

FILMS

Slides, filmstrips, motion pictures, and videos are excellent media to teach Bible stories; to teach Bible background, customs, and geography; to teach practical Christian principles through real-life situations; to train teachers and leaders; to educate in crafts, first aid, safety, special skills, etc.; and to use in club programs at Christmas or Easter. (Take slides of costumed members acting out the Christmas story; make tape recording to fit the pictures and show at Christmas.)

Principles for Use

1. Select filmstrips that fit the age level.
2. Select materials that serve a definite purpose in the class session; projected material should supplement teaching.
3. Preview the film or filmstrip before using.
4. Know how to operate the equipment.

5. Arrive early to set up equipment and check room arrangement.

6. Set up and focus the film before the audience arrives.

7. Make the mechanical operation of the showing as inconspicuous as possible.

8. Remember to bring a take-up reel; be sure it is in gear; don't touch the film with your fingers should it fall to the floor; wind it slowly back onto the reel.

9. Have tape available to splice film if it should break.

10. Don't force filmstrip; sprocket holes are easily damaged.

11. Don't put your fingers on the surface of the slides or filmstrip.

12. Don't place screen too high for children, but put it high enough so they can easily see over heads.

13. Adjust size of image to size of audience. The image should be no larger than necessary for good viewing by those farthest away from the screen. The smaller the image, the brighter it will be.

14. The sound speaker should be placed a little above the heads of the group and pointed toward the middle of the last three rows of seats.

15. Check volume from several spots in the room.

16. Direct attention to the special point of view with which the film is to be watched. Raise questions to be answered in the film; suggest points to watch for and discuss at finish.

17. Follow up film with discussion and action if appropriate.

18. You can use just the audio to vary the presentation of a Bible or character story. Tape the story to play in class. This device is useful when a moving story must be told. Use some of the excellent children's stories of "Bible in Living Sound" records to present the story with sound effects and drama. Discuss the material after it is presented. Prepare the listeners by listing on the chalkboard some questions to be answered by the recorded story.

19. For story sequence and sound effects, tape-recorded sound may be correlated with slides. Practice the production to get it synchronized correctly. (If the slide calls for a lion

roaring, tape enough roars from the sound-effects record to cover the time needed to describe the beast's place in the story.)

20. You may wish to make a tape to go with a filmstrip. The Dukane Projector uses both, simultaneously. Two machines also may be correlated, as for slides.

FINANCE COMMITTEE

The finance committee members should normally have some financial background. They oversee the financial record keeping system of the church, with authorization to make changes as necessary. They take major decisions to the church board, arrange for regular, complete audits by an experienced accountant not involved in the financial record keeping for the congregation, and prepare the annual budget. The chairman should have bank statements sent directly to him for reconciliation.

This committee includes all the financial officers and also other members of the congregation. The congregation's bylaws should spell out the duties and membership requirements.

FINANCIAL MANAGEMENT

Periodically, a church should determine whether it has the best possible program at the lowest possible unit cost. As good stewards of the resources entrusted to them by God and the church membership, the leadership of the church should have a sound financial management policy. A church should have sound financial management to enable it to accomplish its objectives. The management of the church should be interested enough in the mission of the church and its own protection to establish a sound financial system. This management team includes the pastor, church board, financial committee, church treasurer, and financial secretary. Most churches should have people with technical competency in accounting matters or secure outside help. In most states, a church should organize into a corporation to limit legal liability for the church leaders and enable the organization to hold title to assets and enter into contracts.

These guidelines will help financial planning:

1. A church should plan on the basis of its continuing existence.
2. Planners must constantly check the financial statements of receipts and disbursements.
3. Planning some portions of the budget may be done on the basis of projected income through pledges.
4. The establishment of a reserve may cause members to reduce their giving, feeling the church has more money than it can use.
5. The annual budget should be divided into monthly or quarterly periods. Actual income and expenses should be analyzed for the last year on a period-to-period basis to see the pattern of income and expense. Adjustments should be made on this basis.

FINANCIAL SECRETARY

The financial secretary receives, counts, and deposits all contributions. Some other person should be designated to help with the counting. The financial secretary should give duplicate deposit slips, with adequate notations regarding source and fund, to the treasurer promptly.

He also prepares and forwards to any assistant an adequate report of all contributions each week: source, contributor's name, fund, amount, and special instructions. The financial secretary keeps a record of all contributions and deposits. No ledger is necessary, as regular reports fulfill this function. He disburses no funds and has no access to the congregation's checking account.

FINANCING THE LIBRARY/RESOURCE CENTER

Many times the local church votes approval of a library and duly provides suitable quarters. A librarian is chosen, but somehow the project dies a slow death because the appointee receives nothing more than a couple of boxes of old books. The librarian may have the ingenuity to make good use of old books, and some benefit may accrue to the church, but much more is needed to develop a fine and adequate educational resource center within the church.

The best kind of library financing follows church policies and assures a regular, dependable income. Evangelical church policy disallows some fund-raising methods. Ideally the church budget should include money to equip a new library or to increase the inventory and equipment of the already existing one. A Canadian church reported that enthusiasm for its library began to mount after members voted to support the library with 10 percent of the Sunday school offerings.

The following methods and suggestions have been effectively used to raise money to stock the church library.

1. Class or group project. Groups of individuals within the church can often be challenged to help build a library inventory. The librarian can begin by supplying a list of needed books, including volumes for all ages and for varying ranges of interest. Books purchased as a class project will likely reflect the special interests of that class. For example, older adults might select devotional reading, novels, Bible study helps, and other reference books. The younger married and professional people would be interested in books about child care, marital problems, and general psychology from the Christian point of view. There might be a theology or philosophy buff in the group, and he would surely vote for the work of his favorite author. The women's or youth class might provide funds for missionary adventures. The teens will prefer their favorite novelists and books written by prominent personalities, such as athletes and beauty contest winners. Some will want to find Christian classics, and nearly every age group will sooner or later be looking for program helps. Christian educators in the congregation will want to see the shelves stocked with books on teaching and student guidance. Fiction or biography catches the interest of most youngsters from junior high school age down, so that a teacher or department superintendent could challenge his girls and boys to give toward the purchase of some of their favorite storybooks. Teachers might contribute one of the numerous versions of Scripture and make it available for supplementary use in class, along with atlases

and books of art, theology, and geography. The list is as long and varied as are the fields of interest of the congregation.

2. *Library Sunday.* Such a special day might be incorporated as an annual event on the church calendar. The librarian could enlist the help of members in setting up special features for each service on that day.

Here the "wanted list" comes into focus. In preparation for Library Sunday, the day the church asks for special money gifts for books, each member should already have been given a list of books that the library needs, including prices. People could check off the book they wish to purchase and make the appropriate donation. Knowing exactly what their money will buy will elicit greater donations from donors on this special day.

On Library Sunday the librarian or other capable person could be allotted time in the service to review a new or otherwise significant Christian book, preferably one that the library does not already have. Book reviews are also valuable for motivating the congregation to read volumes that are already on the shelves.

3. *Book clubs.* The library could organize a club whose members buy books, read them, and then donate the volumes to the church library. This need not be the type of high pressure group that the word *club* connotes. The advantage for members might simply be that they would obtain books from a publisher or bookstore at a discount. Many companies extend such discounts to churches, but rarely to individuals. This idea will appeal mainly to those who regularly buy and read books, including parents of children who read. Organization of such a club should fit the local situation, possibly being simply a list of people who wish to purchase books for a church at a discount.

4. *Memorial gifts.* Library publicity should occasionally indicate the fact that the church is prepared to accept books given in memory of loved ones, to mark the death of a special person (in the denomination or community), or to commemorate

such events as church anniversaries or a pastor's years in Christian service.

Donations to the library fund upon the death of a loved one must be acknowledged immediately with a letter of condolence to the family. Gifts of books or donations for books given in lieu of flowers must be acknowledged to the donor, and the bereaved family should be notified in writing within twenty-four hours after the arrival of the gift that the donor chose this kind of condolence.

5. *Book showers.* Such a project might be sponsored either by the whole church or by an adult class or department of the Sunday school. A local Christian bookstore would probably be willing to consign a shipment of books that have been selected jointly by the church and store manager. Many folks will not take the time to browse through a bookstore, but if a book table is arranged in conjunction with a church meeting, then such browsing turns out to be a pleasant experience. It can also be profitable for the library—for a book shower is meant to make books available for families to purchase as gifts to the library. Each purchaser is given first chance to check out the book he buys. The book shower gives special impetus to building the library inventory because people will more quickly buy a book that they hold in their hand than one they must choose from a book list.

One church used a gift plan by designating the month of November as "Thanksgiving Month for the Library." The church ordered a consignment of books from a Christian bookseller with the option to return for full credit all unsold books. The advantage of this system is that the librarian has already selected desirable books, yet members can choose those that most interest them.

The theme of the month-long display was "Be Thankful for Written Words." Posters encouraged members to be actively thankful by giving a book to the library. "Progress posters" listed books that had been purchased for the library and their donors. All the books purchased were put on display so that people could become familiar with the new additions and plan to read them after they had been processed. A nameplate in each book designated its donor, and everyone who bought a gift book later received a written thank you from the library committee.

Expenses for this particular book shower came to twenty dollars, paid from the library budget; however, three hundred dollars' worth of books were added to the library.

6. *A bookstore within the church.* A consignment of books stays in the church only temporarily—for Library Sunday, or for the duration of a Sunday school workers' or missionaries' conference. However, some churches have felt the advantages of having their own bookselling corner have far outweighed the arguments against such a venture. Some people feel strongly that no selling should be permitted in the church at any time. But some churches have stocked a book nook and opened it on the Lord's Day, and members are fully convinced that it is a ministry—an effective ministry.

7. *Want list.* The librarian should prepare a list of books (twelve to twenty-four) from which persons may select and purchase books as gifts to the library. He will need to revise this list regularly, deleting acquired books and adding newly published ones. The librarian should also supplement this want list with another comprehensive listing of the titles and types of books that the church library will accept. With this list as a basis, the librarian can kindly but firmly refuse to shelve donations of books that do not enhance the library's purpose of communicating the Christian faith to people.

FLAKE, ARTHUR (1862–1952)

Arthur Flake was a traveling salesman and department store manager who was converted at age thirty-one. He then organized a local church, helped organize the state Baptist Young People's Union and was the state's volunteer Sunday school superintendent.

In 1920 he was placed in charge of the new Department of Sunday School Administration. He developed standards and a philosophy of Sunday school organization and administration on which most future work was based. Among other things, he initiated (1) the enlargement campaign; (2) the five-step formula in building a Sunday school (discover the possibilities, enlarge the organization, provide a place, train the workers, and visit the prospects); (3) *The Sunday School Builder,* a monthly magazine that he edited from 1920 to 1936; (4) books and leaflets on Sunday school work; and (5) the Sunday school clinic idea.

He improved and projected (1) the Training Union administration, (2) the Sunday school Standards of Excellence, (3) the Six-Point Record System, (4) the church library movement, (5) the weekly officers and teachers' meeting, (6) grading and the principle and method of multiplying units—classes and departments, and (7) the associational Sunday school organization.

The most widely distributed of his books was *Building a Standard Sunday School.* More than any other volume, it has given guidance and motivation for the expansion of Southern Baptist Sunday school work.

FLANNELGRAPH

Flannelgraph, intriguing as it may be, if used invariably, becomes monotonous. It can be repeated more often in preschool classes because younger children like repetition.

1. *Board.* A simple board may be made from the side of a large corrugated box. Cut two boards to two-by-three feet and hinge in the center, or make one large board and fold if desired. Reinforce the fold with heavy tape. Staple blue outing flannel to the board and tape around the edges. Or the teacher could make one board in a chart combination with a flannelgraph by covering it with blue flannel. Some teachers of preschoolers wear a "story apron" with flannel pockets. Figures are kept in the pocket and removed as used. If classroom space does allow room for an easel or table, hang a lightweight flannelboard on the wall, at pupils' eye level, tilted slightly forward at bottom.

2. *Backgrounds.* While these may be purchased ready-made, they may also be easily and inexpensively made by hand. With light blue outing flannel as a neutral background, sketch the desired indoor or outdoor scene in colored chalk. Fill in

the details with more chalk. Spray the unfinished scene with hair spray as a fixative.

Some oil stick products, which are brighter, are available at school supply houses. Markal and Sandford's Cra-pas Payons are obtainable at Christian supply stores. If crayons are used, the finished scene should be ironed on the reverse side, to cause the color to penetrate the material and become indelible. Artists may complete a crayon scene with touches of oil paint.

Many Christian publishers' catalogs include both figures and backgrounds. They are also obtainable at Christian bookstores.

3. *Figures.* There are several kinds available:

- Pictograph—Suedegraph. On heavy stock vellum paper, one of the earliest producers of flannelgraph (Scripture Press) has dozens of stories now available.
- Child Evangelism. A complete catalog of stories is available on request.
- World Wide Visuals. Write for descriptive, illustrated price list. Address: World Wide Visual Aids, P.O. Box 1226, National City, CA 92050.
- Scene-O-Felt. Address: Munn Art Studio, P.O. Box 204, Hillsdale, MI 49242.
- Magazines. Back the pictures cut from magazines with vellum paper or flannel and use them to illustrate stories.

4. *Use.* Most commercial flannelgraph sets include the story. The teacher may substitute words that are natural to him. If no suggestions are available, tell the story with enthusiasm and expression, standing at one side of the board with Bible in hand.

The figures then may be used in review. Even preschoolers like to place figures on the board, even though a "man" may float in the sky or fall into the sea. They happily place the leading character of the story or a star in the sky. Allow pupils to take turns if the class is large. At the second retelling, pupils may tell their part of the story as they place the picture on the board.

Object lessons may also be presented on the flannelgraph. Whole books of object lessons are available. Ready-made object lessons for flannelgraph may also be obtained. (Check catalogs for books and lessons.) Such lessons may easily be made by the teacher, using felt, flannel, double knit or construction paper backed with vellum paper.

5. *Memory drill.* Refer to the article on memory work for use of scrambled verses.

Tic-tac-toe may be played on a yarn chart on flannelgraph. As questions are answered, put the symbol in the spaces with squares of flannel.

6. *Story outlines.* Place a few words on each point in a story or lesson on the board as each point is begun. Points covered may be removed.

FLASH CARDS

Large cards, usually in a sequence, are flashed one at a time for review, drill, storytelling, and memory work teaching. They may be used in combination with other aids such as posters, charts, maps, graphs and diagrams.

Effective cards should have large lettering for easy reading and should be held high enough for everyone to see, flashed at the right moment, kept in proper order for easy presentation, exposed long enough for clear comprehension, and as brief as possible.

FLAT PICTURES

These include photographs, clippings, paintings, prints, cartoons, drawings—any picture not projected. They may be obtained from Sunday school magazines and papers, publishing houses, calendars, greeting cards, even catalogs. School supply house catalogs list art pictures.

Pictures may be used with posters, charts, maps, dioramas, flash cards for teaching songs and verses, homemade flannelgraph lessons, review games, Bible-verse matching games, puzzles in presession or review, story wheels, and rebus stories.

F.R.A.N.GELISM

The word *F.R.A.N.* stands for friends, relatives, associates, and neighbors. The program is called F.R.A.N.gelism Follow-up because usually it is F.R.A.N.s who visit a church in response to a relationship. These are receptive-responsive people who can be stairstepped to the gospel.

But some attend church who are not F.R.A.N.s. They don't know anyone in the church. The purpose of follow-up is to network them into a relationship with someone in the church so they can be drawn to Christ.

The Law of Three Hearings

Research shows that the average visitor to church does not come forward during the invitation to accept Christ the first time he visits a church. He will usually visit three or four times before making the meaningful decision to become a Christian.

The Law of Seven Touches

Research shows that a person usually makes a meaningful decision for Christ after the church has contacted him seven times. These contacts, or touches, can be initiated by the church through letters, phone calls, visits, or other personal contact.

Why F.R.A.N.gelism Is Effective

1. F.R.A.N.gelism helps in the stairstepping process. Follow-up draws people to the church and is especially helpful in stairstepping people to a decision for Jesus Christ. The follow-up program is called F.R.A.N.gelism because it helps make friends with prospects in order to reach them for Christ.

   Through the drawing process, the prospect is brought into personal contact (networking) with several Christians. When the unsaved prospect comes to one of those difficult places where he is unable to make the next step toward the Lord, and a soul winner can't seem to provide the needed answer, a word from another Christian may be just what is needed. The drawing process enables Christians to become laborers together with one another as well as with God. The strengths of one believer can offset the weakness of others, and this is exactly as it should be (1 Cor. 3:6-8).

2. F.R.A.N.gelism follow-up prepares for the event of new birth. As the unsaved person becomes personally acquainted with different Christians through the drawing process, he is well on the road to understanding Christians and the church. He will come to understand that the Christian life is not a legal system, but true freedom in Christ. He will learn that Christians can experience lasting joy and contentment. He will see that a Christian will have problems but can have victory over sin and the circumstances of life. When he comes to the point of repentance and faith in Jesus Christ, he will understand that what he is gaining is far greater than what he is turning from or giving up (Phil. 3:8).

The apostle Paul experienced the working of this principle in Macedonia and Achaia. The unsaved of that region did not have to be convinced of the value of the Christian life. They were persuaded that the new birth would lead to a better quality of life because they had seen it in the believers of Thessalonica (1 Thess. 1:7-10). They had been effectively drawn by the church of the Thessalonians even before they were saved, and that drawing had helped to prepare their hearts for the event of the new birth.

3. F.R.A.N.gelism follow-up is essential to proper Christian growth and development. Active involvement in the local church is essential to the proper growth and development of Christians. Peter wrote, "As newborn babes, desire the pure milk of the word, that you may grow thereby" (1 Pet. 2:2). Spiritual growth, like physical growth, requires proper feeding, and God has provided for feeding through the ministry of the local church. He has given gifted individuals to the church for the purpose of equipping the saints (Eph. 4:11-12), and these gifted individuals exercise their ministry in local assemblies, or flocks (1 Pet. 5:2-3).

Nature of F.R.A.N.gelism Follow-Up

1. F.R.A.N.gelism follow-up is personal. People resent being

treated as statistics, numbers, or part of the mass. They need to belong to a group, but they also have a desire and need for personal attention and personal identity. The drawing process used in friendship evangelism provides that needed personal touch.

2. F.R.A.N.gelism follow-up is persistent. Surveys have shown that a visitor who attends the church an average of 3.4 times usually makes a responsible decision to become saved or join the church. The purpose of the drawing process is to positively communicate to the visitor the love, care, and concern of the church, so that he will come back an average of 3.4 times. However, statistics also show that when the church contacts a prospect an average of 8.6 times, he usually makes a responsible decision to accept Christ or join the church.

3. F.R.A.N.gelism follow-up is powerful. Because the drawing process used in friendship evangelism is both personal and persistent, it is also a powerful force. Jesus himself pointed out the power of personal persistence in Luke 11:5-8. In that passage, an approach was made on the basis of personal friendship (v. 5). Friendship is a powerful force, but friendship was not enough by itself. However, personal friendship in conjunction with persistence proved to be more powerful than the forces of resistance.

Beginning the Drawing Process

1. When to begin. The process of drawing people to the church should begin with the first contact. Visitors usually attend one of the regular worship services, or they may be brought to some activity, social function, or fellowship meeting. Whatever the contact, it indicates some degree of receptivity on the part of visitors. That openness and receptivity should be stimulated and cultivated, lest it cool and die for lack of care. The time for harvest is when the fruit is ripe.

When Jesus had finished talking with the Samaritan woman, he turned to his disciples and said, "Do you not say, 'there are still four months, and then comes the harvest'? Behold, I say to you, lift up your eyes and look at the fields, for they are already white for harvest!" (John 4:35). Some have suggested that he was referring to the multitude of men coming out of the city. Whether that is true, or whether he was strictly speaking a parable, the application is the same. The harvest cannot be postponed until the convenience of the harvester. The crops must be harvested when they are ripe, and people must be won to Christ and to the church while they are winnable.

If the farmer fails to harvest his apples from the orchard when they are ripe, they will not remain long on the tree. And once they have fallen to the ground, they are lost to rabbits, deer, or other wild animals, and they soon begin to rot.

2. Who starts the process? If a visitor who has no contact with members of the church attends a regular worship service, then the first contact should be made by the pastor. If the visitor attended only Sunday school or came to a function sponsored by some other group or cell, the teacher or the person in charge should make the first contact.

The Drawing Process

The actual drawing process depends upon several variables: (1) whether the visitor knows no one in the church and the first contact is made by the pastor or some other church leader, (2) whether the individual being drawn to the church is already involved in the stairstepping process, or (3) whether the prospect is a F.R.A.N. (friend, relative, associate, or neighbor to someone in the church). While the ultimate goal is the same in each case, each situation must be handled slightly differently.

The key to a correct approach is information. This information is best gained from visitors' cards, conversations with the visitors, and from the church member who brought or invited them to the service. It is helpful to know whether the church member (a Christian) already has the visitor involved in the stairstepping process. It is also helpful to know the visitor's religious background, spiritual condition, and receptivity to the Christian message. All this information will enable the pastor, or the church worker who makes the first contact, to know how to begin drawing the newcomer to the church.

1. Drawing propects—those who initially attend the church for reasons of their own or are invited to church by a member, but are not involved in the stairstepping process.

First touch. On Sunday afternoon, the pastor should phone all those who visited in the morning service. His purpose is not to invite them to visit again. If fact, he should not make an invitation to return; he should assume they will return.

The pastor should attempt to accomplish four things through this phone call: (1) He should determine whether or not they are receptive-responsive people. Some will quickly state that they are members of another church, hence the pastor will know that they are not prospects. Others will give their reason for attending, but they will not want the pastor to visit them. (2) The pastor should sincerely offer his personal ministry and the services of the church. (3) He should express a desire to visit their home and present them with a friendship packet from the church. The packet might contain such things as a Bible, a devotional guide, a cassette tape on Christian family living, an appropriate book on the Christian life, and a Christian lapel pin. The packet should also contain information about the various worship and service opportunities offered by the church. (4) Close the conversation by telling them that the church secretary will phone to make an appointment for the pastor to visit later in the week. He should tell them that he will not drop by unannounced. Do not ask if the secretary may phone; assume that they would appreciate such a call. If they do not want a visit, they will usually say so at this point.

Second touch. Sunday evening, the church secretary should send a personal letter from the pastor to each visitor. A form letter is acceptable only if the church has the equipment to personalize it. If a form letter is used, it should be personally signed by the pastor. The letter should offer pastoral help and remind them that the secretary will be calling to make an appointment for a visit by the pastor, and that he will bring a friendship packet.

Third touch. Monday or Tuesday, the secretary should phone to make an appointment for the pastor to visit in the home. She should indicate that the pastor has several visits to make, and that he will not be visiting in the home all evening. They are more likely to be receptive to the visit if they know it will be brief. She should also remind them of the things the pastor has already shared with them. Then she should offer her personal friendship as well.

The pastor, secretary, and all other church leaders who might be involved in making the first contacts should recognize that some will not be receptive to the church. About half of those who are called by the pastor can be expected to decline a visit, and half of those who do not decline the pastor will do so when the secretary calls. This means about 25 percent of those who visit the church on Sunday will be receptive to a visit from the pastor the following week. But these are prime prospects for membership or to accept Christ.

Fourth touch. The pastor or trained soul winner will make a visit to the homes of all who have made appointments. He should take a moment to go over the material in the friendship packet and give special attention to the Scripture portion. The prospects may prove to be saved people. If so, this will provide the pastor an opportunity to introduce them to the doctrinal beliefs of the church. If not, it will give him a natural opportunity to point out the plan of salvation and explain the gospel. If they are receptive and the Holy Spirit leads, he may give them the opportunity to trust Christ.

Fifth touch. After the pastor's visit, he should send a letter to follow up the presentation given in the home. In this letter he should explain the simplicity with which they could receive Christ and join the church.

The pastor should determine, on the basis of the information he obtained during his visit, which of the classes in the Sunday school might be most effective to influence this particular individual or family for Christ. The prospect's name and pertinent information should be passed along to the leaders of those classes. (The purpose of this will be clarified later.)

Sixth touch. On Saturday evening someone should be appointed to make a phone call to remind the prospect of the Sunday service.

FRIEND DAY

Friend Day is one of the most successful Sunday school attendance campaigns in the church-growth market today. Historically, the Friend Day campaign is attributed to Wendell Zimmerman at Kansas City (Missouri) Baptist Temple, who began using the idea in the late 1950s. Dr. Truman Dollar, who became pastor of the church, improved on the idea. The author further developed the idea, adding church-growth principles and turning it into a tool for all churches.

Friend Day is an evangelistic outreach involving the total membership in a strategy of church growth that uses existing human relationships to reach people. Its success lies in its simplicity; every church member brings a friend. Many churches have used this campaign to double their attendance on Friend Day. Using the campaign follow-up strategy, many churches have experienced a significant and sustained increase in attendance following Friend Day.

The strength of the Friend Day campaign is that it uses a number of principles of church growth, including (1) identifying and reaching receptive-responsive people (qualify prospects), (2) using existing social networks to reach others in the community, (3) using relationships to assimilate new converts to the church, (4) eliminating barriers and ministering to people's felt needs, (5) utilizing people according to their spiritual gifts, and (6) applying the results of church growth research in a workable plan of evangelism.

The purpose of Friend Day is to create momentum in the

minds of the church members. During the worship service, five Sundays before Friend Day, the pastor holds up a letter to the congregation from a town dignitary, who promises to attend as the pastor's friend on Friend Day. This gives credibility and motivation to the rest of the congregation to invite a friend to church.

The following Sunday, members of the church board hold up their letter indicating a friend is attending with them on Friend Day. The third week, Sunday school leaders reinforce Friend Day by displaying their commitment from a friend. This commitment is an enlistment card. A card is then distributed to all church attenders. On the fourth Sunday, each member of the congregation is asked to display commitment cards.

In 1983, the Church Growth Institute of Lynchburg, Virginia, first published a church-growth campaign plan entitled Friend Day. In the next seven years, more than twenty thousand churches used it to reach people for Jesus Christ. Friend Day usually reaches more people than a week-long evangelistic crusade. One denominational office wrote, "Friend Day is the hottest thing going in Sunday school."

The success of Friend Day and widespread interest in a similar follow-up campaign resulted in the recent publication of *The Second Friend Day* by the Church Growth Institute. The new material includes lessons with coloring books for children, sermon outlines, new adult lessons, and two books that help people evangelize their friends.

Both of these resource packets contain all a church needs to conduct a successful evangelistic outreach campaign. They include audio tapes that explain how to use the packet and motivate church boards and Sunday school teachers. Also included are art layouts that can be copied for advertisements and forms to organize and administer the programs. Everything in the packet is reproducible.

A recent survey of four thousand new converts indicated that 70 to 80 percent had chosen a church because they had been invited by a relative or friend. A nationwide survey of both growing and nongrowing congregations revealed that between two-thirds and three-fourths of the members were affiliated with their particular churches because of friendship and kinship ties; and among the members of the fastest growing congregations, a full seven-eighths of the new adult members indicated that they first attended the church at the invitation of a friend or relative.

GIFT ASSIMILATION

This principle means that people tend to assimilate the spiritual gift of those who minister to them; "like produces like." Those with the gift of teaching tend to produce that gift in others. The biblical basis for gift assimilation is, "Therefore I remind you to stir up the gift of God which is in you through the laying on of my hands" (2 Tim. 1:6). As a young man sits in church and hears his pastor exercise his gift of prophecy, the young man learns to preach by that role model. He becomes a "prophet" with a strong ministry of denouncing sin and upholding righteousness.

GIFT CONFIDENCE

Christians who know their spiritual gifts and how to use them are usually the most effective servants of Jesus Christ. They usually make the fewest mistakes, have more confidence in their service for Christ, and have a better attitude about their service. These people do not serve Christ out of guilt, nor are they workaholics. They serve Christ knowing that they are using the spiritual gifts he has given them in a way that they should be used.

Christians should know their spiritual gifts so they will be confident servants of Christ. When one ministers from assurance, he will not be jealous of others; nor will he be anxious about using his own gift in ministry. Also, when others know the biblical teaching on spiritual gifts and have identified their gift, they too can work harmoniously with the whole body. The result is a unified church blessed with God's presence (Matt. 18:20) and power (Acts 2:1-4).

GIFT GRAVITATION

Just as the positive pole on a battery attracts the positive pulse in electricity, so the Bible teaches that "like attracts like." This is seen embryonically in the law of creation, where "each produced after its kind" (Gen. 1:12, 21). Those with the gift of teaching usually find their greatest fulfillment in studying under those who have the gift of teaching. Dallas Theological Seminary is a unique type of seminary that seems to attract young men with an embryonic gift of teaching. They gravitate toward that seminary, where their gift is enhanced, and they graduate to minister their gift of teaching. Certain independent fundamental churches tend to attract people with a gift of prophecy.

GIFT IGNORANCE

Some people are apparently ignorant of their gift and seem to function perfectly well without knowing the technical identification of their spiritual gift. However, the Bible exhorts us to discover our gift (1 Cor. 12:1). While there are many ways to discover our spiritual gift, one that many people have found helpful is by filling out a spiritual gift inventory questionnaire. A number of these spiritual inventory tests may be available at local Christian bookstores. Taking the time to discover or clarify our spiritual gift often saves time and avoids some of the frustrations associated with other trial-and-error methods.

GIFT IMITATION

Gift imitation happens when a Christian tries to implement a spiritual gift he does not have but has seen in others. Some who thought they had found their gift through trial and error, or by emulating someone they admired, may have wrongly tried to minister a gift that they did not have. While these people may produce some spiritual fruit, they may be attempting to serve in a capacity where they do not have the ability to serve God. They are simply imitating a spiritual gift rather than exercising it.

GIFT INTRUSION

Those who are guilty of gift intrusion try to make everyone fit into their mold or to use their spiritual gifts. They try to get people to use gifts that are not theirs.

GIFT MANIPULATION
When one person tries to use a spiritual gift that is not indigenously his, he is guilty of gift manipulation.

GIVING, GIFT OF
The person with the gift of giving has the ability to invest material resources in other persons and ministries to further the purpose of God. The strengths of this gift include (1) the ability to organize his personal life to make money, (2) the desire to give quietly and secretly, (3) a tendency to give out of a sense of need, (4) a sincere desire to see a ministry grow, (5) a sensitivity to quality, (6) an involvement with his giving, and (7) a tendency to become a positive role model for others. Among the weaknesses of this gift are: (1) others may feel he gives for an outward impression; (2) others may feel he overemphasizes money; and (3) he may be perceived as being selfish. The individual with this gift needs to avoid the dangers of (1) pride, (2) measuring others' spirituality by their prosperity, or (3) insensitivity to the needs of others because of their apparent lack of personal discipline.

GOALS, ATTENDANCE
How can a Sunday school superintendent motivate the teachers to carry our the great commission? The superintendent should discuss goals with the teachers individually and corporately in a teachers' meeting. Ask each teacher to set a class goal. This should provide internal motivation for each teacher because it should be a personal goal and external motivation because the attendance goal for each class should be public.

How to Set Goals for Sunday School
Set attendance goals. Usually, a class will not grow unless there is an aim to grow. First, set a long-range attendance goal. Next, set a yearly goal. A goal will keep vision lifted and a challenge before the people. Then set a goal for a high day in the spring or fall.

Usually, one overall attendance goal will not stir all people in your class. That is why it is advisable to set multiple goals during a Sunday school campaign. This gets several things working for you. Each of several specific goals will challenge the specific need to which it is tied, and each will bring about a specific result. Many goals will create momentum and excitement in the church. The following may be achieved during a Sunday school campaign: (1) an all-time attendance record, (2) the highest average attendance for the spring or fall, (3) the highest average attendance for the year, (4) enrollment goals, (5) departmental goals, (6) the greatest number of visitors, (7) the greatest number of visits made by a worker, (8) the greatest number of phone calls made, and (9) the greatest number of postcards written.

Set output goals. Now that goals have been discussed, they need to be refined. Among the goals you set, you will need some output goals. These are the bottom line of expected results. In computer terminology, *output* is the result of what you put into the computer. If your class base is fifteen, set an attendance output goal of thirty. This means you want the class to double during the campaign. When output goals are established, go to the next refinement—input goal.

Set input goals. The second type of goals you need to set are input goals. These are steps that need to be taken to reach a goal. Just as we must recognize certain causes lead to effects, so input goals include the things you need to do to reach your output goals.

One type of input goal is finding and making a list of new prospects. In order for your class to double, attempt to formulate a list of twice as many prospects as your average attendance. When you reach your input goal of twice as many prospects, you have a basis to expect the output goal; that is, the class doubles. This means that if each member suggests two names of friends he will bring to church, the class has reached its input goal. If there are thirty in the class, get sixty names on your prospect list. Success in input goals gives the class a sense of success. This will lead to confidence as it pursues output goals.

Be sure to educate your people to the attendance goals. If you set a goal of thirty in attendance, prepare several posters that display the goal of thirty. Saturate your pupils with the goal.

Advertise your attendance goals. This will help people identify with the goal and will build excitement and enthusiasm as the class works together to reach the goal. Unless everyone accepts the goal, it will not be achieved. Remember, goals must be bought and owned or the goal will not motivate class members to work for growth.

Be sure you are setting reachable goals. Goals that are unreachable discourage people and kill momentum. A missed goal is like a broken bone in the body—it takes a long time to heal. When you set an unreachable goal and fail to reach it, class members will be reluctant to support a reachable goal the next time. Set *smart* goals when you set goals. A *smart* goal is *s*pecific, *m*easurable, *a*ttainable, *r*eachable, and *t*ime table oriented.

Know strengths and weaknesses. Know the strengths and weaknesses of your class before setting your goals. If your class members have a wide circle of friends outside the church, you will have a larger prospect base with which to work. Conversely, if the class is inbred with few contacts outside the class, it will be more difficult to find the needed prospects. Sometimes the class has problems, and it is not the time to reach out. If there is someone who has a recent death or crisis in the family, the members may be preoccupied with these problems and not mentally ready for outreach. Knowing your strengths will help you feel the pulse of your class. Also, if the church has corporately gone through a split, a financial crisis, leadership problems, or any other major setback, it should evaluate carefully when would be the best time for an outreach campaign. Just as there are times when the sick need to go to bed to recuperate, so there is a time for church "*in*reach," not outreach.

Examine past statistics to determine the best time to plan your outreach day, the day you want class members to bring their friends, relatives, associates, and neighbors to the class. Generally, the Sunday with the biggest attendance in the fall of the year tends to be the last Sunday in October (time change Sunday). The Sunday with the largest attendance in the spring is traditionally

Easter. The second-highest attendance in the spring is usually on Mother's Day.

Choose a day that does not have built-in barriers to the unchurched. Don't plan Sunday school outreach for Labor Day weekend or during the Fourth of July holiday, when there is a natural dip in attendance. The minister who tried to have his largest attendance on Labor Day weekend, or the Sunday after Easter, claiming, "Anybody can get a crowd on Easter; I want to build an attendance to show our people love God," had missed the whole purpose of an attendance campaign. A high attendance should do more than demonstrate the loyalty of the faithful. It should reach visitors (preevangelism), electrify everyone when the attendance is doubled, and bring men, women, and children to a saving faith in Jesus Christ. So plan for Sunday school growth when the best results are possible. Then you will be a good steward of time, energy, and money. Therefore, plan to grow on those days when there are the fewest attendance barriers and the unchurched are most likely to attend.

If you are planning a campaign for several Sundays, plan a high attendance on the last Sunday of your campaign. Some criticize this, saying that it only gets a crowd and makes small class teaching impossible. However, the "high day" is only a return to the old-fashioned rally day, where all pupils assembled in the auditorium to "rally" enthusiasm for Sunday school. Most teachers need to break lethargy and infuse the pupils with enthusiasm. A "double day" convinces the pupils it can be done again and again, until the class is permanently doubled.

Pray for God's guidance in setting your goals. Set a goal to do what you believe God wants you to do. Long before you set an attendance goal or choose an outreach campaign, add the item to your prayer list. (1) Ask God to give you wisdom in setting goals and campaigns. (2) Pray over them until you feel comfortable about the goals or campaigns. (3) Consider the problems and barriers before publicly announcing the task. (4) When you finally make a decision by prayer, then get off your knees and make it work out in reality.

The one unique feature of the church leaders of growing churches around the world is that they are people of faith. Just as a church plans an evangelistic endeavor by faith to reach people with the gospel (revival meeting, literature distribution, or youth rally), so leaders can plan a Sunday school outreach campaign, which is a corporate expression of faith. When a person is converted, it is the result of the faith of the leaders and the followers.

Make sure your goals are biblical, that they fit the principles of the Bible. Proof-texting is not enough; goals should grow out of Bible study and be in harmony with the Scriptures. This is always a good procedure when attempting to discern the will of God.

GRADING

Every Sunday school, regardless of its size, should be age graded for growth. Grading recognizes the unique differences between various age groups and the positive potential of peer grouping. By closely grading a Sunday school (one class for each school grade), teachers are able to teach a more relevant Sunday school lesson that meets the particular needs of the students in his class. Also, grading helps Sunday schools grow, as visitors to Sunday school are immediately introduced to a group of people with similar interests.

There are four grading plans for schools of various sizes.

The class Sunday school or the one room Sunday school. In the smallest schools pupils are divided into broad age divisions with a teacher for each group. Each teacher reports to a general director or superintendent of the Sunday school.

Class/Age

Nursery: birth to 1
Toddlers: 1 to 2
Preschool: 3 to 5
Primary: 6 to 8
Juniors: 9 to 11
Young Teens: 12 to 13
High School: 14 to 17
Young Adults: 18 to 24
Middle Adults: 25 to 59
Senior Adults: 60 and up

The departmental Sunday school. In a somewhat larger Sunday school, the Cradle Roll and Home Departments are added. Classes are divided into six groups. In this plan six department superintendents are needed. Some teachers may also serve as department superintendents.

The age graded or closely graded Sunday school. For a still larger school, even more classes and departments are needed, with superintendents who are not teachers. There may be several classes in each department.

The larger, closely graded Sunday school has one or more classes for each age group. The departments are headed by superintendents who are not teachers; therefore, at least twelve department superintendents are needed.

GRAPHS

Graphs are excellent teaching aids for making contrasts and comparisons or presenting complicated facts and statistics. Graphs that are involved and difficult are not as effective. The graph should tell the story at a glance, with little explanation needed.

Types of graphs include:

1. Bar graph—bars arranged horizontally or vertically
2. Pie graph—resembles a pie and is useful for presenting a breakdown or distribution
3. Line graph—useful to depict trends
4. Pictorial graph—tells the story by illustrations; more difficult to produce, but more effective

GROWTH, LAWS OF SUNDAY SCHOOL

The laws of Sunday school growth reflect averages in Sunday school attendance over the years. They are proven by experience and will work in any Sunday school regardless of size, type, or clientele.

1. Enrollment increases in proportion to workers at a ratio of ten to one. Almost every Sunday school has ten times as many students as teachers. Therefore the law necessitates at least one teacher for every ten students in the Sunday school. Generally, when there is a larger ratio of workers, it

CHART FOR GRADING SUNDAY SCHOOLS

Reprinted by permission from United Evangelical Action, *official publication of the National Association of Evangelicals.*

CLOSELY GRADED PLAN

Find Your Present Enrollment and Grade to Grow	CRADLE ROLL (TO 2 YEARS)	NURSERY (2-3 YEARS)	KINDER-GARTEN (4-5 YEARS)	PRIMARY (AGES 6-7-8)			JUNIOR (AGES 9-10-11)			JUNIOR HIGH (AGES 12-13-14)			HIGH SCHOOL (AGES 15-16-17)			YOUNG PEOPLE (AGES 18-24)	ADULTS (AGES 25-UP)
250 AND UP	USE CRADLE ROLL KIT	USE NURSERY LESSONS	USE KINDER-GARTEN LESSONS	GRADE 1 USE FIRST GRADE LESSONS	GRADE 2 USE SECOND GRADE LESSONS	GRADE 3 USE THIRD GRADE LESSONS	GRADE 4 USE FOURTH GRADE LESSONS	GRADE 5 USE FIFTH GRADE LESSONS	GRADE 6 USE SIXTH GRADE LESSONS	GRADE 7 USE SEVENTH GRADE LESSONS	GRADE 8 USE EIGHTH GRADE LESSONS	GRADE 9 USE NINTH GRADE LESSONS	GRADE 10 USE TENTH GRADE LESSONS	GRADE 11 USE ELEVENTH GRADE LESSONS	GRADE 12 USE TWELFTH GRADE LESSONS	COLLEGE YOUNG SINGLE YOUNG MARRIED USE ADULT BIBLE SERIES	GRADED ADULTS WOMEN MEN MIXED USE ADULT BIBLE SERIES
200 TO 250	USE CRADLE ROLL KIT	USE NURSERY LESSONS	USE KINDER-GARTEN LESSONS	GRADE 1 USE FIRST GRADE LESSONS	GRADE 2 USE SECOND GRADE LESSONS	GRADE 3 USE THIRD GRADE LESSONS	GRADE 4 USE FOURTH GRADE LESSONS	GRADE 5 USE FIFTH GRADE LESSONS	GRADE 6 USE SIXTH GRADE LESSONS	GRADE 7 USE SEVENTH GRADE LESSONS	GRADE 8 USE EIGHTH GRADE LESSONS	GRADE 9 USE NINTH GRADE LESSONS	GRADE 10 USE TENTH GRADE LESSONS	GRADE 11 USE ELEVENTH GRADE LESSONS	GRADE 12 USE TWELFTH GRADE LESSONS	COLLEGE YOUNG SINGLE YOUNG MARRIED USE ADULT BIBLE SERIES	GRADED ADULTS WOMEN MEN MIXED USE ADULT BIBLE SERIES
150 TO 200	USE CRADLE ROLL KIT	USE NURSERY LESSONS	USE KINDER-GARTEN LESSONS	GRADE 1 USE FIRST GRADE LESSONS	GRADE 2 USE SECOND GRADE LESSONS	GRADE 3 USE THIRD GRADE LESSONS	GRADE 4 USE FOURTH GRADE LESSONS	GRADE 5 USE FIFTH GRADE LESSONS	GRADE 6 USE SIXTH GRADE LESSONS	GRADE 7 USE SEVENTH GRADE LESSONS	GRADES 8, 9 BEGIN WITH EIGHTH GRADE LESSONS AND ROTATE THROUGH 9TH GRADE			GRADES 11 and 12 BEGIN WITH ELEVENTH GRADE LESSONS AND ROTATE THROUGH 12TH GRADE			COLLEGE YOUNG SINGLE YOUNG MARRIED USE ADULT BIBLE SERIES	GRADED ADULTS WOMEN MEN MIXED USE ADULT BIBLE SERIES

DEPARTMENTAL GRADED PLAN

Find Your Present Enrollment and Grade to Grow	CRADLE ROLL (TO 2 YEARS)	NURSERY (2-3 YEARS)	KINDER-GARTEN (4-5 YEARS)	PRIMARY (AGES 6-7-8)	JUNIOR (AGES 9-10-11)	JUNIOR HIGH (AGES 12-13-14)	HIGH SCHOOL (AGES 15-16-17)	YOUNG PEOPLE (AGES 18-24)	ADULTS (AGES 25 & OLDER)
100 TO 150	USE CRADLE ROLL KIT	USE NURSERY LESSONS	USE KINDER-GARTEN LESSONS	GRADE 1 USE FIRST GRADE LESSONS · GRADES 2, 3 BEGIN WITH 2ND GRADE LESSONS AND ROTATE THROUGH 3RD GRADE	GRADE 4 USE FOURTH GRADE LESSONS · GRADES 5, 6 BEGIN WITH FIFTH GRADE LESSONS AND ROTATE THROUGH 6TH GRADE	GRADE 7 USE SEVENTH GRADE LESSONS · GRADES 8, 9 BEGIN WITH EIGHTH GRADE LESSONS AND ROTATE THROUGH 9TH GRADE	GRADE 10 USE TENTH GRADE LESSONS · GRADES 11 and 12 BEGIN WITH ELEVENTH GRADE LESSONS AND ROTATE THROUGH 12TH GRADE	USE ADULT BIBLE SERIES	USE ADULT BIBLE SERIES
LESS THAN 100	USE CRADLE ROLL KIT	PRE-SCHOOL USE KINDERGARTEN LESSONS		COMBINED PRIMARY LESSONS These books have been especially designed for the smallest church where it is necessary to combine primary grades into one class.	GRADES 4, 5, 6 BEGIN WITH FOURTH GRADE LESSONS AND ROTATE THROUGH 5TH AND 6TH GRADES	GRADES 7, 8, 9 BEGIN WITH SEVENTH GRADE LESSONS THROUGH 8TH AND 9TH GRADES	GRADES 10, 11, 12 BEGIN WITH TENTH GRADE LESSONS ROTATE THRU 11TH and 12TH	GRADES 10, 11, 12 (Or combine 10th with J. H. and 11th and 12th with Young People's Class) BEGIN TENTH GRADE LESSONS ROTATE THRU 11TH and 12TH	USE ADULT BIBLE SERIES

is because the workers are not adequately fulfilling their job as Sunday school teachers to reach, teach, win, and mature their students in the Word of God. In contrast, a church with unusual effort and hard work may lift this ratio for a while, but it is most difficult to maintain large classes for a period of more than a few months unless there are extraneous circumstances or unusual pressure by the teacher.

There are a few large classes in our Sunday schools that are doing the job. But they are the exception rather than the rule. The large classes are usually built around a strong personality. Total Sunday school growth usually comes from new classes, not from old large classes. The first law of Sunday school growth would imply several principles:

a. Begin new classes. A Sunday school, by reducing its ratio of ten to one, will quite often grow. If the possibilities justify this expansion, and if the new units work to reach their neighborhood, the new class will soon be lifted to the ten to one ratio if the other laws of growth are applied. We grow by creating new units and conquering new territory.

b. Teacher training. We cannot create new classes without having trained workers to take over the new classes. Hence, it is necessary to start teacher training classes to provide more workers. Most Sunday schools think that the way to grow is to first get students and then provide the teachers and send them out to enlist new students. Hence, teacher training is important to the growth of a Sunday school.

c. Class average. The average for the entire Sunday school should be a ratio of ten to one. However, the individual class may vary. The average class size for preschoolers is about five; for primaries, seven; for juniors, nine; for young people, thirteen. The average class enrollment for adults varies from fifteen in churches with a more limited constituency to about twenty-five in churches with more people. Some churches have even more when there are many available adults. The average for all the Sunday school is still ten to one when you add the Sunday school superintendent, the department superintendent, and other workers.

2. The building sets the pattern for educational growth. This law indicates the Sunday school takes the shape of the building. It is difficult to put a growing Sunday school into a small building. A Sunday school takes the shape of the building it occupies. A Sunday school that has ten teaching centers will have difficulty growing beyond 100 in attendance (in keeping with our first rule that the enrollment increases in proportion to teachers at a ratio of ten to one). Growth demands new teaching centers with more space for addition of classes.

It is difficult for a Sunday school to grow beyond the capacity of the building. There is a high correlation between the square footage, available space, and the growth of a Sunday school.

Time is needed to provide space. Extra classrooms should be on the preferred list for growth. If your church has come to the decision that it must provide more space to grow, then one of the following plans should be adopted.

   a. If your Sunday school is now constructed on a class basis, plan your space so that your Sunday school may be graded by departments.

   b. If your Sunday school now has one department for each age group, plan space for at least two departments for each age group.

   c. Make plans to move toward a multiple department program.

3. Sunday school units usually reach maximum growth in a few months. Once a new class has been created, the new unit will reach an optimum limit. Then it is time, if the conditions are favorable, to create another new class. To think that a class will grow beyond the suggestions of the laws of growth, even though left over a number of years, is a false concept. Hence, the addition of new classes rather than the expansion of present classes is the way of growth.

Fruit always comes through new growth, and Sunday school enthusiasm, energy, and outreach comes from new classes. Usually these new classes win more to Christ and provide more workers. New classes produce growth in a twofold manner. First, growth comes in the total number of new students; and second, there is growth potential through providing more teachers for other classes.

4. Dividing classes by school grades provides the logical basis for adding new units. Grading a Sunday school means arranging classes for people of the same age or nearly the same age in order to localize needs. Teaching is meeting needs. Grading by ages offers several strengths to the Sunday school: It helps the teacher to meet individual needs, locates responsibility for each period of life, locates and overcomes neglected areas, simplifies the teacher's task, makes the creation of needed classes easy, anticipates a student's advancement in life, and provides a basis for promotion. Grading breaks down social and class lines, preventing a class from enlisting easy prospects and neglecting needy students. It also recognizes the natural stages of life, and it is scriptural because it meets the individual where he is and attempts to lift him to where he should be. Grading makes for Sunday school growth because it puts more teachers to work for Sunday school and for Christ while paving the way to promote the necessary factor in the normal growth of a Sunday school. Students are placed with others their age, and lessons are geared to their needs.

5. Enrollment and attendance increase in proportion to outreach. The other laws of Sunday school growth are useless without evangelism. Soul winning is the practical application of spiritual concern for men. In a good outreach program, there is lay-centered evangelism.

Attendance is increased in proportion to outreach. Statistics indicate that growth follows the number of contacts made with lost people. Recently, a survey indicated that when eight or nine contacts were made with each visitor, he was likely to return to the church and be bonded into fellowship with that church. These Sunday school laws are built on vision, progress, and planning ahead. If you believe attendance increases in proportion to workers at the ratio of ten to one, then you will employ vision, plan ahead, and provide space for growth. If you believe that new classes will reach optimum size in a few months, you will continue to add new classes and become progressive in organizational growth. If you want to keep the students you have, reach those in your area, and teach them all effectively, you will grade them by ages. If you have the vision to believe the above laws will work, you will evangelize the lost and build a Sunday school for the glory of God.

GROWTH, MEASURING SUNDAY SCHOOL

Sunday school growth is measured by five factors: (1) growth in attendance, (2) growth in enrollment, (3) growth in financial income, (4) growth in physical facilities, and (5) growth in programs and services to individuals. Spiritual growth is not immediately implied in these criteria, although it cannot be neglected. Even though some consider spiritual growth as unmeasurable, its resulting change in attitudes, values, and actions can be measured through observation and tests.

HANDCRAFTS

Correlated handcrafts are teaching aids that reinforce the truths of the lesson. These handcrafts are distinguished from busy work by their correlation with the lesson emphasis. Correlated handwork should be creative. The student should be able to detect its purpose. Handwork may include a great variety of things, from drawing to constructing models to keeping notebooks.

Handcrafts should make the truth of the lesson more vivid. They should accomplish this more economically than another technique. They should clarify concepts for the pupil in a way that stories alone could not do.

Advantages of Handcrafts
1. Handcrafts develop mental coordination, manual agility, problem-solving skills, and ability to follow directions.
2. The process promotes unity within the group, yet leaves room for creativity.
3. Completing a craft provides a sense of accomplishment and a feeling of confidence. Crafts could open areas of hobby interest for further pursuit.
4. Handcrafts clarify concepts for pupils and make truths more vivid and real.
5. Handling objects helps to establish a sense of chronology or historical sequence difficult to achieve through storytelling alone.

Weaknesses of Handcrafts
1. Since people work at different rates, some finish before

others and become bored. Also, people are gifted with various abilities. All people are not equally adept at any given project.

2. Most leather and plastic crafts are expensive, and materials cannot be procured easily.
3. Not all crafts are adaptable for all age levels.
4. While handcrafts should be utilized with a definite purpose in mind, often they are merely time fillers.
5. It is often difficult to relate handcrafts to theology, except through relating them to stories.
6. Handcrafts require a lot of working room and storage and display space.
7. Some handcrafts are messy and unsuitable for Sunday attire.

Principles for Use of Handcrafts

1. Provide situations and experiences so that each child grows in creative ability and learns how to work well with a group.
2. Guard against the tendency to make handwork an end in itself. Be sure the activity helps achieve the purposes of the unit of study. Handwork is justified only as it contributes to learning.
3. Handwork should, if possible, be interspersed with mental activities to make a total learning situation. Handcrafts should be a necessary part of the most effective teaching, not something tacked onto the lesson period.
4. The handwork activity should teach something of value that could not be taught more effectively another way.
5. Choose activities suited to the age of the boys and girls and that arouse a desire to discover, to learn, to work in the group, and to share.
6. Motivate expressional activities by using poetry, hymns, Bible verses, pictures, and conversation.
7. Avoid asking the pupils to do something too difficult or too simple. To encourage originality, the work should be within the range of the pupils' abilities.
8. Quality of product should never take precedence over

teaching value. Yet the pupil should think well enough of his project to put forth his best effort.

9. Recognize each child's efforts to create, and help him learn how to improve. Maintain proper balance between the pupil's initiative and teacher help.
10. The teacher is the guide and must make adequate and careful preparation to see that the work accomplishes its purposes.
11. Provide opportunities for constructive criticism so that each child may improve what he does.
12. Give definite directions on how to use materials for the first time, such as how to wipe a paint brush to avoid dripping.
13. Avoid undertaking to guide pupils in projects that you do not know how to do.
14. Prepare and provide all the necessary materials, supplies, and equipment.
15. The pupil should see the value in the work. He should recognize how the handwork furthers the lesson's objectives.
16. Clarify the spiritual values to be realized.
17. Evaluate what has been done in the light of the purpose.

Effectiveness

Whether behavior problems result from poor teaching or from poor child training by parents, the proper use of handwork may eliminate behavioral problems. A teacher noted that the troublemaker in his class was a caricaturist. The child had made a drawing on the chalkboard before class. The drawing depicted the teacher holding the pupils with chains. In the discussion that followed the students complained that they had heard the Bible stories before, and they were never allowed to express themselves. One pupil suggested making a mural like they did in public school. The teacher suggested a mural of the life of David, which they were studying. The troublemaker was appointed adviser of the project. Today he is a dependable layman in the church.

Some pupils make trouble. Others are simply bored. With the proper use of handcrafts, both will respond, becoming involved and committed. They may even show enthusiasm.

Use According to Age Level

The question is not so much what kind of handcrafts should be used for each age level, but rather what use can any particular handicraft have with the age in question. Some things, like models, can be adapted to any age level. The important factors are physical and mental abilities. These vary with the person as well as with the age. The interest of the student is a vital factor in using handcrafts.

1. Preschool—The child is not expected to make something according to adult standards. He should experience freedom and satisfying activity. The child mostly plays, and toys are important at this stage. He draws or models life as he sees it, thus revealing much about himself.

2. Grades 1–2—The child can now draw pictures and is proud of his ability to write. He likes to build models, although he is just beginning. Puppets are popular. He needs much guidance. The home is the center of his life, and projects should be related to this subject.

3. Grades 3–4—Because they need to develop skills, making things is important in their learning process. They need to gain confidence, make something worthwhile, gain a feeling of achievement, and recognize their ability to contribute to a group. They are able to do basic research.

4. Grades 5–6—The teacher ought to think in terms of projects such as notebooks, collections, or writing an artistic work within the scope of a project. The junior can make useful things.

5. Junior high—Projects create interest; however, free choice must be given to the student so he can pursue his own interests. Intermediates can take on responsibility and are very capable. Charts, displays, notebooks, and more complex projects are possible.

6. High school—Service projects can be exploited, for the high school student would be more inclined to make something for someone. Creative writing or artistic expression connected with worship symbols are possibilities. Teenagers are capable of complex projects.

HANDICAPPED, MINISTRY TO THE

Definition

A handicapped child is one who, by reason of physical, psychological, or emotional problems, is unable to benefit from the regular instruction provided to "normal" children.

1. Mentally retarded. (See Retarded, Ministry to the)
2. Slow learner. This child's IQ is just above that of the educable retarded. In most Sunday schools, he is placed in the regular class of normal children.
3. Superintelligent. Some children with an above-average IQ find instruction in a normal routine to be lacking in interest and challenge for them.
4. Hard of hearing. (see Deaf, Ministry to the)
5. Physically handicapped. In this category are children who cannot walk or talk normally due to cerebral palsy, birth injury, polio, or some other disabling disease, and those with an inherent heart weakness or other limiting condition.
6. Blind. While the blind student is usually in a state school for the blind much of the year, he will spend vacation times at home and accompany his family to their regular church. Older blind persons also may attend.

Special Education

The public school has for many years provided classes in special education to meet the needs of children with some type of variation from normality. Such classes may require an environment, equipment, and teaching methods exceeding those for the normal pupils.

1. *Classroom.* The room size and location should be adapted to the need. If a wheelchair patient is to be a regular pupil in a classroom, the room should be large enough so that the wheelchair will not have to be the center of attention. A ramp will be needed for any area of stairs.
2. *Seating arrangement.* A pupil with an impairment of vision or hearing (but neither blind or deaf) may need a seat near the teacher in order to share in the sights and sounds of the lesson.

3. *Room decoration.* Subdued, neutral colors (such as soft green, blue, or buff walls, and a charcoal or green floor covering) will serve as calming factors to children who tend to be hyperactive or easily excitable. Cheerfulness without gaudiness is the rule.

4. *Methods.* In the various articles in this volume on specific teaching methods are many suggestions for visual aids that will help make lessons clear to slow learners. During picture studies, activity games, puppet presentations, role play, or other group involvement procedures, the teacher will need to be sure the handicapped child is able to participate in accordance with his ability. He, too, learns most by doing. In fact, he may learn more than some of his less-afflicted peers. His eagerness may exceed theirs, as may his future use of the knowledge gained.

While most Sunday school teachers are unable to have the special training required for teaching all pupils with a disability, they have God's promise to supply the wisdom needed if they will ask for it (James 1:5).

5. *Counseling.* Handicapped persons, even children, often are well aware that they are different from others. This causes grief to some whose body has not kept pace with their mental growth. The Sunday school teacher may be the one to counsel with parents as well as the child in an effort to impart courage and determination to all. Illustrations abound of handicapped persons who have excelled in life. One need only remember perhaps the most outstanding case of all—Helen Keller—to know that God can use any life truly dedicated to him. He asks no more than an individual is able to give.

HELPERS (See also F.R.A.N.GELISM)

This term is used here, not in a general way, but technically in the F.R.A.N.gelism program. Helpers are members of the evangelism team, probably with the gift of ministry (helps) or administration, who look after the records, getting the right people to the right thing at the right time. They keep records, which include basic data on prospects, sick calls, new converts to follow up, absentees, or those with special problems. Other helpers may work in preparing meeting rooms or catering the fellowship meal.

HISTORY OF SUNDAY SCHOOL

Robert Raikes, of Gloucester, England, the founder of the Sunday school, became a newspaper editor at age twenty-two. He took over *The Gloucester Journal* from his father in 1757. People called him "Buck Raikes, the dandy" because of his immaculate attire. His children grew up in the clean comfort of a good home. They went to church every Sunday. In an effort to improve the beauty of that good home, the publisher went one afternoon to the rough slum district in search of a gardener. He was jostled by a gang of ragged boys and later expressed his shock and pity to the gardener's wife.

"You ought to see them on Sunday, when the factory is closed and they have nothing to do but get in trouble," she responded. Apparently they did everything in the book.

Raikes was a churchman who carried his religion into his business. He had been concerned about the plight of poor men and women who frequently crowded the city jail for the most trivial offenses. He wrote editorials against conditions in the jail. He went to the jail, handing Bibles to the few who could read. Raikes stayed to read the Word to some who could not.

After his rough reception in the slums, Robert Raikes expressed his concern about the children left at home alone while parents served their undeserved sentences. With hate, fear, and ignorance filling their lives, they had no chance to be anything but the half-wild creatures he had seen. Raikes took the problem to the Reverend Thomas Stock.

The pastor collected names and addresses of ninety children in his own parish, and together the two men put on a strenuous visitation campaign. If they expected a warm reception everywhere, they were disappointed. Some of the parents cursed them. But in time the men gathered a class into the kitchen of a Christian woman, Mrs. Meredith. The minister became the first Sunday school superintendent, and Mrs. Meredith at first did the teaching.

Robert Raikes did not start his Sunday school merely by announcing time and place. He went to the homes and brought the pupils. If some did not have sufficient clothing to come, he bought it for them. What was the price of a pair of shoes or a pair of trousers when the investment netted a life in return? Many of his biographers claimed that Raikes marched unwilling pupils to the class with their feet hobbled like animals. One of those pupils later gave an explanation. It was the parents of some of the wild urchins who put on the hobbles to make sure they got to school. Raikes' pupils learned to read, and they read lessons directly from the Bible. Raikes also wrote four textbooks used in Sunday schools.

Robert Raikes thus began planting the seed. His pupils would grow up to become godly parents and, in turn, raise godly children. Thus began the work of lifting the city from the mire of godlessness into which it had sunk. Taught to read and encouraged to read the Word of God, the boys and girls in those first classes began to respond. The Sunday school areas became the most orderly in the city of Gloucester.

Not until three years later did Raikes use his newspaper as a platform to promote the Sunday school. When the evidence was indisputable, he informed his readers that his thesis had been correct. Starting with the children, the lives of the slum-dwellers were being transformed. His enthusiastic report caught the eyes of Christian leaders in other vice-ridden areas; they responded to the plea of Robert Raikes and started Sunday schools throughout the nation. John Wesley urged, "There must be a Sunday school wherever there is a Methodist Society."

The first Sunday school began at 10:00 A.M. At noon they had a break, then returned for another lesson. Then it was time for the whole group to be taken to church. This at first was as disagreeable to the parishioners as to the urchins.

At first only boys were enrolled, but almost immediately both boys and girls were accepted. Discipline problems were many and severe among the lawless scholars. Indeed, the children were so unruly that the first teacher, Mrs. Meredith, resigned from her post shortly. The school's founder himself and a helper accompanied the offenders to their homes, watched while the punishing wallops were administered, and brought the chastened pupils back to class. No doubt the fact that the first teachers were paid for their services and could use the kitchen slightly eased the task.

However, Robert Raikes suggested that instructors, as well as monitors, should be volunteers. (His classes employed the system of using advanced pupils to help teach the younger children.) As Sunday school became increasingly a religious agency, Raikes's conviction grew that the workers should be voluntary.

In a letter Robert Raikes reported that in four years the Sunday school average enrollment reached 250,000 children. The 1785 "Society for the Support and Encouragement of Sunday School throughout the British Dominions" (understandably shortened to "The Sunday School Society") was largely responsible for the rapid expansion of the movement. Their effort and finances founded and financed the schools.

Robert Raikes died in 1811. By the time a statue was erected in his memory in 1831, Sunday schools in Great Britain were ministering weekly to 1,250,000 children.

The American Sunday School Movement

The people of Savannah, Georgia, claim that the Sunday school started fifty years before Raikes, when John Wesley taught the children there on Sunday afternoons. Even though Wesley did instruct children, his classes were not technically considered a Sunday school because his efforts concerned the children of Christians, catechism instruction, and the aim of edification.

A Sunday school has four unique characteristics: (1) it reaches both Christian and unsaved children; (2) its curriculum is the Word of God, rather than the catechism; (3) the purpose is to reach children for Christ through the ministry of teaching, rather than strictly edifying the children of the faithful; and (4) it is operated by laymen, whereas Wesley was a clergyman. The nature of the true Sunday school cancels out Wesley's claim and reinforces Raikes's position as founder.

The first recorded American Sunday school was held in 1785 at Oak Grove, Virginia, by William Elliot. Both whites and blacks were instructed but at separate hours.

The Methodists were among the first to start Sunday schools, hence their phenomenal growth as a denomination in the United States. Francis Asbury established a Sunday school in Virginia in 1786. In rapid succession Sunday schools sprang up in South Carolina, Maryland, Rhode Island, New York, and Pennsylvania. Within eleven years after Robert Raikes began the first Sunday school in England, a new Sunday school society organized in Philadelphia in 1791. Within three months they raised $3,968 for the establishment of Sunday schools. Sunday school societies soon appeared in other cities.

The Sunday schools that mushroomed all over the United States tied heavily to evangelism, whereas the movement in England was tied heavily to general education. Denominations began organizing their own Sunday schools as they saw their children going to interdenominational agencies. The movement grew at first in the established eastern seaboard cities.

From the early days Sunday schools had contests. Robert Raikes gave away books, shoes, and pants for faithful attendance. Once he offered a twenty-dollar gold piece to any boy who could memorize the book of Proverbs. Toward the end of the 1700s the Christ Congregational Church, New York, gave a silver medal to the scholar bringing the most visitors during the year.

Lowell Mason, the songwriter, and superintendent of the Savannah (Georgia) Sabbath School, wrote out this regulation in 1818: "Tickets are given for good behavior in school and in church, for diligently attending to lessons and memorizing Scripture. Extra tickets shall be given for extra lessons, discretionally by the teacher." Mason also wrote, "Anyone who procures a new scholar shall receive a monthly ticket." A ticket was worth one-sixteenth of a dollar and could be exchanged for books.

Around 1825 the Mississippi Valley enterprise captured the imagination of Sunday school leaders on the eastern seaboard. The area west of the Alleghenies to the Rocky Mountains had a population of 4 million people in 1.3 million square miles. The area was almost devoid of religious influence. The American Sunday School Union spearheaded a massive evangelistic thrust. In May 1830 they made a resolution to start a Sunday school in every town in the Mississippi Valley. They wanted to complete the project in two years. Two thousand people voted unanimously and subscribed more than $17,000 to the project. Large gatherings in Boston, Washington, and Charleston kicked off the project, including United States senators, representatives, and notables such as Daniel Webster and Francis Scott Key. More than eighty missionaries were employed and sent out. They planted libraries throughout the Midwest, each costing approximately ten dollars for more than fifty books. It has been estimated that more than one million volumes were thus placed in circulation, giving further momentum to the growth of literacy in the United States.

One of the most renowned of those missionaries was a man in the pioneer territory of Illinois, himself reached for Christ through the American Sunday School Union. "Stuttering Stephen" Paxson had to overcome the double handicap of a limp and a stammer to become a successful hatter—and favorite fiddler for the Saturday night square dance in Winchester, Illinois.

"I'll get a star if I bring a new scholar to Sunday school," said his little daughter Mary one Sunday. She had decided that her father would be her scholar. The tired dance fiddler went, and he found himself sitting in a class of boys who helped explain to him the hard words of the lesson. In a short time he learned that God had a place for music in his program, and Paxson's fiddle added to the enjoyment of the services. It soon became apparent that God had other plans for him in his program.

Through an American Sunday School Union missionary, Paxson caught the vision of the great task the Union had laid out. Moving his little family to the Mississippi Valley, nearer the action, he set out on his horse to establish Sunday schools. Over the next twenty-five years, horse and rider traveled 100,000 miles. The animal habitually stopped to wait for Stephen Paxson to speak to any child they passed. Eighty-three thousand children were reached for God in the 1,314 Sunday schools established by this zealous missionary.

During the next fifty years 80 percent of all the churches in the Mississippi Valley came out of Sunday schools. In one year alone 17,000 people made professions of faith. From 1824 to 1874 there were 61,299 Sunday schools organized with 407,244 teachers and 2,650,784 pupils. The total amount spent on this endeavor was $2,133,364. As one observer noted, never had so much been accomplished for God with such a small down payment. Another stated, "We could not do it today—that is, start a Sunday school for one dollar per person." But there were a lot of people who were willing to sacrifice in those days.

Clarence Benson, writer on the Sunday school, called that era "the Babel period" because there was no Sunday school literature. Each teacher taught the Word of God the best that he could. Many Sunday schools during this period followed the successful technique later used by the *Ten Largest Sunday Schools,* where the pastor instructs his people at the teachers' meeting. On Sunday the teachers give the identical lesson to their pupils.

Sunday schools took a decided upturn immediately after the war between the states. Mr. Vincent, a Methodist minister, published *The Sunday School Teacher* in 1866, in which he called for a curriculum that would comprehensively and consistently cover the Scripture. Out of this grew a curriculum that most denominations followed. *The International Uniform Lesson* came into existence. *The Sunday School Times,* first published in 1866, became the vehicle to spread Sunday school lessons throughout America. At one time it had the largest circulation of any magazine in the United States.

Massive Sunday school conventions also grew after the war between the states, although the conventions had been officially organized earlier. The first international convention was held in Baltimore in 1875. That year 71,272 Sunday schools existed in America. Each year the size of the Sunday school conventions grew. These conventions were unlike modern-day conventions. Today individuals from publishing houses and colleges instruct the layman. Conventions are characterized by small workshops and a few general assemblies. The older conventions were massive rallies, where laymen motivated other laymen to do the work of the Sunday school. Small committees worked on resolutions, strategy, and plans. These conventions paid little attention to practical techniques. They were, in fact, great Sunday school revival meetings. They organized large parades and made a great impact on the cities.

In 1884 the conventions reported 8,712,511 Sunday school scholars in the United States. Their accomplishments were so staggering that many thought the Millennium could be ushered in. Instead of looking to spiritual horizons, the Sunday school movement began to turn academic. In 1903 the Religious Education Association was formed. The Sunday School Convention changed its name to the International Sunday School Council of Religious Education, and in 1924 the name became the International Council of Religious Education. From this organization grew the National Council of Churches.

In the early 1900s, liberalism crept into theological seminaries and sifted down to the churches. Great debates were held regarding the Virgin Birth of Christ, evolution, the higher criticism of Scripture, and the Resurrection. Since liberalism always kills, Sunday school zeal and expansion waned. A cold, professional spirit developed in Sunday school work. The Sunday school, which had been the most important single agency for the work of God in the preceding century, declined after 1916.

During these years most denominations developed their own Sunday school literature. Sunday school lessons lacked excitement because liberalism was closing in on many denominations. In reaction to the growing unrest, an interdenominational movement back to the Word of God developed. Moody Bible Institute was founded in the late 1800s. In the next fifty years God raised up numerous other Bible institutes to answer the problem of growing biblical illiteracy.

God also raised up interdenominational publishing houses such as Scripture Press, Gospel Light Press, Union Gospel Press, and David C. Cook Publishing Company. These publishers were innovative in their dedication to biblical content, evangelistic fervor, and doctrinal orthodoxy. They laid the foundation for a Sunday school revival in the 1950s.

After World War II a new spirit spread across the Sunday school scene. Attendance took a new upturn in most denominations. Since America has experienced revival after every major war, many liberal-oriented denominations were growing along with smaller evangelical denominations and independent churches. But the growth among liberal denominations was a sociological phenomenon. A new interdenominationalism grew up around organizations such as Youth for Christ, World Vision, and other organizations committed to conservative Christianity. Large Sunday school conventions were planned by the National Sunday School Association. The Sunday school contests of *Christian Life* magazine, 1948–1957, gave impetus to Sunday school growth.

The postwar Sunday school explosion occurred around 1965. Mainline denominations began registering declines in attendance and offerings. They stopped building new educational buildings. A Gallup poll reflected a deterioration of public confidence in the church. Articles began to appear in the popular media questioning the effectiveness of Sunday school. *Life* magazine asked, "What Is the Most Wasted Hour of the Week?" *The New York Times* accused Sunday school of being irrelevant and inefficient.

However, the evangelical denominations continued to grow. In 1968 NSSA published a press release claiming a 3.5 percent growth in Sunday school attendance among its cooperating denominations. *Christian Life* magazine introduced the listing of the 100 largest Sunday schools in 1968. Its message got through to the religious world that Sunday schools true to the Word of God were growing in number and vitality. During the early 1970s a mild Sunday school upsurge came to segments of the evangelical world. The causes of growth were Sunday school busing, renewed interest in soul winning, revival of Sunday school contests, saturation advertisement, and a return to biblical education.

The decade of the 1970s has been characterized as the age of the big Sunday schools. When *Christian Life* began its 100 largest listing, only twenty Sunday schools in America averaged more than 2,000 in attendance. Within the next seven years, more than sixty Sunday schools became that large. But what are 100 out of 350,000 Sunday schools in America? Some people ask, "Why be concerned about the large ones?" But these successful schools prove that it is possible to grow, effectively teach the Word of God, produce godly living, and saturate communities with the gospel.

HOME DEPARTMENT

Sometimes called the Extension Department, the Home Department ministers to persons who, through disability, age, or employment, are unable to attend Sunday school. The Sunday school goes to them instead. In the last few years this department has expanded with the increase of senior citizens' homes and nursing homes.

Purpose

1. Provide fellowship. Any department's outreach results in fellowship with other Christians. So the Home Department provides fellowship for persons whose only contact with other believers may be the department visitor's call. Elderly saints who can do little but sit in a wheelchair and pray may feel useless and unwanted by the church. The brief weekly fellowship is a link with the church.

2. Provide instruction. The Extension Department reaches pupils of many levels of understanding, education, and mental capacity. They need personalized, individual instruction. Such instruction may not be as formal or structured as a lesson in the classroom, but it will impart to them fresh insight into the Word of God.

3. Provide opportunity to participate. Shut-ins may feel left out of the work of a church they may have served long and faithfully during their prime years. The home visitor may give the shut-in a chance to contribute the tithe of his small pension. Shut-ins should have the joy of giving as God commanded—and receiving the blessings he promised.

4. Provide assistance in getting medical or material aid. Elderly persons with no nearby relatives may need assistance getting to doctor's appointments, shopping for groceries, or running other errands. A regular visitor will discover the needs and render or secure help.

5. Provide a tie with the church. In the case of a doctor, nurse, shift worker, or other employed person whose hours prevent

Sunday school attendance, the extension department is a tie to the church. Such people sometimes feel isolated from the church. The brief lesson presentation gives the worker a feeling of belonging.

6. Win the unsaved. The home visitor learns the spiritual status of the shut-in during the conversations and study. The quiet talks together about the Word of God are natural openings to make sure the shut-in is right with God.

Procedure

1. Find the pupils. Several avenues of search are open:
   a. The pastor and the house-to-house visitors for the church will know the names and addresses of persons unable to come to services. The roll of the Home Department does not need to include only those on the church roll. The church worker may win unchurched shut-ins to the Lord.
   b. Check the yellow pages of the telephone book for nursing homes and other community institutions where a weekly or monthly meeting or study could be held.
   c. Make a house-to-house canvas. In cities where the church serves a large residential area, volunteers should go from house to house to discover if there are persons who should be ministered to in the homes.
2. Set up a record system. The secretary will make an alphabetical card file and note information regarding the needs or spiritual status of Home Department pupils. Visits and ministry will be recorded.
3. Assign visits to regular teachers. Pupils in the homes expect to see the same teacher each week, just as do pupils in the church. Only when they know and trust a teacher can that teacher be of real spiritual aid.
4. Set the visitation time. The time cannot be arbitrarily arranged by the church. Each teacher must consider the convenience of the shut-in and those who take care of that one. The nursing home and institution schedules must be considered.
5. Choose the curriculum. Unless an Extension Department program is published by the denomination, the superinten-

dent and teachers must plan with the shut-ins for the course of study. An elderly Christian, for instance, may have a preference that should be considered.

6. Secure an adult class sponsor. While the actual visits and teaching will be done by the Home Department, the responsibility for preparing small gifts, planning for large occasions, and preparing food (where needed) should be shared by the members of an adult class. This relieves some of the load from the extension workers and at the same time gives service opportunities for adults who may not otherwise be serving the church.

Personnel

1. The superintendent. Each department of the Sunday school must have a director. The Home Department superintendent will guide the work, evaluate the progress, enlist and train teachers, and help with the visitation.
2. A secretary. The secretary will keep careful card records on each member on the extension roll. The name of the visitor in charge of each enrollee will be stated on the card for quick reference in time of need.
3. Teachers. The number of teachers depends on the number of persons enrolled. Since weekly contacts are best for greatest spiritual help, one teacher should not be expected to visit more than three homes every week—although many extension workers can and do.

Program

1. The curriculum. A denomination's curriculum usually includes study materials in the form of quarterly magazines for both pupils and teachers. If no such literature is provided by the church, the superintendents and leaders should select the Bible book to be studied.
2. The teaching unit. As with any house call, actual teaching is preceded by friendly conversation. If a shut-in is the subject of ministry, often he or she will want to sing a familiar hymn and may join with wavering voice and faulty memory. The actual teaching period usually should not exceed fifteen

minutes, especially in cases of elderly persons. Give pupils opportunity for response. Allow time at the close for exchange of library books.

3. Variations. From time to time arrange for a group of juniors or young people from the church to go along and sing for the extension enrollee. Take a small gift, or even a large gift, at Christmas and birthdays.

4. Provide the pupil a chance to serve. Plan not only to receive any money offering the pupil may present, but give opportunity for the shut-in or employed enrollee to perform tasks within his strength and ability, at home, to help the church. Even wheelchair patients may be able to prepare handwork materials for Sunday school or vacation Bible school, stuff envelopes for church mail-outs, make clothing for missionary projects, make telephone calls for revivals or conferences, and other tasks.

More than any able-bodied church member, the Home Department shut-in pupil needs to feel useful and wanted. The teacher will render the greatest service who succeeds in creating that feeling by giving the opportunity to share.

HYMNS (See CONGREGATIONAL SINGING)

INTERCESSORS (See also F.R.A.N.GELISM)

The general word *Intercessor* "one who prays for another," is also
a technical title in F.R.A.N.gelism. The intercessors are those on
the evangelism team who undergird the evangelistic outreach of
the church primarily through the ministry of prayer. When the
evangelists, equippers, and encouragers leave to make their calls,
the intercessors go to prayer. The helpers give the intercessors
the names of those who are prospects or new converts and those
who have special needs. The intercessors divide into smaller
groups. Then, on their knees, they pray for specific people and for
specific needs.

INTERNATIONAL SUNDAY SCHOOL ASSOCIATION

Begun in 1860 as the National Sunday School Association, the
International Sunday School Association was formally named in
1905. This Sunday school organization was responsible for popu-
larizing the International Uniform Lessons. Originally, the association was led by evangelical lay leadership who worked to avoid
conflict with religious denominations over control of the Sunday
school. In 1922, the ISSA merged with the Sunday School Council
of Evangelical Denominations to form the International Sunday
School Council of Religious Education. The new group was re-
named the International Council of Religious Education in 1924. In
1950, this organization became the Division of Christian Education of the National Council of Churches in Christ in the U.S.A.

J

JESUS, MASTER TEACHER

Our Lord commanded Christians to teach (Matt. 28:19-20). He knew the importance of teaching and left us his example in the Scriptures. Often we read that he taught the people. In Matthew's threefold description of Jesus' work on earth (9:35), he places teaching first. Both Luke and John speak of his teaching before they tell of his preaching. Nicodemus called him "a teacher come from God" (John 3:2). He is the greatest Teacher of all. He has stated our goal, ". . . teaching them to observe all things that I have commanded you" (Matt. 28:20).

There was unmistakable authority in his very bearing and in his absolute assurance of the importance and verity of his message. He had confidence that stemmed from knowing thoroughly both what he would teach and whom he would teach. The scribes might quote at length from rabbis, but the Master Teacher could declare, "But I say to you" (Matt. 5:22, 28, 32, 34, 39, 44). Jesus knew what he was teaching and spoke with conviction. Jesus was familiar with the Scriptures of his day; he quoted them freely and interpreted them well (Matt. 21:13, 16; Luke 4:8).

The love and sympathy of Jesus indicated his complete understanding of human nature. A master psychologist, the Master Teacher built his lessons upon everyday things. He revealed the secrets of his future kingdom in terms of the familiar—the wheat and the tares, the pearl of great price, and the good and bad fish. He promised to change fishermen into fishers of men.

Jesus knew that we are naturally curious. He made use of the curiosity of the woman at the well in Samaria. A Jew asked a

Samaritan for water. Her curiosity grew to interest as Jesus continued. Eventually she brought others to hear him. More deeply rooted within us is a fear of the supernatural. No doubt this element, too, was in the mind of the Samaritan woman when a stranger suddenly began to tell her all about her past life. Through his miracles, Jesus appeals to this part of our nature. We are drawn to explore and examine incidents that we cannot explain.

Jesus knew that emotions are an important part of life, for they color and influence all our thought and action. He used human emotion in his teaching. What greater example could we have than that of his sorrow over the city of Jerusalem (Luke 13:34)? He often spoke to people in sorrow, as he healed them or raised their loved ones from the dead. His attendance at weddings and feasts show his awareness of the importance of joy in people's lives.

People like appeals to both thought and imagination. An appeal to our ability to think flatters us; it can even stimulate us if we let it. Jesus knew too that our minds require a certain logic. Luke 6:9-10 is an interesting account of Jesus' logic. He also asked pointed questions. His listeners could not evade the question in Matthew 22:42, "What do you think about the Christ?"

Imagination is quite the opposite of logic, yet very real. Some of Jesus' parables could send imaginations soaring (Matt. 25:14-30). Imagination makes vivid any story and imprints that lesson more clearly on minds.

Jesus was familiar with the needs and experiences of all the people he taught, old and young. He did not use highly technical terms in his teaching. That would have confused people. He taught about simple, everyday things—weddings, nature, sickness and health, brotherhood and love, home and family, and vocations. These were things the people knew.

Teaching Methods of Jesus

Jesus was aware that there are many methods to use in teaching, and he employed several of them. He used them well and got the desired results.

1. *Lecture.* Perhaps the best known of his lectures is the Sermon

on the Mount (Matt. 5–7). In it Jesus set forth the greatest principles for living ever known. Moreover, he made his lecture colorful by use of examples, touching on things closest to hearts and vital to life.

2. *Question-and-answer.* Jesus didn't use the question and answer method merely to test the knowledge of his listeners, as is often done today. He used it to stimulate their thinking. The questions in Matthew 16:26, "For what profit is it to a man if he gains the whole world, and loses his own soul? Or what will a man give in exchange for his soul?" are used to teach the value of the human soul. Luke 20:1-8 is an excellent example of Jesus' use of a question to answer a question. His questions were inescapable. They prepared the way for a story. They called for a decision.

3. *Experience.* Jesus knew that we learn best by doing. Life's most important lessons are usually learned the hard way. When Jesus called Peter and Andrew, he didn't say, "Come, listen to what I tell you." Rather, he said, "Follow me, and I will make you fishers of men." He called them to action; he had something for them to do. In Matthew 14:24-32, in order to teach faith to Peter, Jesus actually had Peter walk on the water. Jesus didn't tell Peter to watch him walk on the water; he commanded Peter to do it himself. Experience is the best way to learn.

4. *Object lessons.* Jesus often used object lessons. He knew that people remember what they see longer than what they hear. When he taught of God's provision, he pointed to birds in the sky and flowers in the field. He illustrated the characteristics of a kingdom citizen by setting in the midst of his auditors a little child. In Mark 12:13-17, Jesus used an ordinary coin to teach a lesson when the scholars of the temple tried to trick him. In John 13:5-11 Jesus washed the disciples' feet, a lesson in humility they never forgot. John 20:24-29 gives the story of Thomas, who believed after he saw and heard the resurrected Christ. Many of Jesus' miracles, in addition to being miracles, were, in a sense, object lessons.

5. *Storytelling.* Jesus was indeed a master storyteller. Word pic-

tures made his stories so graphic that they were told and retold by his friends after his departure. He used stories about familiar things and people to illustrate concepts previously unknown. A man repeatedly bothered his neighbor for three loaves of bread. He finally got the bread because the neighbor grew weary of his returning. "Keep on praying until your prayers are answered," Jesus was saying. An injured Jew was refused help by two of his own countrymen but was rescued by a member of a hated race, the Samaritans. Thus Jesus answered for his hearers the question, "Who is my neighbor?" (Luke 10:29).

How Jesus Established His Credibility as a Teacher

Jesus led an exemplary life. It is useless to teach one thing and do another. The actions completely negate the teaching. Note how Jesus lived what he taught.

1. *Love.* Jesus taught, "But I say to you, love your enemies, bless those who curse you, do good to those who hate you, and pray for those who spitefully use you and persecute you" (Matt. 5:44). He permitted Judas Iscariot to be one of his chosen twelve, knowing that he would eventually betray him. Remember, also, his prayer for those who nailed him to the cross.

2. *Mercy.* He taught mercy in his Sermon on the Mount when he said, "Blessed are the merciful, for they shall obtain mercy" (Matt. 5:7). Any one of the many miracles Jesus performed was an act of mercy.

3. *Brotherhood.* He taught in Matthew 12:49-50 the meaning of brotherhood. He mingled with all people and was accused of sitting down with publicans and sinners.

4. *Obedience.* He taught obedience when he admonished a young man to "keep the commandments" (Matt. 19:17). He lived a life of obedience. The Pharisees tried to find some fault with him, but failed.

5. *Humility.* He taught humility, warning, "But when you do a charitable deed, do not let your left hand know what your right hand is doing, that your charitable deed may be in secret; and your Father who sees in secret will Himself re-

ward you openly" (Matt. 6:3-4). Jesus often warned those he healed not to tell anyone else about it. And when he prayed, he liked to go off by himself.

6. *Forgiveness.* He told Peter to forgive seventy times seven, and he forgave seventy times seven, and he forgave Peter who denied him.

When Jesus taught, he saw definite results. When he healed a man, that man was really healed. When a man made a decision to follow him, Jesus gained a new disciple.

Look at teaching in its totality. Don't expect everything to change at once. Jesus spoke to thousands, but the Bible doesn't say they all believed at once. True, many came to faith on occasion, but that must have been the exception rather than the rule. The very fact that the writers noted it indicates that it must have been rare. Results often come slowly and are not always visible. A seed has been growing for quite a while before it pushes through the soil. Teachers must sow the seed, water it, and watch it grow. Teaching is a hallowed task, given by God.

JUNIOR DEPARTMENT

When a child dedicates his life to Jesus Christ during his junior years, he forms the basis for the solution of many of the problems of adolescence. Nine- to eleven-year-olds are most easily won to Christ. They are teachable and ready to form good habits. Juniors want the truth and seek it in the lives of their leaders as well as in their lessons. While preparing to lead the church tomorrow, they are engaged in living now.

Juniors are doers. James 1:22 ("But be doers of the word, and not hearers only, deceiving yourselves") is aptly called the junior verse. They also enjoy companionship. They share ideas and fun with their peers. At the same time, they are hero worshipers. Someone has said, "Juniors make you feel they think you are the greatest, even if you are not, while young people make you feel you are not great, while they really think you are."

Juniors are in the "golden age of memory." Teachers can take advantage of their interest and ability to memorize by helping them store the Word of God in their hearts for the Spirit to use for the rest of their lives.

Organizing the Junior Department

Ideally the Junior Department should be graded according to age, all nine-year-olds, all tens, and all elevens in separate classes. Some leaders also insist the age groups be further separated by having boys in one class and girls in another. In small-church situations, however, where such division is not feasible because of few teachers or few pupils, all three ages and both sexes can and do work together. In fact, they seem to enjoy the competition and interaction possible with the larger group.

Some leaders specify that there should be no more than six or seven juniors to a teacher. In a sit-down-and-listen situation, such a plan might be interesting. But juniors are doers, and drama and contest-games are favorite forms of learning for them. If there is a drama, who will watch if all pupils take part? If two of the six are absent, how much of a contest could take place? Many teachers prefer a class of at least a dozen juniors. In superchurches, junior departments use the team teaching method for twenty-five to a hundred boys and girls in one large open-room teaching situation.

Whatever the size or division, the junior class may have officers with regular responsibilities. Officers may be elected every six months to allow more pupils to serve. Some of these may be:

1. Missionary chairman. This person will find and enlist new members, help to keep the "regulars" in Sunday school, visit absentees, and keep a prospect list. He may help develop and work on missionary projects such as making a class map, reading weekly prayer requests for missionaries, making scrapbooks, collecting clothing, and others.

2. Church attendance chairman. This person will encourage all to stay for church services and may keep a record of such attendance. He may announce the sermon topic or make posters to encourage interest.

3. Bible study chairman. With the help of the teacher, this junior can create interest in Bible study, in weekly lesson preparation, and in the memory work program.

4. Room chairman. This junior can be responsible for getting

assistance in keeping the room clean, neat, and occasionally adorned with flowers and pictures. He can bring supplies for the teacher from the place of storage and return them after use. He also can keep the chalkboard clean and supplied with chalk and eraser.

5. President. This person can be called upon to welcome the visitors each Sunday and give them the welcome pin. He should be taught to preside over any class business in an orderly way.

6. Social chairman. With guidance from the teacher, this junior can learn to choose suitable games and plan outings and parties, even directing the games.

Planning a Teaching Session for Juniors

Select the method according to the lesson content. No junior lesson should be without some form of visual aid or action-type presentation. While variety is the keynote for interest, some skeleton of a familiar general outline gives security, while the "meat on the bones" provides variety. A successful outline is:

Presession activity. This may take the form of working together on a group project such as a mural, picture map, topographical map, molded water pots and other Bible-land items, or a sandbox or sand pan scene. It may involve individual solving of a puzzle or coded Bible verse, unscrambling Bible names or verses, or independent sorting of Bible-book cards into divisions. In most groups, some pupils arrive at least half an hour ahead of scheduled starting time. For them, Sunday school should begin when they get there. The presession thus affords that much more teaching time.

Worship service. Suit the choice of songs and Bible reading to the theme of study. Every part of the morning, including the presentation, should stress one chief aim. Limit this worship time to not more than seven minutes. Choose a Bible reading that juniors can handle from the standpoint of vocabulary and pronunciation. Vary the form of the reading. Vary the form in which songs are presented: Flannelgraph, flash cards, charts, pictures, chalkboard, song sheets.

Review game. Let an assistant teacher lead in a review game such as tic-tac-toe, a spelldown, crossword puzzle, or another. All questions should aid in recall of the previous lesson, to lay the groundwork for continuation.

Approach. A story, minidrama, puppet, or personification may lead into the study with a presentation on the junior level of understanding. The approach should not be a mere review of the two Bible chapters that precede the one being studied. Instead, it should consist of the presentation of a contemporary problem or experience similar to the one being studied in the present lesson.

Bible study. Whether the presentation is via flannelgraph, puppets, chalk or whatever, pupils should have their Bibles open to the selected passage and should be given opportunity to answer questions from time to time. These questions should refer juniors to the Scripture verse involved and should call for an answer in a student's own words, not the mere reading of the verse. What the pupil says will be remembered by him seven times as long as what the teacher says.

Application. The story, drama, or discussion used here should reinforce the aim for the entire period. If, for example, the story of Jacob seeks to emphasize the evil of cheating, let the contemporary application story do likewise. Let discussion prove it to the class. Give an invitation in the brief prayer period for salvation or dedication.

Memorize a key verse. Again, an assistant teacher can be assigned to teach a memory verse in one of many interesting ways. Vary the method from Sunday to Sunday. Because boys and girls often do not memorize at home, the Sunday school must help them to do so by making it fun. Inexpensive awards, publicly presented, often are sufficient motivation for extra effort.

Announce other junior weekday activities. Close with a Bible-verse prayer, which, because of its weekly repetition will become hidden in the hearts of all.

Leading Juniors in Worship
1. Preparation. The challenge to the junior worker is to lead pupils to experience true worship. A "worship service," regardless of how well planned and executed, does not guarantee a worship experience.

The junior room should have an atmosphere of orderliness. The leader should be prepared, for he cannot lead where he himself has not gone. Leaders must come from "the secret of his Presence" if juniors are to be led into that Presence. All should share in the preparation by participating in the preprayer service. Teachers should be seated with their classes before the service begins.

2. The junior worship service should contain six basic elements:

Praise. The call to worship may sound the note of praise with the use of Scripture or poetry. Carefully selected hymns will stimulate such emotions as trust, reverential awe, and joy. Music should be chosen carefully to deepen the thought of the worship theme. Music may be used as a prelude, interlude, offertory, or special vocal or instrumental number, during silent prayer and while marching to classes. The element of praise may also appear in prayer, with emphasis on thanksgiving.

Prayer. Pupils should be led to recognize that prayer is talking to God, having fellowship with him, not merely a repetition of high-sounding words and phrases. Pupils should be reminded frequently that prayer includes thanking as well as asking; telling God the things that make us happy or sad; telling God we love him; confessing sin; and talking to him about others. Prayer time should be brief and reverent, and expressed in a language that is understood by juniors.

Scripture. The Scripture selection should be prayerfully and carefully chosen to carry out the theme of the service. Frequent use of Scripture that has been memorized is good. Scripture may be read by an adult leader who has practiced reading the passage aloud, or by a pupil, a group, or the entire class. In any event, the passage should be assigned at least a week in advance and drilled by parent, teacher, or superintendent. Scripture reading may correlate with the theme of the worship service.

Giving. Juniors may be trained in stewardship through the

wise use of the offering. Benevolent impulses will be created as pupils feel financial responsibility for the total program of the church. Juniors may occasionally be given an opportunity to tell how they have earned the money they have brought. Juniors also should be used as ushers for training in churchmanship. And the children should know for what purpose their money is to be used.

Instruction. The time of brief instruction usually is the responsibility of one of the adult leaders. The subjects for instruction in worship may be built around many themes such as Christ, God's love, God's Word, Bible history, missions, or religious art. This feature should be brief, since the class period is for instruction. The material should be selected well in advance to harmonize with the central theme of the worship service. The instruction also should be within the group's experience and comprehension. The methods of presentation may vary: storytelling, talk, object lesson, or demonstration.

Fellowship time. Juniors like to show an interest in others. The fellowship period offers opportunity to welcome new members, make announcements of activities, celebrate birthdays, and recognize achievements.

JUNIOR HIGH DEPARTMENT (See also MIDDLE SCHOOL)

The junior high public schools (grade 7–8) are also called middle schools (grade 6–7). Someone has said that the Junior High Department has more scalps of defeated teachers to its credit than any other department of the Sunday school. While this may be true, it need not be if teachers are dedicated to reaching junior high pupils for Christ and eternity. This age is considered one of the most difficult to teach because the pupils are beginning adolescence, the transition between childhood and adulthood. They no longer manifest the openness of childhood, nor do they possess the maturity of adulthood.

General Characteristics of Junior High Students

1. Change. In the body, there is rapid, uneven growth (and girls often outstrip boys in height). In ideals, the young teen is no

longer an imitator or hero worshiper but full of ambitions, with elaborate plans for the future. His ideas are fleeting; his decisions temporary; his disposition changeable. Probably 85 percent of these teens decide on their life's work.

2. Interest in the opposite sex. Teen boys soon leave the "woman-haters club" of junior years.
3. Behavior. May be silly or flippant, or critical and insensitive. They may ignore friendly gestures.
4. Independence. Junior highs are beginning to establish independence; they want to be grown-up.
5. Activities. These young people enjoy school and church activities. They incline toward cliques.
6. Sunday school behavior. Although they enjoy variety in presentation, junior highs may whisper and appear inattentive. They will confide in a teacher they like and who likes them. Approximately 65 percent of the girls and 75 percent of the boys drop out of Sunday school at this critical age.

Needs of the Junior High Pupil
Salvation. Needs to recognize his need for a Savior and to have the assurance of salvation.

Dedication. Needs to be challenged to put Bible truths into practice.

Activity. Needs Christian activities in which to use some of his energy.

Friends. Needs someone to depend upon; someone to confide in. Also needs adult guidance that is neither "too late, nor too little."

Teaching Aims in the Junior High Department
1. To lead students to a saving knowledge of Jesus Christ.
2. To cause each student to grow and mature in Christ.
3. To show each student how God's Word relates to his or her personal life.
4. To know each pupil as a friend in order to help him with his problems.
5. To involve each student in the lesson and the class activities.

Principles of Teaching Junior Highs

Because new interests emerge suddenly and devotion to one study is often short-lived, adolescent education should include a wide variety of subjects.

1. Stimulate intellectual capacities at this age, for adult life possesses only the improvement of capacities cultivated in early years.
2. Provide social contacts and development for the youth.
3. While the last days of childhood present the most promising and practical period for evangelistic effort, the largest number of conversions that "stick" take place during adolescence.
4. Organized departments should be provided, since the natural social tendency of teens is to form gangs or groups.
5. Keep open the channels of communication—someone may confide in you.
6. Multiply the interests; no real progress can be made until the mental horizon has been widened.
7. Command by counsel. A young person can be guided even when he cannot be governed, directed when he cannot be driven.
8. Control by companionship.

Developing Methods for Teaching Junior Highs

1. Have an interesting and challenging presession activity.
2. Have pupils participate by reading from Bibles, pointing out places on maps, discussing clippings and pictures, and reviewing the lesson. Junior highs respond more to projected visual aids and discussion than to methods used with younger children.
3. Have a good approach. Never begin with, "Does anyone know what our lesson is about today?" Use thought-provoking questions, a challenge, a brief story, or a visual aid.
4. Let students know you are concerned about them and their problems and are available for help at all times.
5. Give recognition and encouragement to each pupil.
6. Have special projects in which the students can participate.

7. Schedule regular social activities to cultivate and mold junior highs into strong Christians.

8. Use a variety of presentations: personal assignments, buzz groups, committee work, storytelling, questions, discussions, circle conversation, testing, projects, memorization, chalkboard outlines, written reports, testimonies, role play, panels.

Organizing the Junior High Department

Classes can be divided by age and sex according to the needs of the local church. A class containing six to eight pupils may be ideal for good Bible teaching, but too small for social interaction. (As for other groups, a smaller membership and fewer teachers will make age and sex separation impractical. Too few in a class can be boring and also discouraging.)

The "master teacher" approach is growing in use. All the junior high students are placed in one room and exposed to the teacher best qualified to meet their need. This teacher should be the youth pastor when he is available because he understands adolescents, can communicate with them, and has a knowledge of the Scripture.

Class officers may include a missionary chairman, church attendance chairman, Bible study chairman, room chairman, president, social chairman and secretary-treasurer.

KEY, FRANCIS SCOTT (1780–1843)

Francis Scott Key was a well-known statesman in history, arguing cases before the United States Supreme Court and conducting diplomatic missions for the United States. But he is best known for writing our national anthem, "The Star Spangled Banner." Key was sent with a flag of truce to a British admiral during the War of 1812. He was detained on an enemy vessel, and that night he witnessed the bombardment of Fort McHenry, near Baltimore, Maryland. During the night, he saw the American flag by the light of bomb explosions, proudly waving over a battered fort. By the early light of dawn, he saw the flag was still flying; thus, he penned the words of our national anthem.

Key was a Christian and taught a large Sunday school class of more than three hundred men. Also, he was one of the founders of the American Sunday School Union and served on its board of directors. In 1830, Key chaired the Sunday school convention in Washington, D.C., when the Mississippi Valley Enterprise was introduced and approved. The Mississippi Valley Enterprise was an ambitious project to plant a new Sunday school in every town between the Allegheny and the Rocky Mountains, or between Pittsburg and Denver. The area comprised one million square miles, with a population of more than 4 million people. Key attempted to raise $40,000 to get the project done. A newspaper called the meeting the most important ever held in the United States. U.S. senators and congressmen addressed the Sunday school convention on behalf of the project. The clerk of the House of Representatives was the secretary.

Led by Stephen Paxson and other hard-working missionaries, the Mississippi Valley Enterprise was one of the most successful projects in the history of Sunday school. More than 61,297 Sunday schools were established with 407,244 teachers and an enrollment of 2,650,784 pupils. They thought they could complete the project in two years, but it took fifty years to complete the mission. They employed approximately eighty missionaries a year and spent a total of $2,133,364.13 on the project.

KOINONITUS (See also PATHOLOGY OF CHURCH GROWTH)

Koinonitus is a pathology of church growth that develops when a church has a real allegiance to itself and its unique doctrinal commitments. If a church or Sunday school makes a secondary doctrine the priority of its existence, it is described as having *koinonitus.* The word comes from *koinonia,* "to have fellowship." But when fellowship becomes more important than the great commission (the aim of a church), then that church is ill with this disease.

LANGUAGE, LAW OF

The law of language states, "Learning is most effective when the language is common to both the learner and the teacher." Unchurched persons who visit Sunday school for the first time often get the feeling they are in a foreign land. They hear the teacher or a class member use an evangelical idiom to describe someone or something, and the expression means something different to them. In a living language, words and expressions come to take on new meanings to individuals and groups. An exhaustive English dictionary may have more than a hundred definitions for the word *run,* and most people who speak English daily may use this word to refer to several different things in a given day. There is an obvious difference between a customer running up a bill, an athlete running around a track, and a tear running down the face of a crying child, but if a person does not recognize these expressions, he may have difficulty understanding what is meant. Communication and learning takes place when both teacher and pupil use words with the same meaning.

Problems in Communication

Several things hinder words from being understood by students:

1. Words with different meanings. The solution for a teacher in the Sunday school lies in part with looking into the faces of class members while teaching them. If pupils look at each other with raised eyebrows, we need to clarify the preceding statement. Whenever we introduce new words, we should define them by using them in a sentence. It is helpful to write

the word and its meaning on the chalkboard, so it may be seen as well as heard. An overhead projector may also be useful in this regard.

2. Polysyllabic (oversized) words. Some six-syllable words are unavoidable in teaching a Sunday school class, for example, *Mediterranean.* If there is any doubt about a choice of words, it is far better to use a simple word rather than a word the class cannot pronounce or define. If there is a one- or two-syllable word that expresses our meaning, we should use it. That way, even the least word-wise student will understand.

Sometimes the less-familiar, long word slips out. When you realize it was a poor choice (you see question marks in eyes), quickly substitute a simple word. If, however, you deliberately use a more difficult word because it says best what is meant, then explain the word in terms of something familiar.

3. Words that sound alike, but have different meanings. An example of this problem is the word *epithet,* which means a word or phrase that insults someone. Occasionally someone will say that word when they really mean *epitaph.* It is funny in this case, because epitaph means almost the opposite; it complements a person. An epitaph is the kind word or phrase often carved on a tombstone.

4. Enunciation and pronunciation. The first term means "to say every syllable distinctly." Words should not be run together, such as "Wherejago?" One should say, "Where did you go?"

Pronunciation, however, refers to emphasis on the proper syllable, and correct short or long sound on vowels. Listen to someone describe a time of great danger. They may say, "I had a narrow *excape,"* when they mean *escape.* A dictionary can help in avoiding such common errors.

Who cares whether we bumble along the best we can or say the words correctly? The students. In classes from juniors on up, some students will be good readers and will know the correct pronunciation. They will have less confidence in our Bible teaching if they hear common words mispronounced.

But, more important, Bible names and places must be said or read aloud during teaching. A self-pronouncing Bible will help because it includes pronunciation marks for all proper names (people and places).

The way the teacher pronounces a Bible word is the way some pupils will say it the rest of their lives. Also, saying it wrong will cause confusion when another teacher says it correctly. The student's choice of pronunciation will depend on which teacher they know or like best.

5. Lack of expression. Although Bible words (Old English words that end in *ith* and *eth*) may sound strange to unchurched ears, their meaning expresses the same emotions as modern-day speech. Therefore, when we read the Bible aloud, we should give it as much expression as though it were a contemporary adventure story. The Bible is full of adventure, anger, humor, and sorrow. Bible people were *people*. When there was danger, they were afraid. When their loved ones died, they cried. When they did wrong, they were rebuked, sometimes by God himself.

6. Lack of explanation. Frequently in Sunday schools new concepts are not explained, especially the different life-style of Bible times. This is illustrated by the story of the child who came home and was asked by his mother, "What did you learn from the Bible today?" He said, "Don't get scared, you'll get your quilt." His mother felt quite sure he had misunderstood, so she later asked the teacher what he meant. He had scrambled up John 14:26-27, where Jesus told the disciples not to be afraid because he would send them another Comforter (the Holy Spirit).

7. Lack of two-way communication. When all the talking in the class is from the teacher to the pupil, it is unlikely that the pupils will recall more than 10 percent of what is taught. When students are encouraged to participate in the discussion, not only will they remember more but they may also communicate their spiritual character and needs.

LAWS OF . . . (See particular laws)

LEADERSHIP, LAWS OF

The inability of leaders to lead is a frequent weakness in the volunteer work of the church. Yet while God is the undisputed Leader of his church, he continues to use human instrumentality to accomplish his work. Keeping in mind that specific leaders may be needed for specific areas, examine some of the general qualifications of a leader.

1. *Poise.* Poise is not a front or a mask. Poise results when a leader knows his subject and the age group to whom he ministers. Poise comes from relying on the indwelling presence and aid of the Holy Spirit. Thus, one's outer manner reflects his inward faith and assurance.

2. *Bearing.* The leader's bearing further reflects his inner attitude through his posture and walk. While his head is raised in confidence, it is not tilted with pride. While he walks with an air of assurance, it is not a strut of vanity. A leader may be recognized by the pleasure and assurance with which he approaches his task—attitudes, again, born of faith as well as preparation.

3. *Projection.* A leader has eye contact and heart contact with those he leads. He reaches out to his listeners with an interest and concern evident in his words and tone. He knows what he is going to say without having to read it, so his eyes constantly scan the faces of his hearers and note their reactions. He knows enough about his subject to be able to present additional facts if his listeners register lack of comprehension or unrest.

4. *Sharing.* A leader does not attempt to perform all the functions in his given sphere of activity. If, for example, he is the general superintendent of the Sunday school, his function is to share his knowledge and give direction for others to follow. He does not constantly push from behind, saying, "You must do this or that." Rather he shares his own knowledge of how to do it and sets an example through his own performance. The superintendent does not teach, but he

usually has the responsibility of training the teachers in his department.

5. *Humility.* Probably this quality differentiates the real leader from the self-styled big shot. The true leader in God's work has the qualification listed by the Lord Jesus Christ, "And whoever desires to be first among you, let him be your slave." Faithful, willing service commends one for consideration for leadership posts. While some persons seem to have inborn leadership qualities, study and practice can improve this ability. Giving of oneself in service to Christ and his church develops a servant of God. The true leader recognizes his constant dependence upon the wisdom, direction, and strength imparted by the Holy Spirit, who appointed him to his task.

6. *Followship.* The leader is essentially a follower—of the leadership of the Holy Spirit of God. The Spirit's direction may be extended through the process of open and shut doors, realization of need in specific area, or a vision of possibilities in a particular field through a message or book.

7. *Example.* The qualities of spiritual devotion that a church has a right to expect from any Christian will be exemplified by the leader. His strength and courage and vision will come from fellowship with God through prayer and Bible study, as well as through service. He has self-discipline. He goes the second mile in unselfish effort. His enthusiasm and other attitudes are contagious. In short, those who look up to him are going to emulate his qualities, so his qualities must be the highest and finest.

Characteristics of a Leader

1. *Vision.* He projects into the future, sees ahead.
2. *Commitment.* Our age of tension—with nuclear war, social revolution, population explosion, automation, moral crises, materialism, and mobility—breeds rootlessness, lack of identification, alienation, and meaninglessness. Persons who have found the purpose of God in Christ should be able to express their convictions in commitment.
3. *Involvement.* A leader does not just talk about commitment;

he does something about commitment. Involvement means concern for life as it is, not what we wish it to be. There is a willingness to help solve society's problems.

4. *Positive self-concept.* A leader has a realistic self-image. He can assess himself objectively, being neither deceived nor discouraged by his limitations nor puffed up by his potentialities. He is not overly self-centered or self-concerned. He admits mistakes, but feels competent despite them.

5. *Acceptance.* He feels others are of worth and is supportive, encouraging, helpful, empathetic. He cooperates rather than competes. Feeling that other people are worthwhile, he is apt to feel that their efforts are worthwhile. He finds it difficult to say no when asked to assist in a worthy cause. He is a giving person.

6. *Perception.* The leader is aware of people, circumstances, ideas, attitudes, and the world outside himself. He sees the world in shades of gray, rather than black and white.

7. *Tolerance.* He tolerates ambiguities and uncertainties. He does not jump to conclusions or insist upon immediate action. He may appear to be indecisive, a "middle-of-the-roader." But he is in reality suspending judgment, knowing that there is a time for waiting and a time for action.

8. *Creativity.* The outworking of his unique self. To be creative is to be authentic, original, and insightful, rather than imitative.

9. *Interdependence.* He relates to others and recognizes his dependence upon them. Other people's individuality and uniqueness make his own life fuller and more productive. He knows his real strength comes from contacts with others. When he accepts and supports others, he builds a better self. His relationships are not characterized by domination or submission, aggression or appeasement. He is magnanimous and forgiving.

10. *Communication.* The leader is open; he does not wear masks. He listens to others and does not dismiss an idea simply because of its source. He is not as concerned with having people agree with him, as with being understood. In

striving to be understood he may try to get through the defensive psychological mechanisms of others by couching his ideas in nonthreatening terms. This is not compromise, for he is tenacious and vigorous in presenting his beliefs when necessary.

LEADERSHIP AND CHURCH GROWTH (See also CHURCH GROWTH WHEEL)

Numerical growth of a New Testament church begins with the power of God. The leader is the length and shadow of the work he builds for God. Using a clown to draw a crowd is not New Testament growth. New Testament growth does not come from Madison Avenue public relations men, but begins with the man of God. In finding biblical leadership, the following criteria must be observed.

Spiritual Factors of Leadership

1. Growing churches have a leader called of God. A person can be assured he is called of God when he meets the following criteria: (a) He has a burden to serve God. (b) He has a desire to serve God. This is a consuming desire that encompasses all of his perspective. (c) He has no alternative but to serve God. When God calls a man to serve him, it is an imperial decree. When God calls a person to teach a Sunday school class, the person may not bargain with God and drive a bus instead. When a person is called of God, 100 percent yieldedness is the only alternative.

2. Growing churches have an effective leader who displays biblical spirituality. A man who is used of God must be filled with the Spirit (Eph. 5:18). To be filled with the Spirit is to be controlled by the Holy Spirit. God can then channel his power through that leader to build a church or to teach a class. The filling of the Spirit leads to soul winning (Acts 2:1-4), answers to prayer (Acts 4:31), joy (Acts 13:52), and fruitfulness (Gal. 5:22-23). To be filled with the Spirit, the church leader must (a) separate himself from all known sin, (b) yield all conscious endeavors to God, (c) seek the leader-

ship of God in all areas of service, and (d) trust God to work through his service to accomplish the results of the Spirit.

3. Growing churches see the power of God work through their leader. There is no formula to secure the empowering of the Holy Spirit. It comes as the leader yields himself to God and exerts every energy in prayer. The leader must be mature and dedicate all of his abilities to serve God. To secure spiritual power, the leader must meet all of the qualifications in the Word of God.

4. Growing churches share the vision of their leader. Just as the Old Testament prophet was called a seer (1 Sam. 9:9), so the biblical leader must see first, see farthest, and see most. He must have a vision of what God is going to do with the church. He must have a vision of growth. Then he must inspire his congregation.

5. Growing churches have a leader with spiritual gifts (Rom. 12:3-8; 1 Cor. 12:1-27; Eph. 4:7-13). A person with a spiritual gift can accomplish spiritual results through the effective use of that gift. (a) Persons with spiritual gifts vary in their ability to accomplish results. Some with the gift of teaching are more effective than others. (b) Some people have more gifts than others. (c) The gifted man has a combination of intensity and a large number of gifts and is able to accomplish more for God than those with fewer gifts. This accomplishment can be in quantity or quality (he can produce a depth of spirituality in his followers and/or a large numerical following). (d) A leader's faithful use of his gifts will result in the growth of his abilities. Either he accumulates more abilities or those he already has become more effective.

6. Growing churches have a leader who aggressively obeys the commands of Christian service. Some leaders are called of God, have spiritual gifts, and have yielded themselves to God, but they are not effective in their Christian service because they have not been seeking places to serve God. Those who aggressively seek to carry out the New Testament commands concerning service are those who experience the power of God in their lives. The Bible tells us to have a vision

(Matt. 10), aggressively reach the lost (Luke 14:23), and preach to as many people as possible (Mark 16:15). Those leaders who actively seek out and obey the commands in the Bible are those who have more blessing of God upon their ministry.

7. Growing churches are the result of the faith of their leader. Faith usually is considered an intangible quality. Like love, if you have it, you know it. Most people go through life exercising many acts of faith every day. We have faith in the chair to hold us, or faith in the airplane to get us to our destination. Biblical faith is centered in Jesus Christ. (a) The more knowledge we have of Jesus Christ, the more we can trust him. (b) A successful act in trusting God for small things leads to greater spheres of faith. (c) Biblical faith is not wishfully hoping God will bless our endeavors. (d) The closer our project is to the will of God, the more effective our faith will be as we trust God for his blessing upon it. (e) If a service project fails, it is not the leader's lack of faith. Either the project or our service was not in keeping with the will of God.

8. Growing churches have a leader who is mature. Spiritual maturity is not an overnight acquisition. Maturity grows through time, successful service, and accumulated experiences. Some Sunday school teachers do not have twenty years of experience; rather they have one year of experience repeated twenty times. Those teachers have not grown in maturity. Every time a person trusts God and gets an answer to prayer, he grows in his ability to trust God for bigger things. The same holds true for his spiritual gifts. Every time he stretches his abilities to their ultimate, his ability grows for future use. Hence, maturity is acquired as a man walks with God and serves him for many years. All things being equal, the young man just out of Bible college cannot build a great church as quickly as the seasoned pastor.

9. Growing churches are built by a leader with resolute determination. This means he must never give up. When he commits himself to building a church, he is not open to a call from other congregations. He feels the burden of God to reach a

certain community. Therefore, he stays in one place and builds the church. When he meets obstacles, he overcomes them and continues to build.

Natural Factors of Leadership

Leadership has been defined as helping people accomplish the goals of the New Testament church. Therefore, a man who builds a great church will help people accomplish the goals of that church.

1. Growing churches employ gifted workers to accomplish the most for God. Every man should be used in the church. However, those who can accomplish the most should be used in strategic places of leadership. The outstanding man, through aggressive outreach, can produce numerical growth. The gifted teacher should be exposed to the maximum number of persons in the largest variety of learning experiences to accomplish the greatest influence in people's lives. This teacher is usually mature, spiritual, and trained. He can lead pupils into greater knowledge of the Scriptures, and their lives can become more Christlike.

2. Growing churches realize that effective leadership produces a multiplication of their ministry (2 Tim. 2:2). When the leader properly carries out his duties, he accomplishes two results. First, the work of God prospers. Second, new workers are trained for the ministry. As the leader performs his task, (a) others are inspired to serve, (b) those he reaches grow and want to help in the ministry, and (c) his ministry duplicates itself through his people.

3. Growing churches spawn leadership ability through a "hot-poker" approach. Just as heat transfers from the coals to the poker, so the qualities and attitudes of effective leadership are assimilated. A recruit should spend time with an experienced leader to: (a) gain self-confidence, (b) develop a proper leadership attitude, (c) avoid making immature mistakes, (d) acquire a vision of his potential production, and (e) understand the overall strategy of the ministry. The best methods for developing "hot-poker" leaders are by a teaching internship; by bringing great educators to your church;

and by taking your staff to seminars, conventions, and training sessions outside your church.

4. Growing churches improve leadership ability through formal training sessions. A growing Sunday school should plan a program of training. This is effective through: (a) a weekly Sunday school teachers' meeting, (b) a specified training class, (c) placing assistants under the master teacher, and (d) providing literature that will increase leadership ability.

5. Growing churches effectively use leadership by providing a consistent, constant interaction between workers. No worker can be expected to keep performing at a high level without constant motivation, evaluation, and reward. Most fast-growing Sunday schools have a weekly Sunday school teachers' meeting. Workers are reminded of their task and motivated to better service. Those who have performed well are rewarded. This face-to-face encounter between leader and worker is a necessity for constant growth.

6. Growing churches give direction to a Sunday school through written standards. Although most fast-growing Sunday schools have not written out their standards, this does not mean they do not have standards. Usually, these criteria reside in the heart of the leader. This "personal" method has worked, but growth is limited to the ability of the leader to communicate directly with his staff. When the standards are written, the leader extends his ministry beyond his oral communication. Written standards give: (a) direction for Sunday school growth, (b) a basis for solving problems, (c) cohesiveness to the staff, (d) a basis for determining why the Sunday school is or is not growing, and (e) practical help to another person when the leader leaves the scene.

LEADERSHIP, GIFT OF (See ADMINISTRATION, GIFT OF)

LEADERSHIP TRAINING

Leadership is the difference between a healthy and a sick church, between a growing and a stagnant church. Dr. Lee Roberson once said, "Everything rises and falls on leadership." By this statement he meant that a person can make a difference in the face of insurmountable odds, difficult circumstances, and limited resources. Leadership makes a difference, and the greatest need in today's church is leadership.

Why Leadership Training?

1. Because everyone has some leadership responsibility. We wrongly think the pastor does the work of the church. This results in Christians who only watch or listen to the pastor's ministry. The Bible teaches that everyone has a ministry (Eph. 4:16). Since everyone has a responsibility to minister to others, everyone is a leader to some degree. Therefore, leadership training is needed to equip everyone to minister in the body.

2. Because people can lead others. No matter how far down the totem pole in age, rank, or education, everyone is a potential leader. Therefore, we ought to train people to reach their potential leadership.

3. Because people can be trained to do their jobs better. Everyone is in the process of change, either toward improvement or deterioration. People can be molded, so we should train them to become more effective leaders to serve Jesus Christ.

4. Because leadership training utilizes unused talent and ability in the church. In the average church, 85 percent are spectators, while 15 percent fill the jobs. Let's train more people for the task. A realistic goal is to enlist 50 percent of every church in service.

5. To carry out the great commission. No pastor can carry out the great commission by himself. He must challenge, recruit, train, and employ others to be leaders. These leaders will help him reach the lost. The average pastor does not need to work harder but delegate the ministry to others. Why do the work of seven men? Instead, get seven men to work for Christ.

How to Train Leaders

There are a number of strategies for developing leadership abilities in ourselves and others, including the following:

1. Orientation. Proper orientation helps a worker do a job better. The first few weeks on the job will be decisive in determining the attitudes and habits of work. Supervisory relationships are best established early.

2. Job descriptions. A job description is a useful tool in orientation and supervision. It needs to be flexible but should spell out duties, relationships, available assistance, and expectations.

3. Observation. Trainees need to observe experienced workers. Observation of the leader in a teaching/learning situation with a chance to discuss the session is helpful to both observer and teacher/leader.

4. Supervisory conferences. Every worker should have the privilege of reviewing his stewardship of teaching with a qualified supervisor. Evaluation and plans for future emphasis should be discussed.

5. Workers' conferences. The regularly scheduled conference of workers provides for face-to-face interchange of viewpoints in a group situation. The conference can be an effective vehicle in keeping spiritual concern before the group, providing training, caring for business that affects the entire group, and providing fellowship.

6. Guided reading, listening, and seeing. Church, public, and personal libraries contain valuable information that workers can study at their own pace. Much valuable material can be circulated among workers. A growing supply of audiovisual training aids is also available.

7. Visits with specialists. Guest lecturers and discussion leaders can meet with your workers and share out of their experience and study.

8. Delegates to conferences. Arrange for representatives to attend gatherings that discuss relevant matters, and allow them to report back to the group.

9. Courses of study. Formal courses of study are a useful

means of improving workers. Because they involve a well-trained leader, require attendance, and prescribe reading, they are a valuable feature of your leadership training program. Some churches require their leaders to attend improvement sessions.

10. Apprenticeship. This ancient method of learning is valuable for moderns. Observing, discussing, attempting, and receiving correction and encouragement is a very effective way to learn.

11. Team teaching and consultation. In the team situation members of the team discuss objectives, evaluate experiences and prepare strategy. Leadership is shared according to the skills of the team members. Consultation is especially valuable at the beginning of a team experience.

LECTURE

The lecture method might be better titled "oral presentation by the teacher." It includes all remarks constituting an extended formal exposition and all remarks made to clarify issues, to elaborate upon pupils' answers to questions, to supplement data already on hand, or to indicate how something is to be done.

Oral presentation is used to a great extent at all levels of instruction. It cannot be avoided, even at the younger ages. It is impossible to eliminate oral presentation, even from methods of instruction that allow greater pupil participation. It must, then, be done effectively and intelligently with an understanding of the laws of the teaching/learning process. Any teacher with a sense of responsibility will wish to master the technique of effective oral presentation.

The Teacher

In the lecture method the success of the educational process lies at the feet of the teacher. He plays a dominant, sometimes exclusive role. He must realize that mere telling is never teaching. The teaching/learning process involves much more than imparting information, more than transferring notes from the teacher's notebook into the students'. The teacher must effectively stimulate the learning process and guide pupil response. He must feel the mental pulse of

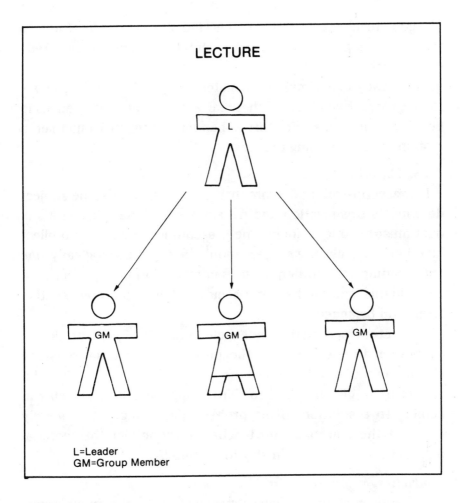

the students and seek to meet their needs. This can be done by the lecture method to some extent, but it involves real planning and work. The teacher must be well prepared. He must have an overall view of the subject and its relationships as well as have a command of the particulars he desires to teach at a given time. In class he must not come across as dogmatic or pushy. The teacher must be a shepherd of thoughts—not one who drives, but one who leads his pupils to pastures of mental feeding.

The Pupil

The pupil's participation in the lecture method is generally minimal. Yet, there can be active participation, at least mentally.

The good teacher can stimulate this kind of interest. The student's mind is not a passive organ into which the teacher pours predigested materials and thoughts from his notebook. The student must digest and assimilate the material himself if real learning is to take place. Keep in mind that real learning involves changes in beliefs and practices. For this to happen the teacher must set in motion the self-learning process.

The Material

In the lecture method, more than in other methods, the subject determines organization and development of material. The student must be able to follow the presentation. Since the intellect functions logically, the subject should be organized logically, one step leading to another, with manifest relationships between parts. In this method the material may be better analyzed, synthesized, and balanced.

The lecture method does not exclude variety of presentation or adaptation to the needs of the pupils. The material must be chosen and adapted to meet the needs of the pupils. The aim should be to get the pupil to think along with the instructor in coming to a solution to his problem. Lecturing is not merely covering the material. The teacher must not let the material obstruct his vision for ministry to his pupils.

Advantages

The spoken word can have a strong impact upon an audience. Spoken words communicate more effectively than printed material. Inflection, emphasis, and explanation make oral presentation an energetic and dynamic method. The lecture conveys the influence of the teacher's personality. Attractive Christian character means much here. The lecture can arouse interest and motivate pupils. The spoken word has the dynamic qualities that draw men.

The lecture saves time. More ground can be covered by a lecture than by any other method. The lecture can be used with a large group better than any other method. It is easier to lecture than to teach by discussion or question. Since not all teachers are well trained in the more difficult methods of teaching, and since many schools find it difficult to enlist and train enough teachers, the lecture is more often used.

The lecture provides opportunity for use of supplementary elements, material that cannot be made available to pupils. Often written material presents only one view, while the teacher with much wider experience can present a broader picture. The lecture provides a means of giving the pupil proper perspective. Immature minds have difficulty making proper evaluations, seeing relationships, and discriminating between what is important and what is not. The lecture can properly interpret and organize the data.

Disadvantages

The lecture limits pupil participation, which is essential to learning. Pupils like activity; the lecture is static. The lecture method tends to encourage passivity and discourage responsibility. This method can stifle the desire to learn if handled without freshness and interest.

The lecture may not be an economical use of the pupils' time. If the teacher merely presents what pupils can get from a text, the time is wasted.

The lecture makes no provision for individual differences among pupils. Selection and coverage of materials, simple or difficult, must be made on the basis of group rather than individual needs.

The lecture requires ability in public speaking possessed by few teachers. However, some teachers can use the lecture method better than any other. Oral communication may be learned and improved. But few lecturers can be at their best constantly.

Teachers are prone to use the lecture method too much. An alert teacher will use more productive methods also.

The lecture may give the pupil more content than he can analyze, understand, or assimilate. The lecture generally gives the pupil only one contact with the material.

Preparing the Lecture

1. Relationship. Review a brief outline of the whole course. See

what part of the course is covered in this lecture and how this lecture relates to the one previous and the one following.

2. Content. Study the subject thoroughly. The more details you master, the more confidently you can present the important ones. Study prayerfully. Remember that the Holy Spirit is the only Teacher who can apply this lesson to the students' lives, and he works in answer to prayer. Study selectively. Out of the mass of available information, select the really essential points to get the lesson across. Determine the aim of the lecture. The aim should be threefold, for the whole personality: (a) What do you want the listeners to know? (intellect) (b) What do you want the listeners to feel? (sensibility) (c) What do you want the listeners to do? (will)

3. Plan. Select all possible teaching aids, and decide when to use them. Write out a complete lesson plan and outline. Assign time limits to each portion of lecture, and calculate the time on the clock when you should complete each section. Write these check times prominently on the lesson plan.

Presenting the Lecture

1. Introduction. Attract attention of the students, gain their sympathy, and set a friendly tone. Tell what you expect to cover in the lecture—the topic, the main points. Tell your listeners why they need to know this information—how they will benefit.

2. Body. Present the subject matter logically, clearly, enthusiastically, sincerely, sympathetically, and humorously (when appropriate). Even serious lectures are improved by a chuckle at intervals. Apply the subject specifically to the students. Don't generalize; give concrete suggestions as to how this can work for them. Be personal; remember that you are teaching individuals.

Evaluate your communication of ideas as you go along by inviting students to ask questions after each point. Test their grasp of each point by asking them pertinent questions. Be alert to their degree of interest. If interest lags, change your tempo, voice, or method; tell a story; produce an object to see; or otherwise regain attention. They will never learn what they don't hear.

3. Conclusion. Review the lesson briefly, summarizing main points. Restate and stress difficult points. When assigning preparation for the next lecture, show how that lecture relates to this one. "Sell it" to them. Challenge the students to make use of this current lesson, beginning now. End on the high note of challenge.

4. General suggestions. Observe rules of good homiletics and speech. Speak slowly, distinctly, and audibly, so that students in the back row understand easily. Use visual aids such as the chalkboard, maps, charts, graphs, pictures, and objects (for object lessons). Use illustrations such as Bible stories, stories from life, analogies, statistics and testimony from experts or authorities. Set some of your material up as a problem to solve. Unless the students are thinking, they are not learning. Observe the time limits set for each section in your lesson plan. Stop when the time is up. Observe the law of learning readiness. Use varied means of stimulating the pupils' thoughts on the subject to be covered. Arrange the room to suit your purpose. Use a center of attention.

When to Use Lecture

1. When the class is large and pupil participation must be limited

2. When pupil background and preparation are limited so as to seriously hamper pupil participation

3. When introducing new or unfamiliar subjects, when giving perspective or summarizing, or in the interpretation of difficult material when the students cannot be entrusted with the responsibility of coming up with the right answers on their own

4. When classroom seating arrangements are not conducive to informal discussion

5. When time is limited. The lecture can be easily altered. When teaching younger children, use the lecture sparingly in conjunction with or in transition between activities and other methods.

6. When the teacher desires to provoke and guide thinking and stimulate imagination and vision, or when students are not accustomed to other methods and reluctant to change
7. When the material lends itself best to coverage by organized lecture

When Not to Use Lecture

1. When it is possible to use other methods or when students are eager to participate, use other methods.
2. When students fall into lazy habits of not preparing for class, make challenging assignments geared to the life of the pupils.
3. When the class is small and well suited for the use of other methods, do not lecture.
4. When the class is below the senior high level, use lectures sparingly and wisely.
5. When practice is a necessary factor in the learning process, there must be demonstration and opportunity to teach. For example, one must teach to learn to teach. Practice perfects theory, and theory perfects practice.

Use of Lecture with Children

With preschoolers, lecture must be interspersed with activities. They have an attention span of two to ten minutes. Avoid extended lecture periods. Lecture must deal with the familiar, making use of the child's vocabulary. Illustrate points with objects and pictures. Lecture must emphasize the present with explanations in terms of the known. Children have a limited concept of space and time.

School-age children must be challenged to think but not be overtaxed. Their attention span is about seven to fifteen minutes. Lecture must provide reasonable explanations for everything, coupled with opportunities for making proper behavior choices. Their logic is developing, as well as their awareness of other ideas and beliefs. Lectures must avoid symbolism and abstraction, because children are literalists.

Use of Lecture with Youth

For early adolescents, lectures must be made interesting with up-to-date illustrations from real life. Strive for pupil participation.

Rapidly growing teens are awkward and restless, unable to find a comfortable position in their chairs. Data in the lecture must be well supported with authority. Allow the pupils to think for themselves. They want a reason for everything and are beginning to question the validity of presented ideas.

The lecture should make use of the increased ability of middle adolescents to reason. They progress to new concepts with less and less initial review because of an increase in memory span.

Lecture to later adolescents should be practical and related to actual problems. They have an insatiable desire for pragmatic knowledge. Lecture must not be dogmatic but should present the rationale behind the argument.

Use of Lecture with Adults

For early adulthood lecture must be used effectively. This audience has reached the peak of intellectual development and reasoning power. They think for themselves and evaluate everything. With this group lecturers must use creative techniques.

The lecture must challenge and motivate those in middle adulthood. Their mental abilities are most productive but will slow down if not used. Lecture must provide a broader outlook because some adults tend to grow opinionated and shallow with age.

Lecturers to older adults must recognize that their listeners have vast knowledge in many areas, good judgment, and many years of experience with life and the world.

LESSON PREPARATION

A lesson plan is a step-by-step arrangement of the content, methods, and procedures the teacher intends to use in order to help students learn and accomplish the lesson aim. There are six steps of lesson preparation that should be followed by both mature and beginning teachers. Each teacher will give different emphasis to each step; nevertheless, each step should be made.

Write the Aim

Sunday school teaching is not grinding out content. Nor is Sunday school teaching like a little boy playing with blocks, stacking them one upon the other in a hit-or-miss fashion. Often teaching is considered stacking blocks of content in the minds of students. When the pile of blocks reaches its limit (the mind absorption limit of the student), then the small boy says he is finished. The purpose of Sunday school teaching is not to communicate content only. "We teach for decisions," the wise teacher says.

Before you begin to teach, have clearly in mind a decision that you want pupils to make. This decision may be to accept Christ, to renounce a certain sin, to practice a certain behavior, or to change a certain attitude.

Try to state your aims briefly in one or two sentences. Determine what you want your students to know (mind), to feel (emotions), and to do (will).

The aims give direction to your study. Too often, Sunday school teaching has poor aims or none at all. Teachers aim at nothing and hit it with precise accuracy. (See also Aims in Teaching.)

Study the Scriptures

After you have completed your overview, you are ready to prepare for next Sunday. The first thing you should do is refresh your thinking about the content.

1. Read the Scriptures first. Ask yourself the following questions:
   a. What is the point of the passage?
   b. What problems do I see in the passage?
   c. What parallel passage in the Scriptures would shed light on this passage?
   d. What are some practical applications in this passage?
2. After you have spent some time thinking through these questions, consult your Sunday school quarterly. First, read the student's quarterly. This is the only material that the students will have at their disposal as they prepare for the lesson. It's important for you to know what the students will know. Teaching begins where the students are and takes them where they should be.

   Second, read over the teacher's manual. Usually, the teacher's manual contains more content explanation. The teacher's manual contains methodology, how to teach the lesson.

Remember, no teacher's manual can make teaching easy. Teaching is hard work. The teacher's manual was written to make you more effective, not to give you an easy time in preparation. The teacher's manual is written by competent authorities who want to communicate the Word of God in the most effective ways possible. Sometimes you may not like their suggestions. However, try to follow them.

3. Then turn to other study helps.

   a. A Bible commentary. This reference book explains the meaning of the verses in the Scriptures.

   b. A Bible dictionary. This reference book will give backgrounds, customs, geography, and the meaning of words in Scripture. You will also find a generous amount of doctrinal explanation in the Bible dictionary.

   c. A Bible concordance. This book will help you find passages of like meaning in Scripture. Suppose you are teaching a lesson on financial stewardship. A Bible concordance will help you find other passages in Scripture that will help you study this topic.

Forget about the dream of studying all day. Most teachers cannot find one large block of time when they can spend three or four hours studying their Sunday school lesson. If you are like the average American, every night is taken with a meeting, TV programs, or business engagements. Do not forget you have family obligations. Try to set aside a little time each day to study your Sunday school lesson. You may feel like this is asking too much, but should a Christian not set aside some time each day to be alone with God? Why not make your Sunday school lesson one source for personal growth? If God speaks to you through the Scripture portion of your Sunday school curriculum, then there is a likelihood he will speak to your students. A little study each day is better than cramming.

The following weekly outline has been suggested at many Sunday school workshops.

■ Sunday afternoon: Evaluate the day's lesson. Read over the next lesson.

- Monday–Wednesday: Study the Bible, using the quarterly and other helps.
- Thursday–Friday: Plan the actual lesson with aim, method and materials.
- Saturday: Gather materials. Review lesson.
- Sunday morning: Review briefly and teach the lesson.

4. Now comes the question of arranging the biblical content into a lesson plan. The Bible is the revelation of God; it tells of Jesus Christ, God's Son. Every revelation demands a response. Therefore, we must present biblical content in teaching for a decision. The question that now faces a teacher is, What content that I have studied should I choose to secure a decision in my pupils' lives?"

Arrange the Lesson in Outline Form

Lesson preparation is not done by writing an introduction. An introduction is a bridge from the student's life to the content, and the teacher must know the content before he builds the bridge. Therefore, the first step is to develop content into an organized whole. It should be sequential, building fact upon fact. Some of the following ways may be used to organize content:

1. A series of questions becomes the lesson outline. As either the teacher or the pupils answer each question, content is filled in. A teacher should write both questions and answers in his lesson plan. If he waits to create questions until he is before the class, the right type of questions may not come. If you try to think of the answers as you stand before your students, you may be caught between home and third. Use more than one type of question. The following list may help you create a variety of questions for teaching:
   a. Factual questions. Usually the pupils can find the fact in the Bible or in other source material.
   b. Interpretive questions. The pupils are challenged to interpret a verse of Scripture.
   c. Discussion questions. An open-ended question will bring out opinions and attitudes of the pupils.
   d. Exploration questions. Some questions take the form of a

project in which pupils are pointed to a problem and given resources for finding the answer.

    e. Opinion questions. At times the teacher will want to involve the pupils by asking them to state an opinion.

2. Use a series of propositional statements. Statements are given to the class, and the students are expected to explore the Word of God to find a biblical basis. If the class is large, perhaps the teacher will have to give the statement and then explain the Scripture that furnishes the proof.

3. List the Scripture verses with their explanation. This is a traditional manner of Sunday school teaching, but it should not be so overused that it becomes boring.

4. Use a modification or combination of the above. The whole lesson does not have to be written out. Sunday school teaching is not a written speech that is read to the pupils. Try reading a speech or the quarterly and you will drive them from the study of God's Word. Be spontaneous in your presentation. Get pupils to discuss and ask questions. You should interact with them. Points in your outline should be like seeds to be sown, rather than full-bloom plants to be admired. Jesus said the Word of God is like seed sown upon the earth. You sow a seed in the mind of your pupils, and God will bring forth a full grown plant in their lives.

However, transitional sentences should be written out in entirety. These are hinges that turn the lesson from one point to another. As you finish the introduction and move into your first point, you want to keep your pupils' interest. The introduction should have captured their attention. Now keep the pupils by a smooth transition.

Write the Conclusion

Teaching without a conclusion is like fishing without a hook. The fisherman may have the best lure and equipment and be a skilled fisherman, yet if he doesn't have a hook, he can't catch fish. If teaching is for decisions, then the conclusion should be designed to have pupils make a decision.

A conclusion is the aim of the Sunday school lesson applied to the life of the pupil resulting in the pupil's decision. The whole element of making a decision should be under the guidance of the teacher.

Some lessons are not concluded, they're just finished. Some teachers talk up to the final minute trying to cram in the last bit of Bible fact, then announce, "we'll take up here next Sunday." This teacher doesn't conclude, he just finishes . . . finishes the opportunity for God to work . . . finishes his opportunity to make a change in the pupil's life . . . and finishes his greatest opportunity in life.

What about the invitation? Should the teacher in the Sunday school class give an invitation, that is, ask children to close their eyes, bow their heads, and raise their hands as an indication they want to receive Christ? In small Sunday school classes, teachers should take the initiative to speak personally to each student about receiving Christ. If teachers don't have the courage to face pupils with the claims of Christ, they shouldn't hide behind the invitation. However, there may be times when God's Spirit works through such invitations, especially when the class is so large that the teacher cannot make a personal contact with each pupil.

A conclusion should summarize your main ideas and refresh the minds of the students. Try to get them to see the unity of the lesson.

Is it all right to have loose ends when you come to the end of a lesson? Loose ends are acceptable if they are live ends. Loose ends drive the student from the classroom to seek answers and resolve issues for himself. These live ends are the very art of teaching. However, loose ends that leave the student confused, perplexed, and frustrated are a manifestation of poor teaching.

When coming to your conclusion, avoid letting interest lag. Do not introduce new material. You are trying to drive for a decision; new materials may sidetrack students' thoughts. Also, do not conclude by apologizing for a poor lesson. If the lesson is poor, the students will know it. If the class has been poor, you may have introduced doubts into their thoughts about the Word of God.

The conclusion should be short, varied, real, personal, pointed, appropriate.

Write the Introduction

The introduction is the last part of the lesson to be prepared. The purpose of an introduction is to bridge the gap from where students are to where they should be. You must prepare your lesson before you can bridge the gap from the student to that content.

A good introduction catches the attention of the pupil, creates a desire to learn, inspires him to action, and becomes a point of contact.

An introduction should promise the students something. However, like a down payment at the department store, when you promise there is more to follow. You lose your investment without the follow-through.

Some of the following types of introductions can be used:

1. A story from everyday life
2. A story from the Scriptures
3. A current event illustrated by a newspaper clipping
4. A question, "Who is the tallest?"
5. Use of a visual aid: for example, a model plane for junior boys
6. A film strip or slides secured from the church library
7. A quotation from a book or significant author, such as Martin Luther
8. A picture: for example, one that reflects the lesson to primary children
9. A drawing on the chalkboard

Choose the Method

The lesson plan is completed. You have planned your material. Now is the time to give attention to methods. Think in terms of two or three methods that can be used with your class. A strategy for choosing the right methods is included in the article Methods of Teaching.

In addition to the above, consider the following in your lesson preparation:

1. Start lesson preparation early in the week, so reading and experiences may be incorporated.
2. Have a central aim in your lesson. Observe the unit aim in your quarterly (if any).

3. Read the background Scripture passages from several versions for clarification.

4. Let the passage soak in by slow, thoughtful meditation.

5. Use commentaries, Bible dictionaries, and a Bible atlas for additional help.

6. Develop a clear outline for the class to follow. Choose from your teacher's manual what you can fit into the class period and what you want to emphasize.

7. Arrange time for prayer, review, Bible study (lesson), Bible reading, discussion, pupil's book, memory work, application, and closing. Be flexible.

8. Remember the needs of individuals in your class (discovered through visitation). Keep in mind that you are teaching persons and not just lesson content. Know the age group.

9. Develop a file with a folder for each topic to add illustrations, outlines, and other teaching aids each year you continue to teach.

10. Know the work required in the pupil's book. Determine how to use it in class review, work period, and discussion.

11. Plan an interesting approach to capture attention. This may be a question to stimulate thought, a problem to solve, a true-life story to illustrate the lesson, a visual aid to motivate interest in the lesson.

12. Plan variety in methods—visuals, object lessons, drama, stories, sword drills, questions and answers, discussion, writing, buzz groups, problem solving.

13. Plan thoroughly what to say or ask to arouse class participation. Mere telling is not teaching; listening is not learning.

14. Develop study questions to cause the pupils to delve into the Bible for themselves—who, what, when, where, why (What does the Bible say? What does it mean? What does it mean to me?).

15. Allow pupils to ask questions. If you don't know the answers, admit it and state you will seek the answer during the week, or assign the question to the class for study.

16. Allow pupils to make applications for themselves. Suggest some applications and let them decide.

17. Prepare the room before the class period, arranging chairs, visual-aid equipment, decorations, objects.
18. Pray for wisdom in preparation, clarity in presentation, and sincerity in application.

LESSON PREPARATION WITH OTHER TEACHERS

Many teachers study the lesson by themselves. While studying alone is necessary and beneficial, there are many times teachers can do a greater job when they plan with other teachers in the department who teach children of the same approximate age or use the same lesson materials. If there is a substitute or assistant teacher (and there should be), plan with them.

Procedures

1. Evaluate last Sunday's lesson.
2. Read together the Scripture passage to be taught the following Sunday.
3. Pray together.
4. Discuss and write out the purpose of the lesson.
5. Share the results of individual home study.
6. Compile a list of learning activities.
7. Consider activities that may be suggested by the children.
8. Practice songs.
9. Fellowship with one another.

All teachers should study the lesson before the planning session. Certainly they should read the teacher's manual and the appropriate pages in the pupil's workbook. Each should bring a list of songs, Scripture verses to be used, topics for conversation, possible related activities, handwork to be used.

1. Evaluation should be a continuing process. Begin by looking at last week. Draw up a series of questions to use in judging the success of class-time activities. Honest answers to your questions will disclose weaknesses, and you may need to guard against developing a negative attitude or a tendency toward discouragement. Learn to profit from mistakes by stepping over them to new heights. Growth, progress, and development come as you climb over obstacles.

You bear the responsibility of guiding others in self-evaluation, but the responsibility of analysis and correction rests with all.

2. Begin each planning session by reading the Scripture passage that will be used. Even though each teacher should have read the passage and studied the teacher's manual before coming to the meeting, each one needs to hear the passage again in order to have it fresh in his mind.

3. Each should have opportunity to lead in prayer. The responsibilities for the total growth of the class belong to each teacher; therefore, each one should undergird the class in prayer. Furthermore, everyone should pray for other teachers.

4. Most manuals state the aim of every lesson. This is an excellent place to begin. Discuss the purpose of the lesson as you see it. Sharpen, redefine, and crystallize the purpose in your mind as you share ideas and make suggestions.

5. As each studies his lesson, he will discover unique approaches to the lesson. In a time of sharing, a teacher can give insight and even teach other teachers. Hence, everyone becomes stronger.

6. Planning is particularly effective in choosing learning activities for the class. Everyone should be encouraged to make suggestions—and all suggestions should be seriously evaluated.

In your final planning, try to anticipate and think through questions the pupils may raise from their study. Determine how each teacher can help the pupils find answers.

Decide on and spell out the specific responsibilities of each person on the team. Write out a lesson plan including the sequence of events and persons responsible for each leadership task.

Team planning usually results in broad plans. Plans should be definite enough that each will be able to proceed with his continued individual preparation, yet flexible enough to allow the pupils' ideas to be incorporated into the lesson.

7. Plan to devote part of the activity time on Sunday morning to

planning with a pupil for the Sunday school lesson. Do not be disappointed if the suggestions made by the pupils are childish, for they are children. The important thing to remember is that a child's suggestions are meaningful to him, and the result is often a true learning experience. Allow some time for his help—but let it be help with your guidance.

Pupils of all ages can share certain responsibilities. Pupils of all ages need some experience in problem solving, decision making, and expressing their own ideas at their own level.

Young children may suggest activities or experiences they enjoy. Listen carefully for children's questions and comments. Note their interests and disinterests as well. Older pupils are able to assume more direct responsibility in helping to determine their own needs and interests by evaluating their own progress in terms of "How are we doing?"

8. Sing the songs and choruses you plan to use. Practice gives confidence to the one leading the singing on Sunday morning. If you plan to use the piano or sing with the record player, practice with it in the planning session. But don't forget that young children can usually sing as well without a piano as they can with one.

The person who leads the children's singing does not need to have a trained voice, but he should possess a clear, well-pitched, pleasing voice. The purpose of singing in church is to worship God. This is not the time to teach the principles of music. Rather, it is a time to teach children the joy of singing from the heart.

Sing songs that are interwoven with the other materials and activities of the Sunday morning lesson. Try to relate the songs to life's experiences and to the lessons found in Scripture. If you have a pianist, ask her to play a new song for the children before you ask them to sing it. (Teachers should learn the songs at the weekly planning session, not during the Bible-school hour.) In teaching a new song to the children, play only the melody. Here are a few additional suggestions to help the leader:

a. Sing gospel songs from memory; teach a song to children only after you know it.

b. Learn the words and teach them correctly.

c. If possible, write the words out before the children for them to see.

d. Use correct pronunciation of all words.

e. Play the music as written without pianistic interpretation.

f. Avoid bass embellishments.

g. Project rhythm in stirring songs.

h. Use proper introductions.

i. Begin at the first stanza of the hymn and end on a tonic chord.

9. In an effective teaching program, each member of the teaching team gives support to the others. The timid teacher should be encouraged to assume leadership when he is ready. Members of the team should offer praise and commendation to other teachers for a job well done. Constructive suggestions should be given and sought, so that each member helps improve the teaching and learning skills of the others.

When You Lead Other Teachers

Can anyone be a lead teacher? What are the duties of a lead teacher? Is it possible to be an effective classroom teacher, but an ineffective lead teacher? May one be a good member of the team, but a poor lead teacher?

There is no simple answer to any of these questions. One person may be a good lead teacher in one church, but a poor lead teacher in another church. Still another person may not make a good lead teacher in any situation.

Duties of the Lead Teacher

1. The lead teacher is responsible for group planning sessions. Sometimes he will lead the group in planning sessions. Sometimes he will delegate leadership to another member of the team. But in the final analysis, a lead teacher will make the greatest contribution to the total class through effective group plannning sessions.

2. The lead teacher may promote harmonious relationships

between parents and teachers. Correlation of home and classroom teaching is important for the spiritual development of children. Some educators view the school as an extension of the home. The good lead teacher develops good parent-teacher relationships.

3. The lead teacher implements policies made on the organizational level. He is the key to communication between the team and the Christian education committee. He fills the gap that might otherwise separate the team from the Sunday school organization.

4. The lead teacher takes the initiative in securing adequate space, equipment, and supplies. While the teacher who acts as secretary may actually order and handle the supplies, the lead teacher should be aware of the supplies that are ordered and see that the budget is respected. When class attendance overcrowds a room, the lead teacher has the responsibility of making the need known to the Christian education committee.

5. The lead teacher helps recruit new teachers for the team. The committee may be responsible for finding and enlisting new teachers, but sometimes the wheels of progress grind slowly. Because of his position on the team, the lead teacher is best qualified to recruit for his department and submit his selections to the committee for approval. He should have the courage not only to seek the best teacher available for his team but to weed out unlikely prospects as well. Not all potential teachers make good members of the team.

6. The lead teacher guides in teacher enrichment. He should encourage team members to attend Christian education conventions and church workers' conferences. Also, he should encourage members of the team to enroll in classes that can help them become more effective teachers. He may plan in-service training experience for the team. In general, the lead teacher should do all within his ability to improve the teaching of everyone on the team.

7. The lead teacher encourages teacher visitation in the home. Team responsibility for children must not discourage indi-

vidual teacher contact with children. Instead, it should encourage a closer relationship. Nevertheless, planning is needed in order to ensure that all children are being visited. The team should frankly discuss the visitation ministry, making sure the teacher with the right personality visits the right pupil.

Conclusion

Teachers must know one another well if they are to work together as a team. Knowing one another means helping one another and sharing experiences. Informal fellowship among the team members is as basic to team teaching, as is serious planning. This is one reason for regular planning sessions. One busy hour on Sunday morning simply does not provide sufficient time to know one another. Light refreshments make the planning more enjoyable, and they may help to establish an informal atmosphere.

In summary, the lead teacher's responsibility is exactly what the title suggests—to lead. The team works together, plans together, prays together, and rejoices together. And in the final analysis, the lead teacher is a member of the team. Together, they serve the Lord.

LEVETT, GUY (1889–1971)

Guy Levett was called "Mr. Sunday School" among the Christian churches of America. For years he served as editor of the *Lookout,* published through Standard Publishing Company, Cincinnati, Ohio, serving the independent Christian churches. Guy Levett wrote *Teach with Success* and *Superintend with Success,* both published by Standard Publishing Company, which became influential among many denominations for its practical approach to running a Sunday school.

LIBRARIAN (DIRECTOR OF RESOURCE CENTER)

The person chosen as church librarian (Director of Resource Center) will be the key to whether or not the library ultimately enhances the total ministry of the church. As in every other department of the church, no library will succeed without an enthusiastic, capable administrator. Nominating elderly or single persons as candidates for librarian simply because they have no other duties in the Sunday school or church is an illogical move. Any preconceived idea that a librarian must of necessity be stodgy and stuffy is equally absurd. If being elderly, or single, or unoccupied is the committee's lone consideration for a librarian, top performance cannot be expected of the person chosen. Neither should possession of fine Christian character or a deep appreciation for books be the sole criteria for choosing a person for your church librarian. The person you choose may have some or all of these traits—none would necessarily detract—yet by themselves they do not qualify a person for the job at hand.

Survey your congregation for someone who meets the following criteria:

1. *Christian character.* The pastor or church officer who displays anything less than the highest spiritual character becomes suspect. The library committee, too, must appoint a person whose life shows that Christ has redeemed him. He may be serving some who attend church but have never met the Lord, as well as new and even unstable Christians.

2. *Cooperative spirit.* Some might say a cooperative spirit is part of Christian character, and ideally it is. But not all persons of fine Christian character have the ability to work closely and well with other people. Some do their best work alone, without giving help or receiving it. The "loner" should probably not be asked to be church librarian, for the position has built into it constant interruptions and requests for help. The librarian must be open to new ideas from church leaders, members, friends, and even little children, since the library will serve them all. Those who are charged with the appointment of a librarian are probably already aware of the men and women in the congregation who seem to have no trouble getting along with others. Shouldn't they be placed on the "prospect" list for librarian to determine if they measure up in other ways? The untried person who holds no other job in the church should also be considered.

The librarian works under the supervision of the church

board and the board of Christian education. Therefore, he must be subject to them and carry out their directions.

3. *An appreciation for books.* This qualification has a twofold meaning. The most helpful kind of librarian loves books for what they can give him personally, but he is also knowledgeable about all kinds of books for all types of people. Stand at the counter of your public library some day and listen to a conversation between the librarian and those checking out books. The librarian has himself read many of the books, or at least reviews of them, and thus converses intelligently with borrowers about their reading material. This eavesdropping proves twice as interesting in the children's section. An interested librarian may be able to tell a child the entire tale in the book the child has just selected, but he never does that. He tells just enough of the story to send the eager child scurrying home, anticipating the wonderful secrets awaiting him inside the covers.

The librarian should know how to stimulate people to read anything and everything good. He realizes that the church library should be equipped to meet the needs of everyone, from its scholars and teachers to the youngest and newest readers in the Sunday school.

4. *Organizational ability.* The librarian must keep his inventory neat and attractive, well supplemented, and cataloged. He is responsible for maintaining regular library hours, whether or not he himself can be there. He also chooses dependable helpers.

5. *Patience and persistence.* Some church members will besiege the library with requests for books both new and old. Others will be thankful if the librarian is not the type to tackle them and tie a book to them; the thought of reading carries absolutely no pleasure for them. But a patient, kind person behind the library desk can get to the most hardened nonreader.

6. *Initiative and leadership ability.* Some may view the church library as a one-man operation that can be safely staffed by an introverted bookworm. He may be so efficient as to have computerlike knowledge of every book and who checked it out. He

may in reality wish that each and every book stood safely in its appointed place on the library shelf. The library needs a broader and more open personality overseeing its operation.

The librarian's initiative will be evident when he introduces new ideas and trends to the attention of church officers. His leadership will show as he implements these ideas for the good of the congregation.

Skills of the Librarian

1. *Knowledge or experience in library work.* The person who has little knowledge of library mechanics, but who does have the time and interest, may quickly compensate by reading or by observing others who do have library skills. The committee may need to give an untried person the chance, if that person meets other requirements. The person who shows efficiency in other aspects of life would probably also be able to run the church library efficiently.

2. *Typing ability.* Lack of typing ability can be a real hindrance to the librarian, but he can compensate by enlisting some clerical help. This might be the place to try out church members who have no other jobs. If they fit in well in this comparatively simple assignment, they could be considered for other jobs.

Duties of the Librarian

The committee should not finalize its choice of a librarian until it has submitted a list of duties to the prospect. The person considering the position must decide whether he is willing and able to perform those duties. He should then meet with the committee, whose chairman would be prepared to again review the tasks that are expected of the church librarian, in order to avoid misunderstanding about the job and its ramifications.

Following is a list of duties of the librarian. The local church library committee will probably want to add to this list.

1. Lead in selecting appropriate books and materials. Particularly good sources from which to make selection of books are the catalogs and publication announcements of Christian publishers. Ask that the name of your church be placed on

their mailing lists, read their notices yourself, and pass them on to the leaders of clubs and other groups in the church to elicit suggestions for possible selection of new materials. Subscribe to Christian education magazines and display them for teacher use. Read reviews of new books from as many periodicals as possible; this will help you choose the best books for your library. Read or skim books that you think the library needs, and know something of their content so that you can answer future inquiries by members. Note books that members request that you buy, and try to fit them into your budget.

2. Supervise the processing and shelving of books.
3. Maintain definite library hours to coincide with the educational programs of the church. This means scheduling your assistants so that a knowledgeable clerk is always on hand to check out books and teaching resources.
4. Supervise the checking out and returning of materials, and issue overdue notices. Inefficiency in these operations will cause a breakdown of the library ministry. Strive to have this operation so firmly in hand that by checking the records, you can quickly ascertain whether or not a certain book is on the shelf. There is no guesswork in the efficient library. The records show who has checked out any book. Always offer to reserve it for someone when it is returned. A church librarian is involved in God's ministry, and this fact should challenge him to be exceptionally conscientious in his work.
5. Give courteous aid. Often library patrons need help in locating books, equipment, and materials.
6. Maintain financial records. Accurate records should be kept of both money received (as gifts, from overdue book fees, from the budget, and from book sales in the church) and funds dispersed for all library expenses. The librarian must also write a proposed budget and submit it to the committee for approval. Categories to be included in the budget are:
   a. Books
   b. Visual aids (slides, transparencies, filmstrips, flannelgraphs, pictures, maps)

    c. Visual-aid equipment (such as screens, projectors, and flannelgraphs) These are costly items, so plan accordingly.

    d. New library equipment (shelves, filing cabinets)

    e. Office and library supplies (such as stationary, typewriter ribbons, records)

    f. Audio tapes

    g. Video tapes

    h. Records: music, stories, and lessons

    i. Periodicals

7. Attend Christian education conferences with the Sunday school staff. Such conferences are excellent sources of information on new equipment and materials, as well as on new educational trends. Be present at all teachers' meetings of the local church, and be prepared to demonstrate the use of teaching aids or to review a new book that will be of genuine value to teachers.

8. Take charge of promotion. The librarian should write library items for local newspapers and the church bulletin, describing library services or new material and equipment.

LIBRARY/RESOURCE CENTER/MEDIA CENTER

The church library is believed by many to be the storage place for storybooks for boys and girls who have time for reading. The church library is actually one of the most valuable educational resources in the church. Today's church libraries are more than books on a shelf; they are media resource centers and include audio and video tapes as well as other resources that may complement the Christian education ministry of the church. This entry will use the traditional term *library*, while realizing other titles are used such as Media Resource Center, or Educational Resource Center.

What's in the Library?

1. *Books.* Variety is the key word in selecting books for any library. The reading preferences of Christians vary as much as their tastes in food and clothing.

    First, there is fiction. Since Sunday school pupils of all ages can go to the public library and find all manner of fiction books, the church library would do well to major on fiction with a distinctively Christian message. More than one life has been changed and strengthened through the influence of a good book. If in doubt about selections, check the catalogs of Christian publishing houses for titles.

In the nonfiction field, the church should seek out biographies of persons who are recognized for their Christian testimony. Boys and girls of junior age often prefer biography to fiction, and through it young people and adults can become acquainted with faithful, outstanding Christians. "Book friends" wield an influence akin to that of human friends, for they represent people's thoughts.

In how-to books, pupils of all ages can learn various crafts and perfect their hobbies. This may be the chief reason for a library visit at first. Looking for self-help books, patrons may be attracted to Christian adventure stories or biographies.

Many Christians cannot afford to buy expensive books, but would like to study the Bible in depth. The church library should aid them by having available Bible dictionaries, handbooks, atlases, commentary sets, books for self-study, and books of Bible background. Christian publishers' catalogs list such books.

A Sunday school member should be able to go to the library and select any book there without feeling unsure as to whether the book is reliable and biblical.

2. *Periodicals.* Magazines of family help as well as Christian magazines for various age levels should be available. Again, people can find secular magazines in the public library. The church can make a greater life investment by assisting people as they become acquainted with the best in Christian literature. Fiction, Bible study, Christian education, and other features are found in leading Christian magazines. The reference department of a city library should be able to provide addresses for specific magazines.

3. *Reference file.* The church librarian should file clippings, stories, articles, and poetry by subject. This will aid teachers

who seek supplementary material for lessons. Some churches file pictures and maps.

4. *Slides, filmstrips, transparencies.* If the church purchases slides or filmstrips for use in a given class or department, the visual aids should be placed in the library after use. This allows other teachers to use materials that are too costly for each class to purchase and use only on rare occasions. Some churches have established video lending libraries making Christian videos available to families in their church.

5. *Video tapes, audio tapes, films.* The modern library-media center will include these resources for teachers.

Who Uses the Library?

1. *Teachers.* "There is no leading without reading," a wise teacher knows. It is impossible for a stagnant pool to give forth fresh water. A teacher can find enrichment and be revitalized by seeking out study or devotional books in the library. The alphabetical clipping file will aid in lesson preparations, as will the file of slides and filmstrips and other materials.

2. *Officers.* The library should have books and periodicals that will help each Sunday school worker do his best work.

3. *Adults.* Avid readers will explore many types of books. The less eager but willing should be able to find a variety from which to choose. The librarian should have a working knowledge of the shelves and be able to guide persons who come. Many do not know how to use a catalogued library and need help.

4. *Youth.* A well-organized library will have a designated section containing books especially geared for teens. If this is impossible, they may need help finding titles most interesting to and profitable for them.

5. *Juniors.* Often the most prolific readers are in this department. A bright-jacketed book of any level may appeal to them—but they can be guided to the best available at their level of understanding. If the library is attractively arranged with some age-level displays, children will easily find their favorites.

6. *New readers.* Happy is the church family that can find books for their youngest readers. Books with large print and graded vocabulary are carefully maintained in the public school and public library. Church libraries should also stock books for young readers.

7. *Preschoolers.* Visiting the library should be a family affair. Pupils in the youngest classes should be able to find picture books that will increase their Bible knowledge and appreciation for God in making his beautiful world. Pictures stimulate thought, leading to questions for which parents can provide Christian answers. Because books of Bible and character stories to be read aloud by parents are not found in every home, the Sunday school library should provide them.

Where Is the Library?

This question should not have to be asked—except in large churches where a guided tour is necessary to find any particular section of the church. In average churches, a library display in the foyer should give easy directions for locating the library.

Every teacher and officer in the church should know where the library is in order to direct pupils and newcomers. If the library seems unknown to the majority of the membership, a quarterly or annual Library Day might remedy the situation. During the evening service, allow a five-minute announcement of available services. The librarian should mention exciting new books available and call attention to a few old favorites. At the close of the service, he may encourage an open-house visit.

The library goes to Sunday school in some churches. Rolling shelves take appropriate books to each class during the first ten minutes of the session, allowing pupils to return borrowed books and check out new ones. This practice keeps the library's riches in the minds of all. Some who would forget to stop in for a book will borrow one brought to class. Additionally, some church libraries take the books to the homes of shut-ins, allowing them to have the pleasure of choosing their favorite reading.

When Should the Library Be Open?

Before or after the regular services, pupils usually find it most convenient to return and borrow books. At churches where a staff is present daily, the library is open at specified times every day. The schedule should be set by the staff.

How Can a Library Be Started?

1. *Church Budget.* A sum may be allocated annually for the purchase of books and library supples.
2. *Donations.* Christian families who have outgrown or completed reading some of their books may give them to the library.
3. *Memorial Gifts.* An increasing number of Christian families are specifying memorial gifts of books instead of flowers at their decease.
4. *Special offerings.* In connection with Library Day, the church may receive a special offering for new books and periodicals.

Why a Church Library?

Doesn't the church have enough expense without stocking a library? Can't people go to the public library and find something to read? These questions are answered in the foregoing sections of this article. The public library may or may not have suitable books for the Christian family. What they have in their section on religion may or may not be biblical. Each church, therefore, is responsible for helping its own people grow and mature in their faith by providing a balanced, nourishing spiritual diet. Reading material is to the mind and heart what food is to the body. Just as the body is weak or strong, depending on the person's diet, so the spiritual life may be weakened or strengthened by the mental diet. The church library can and should be an important source of that strength.

LIBRARY COMMITTEE

The first step in organizing a church library ought to be the appointment by the board of Christian education or the church board of a committee to organize and direct library affairs. The four or five members of this committee should represent all activities and age groups within the congregation (such as Sunday school, youth work, women's missionary group, camp, and club work). This spread of representation will help the library to meet the needs of various groups for source material. An added benefit will be that news of the availability of materials will be carried back to these groups by their representative on the library committee.

Those appointed should have the following qualifications:

1. The ability to discern, recognize, and even seek out the resource materials that are an important part of the modern church library. Schoolteachers, those in publishing or merchandising, or those with an artistic bent, would probably be aware of the trends in Christian resource materials.

2. Familiarity with or experience in library operation. This prerequisite insures that the committee can become active without the need of training recruits. If people with this qualification are not available, someone on the committee should ask for help and advice from the local public or school librarian.

3. An interest and desire to establish and promote a church library. A person who is aggressive in upgrading the church's total Christian education endeavor ought to be invited to serve on the library committee, for he will be more aware of its full potential to aid in communicating the Christian faith through up-to-date methods and materials and through a librarian who will energetically teach and encourage their use.

Committee Duties

Those people who finally do constitute the library committee should understand their duties. These are:

1. To appoint a qualified librarian.

2. To establish policies of and give direction to the library. It must strive to meet effectively the best standards of Christian education and also serve the needs of individual church members.

3. To provide the vision and motivation. The committee will have no trouble fulfilling this duty in a church that is located

in an educationally sophisticated community. However, the speed with which goals are met and the methods used in starting or upgrading the church library will always depend upon the church's geographic location, the available funds, and the spiritual, cultural, and intellectual levels of the members of the church. This is not to say that a church in a poorer community ought to budget a lesser percentage for its library than does an affluent church. Churches in poorer communities actually have greater educational needs. Such a church should probably spend much more money on educational materials, with the special needs of its people as prime criteria for selecting these materials. The spiritual indoctrination of the unchurched or underprivileged child or adult must begin on a much simpler level than for those who at least know the language of the church. The new junior boy in a suburban Sunday school class interrupted the teacher to ask, "What is sin?" At the other extreme of spiritual awareness, a sixth grader in the same Sunday school candidly inquired of his teacher during a lesson, "Is everyone who died before Christ was born now in hell?" Such remarks indicate the wide range of needs with which the Sunday school teacher is confronted. The library committee is indirectly responsible for meeting this range of needs by providing teachers with the proper resource materials.

4. To correlate library services with other agencies in the church. This includes alerting department superintendents, teachers, and group leaders to the supplementary materials that the library has purchased or plans to buy. They should then create opportunities for the librarian to demonstrate these new acquisitions. Library committee members should constantly alert themselves to the needs of groups within the church, then seek ways in which the library can help those groups accomplish their purposes. Committee members can also be active in demonstrating methods and materials. For example, one enthusiastic committee member realized that a tape recorder would be useful everywhere, from the Preschool to the Home De-

partment of the Sunday school. The library purchased a moderately priced, easily operated model. The adult teacher used it first—he taped his Sunday morning lesson to send to shut-ins of the church. This taping idea soon caught on. Preschool teachers taped songs from phonograph records as an aid in class teaching of songs. Another teacher taped her class as they practiced for a special program; thus pupils were able to detect their own mistakes. Teenagers who were using skits to become aware of real life situations in class taped these skits for self-criticism and appraisal of spiritual applications. This church soon found that one tape recorder was not sufficient for its use, and the library committee purchased a second machine.

5. To assume responsibility for selecting books, as well as educational equipment and materials.

6. To oversee the operation of the library. The librarian cannot singlehandedly carry all the responsibility for enforcing rules, managing finances, and supervising the performance of the library personnel. The committee must give assistance in this ministry. It is physically and emotionally impossible for one person to enforce every library rule and still fulfill the job of being a competent, helpful librarian. Others on the committee can set the example of acceptable library conduct and then instruct children, teenagers, and others in the correct use of the church library. Leaders and teachers will be borrowing and returning teaching aids both before and after almost any activity. Committee members should both encourage good library conduct and help to keep the flow of teaching materials operating smoothly.

The library must have efficient help to maintain its strength as the hub of the church educational program. The librarian himself should make clear (probably in writing) just what he expects of his helpers. The committee should also be discreetly aware of library assistants who are not performing well and who may be taking the librarian away from more important duties. If the removal of unsatisfactory help becomes necessary, the committee might work with the board of Christian education to first discover another type of job in the church for that person. Make him feel more needed in another place, and he will probably be relieved to give up the library job. The committee needs patience in forming a competent, congenial team of workers.

7. To act as a sounding board. The librarian should be able to turn to the library committee for advice on new programs and projects that he or other church members propose as an extension of the church's ministry, including such matters as fund-raising, promotion, and any matters that are not specifically written into library policy.

LIBRARY, FINANCING THE (See FINANCING THE LIBRARY)

LIBRARY, PROMOTION (See PROMOTING THE LIBRARY)

LIBRARY RULES

To function as an effective educational arm of the church, the library must formulate some rules that will not only regulate procedures, but encourage library use. A list of rules that has been adopted by the library committee should be printed in a "Guide to the Library." Photocopies are usually sufficient for the average church. Following are guidelines for formulation of rules that will probably be needed:

1. *Hours.* The library should be open at regular, specified times. This factor, plus the attractiveness of the room, will determine the initial response given to the new facility. For example, Sunday school teachers are often encouraged to arrive from ten to thirty minutes before class time to get the classroom in readiness and to greet the students. The clerk or librarian should be on hand during this time to check out materials.

   After church services, two activities will take place in the library. Church members will browse for books and will need help in checking them out. Teachers will be returning materials and perhaps be searching for the items necessary for next week's lesson. The librarian may need to train extra clerks to serve during hours of heaviest traffic, since he himself may not be able to be present all the times the library is open. A church should experiment to find the best library hours for itself.

2. *Use of the library.* Rules for use should indicate who may use the library and when they may use it. The library committee must specify when persons are welcome to use reference sources and check out books. Should this include church members, community members, other pastors, or only those who actually attend the church? Certain benefits come from welcoming community people. The adult who comes seeking a certain bit of information might be attracted to the gospel in numerous ways. School children may ask to use your library while writing a report or term paper. These are opportunities to minister; however, they should not prevent full utilization of library services by those engaged in the Christian education ministry of the church.

It may be necessary to exclude all but teachers before Sunday school, especially if space and help are limited. If such a rule is necessary, Sunday school teachers should encourage the use of the library by students at other times.

3. *Period of loans of books and equipment.* The standard length of a book loan is two weeks; those in current demand may be borrowed for seven days. The librarian maintains a list of those next in line for a book in great demand. Rules for other procedures will have to be established: May a book be renewed? For how long and how many times? May someone (such as a shut-in) borrow or renew a book by telephone? What procedure should be followed in the event a book is returned in poor condition—with missing pages, perhaps, or otherwise marred?

The rules for loaning teaching aids must differ from those for books since the requests for these aids will be frequent. The librarian might post sign-up sheets for each piece of equipment, on which the teacher is asked to sign his name and the date he wishes to use the equipment. Through the sign-up sheet, other staff members will immediately be able to see whether or not a certain machine is available. The same method might be used to distribute seasonal teaching aids, thus eliminating the need for the librarian to search through the records for this information. When the budget allows, the librarian should plan to duplicate equipment that is in constant demand. Although usage should be encouraged, teachers should be discouraged from monopolizing teaching aids.

4. *Overdue fees.* Should there be a charge for overdue books, and if so, at what rate? Individual circumstances may indicate that no charges should be levied. However, a general policy of charging two cents for each day a book is past due (or ten cents a week) would increase respect for library rules. Publicize the fact that overdue book fees go toward replacing books.

Exceptions to the past-due rule may be made in cases of illness, for shut-ins, and in cases where the librarian knows that a book has a special kind of ministry, such as a Sunday school teacher who keeps a book through a quarter to supplement lesson preparation, or the person whose personal spiritual battle is being aided through a particular book.

5. *Books that have been lost or ruined.* If the family responsible for losing or ruining a book does not offer to replace it, the librarian must decide whether or not to buy another copy. Prior circulation of the book will help him determine this. Possibly it would be better to replace it with a new publication. Repeated requests for a volume no longer in the library due to loss or damage would indicate that a new copy should be ordered.

The few remaining rules affect the mechanical operation of the library. The committee may need to consult a professional librarian, or at least a comprehensive handbook on library operation.

LIFE-STYLE EVANGELISM

The basic premise of life-style evangelism is that the unsaved must know more than the words of the gospel because gospel orthodoxy never saved anyone. Your style of life will win them to Christ. First, they must see its message in you. Second, because of your role model, they will desire to have the same kind of life. But in the third place, they will see Christ in you, then identify with him and accept him into their lives. It is built on a valid premise that the life-style of every Christian should be a witness for Jesus Christ (Acts 1:8).

Life-style evangelism tends to be a reaction to what has been called personal evangelism. This is the style of evangelism that is usually taught in courses on soul winning. Personal evangelism is usually (1) confrontational, (2) verbal (giving the plan of salvation), (3) non–church related, and (4) stranger-oriented.

Life-style evangelism swings to the other side, in that it is more (1) nonconfrontational, (2) nonverbal, and (3) friendship-oriented.

Most books on personal evangelism are confrontational in nature, designed to help Christians lead others to a decision to accept Jesus Christ. This approach to evangelism scares some Christians from evangelizing because they are not confrontational in their life-styles. Life-style evangelism allows them to use their nonverbal testimony to influence others for Christ. Some have attacked life-style evangelism because they feel it is too passive for their approach to evangelism. However, do not place a qualitative (right or wrong) judgment on life-style evangelism; look at it quantitatively. It is not the most effective approach to evangelism, but it has a place and some influence.

LISTENING TEAMS

Listening teams are a method of teaching whereby the whole class is divided into teams, or a certain number of students are assigned a task during the lesson and given an opportunity to report their findings. Each listening team should have from four to six people on it; four groups are ideal. In each team appoint a team captain to make a report to the entire class after the lecture. Divide the class into teams by number and instruct them to sit together according to their numbers. This way, teams are not made up of social cliques, and there can be more interaction in the group. If the class is small and cannot have four teams, assign a question to each individual in the class.

Each team is given a listening assignment on a file card before the lecture begins. The value of this approach is that all of the class gives close attention to all of the lecture because the teams don't know when information about their particular assignment will be given.

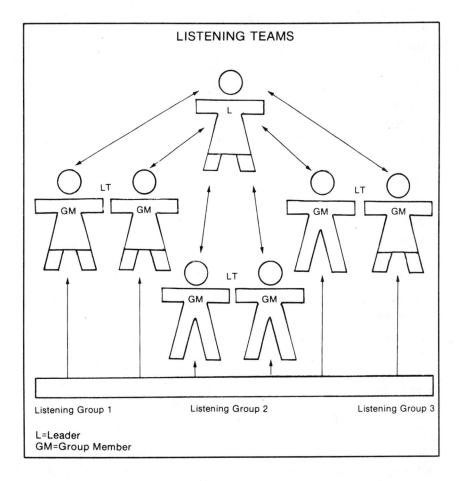

LISTENING TEAMS

Listening Group 1   Listening Group 2   Listening Group 3

L=Leader
GM=Group Member

Be sure to leave time for student discussion, or class members will feel cheated. They will conclude, rightly, that you are just presenting another lecture. Give the listening teams five or six minutes to discuss the answers to their assigned questions. Someone in each team should write a summary of the discussion. As the small groups discuss, write the four questions on the chalkboard. When each listening team is making its report, the other students in the class can see the question that is being discussed. Let the spokesman from each team report. Others on the team may like to amplify what the spokesman has said. A discussion can edify the whole class. Divide discussion time into fourths, allowing equal time for each team.

MAPS

Maps, as teaching aids, can greatly enhance learning. It is sometimes better to draw a map than to use a ready-constructed one. Maps come in many forms—outline, wall, slide, globe, or a collection in a book. They may show the topographical, political, commercial, or economic situation of regions of the world. Globes give a more accurate impression of distances and directions, but are limited to use in small groups.

To be effective, maps should be free from unnecessary detail, should highlight the major emphasis of your lesson, should be readable, must be properly mounted, and must be large enough to be seen easily.

Class use of maps may include these variations:

1. Pupils are called on to come and point out a city or river location.

2. Plastic can be placed over the map to allow pupils to use a grease pencil to trace the movements of story characters.

3. Large maps can be traced onto corrugated board. The pupils can color the map. By punching a hole and putting a paper fastener at each city location, pupils can move yarn from one location to the next each Sunday and trace, for instance, the movements of the apostle Paul or Christ's ministry as he moved from place to place. For several routes different colors of yarn can be used.

4. Picture maps. Instead of paper fasteners and yarn, the pupils can mark city locations with objects symbolic of events,

stuck in place with tape or Plasti-tak. For example, a water jug can be used where water was turned to wine.

5. A parable map following directions, as in number 3. A picture at each parable location will trace the progress of Jesus' ministry.

6. After a series of studies, pupils can be given unlabeled maps with dots for cities. The class should identify cities, countries, and bodies of water.

7. Relief (topographical) map can be used, working on one unit from week to week.

When using the sand table, you should dampen the sand. Use a topographical map as guide and shape hills and valleys; put down foil for seas and rivers.

When making a papier-mâché map, one may obtain a "mix" at a hobby shop or start from scratch. Papier-mâché is made by tearing newsprint into bits and soaking it in hot water. Stir with the hands until paper disintegrates. Stain through cloth to remove excess moisture. Mix paper with a pint of wheat paste. Add flour or starch until thick enough to retain its shape. After shaping the map, you should allow it to dry at least a week. Let pupils paint or spay it the next session. Hair spray may help it hold its shape.

Maps can also be modeled from homemade compounds. Use a mixture of one part salt, two parts flour, and one part water for a molding clay. Or make a sawdust compound by adding wallpaper paste to two quarts of sawdust. Add enough water to achieve the right consistency. Trace a large map, or enlarge one, into a cardboard background. Insert a finishing nail at the location of each city. Pupils should shape mountains with their hands and carefully scrape clay from the area that will be the sea or a river. The following week let several pupils paint the provinces, seas, and rivers. Others may make a label for each nail and tape it on.

MARCH TO SUNDAY SCHOOL IN MARCH

Many individual Sunday schools and denominations have annually used the "marching" theme to get people to march to Sunday school. Therefore, the campaign is usually well received and acted on. To encourage participation, pastors or educational directors may:

1. Offer a small award or gift to each member who brings a visitor and to each visitor who comes.
2. Offer a small gift to each one who attends on a given Sunday. Each person present on the first Sunday of March is given a Bible bookmark with the name of the church and pastor. The only way they can get one is to be there. Many members put them in their Bibles, and one choir member in particular is now glad she did. Ten months after the contest, her Bible—cherished for its long years of use—was stolen from her locked car. The thief decided he could not battle the accusing Book so dropped it by the roadside. An honest man found it, called the telephone number of the pastor named on the bookmark, and the lady was reunited with her Bible—all because she went to Sunday school on the first Sunday of March.
3. Sponsor a parade the Saturday before the first Sunday, featuring appropriate signs of invitation.
4. Sponsor a churchwide visitation, with all classes represented, on the Saturday before the first Sunday, and "march" house to house with invitational handouts.

MASTER-TEACHER PLAN

The master-teacher method is an innovative method of teaching used extensively in fast-growing Sunday schools. Whereas the traditional Sunday school class had the teacher sitting in the center of a small semicircle of pupils, the master-teacher leads large groups of students. Some classes have fifty students, others have two hundred. Whereas past Sunday schools usually taught Bible content through storytelling and lecturing, the master-teacher utilizes emotions, excitement, and sensory perception to teach Bible truths.

Churches have usually structured their Sunday schools to provide one teacher for every ten pupils. The master-teacher approach exposes all pupils to the most gifted teachers, while other adults assist in the teaching process according to their abilities.

Whereas the Sunday Bible school has met in small, self-contained classrooms about ten feet square, under the master-teacher approach, classes meet in large, airy, well-lighted rooms and use the total environment for learning. Master-teachers use the total room for the entire teaching hour, using every teaching technique available, taking advantage of all avenues of learning.

In the traditional Sunday school, if the teacher was exceptional, the class got outstanding results. If the teacher was unmotivated and unprepared, everything (and everyone) suffered. Attendance usually dropped off, and people were seldom won to Christ. No teacher can do it alone. Every teacher needs assistance, especially in his weak areas. He may need someone to lead singing or to tell the story. Every pupil still needs individual attention because each one is different, and every situation is unique.

Advantages of a Large Group

- *Motivation*—built on ability of the teacher to get the pupils excited
- *Teacher-centered*—teacher sets pattern of learning
- *Application*—by identification with the teacher

There are three areas for comparison of the master-teacher plan and the small, self-contained classroom. However, the differences are not that distinct because the master-teacher uses both large and small groups.

1. *Communication.* In the traditional classroom, communication of Bible content is good where there is an adequate teacher. But there are two problems. First, if the teacher is incompetent, communication is marginal. A small class never guarantees effective teaching, nor does a self-contained classroom assure success. Good teachers are the key, not proper size or desirable facilities.

   A second problem is dead orthodoxy. Some pupils have learned Bible knowledge but have done nothing with their knowledge. They need motivation or stimulation to apply the

Bible to life. Just because a pupil knows the Bible does not guarantee he will live its message. He must be motivated to live for God. When a pupil is excited about the truth, he will learn better and apply more of it to his life. The master-teacher approach should create interest in learning.

2. *Teacher-centered vs. pupil-centered.* Education theory has long discussed the merits of both approaches. Many modern-day pedagogues have swung to the extreme of pupil-centered techniques. Yet the teacher can make a difference when his personality is interjected into the teaching process. "The life of teaching is still the life of the teacher." Learning is significantly enhanced by gifted teachers.

The Sunday school is not an either/or situation. Both teacher-centered and pupil-centered classes should be utilized. The master-teacher stands before his pupils (perhaps sixty or more) and communicates the Scriptures; the better his presentation, the more they listen and learn. Then the pupils are divided into small discussion groups. Each teacher-assistant goes through the same lesson again. In the small groups pupils ask questions, review the memory verse, have misunderstandings corrected, and receive personal attention. The master-teacher approach takes the best of two worlds. More can be accomplished when the class emphasizes both teacher-centered and pupil-centered learning.

When a church grows rapidly, where does it get additional qualified teachers? The problem is especially acute when Sunday school buses are added and the classes double. Instead of trying to form more small classes, make large ones where your best teachers are in charge and the others assist them. Some churches are forced into the master-teacher approach because of rapid growth; other churches grow because of the advantages of the master-teacher approach.

3. *Application.* Students identify with the master-teacher and desire to be like him. Visual and sensory inspiration is necessary; the master-teacher can provide a model for their lives. But, at the same time, students learn the most when they rethink and apply truths. As the teacher-assistants discuss

the issues at the table, the pupil "tries truth on for size," much as in a self-service shoe department.

The master-teacher approach recognizes that God has gifted certain men and women with the ability to teach, and it seeks to utilize that gift to the fullest extent.

MATURING

One of the objectives of Sunday school is the maturing of believers. Maturing is bringing a person to completion or making him well-rounded. Sunday school is the maturing arm of the church.

MEARS, HENRIETTA CORNELIA (1890–1963)

Henrietta Mears is considered one of the most outstanding women to influence Sunday school in the twentieth century. She was director of the influential First Baptist Church of Minneapolis, Minnesota, under Dr. William B. Reiley. Then, in 1928, she became the director of Christian education at Hollywood Presbyterian Church. Attendance grew from approximately four hundred to more than four thousand. She taught a weekly collegiate class that averaged more than six hundred. Because she was not satisfied with the Bible content of Sunday school curriculum available, she wrote the entire curriculum for First Presbyterian Church, and out of it grew Gospel Light Publications, one of the largest independent publishers in the world. It is known for age grading, that is, a different lesson adopted for each age throughout the Sunday school. She is known for saying, "I didn't grade them; God did."

Henrietta Mears founded Forest Home Christian Conference that influenced thousands to live for Christ. She pioneered and gave authority to female leadership in an age when women were not always given opportunities of leadership in church circles. In spite of this, she was the primary influence on a number of men who became outstanding leaders of evangelicalism in this century—men such as Bill Bright, who founded Campus Crusade for Christ; Richard C. Halverson, chaplain of the U.S. Senate; Roy Rogers, movie actor; and Billy Graham, evangelist.

MEMORY WORK

Some teachers hold that what is memorized in early years is never really understood and, therefore, unnecessary. They say it is foolish to learn something that cannot be understood, and the result of such learning is merely parrotlike repetition. On the other hand, some argue that is not necessary for children to understand all they memorize. What children learn in early years they will remember longest in life. Understanding will come later and will benefit them then. Further, memorization is good mental exercise.

There is some truth to both sides of this issue. Too much memory work in the Sunday school can bore the children. For children who do not memorize easily, it can become a mental block. Because of the embarrassment they feel over their inability to keep up, they may stay home on Sunday morning. Too much time spent on memory work takes precious time from the lesson period, often too short anyway.

Arguments in favor of memorization are more numerous and more convincing than those against it. Memorization for memorization's sake may not be of much value, but memorization with a purpose as a means to an end is acceptable. Public schools provide motives for memorization. One country schoolteacher required every pupil to learn and recite Edgar Allan Poe's "The Raven" in its entirety. They did it to keep from failing seventh grade.

Why Teach Memory Work?

What motives can Sunday schools offer young people for learning God's Word?

1. *To know what they believe.* Untaught Christians are easy victims for false cults and perverters of Scripture. Christians need to know the Scripture to refute the lies.
2. *To have a pattern for Christian living.* In the world of television and movie idols, young people need a safe and sure guide. Should a Christian be different? How different? Paul urged, "Let no one despise your youth, but be an example to the believers in word, in conduct, in love, in spirit, in faith, in purity" (1 Tim. 4:12). With the aid of a concordance, help the

class select passages that answer questions about dress and conduct. A notebook or poster project would focus the points and aid memorization of them.

3. *To help them win others.* A youth became a Christian at the age of sixteen. He and two pals bought a set of Scripture memory cards and carried them constantly to learn passages answering excuses and problems of the unsaved. They started young to win souls. After the war, the youth barely finished college before he was called to be a pilot of a missionary plane. He won many to Christ before his plane crashed against the mountains of Maracaibo, Venezuela.

4. *To comfort others and to be prepared for sorrow.* Everyone is eventually called upon to comfort a weeping friend, or to face the death of a loved one. Knowledge of God's Word will help one "over the hump" when the time comes. If students are forearmed by the Word of God, they will be able to put up a better fight against the temptation to despair. Dramatize in class the use of these Scriptures. Let someone be the representative of a false cult, and let a Christian answer his arguments with Scripture he has memorized. Role play grief, doubt, or soul winning in the same way.

5. *To know the Lord Jesus Christ more fully.* Christ himself knew the Scriptures. He quoted from them constantly in his earthly ministry, using them as absolute and final authority, thus showing their divine origin. A lesson on how he used the Scriptures will emphasize the need for his children to know how and when to use them. The Lord Jesus used the Scriptures in defense and as a weapon against Satan and his enemies.

6. *External motivation.* A reward can spell the difference between successful memorization and complete indifference to it. The reward may be an award to each one who completes a given passage. Or the teacher might have a 100-percent box, where memory work counts a certain percent, and those who qualify reach into the box and "grab" a wrapped, inexpensive gift. A party or an outing might reward all who complete memory work. A pupil might receive recognition

through a symbolic trophy.

Motivation could come from a multiple-part weekly award, such as a shoe bag of construction paper with a shoe for each verse for each pupil. As each verse is learned, that "shoe" is placed in the bag; bags are taken home at the end of the quarter. Another multiple-part award might be a Holy Land village. Each pupil has a typical Israeli landscape scene. A small square house for each verse is attached to the scene with double-faced tape as a verse is learned. The village scene is carried home when completed. Other multiple-part objects are chains, a verse per link; fans, a verse per section, fastened with a brad; key rings of construction-paper keys with imprinted reference, fastened by yarn or ribbon.

How to Teach Memory in Class

Many pupils will not memorize at home. The following drill games make them eager to learn in class.

1. *Spelldown*. The old spelling-bee method is useful with juniors and older classes. Sides alternate in reciting verses or names of Bible books. When a pupil misses, he sits down.

2. *Scrambled verses*. On squares of felt or blotter paper, print the words of a Scripture verse, and place them on the flannelgraph in jumbled order. Let pupils rearrange the words correctly. Vary by letting one group scramble, the next straighten. Each time a verse is corrected, let the entire group repeat it together.

3. *Magnet board*. Back card rectangles with tiny magnets. Print on each card a word of the verse. Scramble on magnet board and play as flannelgraph game.

4. *Dramatization*. Simple motions portray action of a verse.

5. *Role play and repetition*. Use with preschoolers and young primaries. Climax each dramatization with the correlated memory verse. The action associates the words with their meaning.

6. *Pocket chart*. Cut two-inch strips of cardboard into rectangles. On the top half of each print a word of the memory verse. Make or buy a chart with a number of pockets. Give each word to a pupil to place in a pocket in the order in

which the word appears in the verse. When completed, all read the verse together. The chart may be bought at a school supply store or made of heavy wrapping paper.

7. *Bible baseball.* Questions "batted" are limited during memory drill to statements such as. "Repeat a verse that begins, 'Abstain from . . .'" Or if the drill is on Bible books, "What book comes after Judges?"

8. *Choral reading.* If the group is large, divide into two sides, with solo, duet, etc., for each side. Choose from each group a soloist, quartet, duet, indicating with raised fingers which section is to read. The entire hand indicates all should read. Read the memory passage several times, directing as a choir. Each rereading for improvement impresses the memory.

9. *Progressive recitation.* Let each pupil in turn read one word from the verse. Then each remembers his one word and repeats it from memory the next time around. At each round, increase speed. Finally all repeat each word together.

10. *Clothesline drill.* Attach one-word paper strips to a rope by clothes pins, scrambling the order of a verse. Let pupils unscramble.

11. *Flash cards.* On cardboard rectangles print the first half of each verse. Flash the cards one at a time before the class. Whoever finishes the verse first may hold the card; the one with the most cards win.

12. *Key-word cards.* A flash-card drill, printing only the key word on the card.

13. *Singing Scripture.* Use choruses that are Scripture set to music. (John 3:16 fits into "Silent Night." "John 3:16, John 3:16, For God so loved the world that he . . .", etc.).

14. *King on the throne.* One student on a chair-throne wears a construction paper crown, as king (or queen). Others ask questions limited to memory verses. "What verse ends with *all?*" If the king cannot answer, but the questioner can, the questioner becomes king.

15. *Musical grab bag.* Print on strips of paper the references for

verses learned. (Or print the words of verses, minus references.) Place in a paper bag, which is passed while piano or record player plays. As music stops, player with the bag must fish out a strip of paper. If a reference, he recites verse. If verse, he recites reference.

16. *Fishing*. On fish-shaped pieces of construction paper, print memory verse references. Place on each a paper clip. Put all in a bowl for a "pond." Attach a small magnet to a string tied to a dowel stick for a pole. Pupil casts line into the "pond." For whatever "fish" he catches, he recites the verse.

17. *Matching hide-and-seek*. Print memory verses on paper hearts at Valentine's Day, eggs at Easter, trees at Christmas, and so on. Cut the paper in half and hide the pieces. Pupils must find and match the halves, then partners recite verse together.

MERCY, GIFT OF (See SHOWING MERCY, GIFT OF)

METHODS OF TEACHING (See also individual methods)

A method is an orderly procedure or process. Methods of teaching are only tools of instruction to meet the needs of the student. True teaching includes telling, showing, and doing. Variety is the spice of life, and the key is using various methods of teaching the Bible to create and maintain interest. A number of methods of teaching are discussed in this book under the name of the individual teaching method.

How to Choose the Right Method of Teaching

Some of the following points will guide you in choosing the method to use:

1. Choose a method that is best suited for your lesson aim. If your aim is to get several opinions from the Scripture passage, choose a panel discussion, debate, or forum. If your aim is to indoctrinate, perhaps the best method is lecture or question and answer. If your aim is to communicate feelings and attitudes, then drama may be the best method.

2. Choose a method appropriate for the age level of your students. Do not use flannelgraph with young people or you may

insult their intelligence. Also, do not try debate with primary children since they may not be able to comprehend the logic.

3. Choose a method that is best suited to your classroom and class size. If there are four or five other classes in your room you will have difficulty dividing into small buzz groups or showing a film. Also, you may have difficulty in doing a drama. Perhaps you will have to stick to lecture, question and answer, and some of the other more quiet methods. If you have a large group, then small buzz groups will enhance student interaction.

4. Choose a method within your budget. If your Sunday school is on a small budget, you may have access to films or an overhead projector.

5. Choose a method with variety in mind. Lecture is an excellent way of communicating God's truth, but when it is used every Sunday, it is overused. Variety is the spice of life, especially in Sunday school classes.

6. Choose a method that involves your pupils. Learning is not taking in facts but involvement with facts. Therefore, choose a method that will cause your pupils to interact with the content, interact with other students, and interact with you as the teacher. The Sunday school is a place of mental gymnastics where students wrestle with the Word of God.

MINISTRY

Ministry is the communication of the gospel to people at their point of need. This definition requires that one first understand what is a person's point of need. Second, one must also understand the nature of communication. Finally, one must understand the gospel.

All ministry begins with God and has its eternal existence in God, but there was no need for ministry until God created man. As soon as man was created, a need existed. Man was made in the image of God, which means among other things that he had the ability to reason, express feelings, and act volitionally as an independent being. When man fell to the temptation of Satan, sin produced the greatest need in man.

Several things are now true of all people because of the sin nature that is a part of humanity. First, people are cut off from God. Second, people tend to think of themselves from their own point of reference. Third, they suffer alienation and isolation. Fourth, people tend to be filled with anxiety. Fifth, people are searching for meaning and purpose in life. Ultimately, people are marching inevitably toward death. These consequences of sin represent some of the greatest needs people face today.

The word *communicate* means "to have in common." Ministry is communicating the gospel through relationships. Christianity is a relationship. First, a person must establish a relationship with God through Jesus Christ. After this relationship is established, then people reach out to other people in relationship. A person's worth is measured by the deep relationships he has with other people.

The gospel is the content that is communicated in ministry, but there are two aspects to the gospel: a proposition and a person. The proposition aspect of the gospel is summarized in the death, burial, and resurrection of Jesus Christ (1 Cor. 15:1-4). But the gospel is more than a proposition; it is also a Person, the Lord Jesus Christ. When one receives the gospel, he receives Jesus by faith (John 1:12).

MINISTRY, GIFT OF

The person with the gift of ministry (helps) has the ability to serve God by ministering to the physical and spiritual needs of others. Usually, those in the office of a "deacon" (*diakonos*) have the gift of "ministry" or "service" (*diakonia*). The strength of this gift is demonstrated in the person who: (1) enjoys manual projects or practical service, (2) gets satisfaction from doing a repeatable task, (3) serves without fanfare, but needs to be appreciated, (4) senses physical and financial needs of others, (5) works for immediate goals, and (6) gets satisfaction out of completing projects.

The weaknesses inherent in this gift are demonstrated in one who: (1) seems to be more practical oriented, (2) insensitive to the lack of involvement by prophets or teachers in practical projects and (3) others wrongly interpret their good works.

The individual with this gift needs to avoid the danger of (1) being proud, (2) being critical of nonpractical church leaders, (3) being bitter if not recognized, or (4) being critical of steps of faith that appear unpractical.

MISSIONS EDUCATION

Why are there not enough volunteers to fill the openings on the various mission fields? Perhaps it is because young people are not being faced with the challenge of giving themselves in service in a faraway and often difficult place. If they do not belong to a special missionary organization, many Sunday school pupils—young or old—may not receive specific information on missions.

The logical place for Sunday school members to learn about missions is the Sunday school.

1. *Have a plan.* Unless missions teaching is incorporated in the regular curriculum of a denomination or church, there must be a definite plan to insert it on a regular basis. What is left to hit-or-miss will usually be missed.

   a. Appoint an assistant teacher within each department to be responsible for the missionary teaching.

   b. Choose a regular time—weekly or monthly—when the missionary story or facts will be presented.

   c. Choose specific mission fields for study to be sure the teaching is thorough, rather than presenting sketchy information about many places and people.

2. *Have a program.* Suggest that the missionary chairman select others to serve as a committee to build a definite program.

   a. Select the fields for study.

   b. Find books, pictures, maps, filmstrips, and other necessary materials on those fields.

   c. Make available pictures of the missionaries on those fields for the pupils to "meet" during the study.

   d. Select songs or games and occasionally a food typical of the land being studied.

    e. Use the national costume during presentation of the material if possible.

    f. Display articles from the land under study.

3. *Develop missionary projects.*

    a. Let the pupils work on a missionary map. Some who are artistic can enlarge a map of the area being studied. Let pupils add the names of towns, using the small map as a guide. From time to time (weekly or monthly), let a small representative picture be placed on the map at the location discussed in class.

    b. Prepare a missionary box. Fill the box with pictures, books, games, or puzzles that missionaries can use in their teaching. If possible, make certain that the missionaries can use the materials being sent. Missionaries in certain primitive areas find Sunday school paper pictures useful as awards to boys and girls who otherwise would never see such a picture. Classes may prepare scrapbooks of Bible pictures and stories for the missionaries. Adult classes may make garments to send to hospitals for new babies or supply medical needs.

    c. Make a class scrapbook. While all pupils may contribute pictures and write articles to go in the scrapbook, select a committee to be responsible for planning and arrangement of the contents.

    d. Write to the missionary. Appoint a committee of pupils to correspond with boys and girls on the mission field. Letters from the missionaries may be added to the scrapbook.

    e. Make teaching devices for missionaries who are in education work. Classes of juniors through adults can make posters, puppets, charts, story wheels, and other aids to use in teaching. Such aids are expensive to take in a missionary's luggage and hard to make from materials available on the field. Again, find out in advance if the materials will be useful.

    f. Have a systematic missionary offering. Pupils often give with more concern to those with whom they are acquainted. While the church may have a missionary budget, pupils will feel more personally involved in giving if an occasional special offering is received for missionaries about whom they have studied.

4. *Extend the missionary challenge.* After a missionary presentation, opportunity should be given for pupils to make a definite commitment to service if God has laid it on their hearts. A public acknowledgment of dedication increases the responsibility of the pupil making the decision.

MODELS

A model is a teaching aid that enhances learning by giving the student a three-dimensional view of the subject being taught.

Older primaries and juniors can learn the boxlike architecture of the Palestinian house by making a village of such houses out of folded heavy brown sack paper. Add a paper "fence" around the roof; cut a door and window. Accordion-fold stairs may be added at the side. The following are several "recipes" for materials you may wish to use in making models with your pupils.

Papier-mâché Mixture

1 pint ordinary sawdust
1 pint plaster
1 cup school library paste

Dissolve paste in just enough water to thin slightly. Add plaster, then sawdust, and knead until you achieve the desired consistency of the dough.

Cornstarch Modeling Material

1 cup of salt
½ cup cornstarch
½ cup boiling water

Mix ingredients in a pan and set over low heat. Stir constantly until mixture is too stiff to stir. When cool, knead until smooth.

Salt and Flour Modeling Material

Use twice as much salt as flour and enough water to form an easily handled dough. Heat in a cooking pan, stirring constantly, adding water as needed.

MOODY, DWIGHT L. (1832–1899)

It is said that Dwight L. Moody is said to have "shook two continents for God." The foundation for his worldwide ministry came through Sunday school.

As a young boy, his Sunday school teacher came into the shoe store where he was working and led him to Jesus Christ. After that, Moody moved to Chicago and joined the Plymouth Congregational Church. He rented five pews and filled them with young boys he brought in off the street. But he realized he could do more to reach Chicago for Christ. Moody started a Sunday school in a former saloon in the vice-ridden section of Chicago called "little hell." When this small room could not accommodate the pupils, Moody moved it to North Market Street, and it eventually became the largest Sunday school in Chicago.

Moody spread his enthusiasm through Sunday school conventions from 1859 to 1864. In Springfield, Illinois, he remarked, "This thing [the convention] so far has been a dead failure." He began a prayer meeting with a few people, and within a few days the entire convention experienced revival. Sunday school delegates returned home to revive Sunday schools across Illinois. Out of the prayer meetings in that convention came the great Sunday school leaders: Jacobs, Eggleston, Tyng, P. B. Bliss, and others.

Because of his passion for education, Moody founded other educational endeavors for Christ, such as Northfield Schools. Next he founded the Moody Bible Institute in 1882, one of the first Bible institutes in America. Out of MBI came the Moody Colportage Series, an organization to provide inexpensive Christian literature, *Moody Monthly* magazine, and Moody Press. Today the organization founded by Moody has extensive ministries around the world.

Moody eventually went into city-wide evangelistic crusades that brought hundreds of thousands to Jesus Christ.

MOTIVATING PUPIL INTEREST

If you want to be a better Sunday school teacher, you must learn to motivate your pupils. Why? Because the success of your teaching is not just measured by what you know or how well you present the lesson; your success is measured by what they learn. Pupils mostly learn what they want to learn. Therefore you must make them thirsty to learn. They find answers to their questions whether or not you do a good job of teaching. But if you motivate them, learning multiplies. Remember, 90 percent of teaching is motivation.

Motivation is not yelling; nor is it telling funny stories. Motivation is not begging them to pay attention. Motivation is putting salt on their tongues and showing them where to find water. To be a good motivator, you need a proper mind-set.

Twenty Techniques to Motivate Pupils

If you have the proper attitude, the following twenty suggestions will make you a better teacher.

1. *Tag the name.* Obviously, a good teacher will know the name of his pupils. But the teacher needs also to help pupils know one another. Have name tag day when every pupil is registered with a gummed label.

   Play games with names. Have a child find someone who has the same name or find someone whose name begins with the same letter. Those who first raise their hands together are winners. On another occasion have the pupils find someone with the same number of letters in their names, such as John, Mary, Mark, and Ruth.

2. *Investigate their name.* You have heard the question, What's in a name? Find out what your pupils know about their names. Ask: "For whom were you named?" or, "What does your name mean?" Stay away from impersonal tags such as "sweetheart," "pal," or "son." Those tags may sound cute, but they are impersonal.

3. *Mirror yourself.* Make your room reflective of your life. You ought to have a picture that is personal to you, a vase of flowers, or if you have a desk, your name plate. When you identify with your room and make it personal, the pupils will follow your lead. At the office, Dad has a picture of his family on his desk; why should you not have one in Sunday school?

4. *Create a spiritual mug book.* Ask each of the pupils to bring

one of their little school pictures. Paste them in a scrapbook to remind you to pray for them, or place them on a poster on the wall. If they do not have a school picture, use your Polaroid to take a picture of each pupil. Perhaps you can bring them all together for a group picture. If you do that, go one step farther and have a print made for everyone in the class. Then ask them to take them home and place them on their mirrors so they can be reminded to pray for one another.

5. *Be a handshake and hello person.* At the beginning and end of the class, station yourself at the door to greet your pupils with a friendly hello and a shake of the hand. Call them by name and follow up with a sincere question—because you are interested in them. If you are interested in them, then perhaps they will get interested in Jesus Christ.

6. *Use the third person.* Those who use the first person are interested in "I." Be a "first-person-plural" teacher. Use the word *we* or *us* in speaking to your class. The phrase, "We have work to do" is better than, "You have work to do." When you say, "We are having a good time," perhaps everyone will. When you begin all of your sentences with *we* perhaps there will be unity in learning.

7. *Make taste buds your buddy.* Giving your pupils a candy mint at the beginning of class may not be the answer to a poor teacher, but for a moment your pupils will like you because their taste buds are stimulated. Now, follow through with spiritual and intellectual teaching.

8. *Be a pupil booster.* You know the phrase "band boosters," and "team boosters." You be a "student booster." Let your pupils know that you appreciate anything they can do for you. "Thank you for taking the offering, Billy," "Thank you for keeping your hands in your lap, Debbie." Anytime the children do something that you have asked, show appreciation. If you boost them, they in turn will boost you.

10. *Make the telephone a tool.* According to statistics, a person can contact eleven people per hour by use of the telephone. Perhaps a quick call to a pupil will get him motivated to

study a particular lesson, remind him to bring a Bible, or remind him of a special speaker. Then if you give a phone number to every pupil you call, and he calls another pupil, you could reach twenty-two in one hour. Whereas it might take one hour to visit in a home with one pupil, you have the potential of reaching twenty-two in one hour through the telephone tool.

11. *Hang out your shingle.* Some pupils do not remember the name of their Sunday school teacher, and yours might not be an exception. If it is possible that your pupils do not know your name, make certain they do. Place your name discreetly on the door leading to the class, but not so discreetly ᴛʜat people will miss it. Then inside, write your name on the chalkboard or on a permanently posted area. Then another small name plate should be on your desk. Finally, to reinforce your "handle" wear a name tag. If you teach adults and you want them to call you Bob, put that on the name tag.

12. *Invest a penny.* Discussion is important, but it is never automatic. If you want your pupils to discuss your lesson at home, they must discuss it in the classroom. And if you want them to discuss it in the classroom, you must plan for it. Paste a penny on a card, and at the top write, "A penny for your thoughts"; then on the other side write the question that you would like them to discuss.

13. *Think four steps.* Pupils learn when they are involved in four steps: first, seeing; second, touching; third, talking; and fourth, hearing the lesson. Therefore, "think four steps" with every lesson. Go back to last week and check your lesson plan. Did you appeal to all four? First, was there something that they could see on the chalkboard, overhead projector, or the flannelboard? Then was there something for them to touch? Let them handle a lesson handout or a questionnaire for them to fill out. A great teaching tool is the workbook pictures or a portion of Scripture. When God asked Moses, "What is that in your hand?" (Exod. 4:2) the Lord was using an effective teaching tool. Did your class

have some place for the pupils to talk? They should discuss the question, apply it, explain it, or show appreciation. Even Jesus, who used object lessons, lectures, and stories, allowed time for questions. One hundred and four questions that Jesus used are recorded in the gospels. Finally, most teachers need to get the pupils to hear the lesson. Most learning is listening. But make sure they hear properly, excitedly, and repeatedly.

14. *Leave mental footprints.* Your hour should be so organized that your teaching leaves mental footprints, impressions you left in the pupil's minds. Since organization is the channel of thinking, your students will think with you if you are organized. Most teachers plan their lesson content but never plan their questions, experiences, or activities. Write out a well-planned lesson presentation. A written lesson plan is a teaching tool.

15. *Wear a happy smile.* Toothpaste is sold by testimonials because people buy what helps others. Therefore, if the teacher is happy, the pupils will be excited. If you look forward to next week, they will come back. Not only must you be excited, you must tell your pupils that you are and why. Next Sunday tell your class five times, "I love this Sunday school class."

16. *Let helping hands help you.* There are many small tasks that you do in the classroom that your pupils could do for you. According to their age and responsibility use your pupils to take roll, pass out paper, collect the offering, distribute material, prepare chalkboards, put figures on the flannelgraph, or paste stars on the attendance charts. Anything your pupils can do—let them.

17. *Let the eyes have it.* Pupils have a hard time ignoring teachers who look deeply into their hearts. When you are teaching, do not look at the corner of the room or stare off into space. Let your eyes travel from one pupil to another, and talk to them as though you are talking to only one pupil. Chances are, if you are communicating effectively with one, you are communicating to all.

18. *Let the walls have a voice.* The old cliché is, The walls have ears, but also, The walls have a mouth. So let it help you teach your lesson. Turn an entire wall into a poster. If you have an entire wall, it can be a large "highway billboard" made with huge letters cut out of paper. Arrange a verse on the wall beginning almost at the ceiling, and spread out the verse from corner to corner. The memory verse will be impressed in their minds if you make it the most dominant visual aid in your room.

19. *Play a happy tune.* Bring a cassette recorder or record player to Sunday school, and fill the room with music before the first pupil arrives. Make sure it is a happy Christian melody, and you will create a warm feeling even before your lesson begins. Remember, you begin to teach when the first pupil arrives.

20. *Leave on a high note.* Many teachers do not conclude their lessons, they just stop when the bell rings. How dreary for the pupils to hear, "We'll take up the lesson here next week." Plan to leave your pupils on a high note; if they leave wanting more, they have reason to come back next week. Be ready to play a song as they leave, give them a cup of Kool-Aid, or save your best story till last. Go to the door and have a personal word for each pupil as he leaves. Perhaps you might promise to tell them a secret or have a gift for each.

These twenty techniques will not work if they are substituted for thorough preparation or prayer. Also, these suggestions will not take the place of love and concern, but if you truly love your pupils, you will try to make your class as interesting as possible.

MULTIMEDIA PROJECT

A multimedia project is a teaching technique that will enhance learning by involving students in creativity, involvement, and application. A slide production project takes advantage of the current interest in photography, media, and sense perception. Usually young people undertake this kind of project with the aim of describing the gospel to their non-Christian friends. Music and the media tell the story. Because the medium stimulates thought and involves the viewer visually and audibly, it has great impact. The slides may have familiar scenes of the community, with youth involved in different activities. The slides flash on to blares from speakers. A discussion and question time follows the slides.

The group effort tends to knit the young people together. The youth group should strive to involve the whole group by using each individual's talents. Some can write and others handle the technical aspects of the production. They will see how the church can use everyone's talent in expressing the gospel to the world. If they can view the project as an expression of their own lives and faith, it will build unity in the group. They may begin to think in terms of new and creative ways to tell the Good News.

Personnel

Each aspect of the project demands special talents and interests. For this reason each young person's abilities should be explored and utilized. The project does not require professionally trained people to be a success. Sometimes inexperienced youth come up with creative and effective ideas. The project, after all, is an expression of the youth group, not a professional movie studio. Do not be surprised at the finished product, however. It may look quite professional, even though you thought it would never work.

1. *Cameramen*. Almost anyone can take slide pictures. Choose one or two persons in the group who can take good pictures to head this committee. Anyone in the group can submit pictures taken on vacations or at school. Get casual and real-life pictures that best tell the message.

2. *Script writers*. Select people who are creative and able to write well. This committee determines the application of the message to the medium. The committee should not have more than four or five members. Too many ideas make for disharmony and confusion.

3. *Music editors*. This committee should not have more than two or three members. They should select music with a direct relationship to the message. Music editors should know both popular and Christian music. They should look for music and words to reflect the script.

4. *Sound and lighting crew.* This committee should have members who know how to tape record and to wire the speakers for effective sound. Two or three people are usually sufficient. If no one in the group has such talents, ask those who have an interest in this aspect to work with an experienced adviser or parent.

5. *Projector crew.* Members of this committee do the actual showing of the slides. The number on this crew depends on the number of projectors used. The projectors must be coordinated with each other and with the music and script. One member serves as coach to help each person running a projector. The coach directs the slide sequences to begin and end at the proper place in the script.

6. *Ushers.* This committee plans the arrangement of chairs and helps coordinate the program activities. They usher the audience into the rows, making sure all are in the best position to see all the screens and hear the music. If tickets are used, they can be collected also.

Materials

One important feature of this project is that most materials are common both to the church and the home. It is not necessary to have the most modern and expensive equipment. Usually equipment used in church or home is adequate.

1. *Camera.* Most cameras take slide pictures. A camera with a wide-angle lens or telephoto lens will improve the quality. Since film is expensive, it is important to make sure the camera works and the flash bulbs operate correctly. Film should have twenty or more exposures to take sequential pictures. Ask parents and photographers to get film developed inexpensively.

2. *Script materials.* Material used depends on the theme or script idea. If the group wants to base the production around a biblical portion or character, then information may be needed from a Bible dictionary or from the Bible itself. The group may desire to select reading material expressing thoughts of young persons today. Magazine, newspaper, and editorial articles may provide suitable material. The commit-

tee should look for pictures in magazines and newspapers, as well as posters hanging in shops and coffee houses.

3. *Records, tape recorders, speakers*. Electrical equipment, properly used, gives a professional touch. Select records on the basis of their message and sound quality. Good speakers can make the music sound alive. Usually the young people have good stereo records, compact discs, and/or tapes in their home.

4. *Projectors and screens*. Most slide projectors work well for this project. The number of pictures taken and the number of screens used determine how many projectors will be needed. In the beginning it is advisable to have no more than three projectors. Each projector can use different types of trays or carousels. The bigger the carousel, the more slides it will hold. Large carousels reduce or eliminate the need for changing during performance. Make sure the projectors don't skip slides or stick and that there are plenty of outlets for the cords so that the systems don't overload the electric circuits. Bring extension cords if necessary. Provide an extra projector bulb for each machine. An extra projector is advisable for emergencies.

Production

1. *Determine the theme or message*. This becomes the basis for the whole slide presentation. Music and script are selected to convey this message. Music can be used as the basic script. The message would then be in the music, and the slides would be coordinated with the music. In many ways this type of production is easiest, since the words to the music help determine the type of pictures needed.

Another alternative to script writing is to find a Bible verse or portion that could be used for the theme. Music would be selected as background or to further the story. Slides can be taken in contemporary situations to help the audience visualize the meaning of the Scripture. The Scripture can be read phrase by phrase with a few seconds between readings.

Some groups find it difficult to decide on one theme. In this case, a more unstructured script may be written. Music with

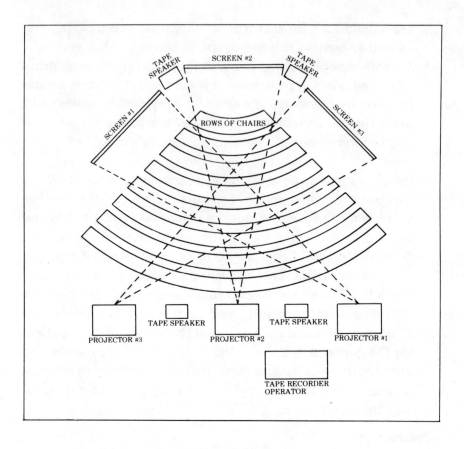

a message would be selected. Random photos taken to present important thoughts would be shown in series while the music plays, without relationship between music and slides. Slides of captions or signs could be taken. The script could be woven around these visual readings without narration.

2. *Determine the kind of pictures needed to illustrate the script.* The script writers should list ideas or places to go for each record or for the theme. This also will aid in taking good and relevant pictures.

3. *Collect relevant magazine pictures and captions.* Many times the pictures found in magazines can be photographed and shown as slides. There is opportunity for creative work with sayings or titles. This is a great source for theme material.

4. *Begin to take pictures.* Unposed action shots are best. Individ-

uals in the youth group can be the subjects. Sometimes pictures of crowds or buildings add a special dimension. It is good to try and take photographs of everyone in the group. Pictures should be taken everywhere the group goes. Variety makes for interesting photographs. While the script is the guide for taking pictures, always have a camera ready to capture that unusual picture.

Approximately seventy-five to one hundred slides are needed for three projectors. The amount will vary depending on the capacity of each projector. Usually the older projectors will hold twenty-five slides, but new carousels can hold seventy-five slides.

If the pictures were taken with the script in mind, editing the slides will be simplified. Group pictures should fit into themes according to the script. Then place the pictures in order of presentation. Words of the music or script should be studied by the script committee as they choose slides for the presentation.

After the slides are arranged according to theme and sequence in the script, divide each group between the three projectors to be used. Put one picture from a group into the tray or carousel of each projector. The idea is to have each projector showing part of the same theme in sequence. This enables the three projectors to show a panorama of thought, much like a film.

Once the slides have been placed in the projectors, the basic work is done. The next step is to show the slides on the screen without music, in order to make final arrangements of the slides and to be sure pictures are right-side up with words and captions readable.

After checking out the slides in the projectors, add the music. It is best to start the tape recorder and play just one song or theme. A system of alternating the projectors should be determined. For example, projector #1 shows the first slide. Projector #2 waits for the right time and then shows a slide. There are now two pictures on two different screens. Projector #3 adds a picture to the third screen. Once all screens are filled, the projectors can follow the same system to progress the theme. The system of showing slides can be varied so the sequence is not so noticeable. Someone should direct the three projectors, much like a music director. It is best to stay with an easy system at first.

If each song or theme can be worked separately, the projector operators can decide how fast to change the slides. They must complete each song or theme without running out of slides or having slides left over when the music ends. Much practice and coordination is needed. A director or sponsor could help in directing the slide timing and changing. Gradually the presentation will look more like a motion picture than a slide presentation. Because of the limitations of conventional equipment, it is not possible to change the slides in rapid sequence. As a matter of fact, with three screens to look at, the audience will need to think about each picture and why that particular slide was included.

Performance

To make the performance run smoothly, it is essential to go through the whole production. Usually the production will run fifteen to twenty-five minutes, depending on the number of pictures taken and songs recorded. Last-minute adjustments should be made before the showing rather than have embarrassing incidents in the final performance.

The size of the room and facilities will dictate the precise arrangement needed. The sound should not be too loud or too soft. The media of sound and slides should not compete for attention but should be combined for the total experience. Since the projectors are in the rear of the room, they must be elevated above the heads of the audience. Any kind of platform or elevated table will raise the projector to the desired height.

MUSIC (See also CONGREGATIONAL SINGING)

Music has many purposes in the Sunday school, such as worshiping of God, producing unity, developing talents allowing expression; but perhaps most important, music is a learning technique that uses the student's mind, emotion, and total personality. Music used to be the means of occupying the punctual Sunday school scholars while they waited for the tardy superintendent. It didn't matter what songs were chosen—just as long as the pianist could play them and the often unwilling song leader could sing them. But today's teachers are aware of music's contribution to learning.

1. The melody often makes the message memorable. Television commercials usually are tuneful. The youngest members of the family can at least hum the tune and may even lisp the words, heedless of any unworthy message. This should be true of Sunday school tunes also.
2. The correlated message of the song should add to the total impact of the aim.
3. An appropriate tune should set the mood for the lesson.

What Type of Music?

1. *Graded.* Not every song is suitable for every age level. Little children would have difficulty relating to the message of "How Firm a Foundation," while teenagers could not be bribed to sing "Jesus Loves the Little Ones like Me." With many fine compilations of songs for each age level, there is little reason for errors in judgment along that line. With songs, as with teaching or stories, children are literalists. As a rule, preteens do not readily grasp symbolism. While preschoolers may enjoy the lilt and motions of "Deep and Wide," its meaning is lost to them.
2. *Correlated.* Besides singing "with understanding," pupils should sing words that emphasize the theme of study for the day. If the Good Samaritan is the story for juniors, a song like "Help Somebody Today" is reinforcing. This technique can provide adequate expression for teens and adults, too. If preschoolers through primaries are learning how God made everything, they can carry away the message of God's power in the singing of "God Can Do Everything."
3. *Suitable melody.* Slow tempo and low volume should be appropriate for a sad or warning song, while a faster rhythm and loud tone would express a militant song. Though the author may have exclaimed with joy and gratitude, "What a Friend We Have in Jesus!" many churches tend to make it

more of a question, by dragging it in sorrow. It would be equally unsuitable to rush through an invitational number such as "Just As I Am," when words and tune show that it is expressing deep contrition and humility. Occasionally so-called children's choruses have unscriptural words added to peppy tunes, rendering them popular with boys and girls—particularly when the leaders have not analyzed the words or explained them.

4. *Praise choruses.* The new reformation in worship centers on "singing to God," rather than just singing one's testimony or singing about God. Even the smallest child in Sunday school can magnify God as the class glorifies him with a praise chorus.

When to Use Songs

1. *In worship.* The term *worship* is a misnomer, for in many services two or three songs are hurried through, supplemented by a few unrelated verses of Scripture and a prayer. Well-chosen songs can help to set the atmosphere of worship, but it is not accidental. With the aid of a topical index or the leader's knowledge and discretion, songs should be chosen that will draw the class or department into prayer and praise.

2. *Before the lesson.* During the time immediately before the lesson, a song may be used to introduce the theme. If the lesson stresses obedience, for example, the message of "Trust and Obey" would be excellent. If the theme is the power of the tongue, "Angry Words, O Let Them Never" has appropriate words.

3. *To exercise.* More than once during the preschool class period, a song can and should be inserted. Not only will it aid the understanding of both story and song, it will afford a time to stretch cramped muscles and enable pupils to give better attention to what follows.

4. *In making application.* A song can allow a class to express thanksgiving, praise, faith, dedication, or other decisions, through its well-chosen words. Many young people have dedicated their lives while singing "Living for Jesus" or

"Wherever He Leads, I'll Go." Others have volunteered for missionary service through "I'll Go Where You Want Me to Go."

How Many Songs?
The answer to this question depends on:

1. *Time available.* If the worship or lesson preparation period is brief, limit the songs accordingly. Usually one or two stanzas from several songs are better than five stanzas from only one. Variety allows more worshipers to respond. Words and melodies that appeal to one person may not appeal to another.

2. *Choice available.* Some doctrines have not often been expressed in music. There may be only one song available that really expresses the truth that needs to be reinforced. In such case, a group may sing the first stanza before the Bible reading and prayer and intersperse another stanza before a brief story or object lesson. The class period may then be closed by singing the last stanza.

3. *Singers available.* In small classes, the assembled group may have so few who can sing at all that a prolonged song service proves embarrassing. On some occasions it may even be preferable for the group to read aloud the words of two or three stanzas instead of attempting to sing them. Those who feel unqualified to sing will thus have opportunity to express the message aloud.

Special Music
Should solos, duets, and other ensembles or instrumental numbers be used in Sunday school? There are several reasons for an affirmative answer:

1. *The singer will remember.* A young person given opportunity to sing a solo will remember the message—much longer than anyone listening. (The same is true for participants in ensembles.)

2. *Participants will use talents.* Allowing musical youth to render a service to the Sunday school through song is a means of encouraging them to develop their God-given talents and use

them for his glory. These same youth are freely called on by the public school and expected to give their time in rehearsals and performance. The Sunday school should expect them to do as much for the church. It often is true that boys and girls do for the church just what is expected of them. If nothing is expected, little is volunteered.

3. *It is scriptural.* While some church groups have felt that the use of instruments in a church is not fitting, there are Scripture passages that show otherwise. Psalm 150 exhorts that many different kinds of instruments be used in praise of God. Young people learn to play instruments in a school band, but they may never be invited to dedicate that talent to God. It is not surprising that they may form combos to play for parties and dances—their gifts and training are not appreciated nor claimed by the church. Instruments dedicated to God and his service are not so likely to be given to worldly entertainment.

The Song Leader

While smaller churches may consider themselves fortunate if anyone at all is willing to stand up and announce the songs, there are qualifications for this important person that should be considered when a choice is possible:

1. *Consistent Christian testimony.* Anyone in a position of leadership is a reflection of the church and the Savior. If the witness is negative, the work is hurt.

2. *Enthusiasm.* A person of minor talent with this trait can render leadership more effectively than can a gifted person lacking enthusiasm. Knowledge of the words of the song and the value of the song, added to the leader's joy in the Lord, can produce enthusiasm. "Like leader, like people." The response will be enthusiastic.

3. *Good musicianship.* While the need for enthusiasm remains true, a leader should know the tune of the song and should know how to keep time—whether or not he knows how to use the correct arm motions. If the pianist is capable of keeping good time, a less efficient song director can (and usually does) follow the lead of the piano. Given a place of musical responsibility, the lay leader can always improve his

knowledge and ability by seeking instruction. School musicians may be willing to instruct him if assistance cannot be found in another church. Instead of doing only "the best he can with what he has," the church musician should seek to improve in order to serve better.

NAMING YOUR CLASS

Over the years, it seems that giving names to Sunday school classes has gone full cycle. Fifty years ago and beyond, all adult classes had names. Then, generic titles or identifications were given, such as Men's Class, ages 30–35. Now names are coming back into popularity because they give identity and *esprit de corps* to a class. The following are some suggested names for adult classes: Faith-Way Class, Pioneers, Bible Seekers Class, Bible Lovers Class, Genesis Class (newly married), Rebuilders Class (single parents), Single Vision Class (singles), New Life Class (recent converts), Overcomers Class, and Sonship Class.

NEWSLETTER/NEWSPAPER

With the availability of a photocopier or instant print service, it is possible to make copies of a one-page newsletter inexpensively. Every class should have a written communication to its members. Even a very small class could produce a class newsletter regularly during a special attendance building campaign.

How to Prepare a Class Newsletter

A newsletter is not hard to prepare. If you have never issued one, simply write a one-page letter giving the news of the class. Then type the letter in two columns to make it look like a newspaper, and put a headline across the top. Fill the newspaper with the names of students, their accomplishments, and what you expect to do for God. In preparing your newspaper, you will want to include many of the following items:

Statistics. Include class statistics about the offerings, attendance, and new members.

Names of visitors. Publishing the names of visitors to the class in the newsletter will help class members identify and call newer members by name. This will demonstrate to visitors they are viewed as more than just statistics.

Special events and projects. Use the newsletter to advertise upcoming events and projects of interest to the class.

Message from the teacher. You may also want to include a brief devotional message from the teacher. Here the teacher will give direction to the class. The newsletter will help him to pastor his flock corporately.

NURSERY

The Nursery Department has been called "the handshake of the church." Parents appreciate adequate facilities and specialized care for their children and show their appreciation by faithful attendance at church.

The nursery is responsible for children from the first time they come to the church as infants to their third birthday. There are varied needs to be met in these short years.

Crib babies must be attended by a capable and trained person. Confidence is felt by parents who know their child will be safe with the attendants. Ideally, a nurse should be employed to supervise the Nursery Department. Accidents can be prevented, minor injuries treated, and illness recognized.

Toddlers (one to two years of age) need special attention, as they still tire easily. The walker-talkers (two to three) will need a room all to themselves, as they cannot be trusted near babies and are old enough to be taught definite Bible truths.

The Nursery Department ideally should be on the main floor, near the entrance and, preferably, close to the Adult Department, where parents will be.

The room should be well ventilated, bright, and spacious. Where there is only one large room, it should be partitioned to accommodate the three divisions as needed.

What Can a Nursery Child Learn?

The nursery child can comprehend that God is in heaven, that he made all things, and that he loves everyone, cares for the individual child, hears prayer, and knows what is good for each child.

Even toddlers can grasp that Jesus is God's Son and that God sent his Son to earth; that Jesus was once a child and grew as other children grow; that Jesus is now in heaven with God; and that Jesus loves them and is their Friend.

Little ones are taught by word and example that the Bible is God's Book; the Bible tells about God and Jesus; the Bible is a Book of true stories; and the Bible tells us how to do right.

Children understand that the church is God's house. They have happy times at church and learn that this is "my" church, and that we learn about God at church.

Young children can be taught that God gave him a home, parents, and brothers and sisters. They can learn to help at home.

Little ones learn basic good behavior by hearing that God wants them to be kind and share toys; to love everyone, and to obey parents.

This is the time to help children know that God loves all the children of the world; that some children do not know about God; that they can pray for other boys and girls and for missionaries; and that they can give money to help other children know about God.

How to Teach in the Nursery

Calmness begets calmness. Speak slowly and distinctly, with clear enunciation in a pleasing, well-modulated voice. Show your enthusiasm for the story. Sense the humor and laugh with the children. Display pictures. Make lessons suitable to the level of understanding. Employ frequent repetition.

Have an attractive Bible in the department, with pictures. Keep it in a special place, and treat it carefully and reverently. Hold it during the Bible stories, and often repeat parts of verses.

For this age, songs should have repetition and a good melody and be only one or two lines long. Songs may express ideas, provide relaxation and change of position, or help children change from one activity to another. Often it is wise to use a record player rather than have a piano crowd the room.

When praying, stress one idea at a time. Pray for the children, not about them. Use few names for God, with simple vocabulary.

Use stories. For these wigglers, stories should be only two or three minutes long, with repetition and simple words. They like rhyme and alliteration.

Use pictures. Pictures for this age group need a clear outline and few details. Display on their eye level. Pictures gain and hold attention, explain words and ideas, and recall stories and verses.

Suggested One-Hour Session in the Nursery

First fifteen to twenty minutes: arrival, offering, activity centers, and putting away materials.

Next twenty-five to thirty minutes: songs, welcomes, birthdays, prayer, Bible story, and picture study.

Last fifteen minutes: rest, Bible story activity, handwork, good-byes.

During the first fifteen minutes, let a helper at each interest center (book center, nature center, home living center, blocks, toys, and puzzles) guide the children in learning from it. Place a bulletin board and suitable pictures at their eye level.

Make space available for activities by using hinged tables or by putting flannelboards and chalkboards on the wall.

The nursery program provides a child's first impression of church, and it should encourage an atmosphere of love, security, and pleasure. Children will associate experiences with God's house. Far from a baby-sitting ministry, it is an opportunity to lay life foundations.

It must provide for activities to stretch restless muscles. Besides games and action centers, use rhythm instruments such as bells, sticks, detergent bottles with beans to rattle, and oatmeal boxes.

Make the moments count toward impressing one main aim. Use stories, songs, activity games to stress that aim. Teach Christian conduct by inserting a memory verse in stories and activities. Link God's love and care with daily life. This enables tots to sing, give, pray, and worship with understanding.

OBJECTIVES IN SUNDAY SCHOOL (See AIMS IN TEACHING)

OBJECT LESSONS

An object lesson is a teaching aid that tangibly communicates the lesson to the pupil. Simple object lessons are effective teaching tools. They focus attention and aid memory. The object should be familiar, and the illustration drawn from the object must be simple and easy to understand. Many simple object lessons use everyday objects, such as a hammer, pen, pins, potatoes, and others.

The object should be secondary; the lesson is primary. Unless the object brings out the point of the lesson, it has no teaching value. An object unrelated to the story only scatters the lesson's impact. Use only one object to teach one truth, for more may confuse. One lesson should have one chief aim, toward which the whole presentation is geared. For younger children use objects that are not symbolic and whose value is real. Children who are early juniors and under do not understand symbolic lessons.

Trick object lessons and many chemical object lessons are not usually effective in teaching a truth because attention may center on the trick. These are most useful as entertainment. Evaluate the effectiveness of a magic lesson by recall the following week. Note which points are recalled—the trick or the message of the application.

OLMSTEAD, BENJAMIN L. (1886–1960)

For twenty-nine years, Benjamin L. Olmstead was editor in chief of *Sunday School Literature* of the Free Methodist Church of North

America. Olmstead was born in Cedar Springs, Michigan, September 14, 1886, and graduated from Wheaton College (A.B. and A.M.) and McCormick Theological Seminary (B.D.). In 1911 he entered the graduate school of the United Free Church College, Glasgow, where he had as teachers two of the world's great biblical scholars, James Orr and James Denney. He took additional work at Oxford University. Dr. Olmstead began his ministry as pastor in Glen Ellyn, Illinois. Later he worked as dean of theology at Greenville College. His work as an editor of Sunday school material is well known throughout the Free Methodist Church and many other denominations. His exact scholarship and positive convictions have strengthened immeasurably the cause of Christ.

For twenty-nine years he edited the popular *Arnold's Sunday School Commentary,* an annual commentary on the International Uniform Sunday School lesson. He also wrote several books and booklets.

ONE-ROOM SUNDAY SCHOOL (See CLASS SUNDAY SCHOOL)

ORGANIZATION

To organize the Sunday school is to form it into a whole consisting of interdependent parts, giving it unity, harmony, and direction toward one purpose. Organization is the breaking down of group responsibility into parts, which can be assigned to individuals and committees. Organization assures orderly planning, work, and problem solving. It will help the church carry out the plan and purpose of the church—presenting the message of Christ to the world in the most effective way. The Sunday school must be properly organized for an effective spiritual thrust into its community.

Why Should a Church Be Organized?

Organization will contribute to the church in six important areas. It (1) makes planning possible, (2) identifies areas of responsibilities, (3) identifies problems, (4) charts the future, (5) provides a channel of communication, and (6) makes for cohesiveness.

Basic Principles of Organization

Denominations differ in the patterns of organization; even churches within a denomination differ in some details. There are, however, some basic principles for church organization. First, the pastor is the leader of the church as Christ's representative and should not be the errand boy of any member. He is the shepherd of his flock and, depending on individual church constitutional rule, a member—official or unofficial—of all boards. Second, each department should have goals to meet specific needs. Third, organizations should be directed and supervised by duly elected officials, all of whom are members of the church. The different boards should be coordinated in an executive board of the church. Also, boards should at specified times report their activities to the general membership, as they are ultimately responsible to the congregation.

As a church grows, pastors and church boards will need help in coordinating the educational program. One means of accomplishing this task is to establish a board of Christian education to help ensure the continued growth and efficiency of the church (see article on Board of Christian Education).

ORGANIZATION AND CHURCH GROWTH (See also CHURCH GROWTH WHEEL)

Most people who want to build a New Testament church give attention to the spiritual growth principles in the Word of God but neglect the natural factors of good organization and techniques. These principles built on common sense cannot be ignored if you want to build a New Testament church, but as demonstrated in the Church Growth Wheel, there are spiritual factors of organization. The natural and spiritual factors fit hand in glove. It is possible to get numerical growth by using circuses or Bozo the Clown. This is not biblical—even though the end result has been salvation of souls. Leaders in each church will have to prayerfully consider the "means to the end."

Spiritual Factors of Organization

1. Churches grow when they meet the biblical qualifications for a church. Not every group calling itself a church is in fact a church. Many organizations go by the generic term *church,*

yet do not meet New Testament criteria. The following principles describe a New Testament church: (a) a church is a group of baptized believers (Acts 2:41; Rom. 6:3-6), (b) a church has the presence of Jesus Christ in its midst (Rev. 1:13, 20; 2:1, 5), (c) a church places itself under the directives of the Word of God (Acts 2:42-43; 1 Tim. 3:15), (d) a church is organized to carry out the great commission (Matt. 28:19-20; Acts 5:42–6:5), (e) a church administers the ordinances, and (f) a church is evident when there is a manifestation of the spiritual gifts of leadership and service (Acts 11:22-26).

2. Churches grow when their leaders are truly called and led of God. Dr. Lee Roberson says, "Everything rises and falls on leadership." The greatest factor in church growth is the leader. The pastor must assume his biblical position of leadership within the flock (Acts 20:28): (a) the pastor leads by example (1 Pet. 5:3), (b) the pastor leads by preaching (Heb. 13:17), (c) the pastor leads by watch care (Acts 20:29-31), and (d) the pastor leads by wise decision making (1 Pet. 5:2).

3. Churches grow when laymen have their proper places of responsibility. Committees, councils, and boards are biblical means of organization. Some fast-growing churches have neglected committees. These churches have strong pastors who make all of the decisions, and while this may be effective, there are liabilities. The church becomes only as stable as the personality of its leader. Only a few leaders are talented enough to become the organizational personification of the church.

A pastor of a growing church needs assistance from his people. Laymen can and should help the pastor in the leadership of the church by serving on organizations such as the finance committee, the board of Christian education, the building committee, and the Sunday school council.

The Scripture illustrates organization:

The twelve tribes were organized around the tabernacle. Jesus fed the five thousand after they were organized into groups of fifty. A committee of seven (deacons) were organized to look after the material needs of widows. Paul organized churches in Asia Minor.

The church was commanded to produce the results of organization: "Let all things be done decently and in order" (1 Cor. 14:40).

The nature of God is consistent and orderly.

The nature of the church demands organization. The church is people, each one working to carry out the great commission, not watching from the pews while the pastor performs his ministry. A good pastor leads all the congregation into Christian service. The best way to get everyone involved is through an organized program. When a congregation organizes itself for service, it is carrying out the purpose for which the church was constituted.

Natural Factors of Organization

The Southern Baptists built the largest Protestant denomination in America by organizing their evangelistic outreach. This is still the secret to church growth.

1. Growing churches allow the pastor to exercise leadership. If a pastor goes in a direction and the people do not follow, he is not a leader. Or, if he runs beyond their ability to follow, he is not a leader. And it must be remembered that the pastor is a leader—not a dictator. There are dangers in a pastor-dominated church, but there are also dangers in a board-dominated church. Dictatorial abuses by pastor and deacons abound. Neither can be successful without the cooperation of the other.

2. Growing churches have workers who assist the pastor through service, prayer, and encouragement.

3. Growing churches are organized to meet the needs of the congregation. Never organize a committee or agency before it is needed. And when the organization is no longer serving the needs of its members, disband it.

4. Growing churches employ qualified people to carry the work forward. Committees do not get jobs done—people do. Too often committees are regarded as personalities. In fact, a committee is only the sum total of people. The following principles will help solve this point of irritation: (a) never give a job to a committee that can be done by one

person; (b) never allow productive people to be tied up in committee work that hinders their leadership or efficiency; (c) committee work is most effective for opinion gathering, policy decisions, and input from the masses; (d) an individual may learn leadership by effectively serving on a committee; (e) excessive committees bog a church down in bureaucracy; (f) the gifted person should be exposed to a great number of people in the largest variety of ministries to accomplish the greatest good for the total church.

This last principle applies to both organization and teaching. The most gifted man might be the Sunday school superintendent, and the most gifted woman may teach a large class. People should be used according to their ability. Find your key people and use them.

5. Growing churches can pinpoint their needs to best solve problems. The sharper the aim of an organization, the more it can accomplish. As a result of this principle, pupils should be grouped by age in Sunday school for efficient teaching.

6. Growing churches get more people involved in the organization and administration of the Sunday school than the average church. Traditionally, the Sunday school has attempted to get one worker for each ten pupils. This law is still effective when kept in balance with the law of the master-teacher. The gifted teacher should be allowed to instruct large classes, but he needs many assistants to take care of follow-up, visitation, record keeping, and counseling. The master-teacher is most effective as a lecturer. However, it is impossible for him to be a pastor-counselor of a large class. He needs many undershepherds.

7. Growing churches build loyalty to the organization on the part of the pupils. We live in a changing society where people have few loyalties. The one characteristic of change is that it rearranges priorities and disassociates the past. A church should be built on stability, for God does not change. Sunday school organization should be stable to reflect the unchanging God. However, this does not say the

organization should be fossilized.

Note the following application of this principle:

a. Assign a name to each class.

b. Attempt to develop loyalty to the class.

c. Try to keep classes in the same room for as long as possible.

d. Appoint teachers to a class on a permanent basis. The traditional law of Sunday school growth suggest that teachers be appointed on a one-year basis so they will not grow stale. However, teachers can be kept fresh by a consecration service at the beginning of each Sunday school year. Here they are challenged and make a commitment to carry out their responsibilities for the coming year.

e. Allow a gifted teacher to build the class as large as possible. The traditional law of Sunday school growth maintains that dividing and multiplying is the path of growth, and classes are kept small. This has not always proven effective. Some churches have grown through dividing their classes, while others have been fragmented. The master-teacher might build the class from fifty to four hundred. When the gifted teacher reaches his highest growth potential, then the class should be divided. The highest growth potential is determined by the size of the room, the teacher's ability to communicate, his ability to follow up, and the logistics of the situation.

8. Growing churches reflect the normal Sunday attendance curve. In the area of statistics, there is a bell-shaped curve. Over a period of years, the following curve indicates a healthy Sunday school:

Nursery	5 percent
Preschool	6 percent
Primary	12 percent
Junior	15 percent
Junior/Senior High	12 percent
Adult	51 percent

Some churches with large busing programs have more in the children's program. This often results in an instability of finances and leadership. Many downtown churches, on the other hand, have an exorbitant number of people in the adult division, especially senior citizens. If the curve falls off sharply with young adults and correspondingly with small children, the church usually has a leadership problem, although it has little trouble with finances. And without children, a church has no future.

9. Growing churches are measured by attendance, financial support, and member involvement. A Sunday school is healthy when people attend, give money, and involve themselves in its service. Therefore, a growing Sunday school ought to incorporate (a) an active program to foster consistent attendance, (b) an active program to get new attenders, (c) curriculum content to bolster attendance, and (d) external stimulation to encourage attendance.

    Many have accused churches of money grabbing. As a result, some leaders feel unspiritual when they talk about money. The opposite is true. When a leader does not mention stewardship, he is not obeying God (Mal. 3:10-11). The average American churchgoer gives $525 per year (1990) to his church. This averages out to approximately $10 per week per attender. When a church gets more than $10 per person, it is healthy. Therefore, a church ought to (a) teach stewardship in its curriculum, (b) provide an organizational program for its members to give, (c) motivate everyone to give, and (d) keep careful records of all income.

10. Growing churches construct buildings and educational space to reflect the purpose of the Sunday school. The traditional laws of Sunday school growth indicate there must be ten square feet per pupil. Since it also holds that there should be only ten pupils per class, classrooms were approximately a hundred square feet. These classes were ideal for small-group discussion. The trend today is to build classrooms the approximate size of public schoolrooms. The reasons for larger rooms are: (a) the master-teacher

can expand attendance; (b) the larger class can provide more motivation to pupils; and (c) many adults would rather not visit a small class but prefer a larger, more impersonal group where they can listen to the Word of God. Keep in mind that the Sunday school is for reaching people and teaching the Word of God. The Sunday school is not a minichurch for liturgy. Neither should the Sunday school be a lounge area with the appearance of a large furniture store. The Sunday school should have rooms constructed for class instruction.

11. Growing churches use their building as a major means of publicity. Many people choose a church for its physical facilities.

    a. The church should have visibility in the community. It should be located on a major thoroughfare. Place the building on the property so it can be seen by those passing by. Its prominence in the community will determine the likelihood of attendance.

    b. Visitors tend to frequent a church that is convenient and easily accessible.

    c. Exposure to the masses is also important. Place your church near the shopping center, business district, high school, or some other place where people can easily see the building. The rule of thumb for attracting shoppers is that a store should be seen by the family on their way to work and school in the morning, then again in the evening as they return home. The same rule holds for attracting prospective church members.

12. Growing churches have expandable, convertible, and interchangeable educational space. A church should get maximum use of its educational space.

    a. Rooms should be constructed so they can be expanded when a class grows in size.

    b. Rooms should be convertible. When the adult class goes from fifty to one hundred, children should be able to use the facilities with very little remodeling.

    c. Space should be interchangeable for activities. When a

gymnasium is built, it should be usable for recreation, education, and banquets, if necessary. Multipurpose facilities can better serve the congregation, and they cost less.

13. Growing churches are reflected by expansion of buildings. If a church never builds or adds to its present facilities, it communicates to the community that it is not growing. Therefore, a pastor is counseled to build a little every few years rather than to initiate a massive construction project every fifteen years.

14. Growing churches economize on building use. The traditional Sunday school had a "three chair" philosophy. The child was provided a chair and space for the traditional opening exercises. This took approximately twenty minutes. This space had to be heated, cleaned, insured, and painted. After opening exercises, the child was sent to a second chair in his small classroom. This space had the same overhead costs as the first. Finally, the child was sent to the sanctuary where a third chair, the pew, was provided for him. Hence, within a three-hour period, the house of God had provided three chairs for the child. This is no longer thought to be a wise use of space.

OUTREACH AND CHURCH GROWTH (See also CHURCH GROWTH WHEEL)

Spiritual Factors in Outreach

As demonstrated in the Church Growth Wheel, there are both natural and spiritual factors to each dynamic that holds a church. The same is true with outreach. Some churches seem to naturally grow in numbers, reaching the community. These churches do not have organized visitation, nor do they use promotional campaigns. Yet visitors come to their services, new members join their ranks, offerings climb, and enrollment indicators go up. God has a plan for growing churches. This plan is found in the Word of God. Growing churches in the book of Acts were characterized by the following spiritual factors.

1. *Churches grow when they have New Testament aims.* The aim

of the church is to go and make disciples of all nations (Matt. 28:19). The early church practiced soul winning, going to every house in Jerusalem (Acts 5:42). Paul went to every home in Ephesus (Acts 20:20) and reached every person in the city (Acts 20:31). God expects a church to grow.

2. *Churches grow best through the Sunday school.* The aims of the church are the aims of Sunday school. The Sunday school does the work of the church in reaching, teaching, winning, and training. Some think Sunday school is for kids at 10:00 A.M. and that preaching is for adults at 11:00 A.M. Both Sunday school and the worship service fulfill the aims of the church.

3. *Churches grow when they aim to carry out the great commission* (Matt. 28:18-20). Followers of Christ are to make disciples of as many persons in the world as possible (Matt. 28:19) (a) by showing compassion on the needs of man, (b) by having a vision of what God can do for the lost, (c) by bringing the lost under the hearing of the gospel, (d) by sharing their Christian experience with the lost, (e) by communicating the gospel to all men, and (f) by persuading the lost to accept the gospel.

Second, they are to identify each Christian with a local church (Matt. 28:19) (a) by getting each Christian under the teaching of the Scriptures, (b) by using the total abilities of each Christian for God's purpose, (c) by encouraging fellowship among Christians so they may strengthen one another, (d) by producing corporate worship and motivating Christians to private worship, (e) by becoming the focus for an organized outreach into the community, and (f) by administering the church ordinances.

Third, they are to teach each Christian to be obedient to the Scriptures (Matt. 28:20) (a) by communicating the content of the Word of God, (b) by training each Christian to use his skills to carry out God's plan for his life, (c) by inculcating Christian values and attitudes in all believers, (d) by motivating Christians to live a godly life as taught in the Scriptures, and (e) by supporting the aims and sanctity of the family.

4. *Churches grow by soul winning.* Philip won the Ethiopian eunuch; Peter preached to Cornelius; Paul witnessed to Ser-

gius Paulus. Churches grew through winning souls to Christ. Evangelism is communicating enough of the gospel so that a man can become saved, then persuading the man to accept Christ. There are two ways of looking at a church's outreach.

First, *church evangelism*, as the examples of the churches in the book of Acts. Congregations systematically canvased their communities, reaching lost people with the gospel. Note the ministry of Paul in Ephesus: "And this [ministry] continued for two years, so that all who dwelt in Asia heard the word of the Lord Jesus, both Jews and Greeks" (Acts 19:10).

A second form is *saturation evangelism,* which involves the communication of the gospel by every available means to every available person at every available time. The goal of saturation evangelism is to completely immerse an entire community in the gospel. In the early church, the disciples had so saturated Jerusalem with the message that the high priest asked, "Did we not strictly command you not to teach in this name? And look, you have filled Jerusalem with your doctrine" (Acts 5:28). The result of saturation evangelism was that Jerusalem was "filled" with the gospel.

5. *Churches grow by a program of evangelism.* Saturation evangelism results from an organized program. The city of Jerusalem was filled, and every house received the gospel (Acts 5:42), the result of a systematic, comprehensive coverage of the city. In other words, they had a master plan to reach Jerusalem. Today, some suggest that evangelism should be spontaneous, and argue against revival meetings, Sunday school growth campaigns, visitation programs, or Sunday school busing. However, a master program of outreach is necessary for New Testament evangelism (a) because the church is an organization (organism) with the specific goal of reaching its "Jerusalem," (b) because of the evidence of a program in churches in the book of Acts, (c) because the average Christian does not win souls unless motivated; and goals, requirements, examples and programs will motivate him, and (d) because the Lord is a God of order and rational-

ity. Just as the universe is governed by laws, the spiritual world is governed by laws; and the church should have organization, procedures, and goals commensurate with the laws of God.

6. *Churches grow through revival.* When the church is in a general state of revival, God blesses its outreach. "If My people who are called by My name will humble themselves, and pray and seek My face, and turn from their wicked ways, then I will hear from heaven, and will forgive their sin and heal their land" (2 Chron. 7:14).

7. *Churches grow through public preaching and teaching.* There is an emphasis in the twentieth century on home Bible studies. Evangelistic preaching has been deemphasized. However, the early church believed in preaching in the open and house-to-house (Acts 2:14-38; 3:12-26; 5:42; 20:20). The Bible is a dynamic book (Heb. 4:12), and it changes lives. New Christians (2 Cor. 5:17) will attract the interest and attendance of the unsaved. When the Bible is properly preached, the unsaved will want to attend and hear its message.

8. *Churches grow by prayer and biblical conviction.* We do not usually think of prayer as a principle of outreach, at least in a casual manner. However, a praying church is a growing church.

   Here are basic prayer concerns:
   a. Pray that the lost will be convicted.
   b. Pray that God will use the preaching of the Word to accomplish his purpose.
   c. Pray for spiritual growth and revival.
   d. Pray for changed lives.

   As a result of answered prayer, outsiders will come into the church, producing growth.

Natural Factors in Outreach

God's program for the church to communicate the gospel does not break the natural laws of communication. As a matter of fact, because all truth flows from God, we can count on him to bless it, no matter what form of communication we use: newspapers, radio, TV, or magazines. The natural principles of church growth, as well as the spiritual factors of outreach, stem from God.

1. *Growing churches project an aggressive image.* A pastor must determine the type of church he believes will best communicate to his community. This will establish an image, which may be defined as "the sum total of the impressions that a church wants to make on the community." Churches may be known as busing churches, youth churches, foreign mission churches, or Bible-teaching churches. When a pastor comes to a community, he should have a clear statement of aims and objectives. He should know what he wants to accomplish. Whether or not these are written down is unimportant. These aims will determine the church's image. The pastor will communicate this image to the entire community.

2. *Growing churches determine what clientele they can reach.* Many publics surround a congregation. A clientele is a natural grouping of people with one factor in common. The church can reach them through this common interest.

   First, the church must identify these people, determine their need and adapt advertisements to reach them with the gospel. Factors that help determine a church's clientele are (a) the friends of regular attenders, (b) the relatives, (c) neighbors who would not be called their friends, (d) neighbors to the church, (e) those living in the community who are unchurched, (f) unsaved people in other churches, (g) visitors who drive a distance to the church, and (h) new residents to the community.

   In addition to the above clientele, each of the areas can be further broken down into (a) new couples, (b) singles, (c) the divorced, (d) servicemen, (e) middle-aged couples, (f) senior citizens, and (g) college students.

   No single advertising campaign can reach every clientele. The church must appeal to the needs of each group it wants to reach. Then the church must communicate to each that it is able to meet their needs by its program of ministry.

3. *Growing churches determine to reach every person in the community.* The more persons to whom you present the gospel,

the larger the crowd likely to attend the church. This is the principle of sowing and reaping.

Never be satisfied when only one person comes for salvation. Rejoice with those who are saved, but keep seeking others. And don't be discouraged. Some soul winners lose their zeal when their young converts drop out of church.

The more fully a person commits himself to Jesus Christ at the moment of his salvation, the more likelihood of his follow-through in the Christian life. Therefore, preach repentance. Let a new convert know his obligations to the church in witnessing, attendance, tithing, Christian service, baptism, visitation, and prayer meeting.

The secondary motive that often causes a man to make a decision for salvation results in a primary action. Some go to church because they are lonely, others to satisfy parents; others attend because it is the thing to do or to make business contacts. Some go forward to commit their lives to Jesus because they want to please a wife or husband. Others go because of the pressure of circumstances. However, if they sincerely receive Christ at the altar, they receive eternal life. This principle reveals that people may go to church for secondary reasons; but when the gospel is preached, their primary need of salvation is met.

4. *Growing churches use every advertising media possible.* The following attitudes toward advertisement will make your Sunday school outreach successful:

Advertise in keeping with your image.

Make your advertising personal to each different clientele. A general poster or announcement to everyone is not as effective as a personal announcement regarding a specific need of a small clientele.

Use advertisements to lead to personal contact. People may not go to church because of impersonal advertisement. They go because of a human contact.

Remember, advertisement begins at home. In a small church situation, spend most of the time and money to reach the officers, the teachers, and the pupils. When these are convinced of the program, they will bring in the outsiders. Advertising is like waves from a splash in a pond—the waves are highest near the splash. Therefore, concentrate your advertisements on those close to home.

Advertising should get everyone involved. If you want to get 500 people to attend Sunday school, try to get 500 people "in" on the special push. This involves contests, delegated work, or other techniques to get them involved.

Use your people to advertise through: (a) personal testimony, (b) personal invitation, (c) skits, (d) phoning, (e) distributing handbills, and (f) writing letters.

Use every church resource to advertise special campaigns: (a) church-planning calendar, (b) church bulletins, (c) church newspaper, (d) pastor's newsletter, (e) church bulletin boards, (f) announcements, (g) posters, and (h) announcements on church radio broadcasts.

Advertise through direct mail. God's people should make their advertisements neat, attractive, and informative. Try church newspapers, letters, postcards, even handwritten letters. Mimeographed or hastily written newspapers have been used effectively by many groups or movements.

Advertise through communication media: (a) purchased advertisements and press releases in newspapers; (b) radio, church programs, community service programs; (c) community bulletin boards; (d) bumper stickers; (e) billboards; (f) posters in store windows; and (g) church announcement boards.

5. *Growing churches are organized to grow.* Many Sunday schools do not grow because the leaders plan to keep them small.

Set attendance goals. A church will not grow unless it aims to grow. First, set long-range attendance goals for a period of years. Next, set a yearly goal. A goal will keep vision lifted and a challenge before the people.

A growing Sunday school will have an attendance chart that looks like a two-humped camel. Growth is experienced in the spring and fall; attendance dips in the summer and around Christmas. Since we know when Sunday schools grow, set attendance goals higher in growth seasons than for other times of the year.

Plan a fall and spring campaign. A Sunday school should schedule its major activities when it will get the greatest results—that is during the fall and the spring peak periods. A Sunday school campaign should mobilize the entire energies of the workers to reach the lost, revitalize the Sunday school, and expand attendance. A Sunday school campaign should have the following characteristics: (a) the lesson content should tie into the theme, (b) the theme should motivate for outreach, (c) the theme should be expressed in a pithy saying, (d) a logo should be chosen that visualizes the campaign, and (e) the campaign should be short enough to sustain interest, but long enough to generate enthusiasm.

Set multiple goals during a Sunday school contest. Usually, one overall attendance goal will not stir all the people. Get several things working. Each of several specific goals will challenge the specific need to which it is tied, and each will bring about a specific result. Many goals will create momentum and excitement in the church.

The following may be achieved during a campaign:

a. An all-time attendance record
b. The highest average attendance for the fall and spring
c. The highest average attendance for the year
d. Class goals
e. Departmental goals
f. Highest average goals for all the buses
g. Highest attendance for an individual bus route
h. Greatest number of visitors
i. The number of visits made by a worker
j. The greatest number of phone calls made
k. A goal for the greatest number of postcards written

The campaign should get as many people as possible involved in outreach. During your fall or spring campaign, plan multiple activities. Some churches will try one idea to gain attendance, such as giving away a Bible, or having a contest with the reds against the blues.

During a campaign, all of the following might be used:

a. A contest of the red against the blue in the adult class.
b. The one bringing the most visitors is awarded a trip to Disney World.
c. A small gift is given to everyone on certain Sundays.
d. Certain giveaways are awarded to bus passengers, such as popcorn, watermelon, goldfish, or cotton candy.
e. Points or prizes are given to those bringing the most visitors.
f. Your church competes against another church in an attendance contest (such as a church in South Carolina against one in North Carolina—"The Yankees versus the Rebels").

Special personalities or musical groups. A segment of your clientele go to church to hear an outstanding speaker, such as a Christian politician. Others will visit your Sunday school to hear a musical group or soloist. Different kinds of musicians will attract different segments of your clientele to Sunday school.

Multiplied saturation produces explosive attendance. An all-time attendance record can be broken when all of the above are used (goal setting, campaigns, contests, guest personalities), plus a saturation of total energies by the workers. The people of the church get excited when they experience more on one Sunday than at any other time. Their excitement generates enthusiasm. When the kids feel the momentum of the big day, they bring their friends. When everyone senses that there will be a big day, the whole project takes on credibility, and other advertisement such as handbills, newspapers, radio, and letters become more effective.

The high day. The traditional Sunday school celebrated Rally Day on the first Sunday of October. Everyone was "rallied" for the coming Sunday school year and met in the large auditorium for a special program. Today this activity is called "the high day" when a church tries to have the largest attendance of the year. If a church uses this strategy every year, an annual expectation is built up. Using the "high day" technique will do the following for your church: (a) it will stir up dead Christians, (b) visitors will see the church at its best and become prospects to be reached for Christ, and (c) the faith of the congregation will increase as they expect God to do even greater things in the future.

OVERHEAD PROJECTORS

The overhead projector is a teaching aid that enhances the learning of the student.

Purpose of Using the Overhead

The overhead projector aids in teaching because it increases understanding by adding the visual element, adds interest, lengthens retention by causing students to use the eyes as well as the ears, and makes teaching more effective. The overhead projector offers a learning experience not easily gained otherwise.

Advantages

1. The teacher can face the class while making presentation.
2. Overhead projectors may be used without turning out lights.
3. Overhead projectors may be used with large audiences.
4. Overhead projectors contribute to clearer and more effective communication by using vision as well as hearing.
5. Other visual aids may be used simultaneously.
6. The instructor may prepare his own materials. Anything that can be traced, photographed, drawn, printed, or typed may be placed on transparency.
7. Materials may be pointed out or added to the transparency while it is being used.
8. Two or more transparencies may be overlaid to give perspective or to superimpose charts, drawings, or maps.

Weaknesses

The chief disadvantage of this aid is its cost, especially for a small school or church. However, if a school or church can purchase a projector and the materials, transparencies may be made on the premises for the occasion. It is not advisable, however, unless the machine will be used regularly. If the church or small school uses visual aids consistently, it would soon absorb the cost of a projector.

Technique for Using

Prepared materials or instructor-made transparencies can be made for practically every teaching situation. The following is a general procedure for making transparencies:

1. Mark on tracing paper the general outlines of the projection area. Then sketch the drawing or words you wish to reproduce.
2. Place a piece of clear acetate (the transparency or pressure-sensitive film) over the "master" and trace it.
3. Color or accent the drawing in the desired colors with felt pens, color tape, drawing pens, or suitable acetate inks.
4. Mount it with pressure-sensitive tape if all the information is on one sheet.
5. Spray it with clear plastic to seal the drawings or letters and prevent running and fading if the transparency is to be used frequently. It may also be mounted in a cardboard frame for easy storage.
6. Make a hinge of pressure-sensitive tape on the face of the mount if films (transparencies) need to be added to the make a progression on a basic picture or frame.
7. Hand out duplicates on regular mimeograph paper for note taking by students. Use pointers or felt-tip pens to add outline or drawing as the presentation proceeds. Other visual aids, such as a slide projector, maps, 3-D models, and the like, can be used simultaneously.
8. Plan a follow-up exercise to ensure understanding of the material presented. This can be in the form of a quiz, discussion, prepared questions, or summary.
9. Evaluate the presentation afterward; write comments or note changes needed in presentation to take into account when the material is next presented.
10. Write out an outline beforehand to ensure coherent and reasonable progress and development of thought.

PANEL DISCUSSION

The panel is a teaching method that allows group discussion by those who have prepared to discuss the topic of the lesson. The method has both advantages and disadvantages to the learning process. Its greatest advantage is that the members of the panel do a great amount of preparation and study on the subject to be discussed. They must do some thorough thinking on the matter, both pro and con. The panel discussion usually deals with subjects that have more than one viewpoint. Some of the panel will speak for the matter, and the other present other views. Its greatest disadvantage is that most of the thinking and discussing will be done only by those on the panel, while the rest of the class will merely listen.

A panel discussion usually begins with the leader presenting the problem, showing several sides of the issue. The various members of the panel, in no particular order, present their arguments for and against the issue. The other members of the panel, however, may feel free to question or to answer any point given by the member speaking. Following the presentation by the panel members, the discussion may or may not be opened to the members of the group. It is, of course, of more value to the class as a whole if they are permitted to ask questions or give opinions. Naturally, the more people who take part, the more thinking will have been stimulated about the subject.

PARAPHRASING

Paraphrasing is a technique by which the teacher motivates all students to apply the lesson by writing the primary Scripture of

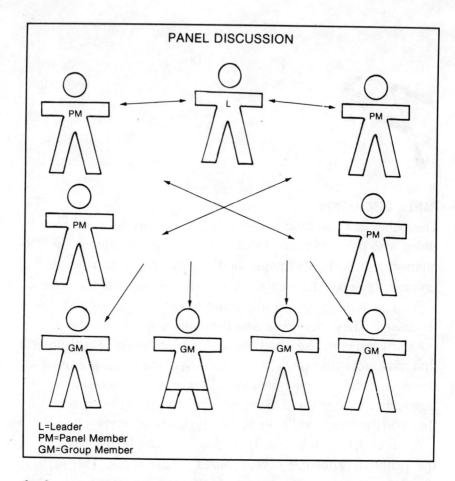

PANEL DISCUSSION

L=Leader
PM=Panel Member
GM=Group Member

the lesson into everyday language. Many classes have found that restating the truths of Scripture in modern idiom is a helpful learning procedure. A person using this technique rewrites in his own words the Scripture verse under consideration. He avoids using the original words of the text, yet the paraphrase must communicate the true meaning of the text. Paraphrasing yields a new understanding to adults who are seriously seeking to study the Scriptures.

The student's ability to paraphrase a passage depends upon his grasp of its basic idea. Many times the King James Version expresses thoughts in archaic language. However, any person who honestly seeks to find the true meaning of Scripture can do so. Perhaps the need of twentieth-century Christians is not for modern translations, but for the healing of their own spiritual blindness so that they can understand God's Word. Occasional archaic language is not the main obstacle in understanding God's Word, though modern translations may have a place in the Christian's library.

The use of paraphrasing as a teaching technique differs from the use of a modern version. Paraphrasing places emphasis on study by the student. Modern versions are used when emphasis is to be placed on the final product.

Paraphrasing is not an attempt to change the meaning of Scripture. In fact, if students change the meaning of Scripture, they have missed the point of paraphrasing. The purpose is to express the meaning of the Scripture passage in a way that will give a clear understanding to each student.

Supply paper and pencils for each student. If possible, provide one or more tables where the students can spread out their Bibles and notepaper. Students must have adequate time to paraphrase the passage, so choose lengths of passage that will enable you to stay within the time available.

Class members will get more out of the Scripture passage if they are given ample opportunity to discuss their written material. Misunderstanding and lack of clarity in thinking show up quickly in such an exercise. Have several student paraphrases read aloud.

Some of the following questions can help you as a teacher to get the most out of paraphrasing: Which words have been misunderstood by various class members? What are the reasons why different class members interpret words differently? What new insights into the Scripture has the class acquired today?

In paraphrasing Scriptures a variety of tools for Bible study will be helpful. Have several Bible dictionaries on hand. An English dictionary will also be helpful. The dictionary gives good definitions for some archaic words. A book of synonyms and antonyms may also prove useful.

The class members together should produce a summary statement composed of the best of the students' paraphrased verses. The first step in arriving at a summary statement is to read the verse from the King James Version. Have those students who feel that their contribution will be significant read their paraphrases to the class. The next step is to write the meaning of the verse in one statement. This method, of course, will not give the meaning supplied to the verse by every class member. But perhaps the class can agree to accept one statement as the best.

After the class has agreed upon a paraphrase for each verse, write the finished product on the chalkboard or on a large pad of newsprint. The teacher might appoint a class secretary to do the actual writing so that he or she may continue leading the class.

Appoint a secretary and discussion leader. Rewrite the paraphrase in prose form, making it about the same length as the verse. You may want to put the same message in a totally different setting. (Try to imagine what sort of situation Christ would use if he were telling this parable today.) Avoid using the same key words as are in the original (such words as parable, householder, vineyard, servants, etc.). Try to get everyone in the group involved. Discuss the various settings that could be used and various ways each thought could be expressed.

PASTOR, THE SUNDAY SCHOOL ROLE OF THE

God's plan for a pastor is found in Acts 20:28—"Therefore take heed to yourselves and to all the flock, among which the Holy Spirit has made you overseers, to shepherd the church of God which He purchased with His own blood."

Notice, the pastor should teach "all the flock," because God has given him responsibility for every person in his congregation.

Technically, this implies the pastor should teach every Sunday school class in the church. But on Sunday morning this is a physical impossibility. Also, it is a psychological impossibility, inasmuch as Beginners cannot be taught with young married couples. Therefore, the pastor must delegate his teaching authority to qualified representatives (see Sunday School Teacher). The Sunday school teacher is an extension of the pastor's role into the life of the students. This means the Sunday school teacher is a shepherd to the Sunday school flock, just as the pastor is a shepherd to the total local church flock.

PATHOLOGY OF CHURCH GROWTH (See also specific pathologies)

The pathology of church growth is the study of the growth-inhibiting diseases of churches, the characteristics and symptoms of those diseases, and the prescriptions to deal with them to achieve the goals of church health and growth. Under separate articles, this encyclopedia considers the following pathologies of church growth: Arrested Spiritual Development, Ethnikitis, Koinonitis, People Blindness, Senility, Sociological Strangulation, and St. John's Syndrome.

PATRIOTIC SUNDAY SCHOOL CAMPAIGN

Patriotism can be utilized to help build Sunday school attendance when utilized in a Sunday school campaign. While patriotic holidays, such as the Fourth of July, are not good attendance days in most churches, many churches feature a "God and Country Day" to encourage others to attend who might not otherwise be present. Other churches use a patriotic theme during their spring or fall campaign with good success. One church adopted the theme "Let Freedom Ring" for a spring campaign running from Easter Sunday through Mother's Day. Each week a different freedom was emphasized, including freedom over death (Easter Sunday), freedom of speech (Loyalty Sunday), freedom of the press (Bible Sunday), freedom of assembly (Friend Day), freedom of worship (May Day), and freedom of prayer (Mother's Day). Each week, a patriotic ribbon was distributed featuring the particular emphasis of that Sunday. Each department had an attendance goal and worked to get people in Sunday school during the campaign.

PAXSON, STEPHEN (1837–1881)

One of the greatest American pioneers did not search for land, rivers, or natural resources. Stephen Paxson was a pioneer who searched for lost souls. During his lifetime he founded 1,314 new Sunday schools with an enrollment of 83,000 students.

Paxson was born with a speech impediment and later was nicknamed "stuttering Stephen." He also was lame, but these difficulties did not prohibit him from doing the work of God.

His little girl begged him to attend Sunday school so she could win a prize. When Paxson got there, they asked him to teach a class of boys. Teaching involved listening to the boys read the Scriptures and simply correcting them when they made mistakes. "Let's go home," he said when they finished reading the lesson. "You are supposed to ask us questions out of the little book," the boys told him.

Paxson was so embarrassed that he did not know answers to the questions that he took a Bible home and read it carefully. He became a Christian by reading the Scriptures and ultimately volunteered his life as a missionary for the American Sunday School Union.

He named his horse Robert Raikes, after the founder of Sunday school. The horse was so well trained that it never passed a child, but waited for Paxson to stop and give out the gospel.

Paxson was a well-known speaker on the East Coast, raising money for Sunday school libraries. He made sophisticated audiences laugh and cry, but more importantly, he got them to give money. They could see beyond his grammatical mistakes to the great vision he had for pioneering the west with the Word of God. As a result, Paxson began Sunday schools in cabins, tobacco barns, taverns, and dance halls.

Stephen Paxson retired to a St. Louis office and died in 1881. He is remembered as "the spirit of Sunday school" because of his great enthusiasm and commitment to the movement.

PEOPLE BLINDNESS (See also PATHOLOGY OF CHURCH GROWTH)

People Blindness is a church growth pathology that refers to the inability of the church to see spiritual, social, and community needs. The key to an effective, growing ministry may be summarized in the expression, "Find a hurt and heal it." Hence, a church must have a "vision" of needs of people and the community, then it must develop a program to meet those needs. A church with a food service for the poor will attract and minister to the poor. Some churches have ministries for the hearing impaired (sign language interpreting) and classes for people with mental retardation, single-parent families, widowed, or newly married. The church that is sensitive to the aches and pains of its people will always have a ministry.

How to Solve People Blindness

1. Create a task force of members to brainstorm the potential community needs not being met by the church.
2. Have the task force brainstorm possible programs to meet these needs.
3. Study the philosophy of ministry in churches similar to yours that minister in neighborhoods similar to yours.
4. Plan special Sunday school classes or Bible studies for "need" groups.
5. Have the pastor preach on the definition of *ministry*: communicating the gospel to people at their point of need.

PEOPLE MOVEMENT

A people movement results from the joint decision of a number of individuals all from the same people group. Such a movement enables them to become Christians without social dislocation, while remaining in full contact with their non-Christian relatives. Such an arrangement enables other segments of that people group to come to similar decisions and form Christian churches made up primarily of members of that people group (source: Donald McGavran, *Understanding Church Growth*).

Types of People Movements

There are several different types of people movements. The following five classifications represent the most common.

1. Lystran movement—a part of the people becomes Christian and the balance becomes hostile to the Christian religion.
2. Lyddic movement—the entire community becomes Christian.
3. Laodicean movement—a movement slows down and stagnates.
4. Ephesian movement—people who desire to become Christians but simply do not know how are provided with the necessary knowledge.
5. Web movement—the gospel spreads through natural friendship and kinship ties.

PLANNING, LONG RANGE

A Sunday school class is like one inning of a baseball game. You have to see the whole to appreciate the parts. Just so, every Sunday school lesson is a part of the whole cycle. Before the students can see the whole, you as the teacher must study and grasp the whole.

The overview is important. At the beginning of a new quarter, scan all thirteen lessons to get the total "overview." Then each lesson is like the spoke in the wheel that completes the cycle of teaching.

Try to visualize the entire quarter's lesson. Can you see the progress of God's people from slaves in Egypt to their conquest of the Holy Land? Can you see the movement of Jesus through the Gospels as he gathers twelve disciples to his ultimate crucifixion on Calvary? Can you grasp the message of justification and the total outline of the book of Romans? If you can visualize the whole quarter, then you can better "fit" each lesson into its part.

The overview will help you gather lesson materials. Perhaps you will need a filmstrip series, a flannelgraph, or a phonograph record. Visual aids are difficult to attain on a Saturday night when you have to teach the lesson the following Sunday morning. An overview will help alert you to needed audio or visual aids, thus making you a better teacher.

POSTERS

Poster making can be a good project for a class. Attractive posters can create a desired atmosphere, teach a new idea, or announce and advertise important events. In an effective poster the message is obvious at a glance, simple and to the point, and large enough to be seen from the farthest possible viewing position. Words, symbols, and pictures are large and familiar. The poster has eye appeal.

PRAYER, PREPARATION FOR TEACHERS

The teacher is not prepared until he prepares himself through prayer. Prayer preparation means more than walking into the class and asking students to bow their heads. Also, prayer preparation means more than asking God to bless the time of study and preparation. The following items will add vitality to a lesson when the teacher uses them as prayer guides.

1. Pray for a teachable spirit. One of the first parts of lesson preparation is asking God for a teachable spirit. Before you can teach others, you must be taught by the Master-Teacher. As a teacher approaches his Scripture lesson he must pray and ask God to guide his study. "Open my eyes, that I may see wondrous things from Your law" (Ps. 119:18). But, along with praying for God to instruct, the teacher must be willing to learn. "If anyone wills to do His will, he shall know concerning the doctrine" (John 7:17).

2. Pray for the teaching ministry of the Holy Spirit. Too often the human teacher sees himself as the only channel in the classroom. Christ has promised, "When He, the Spirit of truth, has come, He will guide you into all truth" (John 16:13). Also Jesus promised "the Holy Spirit, whom the Father will send in My name, He will teach you all things" (John 14:26). This promise referred to the Holy Spirit, who will become our teacher. The Holy Spirit indwells the human teacher and wants to instruct through the human teacher.

   In one sense, your Sunday school has only one teacher—the Holy Spirit. Unless the Holy Spirit works through teachers, students cannot understand the Bible.

3. Pray for guidance in lesson preparation. Anytime you sit down before the Scriptures for lesson preparation, you should ask God to guide your study. Most Christians have a habit of asking God's blessing upon food when they sit for a meal. In the same manner, teachers should establish the habit of asking God's blessing upon the Word of God when they sit down to study. "Trust in the Lord with all your heart, and lean not on your own understanding; in all your ways acknowledge Him, and He shall direct your paths" (Prov. 3:5-6).

4. Pray for your pupils. Teaching the Word of God is earnest business done for eternity. The teacher attempts to change the destiny of each pupil. Lost pupils will be presented with

435

solutions, and backslidden students will be exhorted to repent. The teacher can't effect the Word of God in the pupil's heart; therefore, he must avail himself of God's power. The teacher prays for conviction of sin (John 16:7-11), for the impact of Scripture (Rom. 1:16), and for the moving of the Holy Spirit in pupils' lives (Acts 1:8).

5. Pray for growth. God answers the prayer of those who ask for their ministry to be enlarged, but prayer alone cannot build a Sunday school. God will not do what he has commanded us to do. We are to go and reach people. Classes grow when teachers are busy visiting, phoning, mailing, and praying all week.

PRESESSION

Presession is the time between the arrival of the first pupil and the beginning of opening worship. Remember, Sunday school begins when the first pupil walks in the door, not when the leader announces, "Let's begin," or says, "Good morning!"

Presession activity is a valuable instrument in the hand of the teacher. During this time the pupil is able to: (1) further his love for God by planned and purposeful activities, (2) prepare for the Sunday school hour. The term *prepare,* means: (a) the teacher meets the pupils at the door, which lessens disciplinary problems both before and during class time; (b) the teacher provides the children a chance for fellowship, which lessens extraneous chatter during the Sunday school hour; and (c) the time puts the pupil in an attitude of worship, and seeking God. The time before Sunday school should be used carefully and to its fullest advantage. There are other purposes naturally derived if the presession activity is planned well. (3) It prevents latecomers. (4) It arouses interest and enjoyment for students in their Sunday school experience. (5) Presession is a time to get acquainted. Teacher, do you know your pupils, and do they know you? (6) Presession is a time when wrong motives and misunderstandings can be corrected. (7) Presession is a time when interests are shared between pupil and teacher concerning salvation, ball games, parties, school, and other mutual interests. (8) Finally, presession activities actually teach. Even though the teacher is not talking, learning can take place.

Use presession programs that will encourage the pupils to come early. If you do, presession will naturally lend itself to extra opportunities to teach the Word of God.

Presession activities should be planned to be profitable. Therefore, they require the complete cooperation of every teacher. Each teacher should be present for the presession each Sunday before the arrival of the first pupil. The teachers should greet pupils on arrival. It is very important for each teacher to be with his pupil during this time.

Various activity centers may be utilized on department levels during presession time. Some activities that departments may have are: a book center, a missionary center (primary and older), an art center, a sand table, books, curios, and an interest center with maps. Memory work may be reviewed during this time. In addition to these common interests, various activities may be scheduled according to departments.

Nursery: (1) Wraps will have to be taken off and hung. (2) Toys can be provided for fun and learning to share. (3) A nature center is a sure attention getter and interest holder. (4) A picture Bible should be displayed and used.

Primary: (1) A music center with records, a record player, and a piano. (2) Group projects are also fun.

Junior: (1) A junior choir may be practical; also, records may be listened to, and singing around the piano may be enjoyed. (2) A work center may be set up, where help is given to students with their manuals. (3) Planning time—juniors are full of ideas. (4) Contests may be planned and carried out. (5) Ushers for opening worship may be chosen and duties explained and practiced.

Junior High: (1) Missions can be presented forcibly through a missionary biographical library and mission information. Also, curios and letters from missionaries may be displayed. (2) True worship may be emphasized through discussions. (3) Problems may be discussed and solved.

Senior High and Adults: (1) Prayer groups may be organized. (2) A friendship committee may be employed to greet new students and to make introductions. (3) Talents may be explored with discussions. (4) Various aspects of the church may be explained to those who are not well informed concerning the local church and its operation.

This is not an exhaustive list but is simply a brief outline of programs that may be employed to more effectively use valuable presession time on Sunday mornings. Additions may be made and variations may be adopted to this program to properly adapt it to your own local church situation.

The presession activity should produce a desired result. The result is the changed life of the pupil because of presession activity.

The pupil should learn the Word of God in presession, therefore becoming a stronger Christian. This will help the pupil to take full advantage of the time devoted to the Sunday school hour. He is then an example to those new pupils who may visit from Sunday to Sunday.

This activity instills within the mind of the pupil the fact that punctuality is necessary and that he is not only responsible for himself, but also to be an example to others.

Cooperation, participation, and association is learned at a young age if there is a stable presession activity for everyone from the youngest pupil to the oldest pupil within your church.

PRIMARY DEPARTMENT

The Primary Department is made up of a children ages six to eight years old or first through third grade. Primaries grow and learn at different rates. Primaries use all their senses in learning; they learn by imitating, observing, listening, doing, playing, talking, and moving. Primaries need independence, but they rely on wise, dependable adult guidance. They need to help as well as be helped. They need opportunities for increasing their independence. Wise supervision and a minimum of interference will guide them in getting along with other children.

The teacher must maintain control but be a genuine friend. While the teacher will respect students' ability, they cannot have free rein to do whatever they wish. Limits are set by lesson purpose, abilities, materials, space, and time. The teacher must sometimes say a firm no or yes or, "This is what you must do." Do things with the children, not for or to them. Learning results from shared experiences. Plan experiences that involve the whole personality of the primary.

What Can the Primary Child Learn?

1. The Bible is a very special Book about Jesus and how to please him.
2. God created all things. Sin spoiled God's perfect creation.
3. All have disobeyed God and need the Savior to take away sin. God will forgive if I am sorry and ask him.
4. Jesus died to take my punishment for sin. I can receive him as my Savior. He helps me to know how to live right.
5. God is my heavenly Father, who loved me enough to send his Son to earth for me. He is with me and helps me.
6. God's Son never sinned. He did wonderful miracles on earth. He is coming back again.
7. We can talk to God any time. We should thank him for all his gifts and ask him for what we need.
8. Church is where we feel God near, but we can worship him wherever we are.
9. Because God gave his Son, we give our time and money to him.
10. The Lord Jesus wants to save all people everywhere. He wants me to tell others Jesus loves them, too. I can pray and give money to help children in other lands hear about Jesus.

Developing a Primary Program

1. *Teaching Bible truths.* Memorizing is only one step. Children must understand words and know their meaning. Give them an understanding of the Scriptures to help them develop a proper attitude toward God, Jesus, the Bible, the church, and others.
2. *Activity teaching.* This includes conversation, picture studies, games, visual aids, stories, and songs.
3. *Creating mission interest.* Use a globe, exhibits of dolls or curios from other countries, mission maps, books, Bible verses that stress God's love for all, questions, friezes show-

ing other races, puppets, and dramatization of missionary work.

4. *Using music.* Words of songs must be understandable to this age group. Avoid symbolic language and abstractions. The melody should be simple, with repetition of phrases. Rhythm should be definite. Songs should be correlated with the lesson theme. Christian character and religious attitudes are formulated by use of songs based on Scripture.

Advantages of Open-Room Teaching with Primaries

Several factors indicate that it is wise to use open-room teaching for primaries.

1. Children do not like to be cramped or crowded.
2. Children learn to work, think, and plan together as a group.
3. Much can be learned about children as workers see them work together, expressing themselves in free activity periods.
4. The open room provides opportunities for children to develop plans they and the teachers make.
5. It puts children under the influence of more than one teacher.
6. Small, dark classrooms may dampen the spiritual life of the child.
7. Better and fuller use of materials can be made when all share them in one large classroom.

Proposed Time Schedule for Primary Department

Twenty to thirty minutes, activity time. Five minutes, clean-up time. Twenty-five to thirty minutes, group time. These periods will include:

1. Sharing experiences through conversation
2. Worship experiences
3. Games and activities
4. Fellowship—recognition of birthdays or special achievements
5. Bible story
6. Planning and practicing ways to put lesson truths into life

Learning Activities That Work with Primaries

Types of learning activities include acquiring information, solving problems, appreciation, and handcrafts.

Activities should be chosen because they relate to Bible truths and unit purposes, are appropriate, make the best use of resources, provide for the best possible teaching, incorporate suggestions of children, and provide opportunities for pupil involvement.

Possible activities are: (1) Bible-verse flash cards (verse on one side, reference on the other), (2) Bible-verse jigsaw puzzle, (3) painting, (4) matching pictures to stories and characters, (5) matching pictures to Bible verses, (6) writing a story about a picture, (7) drawing reactions to a story or a problem, (8) dramatization, (9) tours and field trips, and (10) puppet plays.

PROGRAMS FOR SPECIAL OCCASIONS FOR THE SUNDAY SCHOOL

Sunday schools in the past made much of seasonal and sacred holidays. On these occasions, the entire membership met in the church sanctuary for a program—often featuring every class from toddlers through adults. Few cared whether it was a polished performance, as long as almost everyone had a part.

Those programs probably were remembered longest by the performers themselves. And, because of the seasonal association, the spiritual impact was renewed with each recurrence of the season. There is something to be said against these programs, however. Some child psychology experts believe the system exploited the children, to their emotional and mental detriment. If anyone criticized or laughed at their performance, shy children might become more inhibited. At the same time, if a natural extrovert and leader was too highly praised, he might become vain.

Although in the "good old days" families shared church experiences through these programs, in today's well-organized, departmentalized churches, the spiritual progress of many children goes quietly forward without being noticed by parents or grandparents. In the public school, assembly programs afford more opportunity for family awareness than any activity provided by most churches. Perhaps an occasional unified church assembly for all ages would bridge some generation gaps.

Special-day all-church programs also can bridge a gap between parents and teachers who, in very large churches, may never meet. As teachers introduce their pupils, Mother and Dad learn for the first time who Bobby's teacher is.

"Isn't Sunday school for the purpose of Bible study?" Curriculum experts protest. "Why have special-day emphases at all? It interrupts our sacred schedule."

However, God interrupted his scheduled programs for special emphasis involving the family. In the midst of seeing tens of thousands of his people safely across the Jordan River on their way into the Promised Land, he had General Joshua stop and ask a representative of each tribe to take a large stone and put it on a designated pile. Progress was halted while this special program took place. And progress would thereafter be halted at the place whenever a family passed by the stones.

"Why is that pile of stones here?" the children would ask. Then the father would answer their question, explaining the story.

In Old Testament times, observance of special days included the Passover. Annual pantomime of the event kept the memory fresh in the minds of the delivered. So would the Jews' annual drama of the brave Queen Esther and the hanging of Haman. Doubtless the whole family celebrated the event as a group. Other feasts or celebrations were designated by God to be held with regularity.

In the Christian era, Christmas and Easter became occasions for weeks of rehearsal and preparation for an all-church pageant or drama. Most families were involved because a parent or child had a part or helped with the costuming and other duties. Today there are fewer all-church pageants. Junior has too many other activities, especially at Christmas. And Christmas shopping begins before Thanksgiving and continues through the after-Christmas sales.

"People are so busy," say the church leaders, "we don't want to add the burden of rehearsals and programs."

So special-day programs have come to be observed chiefly in the Music Department of the church. Choirs are going to meet every week anyway, leaders say. They can add the seasonal message to song in their regular practice and, with no real extra output of time or effort, can produce a special program. But not everyone is qualified to participate in the music. Persons who could give a good account of themselves in a speech or pantomime must be only onlookers. While children's choirs do not exclude monotones, the youth and adult choirs do, and some who are willing to serve cannot do so when no opportunity is afforded.

A successful program—whether for Mother's Day, Father's Day, Children's Day, Thanksgiving, Christmas, Easter, Promotion Day, or whatever—depends on:

1. *The leader.* Someone must be willing to plan and push the program. Time must be invested in announcing and conducting rehearsals and in arranging for costumes, decorations, curtains, furniture, etc. This leader need not be the one who accomplishes every task, but the one who directs others to do so.

2. *The participants.* With interest and enthusiasm caught from a dedicated leader, those who take part in a program must be willing to memorize any necessary speeches and to attend rehearsals.

3. *The audience.* The majority of the membership should be willing to attend the final production and encourage those who spent hours preparing the program. While a full house may seem frightening, it is also a spur to the participants to do their best. Teachers may prepare children's classes to be good listeners by warning against laughing at performers or attempting to distract them. Sympathy with less-than-perfect performance may help the underachievers try harder next time—or even to attempt a next time.

Where to Find Ideas

1. *Catalogs.* Few teachers have time to spend hours at a bookstore browsing through the program possibilities and making a selection. Catalogs from Christian publishers usually list special-day program collections and describe their contents, so selection can be made by mail.

2. *Publishers of plays.* Three leading publishers of plays for school and community also publish plays, pantomimes, and recitations for church use. They are Baker's Plays, 100 Chauncy Street, Boston, MA 02111; Eldridge Publishing Com-

pany, P.O. Drawer 209, Franklin, OH 45005; and T. S. Denison, 5100 West Eighty-second Street, Minneapolis, MN 55431.

3. *Other churches' programs.* Visit another church's play or pageant. If it seems a possibility for your group, find out where the script is available.

4. *Write it.* Using musical numbers by regular choir groups, a Sunday school leader can put together a program of recitations and Bible passages in chronological order. (Recitations may be obtained through the catalogs mentioned above.) More often than is supposed possible, a leader who knows the abilities of the children, youth, or adult participants, can plan a better program than a printed one that calls for talents not represented in his group. The fact that it is original also can be emphasized in advertising.

PROMOTING THE LIBRARY (See also LIBRARY/RESOURCE CENTER/ MEDIA CENTER)

Any worthwhile Christian endeavor creates and maintains a demand for its existence. The church library is no exception. The librarian and his committee must build the use of this educational facility so that the library becomes an indispensable part of the local ministry. Methods of promoting available services are only as wide as the imaginations of those administering the library. In other words, the methods are endless. If the church can interest an aggressively artistic member in serving on the library committee, it may be guaranteeing acceleration of promotional activity. Even a relatively inexperienced teen who is showing artistic promise through the beginning courses at school might contribute to library promotion, under the direction, of course, of the librarian, who should always lead in promotional policy. Following are a number of suggestions to initiate and maintain interest in the library:

1. Make the opening of a new church library an occasion for special attention. A dedication service involving both library personnel and the Sunday school staff will draw attention to the library. Such a service is most appropriate after the library is furnished and equipped with a basic core

of books. A dedication service provides a definite goal toward which work might be more speedily completed.

2. A library open house might be arranged, complete with refreshments. Give visitors an opportunity to view the newest books, teaching aids, and equipment. The emphasis should be for everyone (not just Christian education leaders) to come and see, rather than to "check it out for use right now"—at least not until the official hours for open house are past. People could use sign-up lists to reserve their choices of books and equipment.

After the library has been inaugurated, teachers and superintendents should arrange to meet with their students for one class session in the library, at which time the librarian can acquaint the different age groups with the kinds of services offered to them.

During the next teachers' meeting, the librarian could present a talk on the audiovisual resources of the library. Materials and equipment should be displayed and demonstrated. The librarian should specifically point out to new teachers the items available for the age groups they are teaching. For such a conference the librarian might secure from the Sunday school supplier enough catalogs so that each staff member may keep one for future reference. Christian publishers are often quite willing to cooperate in this manner.

On the Sunday of an all-church open house for the library (especially for larger congregations), people could be invited to attend in class groups at designated hours. Such an arrangement is advantageous for the librarian because he is then able to emphasize different segments of the library, explaining each more thoroughly.

3. Make new posters at least each quarter. Advertise the library ministry by displaying posters in appropriate, heavily-trafficked areas of the building. Feature seasonal trends, such as winter, when people are generally more confined and may have more time to read.

The Junior Department of the Sunday school may enjoy a

poster-making contest to advertise the ministry of the library. An appropriate book could be awarded as first prize and the posters displayed throughout the church. As the different mothers and fathers view the posters to determine which is best, they will become sold on the ministry of the library in an indirect manner.

4. Place the library bulletin board in a strategic location—as near the main entrance of the church as possible, so that many people will see it. The bulletin board may be utilized to display posters or an arrangement of dust jackets from recently acquired books. The library staff should also post a list of new books on the library bulletin board. News notes, clippings, book reviews, and other media should be used to catch the eye and encourage further reading. Try to add something new every week.

5. Observe special days. On certain days on the church calendar, a display of books can be arranged in the church foyer. The librarian might be present to encourage people to check out books and discover what new books are available. People who are not likely to make their way to the library may check out a book and benefit from reading it. Most librarians would suggest that the exhibit be small. It may include some pamphlets or magazines. The display should tie in with the occasion being observed. For instance, books on missions should appear during the missionary conference, and books on Easter, Christmas, Thanksgiving, or other holidays should highlight those special seasons. If the pastor is giving a series of sermons on a specific portion of the Bible, books relating to this topic could be put in the foyer and checked out by those who want to do further study.

6. Book reviews can and should be used in a number of ways for maximum effectiveness in promoting the library. Making your librarian the only person responsible for giving book reviews has two disadvantages. First, the membership gets acquainted with new books from just one person's point of view. Second, the librarian defeats his purpose of encourag-

ing other people to enjoy books. Let others give book reviews. However, since every reader is not capable of giving oral or written book reports, the librarian needs to be somewhat selective in designating this duty. There are a variety of ways in which book reviews can appropriately be used in the church. Here are a few suggestions:

a. Schedule five minutes during the church service for a review of a significant, newly acquired book. This would be particularly effective if it related to the sermon topic of that day.

b. Schedule five minutes in a department or class for the presentation of a new book for a special age group or one that relates to present lesson material. Teachers have much latitude in choosing books for this purpose. Books reviewed could range from Bible studies to Christian novels.

c. Have someone who has been helped in some definite area of Christian living by a particular testimony.

d. Use book reviews occasionally as part of activities of all groups within the church: youth groups, women's missionary meetings, boys' and girls' clubs and weekend retreats.

7. Book Clubs. Due to the competitive nature of the activity, book clubs probably work best with children and young people. They can probably be used most successfully in the summer when most children are free from school pressures. In a book club, children work against a deadline to read the highest number of books. The child gets credit for a given book by giving an oral or written review to the librarian. At the end of the designated period, first, second, and third prizes (books, of course) are given to the three reading the largest number of books. A book club of this type assumes two things: that a church can supply the necessary books, and that they will be given credit only for Christian books. Caution: Restricting books read to those from the church library will eliminate the use of Christian books given to children by their parents.

8. Library skits. These may be humorous or serious perform-ances, including acting out a portion of a book. This device is best used in youth or women's meetings.

9. Presession activity of the Sunday school. Many children arrive at Sunday school early. To keep these children occu-pied until the Sunday school worship begins, a story "hour" (ten to fifteen minutes in length) might be organized. If there is no room in the library before Sunday school begins, perhaps a room adjacent to the library could be used for this meeting. Someone other than the regular librarian or teachers should be asked to regularly read or tell a story.

10. General and topical book lists can be distributed to the different groups, such as teachers, officers, leaders (espe-cially those newly elected), new members, children, youth, newlyweds, and parents.

11. A library column in the church newspaper. Here book re-views may appear along with news of new books and mate-rials.

12. Promotional book jackets might be used to cover hymnals and books loaned by the library. If well designed and in good taste, such jackets will be effective.

13. Home ministry. Send church library books to those who are sick or shut in. The pastor and others who do home calling have a built-in reason to enter a home if they come bearing a helpful book. It can also guarantee a reason for a return visit to pick up the book. Callers should find out something of the background and interests of the person for whom they are choosing reading material.

PROMOTING THE SUNDAY SCHOOL (See VISIBILITY OF THE SUNDAY SCHOOL)

PROPHECY, GIFT OF (See also SPIRITUAL GIFTS)

The person who has the gift of prophecy has the ability to pro-claim God's truth. The ability to predict the future (1 Sam. 9:9) and to be a channel of revelation (Eph. 2:20) is not operative today. In the exercise of this gift, the prophet "speaks edification and exhortation and comfort to men" (1 Cor. 14:3). The strengths of this gift include (1) sensitivity to the reputation of God, (2) an ability to quickly perceive and denounce sin, (3) an understanding of the sinful motive of man and lack of toleration for hypocrisy, (4) a directness and frankness in his communication, (5) a desire for apparent evidence of conviction, and (6) a discernment of people before considering their message.

The common weaknesses of a prophet include (1) an apparent lack of care for individuals, (2) viewed as being harsh, (3) uncomfortable in a discussion session, (4) difficulty in adjusting to others, and (5) a tendency to be crowd oriented.

Those with this gift may fall into the danger of (1) being dependent on the sermon for ministry, (2) overlooking the needs of others, or (3) being proud.

PROSPECTS

A prospect is someone who is receptive to the church and responsive to the message of the gospel. This is someone who is not a part of your Sunday school but could be reached by your Sunday school.

Where to Find Prospects for Your Class

One key to building a growing Sunday school class is finding prospects for your class. These prospects can be found in several ways. (1) Prospects discovered during visitation should be recorded and systematically followed-up. (2) Anyone who visits the class one Sunday or attends a special class function may be considered a prime prospect for the class. (3) As class members report newcomers to the community, names and addresses should be recorded for future contacts. Other facts can be added to the record following other visits. (4) The friends and associates of your class members are among the best prospects you may have for your class.

PROVIDING ADDITIONAL SPACE

Additional space is a crucial factor in Sunday school expansion. Attendance in many growing churches has leveled off because the building was inadequate. When there is not additional room for new classes, growth usually stops.

Lack of Sunday school space halts attendance growth for many reasons. First, you cannot organize new classes for growth if there is no place to put them. Just as a farmer needs additional acreage to harvest a larger crop, so a Sunday school needs more classrooms to expand its ministry.

Second, attendance levels off then begins to decline when too many children are crammed into a classroom. Packed classrooms hinder efficient teaching, and when pupils are overlooked by the teacher, they become potential dropouts. The farmer knows that planting corn too close together will ruin the crop. In a similar way, an overcrowded classroom ultimately stymies growth.

Third, lack of teaching facilities thwarts teacher initiative. When a Sunday school teacher's classroom is overcrowded, he has little incentive to get more pupils, even when exhorted by the superintendent to "go out and reach the lost." He realizes it is futile to visit when there is no space for new pupils.

Experts are not agreed on the amount of space needed for Sunday school pupils. Some churches build ten by ten-foot rooms for small classes of ten pupils each, but many denominational leaders today recommend twenty-five to thirty-five square feet per pupil. Rooms should be large enough for activity centered learning experiences. Classrooms should look like those in public schools. They should be large, light, and geared to meet pupil needs.

The Bible does not give a blueprint for local churches, nor does it contain an organizational chart on how to arrange people in groups. However, the Bible does tell Christians to gather as a congregation (Heb. 10:25), to teach (Matt. 28:20), and to preach (2 Tim. 4:2). These functions can be carried out only as people congregate. This usually has to be in a specially designed building since most homes are too small. But what happens when the church building is too small? The gospel is preached, people commit their lives to Jesus and want to join the congregation, but there is no room for expansion.

Various congregations have resolved this problem in different ways. Some churches are able to secure nearby buildings that can be easily renovated to provide the needed space for classes. Others may elect to use their Sunday school buses as Sunday school rooms. Still others have changed their approach to teaching, moving from small classes to a master-teacher plan. A fourth response is to begin a second Sunday school at an alternate time to handle the growth. Other churches have moved their youth and adult classes into one large area, thus freeing their former rooms for additional children's classes. A sixth possibility used by some churches is to begin a mission Sunday school in another part of town, sometimes in a former building or other facility.

PUPPETS

A few years ago puppets were thought to be only a game. They were not considered educational. Modern educators claimed that children learned best by their experiences, rather than watching the teacher perform with aids such as puppets. But a revolution has occurred. Sesame Street has used puppets, and it has been proved that children who watch Sesame Street learn better and faster. As a result, a puppet revival has come to American education.

The face of any story character can be painted on a puppet. Papier mâché, styrofoam balls, or stuffed socks are popular and simple bases for a head. The clothing should be colorful and easily changed. Clothing can be made with a basic puppet dress pattern.

The teacher may operate the puppet and then allow the children an opportunity, thus reinforcing the learning experience. On the other hand, children can make up their own actions and words.

Why Use Puppets?
1. To dramatize truth, enabling the child to remember much better.
2. To present information in an indirect but understandable form.
3. To call forth ingenuity and resources at little cost on the part of both teacher and pupil.

4. To encourage participation from all class members, even those too shy to become active in other areas.

5. To encourage creativity.

6. To give a child opportunity to be involved in a role-playing situation. This is a wonderful way for a child to see his own problems and often recognize the answers without a teacher's suggestions. In this type of situation the teacher also benefits by glimpsing the child's feelings, emotions, and outlook on life. This enables the teacher to deal directly with the actual needs of this child, rather than with what she simply thinks are needs.

7. To provide positive reinforcement to attract the pupil to continue attending Sunday school.

8. To discipline indirectly yet effectively. In a puppet presentation, use an actual situation where the children see their own actions reflected, causing no hard feelings toward the teacher for correcting them.

Advantages of Using Puppets

1. Puppets provide anonymity. Many children do not like to display themselves in front of their peers. Puppets allow them to be creative and expressive without embarrassment.

2. Puppets eliminate the need for body movements in drama. Since the child does not need to think about facial expression, gesturing, and stage position, he can better concentrate on the spoken lines that have been assigned to him.

3. Television has made puppets popular and familiar to children. They will be enthusiastic about imitating something they have seen on TV.

4. Using puppets provides in-depth study of a passage or story. By the time the children have made the puppets, studied their lines, and put on the performance, they will be thoroughly familiar with the passage.

5. Making and using puppets may stimulate a reticent child to take part in informal drama later.

6. Use of puppets by the teacher gains the pupils' attention and keeps it throughout the story, whether the class is large or small.

7. Memory retention by the child is far greater when he *sees* the story than when he simply *hears* it.

Disadvantages of Puppets

1. Puppets are time consuming and require talent to create and decorate.
2. The eager actor is denied opportunity to experiment with body movements.
3. The more advanced form of puppetry, such as marionettes, requires handling in a professional manner. Most Sunday school teachers do not have these skills.

Types of Puppets

1. Paper bag. There are two forms of this most elementary kind of hand puppet. In one the bag fits over the entire hand. The face is glued on the bottom of the unopened bag. The top half of the mouth is level with the end of the flap, and the bottom half is glued on the side of the sack. "Wave" the fingers to simulate talking as the story is narrated. This kind of puppet is often included in teaching-aid packets from Sunday school suppliers. For the second type of puppet, the bag fits over the operator's first three fingers and is tied, leaving the thumb and fifth finger for the puppet's arms. The three fingers move the mouth part up and down for speech.
2. Mitten. This uses a mitten instead of the bag, giving the appearance of clothing.
3. Stick. The head (or whole figure) is on the stick that the operator manipulates. Cloth or a sock may cover the operator's hand.
4. Spool. A spool or similar object is used as the foundation of the head, and a sock again covers the hand.
5. Finger. This is usually on a tiny glove-finger end that fits on one finger. Usually it is just the head. Being small, several may be used at once, to have interaction.
6. Shadow. The puppet is silhouetted on a screen, making clothes and distinct facial features unnecessary.
7. Marionettes. This advanced puppetry uses puppets manipulated with strings attached to all movable parts of the body.

The operator is not seen; only his voice is heard. This usually demands a set of well-made puppets. Much action can be presented with these.

Principles for Using Puppets Effectively

1. Keep puppet actions geared to the age level. The younger the children, the simpler the action.
2. Keep the situations familiar to the children.
3. Make sure the situations are true to life, not abstract, since younger children cannot identify with abstract ideas.
4. The teacher must be fully prepared. He must have definite goals in mind and procedures to attain his goals. He should also exercise his creative and imaginative ability, at the same time adhering to the theme of the lesson.
5. The type of puppet should be geared to the age level of the class.
6. Begin with simple puppetry. As you become more experienced, branch out into more advanced and complex forms.
7. While puppets have their greatest value with younger children, other age groups also enjoy them. Their use will require more expertise under the scrutiny of older pupils, however. Of course, a polished performance of puppetry will hold the attention of any age.

Effectiveness of Puppets

1. Puppets are a refreshing change from regular storytelling.
2. Puppets are enjoyable and intriguing for the children, thus encouraging attendance in Sunday school.
3. Puppets give the children a better method of interacting with the subject of the lesson, thus learning the lesson better.
4. Discipline is less of a problem, resulting in fewer dropouts due to hurt pride over correction.
5. Puppet role play for children can be very effective. The puppets act out what goes on at a church service, or in other life situations, showing the children what is expected of them. When they are confident and willing to participate, learning occurs.

QUESTION AND ANSWER

Throughout history the value of the question-and-answer method in education has been recognized. While questioning was used in teaching long before Socrates' day, he made the question method famous. The question lay at the heart of the teaching methods of Jesus Christ. The Gospels record more than one hundred of his questions. Today, much teaching is done by means of the question, either as the chief method, or as a component part of other methods. The use of questions alone does not produce effective teaching, but proper use of the question-and-answer method greatly aids effective teaching.

Why Are Questions So Effective?

They stimulate the natural tendency of the mind to inquire into the unknown. They test the pupil's understanding of the facts and his ability to use facts in a fruitful way. Questions arouse curiosity, stimulate interest, and cause the pupil to think. Questions bring problems to the attention of the hearer and create a desire to find answers. Questions direct attention to the significant elements in a situation, which helps to divide major from minor factors. By questioning, the teacher gets and holds attention because questions require a response. Questions allow the pupil to express his own thoughts and develop appreciations and attitudes. Questions give the teacher information concerning his teaching, revealing whether pupils are learning. If learning is not taking place, the teaching plan must be changed. Questions have value for use in drill and review, for deepening impressions, and for fixing facts in the memory of the pupil.

Properly directed questions can ascertain what the pupils have learned, guide them in further learning, correct misconceptions and imperfect understanding, help them to see interrelationships among facts, aid in organizing thinking, and lead to fruitful expression of learning.

What Makes a Good Question?

A teacher who would teach well must develop ability to ask good questions in the right way. Good questions are logical and developmental. All questions on a given subject should be related. Questions should be full and complete, not merely leading questions that can be answered yes or no. Good questions help pupils learn, keep the whole class actively interested, and give insights. A good question should help pupils see how facts fit together. Make your questions brief, clear, and direct. Address them to the whole class before calling on one pupil. If a teacher addresses a question to one pupil, he may lose the class.

Questions should be a two-way device. A pupil's question may further learning better than a teacher's question. The teacher must be able to answer both good and bad questions in the right way. Learn to say, "I don't know" to some questions.

RAIKES, ROBERT (1736–1811)

Robert Raikes, the crusading editor of the *Gloucester Journal* in England, established one of the greatest lay movements in the history of the Christian church. His first project was jail reform, which wasn't successful. Raikes became convinced that "vice could be better prevented than cured." Therefore he turned to education.

While visiting the slum section of Gloucester, some children jostled him on the street. He became disturbed at their rudeness.

"If you think they are bad, you should come back on Sunday when the worst ones are off of work," an observer told him. Raikes determined to do something and talked with Rev. Thomas Stock, in the village of Ashbury, Berkshire. Out of their conversation came a plan to use laymen to teach the Word of God to children during the best time available—Sunday. They originally planned to reach the children of the streets, not just the children of church members.

Raikes began his experiment in July 1780 when he paid Mrs. Meredith a shilling a day to conduct a school in her home. She began with only boys and listened to the lessons of older boys, who in turn coached the younger pupils. Raikes wrote four text books, which he printed on his presses. As a result, they appeared as large newspapers, which were held up before the class for the students to read. During those early days, Raikes paid for most of the Sunday school expenses.

The Sunday school grew slowly for two years, in and around Gloucester. On November 3, 1783, Raikes published an account of the Sunday school in his paper. Hundreds followed his example and began Sunday schools. Next, news of the Sunday school appeared in *Gentlemen's Magazine* and a year later, another article appeared in the *Armenian Magazine*, published by John Wesley.

The movement that Raikes began grew so rapidly that it left him on the sidelines. Sunday school organizations appeared in every major city, and some towns boasted that every child within its limits was enrolled in Sunday school. Raikes died in 1811, quietly and unnoticed. In 1831 a statue was erected to his memory as the founder of Sunday school. At that time Sunday schools of Great Britain had a weekly enrollment of 1,250,000 children, approximately 25 percent of the population. A second statue of Raikes was unveiled in Toronto, Ontario, near the provincial legislature in 1907 by the International Christian Education Association meeting in that city for a convention.

RECEPTIVE-RESPONSIVE PEOPLE

Receptive people are those who are positive toward the gospel message as a result of social dislocation, personal crisis, or internal working of the Holy Spirit. They are open to hearing and obeying the gospel of Jesus Christ.

We should invest our priority-time reaching those who are responsive-receptive people because: (1) time is short, (2) resources are limited, (3) it follows the biblical example, and (4) through discipleship it produces greater results.

To emphasize ministry to receptive-responsive people is to: (1) try to be as fruitful as possible for Christ, (2) win the winnable while they are winnable, before their receptivity cools, (3) help the church grow faster and larger, and (4) be a good steward of one's time and resources.

In light of his stewardship, the Christian must establish priorities for evangelism. He must be interested in reaching all, but he also must determine where his evangelistic efforts are likely to be most productive and give that area attention. That does not mean he can forget or ignore the rest of the world. It does mean, however, that he should determine which people are likely to be most receptive and responsive to him and then concentrate his efforts on them.

Potential Candidates

For purposes of evangelism, every unsaved person is commonly thought of as a prospect, and rightly so. Every unsaved person is a sinner who needs salvation; there are no exceptions (Rom. 5:12). When Christ died on the cross, he made a provision sufficient for all (1 Tim. 2:6, 4:10; 1 John 2:2), and it is not the will of God that any should perish (2 Pet. 3:9; 1 Tim. 2:4). Therefore, every unsaved person is a potential or possible candidate for salvation, and the church is commissioned to take the gospel to every unsaved person (Mark 16:15).

Likely Candidates

Likely candidates are those who are receptive and responsive to both the messenger and the message. Because they are receptive and responsive, they have a far greater probability of being stairstepped through the process to trust Christ as Savior. Or, they are ready to be saved. Therefore, a responsive-receptive person has the greater possibility of being brought to salvation.

Likely candidates are those who are already in the believer's sphere of influence or those who could be brought into that sphere. Because everyone has a different sphere of influence, every believer has a different group of likely candidates for evangelism.

Targeting receptive-responsive people knows no racial, economic, or social barriers. It does not imply any respect of persons, but, rather, it simply stresses winning the winnable while they are winnable.

Some people become receptive to both the messenger and the message. Naaman is the perfect example of receptivity (2 Kings 5:1, 9-14). He was a highly respected man of position, but he was a leper. In the providence of God, Naaman went to Elisha the prophet of God in search of cleansing. Elisha sent a messenger to tell Naaman that he should go and wash seven times in the Jordan River. Naaman was offended, first by the fact that Elisha sent a servant instead of coming himself, and second by the content of the message. In short, Naaman rejected both the messenger and the message.

When someone pointed out to Naaman that pride was standing in the way of his cleansing, he repented. He responded to the message and was cleansed. But Naaman was not responsive to the message until first he was receptive to the messenger. Receptivity is usually tied to responsiveness.

The Degree of Receptivity Varies

The degree of receptivity varies from one person to another. The most receptive people are usually those to whom a believer is closest. These are his friends, relatives, associates, and neighbors (F.R.A.N.s).

Jesus likened evangelism to sowing the seed of the gospel in four different types of soil, representing four different types of people. He referred to the varying receptivity of the people in terms of four kinds of soil (Matt. 13:3-23).

First, the soil by the wayside represents those who are unreceptive. They hear the message but reject it. Others superficially receive the message; but when tribulation or persecution arises because of the Word, they are offended and fall away. Third, the thorny soil illustrates those who are temporarily receptive but are unwilling to make the changes required of them. Fourth, the truly receptive are represented by the good ground. They respond and become fruitful.

The good soil brought forth fruit thirtyfold, sixtyfold, and a hundredfold. The different amounts of fruitfulness indicate that people respond differently to the message of God.

The degree of receptivity will vary from one person to another. Among one's closest friends there are likely to be some who are indifferent, some who are receptive, and some who are totally unreceptive.

Scale of Receptivity

Unreceptive					Indifferent				Receptive	
-10	-8	-6	-4	-2	0	+2	+4	+6	+8	+10

Receptivity not only varies from person to person, but also from time to time. People change with the passage of time and the change of events. One who is unreceptive today may become receptive tomorrow. Those who are unreceptive or indifferent can be cultivated. Those with a hard heart can become soft to God. Such changes in receptivity are often referred to as "seasons of the soul." Just as there is a season to plant and a season to harvest, so there are times in the seasons of people's lives when they are "ripe to harvest," or they are responsive to the gospel.

What produces seasons of the soul? What makes a person receptive to God? What softens a person who is hardened to the gospel? There are both supernatural and natural factors that make a receptive-responsive person.

The supernatural factors that make a receptive-responsive person are (1) the conviction of the Holy Spirit whereby a person sees his sin and its result, (2) the influence of the Word of God, (3) the guidance of the Lord that brings a man to understand his condition, and (4) the natural revelation of God in the world.

But there are natural factors that make a person receptive to God. Some of these natural factors are transitions of life that disrupt the normal feeling of security a person has, such as (1) marriage, (2) the birth of a child, (3) a job change or bankruptcy, (4) sickness, (5) a death in the family, or (6) being jailed. Any time a person goes through a social disequilibrium or culture shock, he becomes a receptive-responsive person.

When a person moves from one home to another he may become receptive to God, especially if he moves far enough away to disrupt family and friendship roots. A person who has been reared Roman Catholic in another city will attend a Bible-preaching church and become open to its message. This will happen especially if he has a positive relationship to someone in the church. Moving one's home makes a person receptive, also the loss of familiar emotional ties increases his receptivity. The influence of a Bible-believing Christian adds another level of receptivity.

Receptivity must extend to both the messenger and the message. It is possible for a person to reject either the messenger or the message. Jesus warned about this twofold possibility when he told his disciples, "And whoever will not receive you nor hear your words, when you depart from that house or city, shake off the dust from your feet" (Matt. 10:14). The words of that verse translated *receive* and *hear* mean "to approve" and "to give ear." The two possibilities of rejection were (1) the unsaved would reject the messenger, and (2) refuse to listen to the message.

Some people are already receptive and responsive. Most of our friends are open to the gospel because of their relationship to us, yet each one has a different degrees of receptivity. Recognize their receptivity if you want to be successful in reaching them.

A second group of receptive-responsive people are those who have visited the church, but this group is not limited to them only. They may feel a need for change. These are people in whom the Holy Spirit has already been working to bring conviction because they heard the gospel in church. Their hearts are softened to the gospel because of Christian influence. They may have no idea what their real need is, but they are aware that a need exists.

The third group consists of those who are experiencing external changes. God works through circumstances to make them receptive. Some event of joy or sorrow may force them to reevaluate their lives. Transition times, such as graduation, marriage, the birth of a child, separation, or divorce, a move across country, the death of a friend or loved one, may be used by God to make them aware of their need for God.

Many of those receptive-responsive people may not be within the sphere of influence of any Christian. A community search, sometimes referred to as a community census, can help locate such people. The process is simple. It involves going door-to-door throughout the community to locate those who seem receptive to the gospel.

Receptivity can be cultivated. The process of cultivating receptivity begins by winning people to yourself. Before people will hear the gospel from your lips, you must establish credibility by winning them to yourself. You must take the initiative to contact them and begin building a friendship. Paul clearly taught that Christians can contact people for the gospel's sake (1 Cor. 9:20-23).

Once you have won an individual to yourself, you must then win a hearing for the message. That means two things. First, you must demonstrate through your life that Jesus Christ is meeting you needs (2 Cor. 9:8). Second, you must point out that Jesus Christ is also sufficient to meet their felt needs.

RECORDS

Records can be an invaluable aid to measure the spiritual temperature of a church, Sunday school, or class. A church that is growing and keeping records of that growth is often accused of being "numbers conscious." However, awareness of attendance figures is vital for many reasons. The church that knows its past has a future. A wise person can read telltale signs from the records and use records to evaluate progress and develop future goals.

Good records will give the teacher some interesting facts about the students and the teaching. They will help identify faithful students who are probably interested students. They will also help identify absentees and identify the degree of their absence. Some record systems, like the six-point record system, also teach such things as financial responsibility and faithfulness in lesson preparation and Scripture memory.

Specific Values of a Good Record-Keeping System

1. It challenges the entire Sunday school to work.
2. It provides a complete register of pupils and leaders.
3. It provides a basis for evaluation and measurement.
4. It reveals strengths and weaknesses.
5. It makes efficient operation possible.
6. It provides up-to-date statistics for classes, departments, and the total school.
7. It provides a list of prospective new students.
8. It encourages faithful attendance and membership.
9. It helps teachers by revealing spiritual conditions, attendance, and study habits.
10. It teaches pupils good habits, such as reverence, faithfulness, and responsibility.
11. It can be used to guide in curriculum planning.
12. It furnishes the key to budget matters.

13. It furnishes information for ordering supplies.
14. It motivates people.

Principles for an Efficient Record System
1. Records should be simple enough that all workers are able to operate the record system
2. Records should be kept up-to-date.
3. Continuity should be maintained, in spite of a turnover of workers.
4. Records of the past and present and plans for the future should form a complete picture.
5. Inexpensive blanks, forms, and books should provide substantial savings over the years.
6. Books and files should preserve records and materials.
7. A trained and faithful general secretary, along with efficient department and class secretaries, should save time and energy.
8. The same record-keeping system should be maintained throughout the whole school, with few adjustments.
9. All personnel must take part for the greatest effectiveness.
10. Spiritual conclusions reached after an evaluation of the records should be used to challenge the school, departments, and classes to be more like Christ and to serve him more faithfully.

REDEMPTION AND LIFT
Redemption and lift refers to a phenomenon that occurs when a person becomes a Christian and thereby is lifted out of his former environment and separated from it in social and economic respects. The Christian will control himself, work harder, and become more faithful in his home, family, church, and employment. As a natural result, the Christian will rise in his social class. The Christian becomes a better citizen within culture; hence, the natural result of redemption and lift grows out of spiritual causes.

RETAINING WORKERS
The teaching staff of most churches is largely composed of faithful workers who have served in their capacity for many years and

have never considered doing anything else. They are dedicated to the Lord as well as to the church, and temporal rewards are not expected. However, even a consecrated teacher succumbs to the temptation to retreat from the firing line occasionally—or permanently. This tendency may be due to:

1. *Lack of appreciation.* The teacher of children is often the hardest-working, least-appreciated worker in the church. The children themselves rarely say thank you for anything she does—unless prompted—and the parents remain unaware of what goes on in the class, unless a child is displeased with something. The simple device of regular, planned "teacher appreciation" can forestall the retreat of teachers. Teacher appreciation day may coincide with the annual promotion day. A church gift of a helpful methods or devotional book, public recognition and expressed gratitude, or a workers' banquet are ways to say thank you for long hours spent for the lives and souls of children.

2. *Misfits.* Occasionally a volunteer for the teaching corps gets off to a poor start by attempting to serve the wrong age group. Here is a pointed reason for the practice of apprentice teaching. The assistant has opportunity to discover whether or not he can relate to and cope with the students in a given age group.

   Some persons are at ease with preschool children, while others only "talk down to them." Some like the challenge of guiding and keeping up with wide-awake Juniors. Others cannot keep them in control and tear their hair out over the mass confusion. Others find the seeming indifference and inattention of teenagers frustrating or the stoic faces of adults discouraging.

   Through discovering their ineptitude with one group, teachers may be brought to an understanding of their rightful level and be placed where they feel they can do best.

   Lack of proper adjustment is not confined to Sunday school teachers. It also happens in the public school. A first-grade teacher discovered that her young charges "drove her up the wall" to the extent that their talking out of turn once made her lose control and throw a storybook across the room. She resigned from teaching after that first year.

A teacher might not voluntarily come to the superintendent and request a change. For this reason, many churches provide an annual opportunity for teachers to answer a questionnaire, which asks, Are you satisfied to work with the age group that you are now serving? Do you want to continue with the same class the coming year? Would you rather serve elsewhere? If so, where?

3. *Personality clashes.* Not understanding the shyness of a new worker, an experienced teacher may assume responsibilities that could be accomplished by the assistant. The inexperienced one may then feel useless. On the other hand, a new worker may have a spirit of love and enthusiasm that at once endears her to the children, who swarm around her to the exclusion of the regular teacher. The result is hurt feelings on the part of the teacher, who may resent the newcomer. Since people sense a feeling of ill will, the new worker may ask for another assignment or may simply resign from teaching. If a superintendent maintains regular department meetings, problems like this can be aired in a Christian manner. Communication often establishes better relationships. If the regular teacher will not change her attitude, and if that teacher is capable and faithful, the superintendent may have to move the assistant to another department for the sake of the future service of the newcomer.

4. *Inadequate classroom or equipment.* Having completed a course of instruction in good teaching techniques, some new teachers are shocked when they learn that the classroom where they are expected to teach is not large enough for the recommended activities. A more experienced teacher may be able to guide the newcomer over the hump, especially if he has been put in charge of the class by himself. The older teacher can show him how to capture and hold his pupils' attention, even in a noisy situation. The experienced teacher also can suggest substitutions for the plans that had to be abandoned because of the overcrowding. For example, a

resourceful teacher will find ways to enlarge the available space through (a) getting rid of large chairs and using floor mats; (b) hanging chalk and flannel boards on the wall; (c) hinging a work table to the wall, to be pulled down only when needed. Sometimes resourceful teachers will find a junk room in the church that has more space than the assigned room. A simple switch makes everyone happy.

A superintendent or director of Christian education should be careful to maintain good relationships and the best possible facilities (however far from ideal) to keep his staff working together in harmony. He knows that it will be harder to get new workers enlisted and trained if he is unable to keep the ones who already are serving.

With teachers, as with business, "a satisfied customer is the best advertisement." The enthusiasm of dedicated teachers makes others willing to try.

RETARDED, MINISTRY TO THE

"Preach the gospel to every creature" must be construed to mean all persons, in all circumstances. Therefore, the great commission must include a Sunday school class for people with mental retardation.

There are many misconceptions regarding retardation. The most erroneous judgment is that it is mental illness. This is not a proper classification of retardation. The person with mental retardation has not grown at the expected rate of development or has not completed the growth cycle. There are two classes of these "exceptional" people: (1) the trainable have an IQ of 30–55 and (2) the educable have an IQ of 55–80. The public schools usually have special education classes for the educable. At times the educable are found in regular public school classes. If they attend Sunday school, they are usually enrolled in the regular age-level class. Most trainables, however, do not go to school, except in a few cases where there are institutional schools. Only a few churches have classes for the trainable.

Mental retardation is often the result of brain injury at birth, serious illness, or genetic defect. In this broad classification are mongolism, cerebral palsy, retarded emotional growth, and such physical complications as sight and hearing handicaps, slow and incomplete motor-ability development, and mild forms of epilepsy.

The Sunday school is lagging behind in reaching and teaching people with mental retardation even though attempts now are being made to rectify the situation. There are several reasons why the Sunday school has done so little in this area.

1. *Confused parents.* Some parents may shut their eyes to the facts of their child's learning ability. They are so eager to believe the child is normal they will not face the fact that he needs a special kind of teaching. Therefore they subject him to the disadvantage of being placed with others his age with whom he cannot keep up.

2. *Lack of teachers.* Many Sunday schools find it hard to secure enough teachers to staff all classes in the regular age-group divisions. Even if they are aware of the need for a special education class, there is no one to teach it.

3. *Lack of training.* As with other forms of Sunday school teaching, there may be some who are willing to serve as teachers in a special education class, perhaps out of compassion. But because of their inability to express Bible truths on a level where they may be grasped, their efforts are of no avail.

4. *Unkind teasing by other children.* "He's a dummy" may be bluntly stated by a child who sees the slow comprehension of a child with mental retardation. Unfortunately, the slow one often knows he is the object of ridicule. He may shrink from going again to the Sunday school where he was embarrassed.

Remedies

The attitudes can be corrected. Sometimes it is the parents who must make the first move.

1. *Acceptance.* Accept the child for what he is. When parents accept the limitations of their child with mental retardation and love him and make him part of the family's experiences, they go far toward assuring his acceptance by their church friends.

2. *Pastoral influence.* Special recognition may be given to the progress of these special pupils in the Sunday school. When appropriate, the pastor can go far toward reinforcing their

self-confidence by a word of praise—publicly as well as privately. Because he is usually the one who enlists workers for the various classes in the Sunday school, he should also be quick to praise the faithful ministry of the teachers of those with mental retardation.

3. *Training.* A willing Christian may be unable to attend a university for special training in teaching people with mental retardation. She will find much valuable guidance in the book by this author and Roberta Groff, *Successful Ministry to the Retarded.* Suggestions are drawn from its pages.

4. *Compassionate teachers of other classes.* An observant teacher usually has opportunity to learn of the taunting of a slow learner. It is not amiss for the teacher to illustrate this unfairness through a lesson on kindness and Christian love. Telling a story of a similar problem, he can point out the hurt and tell his pupils to avoid being cruel and to use their influence to stop others from unkindness.

Problems of Those with Mental Retardation

While generalizations cannot be made, researchers have found that the chief problems of the trainable people with mental retardation are due to the fact that they have one or more of these groups of characteristics:

1. Shy, fearful, tense
2. Hyperactive, nervous
3. Attention seekers
4. Short in attention span
5. Stubborn, obstinate
6. Poor in communication
7. Poor in motor ability
8. Mischievous, destructive
9. Aggressive
10. Emotionally unstable
11. Withdrawn
12. Infantile, immature

With this imposing list, the question comes, "Who would want to cope with children with these traits?" The answer—"A teacher who realizes that such people have eternal souls, and that many of them can choose between right and wrong."

The Teacher

All the qualifications stated for any Sunday school teacher are required by the teacher of those with mental retardation, plus a double portion of some, such as:

1. *Love.* The retarded one, sometimes unwanted in his own family or perhaps institutionalized, may never have known the touch of Christian love before he came to Sunday school. He is most responsive.
2. *Wisdom.* "Let him [her] ask of God," for the child with the crippled mind reacts to social contacts in an unorthodox manner. Discipline requires knowledge of how to avoid causing frustration, when and how to offer reinforcing praise, even how to cope with a destructive temper tantrum.
3. *Patience.* There is no doubt that patience must be the end product of meeting the challenge of children with multiplied problems. It is also a prerequisite from the start.

The Lessons

1. *Literal.* Like the normal toddler or preschooler, the trainable child with mental retardation can grasp the truths of God's greatness in Creation, his love expressed through his gifts, his desire for obedience through the experiences of Bible characters. However, since this child does not reason, he cannot comprehend the idea of an object representing a truth.
2. *Visualized.* Even more than the normal learner, this child needs visuals as an aid to understanding and to strengthen memory retention.
3. *Undistracted.* Because his attention span is minimal, the child with mental retardation should be in a classroom with the least interruptions. Quiet, neat, and attractive surroundings have a soothing effect. Too much brilliance in color could prove distracting. A carpeted floor would help muffle some of the sound of feet during activities. And the classroom for the special education class should not be in a department

area where other children's classes are in session and where voices carry.

Activities

1. *Music.* The alert teacher will carefully watch the effects of certain songs on her class. If overexcitement propels pupils towards hyperactivity, the tune must be changed. This group of pupils likes music and is responsive. Wise selection of songs can set the tone for a good lesson period.

2. *Handwork.* The criteria for appropriate handwork for these slow learners are (a) simplicity, (b) usefulness, and (c) interest. Great care must be exercised to guide in the making of any article. Much encouragement and praise are needed for children who may have extreme insecurity. Criticism should be positive rather than negative. "Let's do it this way," instead of "Don't do it that way" is the proper way to correct.

3. *Role play.* Like normal fours and fives, the trainables enjoy simultaneous role play, when all the group perform an action in the story. For example, all can stand as angels, arms extended, saying, "Fear not," to the women at the empty tomb of Jesus. All can walk (in a circle) the long road to Jerusalem with the twelve-year-old Jesus. Familiar with make-believe, one child alone often will become brave enough to take a part by himself.

4. *Puppets.* Shy children with mental retardation will find in puppets the same security other children find. They can express their feelings and reactions through the actions and speech of puppets, thereby revealing much about themselves to the teacher.

Can Those with Mental Retardation Be Saved?

While the theological implications of the question have been argued pro and con by church leaders through the centuries, their teachers have found that the trainable as well as the educable usually have a sense of right and wrong. They feel the need of God. Because their understanding is childlike, the gospel must be presented to them as to a very small child. They can be shown that "all have sinned" (Rom. 3:23); that the "the wages of sin is death, but the gift of God is eternal life in Christ Jesus our Lord" (Rom. 6:23); and that "Christ died for us" (Rom. 5:8).

While some may not understand the way of salvation, all should be given the opportunity of a careful, clear explanation.

REVIEW GAMES

Review provides another look at stories and lessons to insure longer retention by pupils. Old-time teaching majored in the play-back of facts drawn out by questions at the close of each lesson. Sometimes the teacher's confidence was bolstered by the expedient of yes or no questions.

Review games accomplish the same purpose as drill, with the added factor of interest. They can review the previous lesson and lay again the groundwork on which the new lesson may be built. The introductory moments of a teaching session should allow five to seven minutes for a review game.

Twenty-two Suggestions for Review Games

The following review games will recall the previous lesson and also reveal to the teacher where the class needs more instruction.

1. *Soldier game.* Put on a table a pile of from five to ten question cards concerning the past lesson for each child. The children are soldiers who, at the teacher's command, march around the table. At the order, "Halt," each child draws a card. If the child correctly answers the question, he keeps the card. Any incorrectly answered cards are given to the teacher. The object is not to let the teacher get more cards than a soldier has. Primaries and juniors like this game.

2. *Classroom basketball.* Make a hoop by attaching a rounded wire coat hanger to posterboard. A pair of socks or wadded-up paper can be the "ball." Prepare questions on recent stories. Divide the group into two teams. Each in turn tries a "foul shot" at the hoop. If he makes a score, he gets to answer a question. He gets five points if he answers correctly. Then the other team has a turn. The first team to reach fifty points wins.

3. *Question spinner.* Make a large posterboard circle. The

pointer should be attached with a paper fastener, with a small circle of cardboard cut like a washer. Make slits around the edge in which to insert small tabbed cards of questions about the previous lesson. (This would also be a good review during the last month of the quarter.) A pupil gives the spinner a whirl. When the pointer stops on a question, he answers. Allow five points for a correct answer. If the class is divided into two or more teams, the first to reach fifty points is the winner. Awards are optional.

4. *Magic pencil.* Make an oversize pencil from an empty cardboard roll with a thumbtack box at the eraser end and a pointed drinking cup as the point. Cover with bright contact paper or construction paper. Put on a label that says, "Magic Pencil." Remove "eraser." Inside have slips of paper with names of Bible stories or characters. The game may be played by individual pupils. If a pupil draws the name of a character, he may act out or tell of an accomplishment of the character for the class to guess. If played by teams, Bible story names may be listed. A team must act out the story it draws, for the other team to guess.

5. *King on the throne.* Confining the questions to lessons studied during the past quarter, select one pupil as "king," seating him on the "throne" in the middle of the room. A construction-paper crown will set him apart and add importance to his position. The others question the king concerning the lessons. As long as he can answer correctly, he stays on the throne. When he cannot answer a question, the one asking it may take his place, provided the questioner knows the answer.

6. *Picture map.* After studying events that took place in Bible lands, place a large outline map of this area at the front of the room. Small pictures identified with each lesson should be cut out or drawn for use. The teacher holds up picture and identifies it. She asks, "Who can pin this picture on the map where the story took place?" Scotch tape may be used instead of pins to make an attractive picture map for future reference.

7. *Pass the basket.* Let each pupil in turn select a folded question from a basket, read it aloud, and give the answer, if possible. Each time a pupil answers correctly, he keeps the question slip. The basket is passed several times, and the one who has been able to keep the most question slips is declared winner.

8. *Spelldown.* As in an old-fashioned spelling bee, pupils line up in even sides facing each other. When individuals correctly answer a question asked by the teacher, they remain in line. When they fail to answer, they must sit down. The winning side is the one with the largest number of players standing at the end of a given time.

9. *Wrong word story.* For each pupil make a copy of the story of the last lesson. Intentionally, insert wrong statements. Ask the pupils to underline each incorrect statement.

10. *Riddle cards.* On one side of three-by-five-inch cards print "Who am I?" "What am I?" or "Who said this?" questions. On the back of the card print the answer. You can use the riddle cards during presession or during review time.

11. *Twenty questions*—or less. List on the chalkboard names of ten characters recently studied. Ask one pupil to stand up while the other pupils ask him questions about the character he secretly chooses to be. If some children have trouble selecting anyone to impersonate, write after each name a Bible reference they may look up.

12. *A matching test.* Write on the chalkboard questions based on the quarter's work. Put the answers on the board, but not in the same order. Pupils then choose the right answers for the questions. Number both lists, so pupils need only to write the number of the correct answer beside the number of the question.

13. *Multiple-choice questions.* Compile questions, each with several answers. Give each student a sheet of paper and a pencil and read each question and its possible answers. Students write down the number of the right answer. Or they may be given a paper with questions printed and be asked to underline the correct answer.

14. *Object box.* An "object box" provides intriguing review for juniors. In a shoe box put objects representing facts in stories. At the close of a study on the journeys of Paul, for instance, objects would represent his experiences. Have an opening large enough for the child's hand to reach in easily and pull out a small article, without exposing the entire contents. Suggested objects are a small boat (the shipwreck), a stone (stoning of Stephen, which resulted in Paul's conversion), a purple crayon (the meeting with Lydia, seller of purple), a piece of chain (prison, or imprisoning of Christians), a silver object (Diana of the Ephesians), a small basket (Paul's escape in a basket let down over the wall), a light bulb or a flashlight (the light that blinded him at conversion), flowers or wreath (Paul and Barnabas being worshiped at Lystra).

15. *A take-home test.* At the close of a lesson give each pupil a paper with a puzzle, sentences with blanks to fill in, or multiple-choice questions. At the top put the Bible references where answers are found. Ask pupils to write the answers down and bring them back the next Sunday. Urging students to keep the papers in their Bibles may prevent the papers from getting lost or misplaced at home.

16. *Build the church.* Draw and cut from heavy paper a large church with two windows and a door. Cut out the windows and door. Cut the church into pieces as follows: left section of church, right section of church, steeple, window, window, and door. Write a question about the last lesson on the back of each part.

    Give the sections of the church building to six members. They may ask the questions of other members. As the questions are answered, let pupils construct the church building by placing the sections on the wall or tackboard, using Plasti-Tak, Scotch tape, or thumbtacks. Bibles may be used, if needed to answer the questions.

    Any large object may be similarly cut up and reconstructed—a piano, house, or car.

17. *Scrambled puzzles.* Jumble and print letters of a Bible name

on a sheet of paper. Put a clue at the bottom. Give one puzzle to each class member and allow time to unscramble the name. Use several different names. Discuss answers.

18. *Grab bag.* Put questions into a paper sack and let each pupil reach in and grab a question. Competition may be individual or team. On teams, members may consult with each other or may be individually responsible for the answers. Play musical grab bag by passing the sack while music continues. When the music stops, the one who holds the bag takes out a question and answers or refers it to the class.

19. *Charades.* This old party game may be given a Sunday school twist. Teams of pupils take turns representing briefly an incident or story in past lessons, and the others guess which one it is.

20. *Matching words.* In one column on the chalkboard put a list of towns, people, or mountains covered in recent lessons. In another column put the event or the name of another person connected with each item in the first column. Jumble the order and let pupils come, one at a time, and draw a line from a name to correct event or place.

21. *Rhyming review.* Draw on the chalkboard two long lines with rhyming words at the end, such as boy and joy. Ask what phrase ending with *boy* will describe something in the last lesson. ("A small lunch in the hands of a little boy") Do the same for the next line (something like "was used by Jesus to bring a crowd joy").

22. *Rebus puzzle.* Draw on the chalkboard simple pictures of objects. Under each picture, put a blank for each letter of the name of the object. Lead the class in filling in the blanks. Show how to cross out letters of words after a minus sign. For young primaries or a class new to the game, make the puzzle only four pictures at first (Example: PLANT + SKATE - TANK = PLATES).

ROLE PLAY

A role is the way one behaves in a given situation. When people role-play, they assume roles in a situation and act them out, trying to reach a constructive conclusion. Role play is a method of teaching to develop more desirable behavior in real-life situations.

It is important to distinguish psychodrama or role play from conventional drama. Role play is not an artistic performance based on a literary text, but an extemporaneous activity in which participants "feel their way through" the situation. Observers question the participants and arrive at an interpretation.

Role play takes various forms. It may seek to apply principles to a hypothetical problem, with an open-ended solution. It may follow historical and literary texts with known outcomes. The first form would apply a Bible passage to a contemporary situation. The second form would involve role-playing a biblical narrative. Among other variants are experimental role play, where the reactions of players to the unexpected are tested; and case analysis, an attempt to act out all important aspects of a large-scale problem over an extended period of time.

Aim of Role Play

1. *Stimulate discussion.* When a group does not care or know much about a topic, it is hard to get a discussion going on the subject. To overcome this problem we often use a speaker to start the process, followed by a good discussion leader. Role play can also serve this purpose. It brings members of a group directly into a situation. Every member has a chance to share in the group feeling, just as an audience reacts at a play. Role play will prompt people to speak spontaneously and stimulate active discussion.

2. *Release emotions.* Some people are reluctant to discuss personal feelings. They do not know how others will react. If the class is to deal with the problems that really trouble members, feelings must be expressed. Emotions need to be dealt with if attitudes are to be affected and learning is to take place.

3. *Bring the problem to life.* At times a group thinks a topic is academic or hypothetical. It may have been put on the agenda by a planning committee or a leader, and the group

considers it unimportant or unreal. Sometimes the members see the importance but deal with the situation in a theoretical way. Role playing brings it to life dramatically.

4. *Train in leadership skills.* An important function of a group leader is helping the group to solve problems. The most significant aspect is giving procedural help—guiding the group to approach a problem systematically. In such an approach the group examines the problem, investigates the information, and draws conclusions. Any group can engage in problem solving, with different members alternately playing the leader. In this way the skills involved in helping a group to approach a problem systematically can be studied and practiced. In problem-solving sessions the person in the leadership role can practice other skills as well.

5. *Other reasons for Role Playing.* To encourage readiness to learn, lessen anxiety by anticipatory rehearsal, provide cross-cultural skill practice, report on a topic, and improve group functioning.

Strengths of the Technique

1. In historical or biblical role play, figures from the past come to life and their problems seem more real.
2. The players often identify with the roles being portrayed, learning to look at a given situation from a different point of view.
3. Students' sensitivities are developed because they learn how it feels to be in someone else's position.
4. Team members with special problems, experiences, or competence can brief the others on particular problems.
5. Role play is flexible and can be tailored to the problem the group is concerned about.
6. It is especially good as an exploratory device when a group is beginning a study.
7. Participants remember the material because they experienced it.
8. Role play leads the class to discuss attitudes they would not normally express with traditional methods.
9. Class members can experiment with new or different re-

sponses without suffering consequences that might be experienced in life.

Weaknesses of the Technique

1. Inexperienced teachers could lose effective control of the class, so new teachers will avoid using role play.
2. Teachers must be oriented to the subject matter and methods.
3. A teacher might lack ingenuity.
4. Dealing with the emotional reactions of participants unknown to the teacher can be dangerous.
5. Undesirable effects can come from putting unpopular people in certain roles.
6. A poorly supervised class may engage in idle, useless discussion. Only superficial opinions and prejudices may be aired if discussion is not well controlled.
7. The class may view role play as a game, rather than an educational experience.
8. Older people tend to laugh and be self-conscious. They may be unable to identify with their assigned roles. Shyness and hesitancy may develop at any age level.

Principles for Use of Technique

1. First, the teacher must present the essential situation to be role-played, including the characters, the setting, the situation or problem, the biblical or literary text.
2. If in the role play a small group acts before a large group of observers, participants should be volunteers with a choice of roles. Time limitations may prevent this for younger pupils.
3. A short briefing session is essential to coach participants on their specific roles. Those who will add the element of surprise should have special briefing unknown to the observers or to other players.
4. The number of characters involved should be limited, to prevent confusion.
5. When possible, provide an open-ended situation where role players must discover solutions.

6. In role-playing a complex problem, the teacher may act as a clarifier by interrupting the action for brief commentary.
7. The observers should evaluate the action at its conclusion, discussing the validity of the emotions portrayed, the facts cited, and the consequences of possible actions.

Examples of Effective Use

1. Bible truths such as the religious and civil trials of Christ are well-suited to role play.
2. Selected students could role-play the meeting of a student with a friend he is trying to win to Christ. The class would then evaluate the visit in terms of its effectiveness.
3. A pastor can deal with problems of adolescents in this framework, giving them a chance to see the problem from two points of view.
4. Role play can be used in teacher training. Effective and ineffective teaching methods may be enacted before the class.
5. The rights and wrongs of church ushering, song leading, and other services could be taught in this way.
6. Visitation procedure can be effectively taught through a role-play situation.

Usefulness at Various Age Levels

1. *Primary.* The uninhibited primary child gives an honest reaction to the situation being portrayed. He thinks literally and simply, so the teacher must choose material that is concrete rather than symbolic. It must be easy to understand. The primary child has a short interest span (twenty minutes); therefore, the role play must be short and interesting. He is concerned about group acceptance, so as many children as possible should be used in the role play.
2. *Junior.* The junior child loves to do things, and the role play gives him a chance to take an active role. He loves true stories. The content can often be historical. Since the junior is a hero worshiper, choose a hero with whom he can identify. The junior still does not understand symbols, so make the content explicit.
3. *Junior High.* The junior high student is starting to be inter-

ested in others and their opinions. For this reason role play is excellent at this age. As the young teen's decision-making power grows, role play can turn him to consideration of Christ's claims. The young teen is beginning to grasp symbols, so include more of the abstract. He is interested in morality, and role play is related to moral issues. Since puberty comes at this time, the psychodrama can take up the problems of sexual awareness.

4. *High School.* High schoolers begin to encounter anti-Christian views, and role play can give advance preparations.

By the middle teens people have formed prejudices, but role play can help them see the others' views on race, culture, or faith. The high schooler can plan role play.

5. *Adults.* Adults have developed a capacity for abstraction. They vary greatly, so role play can be flexible. With adults role play is a good "starter" in a new area of study, as it undermines the copious inhibitions of adults. However, they may have to be sold on role play as a learning technique because of their greater self-consciousness and inability to identify.

ROLL PURGING

Roll purging is a process by which the church honestly reflects its actual membership by removing the names of those who no longer belong on the rolls due to inactivity, transfer to another church, or moving away.

ROOMS, HOW TO MAKE SUNDAY SCHOOL ROOMS MORE INVITING

Some Sunday school teachers are assigned to beautiful rooms with adequate facilities. They should rejoice in the opportunity of exciting teaching experiences. Other teachers are given less adequate facilities. But all rooms can be improved with a little creativity and effort on the part of the teacher. There are certain attitudes that all teachers ought to have toward their assigned rooms. They should be concerned about such things as atmosphere, comfort, cleanliness, and the general appeal of their rooms.

1. *Atmosphere.* The appearance of the children's classroom is

more important than we often realize, for the informal learning that takes place in the life of a child does more to mold spiritual concepts and ideas than does teaching. The room to which a child comes from week to week to learn of God's Word may have as much influence on his life as the teacher's lesson plan has.

First impressions are lasting impressions. Children deserve the best space available in the Sunday school. The Sunday school room does not have to be new, but it should be light and cheerful, and the windows should be low enough for the children to look out. When we stick children in a church basement that is dark and dreary, when we seat them in adult folding chairs that are so high that their feet never touch the floor, when we use second-hand discards for tables, we may be telling children that "anything is good enough for God." Children should be led to think of church as a happy place. If they like church, and love their teachers, they will more than likely love God also, for Bible-school environment has a tremendous effect upon the learning of children.

Plants to water, fish to feed, and flowers to smell bring life into the room. Appropriate pictures placed at the child's eye level and changed often add to the room's appearance and also aid in the total teaching effect.

Is your room as attractive as you can make it? Do you need new furnishings? Are there some visual aids you should have? What changes could be made in the atmosphere of the room to make the children happier and your teaching more effective?

2. *Comfort.* Even when space and facilities are limited, teachers should be concerned about a comfortable place for learning. Rooms should be evenly heated. Floors should be carpeted. Windows should be designed to let in as much light as possible, and so that they may be opened and closed easily. Ventilation is as important as temperature. A hard-to-ventilate classroom may be thoroughly aired before the class members arrive. Be careful to avoid either uncomfortable drafts or stuffy rooms. Take into consideration the body heat

generated by teachers and pupils in an overcrowded room. It is quite possible for teachers who enter an airy, comfortable room to become so gradually conditioned to the rising temperature that they are unaware of the discomfort their pupils may be experiencing. Obviously, an uncomfortable child is not likely to be in the best attitude for learning.

Good lighting is important. If sufficient light is not provided by windows, as is often the case in basement classrooms, be sure to have adequate lighting fixtures installed in the ceiling. Window shades or tinted glass should be provided for those rooms that may be affected by the glaring light of the sun.

3. *Cleanliness.* The children's department in your Bible school should be as clean and neat as you like your rooms at home. Give the walls a new coat of paint as often as needed. Store supplies neatly on shelves. (You may want to make a wooden door or bright curtain door for the shelves.) Keep small pictures, paper, and such articles as crayons, pencils, bottles of glue, and scissors in labeled boxes on the shelves. Discard any materials that are not needed. Bulletin boards should be placed at the children's eye level, and the displays changed frequently.

Students should be given some responsibility in keeping their room clean. The teacher who allows children to leave the room with overturned chairs, paper scraps on the floor, open bottles of glue on the table, workbooks spread out on the shelf, or mud tracked on the floor, is missing a valuable opportunity to teach order and discipline to the children. A good rule is to have a place for everything, and everything in its place.

The children's Bible school classroom should be a room in which they feel at home. Never, never should it be permitted to become either a storeroom or a showplace. Everything in the room should serve a useful purpose. If it does not, it should be removed. Remember, you need at least twenty-five square feet of floor space per child—and that usually leaves no room for storage or show furniture.

4. *An inviting appearance.* A Sunday school room should say, "Come in. This is a room where you can talk to your friends and your teachers, talk about God, and even talk to God." A Bible school room should provide space for working, interest centers for stimulating curiosity, and "room to grow in." Discipline problems often result from crowded rooms. Rooms that provide twenty-five to thirty square feet per child are desirable. When rooms are small (less than twenty square feet per child), activity is often limited to a "talk and listen" situation. Children learn best through firsthand experiences—investigating, exploring, planning, consulting, handling, creating, talking, working, pasting, asking, and moving. Make sure your rooms make such experiences possible.

Overcoming Inadequate Space and Equipment

Adequate space and equipment are not always obtainable. What can you do then? Use your ingenuity and creativity to overcome the problems.

1. *Discuss problems with other teachers.* The process of brainstorming should suggest several ideas to help solve the problem of inadequate room space. When a team of teachers seriously brainstorm, more than one answer to a problem is usually suggested. Thoughts may piggyback on other ideas; that is, one suggestion by one teacher may bring on a new idea or solution from another teacher. In the midst of this exchange of ideas, someone will almost always come up with a helpful, practical way to solve the problem.

2. *Clear the room of nonessential furniture.* Children need space in which to grow and learn. The piano may be too large for the room. Since a piano is not really necessary for good singing, why not give it to an adult class? (They usually need the help of a piano more than children do anyway.) Keep only enough chairs for each enrolled pupil and teacher. Do not allow broken furniture, discarded paper, or storage materials to accumulate in the corners of closets of the rooms. Use the space for good teaching and helpful equipment.

3. *Consider the use of movable screens for additional privacy.* Sheets of plywood, brightly painted and mounted on rollers,

provide excellent screens. Tackboards and chalkboards can be quite easily and inexpensively attached to such screens. Some teachers feel that breaking the sight line is helpful in small-group teaching.

When two teachers conduct class in the same room, the distinct voice and words of one teacher may interrupt the second teacher. However, when more than two teachers use the same room, a class usually hears noise (diffusion of two or more teachers talking) rather than distinct words and sentences. It is well for all teachers to remember that lessons in the same room tend to distract the teachers far more than the pupils. A teacher should work toward the development of such a positive mental attitude toward her class that neither she nor the class will be distracted by the movements or voices of others in the room. Movable partitions may be used to help provide a feeling of separateness for the various groups in a classroom.

4. *Use storage space outside of the small classroom.* Small classrooms should not be needlessly limited by taking away vital teaching space for storage. Instead, look for a place outside the classroom where learning materials can be stored. Or make a set of shelves on rollers and roll them into a place of storage after class.

5. *Use folding chairs and tables.* One small church shortened the legs of a folding game table to a length of fifteen inches. During the activity period the tale was folded and laid against the wall. Folding chairs may also be used when extra space is needed for activities.

6. *Seating mats save space.* Some churches have made seating mats out of squares of carpeting samples. These mats are used by children when listening to a story, singing a song, or participating in large group activities. Other churches use wall-to-wall carpeting. One such church painted two-foot squares on a rug to arrange for the children's seating. "We used to have the children sit on the floor," one teacher explained, "but the boys were tempted to wrestle and roll all over the girls. When we painted the squares and assigned

each child to a square, the children were better disciplined and kept their places more readily."

7. *Church pews may be turned to face each other.* Some churches do not have any classrooms available for children's classes. When this is the situation, two pews can be turned to face each other at the back of the auditorium or at one side next to the wall. Movable screens may be used to block off the view from other classes. A small table placed between the pews will focus attention on the learning activities at the center of the class.

8. *Lapboards may be used in cramped quarters.* In classrooms where space is so limited that there is no room for a worktable, portable lapboards may be used. The lapboard should be from twelve to fourteen inches square and about three-fourths of an inch thick. Some churches use chair seats (minus the backs and legs) for lapboards. The lapboards may be brightly painted to add color and interest. If each pupil has his name painted on the lapboard, he may feel a keener sense of belonging. If you must use boards on church pews for small children, you may need footstools (boxes, cans, or cartons) also.

9. *Make use of available space for displaying pictures and posters.* The insides of doors and movable screens provide excellent areas for displaying pictures, friezes, and murals. Burlap bags or other inexpensive materials may be hung on the walls to serve as tackboards.

Look Again at Your Room

Walk through your Sunday school room and watch for certain items. Yogi Berra said, "You can see a lot by just looking." Do you see . . .

- choir music stacked on top of an old piano?
- a room overcrowded with chairs?
- an exposed light bulb on the ceiling?
- pictures hanging crooked or too high for children to see?
- a bulletin board that hasn't been changed in a month?
- an attendance contest poster left over from last quarter?

- broken crayons in a dirty box?
- an open supply cabinet with ugly bottles of glue, stacks of used handwork, a pile of scissors, unsharpened pencils, and stacks of old take-home papers?
- tables with old, dark paint that are either too high or too low?
- a vase of dusty plastic flowers?
- unmatched chairs of different sizes and different colors, needing repair?

A cluttered room makes the child feel that life is cluttered. A disorderly room makes the child feel uneasy and disturbed. An uncared for room makes the child feel uncared for.

There is no excuse for dirt, disorder, or lack of care. One attractive picture designed to teach children and hung at their eye level is better than a half dozen cheap pictures that carry no meaning. Religious mottoes may be effective, but remember, they are usually phrased in concepts—and children do not think in concepts.

One chair per pupil for the maximum attendance is sufficient. Children need space, not extra chairs. If chairs must be varied in design or size, at least paint them all the same color, and arrange them in an orderly, attractive manner.

Walk around your classroom and look for some of the following things. Do you see . . .

- clean windows and bright curtains?
- bright lights in a fixture hanging from the ceiling?
- matching chairs placed neatly about the study tables?
- low shelves and interesting-looking books?
- inviting art materials that are easily accessible to the pupils?
- a good picture hung at the eye level of pupils?
- neatly arranged supply cabinets with doors?
- something alive—flowers, vines, goldfish?
- enough crayons in good condition for each child?
- storage space for each teacher?
- windows low enough for children to look out?

- a spotless floor—clean enough for children to play on without getting dirty?
- a bulletin board at eye level with materials changed at least every other week?
- a picture file for the teacher?
- a desk for the departmental secretary?
- a record player?
- a well-tuned piano that is painted or finished to complement the room?
- a bookrack with interesting, colorful books?

A room for children should be designed and arranged to make learning about God interesting, enjoyable, important, and lasting.

What Rooms Are Needed for Sunday Schools

Some people think of Sunday schools as a quiet building like a mortuary, where secretaries tiptoe down the hall when they collect attendance books and teachers put a finger to their lips and say, "Shhh." But many classrooms are noisy with students laughing, talking, and moving about.

Do students learn best in solitude or through activities? Traditionally Sunday school has been as quiet as a library, but modern students learn by talking, doing, and interacting—through an active environment.

What happens when you allow thirty to fifty students to talk and work on different activities at the same time? Perhaps these and other similar objections may be partially answered by taking a look at the business world. Walk into any modern office, and you will find people doing business with customers. All around are others at their desks. Some are talking. Some are working on stacks of papers. Some are talking into dictaphones, while typewriters clatter, telephones ring, and people come and go. But the noise is not particularly disturbing. Why? Because the noises are an accepted (and expected) part of the activities at hand. A crowded restaurant is the same. Many groups are there eating and chatting away.

Some teachers who have worked in open rooms report that in the beginning, children who are used to a self-contained classroom may tend to watch what nearby groups are doing. But this habit soon wears off unless the competing activity is particularly attractive (or distracting), in which instance the temptation may be removed by changing locations or activities.

Mark Hopkins said, "A school is a teacher at one end of the log and the pupil on the other." The log is the classroom. The classroom is important because it is the environment in which teaching and learning take place. But does it mean a totally quiet environment.

Some Sunday schools have modern, well-equipped, well-lighted rooms. Other schools meet in poorly equipped, poorly lighted, small basement rooms with low ceilings, tiny windows, and dark woodwork.

Classrooms Should Reflect Teaching

The following questions are given as a guide to help you see what is needed for the most effective instruction in Sunday school.

1. *What is the purpose of Sunday school?* Those who plan Sunday school buildings should ask themselves, What groups of persons will be meeting here? What types of activities will best instruct these persons? What skills need to be developed in order to help people grow to spiritual maturity? How can the building be utilized to impart these skills? Will the Sunday school need facilities for a lecture program or for activities?

2. *How do children learn?* The blueprint of the Christian education plant should reflect the nature of the Christian learner. Do children become better Christians, for example, by learning facts about the Bible, or by involving themselves in activities based on the facts of the Bible? Can doctrine be taught best by drill and recitation, or by having pupils engage in a variety of properly guided, interesting activities? Do pupils learn more by listening to talk, or by being involved in handwork, activities, and interaction with teachers and other pupils? If the emphasis is on indoctrination of Bible facts, a small room where pupils can sit and listen to teachers

is desirable. If the emphasis is on living the lesson, a large activity room should be provided.

3. *How will the Sunday school be organized?* There are three basic types of Bible school organization: (1) single unit Sunday schools, also called the one-room Sunday school or class Sunday school because everything is organized around classes; (2) departmentally graded schools; and (3) multiple department schools, also called closely graded or age graded.

A single unit school has one or two opening assemblies. If the school has two opening assemblies, young people and adults may meet in the church sanctuary for ten to twenty minutes of preliminary activities before going to class, while the children gather in another part of the building for an opening assembly consisting of such activities as stories, object lessons, singing of choruses, announcements, recognition of birthdays, and devotions. The growing single unit school faces the dilemma of building a plant for the present organization while planning for expansion to the departmentally graded school. However, one answer is that the opening worship or opening exercise is being eliminated, with pupils going straight to class. The activities of the opening exercise is spread through the class time or learning experiences.

The departmentally graded school ordinarily provides space for seven or more opening assemblies: for the nursery, kindergarten, primary, junior, junior high, youth, and adult departments. At least seven rooms are necessary for opening worship and perhaps several times as many for individual class sessions. If teaching centers are used for classrooms, temporary dividers may take the place of permanent walls.

The multiple department school is more complex because a separate department is provided for every age level. In fact, very large Sunday schools often have more than one department for each age level.

Planning Rooms for Teaching

When designing a new Christian education building, the architect should be instructed to design the building for maximum flexibility and resource learning.

1. *Classrooms should be expandable.* Provision should be made for increased floor footage when it is necessitated by growth in attendance. This could be provided by additional classrooms, by expansion of present classrooms, or by additional acreage.

2. *Classrooms should be versatile.* Rooms should be purposely designed to accomplish a variety of functions. The same room may well serve as a classroom for Bible study during the week and as an activity teaching classroom on Sunday. It may also be used for club activities during the week, or for kindergarten or Christian day school. To apply the concept of versatility to other areas of the church program, a multipurpose room may be constructed to serve as a gymnasium, an auditorium, or a large dining room.

   A word of warning should be inserted here: Do not make any room so versatile that it is unfit for its primary function—being used as a classroom.

3. *Classrooms should be convertible.* Rooms should be designed for easy and economical change to meet new program needs. A room may need immediate change to reduce or increase space size. Expandability is accomplished by labor and materials outside the school. Convertibility may be performed by pupils or teachers. The use of partitions and dividers will be examined in detail.

   The folding door is a very popular divider for several reasons. Floor tracks are not required. The partition walls usually fold completely out of the way against the wall or into a compartment specially prepared for its enclosure.

   There are, however, certain disadvantages to folding doors. The greatest of these disadvantages seems to be sound penetration. Most folding doors are not soundproof. Also, they are temporary. That is, they do not look or operate well after continued use.

   Movable space dividers are often used to partition off one section of a class from another. They may also be used to divide one class from another before a building is completed.

One of the most popular dividers is a free standing plywood board on wheels, four feet by eight feet in size. Such a divider may also serve as a bulletin board. Chalkboards and/or tackboards may be attached to the sides of the board. The dividers are of sufficient height to provide visual separation between seated pupils in different classes. Plywood or chalkboard dividers are not sound barriers, but soundproofing is not their purpose.

The use of furniture and class equipment as partitions has become popular in many areas. Bookcases may be arranged to form an alcove around a library table. They may even lend atmosphere to library work. Movable storage units with suitable tops designed for work areas make ideal work centers.

Office buildings are modified to suit incoming tenants. This can be done in Sunday school buildings as well. A primary department may have forty-five in attendance one year, and thirty or sixty the next. If rooms can be converted to meet shifting population, there may be economical advantages as well as improved teaching.

4. *Classrooms should allow for frequent change of group size with minimum loss of time.* Proper grouping is one of the keys to successful teaching. Frequent changes between large groups and small activity centers are a necessary part of teaching.

5. *Classrooms should become "identity-security" centers for the pupils.* When a pupil is moved several times, he sometimes loses his sense of identity and security. He may even think of church as a place to visit and observe. For this reason, he needs a spot that is uniquely his. In one Bible school, for instance, each child "belongs" to a certain table (each painted a different color). The child should also think of the classroom as "his" classroom. He needs to have a place to hang his wraps, store his books and supplies, and find his friends and his teachers.

6. *Each teacher needs a home base* much as the pupil needs an identity-security center. A teacher may be teaching in a large room with other teachers. Still, he needs a place where he

can confer with pupils, prepare activity materials, and work work with small groups of children. Most teachers make their activity tables "home base." In a few weeks' time, most pupils identify certain tables as belonging to certain teachers.

7. *Classrooms should make teaching-learning materials available to as many pupils as possible.* Some teaching materials (chalkboards, tackboards, storage shelves, and worship centers) are used frequently by all groups. These should be permanently located where they are easily accessible to all. Teaching materials that are used less frequently—record players, tape recorders, filmstrip projectors, overhead projectors, projection screens, maps, globes, and pictures—will, of course, be movable, and they are usually kept in the church library or resource center.

8. *Classrooms should have an instructional resource center.* It needs a library to supply pupils and teachers with materials and activities for learning. When using a activity concept rather than a lecture method of teaching, the resource center should contain more than just books. Some of the materials that should be available in a resource center are books, periodicals, pamphlets, pictures, slides, records, tapes, maps, charts, a record player, filmstrip and slide projector, puppets, missionary curios, materials for object lessons, flannelgraph boards and materials, parallel readers (several copies of the same book for reading groups), globes, and music.

   The purpose of the resource center is to provide space and materials for both individual and group study. It should not replace the church library; instead, it should supplement it. The church library serves the entire church family. The resource center expands this service by supplying extra materials that are particularly useful for a specific group.

9. *Classrooms should allow for acoustical solutions to the problems of sound distribution.* More than one teacher may be talking in a room at the same time when an activity approach to teaching is used. Pupils will be speaking, asking questions, or reporting to each other in various groups within the room.

While one group is reading silently in the resource center, a second group may be practicing a play. A third group may be working at a table.

Because of the frequent movement of groups, the varying sizes of the groups, and the multiple function of many areas in the room, the sound problem may at times become complex.

Wall-to-wall carpeting is being used in some places throughout the Christian education unit and hallways as well as in the sanctuary. Research has proved that carpeting is actually a rather inexpensive addition.

One approach to the problem of noise is to ignore it. This approach is not really new. A busy working sound surrounding a person may actually help create a better learning atmosphere. Some educators feel that children who regularly work alongside of other working children do not disturb one another.

Self-contained classrooms give privacy to teachers, uninterrupted class time, a sense of belonging to both teacher and pupils, and a quiet setting in which the teacher may instruct the pupils. There are, however, certain limitations. Children are somewhat hindered in social interaction, movement of groups is limited, the resource center and the teaching-learning aids may not be readily available to all, certain types of learning activities are prohibited, sizes of groups are limited, and several small rooms are more expensive to construct and to maintain than one large room would be.

Sunday schools that maintain a lecture approach to teaching seem to be happy with the traditional departmentally graded rooms. Such Sunday schools might not be happy with an activity approach or activity-type learning. Every church should construct a building that reflects its philosophy of education.

ROOM DECORATION CONTEST

A room decoration contest will motivate everyone in the Sunday school to clean up, paint, and fix up their facilities. Such a contest has effectively turned more than one dirty, lifeless Sunday school into a clean, attractive, and exciting learning environment. Not only are the facilities improved, but excitement is pumped into a dying Sunday school.

Why You Need a Room Decoration Contest

1. *Reflect the changing seasons.* A contest will challenge every teacher to make sure his or her classroom reflects the new season of the year.

2. *Develop esprit de corps.* A room decoration contest will motivate class spirit. One Sunday school teacher hung paper flowers from the ceiling. A class member's photo was glued to the center of each flower. Not only were the pupils excited; mothers and fathers came visiting the class to see their child's picture.

3. *Teaching tool.* A room decoration contest will provide an additional means of teaching Bible truth. One teacher wanted to teach his class of Junior boys biblical principles of discipleship. First, the class was given the name "The Disciples," and a large sign with that title was hung over the door. The classroom was littered with paper footprints, each footprint containing a verse on the theme "following Jesus." The boys learned what it meant to be a follower as they thought up ideas to decorate their room. Every Sunday school class should be freshly decorated at least four times a year in connection with a new quarterly theme.

4. *Promoting goals.* Recently a class at the Glen Haven Baptist Church of Decatur, Georgia, was decorated with hundreds of paper tabs, the type used to identify filing folders. Each tab had the class attendance goal lettered in different colors to remind the class members of the attendance goal. In another church a Sunday school teacher had a goal of sixteen visitors. To announce the goal the teacher cut out a block number 16 and hung it with thread from the ceiling. Also, another large block number 16 was attached to the wall.

5. *New life.* Most Sunday school classes need new life every once in a while. Enthusiasm exists when a new Sunday school building is completed. Over the months and years the

excitement of and appreciation for a building is blunted. But a room decoration contest will give a change in appearance and will help restore enthusiasm concerning the facilities.

6. *Growth.* Excitement will help your Sunday school grow. When people get excited about their church, they will begin to talk to others about it. Soon visitors will appear.

7. *Testimony.* Ask yourself, *What do people think about my Sunday school when they visit?* It would be great if they remembered the Bible lesson, good visual aids, spirited singing, and enthusiastic teaching of friendly teachers instead of the dirty bathroom or the broken windowpane. The problem is that people in a church become used to dirty facilities or an accumulation of junk. A room decoration contest may be an important step toward getting people to see their facilities as others see them.

How to Conduct a Room Decoration Contest

If you think a room decoration contest will help you accomplish the objectives of your Sunday school, then you should plan now to take the following steps:

1. *Date.* First, decide on a date. Enthusiasm will spread through the entire Sunday school if every class is freshly decorated on the same date. Do your best to avoid making exceptions. Set a date so that teachers have three to four weeks to plan and organize their classes to help them.

2. *Teachers.* Next, educate your teachers concerning the project. Share some of the reasons why they need the campaign. No doubt you can think of additional reasons applicable to your specific situation. The teachers are the key to organizing their classes. It is important that they are convinced the campaign is necessary.

3. *Students.* You will want full participation in the contest. Every class member needs to be involved in preparing the class. Some classes will decorate the room together as part of a class project. Others may divide the work into various groups assigning one or two people to make the final arrangement of the room a day or two before the final day. Total

involvement of class members is one of the things you will watch for as you choose a winner.

4. *Alternatives.* You may have some classes that for one reason or another cannot decorate their room. This would probably be true of the auditorium Bible class or classes meeting in a gymnasium. In these situations, provide a list of alternatives that will help beautify the building. There may be gardens to plant, sidewalks to repair, and kitchens to clean. You know what could look better if it were cleaner in your church. If a class does not have its own room, it could be assigned space on a wall in the hall or gymnasium. There they could hang pictures, posters, or other things that relate to their theme. A church in Anderson, South Carolina, has many small classes meeting in a large gymnasium. They used a modified approach to team teaching. When it came time to decorate, each teacher decorated the room divider (four-by-eight-foot plywood panels on rollers) that separated his or her teaching space from other classes.

How to Decorate

The possibilities in decorating your rooms are virtually unlimited. The best decorations are the ones that the pupils plan for their rooms, rather than the teacher doing some spring cleaning the day before the rooms are judged.

1. *Pictures.* Several classes have made use of pictures of the entire class or photos of individual class members in their decorations.

2. *Mobiles.* Mobiles are particularly popular among classes of younger children. Strings can be tied from the ceiling, and the mobiles can be dropped to the child's level. The mobiles can be animals, flowers, pictures, numbers, or any other creative idea. For an added effect, a fan in the corner of the room will keep the mobiles moving.

3. *Door entrances.* Again, classes of small children often decorate their room by constructing a special entrance around the door. One class of four-year-olds called themselves "The Bee Hive." The room was decorated with bumblebees hanging from the ceiling. Each bee had the name of a child. The

entrance to the room was shaped like a beehive. A fourth grade boys class called themselves "The Tree House Gang" and built a tree house out of plywood. A child had to climb through the "tree house" to enter the room.

4. *Wall-size posters.* The entire room can be transformed by a colorful mural poster that takes the place of what was formerly a blank wall. The Tri-City Baptist Church in Gladstone, Oregon, had an artist paint life-size murals on the walls of the children's departments. The children could see Daniel in the lions' den and Jacob viewing the ladder to heaven. When planned ahead of time, a mural could serve as a visual aid for the quarter's lesson. Wall-size posters are popping up all over, especially in the youth department.

5. *Logo.* When decorating a room, make sure the pupils follow a theme. Then the room will be judged by their creativity in using the theme in their decorations. The theme for decoration should reinforce the lesson theme. A theme should be expressed in a logo that deals with a biblical theme. (A logo is a pictorial representation of a motto or theme.)

How to Judge a Room Decoration Contest

One of the most difficult tasks in the entire campaign will be choosing a winner. You should also recognize one or two "honorable mentions." When I am asked to judge a room decoration contest, I choose a winner by using the following four criteria:

1. *Creativity.* How original is the theme and decorating? Has the teacher put thought into this or is it simply a rehash of what someone else did? You should encourage the teachers to be creative in preparing for the contest. The best ideas are the ones no one has had yet.

2. *Personal involvement.* The prettiest room could be decorated by an interior decorator, but that is not what you really want. Judge the rooms on the degree of participation by every class member. Your Sunday school pupils will only become excited about their room as they decorate it.

3. *Theme.* The third question I ask myself is, *How closely does this room follow a single theme?* This will help prevent the flea-market look (a little bit of everything and a lot of noth-

ing). One thing ought to capture your imagination in every aspect of the decorated room.

4. *Quality.* At the bottom of the list is quality. I would rather see a class do a poorer job than see a single individual do a first-rate job alone, but hopefully the class can work together to do a first-rate job. Expect the best from your teachers, and consider quality as you choose the best-decorated room in your Sunday school.

Room Decoration

When the winning class has been chosen, a simple recognition service will encourage others to follow their example. You may want to give the teacher a book to help him in his teaching or pay his expenses to an area Sunday school convention. In a smaller community, the local weekly paper may be interested in printing pictures of the winning class and carrying a story about your church. A larger church could do the same sort of thing in the church newspaper. A letter of appreciation should always be sent from the superintendent to the winning teacher for the fine job he did.

SAINT JOHN'S SYNDROME (See also PATHOLOGY OF CHURCH GROWTH)

The Saint John's syndrome is also called the Second Generation syndrome. The first generation usually are pioneers who want to reach lost or unchurched and build the church, but second generation members usually want to settle down on the land. The term comes from Saint John, who wrote the book of Revelation, where Christ challenged the second generation church that had lost its first love (Rev. 2:4).

SALARIES

It is important that the church pay its pastor and staff an appropriate and adequate salary so as to enable church staff to provide for the needs of their families. Often it is difficult for a church to determine what the salary of the pastor should be. The following principles and suggestions may help a church determine what to pay its staff:

1. Salaries vary by denomination, types of church served, educational preparation, and benefits received.
2. The higher the church membership, the larger the minister's salary; the longer the years of service, the higher the salary.
3. The compensation of a minister should enable him to give full time and energy to his task.
4. The minister should not have to be dependent on ministerial discounts and fees for weddings, baptisms, and funerals.
5. The budget should be arranged in two parts: reimbursable expense (funds for all expenses incurred by the minister in

travel for the church, including car expense and cost of additional professional training) and compensation (salary, housing and all utilities, payments toward a pension, and health and accident insurance premiums).

6. As a help in keeping abreast of inflation for salaries of the pastor and staff, the U.S. Department of Labor will furnish you with a cost of living index.

7. Ministers should keep abreast of the rising costs of Social Security; the church should pay this tax, just as other employers do.

SAND TABLE

A sand table is a teaching tool that helps the teacher develop creativity and enjoyment in the lesson. To make it effective, dampen sand and shape rolling hills and a river or lake. Let primaries or juniors make trees (from construction paper or cardboard) and houses (see article on Models) or tents (as for Abram), and place as desired. Add water jars and other accessories. Clothespins or chenille-wire figures may be draped with a square of cloth with a neck hole and tied on with a yarn belt. Construction paper animals, such as donkeys and camels, may be scattered about.

SATURATION EVANGELISM

Saturation evangelism is one method of evangelism (see definition of *evangelism*). It is defined as using every available means to reach every available person at every available time. Some have called this media evangelism, but saturation evangelism is broader, usually including such methods as bus evangelism and visitation evangelism.

SCRIPTURE MEMORY

When Robert Raikes began the first Sunday school, he gave a gold coin to pupils who could recite the entire book of Proverbs. Why such a long passage of Scripture? Because Raikes knew the Bible could change a life when it worked on both the conscious and unconscious mind. The following are some reasons why we memorize Scripture.

First, the Bible will keep us from sin. The world says, "An ounce of prevention is worth a pound of cure." But the psalmist wrote, "Your word I have hidden in my heart, that I might not sin against You" (Ps. 119:11). Since the Bible is pure, it cannot abide where sin reigns. Inside the cover of Dwight L. Moody's Bible were penned the words, "This Book will keep you from sin, or sin will keep you from this Book."

But what if you slip and sin? The memorized Word will come to the rescue. The same psalmist asked, "How can a young man cleanse his way? By taking heed according to Your word" (Ps. 119:9). The Word of God is a spiritual cleanser. Jesus told his disciples, "You are already clean *because of the word* which I have spoken to you" (John 15:3, emphasis added). The apostle Paul explained that Christ died for the Church to "cleanse her with the washing of water *by the word*" (Eph. 5:26, emphasis added). No matter how clean the water is, people won't drink it if it comes in dirty glasses. Every Christian should be concerned about his testimony as he desires to serve God and reach people.

If you want to be a better Christian worker, memorize the Word. What would you think of the carpenter who tried to build a house without a hammer and saw? Many Christians are just as senseless as they attempt to serve God without their tools. Usually the worker who has memorized the most Scripture will be most effective. Every Christian needs a working knowledge of "the sword of the Spirit, which is the word of God" (Eph. 6:17).

But even if you are not a Christian worker, you need to memorize Scripture. Peter advised his converts, "as newborn babes, desire the pure milk of the word, that you may grow thereby" (1 Pet. 2:2). Spiritual growth occurs as we commit the Bible to memory.

Scripture memory will improve your prayer life. Jesus promised, "If you abide in Me, and My words abide in you, you will ask what you desire, and it shall be done for you" (John 15:7). John wrote later, "And whatever we ask we receive from Him, because we keep His commandments and do those things that are pleasing in His sight" (1 John 3:22).

Two words summarize all that is needed to memorize the Bible: repetition and review. Almost everything you have learned since birth came by repetition and review. If you do something enough times regularly, you will form a habit. If you repeat a poem enough times you will remember it. If you will recite a verse enough times, it will be committed to memory. The big question is, How many times is enough? As many times as it takes, then a few more for safety's sake.

Each one has a different ability to learn. Some read a verse once and know it. Others may recite a verse twenty times and forget it the next day. Educators agree children will memorize easier than their parents. This does not mean adults cannot memorize the Scriptures—only that it may be harder for them.

Twenty Steps to Scripture Memory

We can teach memory verses without boring our pupils. How? The answer is not found in any one method or strategy but in the word *variety*. Below is a list of twenty ways to teach and review memory verses. Not all of these methods can be used by every teacher. Some work better with children; others are more effective in adult classes. The effective Sunday school teacher will use many ways to teach pupils the Word of God.

1. *Posters.* Printing the Scripture text on a poster with an attractive picture not only reminds the pupil of the verse but also helps decorate the classroom. You can refer to the poster when reviewing the verse with the class. Also, it will be a subconscious reminder of the verse.

2. *Find the word.* Children especially enjoy solving problems. Write out the verse but reverse a word or phrase. Have the pupils review the verse and correct it. You may want to use this technique near the end of the quarter to review several verses.

3. *Cassette tapes.* Deuteronomy 6:7 gives four times when Scripture memory may be taught in the home. "You shall teach them diligently to your children, and shall talk of them [1] when you sit in your house, [2] when you walk by the way, [3] when you lie down, and [4] when you rise up." Therefore, have the pupils record the passage on a cassette for review. This method is best with long passages. Adults can be encouraged to review the Scriptures as they drive

around town or do housework. The more opportunities pupils have to listen, the more Scripture can be learned.

4. *Testimonies.* A testimony of what a particular verse means to an individual will help motivate your pupils to understand the verse they are memorizing. Taking a few minutes to tell the story behind a verse will be effective if it creates an interest in the pupils to learn the verse.

5. *Achievement chart.* One junior Sunday school teacher motivated his pupils in Scripture memory by posting a chart with a record of the verses his pupils had memorized. Most of us will remember something similar when we were in Sunday school. Because the method has worked for a number of years, it will also work today.

6. *Flash cards.* Use flash cards with children. Recently a class of about twenty pupils finished learning Ephesians 6:10-13, with the aid of flash cards. That may not seem unusual until you realize the pupils were four years old and had begun working on the verses only a week or two earlier. No one is too young to begin learning the Bible.

7. *Group recitation.* Some churches have practiced Scripture memory as a congregation. During the prayer meeting, the pastor has the congregation turn to a verse and recite it several times as a group. This may be the easiest way to teach adults to memorize the Scriptures, and it takes relatively little time in preparation. The best thing about this method is that it works.

8. *Chalkboard.* Print the verse on the chalkboard. Erase some words as the class reads the verse together. When more words are erased, the pupils have a greater challenge to remember the total verse. After all the words are gone, the verse will remain in the minds of the class members.

9. *Explain a word.* The memory verse can be a capsule of everything you want to accomplish in the lesson. Why not teach the meaning of words in the verse during the lesson? Choose songs that relate to the verse. Plan activities relating to the memory verse in presession and group times. If

the pupil remembers only one thing that Sunday, it will be the memory verse.

10. *Word pictures.* Many verses lend themselves to a particular symbol or logo. Make word pictures out of these verses. Verses dealing with the law can be written out on replicas of the two tablets of the law. Love verses could be taught from heart-shaped visuals. Particularly with younger children, the symbolism of the visual aid helps reinforce the theme of the verse.

11. *Prizes.* Sunday school has always conducted contests for various purposes, including a Scripture memory contest to challenge each pupil to memorize a certain number of verses, and giving a prize to the one who memorizes the most. Robert Raikes, as mentioned earlier, gave a gold coin to the pupils who could recite the book of Proverbs. Dwight Moody gave away shoes, coats, and other prizes to the children in his Sunday school for learning hundreds of verses. During Scripture memory month at one church, a boy learned more than six hundred verses to win a free week at camp.

12. *Choral reading.* On those weeks in which the memory verse seems particularly long, the class may learn it better through choral reading. Divide the class into several sections, and have them each learn a part of the verse. Then have the various groups recite their part of the verse together. By rotating the groups, each class member will learn the complete verse. A verse that seems impossible will be known by all in as little as ten to fifteen minutes.

13. *Scripture songs.* A welcome trend in Sunday schools is the singing of Bible verses. Most of us find it easier to learn a new song than recite a poem. A simple melody will not only make it easier to teach the verse, but will also help in review. In the Old Testament, young Hebrew children sang or chanted many of the Psalms, hence learning the lesson and the words.

14. *Flip chart.* The use of a flip chart is a tremendous aid in teaching longer passages. This tool is particularly helpful in

camping and vacation Bible school situations where long passages are learned in comparatively few days. Place part of a verse on each section of the flip chart, then flip the pages as the pupils repeat the verse. The chart aids in both learning and reviewing the verse.

15. *Foreign verses.* A regular missionary conference feature is the festival of sound. Visiting missionaries are each given the opportunity to recite John 3:16 or their life verse in the language of the people with whom they work. Some missions have published verses and gospel songs in foreign languages. People who would not normally memorize a verse at all may memorize verses in several languages due to the novelty of speaking a foreign language. By challenging Sunday school pupils to learn a verse in a foreign language, you are motivating them to learn the same verse in English.

16. *Personalized verses.* Encourage your pupils to apply personally the promises of Scripture. After reading and explaining the verse, have the pupil recite the verse with his name. I would repeat John 3:16, "For God so loved Elmer Towns that He gave His only begotten Son. . . ." Personal application of memory verses is the ultimate objective of teaching Scripture memory, and this method of teaching helps move the pupil closer to that goal.

17. *Puppets.* Puppets can be used to teach memory verses. Many teachers realize their pupils are more interested in what the puppet has to say than what they have to say. Therefore, use a puppet to lead a class in Scripture memory. The puppet can use almost any of the above means of teaching.

18. *Memory project.* What if you didn't have a Bible to teach from next Sunday? In many parts of the world, the only Bible a church possesses is the one existing in the memory of its church members. Challenge a Sunday school class to memorize a book of the Bible during a quarter's study of that book. Divide the book into equal passages of twenty to thirty verses. Distribute the assignments to the class, and

encourage them to do their part to memorize the book as a class. You may want to conclude the campaign by having the class recite the book in a public service. Some larger churches have organized to memorize the New Testament or the entire Bible in a year.

19. *Puzzles.* Many teachers are using presession activities to help prepare students for the morning Bible lesson. Teach a memory verse using a jigsaw puzzle. The verse could be written out on construction paper and then cut into puzzle pieces. As students reassemble the puzzles, they will be learning the verse. There are many different kinds of puzzles that could be used. A creative teacher should be able to produce several puzzles during a quarter.

20. *Memory cards.* Teaching the memory verse does not have to take place only on Sunday morning. When pupils are given Scripture memory cards, they can spend those spare moments each day learning and reviewing Bible verses. Packets are prepared by many organizations, including several youth organizations, Sunday school publishers, and denominations.

Unfortunately, many Sunday school workers have already resigned themselves to believing their class members will not engage in Scripture memory. For those, however, who realize they are doing their pupils a great favor by helping them develop the habit of Scripture memory, the possibilities are unlimited. Children and adults alike can commit the Scriptures to memory. The Holy Spirit can use the Scriptures to cause new Christians to grow (1 Pet. 2:2) or help a child of God mature in the faith (2 Tim. 3:16-17).

Principles for Teaching the Memory Verse
Sunday school superintendents are part of the group God identifies as responsible for the spiritual growth of others: "For they watch out for your souls, as those who must give account" (Heb. 13:17). In light of the solemn responsibility, you will want to do the best job possible. Teaching memory work can be done effectively if you remember four principles:

1. *Enthusiasm spills.* Enthusiasm has been described as twenty gallons of coffee in a tea cup—it spills, leaving its mark on everything it touches. Get enthusiastic about memorizing the Bible. Think of the benefits in your own life. Review the reasons for Scripture memory until you begin Scripture memory yourself. As the Scriptures begin to produce results in your life, let your excitement show. Before long, you will know what they mean when they say enthusiasm is contagious.

2. *Sow a big crop.* One thing is for sure: God will reward our faith (Heb. 11:6). The problem is we do not have faith to expect him to do what he promised. We will get the kind of response we expect. If we want to help our pupils, we should teach Scripture memory expecting results.

   The great British preacher of his day, Charles Haddon Spurgeon, was approached by a younger preacher concerned over seeing people saved in his ministry. When the older pastor asked if results were expected every time, the younger preacher responded, "Of course not."

   "Well, that's why you are not seeing them," counseled Spurgeon.

   As you teach the memory verse, believe God to use his Word to accomplish his results in the life of the pupil.

   If a farmer wants a big crop, he must sow the entire field with the best seed. The Bible teaches we will reap according to our sowing. So, the teacher who gets the pupil to memorize many Scriptures effectively will reap a great harvest.

3. *Work equals wages.* The person who works best should get the most wages. Sometimes it is hard work; other times it is smart work. The degree of success you experience teaching the memory verse will depend on the effort put into the task. Put everything you have into teaching the verse, and do not waste time, or allow for failure. If we devoted as much effort to teaching the verse as we do making excuses for why our pupils cannot learn, we would get better results.

4. *The bottom line.* You are not finished teaching just because the students can recite the verse. The memory verse is not

learned until it is put into life. It is not good enough to know (observe) the verse, Joshua was told to "observe to do" (know and practice, Josh. 1:8). In teaching a memory verse, make sure to pray that God would use it in the life of the class. Then apply the verse to daily life. Finally, trust God to work through the verse in the hearts of your students.

SECOND WORSHIP SERVICE—HOW TO BEGIN

Most church growth today seems to be taking place first in the worship service rather than the Sunday school. When the Second Baptist Church of Houston, Texas, grew by an average of 2,842 worshipers—from an average of 4,146 attending each week in 1985 to 6,988 attending each week in 1986—the primary factor contributing to the increase in attendance was cited as the completion of a new 7,000-seat sanctuary costing approximately $34 million. While adding additional worship space alone will not result in growth, a church cannot grow without space for people.

Just as it is impossible to pour a pot of coffee into a single cup, so it is impossible to crowd 300 people into a sanctuary that seats only 100. Just as coffee spills from the cup and is lost, so an overcrowded sanctuary will spill people into other churches, and potential members will be lost to your church.

Those who are uncomfortable when they visit an overcrowded church usually make a decision, perhaps subconsciously, not to return. The old adage is surely true regarding church visitors: You never get a second opportunity to make a good first impression.

Again, examine the illustration of the overfilled cup; when coffee is spilled, it makes a mess. There is a definite correlation between an overcrowded sanctuary and ongoing problems in a church. First, those who worship in an overcrowded sanctuary are not comfortable to pour their hearts out to God. It is hard to stand in awe of God when standing on someone's foot.

Second, those who worship in overcrowded sanctuaries are not motivated to evangelize their friends. If anything, they have mental barriers to inviting their friends to church. So the overcrowded church is not motivated to grow.

Third, those who have been inconvenienced by an overcrowded sanctuary spread the word. Their criticism makes it hard for other potential visitors to consider worshiping where there are problems.

There are so many problems facing a local church that crowded facilities shouldn't be one of them. Beginning an additional worship service may be a temporary solution to the space problem until the church is able to raise funds for an enlarged building.

Suggestions for How to Begin a Second Service

One of the most frequently asked questions by pastors of growing churches is, How can I go to two worship services? They realize this is the path to growth. In the past, they have usually thought first of a larger auditorium. But a new auditorium may involve other problems, such as higher interest payments on borrowed money, unavailable ground, additional parking needed, etc. Today, the first step to growth is inaugurating multiple worship services.

Some have objected that a second service would divide the church into two congregations. However, multiple services produce a larger attendance with a greater evangelistic outreach. Most churches can't get past the barrier of 100 to 150 in attendance. They are a single-cell church. Adding a second worship service makes the church into a multiple-cell church. The church body grows by the addition of cells.

A second objection is that with two worship services, attenders wouldn't know everyone. However, statistics have proven that the average church attender is on a first-name basis with only fifty-nine people, no matter how large the attendance. So there is no threat to intimacy in two worship services. Many who enjoy the intimacy of a small church should realize they will not lose intimacy with friends. The second service provides a larger outreach, and those in the other worship service will have relationships with those in that fellowship. Remember, the purpose of a church is not that everyone know everyone, but that the church carry out the great commission.

The innovation of multiple services was first introduced by Roman Catholics as early Mass. Later mainline churches began using the multiple services, especially in metropolitan areas. Now churches all over America are beginning to use multiple services on Sunday morning to expand their outreach, solve their crowded conditions, meet the scheduling problems of their people, and reduce their financial overhead.

As you prepare to begin a second service, there are seven questions you need to ask. Answering them will help you know what to expect as you begin, and doing so may diffuse potentially explosive issues before they arise in the church.

1. Why begin a second service? Most begin a second worship service because it provides auditorium space and additional parking for church growth. Some begin a second worship service because of convenience to worshipers, and others want to provide different forms of worship. Probably the greatest reason is to turn the church into a multiple-cell church so that each worship service is a source of ministry and growth. The church with two services is no longer a single-cell church, which can't grow. The physical body and the church, which is a spiritual body, grows by the division of cells.

2. Who will come to an earlier service? Usually senior saints enjoy an earlier service as well as young singles who are not married with children. Families with children usually don't attend, so a nursery is not mandatory when first beginning an additional service.

3. What time of the year should it begin? Begin an additional worship service in early September or early spring when secular culture gives energy to the church schedule. The principle of the two-humped camel indicates attendance will grow at this time of year, contributing to the success of the additional service.

4. Should the new worship service be identical to the existing one? Some pastors have begun a second service to introduce a different type of worship experience (example: a formal liturgical or an informal praise service with audience participation). However, most pastors will lead both services from their hearts, which means they will follow in both services one form of worship. But even then the services will not be

identical. The pastor will preach the same sermon, but the expression will not be identical.

5. Should the same choir be used twice? No, because it tends to diminish their effectiveness. Use other singing groups or solos for special music in the earlier service. Using different groups or individuals will double the number of people serving the Lord through music.

6. Should the same ushers or workers be used? No. Involve more members in serving the Lord.

7. What if the auditorium is not filled? Sometimes space is not the problem that prohibits growth. It could be a lack of excitement, outreach, or limited vision that puts a cap on attendance. A new worship service can provide a step of faith or break the fear barrier. However, do not begin a new worship service in an auditorium that is already too large. The people will rattle like small stones in a box. Use a marriage or prayer chapel that will provide intimacy. If one is not available, redecorate a Sunday school room into a prayer chapel. The renovated room will contribute to church excitement.

SENILITY (See also PATHOLOGY OF CHURCH GROWTH)

Senility is a term used in church growth pathology to describe a church having a disease that keeps it from growing when there is an absence of a workable strategy for growth in a church.

SENIOR HIGH DEPARTMENT

Senior high students usually have vigor and energy, ambition, and enthusiasm. They respond to challenge. They like doing things as a group. As sex interest develops, they enjoy social activities involving the entire department. Like juniors, they are hero worshipers with more discretion—but like younger teens they need understanding and a confidant.

Keeping in mind these particular characteristics, a well-rounded church program for young people should include Bible study, expressional activities (such as Training Union or Christian Endeavor), and social activities.

Organizing a Senior High Ministry

Besides a president, vice-president, and secretary-treasurer, the class needs these committees:

Lookout committee. These young people should lead in contacting absentees and enlisting new members.

Telephone committee. This group should work with the lookout committee. They contact absentees and prospects and give social invitations.

Evangelistic committee. Members should not be afraid to talk to others about Christ and should have a pleasing personality. It is their responsibility to sponsor a reception each year for all who have committed their lives to Jesus Christ during that year.

Publicity committee. These seniors make the announcements in Sunday school concerning activities and are responsible for making posters and getting announcements in the church bulletin and other publications.

Reception committee. Members are stationed at the door to welcome new persons to class or to socials.

Sunshine committee. This group looks after class members who are ill or contacts prospects who are ill.

Social committee. Games, refreshments, programs for dinners, hikes, sports (gymnasium or outdoors), talent night, family night, mother-daughter banquet, father-son banquet, stunt nights—all these and more are the responsibility of this committee.

SEVEN TOUCHES, LAW OF

The newly saved person must be networked into the church if he will remain true to the decision he makes for Christ. Research shows that people are more likely to return for a second and third visit if they are contacted seven times after their first visit; hence the *Law of Seven Touches.* These contacts can be initiated by the church through letters, phone calls, visits, or other personal contacts. These seven touches also include times the prospect sees the church message in the Yellow Pages, billboards, advertisements, flyers, or church newsletter. The obvious conclusion is that the church that contacts the most people the most times will probably have the greatest results. However, evangelistic results never depend on only one aspect, such as the number of contacts a church makes with a prospect or the number of hearings given to the gospel. But when all aspects of evangelism are followed—including the laws of the three hearings and the seven touches—the more likely a person will respond to the gospel.

Suggested Follow-up Bonding Strategy for Your Church

When someone visits the church on a Sunday morning (usually the most common time for a person to make a first visit to a new church), he or she should be immediately followed up in accordance with the law of seven touches. The most important immediate concern of the church should be to get that visitor back the second and third time (see Three Hearings, Law of). To do this, the visitor should be contacted seven times before the next Sunday.

The first of these seven contacts or touches is Sunday afternoon. The pastor or teacher should phone the visitor and thank him for visiting with them. The phone call should establish three things. First, the caller should offer to help the family in any way he can. Second, he will want to mention the special friendship packet the church has prepared for visitors and that someone would like to deliver the packet to the visitor's home. Third, the visitor should be told the church secretary will phone for an appointment to bring the packet to the home.

The next of the seven touches occurs Sunday evening. The pastor or Sunday school teacher should write a letter covering much of what he said during the phone call. This could be a standard form letter that comes off a home computer, which goes out to visitors, but if it is a form letter, each printout of the letter should be personalized to the recipient.

Suggest a time for the visit to their home during the phone call or the follow-up letter. This can later be confirmed by the secretary. Because it is important to win the winnable while they are winnable and reach the reachable while they are reachable, many churches find Tuesday evening a good time for this second phone call. When suggesting a time, be approximate so as to give you liberty to stay longer or leave earlier on other visits you may make that evening. You might suggest you could drop by around 7:00 P.M. on Wednesday evening.

After the Tuesday evening phone call, write a letter to the prospect confirming the time of the visit. (Even though some letters arrive after the visit because of delays in postal service, it is part of the accumulative effect of follow-up.) Again express your interest in being of service to him and his family and assure him he is welcome to visit the church services as often as he can.

On Wednesday or Thursday evening, someone from the church or Sunday school class with which he would most likely attend should visit him. Ideally, it should be the teacher, but if there are a number of people to follow up, it is better that another class officer or member make the visit rather than putting it off several weeks until the teacher can make the call.

During the visit, the teacher should tell the prospect about the class and how he could fit into it. He will also want to be familiar with the rest of the church program that might be of interest to others in the family, such as childrens and youth ministries. The primary reason for visiting the home is to present Jesus Christ to the person. Beyond this, the pastor or teacher should be alert to the need in the home and share the gospel with the prospect if the opportunity arises.

The pastor or teacher should immediately take the time to write a letter to the prospect outlining the next spiritual step he should take. After the visit, the pastor should know if the person needs to accept Christ, rededicate himself, join the church, or whatever. The letter should clearly outline what is expected. The letter should also thank him for allowing the visit and again extend the invitation to visit the appropriate Sunday school class that Sunday.

An informal follow-up phone call on Saturday inviting the prospect to the Sunday school class or service the next day provides the finishing touches to a week of following up a receptive-responsive person. By the end of the week, the casual visitor has met several people from the church and recognizes the church is interested in him. Unless there is some particular reason why he cannot, it is very likely the visitor will return the following week to the church where he knows he is welcome and accepted.

SHEPHERDING, GIFT OF

The person with the gift of shepherding has the ability to serve God by overseeing, training, and caring for the needs of a group of Christians. The strengths of this gift include (1) a burden to see others learn and grow, (2) a high sense of empathy and sensitivity, and (3) a strong others-orientation in ministry.

Among the weaknesses of this gift are (1) a tendency to become overinvolved in ministry, (2) a failure to involve others, and (3) a tendency to become overprotective of people.

An individual with this gift needs to avoid the danger of (1) discouragement, (2) pride, and (3) selfishness.

SHOWING MERCY, GIFT OF

The person with the gift of showing mercy has the ability to locate those in distress and express sympathy and give spiritual help. The strengths of this gift include (1) the ability to empathize with those who have problems that affect their spirituality so that they desire the healing that is available, (2) the wisdom to place greater emphasis on emotional or spiritual needs than the physical needs, and (3) the ability to develop rapport and identity with individuals or groups.

Among the weaknesses of those with this gift are: (1) they are perceived as offering help when it is not wanted; (2) they are perceived as being too intimate with people to whom they are ministering; and (3) they have a tendency to attract to themselves those with emotional problems, those with mental retardation, the handicapped, and social misfits.

An individual with this gift needs to avoid the danger of (1) lacking firmness in dealing with people, (2) basing his life on his emotions or feeling, or (3) resenting others who are not sensitive to the inner needs of others.

SIDE-DOOR EVANGELISM

Side-door evangelism refers to an evangelistic strategy that first networks people with church members, then networks them into the activities of the church and, through these relationships, networks a person to Jesus Christ. There are three steps to side-door evangelism: first, winning the unchurched to the Christian; second, winning the unchurched to the churched; and third, winning a person to Christ.

SMALL SUNDAY SCHOOLS (See also CLASS SUNDAY SCHOOL)

While much is written about the large Sunday schools in America and around the world, the average church in the United States has about eighty-nine members. These churches do not need to feel like they can only have a second-rate ministry, but rather realize they can build on their strengths. While larger churches tend to have a citywide outreach, the smaller church can have a greater impact on a local neighborhood. Also, a smaller church is better able to provide personal pastoral care to the members of the congregation. The educational program of a smaller church can be built on the greater interaction of its members, which should result in better learning. Also, because everyone tends to be responsible for some aspect of ministry in a smaller church, this could lead to greater individual growth spiritually.

Though all agree a church must begin small, not all agree that it should remain small; nor is there agreement as to how large a church should grow. There are problems in the smaller church that can be resolved as the church grows. This growth can be best realized by building on one's strengths as a small church and being willing to adapt to the changes experienced as the church begins growing.

SOCIOLOGICAL STRANGULATION (See also PATHOLOGY OF CHURCH GROWTH)

This condition describes the church with facilities that are not capable of providing for growth. It is impossible to put a hundred pupils in a Sunday school that is designed for fifty. When facilities are not able to service the pupils, ultimately the spiritual condition of the church begins to die because of this pathology or illness.

SPAN OF CONTROL

Span of control is a basic management principle stating one manager should never have more than seven people reporting to him. This is one of the growth limiting factors in the class Sunday school.

SPIRITUAL GIFT INVENTORY

A Spiritual Gift Inventory is a tool that has been developed to help Christians identify their spiritual gift(s). This tool normally includes a questionnaire, completed by the candidate, that tends to identify areas of interest and that suggest the possibility of giftedness in different areas. One of the most popular of these inventories is that developed and distributed by Church Growth Institute in Lynchburg, Virginia, the Spiritual Gift Inventory. Other gift inventories that are distributed through Fuller Theological Seminary include the Wagner Modified Houts Questionnaire, Wesley Spiritual Gifts Questionnaire, Houts Inventory of Spiritual Gifts, and Trenton Spiritual Gifts Analysis.

SPIRITUAL GIFTS

Spiritual gifts are the abilities given to Christians to carry out the work of the church. Usually, spiritual gifts relate first to miraculous or sign gifts and second to serving gifts. Since this encyclopedia focuses on practical helps, emphasis is given to the serving gifts of believers. Also, the number of gifts differ in the list provided by different Christian teachers. The following list comes from the Spiritual Gift Inventory, Church Growth Institute, Box 4404, Lynchburg, Virginia, 24502:

Serving Gifts
- Evangelism
- Prophecy
- Teaching
- Exhortation
- Shepherding (group leadership)
- Mercy showing
- Helps
- Giving
- Administration

The Five Terms for Spiritual Gifts

The five terms for spiritual gifts are used interchangeably or explicitly in Scripture to identify spiritual gifts. These terms each occur in the introduction to the discussion of spiritual gifts in 1 Corinthians 12. An understanding of these terms will give insight into spiritual gifts and lead to a workable definition.

The Greek word *pneumatikon* is an adjective that gives meaning to the thing or person that possesses it. This word is translated "spiritual gifts" in 1 Corinthians 12:1 and 14:1. Hence, when the word is used, the author is emphasizing the spiritual nature of the gift. Therefore, the Holy Spirit, who is the source of a Christian's spirituality and who also dispenses the gift, makes the gift spiritual.

When the Greek word *charismata* is used (1 Cor. 14:1), it is translated "gifts." The root of the word comes from *charis,* which means "grace." Grace is freely given at salvation (Eph. 2:8-9), but when *charis* is used with spiritual gifts it implies a gift that is freely and graciously given. Hence, a spiritual gift is that which is not sought or earned by human initiative, but is bestowed by the Spirit.

The word *diakonia* is translated "ministries" or "administrations," but is also a reference to spiritual gifts (1 Cor. 12:5). A gift is a ministry that is given by the Lord. When the word *diakonia* is used in the context of spiritual gifts, it implies that spiritual gifts are in fact spiritual ministries. Therefore, gifts are for a purpose, to be used in ministry. The verb form *diakoneo* means "to be a servant, to serve or wait upon another person, particularly to wait on tables by serving food to guests." Hence, those who are given a spiritual gift should receive it with the purpose of serving other people. This implies a spiritual gift is not received to minister primarily to oneself, nor is a spiritual gift given to serve itself. A spiritual gift is given to serve others.

The Greek word *energema* is translated "activities" in 1 Corinthians 12:6. Paul uses this term to denote spiritual gifts as the activity produced by God having endued men and women for service. The word is derived from the verb *energeo* from which we get *energy* and implies the power or energy of God to activate or set something in motion. Hence, a spiritual gift is not the natural ability of the individual but a ministry empowered by God.

The term *phanerosis* is translated "manifestation" in 1 Corinthians 12:7 and also describes a spiritual gift. A spiritual gift is a manifestation of the Holy Spirit. The word *phanerosis* comes from the verb *phaneroo,* which means "to make visible or to make clear." A spiritual gift is identified as residing in the believer. When a Christian exercises a spiritual gift, it should be an evident work of the Holy Spirit.

Therefore, a spiritual gift is spiritual in character, sovereignly given by God the Holy Spirit, to minister to others, with an evident manifestation of the Holy Spirit through each Christian as he serves God. Spiritual gifts are the various abilities given sovereignly to believers by the Holy Spirit so that when they faithfully serve the Lord, there are spiritual results in the work of God, and each believer grows in his effectiveness and develops other spiritual abilities of service.

How to Discover Your Spiritual Gifts

1. *Study spiritual gifts.* Those who want to discover their spiritual gifts must understand the basic teaching of Scripture on spiritual gifts. Discovery is dependent upon some degree of knowledge. Therefore, a thorough study of spiritual gifts is the place to begin in an attempt to discover your spiritual gifts.

   During the 1500s, Spanish conquerors began seeking for gold among the Aztec Indians of Mexico. A legend grew up about a land called El Dorado, where gold was as plentiful as sand. Through the centuries, many explorers searched throughout Mexico for the legendary El Dorado without success. The truth is, there was very little gold to be found anywhere in Mexico.

   Those same explorers, however, might have become very rich if they had only looked for silver. Mexico is the world's fourth largest producer of silver and one of the two chief places where pure silver is found. Because they lacked knowledge, those early explorers came away empty. Many

Christians are empty in service because they don't know the riches of the spiritual gifts.

2. *Spiritual Gifts Inventory.* A Spiritual Gift Inventory test is based upon the characteristics of Christians who are known to possess the various gifts. The Spiritual Gift Inventory is provided as a part of the Friendship Evangelism resource packet. Such an inventory will not give conclusive results, but it will provide an indication of which gifts you are likely to possess.

3. *Trial and error.* One of the most important ways to discover your spiritual gifts is to get busy in the work of the Lord. Your proficiency in an area of ministry may indicate that you possess a spiritual gift or gifts. This can be a very rewarding experience, even for those who think they know what their spiritual gifts are. Trying a new area of ministry may uncover gifts that have gone undiscovered for decades.

Remember, the only people who do not make mistakes are those who never do anything. Those who succeed have usually failed many times. It may be necessary to try many things and fail at several before a gift is discovered and developed.

4. *Consult other believers.* Older and wiser Christians sometimes recognize that a believer does not have the gift that he thinks or wishes he had. Solomon referred to the wisdom of seeking the counsel of others (Proverbs 11:14; 15:22; 24:6).

Once the believer has studied all the gifts, taken the test to determine which gifts he is likely to possess, and begun the process of trial and error, he will find great wisdom in seeking the counsel of older and wiser Christians. The first deacons were chosen because the entire church observed that they had the gift of wisdom (Acts 6:3).

STAIRSTEPPING

Stairstepping refers to a systematic and natural approach of bringing people to Christ one step at a time. This is also a joint ministry of the Holy Spirit, who predisposes a person to receive Christ, and the soul winner.

Evangelism—A Process and an Event

1. Salvation (the new birth) is an event. Jesus referred to salvation as a new-birth experience (John 3:3, 5). Peter also used the analogy of birth in reference to salvation (1 Pet. 1:23). John, in his first epistle, indicated that salvation is a birth experience that begins with faith in Jesus Christ (1 John 5:1). Just as birth is an event, so salvation is an event.

   Salvation is like a light bulb; it is either on or off. The lights may gradually become brighter of dimmer, but there is a point when they are turned on. So it is with salvation. Faith may gradually grow stronger, but the exercise of faith in which a person is saved is always instantaneous.

   A birth is always an event. Look at any birth certificate. One baby is not born at all hours of the day and night. The birth certificate may state "Born alive at 2:45 A.M.," "Born alive at 5:18 P.M.," or even "Stillborn at 11:00 A.M." But it will never read, "Born from 6:40 A.M. to 11:02 A.M." A birth happens at a point in time—it is an event.

   But just as there are nine months of preparation before a birth, so a person is prepared for salvation before conversion. This is called stairstepping or preevangelism. The human life cycle begins with an event commonly referred to as conception. That event is then followed by a nine-month gestation period during which time the prenatal development process takes place. That process leads up to the event of birth. After the event of birth, another process begins. This process, called postnatal, includes further growth, development, training, and maturing. In reference to salvation, this is called post-salvation.

HUMAN LIFE-CYCLE CHART

Event	Process	Event	Process	Event
Conception	Gestation	Birth	Maturing	Death

Each contact that the church makes with a lost person should move him closer to acceptance. Just as there are nine months of prenatal growth before a baby is born, so there is usually a period of preconversion influence that brings a person to Christ. This is sometimes called preevangelism, but in Friendship Evangelism it is called "stairstepping a person to the gospel."

2. Evangelism leads to an event. The event of salvation (the new birth) is an indispensable and unalterable part of the process of evangelism. In the human life cycle, the gestation period can be and is often cut short by a premature live or dead birth. Birth, however, is essential to the completion of the life cycle.

Growing churches must not lose sight of the new-birth experience. Stairstepping cannot be completed apart from the salvation of the unsaved. Salvation is neither the beginning nor the end of the process of evangelism, but without it there is no true evangelism. Like the human life cycle, evangelism is a process (preevangelism, conversion, post-evangelism) that consists of events.

EVANGELISM LIFE-CYCLE CHART

Event	Process	Event	Process	Event
Initial Contact	Stairstepping	New Birth	Spiritual Growth	Death

Stairstepping People to a Decision for Christ

1. The process of evangelism. Stairstepping includes all that is involved in reaching the unsaved where they are and influencing them toward Christ. It is moving people through a process, which is accomplished one step at a time.

The following chart shows the entire process. The initial contact could be made with a person at any level. An unsaved person is not required to begin on the first step. Therefore, stairstepping can begin or end with any of the various steps in the process.

CONVERSION

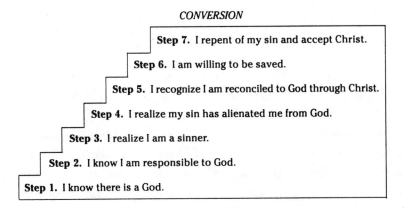

Step 7. I repent of my sin and accept Christ.

Step 6. I am willing to be saved.

Step 5. I recognize I am reconciled to God through Christ.

Step 4. I realize my sin has alienated me from God.

Step 3. I realize I am a sinner.

Step 2. I know I am responsible to God.

Step 1. I know there is a God.

2. Stairstepping is both supernatural and natural. Many things bring a person to Christ; such as the power of the gospel, the convicting work of the Holy Spirit, and the drawing of the Father. The power of God that brings salvation resides in the gospel, not in any human program or humanly devised scheme (Rom. 1:16). Only the Holy Spirit can convict the sinner (John 16:8ff.), and every possible precaution must be taken to see that no conscious or unconscious attempt is make to replace spiritual conviction with psychological pressure or human manipulation. Regardless of human effort, only God can draw sinners to himself (John 6:44).

At the same time, it is neither logical nor biblical to expect a "God-hater" to be saved without taking some intermediate steps in his understanding and acceptance of the person of God. Before he can exercise faith in Christ, he must understand the provision Christ has made for his redemption (Heb. 11:6).

In evangelism, the decision to trust Jesus Christ by faith is usually preceded by many other decisions. Some of those decisions may be subconscious, or they may come so early in life that the person has forgotten that he made them. An unsaved person does not repent and trust Christ until he sees his need for the gospel. Looking at the stairstepping process, it is obvious that each step is dependent upon the one before it. Stairstepping is natural to Friendship Evangelism.

3. Entry level to stairstepping. The first step of an individual toward God is determined by his need. As previously stated, that could be on step five, six or even seven of the stairstepping process. The important thing is that the process begin at the sinner's understanding of the gospel. Then he must proceed to salvation.

Stairstepping is nothing more than a systematic and natural approach of bringing people to Christ. It allows the Christian to keep the ultimate objective in clear focus and, at the same time, see where he is in the process of evangelism. The unique quality of stairstepping is that it takes the guesswork out of evangelism and provides an objective means of measuring progress.

All Christians must be aware of the stairstepping goal. They will come in contact with people on different steps. Their aim is to network people into the church and stairstep them to a meaningful decision for Christ. Barriers must be removed. The unsaved must hear the gospel often so they will become more receptive to it.

The key to getting started is determining where the prospect is in relationship to God. Then, the believer must know what entry level to make in witnessing to him. Once a relationship has been made, the process of evangelism is a matter of stairstepping the prospect toward faith in Christ.

STANDARDS, SUNDAY SCHOOL

Policies

The Sunday school should have definite governing principles so that it may function efficiently and effectively. It should be:

1. A Sunday school organized to teach Bible content.
2. A Sunday school organized to change the life according to New Testament concept.
3. A Sunday school constituted to promote fellowship of believers one with another.
4. A Sunday school administered to work in harmony with the Christian home.
5. A place where people can administer their spiritual gifts.
6. A Sunday school composed of teachers grounded in the

Word of God and trained to meet the needs of individual pupils.

7. A Sunday school designed to have an evangelistic thrust into the community.
8. A Sunday school founded to nurture the spiritual growth of teachers and staff.
9. A Sunday school departmentalized to meet each pupil on his own age level.
10. A Sunday school planned for expansion.
11. A Sunday school informed concerning the denomination and ready to cooperate with it.
12. A Sunday school established with a definite financial budget.

Personnel

The Sunday school should have definite policy concerning the spiritual and academic standards of the personnel responsible for its ministry. Besides being saved, the Sunday school teacher should have the following qualifications:

1. The gift of teaching (Eph. 4:11)
2. A thorough knowledge of the Word of God (2 Tim. 3:15-17)
3. Daily devotions consisting of prayer and Bible study
4. Regular church attendance (Heb. 10:25)
5. Planning and administrative ability
6. Leadership qualities; the ability to inspire confidence
7. Vision—ability to view the job objectively and not become discouraged in it (Phil. 3:13-14)
8. Ability to communicate—to express himself or herself
9. A cheerful, radiant personality
10. A manifested love for children
11. Patience
12. The ability and desire to counsel
13. Originality; ability to create an interesting and diversified class session

The teachers duties would be:
1. Regularity in teaching the class
2. Visitation of the pupils' homes
3. Arrival in class fifteen minutes ahead of time

4. Attendance at Sunday school teachers' meetings
5. Acquaintance with pupils through socials, etc.

The Sunday school should have a regular progress evaluation for the teachers. The above qualifications are desirable for substitute teachers where possible.

Pupils

The Sunday school should have definite plans for the conversion and spiritual growth of each pupil. These plans are as follows:

1. Salvation of every constituent Sunday school pupil
   a. Need of salvation
   b. Provision of salvation
   c. Acceptance of salvation
   d. Consequence of salvation
      (1) Dedication
      (2) Consecration
2. A systematic program to develop full growth into Christian maturity.
   a. Teach pupil to grow to maturity in Christ.
      (1) Bible study
      (2) Prayer
      (3) Witnessing
      (4) Memory Work
   b. Church membership
      (1) Instruction in church membership
      (2) Baptism
      (3) Reception of members
   c. Church education
      (1) Sunday school administration
      (2) Teacher training
      (3) Personal evangelism
3. Development of a social life that is honorable to God
   a. Teacher-pupil relationship
   b. Participation in wholesome social activities
4. Development of a friendly relationship between the home and the Sunday school

Progress

The Sunday school should make definite plans for progress. Increased attendance, improvement of organization, and the addition of equipment should all contribute to the salvation and spiritual progress of the student. To ensure progress in the Sunday school, the following are required:

1. Teacher training for the new teacher and in-service training
2. Promotions each year for greater interest and incentive at all age levels
3. Evangelistic outreach within the Sunday school
4. Mission program to broaden the vision of the home church
5. Prayer
6. A Home Department
7. Division of departments as Sunday school grows
8. A board of Christian education made up of department heads and Christian education director
9. Training in the use of audiovisuals
10. Extension work, ministry to prisons or hospitals, mission work, youth groups, mission Sunday school, visitation

Public Relations

The Sunday school should use varying methods of serving its students and reaching its community by means of visitation, advertisements, and transportation. Such a goal would call for:

1. A well-organized visitation program
2. A follow-up program for absentees
3. Transportation for those who desire to come but have no means
4. A well-organized publicity campaign to make the church and community aware of the events of the Sunday school
5. Attention given to the total image of Sunday school in the mind of the public
6. A well-planned church calendar to coordinate special events and meetings in the church

Property

The Sunday school should maintain adequate facilities and

equipment for effectively housing and teaching its pupils. Ideally Sunday schools should have:

1. Twenty-five square feet per pupil per building or ten square feet of prime educational space per pupil
2. Strategic location in the center of its locale
3. Separate classrooms for each class and separate rooms for departmental activities
4. Windows in each room if possible
5. Adequate heating (72° F), lighting (natural if possible), and ventilation (air-conditioning)
6. Decorations—inner decor should create a cheerful, pleasant atmosphere
7. Adequate washroom facilities, including facilities for younger children as well as adults
8. Nursery Department equipped with cribs, washable toys, baby-bottle warmer, separate wash room
9. Equipment suited to each level, with chairs, tables, shelves, pictures, bulletin boards adapted to height of the children
10. Projectors, screens, flannel boards, chalkboards, record player, and other visual aids available. A visual aid file would be helpful.
11. A library with a good selection of books for all ages
12. Cloakroom space provided for each department
13. A piano available in each department area
14. Storage space provided for all equipment, which should be organized and labeled
15. Proper fire exits and equipment available, and attention drawn to them frequently
16. Kitchen facilities to provide for socials, programs, and other needs
17. A Sunday school office with sufficient space for workers, records, filing system, Sunday school materials
18. First-aid kit available in Sunday school office
19. Wastepaper baskets in each room and arrangements made for proper method of garbage disposal

STANDARDS FOR SUNDAY SCHOOL WORKERS

Standards for Sunday school workers are the minimum requirements that might be expected of anyone who holds an elected or
appointed office in the Sunday school. Prospective Sunday school
workers who do not measure up to the church's minimum standards should be challenged to take steps to do so prior to being
enlisted. Because each church is different, the specific standards
in each church will be different. A sample statement outlining
standards for workers that is used by many churches is, "All
elected and appointed workers in this Sunday school shall be
saved, active members of the church in agreement with the doctrinal position of the church, tithers, soul winners, loyal to the
pastor, and living a separated Christian life." (See also Standards,
Sunday School.)

STEWARDSHIP CAMPAIGN

Most churches hold their stewardship campaigns in the month of
November or January. During this month attention is focused on
stewardship. Usually, Sunday school lessons emphasize the Christian's stewardship for God. Then letters are mailed from the
church, reminding people about the church budget, the stewardship theme of the year, and the person's responsibility to tithe.
The pastor usually preaches a series of sermons on stewardship.
Then, lay people are asked to give testimonies in the church
service about why they tithe. This is a stewardship campaign
centered around a theme such as "God Is Able" or "Tithing Is
Christian." The intent is to get every person in church to be aware
of his responsibility to God and to be obedient in giving through
the church.

Whereas some churches emphasize money almost every week
of the year, this is not the path to successful stewardship. A pastor
correctly noted, "I teach stewardship once a year, then our people
give faithfully for the rest of the year. I don't mention giving until
next January."

Church campaigns are biblical. Just as a church has a campaign
for soul winning, foreign missions, or a campaign to especially
emphasize Bible reading, a church ought to emphasize steward-

ship during a designated time of the year. The biblical basis is that whatever God has commanded his people to do, the pastor and church ought to motivate the congregation to perform. A stewardship campaign is an organized program to educate and motivate everyone to faithfulness.

Many mistakenly think that stewardship is just fund-raising. They often think that a stewardship program in a local church is raising money much as a community agency raises money. Even though money is raised during a stewardship campaign for the church budget, that is not the bottom line. Stewardship is not talking people out of their money. It is teaching people how to use their money properly. *Stewardship* is a biblical term that Jesus used to emphasize our obligation to him.

A steward is a money manager, usually a servant who manages the household for the owner of the house or the farm (managing money, time, resources, and personnel). Jesus used the illustration of good stewards and bad stewards to teach how we should be stewards for him.

A Christian should manage his time (schedule), talent, and money for God. Part of a stewardship campaign is to teach that all money belongs to God, not just 10 percent (the tithe), because God wants all of our money to glorify him. A Christian should spend all of his money wisely, find more bargains, and get more out of life; but first, he should automatically give 10 percent to God.

A stewardship campaign is not to get money for the church; it's to teach believers how to live the abundant life. When Christians obey the financial principles of the Bible, their lives will be lived more abundantly, and God's work will be financed.

Why a Stewardship Campaign

1. *To help strengthen Christians.* The purpose of stewardship is to strengthen every believer in the local church. Every person should be taught how to handle money—from a child who may have an allowance of one dollar a week, to a senior saint who may have little to give.

   Stewardship emphasizes that all money belongs to God. If we realize we do not own our money, it is easier to give it back to God. As an illustration, if we drive a company car, we know that it is not our car, but is to be used for business. That attitude is how God wants us to treat our possessions. God is letting us use the money he gives to us for his business. A Christian's business is God's business. Just as a company gives a salesman rules and limits how the company car is to be used, God has instructed us how to use our time, talent, and treasures. Therefore, a stewardship program should educate church members how to manage their time, talent, and treasures for the glory of God.

A Christian is called to be a disciple, which means one who lives a disciplined life. Since stewardship is management or discipleship, it is an expression of the Christian life. Stewardship does not just involve money, it involves something deeper. It involves our discipleship to Jesus Christ, which can be expressed in the way we use our money.

2. *To help all Christians become obedient.* During January, a campaign is conducted to help every Christian obey God in managing his time, talent, and treasure. That is why stewardship letters are mailed to every person in the congregation. Some marginal members will not attend church to hear the stewardship sermons and see the stewardship posters. Also, a phoning campaign is initiated to contact every person in the congregation. Why? Not just to get money, but to help everyone to obey God and become a steward of his resources.

A Christian cannot become spiritual without being obedient. Therefore, a stewardship campaign cannot be viewed as something carnal because it involves money. The campaign should be viewed as the highest expression of spiritual ministry in the Sunday school year. If conducted properly, more people will obey Jesus Christ and follow his lordship.

3. *To identify and help backsliders.* During a stewardship campaign, every person in the church is contacted. One hardened church member once complained, "The only time you contact me is during a stewardship campaign." While the visitors or those who make the telephone contacts should do more than talk about money, the man complaining should be

grateful that someone was concerned about his spirituality. Lax church members are contacted for that reason, because they are lax. Too often the faithful are exhorted to give money, and they are already doing it. In a stewardship campaign, those who need to become faithful are exhorted to become stewards.

4. *To share our blessings.* God does not ask those who have nothing to give to him, nor does God ask for a fixed amount. God only asks for stewardship after he has given to us. In the different parables of the vineyard, the landowner came for his share after there was fruit on the vine. The workers were expected to manage a vineyard for the owner. But once there was a harvest, the owner wanted his share of the harvest. As Christians, we are the workers, and God is the owner. Our stewardship is to manage the vineyard for him. Everything in this world belongs to God, who created it and redeemed us.

The psalmist recognized the source of all of his benefits and responded, "I will praise You, for I am fearfully and wonderfully made; marvelous are Your works, and that my soul knows very well" (Ps. 139:14). When Christians see how much God has given to them, it is embarrassing to see how little they return to him. A good steward will manage his resources for his master's best interest.

5. *To reveal our hearts.* The problem with possessions is that they possess us, rather than our possessing them.

On many occasions, partners have gone into business and have enjoyed working together until there was a profit, or money on the table to be divided. The best friendships have been destroyed when there was money involved.

Many children weep together at funerals because of the loss of a parent. But when it comes time to divide the inheritance, their greed becomes evident. They argue, fight, and take one another to court. Harvesttime reveals the selfish hearts of people.

A stewardship campaign will touch the nerve of Christians in the church because it touches their money after they make it. When money possesses the Christian, he is in a dangerous position. So, once a year during a stewardship campaign, every Christian is reminded that all of his money belongs to God.

A wealthy man went from church to church telling how he gave his last twenty dollars to God. He testified that because he sacrificed all, God made him a multimillionaire. A lady stood in one of his meetings and asked, "Why don't you do it again?"

"What do you mean?" the millionaire asked.

"Why don't you give your last million to God now?" the lady responded. The millionaire was embarrassed.

A stewardship campaign reveals the heart of all Christians because they are brought to the place where they must account for the way God has blessed them during the past year. It is a time of self-evaluation, commitment to God, and potentially a time for revival.

6. *To give to God.* Like any investment-oriented businessman, God expects a good return on his resources. He has placed Christians in control of his business—his ministry in the world. In the parables of Jesus, it is significant that whenever the master went on a long journey, he always came back looking for a return from his farm. In application, God created us in his image and likeness. He has given us a good mind, a strong will, and the opportunity to make something of our life for his glory. God now comes and wants us to use our gifts and abilities for him. During a stewardship campaign, every Christian should be reminded that he should return finances to God so that the work of God may prosper.

7. *To teach judgment.* Once a year, the church teaches stewardship to all its people. Again, it is not primarily to get money from its people. Christians should know that they will be judged. That judgment is based on stewardship. In the parables of Jesus about landowners, they judged their managers based on their faithfulness. When the owner delegated the vineyard to a steward, it did not mean that the steward owned it. Even though the workers developed an emotional attachment to the vines and the vineyard, the farm still did

not belong to them. The workers always treated the farm as if it were their own. The issue is always ownership. Who owned the vineyard?

Once a year during the stewardship campaign, Christians need to be reminded "who owns the vineyard." That means they are reminded who owns their house, their bodies, and their investment portfolio. If God is the owner of all things, and he allows Christians to manage them for his glory, then there is coming a judgment day.

God will judge Christians based on their stewardship (management). They will not be judged for what they did not have, but for what they have done with what they have been given. Some sit in a pew and think that God doesn't need their possessions. That is not the issue. Others think that they need to give God some money to get the church through the week. Christians treat the church like an automobile. They put enough money in the plate to buy gas and to get God through this week, and then they will help God out again next Sunday. We do not give money to God to help him out. He owns our resources, we manage them for him. We give back to God what is his.

First, every Christian needs to settle the issue of ownership. Does God own him? Second, every Christian needs to settle the issue of trust. Is he going to trust God with his money, or is he going to trust himself?

The bottom line of a stewardship campaign is faith. People actually have difficulty in trusting God.

Jim Elliott, a missionary martyred in South America by primitive tribesmen that he sought to reach with the gospel, once observed, "He is no fool who gives what he cannot keep to gain what he cannot lose." What we keep selfishly for ourselves we eventually lose.

Different people respond to stewardship in different ways. Some people learn the lessons of stewardship, prosper, and evangelize properly. There are always those who complain and say, "The church is after money." We must be careful to deal with the problem of criticism before it turns into the poison of bitterness. When a person is cut and injured, there is pain associated with the wound. We never doubt the wisdom of the doctor who inflicts more pain on the already sore area by applying a painful medication or antiseptic to the wound. The doctor doesn't do it to needlessly hurt but to help in the healing process. Without the medication, there would be the risk of infection. Without the teaching on stewardship, Christians risk the infection of selfishness, materialism, and worldliness.

STEWARDSHIP, FIVE POCKETS

There are five motivations for giving to the church. These are called "Five Pockets." These "pockets" are not literal but are symbolic pictures representing the five major motives of church members in giving to their church. When church leaders understand the nature and source of their financial income, they can better plan a strategy for outreach and growth.

In the first pocket there is money for "light and heat bills." This represents the desire to contribute to the general fund. Members are motivated out of concern to give for the operating expenses of the church. The "light-and-heat" pocket represent salaries, supplies, utilities, and general maintenance.

The second pocket has money for "missions." Certain members want most of their money to go to foreign missions, and often members want at least some money to go to outreach, usually out of their concern for the great commission.

The third pocket has money to buy "ivy walls." Because some church members value higher education, they direct their money to build college classrooms, libraries, or equip science laboratories.

The fourth pocket contains money for the "cup of cold water." These members have compassion for the needs of their hurting brothers. They give to feeding projects, hospitals, and to provide housing and emergency relief.

The last pocket contains money for "brick and mortar." This is money specially earmarked for church buildings. Some will give large amounts here and usually will fund no other project. However, almost all members want to give something for their church building project.

Some church leaders hesitate to enter a stewardship campaign because things are tight in the "light-and-heat" pocket. A church's inability to properly meet its operation needs is not a proper reason to hold back a building campaign. However, understanding the following principle should overcome that heresy:

First, money in one pocket usually will not go for projects of another pocket. Even though a church has no excess finances to pay bills does not mean it cannot raise excess money for a new sanctuary, for missions, or to support its denominational college. The emotional or spiritual commitment of members usually does not transfer from one project to another.

Second, money in the "brick-and-mortar" pocket that is not collected will be lost to the church. Finances that are not given to local church members will usually go to an interdenominational or humanitarian agency. Therefore to postpone a capital fund project means the church is losing money it could otherwise use.

Third, church leaders are not aware of what members have in their pockets until the members are presented with a financial challenge. People give in response to a challenge, and their preference is unknown until they give. Therefore, a capital stewardship campaign may be a step of faith because the church has no history of giving to a building fund. It is, however, a step of faith based on the fact that Christians have a "brick-and-mortar" pocket.

Fourth, once a member's pocket is opened, he will give again from that same pocket with the same motivation to the same type of need. Just as members give their tithes and offerings regularly for the ongoing church expense, so those with a "brick-and-mortar" pockets will continue to give because that preference fulfills their need.

In conclusion, knowledge of giving habits by church members will help church leaders plan a healthy continuous strategy for financial enlargement that will provide for church growth.

STORYTELLING

Storytelling is effective from the beginning stages of learning to the adult level, although its greatest value may be with teaching children. Stories can usually be used anytime and anywhere. They can be used as a part of a lecture, as illustrations during the discussion, as a part of worship, or as "filler material" if the lesson is too short. Choose stories carefully. Make them an integral part of the lesson or worship. Because everyone loves stories, use them well.

A story may be used to present salvation, create and hold interest, introduce new ideas, or enable listeners to put themselves into real-life situations. A story can help to clarify wrong ideas, give solutions for existing problems, and train in moral conduct. It can create desirable attitudes or receptivity to new truths and experiences. A story develops the imagination, cultivates a sense of humor, and tends to relax the listeners. People will remember a story when they have forgotten everything else. A story wraps up abstract truth in life experiences that are easily understood.

A story is a narrative about persons or events that should arouse interest from the start and sustain it through the climax. A story is not a report, a series of descriptions, or a succession of events. A story should have an introduction that captures interest and establishes the problem. It should have a logical order of events, a climax, and a conclusion that leaves no questions or loose ends.

Choosing a Story

1. *Occasion.* When choosing a story, keep the occasion in mind. For example, do not choose one of the hair-raising Old Testament battle tales for a worship period. If the story is part of a lesson, be sure the point of the story is the same as that of the lesson. Some stories can be used to illustrate more than one type of lesson, but don't stretch the application too far.

2. *Length.* Keep in mind the length of the story. Be guided by the amount of time for a lesson. You would not want to take the whole period in telling just the story. If you don't know how much time you will have, choose a story that can be easily lengthened or shortened in the telling. The age group will help determine the length of the story. Very small children would usually rather hear two or three short stories than one

L=Leader
GM=Group Member

long one. The interest span of a four-year-old is much shorter than that of a ten-year-old.

3. *Age group.* The age of the listeners will also determine many other factors. For very small children choose stories within their sphere of experience. The details should not be lengthy, and there should be a minimum of description. Juniors and intermediates love "hero" stories and a great deal of action. Teenagers and grown-ups alike want details, realism, little repetition, and a strong climax. Perhaps one exception to the limit on repetition is the story of Tiki-tiki-tembo, where the repetition of the long name becomes an integral part of the plot. Use vocabulary suitable to the audience. Big words only bore children and impress few teenagers. Moreover, if listeners do not understand the words, they lose some of the story. The continuity is broken.

Preparing the Story

1. *Read it.* Read it through several times to acquaint yourself thoroughly with it, until all names and places are familiar. If there are unusual names, check pronunciation in a dictionary. Practice saying them aloud until they give no trouble. Stumbling on words causes children to giggle or become annoyed.

2. *Outline it.* When you are well acquainted with the story, outline it on paper. Beginning with the first incident, number the incidents in order, and then learn the outline thoroughly. There is nothing that can throw you off more quickly than to forget an incident, only to discover later that you have no explanation for some result. Children sense this quickly and are puzzled. The same holds true for characters in the story. To have some unknown and unmentioned person suddenly figure in the climax can throw the listener off the track and lessen the effect of the climax.

3. *Find the climax.* Find the climax of the story, and let all that comes before build toward that climax. When the climax has been reached, draw the story to a quick end. Dragging a story out leads to moralizing, which simply bores the listener.

4. *Fill in the details.* Color and suspense depend on the details. Too many will deaden your story, but the right amount will help listeners picture the scenes and will add to the suspense. Times and places are important, as are names and relationships.

5. *Practice your story.* Always practice your story before you tell it. It is easy to think it through and decide you know it, but it is something else to get up and tell it. Listen to your tone patterns. A singsong voice annoys a listener as much as a dead voice. Practice in front of a mirror to see how you appear to your audience. Check nervous habits. For example, if you sway from one foot to the other you will make your listeners dizzy. Or you may have a furious scowl on your face as the action becomes more intense. If some youngster is handy, practice the story on him. His reaction will reveal the success you are likely to have on a group of children of the

same age. If he becomes bored, check the story for action. If he loves it, leave it alone.

Telling the Story

1. *Be natural.* Be relaxed at all times, and do not be afraid to use motions to illustrate the action. To point "far down the road" helps children sense distance; but to stomp your feet for "the sound of many feet passing by" will probably disturb the listeners, or set off little feet stomping with you. Action is one of the best tools in storytelling. To say someone is coming, running or walking is far more interesting than merely to say someone is there. To put the stone into David's slingshot, whirl the sling, and let the stone fly will set children on the edge of their seats. But merely telling them David killed the giant with his slingshot may seem funny or even impossible to them.

2. *Speak directly to the audience.* If you look at them as you speak, they will respond more than if you gaze at the ceiling or the back wall. If you look in one direction for a long time, children may turn and look in that direction. Look at the audience; be interested in their reactions. They will, in turn, be more interested in you and your story.

3. *Use color and action when you tell a story.* A certain amount of description is good, but too much can deaden the story. For example, the description of the court in the story of Queen Esther will fire the imagination of any child. Giving the color of objects in the story stimulates the imagination of the listener and heightens the interest.

4. *Be enthusiastic.* The persuaded persuade. Your own interest in the story and the way you tell it determine how it will be received. If you are enthusiastic, the listeners will be enthusiastic, for enthusiasm is contagious. Your tone of voice will indicate your interest. A period or question mark where an exclamation belongs will not inspire your audience. Check tonal habits again. Use the range of your natural voice—loud or soft for emotional variations, rising or falling at the right place.

SUNDAY SCHOOL—DEFINITION

Because our society is changing, some have suggested the age of the Sunday school is past. However, the future of Sunday school is bright, and God will continue to use the Sunday school as the evangelistic and educational arm of the church. Still, the Sunday school must adapt to continue its influence. The Sunday school must not change its purpose, but it must go back to the basics.

The Sunday school is not an agency separate or apart from the church, but it is perhaps the best structured agency in the church for carrying out the ministry of Christ most effectively. The Sunday school is defined as the reaching, teaching, winning, maturing, or nurturing arm of the church.

Some people have the wrong idea about Sunday school and as a result fail to see its importance in the revitalization and growth of their church. They think Sunday school is only for kids, or that it is an outdated method. Others think of Sunday school as a place where contest losers are rewarded with a pie in the face. Someone repeating this tortured view said, "When is a school not a school? When it is a Sunday school."

Just as the New Testament church was built on teaching and preaching, so the modern biblical church must be built on Bible study in Sunday school and exhortation in the preaching service. Sunday school is still functionally defined as the reaching, teaching, winning, maturing arm of the church. This fourfold nature of Sunday school is perhaps best expressed in an Old Testament verse that has often been used in the historic Sunday school conventions to express the nature of Sunday school: "Gather the people together, men and women and little ones, and the stranger who is within your gates, that they may hear and that they may learn to fear the LORD your God and carefully observe all the words of this law" (Deut. 31:12). This verse reflects the four distinct areas of Sunday school ministry.

Sunday School Is the Reaching Arm

First, Sunday school is the evangelistic reaching arm of the church. Reaching is defined as making contact with a person and motivating him to give an honest hearing to the gospel. Since evangelism is giving out the gospel, reaching is basically preevangelism; for it is what we do to get people to listen to the gospel. In Deuteronomy 31:12, reaching is expressed in the word *gather.* Note those who are gathered: (1) men, (2) women, (3) little ones or children, and (4) the stranger. Most church members have someone within their sphere of influence who is a stranger to the church who could be gathered into the church.

Sunday School Is the Teaching Arm

Second, Sunday school is the teaching arm of the church. Teaching is guiding the learning activities that meet human needs. The first step of teaching is expressed in the words of Deuteronomy 31:12, "that they may hear." The ultimate step of teaching is "that they may learn."

Sunday School Is the Winning Arm

Sunday school is also the arm of the church that wins people to Christ. Winning is defined as communicating the gospel in an understandable manner and motivating a person to respond to Christ and become a member of his church. The expression "fear the Lord" found in Deuteronomy 31:12 means "bringing a person to reverential trust." It is a concept of salvation. Today we might describe "fear the Lord" as a person getting saved, receiving Christ, or trusting the Lord for salvation.

Sunday School Is the Maturing Arm

Finally, Sunday school is the maturing arm of the church. Maturing is bringing a person to completion or making him well rounded. One of the objectives of every Sunday school should be the nurturing of every member so that each "carefully observes all the words of this law." Some call this nurturing, others call it training.

Sunday school is the reaching, teaching, winning, maturing arm of the church. However, this definition becomes a mosaic when applied to individual churches. Just as it takes all the pieces of tile to make up a mosaic picture, so it takes all four aspects of the definition to describe a beautiful Sunday school. But some destroy the beauty when they focus on one section of the tile and lose the whole picture. This happens when some have a strong reaching dynamic resulting in an abundance of visitors, such as a Sunday school with a dominant busing outreach. These focus on numbers so much that they lose the total perspective of ministry. Some are strong teaching Sunday schools with a deep commitment to Bible mastery. Other Sunday schools are committed to soul winning, and their success is measured by how many they have won to Christ or prepared for church membership. Finally, some Sunday schools are maturity oriented. These are committed to nurturing and caring for pupils. They measure their effectiveness by the quality of change in the life-styles of their pupils.

From generation to generation there seems to be different emphasis on the character of Sunday school. In the early seventies, the emphasis was on reaching with attention given to Sunday school busing and Sunday school contests. The correct emphasis is on the teaching arm. The Sunday school was the steeple, but it is becoming the foundation. The steeple is the most visible part of a church building and its most symbolic emblem. The teaching foundation of the Sunday school will give the church of the twenty-first century stability and direction. In keeping with this shift in emphasis is an obvious attendance pattern. Visitors attend the preaching service first, not like past years when they visited Sunday school first. The modern American Sunday school runs 24 percent under the attendance of the average church service.

Vince Lombardi, former football coach in the National Football League, was described as beginning each season by emphasizing the basics. He would hold up a football before his veterans and announce, "This is a football." Then he would point to the yard markers on the field and explain how they would hike the ball, block the opponent, and then run and pass the ball over the goal line for a touchdown. Winning football began when a team mastered the basics. A winning Sunday school begins when the superintendent and teachers master the basics. The great commission tells us to reach the lost, teach them God's Word, win them to Jesus and mature them in the faith. This is the formula for a growing Sunday school.

SUNDAY SCHOOL OFFICERS (See also specific officers)

A well organized Sunday school gives specific responsibilities to its workers and effectiveness to its ministry. These workers or

Sunday school officers include the Sunday school superintendent, department superintendents, teachers, the curriculum secretary, and other such workers as the unique needs of a particular Sunday school may require.

SUNDAY SCHOOL TEACHER

Inasmuch as there is no institution in the world like the Sunday school, we cannot define a Sunday school teacher by comparing him to anyone else. We must go to the Word of God for a description.

The Sunday school teacher has the same responsibility to his class as the pastor has to his flock. We can define a Sunday school teacher as the extension of pastoral ministry into the life of the class. Therefore, to understand the duty of a Sunday school teacher we need to examine the role of the pastor (see Pastor).

Everything a pastor is to his congregation, the Sunday school teacher should be to his class. As the pastor is an example, so the Sunday school teacher is an example. As the pastor must teach the Word of God, so must the Sunday school teacher. As the pastor must visit, so must the Sunday school teacher.

Notice the three responsibilities of the pastor in Acts 20:28-30. These are the responsibilities of a Sunday school teacher.

1. *To lead the flock*. Paul told the elders at Ephesus that they were to take heed to themselves and the flock that God had permitted them to oversee. The leader must lead by example. He must lead by making the correct decisions. He must lead by motivating his people to follow. A Sunday school teacher is first and foremost a spiritual leader.

2. *To feed the flock*. Just as the pastor is to feed all the flock, so the Sunday school teacher should give the Word of God to the pupils. He teaches by lecture, by questions and answers, by visual aids, by repetition, and by explanation. The teacher should use every means possible to reach every pupil.

3. *To protect the flock*. Paul warned the elders that savage wolves would come from the outside and enter the flock. Therefore they were to be watchful. Also, he warned of some arising from within the flock to tear it apart. Just as a shepherd must protect his sheep, so a pastor must protect his

congregation. Following this example, the Sunday school teacher must protect his flock. This means visitation. If a young girl is absent two weeks in a row, the teacher should mail a card, contact her by phone, and/or make a personal visit. Some teachers have the mistaken notion that visitation is an American publicity device to balloon attendance. Not so. A teacher visits to protect straying lambs. Even those who are sick need a "protective call" to encourage them in the faith. The old adage remains true: A home-going teacher makes a church-going pupil.

Qualifications of a Sunday School Teacher

A Sunday school teacher not only must be a born-again believer, he must have experienced a spiritual change in his life. To be qualified to present the gospel of Jesus Christ to the unsaved, he must have the assurance of his own salvation. His spiritual life must be established on a good foundation. He must be wholly separated (set apart) from the lusts of the world.

The Sunday school teacher can maintain a consistent spiritual life by daily yielding himself to the Spirit of God. He must daily feed himself from the Word of God to mature in Christ.

The Sunday school teacher must agree with the local church in theology so that there will be no conflict of purposes: Pupils will be taught the same biblical doctrines in both Sunday school and worship services.

A Sunday school teacher must be faithful and regular in church and class attendance, unless ill. If ill, he must inform the superintendent so that he can get a substitute teacher. As a member of the church, he must participate in its activities as well as in the activities of his own class.

A teacher is a builder; each pupil, a temple. Therefore the teacher's construction work is most important. First, it consists of leading each pupil to accept Jesus Christ as Lord and Savior. Second, it is building upon that foundation a life free and wholesome—a life that seeks to become everything that God intended, through his grace and power.

Some of the requirements of such a teacher are:

1. *Purpose and perseverance.* The first essential characteristic

of any builder is dedication to the job. Unless personal consecration has been made, it will be impossible to rightly shoulder responsibilities as a Sunday school teacher. There will be no experience to draw upon to help others build their Christian lives.

A teacher must be able to say with Paul, "Brethren, I do not count myself to have apprehended; but one thing I do, forgetting those things which are behind and reaching forward to those things which are ahead, I press toward the goal for the prize of the upward call of God in Christ Jesus" (Phil. 3:13-14).

A life thus consecrated to the will of God is ready to be used of him, ready to help build those temples which, for a short while, have been entrusted to his labor. This consecration needs to be daily. It needs to be the prayer before every period of preparation and before entering every class. Only with daily instruction from the Master Builder can a teacher rightly build his own temple—and help build someone else's.

2. *Inspiration.* A teacher needs ability to inspire those with whom he works. He can't inspire anyone else unless he is inspired. The teacher who matter-of-factly presents the lesson, with little enthusiasm, will never receive the response from the class that the vibrant, enthusiastic teacher arouses.

There also must be a zest for living in the heart of the teacher, a wholesome interest in life, and a sense of wonder. Vibrant, exuberant Christianity is contagious. Try it on pupils. Take them into God's outdoors. Few children are too young or too old to be awed by the beauties of nature.

Take time to let Psalm 19 sink in. Let childhood wonder take over; let pupils send your spirit soaring. Then bring that wonder and thrill to class. Let pupils know the thrill of trying to behold the love of the Father. If a teacher is completely inspired, captured in mind and spirit, that thrill is transmitted to the class.

3. *Experience.* Another requirement of a builder is experience, for we teach best out of our own experiences. We may be prone to shrink from experience, not knowing whether or not it will be pleasant. But Jesus never shrank from experience.

He welcomed it. He seized all opportunities. He went into the wilderness, knowing he would have to face both physical and spiritual hardships, some new to him. Yet he went willingly, knowing that what he would endure there would equip him for his ministry.

In our quest to become wise master-builders, we must seek experiences to enrich life and make teaching come alive. Illustrations then will crowd in upon us, and extensive research will be unnecessary.

Our experiences may not be sensational, but through them our Christian life will be deepened and our character strengthened. A study of the lives of many great saints also can be of great value, for their problems and experiences parallel contemporary ones.

4. *Knowledge.* A builder also needs to study, to know his materials and tools. A teacher must be a scholar and constant seeker for knowledge even though the field is so great the course cannot be completed in a lifetime.

Many teachers think that with a knowledge of the Bible, they are well-advanced in the field of teaching. True, a Sunday school teacher needs to know what is in the Bible. But he also must know how to interpret those truths and how to translate them into the everyday experiences of class members, to make them meaningful and significant.

Every teacher needs to know where to find help in understanding difficult portions of Scripture. He or she will seek such aids as pictures, filmstrips, stories, and the like, to make the lesson more vivid and real.

The wise teacher will seek to know the particular needs of the age group with which he is working, to know how best to reach the pupils. He needs to study the psychology of the age group; to understand the children and their reactions. An interested teacher will learn the background of each pupil, understand his personal needs, and help him adjust to his particular environment.

5. *Curiosity.* A teacher must possess an inquisitive or exploratory nature. If he doesn't happen to possess this charac-

teristic, it can be developed. One of the first steps in learning is a healthy curiosity. This is true in teaching. Teaching is both exploration and discovery. Second Corinthians 4:7 says, "But we have this treasure in earthen vessels, that the excellence of the power may be of God and not of us." This can be interpreted to mean that there is a treasure in every individual, placed there by God. It is the privilege and duty of the teacher to help the pupil find that treasure so that it may be used to the glory of God.

SUNDAY SCHOOL TEACHERS' MEETING

The Sunday school teachers' meeting is a tool for leadership education. It brings workers together at regular intervals for conference, study, fellowship, business transactions, and inspiration. One leading Christian educator has described it as "an educational session of the school's workers for the purpose of exchanging ideas, receiving inspiration and instruction, and achieving unity in common objectives and programs." Another adds the idea that it is held "with a view to improving [their work]."

It is in the teachers' meeting that: (1) problems are presented and considered and (2) a solution is sought; (3) new plans of work are talked over; (4) failures are faced and the causes are discovered; (5) successes are reviewed and the reasons found; and (6) programs of action are formulated. It is a democratic meeting where each has a voice, and all have the common interest of the church and its school at heart.

While the meeting emphasizes teacher improvement, the devotional, educational, and fellowship aspects also are recognized as important. Workers need constant training to keep abreast of the times. They also need incentives and inspiration to accomplish the best results. They grow under the challenge to faithful, sustained effort, brought about by contact with fellow workers under conditions that stimulate and quicken interest, cement friendships, enlarge visions, deepen their sense of responsibility, strengthen loyalty, and motivate them to do the best work possible.

Purpose of the Teachers' Meeting

The primary purpose of the teachers' meeting is educational. It is the means whereby workers learn to plan and carry on a better program of teaching. It must be a cooperative study and effort with a common understanding about major aims and the elements of a good program. Each worker should examine his own area and recognize the need for improvement. An underlying reason for such a meeting is to provide an opportunity for workers to understand and solve their problems.

The teachers' meeting is not to be confused with the education committee meeting. The purpose of the latter is to give general oversight to the educational work of the church as a whole and to build it into a total comprehensive program. It sets up standards, goals, forms policies, chooses leaders, and sees that the heads of organizations carry out the plans delegated to them.

Not all Sunday schools teach the lesson to teachers at the weekly meeting. Those who do not should have these goals: (1) fellowship, (2) inspiration, (3) information, (4) instruction (practical messages). Or, stated in another way, the goals should be: (1) a smooth-running school, (2) a spiritual school, (3) an evangelistic school, and (4) a growing school.

Some reasons for a teachers' meeting include the following:

1. *To gain a vision of the whole task.* Concentration on the separate details of a picture blurs the effect of the whole. There is a definite need to get a broad view of the work of the Sunday school. The workers should have a common understanding about the large general goals, including the elements that make up a comprehensive program. Each worker should know what is being accomplished by the others.

2. *To see the place of one's individual work.* Each worker should see the relationships and interdependence of the various parts. He should also see clearly the true perspective, sense of proportion, and proper relationships of his work to the whole. Lack of cooperation at any point or in any phase of the work weakens the whole program.

3. *To serve as a means for solving problems.* Many problems are best solved through cooperation of the workers. As the adage says, "Many heads are better than one." Ideas will surface in a group that one person alone would not think of.

4. *To reach more with leadership training.* Only a few workers can arrange for trips to teachers institutes, conventions, or meetings, while many can attend a church's once-a-month meeting.
5. *To make possible democratic planning.* Workers understand more fully those plans they have helped to formulate, and they know better how to put them into effect. They are then more able and willing to carry the work forward.
6. *To keep up to date.* The latest educational methods and materials should be explained and distributed at the teachers' meeting.
7. *To promote fellowship and deeper consecration.* Thinking together and other teamwork help draw the departments together. Their cooperative worship and prayer bring the blessing of the Lord.

God's Word has all the principles we need to serve him effectively. In Proverbs 15:22 we read: "Without counsel, plans go awry, but in the multitude of counselors they are established." God's blessing always is on those who obey his Word and the advice in it.

Organizing the Teachers' Meeting

1. Although teachers' meetings may be initiated by anyone who has the firm conviction that they really are needed, and who has a knowledge of the purpose of such meetings, it is really the pastor's or Sunday school superintendent's duty to start them. Then it is up to this conscientious "starter" to create interest among teachers and officers.
2. Next, a committee should be appointed to look into the different aspects of the teachers' meeting and to list the pros and cons. This committee should report to all the workers and receive approval or disapproval of the program. Teachers and officers must be enthusiastic about such a conference before it is launched, for only as the entire staff works as a unit will the Sunday school operate efficiently.
3. The superintendent of the Sunday school should be responsible for planning and directing the teachers' meeting, although any qualified teacher could handle this position. He

should serve as general chairman of the meeting and should conduct the business sessions. However, he should delegate most of the other duties. Wide participation by workers means greater interest and educational growth. He should appoint a committee to plan the program, another to conduct it, and another to put into operation the plans for improvement. The director should give guidance and supply needed materials. He is somewhat like a liaison officer, bringing recommendations of the committee to the conference and taking the problems and requests of the conference to the committee.

4. A secretary should be elected to keep notes of all business and to see that photocopies of the minutes are given to all members, including absentees. A treasurer should be elected to care for all financial matters.

5. To run efficiently, the teachers' meeting should be planned well in advance. it should be organized with a carefully arranged time schedule, to accomplish the maximum results in terms of the total work to be done. Consideration should be given to the following: (a) a theme for each month's meeting, (b) a variety of methods of presentation, (c) items that need to be covered throughout the year, (d) content of the instruction periods, (e) special speakers, and (f) program participation. These meetings can be planned by a committee working with the pastor, the superintendent, and the chairman of the board, or the board can plan the meetings.

Program of the Teachers' Meeting

Many long hours of planning are put into the teachers' meeting to make it interesting and efficient. Therefore, explicit care must be exercised in advertising the meeting. When a meeting is called, every effort should be made to assure attendance.

Since punctuality is vitally important, the meeting should begin promptly at the designated time—and end on time. Also of great importance is the order of the meeting. Many churches find it difficult to plan a specific order, hence the following pattern is suggested:

1. *Devotions.* This includes one or more hymns, Scripture reading, and prayer.
2. *Reports.* Minutes of previous meeting, treasurer's report, and departmental reports.
3. *Unfinished business.* Reports on activities planned at previous meetings.
4. *New business.* Action on recommendations made by departments or committees; also plans for coming events.
5. *Educational feature.* Instruction, various speakers, or films.
6. *Fellowship.* Sometimes the meeting is preceded by a fellowship supper. However, for the best results, a fellowship supper should be given only once a quarter. Some groups serve refreshments during a period of informal fellowship at every meeting.
7. *Departmental meetings.* Some churches have departmental conferences before the fellowship supper. After the supper they present reports and recommendations at the general meeting.

The opening devotional service has a fourfold purpose: (1) to recognize God's presence and guidance, (2) to bring the spirit of worship into the conference, (3) to train the workers in the expression of spiritual aspirations, and (4) to prepare the hearts and minds of those present to get the most out of the session.

In the business session, *Robert's Rules of Order* should be followed. The chairman should be familiar with these rules and should enforce them. Business at the teachers' meeting includes a roll call, the reading of the minutes, the attendance report, the treasurer's report, and departmental reports. Unfinished business should follow. New business is then considered. Action is taken on requests submitted in the departmental reports.

The educational part of the program is a period of instruction or training. This may effectively be presented by means of reports, visual aids, panel discussion, forums, or demonstrations.

If the meeting includes a lesson-planning time, the potential of the lesson can be stressed. The teachers may question some point in the lesson, which then can be explained by an appointed instructor. A speaker who is an authority on a specific subject covered in the lesson would be of great help to the teachers.

After the educational program, points of interest and new ideas should be discussed. The leader should be careful not to let the discussion become irrelevant. If different viewpoints are presented, the leader should give attention to all and bring the group to a definite conclusion.

The social hour should be considered an important part of the conference, and it should be directed by a competent committee, whether there is a fellowship supper or not. A decorated room often adds a desirable atmosphere.

Departmental meetings also are necessary. They should focus on aims, problems, subjects, and methods of special concern to each particular department. The study and planning should be geared to the age group being taught. Lesson applications and teaching methods should be stressed. The superintendent of the specific department should be in charge of the departmental meetings.

Matters not important enough for the general teachers' meeting can be discussed and settled in departmental meetings. A conclusion should be reached as to recommendations to be submitted to the general meeting or education committee.

The departmental meeting could meet either before or after the general meeting, depending on the needs of the local Sunday school. If the departmental meeting is first, special problems can be brought up later in the general meeting. However, there is some advantage in first meeting together in a large combined group, then planning in detail in separate groups.

If each program is well planned and interesting, the workers will continue to attend and will receive inestimable help. Some suggested topics for discussion at the teachers' meeting are:

1. How can we increase average attendance?
2. What can be done to make the worship period more meaningful?
3. What can be done to enlist and train more workers?
4. How can we make the visitation program more effective?
5. How can we overcome absenteeism and encourage latecomers to be on time?

6. How should a lesson be prepared?
7. What is the proper use of the Bible in Sunday school?

The sevenfold purpose of the teachers' meeting shows the necessity of continuing such a program after it has been put into operation in order to have a successful, growing Sunday school. Restated, this sevenfold purpose is:

1. Initiate with fellowship.
2. Inspire with worship.
3. Inform with facts.
4. Instruct with practical studies.
5. Involve in departmental groups.
6. Interest with year's program for Sunday school.
7. Intercession through prayer.

A suggested program has been presented incorporating the sevenfold purpose, which may be changed to suit individual needs. Variety is not only good, but essential for worthwhile meetings.

God's Word includes principles regarding every attempt his children make to serve him. In Proverbs 11:14, we are told, "Where there is no counsel, the people fall; but in the multitude of counselors there is safety." And in Proverbs 13:10, God reminds us that "by pride comes nothing but strife, but with the well-advised is wisdom."

This conclusion may be drawn: As the teachers' meeting goes, so goes the Sunday school. A successful Sunday school teachers' meeting, supported by hard work and fervent prayer, will help bring about a successful Sunday school to the glory of the Lord Jesus Christ.

SUPERAGGRESSIVE EVANGELISM

Superaggressive evangelism is the attitude that the Christian should be energetic and innovative in giving the gospel to every person. Superaggressive evangelism is built on the premise that all are lost (Rom. 3:23) and Christ died for all (John 1:29; 3:16; 1 John 2:2). Therefore the Christian ought to be aggressive in spreading the gospel to all.

SUPERINTENDENT, ADULT (See also SUPERINTENDENT, DEPARTMENT)

Often there may be several adult superintendents in a church (young adults, middle-age adults, senior saints, etc.), but the qualifications are similar for every adult superintendent. He must know and love his age group. He must be able to communicate with the students to meet the specific needs in the lives of each separate group. This responsibility increases if the department includes all ages of adults. Also, he must know and love the Word. He should be ready to help sincere seekers untangle the mass of erroneous ideas they may have and be able to prevent deliberate troublemakers from leading other adults into error.

SUPERINTENDENT, BEGINNER (See also SUPERINTENDENT, DEPARTMENT)

The superintendent of the Beginner Department needs specialized training for this age group, which will enable him or her to understand these young children and know how to effectively communicate to them. Also, he or she should be aware of the abilities and limitations of children this age and what teaching methods are most effective. He or she should also have some understanding of how to cope with the unique problems experienced by and with children this age.

SUPERINTENDENT, CRADLE ROLL (See also SUPERINTENDENT, DEPARTMENT)

In addition to the basic requirements for a department superintendent, the cradle roll superintendent should have a fondness for babies. While a baby cannot express to its parents its preference in churches, a mother is quick to sense whether her baby is contented in the nursery. If unusual crying and fear are manifested, a parent may well try out the nursery of a different church. A worker's love for babies will beget a response of security.

The cradle roll superintendent should also be alert. Soon after the baby first arrives, the superintendent should visit the home and express the interest of the Sunday school in the new life. The child's name should be put on the cradle roll and an appropriate symbol given to the parents, together with a letter or leaflet explaining the church's concern. There should be an invitation to bring the baby each Sunday to the church nursery, where an adequate staff will take care of him so that parents can attend services.

Since a baby nursery requires more than one worker, the superintendent should have the ability to direct a staff. Both the superintendent and nursery staff should have cheerful dispositions. The superintendent needs to be a person of tact and discernment in enlisting and selecting mothers and fathers to work in the nursery.

The cradle roll superintendent should also be concerned about the hygiene of the nursery and nursery workers. Mothers are made aware of the need to protect infants from exposure to germs. The superintendent should be equally aware and take steps to protect all babies from this danger. A plan should be adopted whereby mothers can leave the infant's bottle, with any necessary instructions regarding feeding. Also, laundry and house cleaning should be carefully and regularly accomplished by the nursery staff.

SUPERINTENDENT, DEPARTMENT (See also SUPERINTENDENT, SUNDAY SCHOOL)

In a large Sunday school, the department superintendents are responsible to the general Sunday school superintendent who will work through him with the teachers. The duties and qualifications of the department superintendent will depend to some degree on the needs of their individual departments. At the same time, there are certain generic qualifications of every superintendent in the Sunday school. He should be dedicated to his job in the Sunday school, viewing the task as a definite call from God. He must know the characteristics, needs, and how to minister to the age group to which he is called. He should be a leader, not a driver. The department superintendent needs to be as much aware of the praiseworthy accomplishments of his teachers as of areas where improvement is needed. Also, he should have a genuine Christian character as one who represents the Lord and his Church to a department of teachers and pupils.

SUPERINTENDENT, JUNIOR (See also SUPERINTENDENT, DEPARTMENT)

In addition to the normal requirements of a department superintendent, the superintendent of the Junior Department should be (1) flexible in teaching methods; (2) alert and growing as he provides leadership for the most active department in the Sunday school; (3) actively involved with juniors in extra-class outings, such as hikes, wiener roasts, or ball games; and (4) able to lead his students to Christ since this is the most responsive group in the Sunday school to the salvation invitation.

SUPERINTENDENT, JUNIOR HIGH (See also SUPERINTENDENT, DEPARTMENT)

The junior high superintendent must be a listener. Junior high students have unique problems and need adult counselors who will listen to their problems, give advice, and help them find solutions. Also, the superintendent must be innovative. Junior high students may be bored with presentations where the teaching methods are similar to those used in the junior department. The Junior high superintendent must master ways to get and hold their attention, or enlist the aid of someone who can. Third, this superintendent must be a learner, able to give biblical guidance to students who come to him with their doubts and fears. Finally, self-control in emotional situations is vital. Shock, anger, and tears should be kept in check, though the words and acts of the teens may provoke all three with frequency.

SUPERINTENDENT, PRIMARY (See also SUPERINTENDENT, DEPARTMENT)

In addition to meeting the normal qualifications of a department superintendent, the superintendent of the Primary Department should know how to lead a child to Christ. Primaries readily respond to the invitation for salvation, and the Primary superintendent and teachers should know how to respond. Also, the superintendent should understand the unique needs of primary students in the department. Since the superintendent will probably be the master-teacher during worship time, he must know the children.

SUPERINTENDENT, SENIOR HIGH (See also SUPERINTENDENT, DEPARTMENT)

Senior high students are eager to be led in putting feet to the faith. Therefore, the Senior high superintendent needs to be need-conscious. In his search for ways to involve senior high students in service projects, the superintendent will seek out areas where there is a need they can meet. He will contact various church and community agencies to discover what aid can be extended by the church. Also, this superintendent should lead by example. Many senior high students lack adult leadership in the home and will emulate the life of their church leader.

SUPERINTENDENT, SUNDAY SCHOOL

Because of the vital role of the Sunday school in the growth and training of the membership of the church, the general Sunday school superintendent is often considered second in importance to the pastor. Indeed, in some churches the pastor assumes the position of the general superintendent of the Sunday school, overseeing its program and personnel. Since the pastor is responsible for leading, feeding, and protecting all the flock (Acts 20:28), he has the general administrative oversight of the congregation, including the Sunday school. Therefore, the Sunday school superintendent is the extension of the pastoral responsibility of administration and organization in the life of the Sunday school. The superintendent is the spiritual leader of the Sunday school, the pacesetter in dedication, faithfulness, and zeal.

What to Look for in a Sunday School Superintendent

As a leader in the church, the Sunday school superintendent should meet the general standards for leadership required by the church. In addition, the superintendent should view his task as a call to that particular area of service. He should know Sunday school work, preferably having been a teacher or officer. He should be able to work with department superintendents as part of the leadership team in the Sunday school. Because of his position and rank in the work of the church, the general superintendent should be of impeccable character.

What Are the Duties of the Sunday School Superintendent?
The duties of the Sunday school superintendent include (1) promotion, (2) superintending, (3) training, (4) recruiting, and (5) improving the Sunday school. The enthusiasm of the superintendent should be apparent in his effort to make the church and community aware of the activities and accomplishments of the Sunday school. He will see opportunities for growth through a program of visitation and religious census. He will set the example of concern for the unreached through his own participation in such activities. Also, he should oversee and direct the work of the teachers and officers of the Sunday school. In consultation with them he evaluates and constantly seeks to improve the program and policies. He maintains careful records of absentees so that concern may be extended. If records show consistent absenteeism, he seeks to determine causes and to make the necessary changes. Further, the superintendent will guide the teachers and officers in maintaining a definite program of in-service training and of training prospective teachers.

SUPERVISOR
In some large churches, departmental supervisors administer several departments and serve as an intermediate administrative officer between the age-group ministry director and the superintendents of several departments of a specific age group. For instance, the junior supervisor might act as an intermediate officer between the children's ministry director and the superintendents of several Junior Departments in the Sunday school. The following is a sample job description for a Sunday school supervisor:

Sample Job Description for a Sunday School Supervisor
General responsibility. The supervisor will be responsible for all church programs for a specific age. The supervisor will work under the age-group ministry director and will direct all superintendents in the specific age group for which he or she is responsible.

Specific duties. The specific duties of the supervisor includes the following:

1. To direct the work of each superintendent in the assigned age group. This would involve helping with planning, programs, finding materials, training workers, evaluating results, and solving problems.
2. To provide curriculum and curriculum materials, including all supplementary supplies and teaching materials.
3. To provide all teaching and craft supplies used by teachers under their indirect supervision.
4. To maintain a personal visitation program of workers and children in the age group, and assist in planning and implementing a visitation program for all the workers in the departments.
5. To assist with the recruitment of new workers for the age group.
6. To provide in-service training during regular workers' meetings.
7. To plan, direct, and coordinate special activities for the age group.

SYMPOSIUM

This method of teaching is not often used, as it is even more limiting than the panel discussion. As a general rule, it consists of three or more members of the class, each discussing some point or problem. Generally, the problem is not controversial. In other words, the symposium is usually a lecture broken up into several small sections, a different class member leading each section.

TAUBMAN, GEORGE PRIMROSE (1869–1947)

George Primrose Taubman was minister of the First Christian Church, Long Beach, California, where he served from 1915 to 1939 as minister and director of the Bible school. Taubman organized the Taubman Bible class after becoming minister of the church and saw it reach an enrollment of 3,000 men, all active. He claimed to have the largest membership of its kind in the world. For more than five years, the Sunday school averaged more than 1,500 men, and on two special occasions there were 25,000 (September 30, 1928) and 31,856 (September 21, 1930), to that date the largest single day attendance for a Sunday school. This outstanding Sunday school for years had a record attendance of approximately 5,000 every Mother's Day and Armistice Day. Taubman took advantage of the patriotic fervor of men in the greater Los Angeles area who rode the red trolley cars to Long Beach so they could attend Sunday school and march in a gigantic Sunday school parade. When Taubman became minister of the church there were 400 members. That had increased to 4,200 by the time he left. Taubman was born June 30, 1869, and died March 12, 1947.

TEACHER (See SUNDAY SCHOOL TEACHER)

TEACHER REPORT FORM

A teacher report form is an effective tool in improving the quality or standard of teaching in the Sunday school. However, do not try to use a report form every week, or it will lose its impact. The report form should be used during the spring and fall attendance campaigns. As every good personnel manager knows, people do not always do what is expected, they are more likely to do what is inspected. But even something as effective as a teacher report form can lose its punch and impact if used all the time. That is why it is recommended it be used only during the attendance campaigns to insure the highest quality of teaching at those times. Also, many teachers who get into the habit of teaching up to a higher standard during a campaign will continue to be better teachers even when the campaign is ended.

Sample Teacher Report Form

1. Were you in class on time? (15 minutes early) _____
   What time did you arrive? _____
2. How much time did you use in preparing the lesson?
   1, 2, 3, 4 hours?_____
3. How many teaching methods did you use in presenting the lesson? _____
   List them:
   a. _____
   b. _____
   c. _____
   d. _____
   e. _____
4. How many absentees did you contact and try to get back in church? _____
5. How many times did you present the gospel this past week? _____
6. What results did you have in your class today? _____
   _____

TEACHER'S COVENANT (See COVENANT, SUNDAY SCHOOL TEACHER'S)

TEACHING—DEFINITION
The importance of Sunday school teaching lies in its definition.

Teaching in Sunday school is the preparation and guidance of learning activities. The ultimate purpose of teaching is that the gospel will change the lives of its hearers. Obviously, teaching is much more than just presenting truth. It is a process that involves the teacher and pupil with the Word of God. Therefore, it is imperative that Sunday school teachers properly teach the Scriptures if the class is going to grow according to New Testament standards.

Teaching by Explaining the Word of God

The Word of God is the source of the Christian life. In Sunday school, the teacher should use as many methods as possible, but the foundation of instruction is explanation of the text of the Bible.

The Word of God gives a foundation of doctrine (2 Tim. 3:16); it cleanses the life (Ps. 119:9-11); it gives power (Matt. 4:6-10); it comforts (Jer. 15:16); it gives direction for living (Ps. 119:105); and is the source of eternal life.

There is a special place for teaching the Word of God to the unsaved. The Bible will convict them of sin (Jer. 23:29); it will point them to Jesus Christ (John 1:36); it will give them a new nature (2 Pet. 1:4); and will be the instrument that causes them to be born again (John 1:12; 1 Pet. 1:23). Therefore, explaining Scripture is the foundation of Sunday school.

Teaching through the Use of Activities

Children are eager to learn. Their active, growing bodies need opportunity to move and explore. Children need to be able to walk about the classroom. They should feel free to ask questions about what they see.

Movement in and of itself is not enough. A Sunday school must provide ways for preschoolers to explore the lessons they are learning. Elementary students need to use their hands and feet for involvement. Older students use their minds to interact with one another.

Children are not good sitters, nor are they good listeners, but they are excellent learners. They like to learn from books, pictures, and posters on the wall. They like to learn by asking questions and by seeing different things. Because children are dynamic growing personalities, they learn "beef-stew" style. They learn many lessons at the same time. They acquire skills, memorize verses, imitate the teacher's life, and learn how to get along with other children. All these lessons may come in one learning process.

Sometimes the active involvement of children makes adults uncomfortable. They want the pupils to sit still and be quiet, but the little ones are not made that way. Of course, there should be a time and place during the session for them to sit still and listen as the teacher explains the Bible. However, organized informal learning takes place all during the session through the children's activities.

Teaching by Meeting Needs

Involvement for the sake of involvement can become just "busy work." Listening to a lecture may just be "routine." Also, coloring or pasting may become unexciting. A teacher can go through all the motions of teaching, but until the students' needs have been met, the lesson has not been taught. Facts about the Bible and words from the manual may be quickly forgotten, but when the Bible meets the needs of the pupil, the lesson will stick to his life.

The teacher who meets needs has to deal with the rapid learner who explores much more than the child who is rebellious. The teacher who meets needs tries to motivate the pupil who is uninterested. The teacher needs to know the pupils in order to help all of them.

The purpose of the Sunday school is spiritual growth. Children grow as their inner problems are solved and their needs met. Teaching a baby how to walk illustrates this point. We do not lecture to him on the principles of walking. Nor do we give him a demonstration of how to walk. Watch how a father teaches his child to walk. He takes the baby by both hands, holding and guiding his every action. Sometimes the father will tenderly pull the left hand forward, causing the baby's left foot to take a step. Then he repeats the process with the right hand. The ultimate aim is that the child might walk without the help of the father.

Sunday school is helping pupils walk in the Lord. Teachers can be most effective when they work with individuals helping them take one step at a time. Suppose a child took his first step and the father was disappointed because he did not run. The father's disappointment could destroy the initiative of his son. When pupils take a spiritual step, the teacher should show them love and support in every step. A sense of achievement and direction is part of learning; the teacher must give this to pupils.

Teaching by Example

The teacher determines what learning will go on in the classroom. The teacher who loves the Word of God is committed to communicating it to his pupils. And the teacher who loves children is committed to helping meet their needs. But in the final analysis, the teacher's most important lesson is himself. The teacher who is called of God will want to provide the best example possible for his pupils.

Identification helps to change lives. Young boys learn their role in life by identifying with their father. Later on, they identify with other adult men, hopefully with godly Christian men. The same forces are at work in the lives of young girls. All children should have a godly Sunday school teacher who loves Jesus Christ so that they will be influenced accordingly.

More and more children are coming from broken homes. They do not have a father or mother after whom to pattern their lives. They should be able to find in their Sunday school teacher a substitute father or mother who has the qualities of Jesus Christ. Children who have never known a Christian father can begin to appreciate the loving care of their heavenly Father through their Sunday school teacher.

A teacher imparts more by actions than by words. Sometimes the way that a teacher squeezes a child's hand says, "I love you" much more than the figures she puts on a flannelgraph board. Both the words that are spoken and the actions that are symbolized must, of course, reinforce each other.

A teacher must be careful that she uses the right words, involves the pupils in learning, reaches them through their activities, and makes sure their needs are met. Beyond all of this, her life must be a godly example to her pupils.

TEACHING, GIFT OF (See also SPIRITUAL GIFTS)

The person who has the gift of teaching has the ability to accurately make clear God's truth so all can understand it. The strengths of this gift include (1) a desire to study and classify truth; (2) a feeling that this gift is foundational to others; (3) a tendency to present truth systematically; (4) a concern about learning; (5) a concern for the accurate communication of Scripture and lack of tolerance for its misinterpretation; (6) a tendency to listen to those who have correct knowledge; and (7) a sensitivity to use biblical illustrations in his teaching.

Among the common weaknesses associated with this gift are (1) a greater interest in interpretation than application, and (2) the absence of practical faith.

Those with this gift may fall into the danger of (1) being proud about knowledge; (2) concentrating on details rather than the broader issues of life; or (3) having a greater concern for truth than individuals.

TEACHING METHODS (See individual teaching methods)

TEAM TEACHING

Some churches have revolutionized their Sunday schools by changing to team teaching. Others have modified this approach to teaching and use a master-teacher plan in the classroom (see Master-Teacher Plan). These approaches to teaching have been common in vacation Bible school for years, although they have only recently been widely used in Sunday school.

What Is Team Teaching?

The team approach to teaching calls for two or more persons to guide the learning, growth, cooperation, and evaluation of the classroom experience. Sharing of responsibility is vital to the team approach.

No one person can or should be responsible for the spiritual life of a child. In the one-teacher-to-a-classroom approach, the teacher has responsibility for all the praying, teaching, guiding, encouraging, and counseling. But every child is different, and every class is unique. Needs change from child to child and from age to age. Several teachers should pray, teach, visit, guide, and direct the pupil. These teachers form a team.

Team teaching is not entirely new or untried in the Sunday school. For many years the church nursery and kindergarten classes have had two or more teachers. Also, the vacation Bible school has used teaching teams in beginner and primary classes. Some of the older denominations have been using the team approach in these classes also.

What Are the Advantages of Team Teaching?

Sunday school conventions and Christian education literature have begun stressing the advantages of team teaching.

1. The emphasis is on the group. The church has come a long way in understanding how learning takes place. Once people thought that knowledge resided in the adult teacher, parent, or camp counselor. This knowledge was passed from the adult to the child as apples are passed from one basket to another.

   Now educators recognize that children do their own learning. The teacher only guides the learning experience. We know that boys and girls teach one another through sharing mutual experiences. This interaction has as great an impact on their total learning as the adult teacher. Thus, team teaching emphasizes the group and recognizes the way children learn.

2. Team teaching increases learning possibilities. Team teaching permits larger classes because two or more teachers share in the leadership. More children in a group mean more possibilities for rich learning experiences.

3. Team teaching makes teacher recruitment easier. People join the teaching staff more readily if they know that the responsibility will be shared. In a team-teaching approach the new teacher is not "on his own." The beginning teacher enters into group planning, sharing, and evaluation. He learns from the older, more experienced teachers in the classroom. Still, teaching must be "caught" rather than "taught." New teachers learn to teach by actually teaching with other teachers.

4. Team teaching offers more possibilities for teachers to grow. In a team teaching approach several teachers work together in a group. They help one another grow and learn. They share

insights from the Scriptures. They encourage one another to try out new ideas. With such support a teacher finds it easier to attempt new methods and try different materials.

When one teacher is isolated in a classroom, outside evaluation is limited. Usually the pupils are the only judge of teaching. Mistakes are perpetuated. Poor teachers do not usually improve their methods except by trial and error. However, the errors have eternal implications. Team teaching helps to minimize mistakes and enrich teaching.

5. More specialized skills can be utilized. With more teachers present, more skills are likely to be available for class enrichment. A Sunday school teacher with a specialized skill may join a class for a short time. For instance, the team may feel the need for help with audiovisual aids or a children's choir. A teacher with these special skills may join the team. The new teacher participates in the planning, works in the session, and shares in the evaluation. The new teacher's special skills contribute not only to the children but to other teachers. Thus, every Sunday school classroom can become a training laboratory for teachers. Teachers continue to grow through a team-teaching approach.

Who Is on the Team?

Everyone associated with the class is on the team. This includes the pianists, class secretary, and others with specialized responsibility. All team members—whether teacher, pianist, or superintendent—are thought of as teachers.

The adults are responsible for initial planning and preparation for the learning situation. However, the boys and girls can help plan in the classroom. They can suggest things they want to learn. Especially in the older grades pupils can share responsibility for what is happening in the classroom. Team teaching means that everyone in a group is teaching.

How Team Teaching Operates

One person on the team should be designated as the lead teacher. He carries the administrative responsibility—scheduling the planning meeting, administering the planning, ordering supplies, and caring for some of the details. The lead teacher may serve as chairman of the planning sessions. Or other teachers may serve in this capacity. Some teams rotate the chairmanship of planning, with each teacher in the group taking turns.

How a Team Plans a Lesson

Certain steps should be followed in planning a unit and in carrying out the plans.

1. All teachers must be fully acquainted with the area of study. All teachers should read the entire unit—the teacher's manual, the pages in the pupil's quarterly, and other related materials. Each member of the team should make a list of songs, Scripture verses to be used, topics for conversation, activities or projects, handwork, and other suggestions appropriate for the units.

2. The team must meet for planning. The planning session should meet at least two weeks before the lesson is taught. The lead teacher schedules the meeting. The chairman for planning presides at the session. Each teacher should share his list of learning materials and activities. Together they may:

   a. Think through questions the pupils may raise from the study. Determine how to help the pupils find answers.

   b. Consider the aims and purposes of the lesson and make a list of the needs of the pupils. The specific aims should meet immediate needs. However, the pupils may have additional purposes to add.

   c. List all possible activities in which their pupils may be engaged for learning and growth.

   d. Determine the specific responsibilities for each teacher on the team.

   e. Practice the teaching skills each will need during the lesson.

   f. Write out a specific lesson plan. Include the sequence of events and persons responsible for each leadership task.

   The team makes broad plans. However, the plans should be specific enough so that each teacher can proceed with his individual preparation, yet be flexible enough so that the pupils' ideas can be incorporated.

The success of team teaching depends on team planning. Where all teachers share the planning, all share an equal responsibility for the results. The team should consider the suggestions of each member of the team. No one dominates; no one just listens; all participate.

3. All members of the team work together during the class. Even though a teacher may not be in direct command of the class, he should not sit back and take a mental vacation. The silent teacher may be observing the pupil's responses, evaluating an activity, or giving support to the guiding teacher. Each team member, whether teaching or observing, should feel responsible. Then at times the class will be divided into small groups with each teacher working with a group.

4. Each team member supports the others on the team. All teachers should help one another to grow and improve. The timid teacher should be encouraged to assume leadership when he is ready. Team members should give and seek constructive suggestions.

5. The pupils share responsibility. Pupils of all ages can share responsibility to some extent. All pupils need experience in solving problems, in making decisions, and in expressing their own ideas at their own level. All pupils should be able to help choose what they want to learn, under the teacher's guidance, of course.

Younger children can suggest activities or experiences they enjoy. The teacher should listen carefully for each child's questions and comments. Student interest or disinterest will tell a teacher whether he is meeting needs.

Older students can assume more responsibility for helping determine what needs to be learned and how to carry out work. They can help evaluate progress in terms of "how are we doing?"

Members One of Another

One must know a person in order to help him or her. This takes time. Knowing one another means sharing many experiences.

Teachers must know one another well. Informal fellowship among team members is as basic to team teaching as serious planning. This is one reason for regular sessions. One hour on Sunday morning does not provide sufficient time to know one another. Through-the-week activities make possible a variety of experiences.

Not only must teachers know one another, they must know their pupils. Teachers should phone their pupils, write cards, and make personal visits. Every pupil should be able to say of his class at church, "This is my group. I really belong here. My teacher really cares about me. The other pupils care about me, too. I like my class."

Problems in Team Teaching

Many difficulties beset the forming of a team. The shy, timid teacher may withdraw and not make a contribution to the group. The aggressive teacher may manipulate the other team members. The end product in either case is not a team effort.

Problems in personal relationships may arise. Any time two people work together these difficulties may develop.

Lack of time may be a problem. It takes time for all members of the team to make their suggestions. One or two talkative members may dominate the conversation in the time available. The group needs to take extra time to draw out points from all members. Progress may be slow. However, the team that is willing to move slowly at first in order to be a "team," may later move more rapidly.

Another difficulty in team teaching is personal reticence. "I wouldn't want to tell the story with Mrs. Hesselgrave in the room!" As members of the team support one another, they may overcome this fear.

Misconceptions about Team Teaching

When considering team teaching, people often ask, "If you have thirty-seven children in the room, won't you lose personal contact?" Past experience with team teaching has proven the contrary. Team teachers usually have deeper insight into individual students because of shared observations. In the one-teacher classroom the teacher may overlook Sally because of personal reasons. However, when the team evaluates Sally, three other teachers can share their observations on her progress. "In the multitude of counselors there is safety" (Prov. 11:14). Also, when more than one teacher is in the room, they can observe Sally in a variety of activities and relationships. Thus they get a better overall understanding of her.

Another misconception relates to teacher recruitment. People often remark, "Team teaching is so difficult, how could we get anyone to serve?" Once again, experience overrules the objection. Teacher recruitment is easier when the candidate knows he will receive in-service training and help in the classroom. The learn-as-you-work approach removes the threatening aspect of teaching. Also, people like the idea that they will not have to assume sole responsibility for the class.

The team teacher is like a member of an orchestra. Each one must follow the conductor, be on key and able to carry out the assignment, and have a knowledge of the responsibilities of others. So it is in team teaching. Each teacher must come to class prepared, able to carry out his assignment, have a knowledge of what other teachers are doing, and work in harmony with others. Just as the orchestra produces the full and complete symphony, so the team of teachers produces well-rounded, mature students—to the glory of God.

TEN LARGEST SUNDAY SCHOOLS (See also APPENDIX 2: FIFTY LARGEST SUNDAY SCHOOLS)

The first listing of the ten largest Sunday schools appeared in the listing of the largest Sunday schools in 1968. From the listing a book was written, *The Ten Largest Sunday Schools and What Made Them Grow* (Baker Book House, 1969). The volume made the list of best-sellers in the *The Christian Bookseller* for three months, and the book went through nine printings, plus 7,000 prepublication copies of a special edition. The original listing included:

Sunday School Attendance in 1968		The Ten Largest Sunday Schools in 1991:	
1. Akron Baptist Temple Akron, Ohio	5,762	1. First Baptist Church Hammond, Indiana	20,000
2. Highland Park Baptist Church Chattanooga, Tennessee	4,821	2. Willow Creek Community Church South Barrington, Illinois	11,743
3. First Baptist Church Dallas, Texas	4,731	3. First Assembly of God Phoenix, Arizona	9,685
4. First Baptist Church Hammond, Indiana	3,978	4. Thomas Road Baptist Church Lynchburg, Virginia	9,000
5. Canton Baptist Temple Canton, Ohio	3,581	5. Metro Assembly of God Brooklyn, New York	8,057
6. Landmark Baptist Temple Cincinnati, Ohio	3,540	6. First Baptist Church Dallas, Texas	7,615
7. Temple Baptist Church Detroit, Michigan	3,400	7. First Baptist Church Jacksonville, Florida	6,272
8. First Baptist Church Van Nuys, California	2,847	8. University Presbyterian Church Seattle, Washington	6,004
9. Thomas Road Baptist Church Lynchburg, Virginia	2,640	9. Bellevue Baptist Church Cordova, Tennessee	5,200
10. Calvary Temple Denver, Colorado	2,453	10. Second Baptist Church Houston, Texas	5,181

TESTIMONY EVANGELISM

Testimony evangelism can be used in a "side-door" approach to evangelism. This is verbal evangelism where the believer shares his experience. Some Christians cannot give the plan of salvation to a lost person. They think that is preaching, or they think it is salesmanship. But anyone can tell what has happened to him. Testimony evangelism is sharing our experience in Jesus Christ with other people so that they too will want to experience what we have in Christ.

First, a witness should share what he has seen about Jesus Christ, "That which was from the beginning . . . which we have seen with our eyes, which we have looked upon" (1 John 1:1).

There are two areas that we want to share as a result of our looking. First, what we have seen in Jesus Christ. The two disciples on the Road to Emmaus were first blinded to Christ, but he gave them spiritual sight. The Bible says, "Their eyes were opened and they knew Him" (Luke 24:31). When we know Christ, we want to share him with our friends.

In the second place we see a difference in our life. We see how our desires have changed and our life is different. Then we want to share with our friends what Christ has done for us.

A witness should share what he has heard about Jesus Christ. When Peter and John were called before the Sanhedrin for their preaching, they confessed, "For we cannot but speak the things which we have seen and heard" (Acts 4:20).

When a person is called as a witness in a legal trial, the judge will not permit his opinion, but only what he has seen, heard, or experienced. A witness should share what he has experienced in his relationship with Jesus Christ. In Acts 4:1-20, a healed man who had been lame from birth stood with Peter and John. He gave his testimony as to what had happened to him: "And seeing the man who had been healed standing with them, they could say nothing against it" (v. 14). Testimony evangelism is an effective evangelistic strategy because it gives credibility to the message.

THINK TANKS, USING TO GATHER DATA

More and more businesses, charitable institutions, and churches are using a committee drawn from various segments of their constituents to help gather current and accurate information needed to make good decisions and give the organization better direction. Inasmuch as it is expensive, difficult, and sometimes time consuming to get a valid statistical survey, a church can carefully choose a group of designated people for controlled discussion of a specific topic to help the leadership in serving its members.

Think tanks are a method of gathering data for use by leadership. A think tank is also called a task force or focus group.

Think tanks can also be used where primary research is needed, but the leadership has little experience or background in research methodology. The use of a think tank can help solve problems, refocus aims, make decisions, or revitalize dead programs.

Usually a think tank has approximately eight to fourteen people, their purpose being to gather, analyze, and systematically classify qualitative information into a written report. Also, a think tank can be used to explore the different responses people will make to changing conditions or a new program in a church. They can even evaluate the members' likely response to new situations.

A think tank should be clear in its methodology:

1. The group should state specifically what information is needed and what facts should be gathered from the process.
2. It should select a seasoned moderator who can direct the group toward its objective.
3. It should select people from various audiences within the church—those who bring expertise or objectivity, who have demonstrated good rational processes, and who are loyal to the institution.
4. It should determine how the conclusions will be used after the think tank is over.
5. It should put in place safeguards that will insure objective information.
6. It should list the discussion questions ahead of time to give direction to the group process.
7. It should assign an approximate time for group discussion on each question.
8. It might make an audio tape of group discussion.
9. It should produce a written summary of the various opinions, observations, and suggestions.
10. It should draw conclusions from the results of the discussion.

There are many areas where a think tank can give good information to a local church. Because a church cannot make good decisions on bad information (bad decisions are made on bad information), churches need superior information to make superior decisions. A church should consider the possibility of a think tank before proceeding to make a decision on adding services. Also, a think tank can explore issues about a new building, new areas of ministry, the addition of new ministerial staff, or can evaluate the strengths or weaknesses of existing programs.

Things to Avoid

Do not use people who represent authority positions to lead discussions, such as a pastor, youth pastor, chairman of the deacons, or others in positions of authority. People are usually not objective in responding to those who represent power. On some occasions there is strong motivation for people to give only a positive or acceptable answer rather than to be realistic. Some people are so positive about their local church that they cannot realistically face its problems when talking with the chairman of the board or one of the pastoral staff members.

Second, do not allow any individual to monopolize the conversation to the detriment of the rest of the group. A strong moderator is necessary to control the group by assuring that everyone's opinion is heard.

Third, avoid hasty conclusions. People often want to arrive at the "right" answer and usually want to vote on it. A good moderator must inform the people that there may be no right or wrong answers but that all opinions, issues, and problems must be put on the table. Usually, a think tank does not solve a problem but gives all opinions and weighs them accordingly; then some other group can solve the problem. The strength of a think tank is in its ability to explore an issue, not necessarily solve it. People are more likely to fully discuss an issue when they know there will be no vote taken to approve, disapprove, or spend money.

Fourth, the moderator should not move toward consensus to get everyone to agree, or even to accept one another's ideas. The examination of the issues is foremost on the agenda. That means the moderator must encourage people to disagree without being disagreeable. This also means that people should not try to persuade each other to their opinion or dissuade them concerning things that are being discussed.

The report should not try to project percentages, such as "50 percent of the committee said . . ." The percentages of the think tank are not valid for decision making, nor are they necessary. The success of the think tank is not in how many agree with an issue, but in exploring the issue and determining its strength and weakness.

Finally, avoid the tendency to use only one think tank to attack a problem. Perhaps three think tanks, each one looking at the problem from a different focus or a different perspective, will come up with more facts for better decision making. Because there is always the danger that one group of people can be misled or arrive at a conclusion with insufficient data, use more than one think tank to explore an issue. Perhaps an opinion that needs to be heard was not represented in a particular think tank.

As the church moves into the next century, it is seeking to give a more clear voice to its people in problem solving, decision making, and shared leadership. The use of think tanks is another way it is accomplishing more people involvement.

THOMPSON, HORACE E. (1865–1952)

A leader in the Advent Christian church was H. E. Thompson, who served as editor of the *World's Crisis, Young Pilgrim,* and *Blessed Hope Quarterlies.* He was business manager of the Advent Christian Publication Society, principal of the Boston Bible School (now Berkshire Christian College), and president of the General Conference. He also served as pastor to some of the most important churches in the Advent Christian movement.

Thompson was born in 1865 at Limerick, Maine. At the age of fourteen he began working in a shoe factory in Massachusetts, was converted, and started spending spare hours in evangelistic and Sunday school work. In 1894 he accepted the pastorate at Fall River, Massachusetts, and was ordained the following year.

Horace lacked formal training for the ministry, but he thirsted for more knowledge. One day he read in a newspaper that the Primitive Methodists were starting a Non-Resident School of

Theology. Thompson enrolled, earned a diploma, and pursued three years of post-graduate work. His Ph.D. was earned from Taylor University, Upland, Indiana.

Thompson believed that Christian workers in the Advent Christian church could benefit from a similar correspondence program, so he organized a Christian workers course that evolved into the Bible School Correspondence Institute. By the turn of the century more than one hundred men and women received instruction. Eventually the course became an extension program under Mendota College (now Aurora University). Sunday school teaching methods were an important part of Thompson's curriculum.

In 1899 Dr. Thompson introduced a series of children's stories to the *Young Pilgrim,* a popular take-home publication. Six years he was named editor. From 1905 to 1920 "Uncle Pilgrim" brought inspiration to a generation of Advent Christian Sunday school students.

Over the years Dr. Thompson served his denomination well as its representative on the International Lesson Committee and was a respected figure in interdenominational Sunday school work in New England.

THREE HEARINGS, LAW OF
Research shows that the average visitor to a church does not decide to accept Christ or join the church the first time he visits. A person will usually attend a church 3.4 times before making a meaningful decision to become a Christian or unite with a church. It is similar to the process of a person purchasing a new suit: the more significant the purchase, the longer it takes some people to make up their minds. This does not mean that some are not saved the first time they visit a gospel-preaching church. The time it takes to get someone saved depends on his receptivity to the gospel and responsiveness to the church.

"TITHING IS CHRISTIAN" STEWARDSHIP CAMPAIGN
"Tithing Is Christian" is a four-week campaign designed to teach the principles of storehouse tithing to members of the church. For one month the church is engaged in teaching and preaching

tithing. The campaign includes posters to remind people to tithe. The theme is reinforced through letters and tracts. The spiritual basis for giving money to God and scriptural explanations for tithing are detailed in a student book entitled *Tithing Is Christian.*

This campaign is aimed at total saturation and education of your church. Sunday school lessons on tithing will be taught to all departments. The pastor will preach messages on stewardship. Laymen will give testimonies in the service on the blessings God has given them because they tithe. Letters will be sent to every member.

Everything is aimed toward a great climax at a stewardship banquet during the third week. The banquet is exciting and uplifting as people rejoice in the blessing of God. Faith promises received that evening and on Over-the-Top Sunday, the final Sunday of the campaign, help subscribe the church budget. The hidden blessing of this approach is that a church determines its financial needs for the coming year, educates its people, and commits everyone according to his or her ability. Most people will give what they promise, so that the minister does not have to plead weekly for money. The whole church can get on with the task of soul winning and teaching. The church offering then becomes part of the worship experience of every member.

TRAINING WORKERS

When anyone volunteers to teach in Sunday school, that person may not be equipped to teach. He needs to be trained to teach. Churches may provide needed guidance to volunteers in a number of ways.

1. *Apprenticeship.* It works in the public school, and it works in churches. An inexperienced teacher may be chosen as an assistant in the age group of expressed interest and preference. Such a person may be of real help to the teacher by arranging chairs, setting up and putting away materials, recording absentees, perhaps playing the piano, or leading the singing. The apprentice is in the room to help when a child needs attention (going to the wash room, sustaining an injury, removing or putting on wraps, misbehaving). At the same time, she can observe the regular teacher's methods

from week to week. After a time, the apprentice should be asked to be responsible for a specific part of the weekly program: the character or mission story, an object lesson, the songs, a puppet. When she is confident of handling an entire lesson, she should be given additional responsibility.

2. *Training classes.* A continuing training class during the Sunday school hour provides training at the time when the most workers can be present. Some churches have an ongoing training class during the training hour preceding the evening service. This class is not a class in Bible content but a study of teaching methods. Inexperienced teachers (and that, unfortunately, could include a large percentage of the regular teaching staff of many churches) should attend eight or twelve weeks of sessions covering various ways of presenting the lesson, maintaining good discipline, capturing and holding attention.

3. *Saturday workshops.* Bring an outside speaker who can effectively demonstrate a variety of approaches to teaching. Invite all teachers and prospective teachers to come for a Saturday afternoon (or a 10:00 through 2:00 session, including potluck lunch) for training in the use of techniques. This should never be a "sit and listen" affair, where the speaker merely lectures and everyone goes home none the wiser. It should be a demonstration and participation time, when workers are involved in learning by doing.

4. *Workers' banquet.* Prospective workers and regular teachers may be invited to a banquet. The after-dinner program may be a couple of hours of training, discussion, and demonstration.

5. *Taped training.* Video and audio cassette tapes of teaching motivation and ideas may be circulated individually to new teachers, for their study at home in conjunction with an illustrated manual of instruction. Or the tapes may be played during a group meeting of all such teachers, followed by demonstration and discussion. (Check Christian supply catalogs for such tapes.)

6. *Books.* Provide each new worker with a good book of many methods of teaching. If this is financially impossible due to

large numbers of teachers, secure several copies of such a book for the church library, and make it available for new workers for two weeks at a time.

7. *Regular workers' meetings.* Many churches have a weekly meeting of all teachers—including assistants and prospective teachers. A period is devoted to discussion of the Bible content for the forthcoming Sunday, after which individual departments assemble to plan and demonstrate methods on the various levels.

8. *Conventions, conferences.* Arrange for the church to sponsor new teachers as delegates to a statewide or national Sunday school convention, where training in each age group is available. The importance of the task is magnified by the enthusiasm of large numbers of teachers dedicated to the same task.

TREASURER

The church treasurer (1) reports to the finance committee and board; (2) is responsible for establishing a sound bookkeeping system and insuring its accuracy; (3) should set up procedures to safeguard the assets of the church; (4) advises the board and membership on financial matters; (5) may present a forecast of financial plans of the church; (6) pays, by check only, all disbursements authorized by the budget or church board; (7) makes no deposits of funds; handles no loose cash; and disassociates himself from responsibility for counting or receiving any of the church's offerings; (8) prepares a regular report comparing expenditures to budgeted amounts; (9) keeps a record of checks issued in a cash disbursements journal; and (10) periodically lists assets at cost and replacement values, listing liabilities and their terms for repayment and interest rates.

TWIN SUNDAY

This one-Sunday promotional effort is effective as a means of making the church and its ministry known to those who are invited to make a first-time visit. The pastor usually plans to literally feature twins in the church, or even in the entire community, during the service through special recognition and perhaps an inexpensive gift. This assures the attendance of many babies, children, and parents, as a starter.

For this big day, everybody can have a "twin"; any visitor brought by a member is considered that person's "twin" for the day. Double cards are provided for each participant. One side of the perforation reads, "I have a twin," while the other says, "I am a twin." The member gives the latter to the visitor to wear. Furthermore, a participant may have more than one "twin" on this occasion. He may give out as many twin cards as he is able to bring visitors. Each is his "twin" for the day.

Churches that have used this emphasis report good cooperation on the part of neighbors, friends, and relatives who are willing to please someone by coming. Happily, some members of cold, dead churches are exposed to the Word of God through the visit. The long-range result has been, in some cases, the salvation of souls.

TWO-HUMPED CAMEL, LAW OF THE

The demographical attendance graph over the course of a year is described as the "law of the two-humped camel." Sunday school attendance will have two attendance bulges that look like two humps on a camel. Growth is experienced in the spring and fall; attendance dips in the summer and winter (unless the area is impacted by holidays and vacations). This is another way of describing the fact that secular culture influences Sunday school attendance. Since we know when Sunday schools grow, set attendance goals in the growth seasons, not at other times of the year.

There are thirty-six or thirty-seven weeks in the Sunday school growth year (the Sunday after Labor Day until the Sunday before Memorial Day weekend). Plan growth in the fall and spring, the primary growth weeks in the Sunday school.

TYPES OF CHURCH GROWTH/WORSHIP STYLES

In *The Complete Book of Church Growth*, the author identified six basic types of church-growth or worship styles. Each of these six types of church growth represents an essentially different worship style.

1. *Evangelistic churches.* Characterized by organized evangelistic outreach (soul winning) and individual religious response, pastor-led churches, revivalistic preaching, education that indoctrinates, dependence on literal church principles for administration, with emphasis on numbers as evidence of biblical credibility, and ethics that magnify personal purity and separation of the church from carnal influences. Emphasis is on such methods as evangelistic visitation, busing, public invitation for salvation, etc.

2. *Body-life churches.* Characterized by cells, small groups, or an emphasis on *koinonia*. These churches are known by love as a life-style, servant leadership, and ministering laity. Church growth is initiated by personal concern (not organized or manipulative).

3. *Renewal churches.* Characterized by emphasis upon the supernatural power of the Holy Spirit (this could or could not include signs and wonders), sharply altered style of living as a result of spiritual gifts, extreme enthusiasm, priority of experience, worship of God through praise music, and emphasis upon the organism of the body rather than the organization of the church, resulting in church growth. Emphasis in the worship service of raised hands, applause, positive practiced preaching, and revival atmosphere.

4. *Bible expositional churches.* Characterized by strong Bible teaching and emphasis on the edification of believers. The pastor equips the saints to do the task of evangelization; leaders are discipled by the pastoral staff; an intense caring spirit is manifested; and there is a plurality of godly leaders. Emphasis in the worship service on expositional preaching, use of the overhead projectors, reference Bibles, and distribution of outline notes.

5. *Congregational churches.* Characterized by using laity in ministry throughout the local body and a well structured organization of the total church. The church has detailed training for staff and teachers and an effective visitation program for outreach and growth. Emphasis on worship forms, such as gospel songs, extemporaneous preaching (rather than read-

ing sermons), congregational response, lay preaching, and spontaneous programming.

6. *Liturgical churches.* Characterized by an emphasis on liturgical (traditional) worship, nurture of members, social service outreach, and attention to internal programs. They are accepted by the community and are usually not outwardly evangelistically nor church-growth oriented. Emphasis is on worship forms, such as printed prayers, the Doxology, the Lord's Prayer, and the Apostles' Creed.

VACATION BIBLE SCHOOL

Vacation Bible school (VBS) has been defined as everyday Sunday school. VBS offers an unequaled opportunity to supplement the Sunday school coverage of Bible subjects. VBS is usually conducted during the morning, afternoon, or evening for one or two weeks during the summer months when the public school is dismissed for vacation. VBS is correlated with the Sunday school in that it continues studies of subjects, characters, or passages that strengthen the foundation laid in Sunday school.

How to Conserve the Results of Your VBS

In many churches, VBS is announced and open to boys and girls from any church or no church at all. It is viewed as a missionary opportunity. Often these churches may reach a large number of children not involved in a Sunday school. Several things can be done to conserve the results of a VBS outreach and increase the attendance in Sunday school.

If the children are not enrolled in a Sunday school when they come to vacation Bible school, their names and addresses should be provided to the proper department superintendent or teacher. Also, if children accept Christ or dedicate their lives for service during VBS, this fact should be passed on to their teachers. Home visits are needed before children join the church and are baptized.

The Sunday school teacher should follow up on the new children in VBS by visiting in the homes. Interest thus expressed may result in a family won for Christ. Also, the Sunday school teacher should learn and use the new songs taught during VBS and refer to the characters and stories studied in VBS to aid in bridging the

Sunday school and VBS in the minds of the children. Sunday school and VBS should be complementary rather than competing ministries of the church.

VACATION BIBLE SCHOOL TEACHERS

The main vacation Bible school (VBS) teachers are usually the regular teachers in the Sunday school. They are best acquainted with the children and the work of the department, so are best qualified. Occasionally, a teacher wants to change his place of service, feeling he might relate better to the pupils of a different group. A brief time with another age group provides a chance to discover whether or not he can work well with the new age level.

Assistants are needed in each department of VBS. The daily teaching periods afford excellent opportunity for willing but untrained workers to become apprentices. Taking a small but regular responsibility, they observe and learn from the teacher. An assistant may take records, take charge of the games at recess, tell the daily missionary story, lead the singing, play the piano, or help with handcrafts. This is a vital and necessary role. At the same time the assistant is preparing for greater service in the Sunday school and in any future VBS.

Superintendents in VBS departments have opportunity to see the apprentice teacher in action. At the close of the school, they may invite the new worker to become a regular assistant in the department, or they may alert the superintendent or nominating committee that the apprentice is a good worker and should be called upon to serve.

VISIBILITY OF THE SUNDAY SCHOOL

There are many reasons why people don't come to Sunday school. Perhaps one of the main reasons is that your Sunday school does not have high visibility—outsiders don't know about it. Absentees are not reminded of it. Casual members are not motivated to attend. Because no one gives Sunday school much thought, attendance goes down. If your Sunday school were given higher visibility, perhaps people would see its importance and give it priority in their schedule.

For the past twenty years worship service has been growing in attendance while Sunday school attendance was diminishing. Prior to the early seventies, Sunday school was larger in enrollment and attendance, and the worship service was smaller. However, recent research tells us that people visit the worship service, not the Sunday school. Why? First, they can visit the worship service without making a deep commitment or getting involved, which is not true of Sunday school. Second, worship is experience oriented with touch, feel, and the expression of "worship" through singing, prayers, and praise. A third practical reason is that people like to sleep late on Sunday morning. (The number one reason given in polls why people don't attend Sunday school is the early hour in which it is held.) Fourth, the pastor gets immediate affirmation from the worship service; therefore he gives it high visibility. Because people look into the pastor's face, some shout Amen, and everyone feeds on the Word of God as he preaches; the pastor gives the worship service attention because of its immediate reinforcement to him. Usually, it is difficult for a pastor to get affirmation when he delegates ministry to Sunday school teachers. Teachers are his representatives and help to bring maturity to his church members, but the pastor has little involvement in the process. The pastor gets affirmation by training ushers to run an efficient program, he gets affirmation from worshipful music that builds a platform for the sermon, or by raising money for an expensive sound system, pews, and sanctuary. The pastor becomes personally involved in the worship service; hence he gives it visibility.

The Sunday school teacher is the extension of the pastor's ministry in the life of his class. That is another way of saying the Sunday school teacher is the shepherd to those in his flock, just as the pastor shepherds the entire flock. However, since the pastor doesn't see all of the sheep (in Sunday school) and get a chance to feed them, he doesn't give Sunday school the center of his attention. The Sunday school needs higher visibility.

How to Get More Visibility for the Sunday School

The Sunday school needs more attention from everyone in the church. The following points can help give Sunday school the visibility it needs:

1. Establish Sunday school visibility in the worship service. Print Sunday school enrollment and attendance figures in the bulletin. Also, point out the content of Sunday school lessons in advertisements. Announce special Sunday school events in the worship service. The pastor should be the cheerleader for the Sunday school, realizing he cannot pastor his people better than through the teachers who are the extension of his ministry.

2. In many Southern Baptist churches, the Sunday school superintendent announces the attendance of Sunday school at the beginning of the worship service. Its priority is evident.

3. To establish a visitors' center with tables, hostesses, greeters, and necessary signs to inform people about Sunday school. The purpose of a visitors' center is to give a warm greeting.

4. Make an entrance map. The Calvary Nazarene Church of Oklahoma City, Oklahoma, drew up a map of "seven touches" showing a planned route for visitors from the parking lot to their final seat. This involved curbside greeters, sidewalk greeters, door greeters, hosts and hostesses, ushers to walk with visitors to their seat, and greetings from those sitting around visitors.

   Your average grocery store, department store, and variety store all have an "entrance map" that is an organized series of experiences as one enters the store. Obviously, their purpose is sales, our purpose is the great commission.

5. Teacher of the year. Establish standards and means of measurement to determine which teacher in the Sunday school has done the best qualitative and quantitative ministry during the past year. Then recognize that person in the morning service. Perhaps have a testimony from a pupil telling what he has gotten out of the class, or allow the teacher of the year to tell of his or her passion to teach Sunday school.

6. Sunday school teacher appreciation banquet. Even though this is not held during the Sunday morning service, a banquet to recognize teachers should be given high visibility.

First, give it visibility in the budget so that it is paid for by the church. Second, give it visibility in the schedule so that all know it is being held. Third, give the event and speaker of the banquet visibility. Fourth, results from the banquet should be shared with the entire congregation. Every member must know that the Sunday school teacher represents him as his ambassador to teach the Word of God to children and adults.

7. Sunday school teacher dedication. At the beginning of each Sunday school year (usually the first Sunday in September) teachers should be brought to the front of the auditorium during the worship service and dedicated for their ministry. Just as a commissioning service is held for missionaries who go to the mission field, so Sunday school teachers should be committed to the Lord's ministry among the church's children, youth, and adults. They can kneel at the altar or bow in prayer in an act of consecration. A series of questions can be given to them from the Sunday school teachers' covenant. (1) Will you accept this responsibility as a calling from the Lord? (2) Will you faithfully prepare the lesson each week? (3) Will you live a godly life of example to the students? (4) Will you pray for your students that God's Word may work in their lives? (5) Will you follow up all absentees and dropouts with a view of getting them back in the fellowship of the church body? (6) Will you try to win every person in your class to Jesus Christ who is not saved?

These questions should be asked the teachers publicly, and together all can answer in the affirmative. At the end of their commitment, someone should be called to the pulpit to dedicate these teachers and their ministry for the coming year.

8. Change the role designation of Sunday school teachers. A large Bible church in Lancaster, Pennsylvania, changed the title *teacher* to *leader*. The church's rationale was that the word *teacher* was tied to curriculum and content, whereas

the word *leader* was tied to people and action. This church wanted everyone to know that their Sunday school teachers were outreach leaders, spiritual life leaders, Bible study leaders, and pastoral care leaders. The word *leader* means "one who is in front of people to lead them." They wanted everyone to know that Sunday school leaders were in front of their classes, leading people into the Word of God every week.

9. Change the name *Sunday school* for one outreach campaign. I do not mean the words *Sunday school* should be dropped. However, enroll people in Bible study for an outreach campaign. Use the action phrase *Bible study* instead of the name *Sunday school*. Many secular minds think Sunday school is for small children, or that the Sunday school is attached to some juvenile method of teaching. By changing the name to *Bible study,* people will know they are becoming involved in the study of the Word and that the Bible is the focus of attention. After this outreach campaign is completed and people are enrolled in Bible study, obviously the name *Sunday school* would be retained.

10. Have a Friend Day. A Friend Day is when every person in the church is encouraged to bring his or her friend to Sunday school and church on a designated Sunday. This campaign is discussed in a separate article.

11. Dedicate your Sunday school to God. Perhaps Sunday school does not have high visibility in your church because it does not have high visibility in your Christian life. Perhaps you need to dedicate your relationship to your Sunday school to Christ. Perhaps you need to ask God to give you a new vision of the Sunday school. When it has a high priority in your vision, then you can communicate that to other people.

VISITATION PROGRAM (See also F.R.A.N.GELISM)

Visitation is the one area of Sunday school about which it may be said, "Everybody's job is nobody's job." Experiments in hit-or-miss visitation compared with an organized plan have proven that a planned program reaches the most people.

Who Visits?

1. *The pastor.* Just as he must set the spiritual pace in other areas of church life, the pastor sets the pace for the visitation program by his own example of regular visitation. Some churches feel they have hired a church visitor when they pay the pastor's salary. Visitation is only one of the pastor's many responsibilities, and it should be shared with others.

2. *The teachers.* Teachers best show their interest and concern when they visit in the home of every pupil at least once during the year. In a very large class, the responsibility may be shared with assistants. There is no substitute for a home visit to help a teacher become really acquainted with the background and the interests, hopes, and fears of the pupils—be they young or old. Until something of the spiritual status and needs are known, there cannot be effective ministry.

   Not only should a teacher visit those on the roll, but special visits should be made to pupils confined to home or hospital with extended illness. The teacher also should visit homes of new church attenders who have children of her class's age level.

3. *The deacons.* Deacons usually represent the church rather than the Sunday school when they visit. But they should be interested in the Sunday school to the extent that they will encourage attendance on the part of any who may be lax.

4. *Church officers.* Paid or unpaid workers in the church should visit absentees and prospects, particularly non-Christians in the Sunday school or in the community.

5. *All Sunday school members.* Any Christian should be willing to express interest in an absentee by making a visit. All Christians should be willing to go to the home of newcomers and extend an invitation to Sunday school. Older Christians should seek to win the lost to Christ during such visitation as the Lord opens the way and reveals the need.

When to Visit

1. *At a designated time.* Set aside a night or afternoon when all visitors meet at the church to pray and to receive visitation assignments. It encourages all present to see that others are concerned.

2. *Whenever possible.* Sometimes employment schedules do not allow some teachers or members to visit at the time set by the church. Their visit at another time may be even more fruitful. Unchurched people in a community often discover the scheduled time for church visitation and leave home to avoid the visitors. When an unscheduled visit is made, they are caught by surprise.

3. *At times of special need.* Bereavement or illness in a family may not coincide with the visitation program. Visits at those times are usually opportunities to extend the greatest help because hearts are the most open to the Word of God.

4. *In case of absence.* When the pupil is absent one Sunday, phone him and let him know he is missed. Everyone likes to know someone cares. When he is absent two Sundays, visit in the home. After he is absent three Sundays, the departmental superintendent should visit in the home. If he is absent four Sundays, the Sunday school superintendent and pastor should do all they can to solve the problem and to reach this family for Christ. Prayer for the pupil should increase with each absence.

Where to Visit

The answer at first glance would seem to be, in the immediate area around the church. However, the outlook of most churches has changed regarding this practice. Once a church could say, "This is my territory." Now, with church buses often bringing riders from a radius of twenty-five miles or more, many churches feel that the field is wide open to any and every church, and that any effort is justified.

There are some ethical restrictions to this freedom, however:

1. *Overlapping by biblical churches.* Some church bus directors have gone overboard for numbers of riders to the extent they visit in the homes of those who are faithful and regular members of a sister church. They seek to persuade even those faithful workers to change their allegiance and ride the bus to a different church. This has resulted in ill will among fellow Christians. Sheep stealing is never viewed kindly by another church. Proselytizing has been frowned upon since the times

of the Galatians. Christians are to love one another; it is difficult to love a Christian who seeks to undermine the work you have done, and many view sheep stealing in that light.

Such a practice has also resulted in some families being confused. In some communities with a multiplicity of church buses covering the territory, the parents may ride to one church, the teenagers to another, and the small children to still a different one. The family is divided, and the religious education is haphazard and confused. On a given Sunday, the little children may choose to go with the parents because of a special program or a special reward. They break the continuity of their lessons and view the Bible as disjointed stories. The teens will be without parental supervision in church. They may feel free to cause disturbance by talking, which they would not do with the parental eye upon them.

2. *Wasted time.* While visitors are spending time calling in homes already reached by a church of like faith and practice, they are using valuable hours needed to go out into an area where no one has visited. Such areas are to be found in nearly every county.

3. *Wasted money.* The car expense of the visitor is wasted when the visit is made to an already churched home. When it is clearly known that the family is regularly attending a church of like faith, it is deliberate waste. Bus drivers who make an effort to secure riders in an area already reached by a sister church waste the Lord's money when they use the bus to pick up a few children from a home where parents already attend a similar church.

4. *Scorn of the unchurched.* Viewing the competition of Christians who pretend to love one another, unbelievers feel their concern is only to solicit members. They may choose to go where they will get the most material gain.

How to Visit

Sometimes new Christians are willing to visit on behalf of the church, but are timid. "I don't know what to say" is their reason for not taking part in the visitation program. Courses discussing soul winning may provide some answers. New Christians may and should visit in the company of an experienced visitor. The visit on behalf of Sunday school (or church) should be viewed as a friendly visit. Going with the hand of friendship extended can put a different light on the conversation. Encourage the one visited to express his interests, views, and needs by asking questions rather than expecting to dominate the conversation. A visit may be opened by:

1. *A leaflet.* A teacher can make friends in a home by taking an absentee member a Sunday school paper or picture card. This small token shows concern and often will open the heart of the recipient.

2. *An illness.* Go to the home of a sick member and take a cheery bouquet, a book, a magazine, or some other gift for the one who must spend many days in bed. Expression of interest is all the approach needed. People in the home most often will welcome the friendly overture.

3. *A welcome.* Newcomers are made to feel less lonely when the Sunday school has expressed its interest by a visit—especially if the visitor has brought a plate of cookies, a hot dish, or a cake. They are more open to an invitation to services when it is extended by someone who cares.

4. *A spiritual need.* A teacher needs only the knowledge of a sorrow or great problem to have a reason to make a visit to extend sympathy and offer assistance.

5. *A census.* A visit may be made, stating that the Sunday school is seeking to get acquainted and requesting the names, ages, and church affiliations of family members. Such a brief visit will open the door for a teacher to call upon children in the age group of her class. First-time visitors need only introduce themselves, tell what church they represent, state the wish to get acquainted, and record the information. If the family is cordial, they may visit longer.

How Long to Visit

1. *Briefly.* If the family is just arriving home with the week's groceries or from a funeral, it is seldom appropriate to detain them by a long visit. Express interest and concern and depart.

2. *Not at all.* If the person visited is hostile to the church and argumentative, say good-bye quickly. There is nothing to be gained by argument.

3. *A few minutes.* A sick person usually welcomes visitors but may tire quickly. A stay of ten or fifteen minutes usually is sufficient to learn how the person is, to give spiritual comfort and help, and to pray with him.

4. *As long as need be.* Occasionally the Sunday school visitor encounters a spiritual need that cannot be met in a brief conversation. When the needy one expresses a wish for help, sit down with him, open the Bible, and stay until the need is met or the person has found the strength and comfort sought.

VISUAL AIDS (See also specific visual aids)

Visual aids may be defined as objects, symbols, materials, and methods that appeal to the sense of sight. Their purpose is to clarify thought by making the abstract concrete. Visual aids are valuable in the teaching-learning process. Proper use of visual aids will help clarify the material, illustrate difficult points, make learning more lasting since a child remembers 50 percent of what he sees, complement other teaching methods, motivate change, speed learning, get attention, improve behavior, make learning more enjoyable, and provide eye appeal as an avenue to the soul.

1. Problems of visual aids. Use of visual aids can be a hindrance to good teaching if:

   a. They become lessons in themselves.

   b. They become a substitute for traditional teaching methods.

   c. They are limited to one kind.

   d. They become mere entertainment.

   e. The instructor is not fully versed in the use of the aid.

   There are some disadvantages and limitations to the use of some visual aids:

   a. The cost of some visual aids makes use prohibitive.

   b. Some upkeep of mechanical aids and replacement of materials is expensive.

   c. Storage space is required for large mechanical aids.

    d. Small visual aids may only be viewed by a small group.

    e. Projected visual aids require room space for seating, good acoustics, and good lighting.

    f. It takes time to set up and take down visual aids, write script for them, and train people in their use.

    g. Packaged visual aids are not always edited and may be inappropriate.

2. Principles for visual aids. Some guidelines in selection and use are:

    a. Be familiar with the field, especially the latest developments in methods and effective uses. A teacher should read periodical reviews of literature in the field, invite resource experts in the field to demonstrate use of an aid, have group discussion and periodic reports on the subject, offer courses in the effective use of visual aids, and secure catalogs or price lists from many companies.

    b. Be careful in selecting your visual aids. Select the aids requested by the teacher who will use them. Select aids in your price range and with which you are familiar—or become familiar. Choose aids that are durable, attractive, professionally made, and that present an effective message. Select the aids you know how to operate or those with clear instructions for use. Check to be sure the aids are free from false doctrine or undesirable elements.

    c. Choose aids appropriate to your teaching situation. Use aids that are interesting and understandable to each age level, accurate, authentic, realistic, educational rather than entertaining, able to accomplish the desired purpose, stimulating, and easily transported.

    d. Be intelligent and efficient in the use of visual aids. Have all equipment set up and tested beforehand. Plan and practice all mechanical procedures thoroughly. Be sure of visibility of the aids from all parts of the room. Plan a smooth transition into use of the visual aid. Apply the lesson of the visual aid to the lives of the students.

VITAL SIGNS OF A HEALTHY CHURCH

There are certain signs of life that are normally found in healthy and growing churches. Seven vital signs commonly recognized are (1) the pastor, (2) the people of the church, (3) church size, (4) structure and functions, (5) homogeneous unit, (6) methods, and (7) priorities.

WALKER, ROBERT (1912–)

Robert Walker was editor of *Christian Life* magazine from 1929 to 1984. He used the pages of the magazine to influence the Sunday schools of America. The first significant project was the Annual Christian Life Sunday School Growth Contest, which began in the early 1950s. There were four attendance levels so that each Sunday school competed with those of the same size. The contests were more than just attendance, so that total involvement of the church, ingenuity, community impact, and gains were judged. Each Sunday school constructed a scrapbook presentation. Because of the national recognition of the contest, most major Christian publishers and suppliers of related services offered their products to the winners. Some of the attention involved an armada of boats representing the Sunday schools of Seattle, Washington, that invaded the city from the harbor. Roy Rogers registered his horse, Trigger, in the Sunday school of First Presbyterian Church, Hollywood, California.

The second project by Walker was the publishing of the list of the 100 largest Sunday schools in America, which was printed from 1967 to 1976. This project demonstrated optimism, i.e., that Sunday schools were growing.

The third project was the publishing of the list of the fastest-growing Sunday schools in each state. This project began in 1975 and continued till 1984.

Walker was born in Syracuse, New York, and was on the staff of a daily newspaper in Michigan. He moved to Wheaton, Illinois, to join the staff of Scripture Press, Inc. From there Walker took on the once-struggling publication named *The Sunday School* magazine. Instead of allowing the management to drop it, he published it out of his home, changing the name to *Christian Life* magazine. It became the most influential evangelical magazine to report the trends and news in the Christian world during four decades, from the forties to the seventies.

WANAMAKER, JOHN (1838–1922)

John Wanamaker, founder of the commercial empire that bears his name, Wanamaker Stores, was one of the more influential lay leaders in the Sunday school movement of his day. Born in Philadelphia, Wanamaker grew up in a strict religious environment but received little formal education. He was converted at age eighteen at Philadelphia's First Independent Church, where he later began teaching Sunday school. He participated in the 1857 prayer revival and the next year began the Bethany Sunday school in a rough neighborhood. He also became the first full-time secretary of the YMCA in the United States.

In 1861, he resigned his position in the YMCA to begin his business empire, although he remained a national figure in that movement throughout his life. Wanamaker was also instrumental in the evangelistic ministries of Dwight L. Moody and Billy Sunday in Philadelphia and helped establish *The Sunday School Times* and *The Scholar's Quarterly*.

Wanamaker remained superintendent of the Bethany Sunday School for more than sixty-years. Under his leadership, the Sunday school became the largest Sunday school in America and served as a model for similar ministries in other churches. When appointed U.S. Postmaster General, he took the job with the condition he could return home each weekend to lead his Sunday school. Wanamaker achieved his success in Sunday school by applying many of the same promotional and entrepreneurial principles that led to his success in business.

WASHBURN, ALPHONZO VICTOR (1912–1978)

Alphonzo Washburn was the Sunday school secretary of the Sunday school board of the Southern Baptist Convention from 1957 to 1978. He served the Sunday School Department during its golden years of growth after World War II and when growth slowed down during the turbulent sixties and seventies. The Action Program was introduced to Southern Baptist Sunday schools under his leadership.

WELSHIEMER, P. H. (1872–1957)

P. H. Welshiemer pastored the First Christian Church in Canton, Ohio, and was recognized as having the largest Sunday school attendance in the fellowship of Christian churches with more than 3,000 attending weekly. As a pastor he was noted for putting emphasis on the Sunday school as the most significant agent for evangelism and church growth. He came to Canton January 1, 1902, and stayed for fifty-six years with the same congregation.

WESLEY, JOHN (1703–1791)

The people of Savannah, Georgia, claimed that John Wesley began the first Sunday school in their city in 1736. Wesley came to Georgia as a young Anglican clergyman to preach to the Indians in the new colony. Careful study shows that Wesley taught the catechism to the children of his parish on Saturday and Sunday afternoon. This religious exercise does not fit the technical description of a Sunday school. But the desire of Wesley to reach all children with the gospel was later manifested in the Sunday school movement.

Wesley returned to England and was converted at Aldersgate. The impact of his conversion resulted in a new movement. At first Wesley and his followers were sarcastically called "methodist" because they used innovative methods to reach the masses.

Wesley divided his followers into small classes, predictive of the Sunday school that was later to come. Wesley wrote more than 300 books in his lifetime, aimed at helping lay preachers give out the Word of God, again predictive of the Sunday schools that provided literature for the lay public. Wesley also worked with the masses outside of the established church, once again, a glimpse of Sunday schools that began outside of church buildings in view of reaching the children of the street.

Obviously Wesley never claimed to begin Sunday school. In his journal he shows surprise when he visited a Sunday school. Wesley called them "nurseries for Christians." Wesley showed delight with the new movement as he wrote in his journal (1884) after visiting Leeds, England. The town had twenty-six Sunday schools, two thousand scholars and forty-five teachers. Wesley realized he could use the Sunday school to expand his movement, so he called them, "Methodist Sunday Schools." He wrote, "There must be a Sunday school where ever there is a Methodist society." John Wesley is the forerunner of Sunday school because he planted the seeds of the movement thirty years before Robert Raikes began the first Sunday school.

WORSHIP STYLES (See TYPES OF CHURCH GROWTH/WORSHIP STYLES)

YOUTH PASTOR—YOUTH DIRECTOR

The youth pastor is to the youth of the church and their families what the senior pastor is to the church. He should be able to understand, communicate with, counsel, and lead youth. He should have a genuine love and concern for all young people and be able to train and develop youth in their Christian life for effective ministry. He is normally responsible for any ministry of the church directly involving youth.

Sample Job Description for a Youth Pastor

The youth pastor is generally responsible for the youth ministry of the church from junior high through college and career age. He is expected to select, recruit, train, supervise, and assist a lay staff of youth workers in the various youth activities of the church. He should correlate and coordinate the total youth program with other church activities. This will involve the preparation of a calendar of events and coordination of the same with the master calendar of the church.

The youth pastor should be alert to the activities of schools, community groups, other churches, and parachurch youth ministries. He should remain current on contemporary thought regarding youth through the study of suitable books and periodicals and involvement in youth ministry conferences and clinics.

The youth pastor should have continual open communication with the senior pastor and other church staff as part of the ministry team. Final decision-making authority in areas of staff relations rests with the senior pastor from whom counsel and guidance should be sought. The youth pastor should report on general activities, needs, and plans and share in general pastoral staff functions and responsibilities.

The youth pastor should adhere to office schedules, appointments, and procedures. He is expected to regularly attend all meetings of specific church boards and committees in which the youth pastor is involved.

QUESTIONNAIRE I
How to Survey the Sunday School

EDUCATIONAL PRACTICES
AND
PROCEDURES OF THE CHURCH

Name of church _____ Phone _____

Address _____ Denomination _____

Mr.
Your   Name: Mrs. _____
Miss
Your position in the church _____
Please be as exact as possible in giving your answers. Be conservative where you may have to approximate. The information you give can help your church accomplish the task Christ intended. This questionnaire will be one of the sources to help formulate a three to five year plan of growth. Your help is greatly appreciated.

****

I
THE CHURCH AND ITS COMMUNITY

A. The church
1. When was the church begun? _____
2. List all of the pastors of the church since its inception.

Pastor   Years in Office
_____ From _____ 19____ To _____ 19_____
_____ From _____ 19____ To _____ 19_____
_____ From _____ 19____ To _____ 19_____
_____ From _____ 19____ To _____ 19_____

3. During the term of which pastor did the church see the most numerical growth?
_____

4. What is the reputation of the church in the community? (You may check more than one item)
_____ Bible preaching   _____ stodgy
_____ fundamental   _____ cliquish
_____ separatist   _____ other (specify)
_____ friendly   _____
_____ evangelistic   _____

5. What number of the church members who are family heads or single adults are in the following occupation?
_____ (1) professional and proprietors of large businesses
_____ (2) semi-professional and smaller officials of large businesses
_____ (3) clerks and kindred workers
_____ (4) skilled workers
_____ (5) proprietors of small businesses
_____ (6) semi-skilled workers
_____ (7) unskilled workers
6. What number of the church members who are family heads or single adults have the following sources of income?
_____ (1) inherited wealth
_____ (2) earned wealth
_____ (3) profits and/or fees
_____ (4) salary
_____ (5) wages
_____ (6) private relief
_____ (7) public relief
_____ (8) other

7. What number of the church members who are family heads or single adults live in the following house types?
_____ (1) excellent houses
_____ (2) very good houses
_____ (3) good houses
_____ (4) average houses
_____ (5) fair houses
_____ (6) poor houses
_____ (7) very poor houses
8. What number of the church members who are family heads or single adults live in the following types of dwelling areas?
_____ (1) very high: north shore, etc.
_____ (2) high: the better suburbs and apartment areas, houses with spacious yards, etc.
_____ (3) above average: areas all residential, larger than average space around the houses, apartment areas in good condition, etc.
_____ (4) average: residential neighborhoods, no deterioration in the area.
_____ (5) below average: area not quite holding its own, beginning to deteriorate, business entering, etc.
_____ (6) low: considerably deteriorated, run down and semi-slum
_____ (7) very low: slum
9. Name or give other identifying phrase (beyond the tracks, etc.) for each neighborhood area in the community. List the number of church members from each neighborhood area.

      Neighborhood   Number of members

_____
_____
_____
_____

10. Which of the above neighborhoods have special needs or social problems? Describe the specific need or problem.

      Neighborhood   Problem

_____
_____
_____
_____

11. How many members of the church participate in the following civic activities?
_____ (1) high elected office (mayor, councilman, etc.)
_____ (2) elected office (school board, etc.)
_____ (3) P.T.A., neighborhood association, etc.
_____ (4) civil defense, rescue squad, volunteer fireman, etc.
_____ (5) service or fraternal organizations (Rotary, Lions, etc.)
_____ (6) other (specify)

_____
_____

12. In what community activities is the pastor involved (ministerium, Rotary, etc.)?

_____
_____

B. The community

Information for this section may be obtained from:
_____ Chamber of Commerce
_____ School Board
_____ welfare and social agencies
_____ public library
_____ city planning commission
_____ urban renewal agency
_____ Census Bureau
1. When was the community first settled? _____
2. Is the community conscious of its history and heritage?

_____ very traditional
_____ traditional
_____ average
_____ progressive
_____ very progressive

3. Rate the occupation of the average family head (single individual in each of the neighborhood areas mentioned under "The church" question 8. Using the following rating system list the neighborhood name or designation, and the rating number.
   (1) Professional and proprietors of large businesses
   (2) Semi-professional and smaller officials of large businesses
   (3) Clerks and kindred workers
   (4) Skilled workers
   (5) Proprietors of small businesses
   (6) Semi-skilled workers
   (7) Unskilled workers

   _____
   _____
   _____
   _____
   _____
   _____

4. In the same manner as the above question, rate the sources of income of the average family head or single person in the neighborhood areas.
   (1) Inherited wealth
   (2) earned wealth
   (3) profits and fees
   (4) salary
   (5) wages
   (6) private relief
   (7) public relief
   (8) other

   _____
   _____
   _____
   _____

5. In the same manner rate the type of housing.
   (1) Excellent houses
   (2) Very good houses
   (3) Good houses
   (4) Average houses
   (5) Fair houses
   (6) Poor houses
   (7) Very poor houses

   _____
   _____
   _____
   _____
   _____

6. In the same manner rate the neighborhood as a dwelling area.
   (1) very high: north shore, etc.
   (2) high: the better suburbs and apartment house areas, houses with spacious yards, etc.
   (3) above average: areas all residential, larger than average
   (4) average: residential neighborhoods, no deterioration in the area
   (5) below average: area not quite holding its own, beginning to deteriorate, business entering, etc.
   (6) low: considerable deterioration, run down and semi-slum

(7) very low: slum

_____
_____
_____
_____
_____
_____

7. What zoning classifications exist in the immediate vicinity of the church? Please give an explanation of the local zoning code's symbols.

_____
_____
_____

8. Indicate by a check the nature of any current land development in the community. In the blanks to the right record the distance in miles of the development(s) from the church.
____ (1) very high residential _____
____ (2) high residential including better apartments _____
____ (3) above average residential and apartments _____
____ (4) average residential _____
____ (5) low income housing _____
____ (6) clean industrial _____
____ (7) industrial _____
____ (8) business _____
____ (9) shopping center _____

9. Is there undeveloped land with potential for a residential area within a one mile radius of the church? ____ yes ____ no

10. Has the church delineated a particular geographical area for its specific responsibility? ____ yes ____ no. If so give the boundaries of that area. _____

11. Is a map of the public transportation system of the community attached to this questionnaire? ____ yes ____ no

12. What is the population of the community?
Census of 1960 _____
Census of 1970 _____
Now _____

13. What population is projected for 1980? _____ 1985? _____

14. What is the population of the particular geographical area of the church's specific responsibility? _____

15. What is the population of the county?
Census of 1950 _____
Census of 1960 _____
Census of 1965 _____
Now _____

16. List the racial and/or ethnic groups living in the community, giving the population of each.
_____

17. What is the population of the following age groups in the community?
(1) children 0-12 _____
(2) youth 13-20 _____
(3) young adult 21-40 _____
(4) middle adult 41-60 _____
(5) older adult 60- _____

18. What is the percentage of annual population turnover in the community?
_____

19. What are the percentages of annual population turnover in the neighborhoods in the geographical area of the church's specific concern? _____

20. In what neighborhood is the population the most stable? _____

21. Are young adults remaining in the community in any sizable amount?
____ yes ____ no. Of what occupational class(es) are most of those who are remaining?
_____

22. What is the current form of taxation at the local level?
_____ personal
_____ property
_____ real estate
_____ sales
_____ income
_____ other (specify)

23. State in percentages the current dispersion of the tax dollar.

24. What are the principal industries of the community?
    Industry   Approximate number of employees

25. What percentages of the working citizens are employed within the community?

26. How many people work in the community but do not live there? _____
27. What is the current rate, in percentage, of unemployment? _____
28. How many families are there on welfare rolls? _____
29. How many of the industries are union shops?
_____ very few
_____ some
_____ about half
_____ most
_____ all
30. Are the unionized industries open _____ or closed _____ shops?
31. What vocational training is offered the youth in terms of trades and other skills?

32. List the denominations represented in the city. _____

33. List the churches within the geographical area of the church's specific concern and their approximate membership.
    Name   Denomination   Membership

34. Name any other religious agencies in the geographical area of the church's specific concern.

35. Name the governmental social agencies in the community.
    Agency   Level of government (county, etc.)

36. Name the private social agencies in the community.

37. Are there psychological services for low income families? _____ yes _____ no. Is family counseling available for low income families? _____ yes _____ no. Check the other professional services available for low income families.
_____ medical
_____ dental
_____ recreational
_____ legal
_____ other (specify)

38. What is the form of government in the community?
_____ mayor
_____ council
_____ city manager
_____ county board
_____ other (specify)

39. Is an annual report from the local police department attached to this questionnaire?
_____ yes _____ no

40. What recreational facilities are readily available?
_____ swimming pools
_____ gymnasiums
_____ parks
_____ youth centers
_____ tennis courts
_____ garden clubs
_____ senior citizens clubs
_____ other (specify)

41. How many of the following amusements are there in the community?
_____ bowling alleys
_____ spectator sports
_____ bars
_____ pool halls
_____ museums
_____ theatres
_____ golf courses
_____ casinos
_____ zoos
_____ parks
_____ road houses

42. Is an annual report from the Board(s) of Education attached to this questionnaire?
_____ yes _____ no

II
ENROLLMENT, ATTENDANCE AND RECORDS

1. What is the present enrollment of your Sunday School? _____
2. What was the enrollment one year ago? _____
3. What was the enrollment five years ago? _____
4. What was the average attendance one year ago? _____
5. What was the average attendance five years ago? _____
6. At what age do most children enroll in Sunday School? _____
7. At what age do most students drop out of Sunday School? _____
8. Are drop-outs increasing _____ or decreasing _____?
9. If there has been an increase or decrease in attendance, how do you account for it?
_____

10. What is the local church membership? _____
11. Who is responsible for the attendance records and other related records of the Sunday School? _____
Who is responsible for other agencies such as clubs, young people's, etc.?
_____

12. Is there a master file in the Christian Education office, or another centrally located place, that covers all church activities of each person? _____

13. Check what information is recorded about each attender.
_____ attendance
_____ Bible
_____ offering
_____ on time
_____ church
_____ study lesson

_____ visitor
_____ other (specify)

14. Check what use is made of the records.
_____ follow up
_____ building project
_____ attendance
_____ evaluation of growth
_____ personal evaluation of individuals
_____ other (specify)

15. Are the records used regularly? _____ yes _____ no
16. Check what recognition is made for perfect attendance.
_____ cross and crown
_____ yearly pins
_____ cups
_____ Bibles
_____ other (specify)

17. Are student records kept up-to-date? _____ yes _____ no
18. Are the figures compiled and distributed weekly _____ monthly _____
quarterly _____ or yearly _____
19. Who has access to these records? _____
20. Is there any kind of confidential file that would describe in depth the activities of each individual student? _____ yes _____ no
If so, check what is included.
_____ conversion
_____ full time service decision
_____ emotional background
_____ family background
_____ date of baptism
_____ date of membership
_____ offices held
_____ personal achievement
_____ other (specify)

21. Check other sets of records that are kept.
_____ financial
_____ audio-visual
_____ library
_____ other (specify)

22. Is there a church historian? _____ yes _____ no
23. How are records preserved?
_____ record books (bound)
_____ card files
_____ loose leaf forms
_____ other (specify)

24. When is a student's name added to the Sunday School roll? _____

25. When is a student's name removed from the Sunday School roll? _____

III
ADMINISTRATION

1. Do you have a general Sunday School superintendent? _____ yes _____ no
2. Do you have departmental superintendents? _____ yes _____ no
Check the departments for which you do have superintendents.
_____ Cradle Roll
_____ Nursery
_____ Kindergarten

_____ Primary
_____ Junior
_____ Junior High
_____ Senior High
_____ College and Business Youth
_____ Young Adults
_____ Adults

3. Does the entire Sunday School staff meet together? _____ yes _____ no
   How often? _____
4. Does the Sunday School Executive Committee meet? _____ yes _____ no
   How often? _____
5. List in order of priority the matters handled when the Sunday School teachers meet. (Use 1 for most important to 8 the least important.)
   _____ Sunday School business
   _____ instruction on how to teach
   _____ inspiration
   _____ devotional approach
   _____ evaluation of past effectiveness
   _____ discussion of Sunday School lesson
   _____ information on local church educational resources, materials, etc.
   _____ planning for the future
6. Do you have the following appointed officers (please check)?
   _____ librarian
   _____ registrar
   _____ visitation chairman
   _____ assistant Sunday School superintendent
7. At what time of year do you have promotion? _____
8. Do you have a printed handbook telling the aims, duties, qualifications, etc., for Sunday School teachers? _____ yes _____ no
9. How often is this printed copy given to Sunday School teachers?
   _____
10. What do you consider to be the best new idea practiced in the administration of the Sunday School in the past two years? _____
11. What do you consider to be the main administrative problem in your local Sunday School?
   _____

IV
ORGANIZATION

Sunday School
1. Indicate the departmental attendance in your S.S. and how many classes are in each department.
   _____ _____ Cradle Roll
   _____ _____ Primary
   _____ _____ Senior High
   _____ _____ Adult
   _____ _____ Nursery
   _____ _____ Junior
   _____ _____ College
   _____ _____ Kindergarten
   _____ _____ Junior High
   _____ _____ Young Adult
2. Are all the departments closely graded? _____ yes _____ no
3. What is the average size of a single S.S. class? _____
4. Do S.S. departments meet together as departments for the opening activities?
   _____ yes _____ no
5. Does the whole church meet together for opening activities? _____ yes _____ no
6. What is the primary aim of the S.S.? (rate from 1 to 3)
   _____ evangelism _____ Bible knowledge _____ Christian living
7. How many are there on the total volunteer S.S. staff?
   _____ teachers _____ staff workers
8. How are teachers elected to their position?
   _____ S.S. board

614

_____ church board
_____ Christian Education Board
_____ pastor
_____ other (specify)

9. How are substitutes elected? _____

10. Are the substitutes required to work closely with the regular S.S. teachers?
_____ yes _____ no Sit in the class? _____

11. What are the specific aims for the S.S. classes? _____

12. Are the regular teachers given at least one Sunday per quarter off? _____ yes _____ no

13. What percentage of the teachers usually attend teachers' meetings?
_____% of the substitutes _____%

14. Are teachers required to be present and sit with their class for opening activities?
_____ yes _____ no

15. Are the teachers appointed for a regular length of time?
_____ yes _____ no How long? _____

16. Who decides which teachers should be reappointed? _____

17. Can teachers be reappointed to the same class? _____ yes _____ no

18. To whom are teachers directly responsible?
_____ S.S. superintendent
_____ Christian Education Director
_____ pastor
_____ other (specify)

19. Are parent-teacher meetings used? _____ yes _____ no If so, how often? _____

20. Do teachers actively contact absentees? _____

21. Are regular reports made in writing?
from teacher to the S.S. superintendent _____
from the S.S. superintendent to the C.E. Board _____

Church Organization

1. Is the job of S.S. Superintendent separate from the job of chairman of the C.E. Board?
_____ yes _____ no

2. Is there a church calendar? _____ yes _____ no If so, when is it constructed? _____

3. Are all church organizations required to clear their activities on this calendar?
_____ yes _____ no

4. What persons are represented on the Executive Board of the church?
_____ pastor
_____ treasurer
_____ financial secretary
_____ Christian Education Director
_____ Chairman of Trustees
_____ Chairman of Deacons
_____ moderator
_____ church clerk
_____ S.S. superintendent
_____ other (specify)

5. Is the pastor also the moderator? _____ yes _____ no

6. What is the primary aim of the church? _____

7. Are new members of the church required to enter a membership class? _____ yes _____ no

8. Do new members sign a covenant? _____ yes _____ no

9. Is any member allowed to hold more than three positions of responsibility in the church?
_____ yes _____ no

10. Who decides matters of policy in the church? _____

Training Courses

1. Does your church require training courses for all teachers? _____ yes _____ no
For all substitutes? _____ yes _____ no

615

2. Is it required for leaders in church organizations? _____ yes _____ no
3. Is training made available to all interested members? _____ yes _____ no
4. Has the opportunity of the present training program been presented to the entire congregation? _____ yes _____ no
5. Are any requirements prescribed for teachers? _____ personal _____ spiritual
   For officers? _____ personal _____ spiritual
6. Does your church provide inservice training for teachers?
   _____ yes _____ no
7. Is there organized presentation of methods of leading people to Christ? _____ yes _____ no
8. Does your S.S. cooperate with local or regional S.S. conferences or workshops?
   _____ yes _____ no
9. What percentage of your teachers attend at least one conference or workshop a year?
   _____

10. In your training course:
    a. Are there regularly scheduled classes   _____ yes _____ no
    b. Is the teacher well prepared   _____ yes _____ no
    c. Are achievement awards given upon completion of the course   _____ yes _____ no
    d. Is attendance required   _____ yes _____ no
    e. Are tests given for successful completion of the course   _____ yes _____ no
    f. Is there specialized training for each age group of the S.S.   _____ yes _____ no
    g. Is observation of good teachers a part of the training program   _____ yes _____ no
    h. Does the church library have sufficient reference material for this training
                                                                                 _____ yes _____ no
    i. Is a visual-aid program outlined   _____ yes _____ no
    j. Is Bible content knowledge tested   _____ yes _____ no
    k. Is Scripture memorization required   _____ yes _____ no

V
SUPERVISION

1. Are Sunday School departmental superintendents and heads of other agencies appointed by the Board of Christian Education? _____ yes _____ no
2. Does the Board of C.E. replace these people? _____ yes _____ no
3. Is there a systematic method of evaluation for these people done by the Board of C.E.?
   _____ yes _____ no Explain _____

4. Are Sunday School departmental superintendents responsible only to the Sunday School superintendent? _____ yes _____ no
5. Do the heads of other agencies know who they are specifically responsible to?
   _____ yes _____ no
6. Is there confusion in some agencies over who is really in charge? _____ yes _____ no (If yes, explain) _____

7. What is the title of the person that represents the Sunday School on the Board of C.E.?
   _____ Is he a voting member? _____ yes _____ no
8. Is there a board member assigned to oversee the youth activities? _____ yes _____ no
9. Does each member of the Board of C.E. have a specific agency to oversee and report to the Board on? _____ yes _____ no Explain _____

10. Do some agencies have little voice or representation on the Board of C.E.? _____ yes _____ no
    Explain _____

11. All Sunday School departmental superintendents have attended some form of leadership training in supervision. _____ yes _____ no (If no, what percentage have not?) _____ %
12. Have the heads of other agencies been trained in leadership directly related to their agency?
    _____ yes _____ no Explain _____
13. Do your supervisory personnel attend additional leadership training sessions?
    _____ yes _____ no
14. Do the departmental superintendents meet regularly to evaluate and plan? _____ yes _____ no
    How regularly? _____

15. Do the supervisors within other agencies meet regularly to evaluate and plan? ____ yes ____ no How regularly? _____
16. How far ahead do most agencies plan their program? _____
17. Do most agencies evaluate past activities to build a better program for the future? ____ yes ____ no In what way? _____

18. Does the Sunday School maintain a 12 month calendar of activities? ____ yes ____ no
19. Do other agencies maintain 12 month calendars of activities? ____ yes ____ no Which do not? _____

20. Must agencies clear their dates for activities through a proper channel? ____ yes ____ no What channel? _____
21. Are there times during the year when there is competition among agencies due to too closely scheduled activities? ____ yes ____ no Examples _____

22. Is there a "fair" method of sharing important dates or services (i.e. Sunday night before Christmas) among agencies, or does one group always "get what they want"? Explain __

23. Does the Board of C.E. or the D.C.E. know what curriculum each agency is using? ____ yes ____ no
24. Is there an attempt made among agencies who serve the same age group to work together in planning the curriculum? ____ yes ____ no
25. Do Sunday School departmental superintendents ever meet together to evaluate the total curriculum of the Sunday School to point out strengths and weaknesses at various age levels? ____ yes ____ no
26. Does the curriculum of each agency require the approval of the Board of C.E.? ____ yes ____ no
27. Are there any specific weaknesses in the curriculum of any agency at the present time? Explain _____

28. Does the Sunday School superintendent confer with the departmental superintendents with regard to budget allocations? ____ yes ____ no
29. Does the head of each agency submit a budget to the C.E. Board only after he has conferred with his staff? ____ yes ____ no
30. Do the Sunday School superintendent and departmental superintendents frequently offer help and advise in problem areas? ____ yes ____ no Explain _____

31. Are there any noticeable problems in the working relationship between supervisory personnel and general workers? ____ yes ____ no Explain _____
32. Does the pastor cooperate readily with the C.E. Board? ____ yes ____ no
33. Does the pastor cooperate with and advise the S.S. superintendent? ____ yes ____ no
34. Does the pastor's relationship with general workers emphasize a spirit of helpfulness and cooperativeness? ____ yes ____ no Explain _____
35. Describe the relationship between the D.C.E. and the C.E. Board. _____
36. Describe the relationship between the D.C.E. and the S.S. superintendent. _____
37. Describe the relationship between the D.C.E. and the heads of the various agencies.

38. Does the D.C.E. have a written job description? ____ yes ____ no (If so, attach a copy)
39. Does the S.S. superintendent have a written job description? ____ yes ____ no
40. Does each agency head have a written job description? ____ yes ____ no
41. List the supervisory personnel who do not have job descriptions written out for them.

42. Do those who have written job descriptions follow their responsibilities stated therein? Explain _____

VI
BUILDINGS AND EQUIPMENT

1. How many teaching centers do you have that are used for Sunday School rooms? ____

NOTE: A teaching center is an area where a teacher meets with his class during the lesson time.
2. How many rooms do you have that could be used for Sunday School teaching centers? _____
3. What is the total educational floor space in your building? (Do not count halls, offices, and stair wells in computing floor space footage) _____
4. Please diagram the floor plan of your present building(s), specific purpose(s) for each room.
5. Have you increased floor space in your educational unit in the past two years? _____ yes _____ no How many square feet? _____
6. What is the size of your plot of ground? _____ Draw a rough scale of the plot.
7. What are your plans for future expansion? _____

Where will you put the new building? _____

What will be the purpose or function of the new building? _____

How many square feet will be in the new building? _____ How many additional persons will the new building accommodate? _____
8. What building material was used for construction of your present plant? _____

9. How many toilets do you have in your present system? _____
10. Approximately how much square floor footage do you have for storage? _____
11. In the columns below, please indicate the number and size of tables and chairs in the various departments. NOTE: The number indicated under the line is that recommended by the National Sunday School Association (NSSA).

Department	No. Chairs	Height (avg.) Chairs	No. Tables	Height (avg.) Tables
Cradle Roll	_____ (cribs)	_____	_____	_____
Nursery	_____	_____ (8″)	_____	_____ (18″)
Beginner	_____	_____ (10″)	_____	_____ (20″)
Primary	_____	_____ (12-14″)	_____	_____ (24″)
Junior	_____	_____ (16″)	_____	_____ (26″)
Junior High	_____	_____ (18″)	_____	_____ (28″)
Senior High	_____	_____	_____	_____
Adult	_____	_____	_____	_____

12. Do you have at least one chair per pupil? _____ yes _____ no
13. Please list the number of items that are now used or accessible in the department indicated.

Cradle Roll
_____ cribs
_____ refrigerators
_____ bottle warmers

_____ rocking chairs
_____ change tables
_____ storage areas

Toddlers (birth-2)
_____ coat racks
_____ storage areas
_____ rugs
_____ toy boxes
_____ toys

_____ blocks
_____ pictures
_____ Bible picture books
_____ Bibles
_____ cuddle toys

NSSA indicates that there should be between 25-30 square feet per person. How many square feet do you have? _____

Nursery (2-3)
____ low clothes hooks
____ storage areas
____ display tables or
    interest centers
____ books
____ blocks

____ dolls
____ puzzles
____ picture display areas
____ rugs
____ bulletin boards on eye level
    of pupils

NSSA indicates that there should be between 25-30 square feet per person on the first floor near a bathroom. How many square feet do you have per person? _____
Where is it located? _____

Beginner (4-5)
____ low clothes hooks
____ storage areas
____ pianos
____ interest center
    tables
____ crayons
____ blunt tipped scissors
____ Bibles

____ books
____ rhythm band instruments
____ bulletin boards
____ rugs
____ papers
____ flannel boards
____ chalkboards

NSSA indicates that there should be between 25-30 square feet per person on the first floor near a bathroom. How many square feet do you have per person? _____
Where is it located? _____

Primary (6-8) (Grades 1-3)
____ clothes racks
____ storage areas
____ piano for department
____ teaching pictures
____ display tables
____ flannel boards

____ Bibles
____ crayons
____ pencils
____ scissors
____ teaching aids suggested in
    curriculum
____ chalkboards

NSSA indicates that there should be between 20-25 square feet per person. How many do you have? _____

Junior (9-11) (Grades 4-6)
____ coat racks
____ storage areas
____ piano for department
____ pencils
____ paper
____ hymnals
____ display tables
____ bookcase with Bible
    dictionary
____ concordance

____ pictures
____ flannel boards
____ bulletin boards
____ chalkboards
____ maps
____ charts
____ teaching pictures
____ Bibles
____ other teaching aids suggested
    in curriculum

NSSA indicates that there should be between 15-20 square feet per person. How many do you have? _____

Junior High (12-14) (Grades 7-9)
____ coat racks
____ storage areas
____ piano for department
____ hymnals
____ bulletin boards

____ chalkboards
____ reference books
____ teaching aids suggested
    in curriculum

NSSA indicates that there should be 10-15 square feet per person. How many do you have? _____

High School (15-17) (Grades 10-12)
____ coat racks
____ storage areas
____ piano for department
____ hymnals

____ chalkboards
____ teaching aids suggested in
    curriculum
____ bulletin boards

NSSA indicates that there should be between 10-15 square feet per person. How many do you have? _____

Young People (18-24) (College, etc.)

_____ coat racks
_____ storage areas
_____ piano for department

_____ hymnals
_____ chalkboards
_____ teaching aids suggested
in curriculum

NSSA indicates that there should be 10-12 square feet per person. How many do you have? _____

Adults (25 and up)
_____ coat racks
_____ storage areas
_____ piano for department

_____ hymnals
_____ chalkboards
_____ teaching aids suggested in
curriculum

NSSA indicates that there should be 10-12 square feet per person. How many do you have? _____

14. How often is equipment examined for need of repair or replacement?
_____ 6 months   _____ 12 months   _____ 2 years

VII
TEACHING AIDS

1. Please list the number of teaching aids below that are available for use in the church.
_____ 16 MM projector
_____ 8 MM projector
_____ flannelgraph file
_____ flat picture file
_____ slide projector
_____ slide file
_____ filmstrip projector
_____ filmstrip file

_____ tape recorder
_____ tape file
_____ record players
_____ records
_____ other
_____
_____
_____

2. Name the audio-visual aids (other than those listed above) which you have used this past year (rent or borrow). _____

3. Where are the audio-visuals kept? _____

4. Is one person designated to be in charge of all "teaching aids"? _____ yes _____ no

5. How is this person designated into office? _____

6. Is he/she instructed as to the use, care and maintenance of the various pieces of equipment?
_____ yes _____ no

7. What check-out process is followed for use of an aid? _____

8. What procedure do you follow to add to the present audio-visual aids? _____

9. What percentage of teachers would use an aid each Sunday? _____

10. What visual aid is most generally used in classroom teaching? _____

11. Do you have files on the following available to teachers? (Indicate by a check)
_____ flat pictures
_____ object lessons
_____ maps

_____ film strips
_____ flannelgraph lessons

12. How many volumes are contained in your library? _____

13. What system of classification is used? _____

14. What are the major division headings of your books? _____

15. Do you have written guide lines or procedures for your library? _____ yes _____ no (If so, please enclose a copy with this report)

16. Who is in charge of the library? _____

17. To what board or committee is the library accountable? _____

18. What is the annual budget of the library? _____

19. What other method do you use to acquire books? _____

20. How many books are checked out each month? _____

21. Is the library considered an educational arm of the church? _____ yes _____ no

VIII
CURRICULUM

1. List those experiences which are available to students in your Christian education ministry in order of frequency. (Mark most frequent 1, next frequent 2, etc.)
_____ service opportunities   _____ leadership opportunities
_____ worship   _____ programs for the family together
_____ doctrinal teaching   _____ Bible content teaching
_____ memorization   _____ denominational doctrine
_____ social work   _____ witnessing
_____ missions   _____ prayer
_____ use of talents (music, etc.)   _____ other

2. Who designs or chooses the curriculum in the Christian education ministry of the church?

3. Who designs or chooses the curriculum of the Sunday School? _____

4. How often is the curriculum of the Christian education ministry reviewed?
_____ yearly   _____ other (specify)
_____ semi-annually   _____
_____ every five years   _____

5. Are the curricula of the other church's agencies besides the Sunday School reviewed at the same time as above? _____ yes _____ no
6. Has the curriculum material been changed in the last five years? _____ yes _____ no If so what was used before? _____
Why was the change made? _____
7. What publishers does your denomination suggest? _____

8. Why are you or why are you not using that material? _____

Does the Sunday School use printed materials? _____ yes _____ no List the publishers used by departments:
Cradle Roll _____
Nursery _____
Kindergarten _____
Primary _____
Junior _____
Junior High _____
Senior High _____
Young Adult _____
Adult _____

9. How is the quarterly used in the Sunday School? (You may check more than one item)
_____ printed scripture portion read from it
_____ teacher teaches from quarterly
_____ students do homework
_____ used for lesson preparation
_____ not used in the classroom
_____ other (specify)
_____
_____

10. Are materials purchased to assist the leaders of worship time in the Sunday School?
_____ yes _____ no Do the materials purchased suggest activities for pre-session?
_____ yes _____ no _____ sometimes
11. What material do you purchase for each student?
_____ pupil quarterly (workbook)   _____ other (specify)
_____ activity packet (handwork)   _____
_____ take home papers   _____
_____ none

12. What additional materials will the Sunday School purchase at the request of a teacher?
_____ handwork
_____ visual packet
_____ films
_____ filmstrips
_____ records
_____ tapes

_____ other (specify)
_____
_____
_____

13. Is there an official version of the Bible in the Sunday School? _____ yes _____ no
If so, what is it?
_____ King James
_____ Revised Standard
_____ Other (specify)
_____

_____ American Standard
_____ New English

14. What is the view of the Bible in your Sunday School? (You may check more than one item)
_____ good literature
_____ myth
_____ not to be taken literally

_____ Word of God
_____ normative for faith and practice

15. Who is Jesus as taught in the Sunday School ? (You may check more than one item)
_____ a good man
_____ The Messiah
_____ truly human
_____ a living Savior

_____ a great teacher
_____ the Son of God
_____ a dead person
_____ other (specify)
_____
_____
_____

16. Is there a Bible memory program for _____ children, _____ for youth, _____ adults.

17 In your experience how often is application to the pupils' lives made of the daily lesson in your Sunday School?
_____ very seldom
_____ rather often
_____ always

_____ not very often
_____ very often

IX
OUTREACH

1. Is there a coordinating committee of some kind that has the overall responsibility for visitation? _____ yes _____ no What positions in the church are on the committee? _____

2. Do the visitation efforts of the church come under the direction of the Board of C.E.?
_____ yes _____ no

3. Do agencies which serve the same age group cooperate together in visitation efforts?
_____ yes _____ no

4. Has there been a duplication of visitation efforts in the past? _____ yes _____ no
Explain _____

5. Are visitation records kept and promptly turned in after each visit?
_____ yes _____ no

6. Are the visitation records made available to the various agencies? _____ yes _____ no

7. Is there a systematic procedure within each agency, or with the visitation committee, whereby visitation assignments are made available and/or recommended?
_____ yes _____ no Explain

8. Does each agency have a systematic plan of informing workers when an absentee student should be visited? _____ yes _____ no Explain _____

9. Is there a standard policy in the school as to how many times a student may miss before he should be visited? _____ yes _____ no

10. What other methods are used to contact absentees besides personal visits?
_____

11. Does each agency have a systematic plan of visiting prospects (people who have indicated an interest in attending)? _____ yes _____ no Explain _____
_____

12. Are visitation assignments made available to laymen who are not directly involved within an agency? ____ yes ____ no
13. What other methods are used to visit prospects? _____
_____

14. Does every person who visits attempt to introduce the person to Christ? ____ yes ____ no Explain _____
15. Are visitation workers trained in personal evangelism? ____ yes ____ no
16. How many people have received Christ through the specific efforts of visitation (within the last year)? _____
17. Does the church hold any special visitation for evangelism emphases during the year? Explain _____
18. Is there a simple, but effective way for church members to turn in the names and information about possible prospects? Explain _____
_____

19. Do church members turn in the names of people they are witnessing to? ____ yes ____ no
20. Is any use made of community programs that serve new arrivals in the community (i.e. Welcome Wagon, Junior Chamber of Commerce, etc.)? ____ yes ____ no Explain _____
21. Is there a periodic canvassing of the community made to determine new prospects and make the community aware of the church? ____ yes ____ no How often? _____ Explain _____
22. When was the last canvass done? _____ What were the results? _____

23. Do the church and the various agencies of the church feel responsible for locating prospects? Explain _____
24. Is there a good core of witnessing Christians in the church? ____ yes ____ no
25. Are the results of individual witnessing seen by an increase in church attendance? Explain

26. Is there an emphasis by each agency of the church to encourage, train and challenge Christains to witness? ____ yes ____ no Give the strong and weak areas of this:
_____
_____
_____

27. Does each agency receive C.E. Board approval (or its properly appointed committee) before publicizing an activity in the community? ____ yes ____ no Explain the procedure
_____
_____

28. Does the public relations committee seek to develop a year-round program of consistent and regularly spaced promotion to the community? ____ yes ____ no
29. Who is included in the public relations committee? _____
_____

30. Place a check by the image (or images) that you think best represents the church as you see it.

____ Bible-believing
____ fundamental
____ evangelical
____ liberal
____ social
____ lower class
____ middle class
____ upper class
____ conservative
____ strict
____ friendly
____ youthful
____ Republican
____ socially concerned
____ bigoted
____ biased
____ prejudiced

_____ warm
_____ community conscious
_____ politically involved
_____ growing
_____ dying
_____ religious
_____ old-fashioned

Place a zero (o) by the image (or images) that best represents the church as the community sees it.

31. What is being done to improve the image of the church? _____

32. Is there general agreement among the various agencies what the image of the church should be? Explain _____

33. Please indicate, in order of importance (1, 2, etc.) the methods and media used to promote the various programs and activities of the church to the community.
_____ visitation
_____ newspaper stories
_____ newspaper advertisements
_____ radio
_____ posters
_____ direct mail
_____ telephone contacts
_____ church newsletter
_____ weekly bulletin
_____ pulpit announcements
_____ door to door flyers
_____ television
_____ parades (floats)
_____ yellow pages listing
_____ school publications
_____ city directory listing
_____ door to door
_____ booths at fairs, etc.
_____ airline terminals
_____ bus terminals
_____ train terminals
_____ hotel and motel lobbies

34. What kinds of contests or special events have you used to attract outside attention? _____
_____
_____

35. Please list a typical plan of the outreach thrusts of the various agencies of the church. (Visitation, Promotion, Special Meetings, Contests, etc.)
September _____
October _____
November _____
December _____
January _____
February _____
March _____
April _____
May _____
June _____
July _____
August _____

36. Do all of the agencies of the church cooperate successfully in the total outreach thrust of the church? _____ yes _____ no Explain _____

37. Is there a 12 month calendar that is actually used to plan for public relations, etc.? Explain _____

38. Is there a general budget for outreach? _____ yes _____ no Explain _____

39. Must all outreach expenditures be approved by the public relations committee?

Explain _____

40. How much money is spent annually for outreach? _____
   By the Sunday School? _____ By the general church promotion? _____
   What percentage of the budget is the total outreach spending? _____
41. Has the Board of C.E. determined any goals for the outreach program of the church?
   _____ yes _____ no Explain _____
42. Have numerical goals been established for the Sunday School or other agencies? Explain
   _____
43. How many people received Christ as Savior last year as a result of the outreach program
   of the church? _____
44. Is there a transportation committee in the church or within any agency? Explain _____
   _____
45. What kind of transportation is available, and for what agencies? _____
   _____
46. Is the community aware of the available transportation? _____ yes _____ no
47. Are there agencies which suffer because of the lack of transportation for prospects?
   Explain _____
48. Do church members know who to contact to arrange transportation for people?
   _____ yes _____ no Who? _____
49. Is any remuneration given to those who provide transportation? Explain _____
   _____
50. Does the burden of providing transportation fall on the shoulders of just a few (i.e. pastor,
   D.C.E., youth sponsors, etc.)? _____ yes _____ no
   Has anything been done to rectify the situation, if no? _____
51. Are buses used to transport students to and from the church? _____ yes _____ no
52. How many buses are used? _____
53. How many are brought to Sunday School each week on these buses? _____

PARALLEL INFORMATION

To do a thorough job of evaluating your church and constructing a 3-5 year plan of growth, as much
information is needed as is available. Please attach to this questionnaire the following:
   1. Church Constitution
   2. Annual Budget
   3. Sunday School Teachers' Handbook or Constitution
   4. Copy of the Annual Report
   5. Sample copies of Church Brochures or Publicity Items
   6. Other printed matter that reveals the educational nature of your church

QUESTIONNAIRE 2
How to Survey the Sunday School

Name of Church _____ Denomination _____

Address _____ Phone _____

Your Name:
Mr.
Mrs. _____

Miss

Your position in the church: _____

This evaluation should be filled out *after* you have completed the Questionnaire (Q-1). Please rate your church's level of efficiency on each item from 1 to 5. Try to be as objective as possible. This information will be used to construct a 3-5 year plan of growth for your church. Use the following scale to rate your church:

1. This item is *never* found in our church.
2. This item is *occasionally* found in our church.
3. This item is *average* in our church.
4. This item is *above average* in our church.
5. This item is one of our *strong* qualities.

Do not leave any item blank. If you leave an item blank, the scorer will assign a #1.

****

I
THE CHURCH AND COMMUNITY EVALUATION QUESTIONNAIRE

	1	2	3	4	5

1. Our church is concerned for the needs of our community.
2. Our church is actively involved in the affairs of our community.
3. Members of our church are active in the civic affairs of our community.
4. Our church is involved in ministering to the people in needy neighborhoods.
5. The pastor's activity in the community satisfies the members.
6. The reputation of our church in the community is what it should be.
7. Our church fulfills its role of calling attention to sin in the community.
8. The racial attitudes of our church are Biblical.
9. Our church has properly defined the specific neighborhoods for which it is concerned.
10. Our church has had a consistently Christian testimony in business and financial affairs.
11. Leadership in our church is open to anyone who is qualified.
12. Our community has opportunity for further growth.
13. Our community is a stable community.
14. Our community has been faithful to the vision of its founders.
15. The industries in our community are adequate for assuring the stability of the community.
16. Our community has an equitable tax system.
17. Our community's religious attitudes are healthy.
18. The religious nature of our community is such that our church has opportunity for growth.
19. There are enough social agencies in our community.

627

20. Our community is attempting to help the minority groups (racial, ethnic, and needy) who live there.
21. The racial attitudes of our community are in line with the view of Scripture.
22. The teenagers in our community are clean cut and well mannered.
23. Our community is involved in planning the future.
24. The government in our community does a good job.
25. The government of our community is honest and lawful.
26. The police department in our community does a good job.
27. The rate of crime in our community is fairly low.
28. There are adequate recreational facilities in our community.
29. Amusements in our community are constructive.
30. The schools in our community are giving our children a fine education.
31. Our community spends money on schools at a rate that is on a par with neighboring communities.
32. Our schools offer a constructive program of extra-curricular activities.
33. An adequate percentage of our high school graduates go on to college.

II
ENROLLMENT, ATTENDANCE AND RECORDS

1. Our attendance is stable and consistent.
2. Our past attendance growth has been steady.
3. We have a healthy outlook on expansion and attendance growth.
4. Our teachers have a desire to win the lost to Christ.
5. Sunday School contests are important to attendance growth.
6. Our Sunday School enrolls students at the right time of their growth. (Score less if you think the Sunday School enrolls too young or waits too late.)
7. Our church has a drop-out problem.
8. The Sunday School staff has a healthy attitude in dealing with the drop-out problem.
9. Our church enlists Sunday School pupils at the right age for church membership.
10. Our church has adequate plans to prepare people for church membership.
11. Membership in our church has meaning to our members.
12. The church has the right (general) attitudes toward the Sunday School.
13. The records and files are all centered in the responsibility of one person.
14. There is a master file that covers all church activities of each person.
15. Records are used to pin-point weak areas and realize growth.
16. Consistent attendance is important to pupils.
17. Each agency has their own set of records.
18. The records from each agency are transferred to the master file once a month.
19. The pupils are aware of the record kept on their progress.
20. All records are current and accurate.
21. The Sunday School and other agencies maintain a definite visitor and absentee record and follow-up system.
22. The congregation is satisfied in supervision of financial records.
23. There is a confidential file on each active attender kept locked in the pastor's office.
24. Records are important to all key personnel.

III
ADMINISTRATION

1. The Sunday School superintendent is given enough direction and guidance to do his job efficiently.

628

	1	2	3	4	5

2. The Sunday School teachers know what is required to perform their task properly.

3. The qualifications for teaching in our Sunday School are strictly kept.

4. The aims, duties and qualifications of Sunday School teachers are revised often enough to be up-to-date.

5. We have enough departmental superintendents to guide our Sunday School.

6. The department superintendent is given enough direction to do his job efficiently.

7. The regular Sunday School staff meeting is meaningful to teachers and necessary in the growth of the Sunday School.

8. The administration of our Sunday School welcomes and easily implements new ideas.

9. The administration of our Sunday School deals with problems in a satisfactory manner.

10. Promotion of pupils is given adequate attention by the administration.

11. When teachers are absent from class, the matter of obtaining a substitute is adequately handled.

IV
ORGANIZATION

1. Opening exercises (departmental worship) is meaningful on the whole to the students in our Sunday School. Rate each department:
Nursery
Kindergarten
Primary
Junior
Junior High
Senior High
College and Business Youth
Young Adults
Adults

2. The individual Sunday School classes are the right size for effective teaching (rate low if classes are too large or too small).

3. The organization of the Sunday School instills a spirit of cooperation and comradeship among teachers.

4. The substitute teacher system is adequate for our Sunday School.

5. The staff personnel for running the Sunday School is adequate in keeping with the number of teachers we have.

6. The system by which new teachers are appointed is efficient.

7. The system by which former teachers are re-appointed is adequate.

8. The instruction given to prepare teachers for their positions is sufficient.

9. The instruction of *inservice training* given to those already teaching is adequate.

10. Our Sunday School benefits from denominational or interdenominational workshops and/or conferences.

11. We receive inspiration from such workshops.

12. We receive practical and helpful instruction from workshops.

V
SUPERVISION

1. The Board of C.E. usually makes wise choices in its appointment of individuals to various agencies.

2. The Board of C.E. has an adequate method of replacing vacancies within agencies.

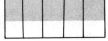

	1	2	3	4	5

3. The Board of C.E. has a systematic and effective method of evaluating personnel.

4. The S.S. departmental superintendents know who they are directly responsible to.

5. The heads of the various agencies know who they are directly responsible to.

6. The S.S. is adequately represented on the C.E. Board.

7. The Board of C.E. delegates one of its members to oversee the youth activities and consequently stays alert to its program.

8. Other members of the Board of C.E. have similar responsibility with other agencies and also stay alert to their programs.

9. Some agencies are seldom represented fairly on the Board of C.E.

10. Departmental superintendents have received adequate training through leadership sessions they have attended.

11. The supervisory personnel of other agencies are also well trained through the leadership sessions they have attended.

12. All supervisory personnel attend additional leadership training sessions of great value to them.

13. The regular meetings of the departmental superintendents usually prove to be quite valuable to the total program of the S.S.

14. The supervisory personnel of the various agencies find that their regular meetings together help them to do their own work more effectively.

15. Advance planning for future activities for most agencies is done quite successfully.

16. The systematic evaluation of past activities helps the various agencies to plan more effectively for future activities.

17. The planning of a 12 month calendar by the S.S. enables personnel to avoid unnecessary conflicts with dates.

18. The various agencies also make successful use of a total church 12 month planning calendar.

19. There is a simple, yet effective method for the clearing of dates for the general calendar.

20. There is careful planning done to avoid the scheduling of activities too close together.

21. The most important dates and services of the year are successfully shared with the various agencies over a period of several years.

22. The Board of C.E. or the D.C.E. maintains a careful watch over the curricula of the various agencies.

23. The cooperation among agencies who serve the same age group enables the supervisory personnel to plan the curriculum jointly.

24. The S.S. departmental superintendents find it helpful to meet together at times to discuss the strengths and weaknesses of the curriculum.

25. The curriculum of each agency is always approved by the Board of C.E.

26. The overall curricula of the total church program generally meets the needs of the people.

27. S.S. departmental superintendents are able to have a strong voice with regards to their yearly budget allocations.

28. All supervisory personnel confer with their staff members before submitting a budget to the C.E. Board.

29. The S.S. superintendent and the departmental superintendents are quite helpful to their staff members.

30. There is a good spirit of cooperativeness among supervisory personnel and general workers.

31. The pastor and the C.E. Board have a good working relationship.

32. The pastor is very cooperative with the S. S. superintendent.

33. The general workers in the various agencies enjoy the help and advice of the pastor.

34. The D.C.E. and the C.E. Board enjoy a good working relationship.

35. The S.S. superintendent and the D.C.E. are able to work closely together.

	1	2	3	4	5

36. The D.C.E. and the heads of the various agencies work well together and the D.C.E. serves them primarily as a resource person.
37. There is an adequate job description for the D.C.E.
38. The S.S. superintendent has an adequately written job description.
39. The heads of the various agencies have adequate job descriptions.
40. There are some supervisors who do not have written job descriptions.
41. Most supervisory personnel know their job requirements and successfully fulfill their responsibilities.

VI
BUILDINGS AND EQUIPMENT

1. The church building is located geographically in the center of where the church members live.
2. The church is easily accessible from public transportation or private cars.
3. There is no traffic hazard in reaching the church.
4. The church is in a suitable environment. (It is away from noise, offensive odors, and undesirable influence of taverns, industry, etc.)
5. The landscape is neat, attractive, and adds to the purpose of the church.
6. There is enough parking for the congregation (one lot for each four in attendance).
7. The building's height is in keeping with the surrounding neighborhood. (Score low if height is out of proportion to situation and type of construction.)
8. There are at least two means of exit from every Sunday School room to the outside.
9. There are fire extinguishers available.
10. The building is considered safe from fire hazards.
11. The building is kept clean.
12. The building is properly designed for the control of sound.
13. The maintenance is adequate (score low for broken windows, unreplaced light bulbs, etc.).
14. There is adequate heating for good education.
15. There is a good amount of storage space (apart from educational materials) in the building.
16. The classroom provides natural light.
17. The classrooms are open and clean as opposed to cramped, dark, damp quarters.
18. Most of the educational rooms are flexible so that they may be adapted for use by other agencies.
19. The classrooms are so arranged that class will not be interrupted by late comers.
20. The artificial lighting is adequate.
21. The color scheme is bright, pleasing to the eyes and lends itself to creating the atmosphere of study.
22. Each teacher or at least department has its own storage unit for supplies.
23. There is adequate space for wraps and overcoats of the pupils and these are at the correct height according to student needs.
24. There are enough chairs for all students.
25. The chairs are of the correct size for the students.
26. There are enough adjustable tables for the teachers.
27. The equipment of our church is up-to-date and adequate.
28. There are plans for increasing the audio-visuals in the church.

VII
TEACHING AIDS

1. Our Sunday School has an adequate number of audio-visual teaching aids.

	1	**2**	**3**	**4**	**5**

2. The teaching aids are stored where they are easily accessible to all the teachers.
3. We have an adequate method of securing up-to-date audio-visual aids.
4. The Sunday School teachers make good use of audio-visual aids.
5. The church library is adequate for our needs.
6. The library has good procedures for securing additional books.
7. The average person can find a book easily in the library.
8. The teachers make good use of the library.
9. The average pupil makes good use of the library.
10. The library has efficient administration.
11. The library is considered an educational arm of the church.
12. The library has a well-rounded service (biographies, commentaries, encyclopedias, teaching aids, fiction, youth, children's material, soul winning helps, etc.).

VIII
CURRICULUM

1. The Bible is the central text in the Sunday School.
2. The teachers stick to the assigned lessons in the quarterly.
3. The pupils do the assigned homework in the quarterly.
4. The teachers write out lesson plans at home to be used in the classroom.
5. The teachers know how to use their quarterlies and other materials.
6. Our Sunday School is satisfied with our present curriculum materials (publishing house).
7. Our Sunday School uses the present material out of choice and conviction.
8. The take home material is meaningful and used by the students.
9. Take home papers are considered part of the total teaching material.
10. Our Sunday School teachers consider practical application as important as Bible knowledge. (If one is overemphasized score low).
11. The pupils' understanding of the passage is emphasized in memory work.
12. Play activities are used to teach the younger children Christian living. Rate each department:
    Crib Room
    Nursery
    Kindergarten
    Primary
13. Handwork among the children is considered educational and helpful to cause children to grow in Christ.
14. Memory work is considered important with children.
    Memory work is considered important with youth.
    Memory work is considered important with adults.

IX
OUTREACH

1. The visitation program is effectively coordinated by a committee.
2. The Board of C.E. has careful supervision of the total visitation program.
3. There is a good cooperative effort among agencies serving the same groups toward an effective visitation program.
4. Careful planning has avoided the problem of duplication in visitation assignments among the various agencies.
5. There is an adequate system of record keeping for the visitation program.
6. The various agencies make good use of the visitation records.
7. Visitation assignments are effectively given out to the various agencies and/or staff workers.

	1	2	3	4	5

8. Each agency has a good plan whereby workers are informed of absentees who should be visited.

9.There is a general policy regarding how many times a student may miss before he should be visited.

10. There are a variety of methods used to contact absentees.

11. Each agency employs a systematic and effective plan of contacting prospects.

12. Laymen not directly involved with any agency have ample opportunities to be involved in visitation.

13. A variety of methods are used to visit prospects.

14. An attempt is made to introduce Christ to every person visited.

15. All visitation workers are effectively trained in personal evangelism.

16. There have been a good number of people who have received Christ through the visitation efforts within the last year.

17. Special emphasis on visitation for evangelism proves to be effective each year.

18. Most church members know who they should see about turning in the name of a prospect.

19. Most church members inform the pastor or someone else about specific individuals they are witnessing to.

20. The church takes advantage of community programs geared to welcome new arrivals in the community.

21. The periodic canvassing of the community provides the church with an effective way of finding prospects.

22. The latest canvass was done within the last year.

23. Church members are generally looking for opportunities of finding prospects for the church.

24. The church has many members who are regularly sharing their faith.

25. Church attendance is climbing due primarily to the effective witnessing of its members.

26. The church's programs emphasize the need for its members to be witnessing Christians.

27. The public relations committee must approve all promotion of any agency which desires to promote activities in the community.

28. The public relations committee has set up an effective year-round program of consistent promotion to the community.

29. The public relations committee is made up of a good representation of the various agencies of the church.

30. The church has a very favorable image in the community.

31. The church is constantly seeking to improve its image.

32. The agencies of the church are in agreement as to the image they would like to present to the community.

33. The public relations committee effectively uses the best methods and media (to publicize activities) which are best suited for the community.

34. Generally, the contests and special events in the church have helped to increase attendance and promote community awareness of the church.

35. The special emphasis of the various agencies are planned with a total 12 month impact in mind.

36. All of the agencies of the church play an effective role in the total outreach program.

37. The outreach activities of the church are coordinated by the use of a 12 month planning calendar.

38. There is an adequate budget for the outreach program.

39. The public relations committee has general control over the spending of money for outreach purposes.

40. The Sunday School has a sufficient portion of the outreach budget for its specialized outreach efforts.

41. The C.E. Board has written aims and objectives for the total church outreach program.

42. Numerical goals have been set as a future achievement to strive for.

43. A good number of people received Christ as Savior last year due to the effectiveness of the outreach program.

	1	2	3	4	5

44. A transportation committee functions cooperatively with the outreach program of the church.

45. There is a sufficient amount of transportation available to those who need it.

46. The community is aware of the available transportation.

47. Every agency within the church is able to acquire the necessary transportation when needed.

48. Church members know whom they should contact when some transportation is needed.

49. Those who provide transportation are reimbursed for any personal expenses incurred in providing transportation.

50. The providing of transportation is shared by a large number of people preventing the work from falling only to a few.

THE FIFTY LARGEST SUNDAY SCHOOLS IN AMERICA
1989–1990 Sunday School Attendance

S.S. Attend.	Church	City, State	Aff.	Pastor
20,000	First Baptist Church	Hammond, IN	IB	Dr. Jack Hyles
11,743	Willow Creek Community Church	S. Barrington, IL	IND	Rev. Bill Hybels
10,077	First Assembly of God	Phoenix, AZ	AG	Dr. Tommy Barnett
9,111	Metro Assembly of God	Brooklyn, NY	AG	Rev. Bill Wilson
9,000	Thomas Road Baptist Church	Lynchburg, VA	IND	Dr. Jerry Falwell
7,558	First Baptist Church	Dallas, TX	SBC	Dr. W. A. Criswell
6,401	First Baptist Church	Jacksonville, FL	SBC	Drs. H. Lindsay, Jr. & J. Vines
5,316	Bellevue Baptist Church	Cordova, TN	SBC	Dr. Adrian Rogers
5,314	Second Baptist Church	Houston, TX	SBC	Dr. H. Edwin Young
5,006	Capital Christian Center	Sacramento, CA	AG	Dr. Glen D. Cole
4,820	First Baptist Church	Houston, TX	SBC	Dr. John Bisagno
4,400	Calvary Temple	Springfield, IL	AG	Dr. Mitchell Johnson, Jr.
4,341	First Assembly of God	Grand Rapids, MI	AG	Rev. Wayne M. Benson, Sr.
4,307	North Phoenix Baptist Church	Phoenix, AZ	SBC	Dr. Richard Jackson
4,207	Prestonwood Baptist Church	Dallas, TX	SBC	Dr. Jack Graham
3,800	Trinity Baptist Church	Jacksonville, FL	IB	Dr. Bob Gray
3,750	New Life Church	Philadelphia, PA	AG	Rev. Anthony McCreary
3,700	Grace Community Church	Sun Valley, CA	BIB	Dr. John MacArthur
3,601	First Baptist Church	Orlando, FL	SBC	Dr. Jim Henry
3,601	Idlewild Baptist Church	Tampa, FL	SBC	Rev. David Brock
3,500	Calvary Church	Santa Ana, CA	IND	Dr. David Hocking
3,322	First Baptist Church	Atlanta, GA	SBC	Dr. Charles Stanley
3,060	Hyde Park Baptist Church	Austin, TX	SBC	Dr. Ralph M. Smith

S.S. Attend	Church	City-St.	Aff.	Pastor
3,042	Mt. Paran Church of God	Atlanta, GA	COGC	Dr. Paul L. Walker
3,007	First Baptist Church	Midland, TX	SBC	Dr. James Denison
2,896	Green Acres Baptist Church	Tyler, TX	SBC	Dr. Dennis Parrott
2,819	First Baptist Church	Arlington, TX	SBC	Dr. Charles R. Wade
2,800	Peoples Church	Fresno, CA	AG	Dr. G. L. Johnson
2,800	Peachtree Presbyterian Church	Atlanta, GA	PCUSA	Dr. Frank Harrington
2,794	First Baptist Church	Euless, TX	SBC	Dr. Jimmy Draper
2,771	Central Church	Memphis, TN	IND	Dr. James Latimer
2,371	Ward Evangelical Presbyterian	Livonia, MI	EP	Dr. Bartlett L. Hess
2,730	Fairlane Assembly of God	Dearborn Hts., MI	AG	Rev. Paul F. Bryant
2,700	Belmont Church	Nashville, TN	IND	Dr. Don Finto
2,684	Champion Forest Baptist Church	Houston, TX	SBC	Dr. O. Damon Shook
2,600	Highland Park Presbyterian Church	Dallas, TX	PCUSA	Dr. B. Clayton Bell
2,596	Skyline Wesleyan Church	Lemon Grove, CA	WES	Dr. John Maxwell
2,569	First Baptist Church	Jackson, MS	SBC	Dr. Frank Pollard
2,536	Sagemont Baptist Church	Houston, TX	SBC	Dr. John Morgan
2,529	Assembly of God	Pace, FL	AG	Rev. Glyn Lowery, Jr.
2,507	First Baptist Church	Springdale, AR	SBC	Dr. Ronnie Floyd
2,500	First Baptist Church	Modesto, CA	IB	Dr. William E. Yeager
2,500	Park Cities Baptist Church	Dallas, TX	SBC	Dr. James Pleitz
2,468	Rehobeth Baptist Church	Tucker, GA	SBC	Dr. Richard G. Lee
2,466	Lake Avenue Congregational Church	Pasadena, CA	CCCC	Rev. Jerry Johnson
2,443	Southeast Christian Church	Louisville, KY	ICC	Dr. Robert L. Russell
2,400	Longview Baptist Temple	Longview, TX	IB	Dr. Bob Gray
2,380	Shades Mt. Baptist Church	Birmingham, AL	SBC	Dr. Charles Carter
2,374	Saddleback Valley Community Church	Mission Viejo, CA	SBC	Rev. Rick Warren
2,323	Graceland Baptist Church	New Albany, IN	SBC	Rev. Steve Marcum

SELECTED BIBLIOGRAPHY

Anderson, Clifford V. *Count on Me!* Wheaton, Illinois: Victor Books, 1980.

Anderson, Leith. *Dying for Change.* Minneapolis, Minnesota: Bethany House Publishers, 1990.

Arn, Charles, Donald McGavran, and Win Arn. *Growth, a New Vision for the Sunday School.* Pasadena, California: Church Growth Press, 1980.

Barna, George. *The Frog in the Kettle.* Ventura, California: Regal Books, 1990.

———. *Marketing the Church.* Colorado Springs: Navpress, 1988.

Beal, Will, comp. *I'm My Own M.E.! For the Pastor without a Minister of Education.* Nashville: Convention Press, 1985.

Bedell, Kenneth B. *The Role of Computers in Religious Education.* Nashville: Abingdon Press, 1986.

Bellah, Mike. *Baby Boom Believers.* Wheaton, Illinois: Tyndale House Publishers, Inc., 1988.

Bowman, Locke E., Jr. *Teaching Today.* Philadelphia, Pennsylvania: Westminster Press, 1980.

Brown, Lowell E. *Sunday School Standards. A Guide for Measuring and Achieving Sunday School Success.* Ventura, California: International Center for Learning, 1980.

Conaway, John. *Teaching the Bible. How-to Methods for Every Age Level.* Elgin, Illinois: David C. Cook Publishing Company, 1982.

Cully, Iris V. *New Life for Your Sunday School.* New York: Hawthorn Books, 1976.

Daniel, Eleanor, John W. Wade, and Charles Gresham, *Introduction to Christian Education.* Cincinnati, Ohio: Standard Publishing Company, 1980.

Edge, Findley B. *The Doctrine of the Laity.* Nashville: Convention Press, 1985.

Evette, Ray F., comp. *The Ministry of Childhood Education.* Nashville: Convention Press, 1985.

Gangel, Kenneth O. *24 Ways to Improve Your Teaching.* Wheaton, Illinois: Victor Books, 1986.

Glaser, John, ed. *Caring for the Special Child.* Kansas City, Missouri: Leaven Press, 1985.

Hadaway, Kirk C., Stuart A. Wright, and Francis M. Dubose, *Home Cell Groups and House Churches.* Nashville: Broadman Press, 1987.

Hall, Terry. *Dynamic Bible Teaching with Overhead Projectors.* Elgin, Illinois: David C. Cook Publishing Company, 1985.

Hanson, Grant W. *Foundations for the Teaching Church.* Valley Forge, Pennsylvania: Judson Press, 1986.

Hawkins, O. S. *Revive Us Again.* Nashville: Broadman Press, 1990.

Hendricks, Howard G. *Teaching to Change Lives.* Portland, Oregon: Multnomah Press, 1987.

Hendricks, William L. *A Theology for Children.* Nashville: Broadman Press, 1980.

Huitsing, Betty, Elsiebeth McDaniel, Betty A. Riley, and Mary Tucker. *Adventures in Creative Teaching.* Wheaton, Illinois: Victor Books, 1986.

Jones, Bruce W. *Ministerial Leadership in A Managerial World.* Wheaton, Illinois: Tyndale House Publishers, Inc., 1988.

Kesler, Jay, Ron Beers, and LaVonne Neff, eds. *Parents and Children* Wheaton, Illinois: Victor Books, 1986.

Kiser, Wayne. *Getting More Out of Church.* Wheaton, Illinois: Victor Books, 1986.

LeFever, Marlene D. *Toward Freedom, a Teacher's Guide to Helping Teens* Elgin, Illinois: David C. Cook Publishing Company, 1979.

Lynn, Robert W., and Elliott Wright. *The Big Little School, 200 Years of the Sunday School.* Birmingham, Alabama: Religious Education Press, 1980.

Mayes, Howard, and James Long. *Can I Help It If They Don't Learn?* Wheaton, Illinois: Victor Books, 1977.

McBride, Neal F. *Teacher! A Christlike Model for Students.* Elgin, Illinois: David C. Cook Publishing Company, 1982.

McGavran, Donald A., and Peter C. Wagner, *Understanding Church Growth.* 3d ed. Grand Rapids, Michigan: Eerdmans 1990.

Murren, Doug. *The Baby Boomerang.* Ventura, California: Regal Books, 1990.

Richards, Lawrence O., and Clyde Hoeldtke. *A Theology of Church Leadership.* Grand Rapids, Michigan: Zondervan Publishing House, 1980.

Schaller, Lyle E. *The Change Agent.* Nashville: Abingdon Press, 1972.

Smith, Sid. *10 Super Sunday Schools in the Black Community.* Nashville: Broadman Press, 1986.

Stewart, Ed, and Nina Fishwick. *Group Talk! A Complete Plan for Leading Adult Bible Discussion Groups.* Ventura, California: Regal Books, 1986.

Stubblefield, Jerry M., ed. *A Church Ministering to Adults.* Nashville: Broadman Press, 1986.

Taulman, James E. *Encouragers: The Sunday School Worker's Counseling Ministry.* Nashville: Broadman Press, 1986.

Towns, Elmer. *How to Grow an Effective Sunday School.* Denver, Colorado: Accent Books, 1979.

————. *154 Steps to Revitalize Your Sunday School.* Wheaton, Illinois: Victor Books, 1988.

————. *10 of Today's Most Innovative Churches.* Ventura, Calif.: Regal Books, 1990.

————. *The Successful Sunday School and Teacher's Guidebook* Carol Stream, Illinois: Creation House, 1976.

Towns, Elmer L., John N. Vaughan, and David J. Seifert. *Book of Church Growth.* Wheaton, Illinois: Tyndale House Publishers, Inc., 1981.

Wagner, C. Peter, *Church Growth: The State of the Art.* Edited by Win Arn and Elmer Towns, Wheaton, Illinois: Tyndale House Publishers, Inc., 1986.

————. *Strategies for Church Growth.* Ventura, Calif.: Regal Books, 1987.

Walrath, Douglas Alan. *Creative Leadership Series.* 2d ed. Nashville: Abingdon Press, 1980.

Wilbert, Warren N. *Teaching Christian Adults.* Grand Rapids, Michigan: Baker Book House, 1980.

Wilhoit, Jim. *Christian Education and the Search for Meaning.* Grand Rapids, Michigan: Baker Book House, 1987.

Willey, Ray, ed. *Working with Youth.* Wheaton, Illinois: Victor Books, 1982.

Willis, Wesley R. *Make Your Teaching Count! A Guide to Improve the Ouality of Your Sunday School Teaching.* Wheaton, Illinois: Victor Books, 1985.

Zuck, Roy B., Robert E. Clark, and Joanne Brubaker. *Childhood Education in the Church.* Chicago: Moody Press, 1979.